PSYCHOLOGY

STEPHEN F. DAVIS • JOSEPH J. PALLADINO

For the Students of Ivy Tech State College

Taken from:

Psychology, Fourth Edition, Media and Research Update
by Stephen F. Davis and Joseph J. Palladino

Study Guide
by Scott A. Bailey
for *Psychology*, Fourth Edition
by Stephen F. Davis and Joseph J. Palladino

Taken from:

Psychology, Fourth Edition, Media and Research Update
by Stephen F. Davis and Joseph J. Palladino
Copyright © 2005, 2004, 2000, 1997, 1995 by Pearson Education, Inc.
Published by Prentice-Hall
Upper Saddle River, New Jersey 07458

Study Guide
by Scott A. Bailey
for *Psychology*, Fourth Edition
by Stephen F. Davis and Joseph J. Palladino
Copyright © 2003 by Pearson Education, Inc.
Published by Prentice-Hall

This special edition published in cooperation with Pearson Custom Publishing.

Printed in the United States of America

10 9 8 7 6 5 4 3 2 1

ISBN 0-536-95864-5

2005500079

BK

Please visit our web site at *www.pearsoncustom.com*

PEARSON CUSTOM PUBLISHING
75 Arlington Street, Suite 300, Boston, MA 02116
A Pearson Education Company

BRIEF CONTENTS

Taken from:

Psychology, Fourth Edition, Media and Research Update
by Stephen F. Davis and Joseph J. Palladino

RIEF CONTENTS

Taken from:

Study Guide
by Scott A. Bailey
for *Psychology*, Fourth Edition
by Stephen F. Davis and Joseph J. Palladino

Part 1

Taken from:

Psychology, Fourth Edition,
Media and Research Update
by Stephen F. Davis and Joseph J. Palladino

Stephen F. Davis is Professor Emeritus of Psychology at Emporia State University in Emporia, Kansas. Most recently he served as the 2002–2003 Knapp Distinguished Professor of Arts and Sciences at the University of San Diego. He received his bachelor's and master's degrees in psychology from Southern Methodist University and his Ph.D. in experimental psychology from Texas Christian University. His research, which always includes student assistants, has investigated such diverse topics as academic dishonesty, learning versus grade orientation of students, Type A personality, and the behavioral effects of ingesting toxic metals. He is the author of more than 250 journal articles, 10 books, and more than 800 convention presentations.

Steve's teaching abilities have drawn acclaim on the national level. In 1988 he received the National Distinguished Teaching of Psychology Award from the American Psychological Foundation. He was awarded the Teaching Excellence Award from Division Two (Society for the Teaching of Psychology) of the American Psychological Association in 1989. His professional accomplishments also include serving as president of the Southwestern Psychological Association, the Southern Society for Philosophy and Psychology, and Division Two of the American Psychological Association. He also served as the National President of Psi Chi (the national honor society in psychology). He has been elected as a Fellow of the American Psychological Association, the American Psychological Society, and the American Association of Applied and Preventive Psychology.

Joseph J. Palladino is Chair and Professor of Psychology at the University of Southern Indiana in Evansville, Indiana. He received all his academic degrees from Fordham University, including his Ph.D. in general theoretical psychology. His numerous articles and presentations have covered topics such as sleep and dreams, the death penalty, extra-credit opportunities, teaching methods, and techniques to encourage research by undergraduate students.

Joe founded the Mid-America Undergraduate Psychology Research Conference in 1982. The Mid-America Conference for Teachers of Psychology, which he founded in 1984, has become the model for regional teaching conferences. His contribution to the continuing education of teachers was recognized by the Faculty Service Award presented by the National University Continuing Education Association in 1991. In 1990 he received the Teaching Excellence Award from Division Two (Society for the Teaching of Psychology) of the American Psychological Association. He was elected to Fellow status in the American Psychological Association in 1989 and served as the president of Division Two in 1991–1992. He has also served Division Two as a consulting editor and the Methods and Techniques editor of Teaching of Psychology, and as chair of the program committee. In 2000 he received the University of Southern Indiana Alumni Association Faculty Recognition Award. He served as midwestern Vice President of Psi Chi, The National Honor Society in Psychology (2000– 2002). In his spare time, he enjoys writing the column "On the Light Side" with Mitch Handelsman of the University of Colorado at Denver and speaking to faculty on "The Humor of Teaching; the Teaching of Humor." "On the Light Side" appears in the Psi Chi newsletter, *Eye on Psi Chi*. In addition, he creates cartoons to accompany the column, and several of these now appear in this textbook.

PREFACE

TO THE INSTRUCTOR

We began the first edition of this text with the premise that introductory psychology may be the only psychology course your students ever take. With that in mind, we set out to write a text that would make the beginning psychology course an engaging, relevant, and interactive experience. We have maintained this philosophy in all four editions of this text.

Between the two of us, we have taught introductory psychology for over 50 years. Our experience has taught us that students would rather be "talked with" than "talked to." We hope that as students read the fourth edition of this book they will have the feeling they are engaging in a conversation with us. We have also attempted to convey the excitement and love of psychology that we hope characterize our own classes.

OUR OBJECTIVES IN THE FOURTH EDITION

Our objectives for this edition were to make the book as **accessible** as possible to students; to encourage **active learning** through the design and features of our text; and to help students **apply** what they learn in this class to their own lives.

Accessibility   As in the first three editions of this text, our first objective is to make our book intellectually and financially accessible to students. We've worked hard to develop a conversational and interactive style of writing that will appeal directly to students. Rather than trying to impress colleagues with our command of the material, our primary interest is always making sure that the student comes away with a clear understanding of key principles. We're also very conscious of the fact that the cost of college tuition and textbooks can put a strain on students' (and parents'!) finances. That's why this book is priced significantly lower than most comprehensive, hardcover introductory psychology texts; and, in addition, every copy of the fourth edition comes automatically packaged with a free copy of the Study Guide. We, along with Prentice Hall, are committed to providing students a quality educational package at the lowest possible price.

Active Learning   We believe that students learn better when they are actively engaged in the process, so we've built several features into each chapter that are designed to facilitate active learning. Each major section begins with a brief **vignette** that includes questions to spark interest and anticipation for the content to come. Several times within each chapter, **Psychological Detective** features ask students to consider a question about the topic under discussion. The question may deal with issues such as research ethics, how to conduct research, or the importance of a particular research

finding. The student is asked to supply an answer to the question before reading further. **Hands-On** questionnaires and exercises bring your students into direct contact with the material presented in the chapter. Each chapter also includes **Check Your Progress** quizzes after each major section. These allow students to test their mastery of the material they have just read and to prepare for exams.

Helping students succeed is the goal of every instructor; and toward that end we have incorporated two new instructional aids in this edition. A new "To the Student" study skills section (pp. xxii–xxvii) helps students assess their own learning styles and apply them in the areas of note taking, reading, memory, and test taking. We have also added new "Study Tips" in the margins of each chapter, which offer students specific strategies on how to master key concepts in the course.

Applied Knowledge   Psychology is a dynamic discipline that is constantly seeking new ways to apply knowledge gained from research. Within each chapter, we stress the wide range of practical applications of psychological research. Based on a thorough coverage of research methods and in the interest of making students better consumers of psychological information (see Chapter 1), we present these applied findings throughout to demonstrate the relevance of research to everyday life. Examples dealing with sleep problems (Chapter 4), efforts to determine if people are telling the truth (Chapter 6), determining if individuals have problems with alcohol (Chapter 4), improving your memory (Chapter 7), and using personality tests in employment situations (Chapter 16). In addition, we have expanded our final chapter (Chapter 16) to include more areas of applied psychology, showing students how psychology applies to work and the workplace, forensics, and sports.

WHAT'S NEW IN THE FOURTH EDITION?

Revised Organization   As in prior editions, we believe that the most effective approach is to continue to provide an interactive framework, numerous illustrations, and pedagogical aids designed to help students study and review material as they progress through each chapter. The 16 chapters of this text follow the sequence that has become standard in introductory psychology textbooks, beginning with the nature of psychology and its biological foundations and ending with maladaptive behaviors, therapy, health psychology, social psychology, and industrial/organizational psychology. One chapter not always found in other texts is Chapter 10, Sex and Gender. We believe that this topic is important enough in today's world to warrant an entire chapter.

Although a chapter on Sex and Gender is not always included in introductory textbooks, we decided to continue to include it for several reasons. First, reviewer input was positive on its coverage and supportive of its continued inclusion. Second, we believe the topics in this chapter (e.g., sex role stereotyping, sexual harassment) are important for understanding both the individual and society. Third, many of the topics in this chapter are not only inherently interesting to students (e.g., sexual behavior), it is very likely that they receive limited attention in other classes.

Based on the recommendations of our expert reviewers, we have made several organizational changes in the fourth edition. We have combined the two chapters on developmental psychology into one, to make this topic easier to cover in a typical 15-week semester. We have also reordered the chapters on states of consciousness, basic principles of learning, and motivation and emotion to provide a more logical flow of the material and to enhance student's understanding of the material.

New Material in Each Chapter In preparing the fourth edition, we streamlined our presentation in all chapters, enhanced our coverage of several key topics, updated research examples, and introduced relevant and exciting new material. We also added additional photos and figures throughout to motivate the reader and amplify the exposition. Specific changes to the fourth edition include:

Chapter 1—Psychology, Research, and You

- New material on work settings for psychology degree recipients.
- New material on employment trends in psychology.
- Additional discussion of the evolutionary perspective in psychology.

Chapter 2—Behavioral Neuroscience

- Refreshed and improved art program for this chapter, including "talking graphics" that lead students step-by-step through key illustrations.
- New material on neurogenesis.
- Expanded material on the endocrine system as befits its key role in all aspects of our lives.
- Additional material on disorders such as Alzheimer's Disease.
- Expanded coverage of the neurotransmitters and how they are affected by various drugs.
- New coverage of brain surgery, including the impact of removal of an entire hemisphere.

Chapter 3—Sensation and Perception

- New table depicting signal detection theory outcomes.
- New random dot stereogram to facilitate understanding of binocular disparity.
- New general section on somatosensory processes.

Chapter 4—States of Consciousness

- New material on SIDS, the cause of narcolepsy, and drug treatment of insomnia.
- Reformatted and expanded the already comprehensive summary of the actions of drugs.
- New information on ecstasy and marijuana.

Chapter 5—Basic Principles of Learning

- Reorganized chapter to improve the flow of the material.
- New material, including new graphics, on biological preparedness, illustrates the evolutionary perspective.
- Expanded coverage of shaping and the Premack principle.

Chapter 6—Motivation and Emotion

- Moved material on eating, hunger, and obesity to this chapter.
- Continued focus on the usefulness and interpretation of the body mass index and new graphics material.
- Revised and simplified material on theoretical views of motivation to provide a solid foundation for the specific motives that follow.
- Updated material on emotions, including polygraphs, sex differences in emotion, and Plutchik's model.

Chapter 7—Memory

- Added material on the stages-of-memory model.
- New material on the use of brain-imaging techniques to locate brain areas that are active during various types of memory.
- New material on flashbulb memory.

Chapter 8—Thinking and Intelligence

- New material on language in this chapter.
- Expanded number of problem solving exercises to give students more opportunities to apply their knowledge.
- Expanded material on framing and new graphics.
- New material on giftedness, savants, and the myth of birth order and its relationship to intelligence.
- Additional material on educating children with special needs.

Chapter 9—Development across the Lifespan

- Combined previous two chapters to create a single lifespan developmental chapter.
- New material on male and female age expectancies into the 21st century.
- New material on child care.
- New material on Alzheimer's Disease and behaviors that can help prevent it.

Chapter 10—Sex and Gender

- Expanded material on stages of sexual arousal.
- Expanded material on risk factors for sexually transmitted diseases.

- New material on age differences in sexual behavior.
- Included Steele's work on stereotype vulnerability.

Chapter 11—Personality

- New discussion of alternatives to the Big Five model.
- New material on inherited components of personality.
- New material on individualistic and collectivist societies and the sense of self.

Chapter 12—Psychological Disorders

- New material on the etiology of schizophrenia and depression.
- New table summarizing the major personality disorders.
- Updated material on the Genain quads and identifying depression in children and adolescents.
- Updated material on the prevalence of disorders based on recent reanalysis of past surveys.

Chapter 13—Therapy

- New material on the "Integrative Approach."
- New discussion of the issues associated with doing psychotherapy with homosexual clients.
- New material on recent improvements in electroconvulsive therapy.

Chapter 14—Health Psychology

- New data on the prevalence of HIV/AIDS.
- New material on obesity.
- Additional material on women's well-being and work.
- New research on the relationship between level of stress and type of business organization.

Chapter 15—Social Psychology: The Individual in Psychology

- New discussion of the door-in-the-face technique.
- New material on the effects of stereotypes.
- New material on the just world belief.
- New discussion of procedures designed to avoid groupthink.

Chapter 16—Industrial/Organizational and Applied Psychology

- Broadened chapter focus to include other areas of applied psychology, such as forensics and sport psychology.
- Updated material on the use of psychological tests in evaluating candidates, interviewing, and design of equipment.

DESIGN AND PEDAGOGY FOR ACTIVE LEARNING

In keeping with our goals of making this text accessible and encouraging active learning, we have devoted a great deal of attention to the text's design and pedagogical aids. Our experience in the classroom tells us that students tend to skip over material that is boxed or separated from the main narrative, viewing it as less important and not likely to be on the test. We have therefore made a deliberate decision not to include long sections of boxed material. Instead, we offer very brief features within the body of the text that encourage students to read actively, review often, and apply concepts immediately.

NEW: Focus on Study Skills   We have added an entirely new "To the Student" section at the beginning of the text to help students develop better study skills right from the start. This section includes an assessment tool by Dr. Joyce Bishop to help students become aware of their own learning styles, as well as specific strategies for improving their skills in the areas of note taking, reading, memory, and test taking. We have also added brief "Study Tips" in the margins of each chapter which offer specific suggestions for studying key concepts in the text.

Chapter Outline   Each chapter begins with a detailed chapter outline that lets students know what to expect in that chapter.

Chapter in Perspective   We open each chapter with a brief discussion of how the material fits with the "big picture." As we progress from the chapters that emphasize basic processes to those that deal with more complex behaviors, we show students how chapters build on one another to create a more complete understanding of behavior.

Opening Vignettes   Each major section begins with a brief **vignette** that includes questions to spark interest and anticipation for the content to come.

Psychological Detective   Every chapter includes several **Psychological Detective** features that ask students to consider a question about the topic under discussion. The question may deal with issues such as research ethics, how to conduct research, or the importance of a particular research finding. We ask the student to supply an answer to the question before reading further.

Hands-On   We now include at least one **Hands-On** activity in every chapter, which features a questionnaire or similar interactive exercise. These activities bring the students into direct contact with the material presented in the chapter.

Myth or Science   These brief sections compare the findings of psychological research with widely held popular notions, and help students evaluate "pop psychology" claims.

Margin Definitions   Since so much of the terminology in this course is new to students, we believe it is important to provide instant access to definitions. We therefore include the definition of each key term in the margin on the page where that term is introduced.

Review Summaries and Check Your Progress Quizzes
Students learn material more effectively when it is presented

in smaller "chunks" of information. We have therefore included **Review Summaries** and **Check Your Progress Quizzes** at the end of each major section within chapters. These "intellectual speed bumps" ask students to slow down, review what they have just read, and quiz themselves to determine if they have understood the previous section before moving on to the next. The total number of items contained in the **Check Your Progress** sections has been expanded to provide more comprehensive coverage of the material in each section.

NEW MEDIA FOR ACTIVE LEARNING

In this fourth edition, we have streamlined and significantly enhanced the **Companion Website** to provide students with the tools to understand and master the basic concepts. For each chapter, students will find numerous online quizzes with instant scoring and feedback, interactive lectures that help students review the key concepts, flashcards for drilling themselves on key terms, and an exciting new component called *Live!Psych*.

Live!Psych is a series of highly interactive media simulations, animations, and assessments found on the Davis & Palladino Companion Website. All *Live!Psych* modules were created in consultation with psychology instructors and carefully reviewed by a board of experts to ensure accuracy and pedagogical effectiveness (see list of contributers below under "Student Supplements: *Live!Psych* Modules"). The modules focus on the concepts students find most challenging, such as the major brain structures and functions; neurons and neural impulses; the structures of the human eye and ear; stages of sleep and brainwave patterns; the classical and operant conditioning processes; and many others. *Live!Psych* helps students master these difficult concepts by allowing them to see and experience them in a more interactive format than can be achieved in any textbook. *Live!Psych* icons appear in the margins of the text to indicate that there is an interactive module available on the website for the concept just covered. All of the material on the Davis & Palladino Companion Website, including the *Live!Psych* modules, can be accessed without restriction at **www.prenhall.com/davis**.

SUPPLEMENTS

Print Supplements for Instructors

Instructor's Resource Manual   We believe that you will find a wealth of helpful information and other resources in the Instructor's Manual written by Alan Swinkles (St. Edwards University). This experienced teacher brings a number of innovative ideas to the IRM for our fourth edition, including expanded "Lecture Enhancers" as well as demonstrations, activities and student assignments. Each chapter describes how students can use resources on the Companion Website and the *Video Classics in Psychology*

CD-ROM as homework assignments or activities. The manual also offers a number of cross-cultural and multicultural resources and teaching ideas for each chapter.

Test Item File   The authors' involvement in all aspects of the ancillary program for the fourth edition is clearly illustrated in the Test Item File, which was written by Joe Palladino. Drawing on his experience as a graduate student in Dr. Anne Anastasi's Test Construction class at Fordham University, Joe has carefully reviewed and rewritten the items to improve clarity and coverage of the material and to ensure that the vocabulary level is accessible to students. Joe continues to teach and do research in the area of Psychometrics.

The total number of items has been expanded for the fourth edition, and an increased number of items are now written in the question format rather than the incomplete stem format. The items continue to be coded as either definitional/factual or applied/conceptual.

PH Color Transparencies for Introductory Psychology (0-13-041840-4) This set of over 130 full-color transparencies offers a wealth of illustrations, figures, and graphs from the text, as well as images from a variety of other sources.

Media and Online Resources for Instructors

Instructor's CD-ROM (0-13-182747-2)   This valuable, time-saving supplement brings together all of the Davis & Palladino instructor resources in one convenient place. The CD-ROM offers presentation resources, including PowerPoint presentations customized for this text. It also includes Word files for the Instructor's Resource Manual and the Test Item File.

PH Test Manager (0-13-049241-8)   One of the best-selling test-generating software programs on the market, Test Manager is available in Windows and Macintosh formats (both of which are included on one CD-ROM). The Test Manager includes a Gradebook, Online Network Testing, and many tools to help you edit and create tests quickly and easily.

PsychologyCentral Website (www.prenhall.com/psychology) This site is password-protected for instructors' use only and allows you online access to all Prentice Hall Psychology supplements at any time. You'll find a multitude of resources (both text-specific and non-text-specific) for teaching introductory psychology—and many other psychology courses, too. From this site, you can download the Instructor's Resource Manual and Test Item File for Davis & Palladino's Fourth Edition. Contact your local sales representative for the User ID and Password to access this site.

PowerPoint Presentations (on the Instructor's CD-ROM and the PsychologyCentral Website)   H. Lynn Bradman of

Metropolitan Community College has created PowerPoint presentations for each chapter to give you even greater flexibility in your lectures. The presentations highlight all of the key points in each chapter of the text and include many graphics and tables from the text.

Online Course Management For instructors interested in using online course management, Prentice Hall offers fully customizable courses in BlackBoard, Course Compass, and WebCT to accompany this textbook. These online courses are preloaded with material for Davis & Palladino's fourth edition, including the test item file. Contact your local Prentice Hall representative or visit **www.prenhall.com/demo** for more information.

Video Resources for Instructors

NEW: Prentice Hall's Lecture Launcher Video for Introductory Psychology Adopters can receive this new videotape that includes more than 20 brief video segments covering all major topics in introductory psychology. The segments have been carefully selected from the *Films for Humanities and Sciences* library, and edited to provide brief and compelling video content for enhancing your lectures. Contact your local representative for a full list of video clips on this tape.

The Brain ***Video Series*** Qualified adopters can select videos from this series of eight 1-hour programs that blend interviews with world-famous brain scientists and dramatic reenactments of landmark cases in medical history. Programs include The Enlightened Machine; The Two Brains; Vision and Movement; Madness; Rhythms and Drives; States of Mind; Stress and Emotion; and Learning and Memory. Contact your local representative for more details.

The Discovering Psychology ***Video Series*** Qualified adopters can select videos from this series produced in association with the American Psychological Association. The series includes 13 tapes, each containing two half-hour segments. Contact your local sales representative for a list of videos.

ABC News Videos for Introductory Psychology, Series III Qualified adopters can obtain this series consisting of segments from the *ABC Nightly News with Peter Jennings, Nightline, 20/20, Prime Time Live,* and *The Health Show.*

Films for Humanities and Sciences ***Video Library*** Qualified adopters can select videos on various topics in psychology from the extensive library *Films for the Humanities and Sciences.* Contact your local sales representative for a list of videos.

Supplements for Students

Study Guide (0-13-049242-6) Prepared by Scott Bailey of Texas Lutheran University, this study tool is provided at

no charge with the purchase of each new text. It encourages students to reinforce their learning by providing chapter reviews and self-tests. Each chapter opens with a "Do You Know" section that piques student interest by expanding upon the information presented in the text and presenting it in different ways. After the review and testing sections, each chapter concludes with a useful tip for developing useful study habits that students can take well beyond their introductory psychology course.

Companion Website (**www.prenhall.com/davis**) All of the online resources on Companion Website have been carefully created and selected by H. Lynn Bradman of Metropolitan Community College to reinforce students' understanding of the concepts in the text. Students can take online quizzes and get immediate scoring and feedback, and go through an interactive lecture that helps review material from the text. An exciting new addition to the fourth edition website is *Live!Psych*, a series of interactive animations and demonstrations (described below). Davis & Palladino's fourth edition Companion Website is found at **www.prenhall.com/davis**, and access is unrestricted.

Live!Psych ***Modules on the Companion Website*** This series of highly interactive media simulations, animations, and assessments reinforces the more difficult concepts in introductory psychology, making them more accessible to students with different learning styles. The modules are integrated with the text through marginal icons, indicating when students should go to the Website for a *Live!Psych* module that corresponds to concepts just covered in the text. All *Live!Psych* modules have been created in consultation with psychology instructors and carefully reviewed by a board of experts to ensure accuracy and pedagogical effectiveness. Lynne Blesz Vestal has served as the primary content provider, and the review board includes: Kim Ainsworth-Darnell (Georgia State University); Eric J. Chudler (University of Washington); Margaret Gatz (University of Southern California); Karen Hoblit (Victoria Community College); Gail Knapp (Mott Community College); John Krantz (Hanover College); Nancy Simpson (Trident Technical College); and Chuck Slem (Cal Poly–San Luis Obispo).

Video Classics in Psychology **CD-ROM** Using the power of video to clarify key concepts in the text, this CD-ROM offers original footage of some of the best-known classic experiments in psychology, including Milgram's obedience study, Watson's Little Albert, Bandura's Bobo doll, Pavlov's dogs, Harlow's monkeys, and others. In addition, students can see interviews with renowned contributors to the field like B. F. Skinner, Carl Rogers, Erik Erikson, Carl Jung, and others. Each video is preceded by background information on the importance of that experiment or researcher to the field, and is followed by questions that connect the video to concepts presented in the text. The *Video Classics* CD-ROM can be packaged *free* with Davis & Palladino's fourth edition. Contact your local representative for the value-pack ISBN.

Mind Matters *CD-ROM* Free when packaged with a new text, *Mind Matters* features interactive learning modules on history, methods, biological psychology, learning, memory, sensation and perception. Each module combines text, video, graphics, simulations, games and assessment to reinforce key psychological concepts.

***Research Navigator*™** This website features three exclusive databases full of source material, including:

- *EBSCO's ContentSelect Academic Journal Database* organized by subject. Each subject contains 50 to 100 of the leading academic journals for that discipline. Instructors and students can search the online journals by keyword, topic, or multiple topics. Articles include abstract and citation information and can be cut, pasted, emailed, or saved for later use.
- *The New York Times* Search-by-Subject One-Year Archive, organized by subject and searchable by keyword, or multiple keywords. Instructors and students can view the full text of the article.
- *Link Library*, organized by subject, offers editorially selected "best of the web" sites. Link Libraries are continually scanned and kept up to date providing the most relevant and accurate links for research assignments.

To see for yourself how this resource works, take a tour at **www.researchnavigator.com**, or ask your local Prentice Hall representative for more details.

SUPPLEMENTARY TEXTBOOKS AVAILABLE FOR COURSE PACKAGING

A variety of Prentice Hall textbooks are available for packaging at reduced prices to enhance the introductory experience:

The Psychology Major: Careers and Strategies for Success, **second edition,** by Eric Landrum (Boise State University), and Stephen Davis (Emporia State University). This 160-page paperback provides valuable information on career options available to psychology majors, tips for improving academic performance, and a guide to the APA style of research reporting.

Forty Studies That Changed Psychology, **fourth edition,** by Roger Hock. Presenting the seminal research studies that have shaped modern psychological study, this brief supplement provides an overview of the environment that gave rise to each study, its experimental design, its findings, and its impact on current thinking in the discipline.

How to Think Like a Psychologist, **second edition,** by Donald McBurney. This unique supplementary text uses a question-answer format to explore some of the most common questions students ask about psychology.

The Psychology Student Writer's Manual, **second edition,** by Jill Scott, Russell Koch, Gregory Scott, and Stephen Garrison. This clear and functional handbook shows how to research and write in psychology, offering assistance in writing research reports and term papers.

ACKNOWLEDGMENTS

No textbook is the product of the authors' efforts alone. In preparing this fourth edition of *Psychology*, we have benefited from the insights of many colleagues in the discipline. First, we would like to thank the following colleagues who provided expert feedback and detailed suggestions for several key chapters of the fourth edition:

Lois Attore, *Orange Coast College—Chapter 2, Biological Foundations of Psychology*
Julie Evey, *University of Southern Indiana— Chapter 3, Sensation and Perception*
Sid Hall, *University of Southern Indiana—Chapter 16, Industrial, Organizational, and Other Applications of Psychology*
Patricia Puccio, *College of DuPage—Chapter 9, Developmental Psychology*
Elane Rehr, *Diablo Valley College—Chapter 10, Sex and Gender*
Lauren Scharff, *Stephen F. Austin State University— Chapter 3, Sensation and Perception*

Next, we would like to thank the following reviewers who offered their insights and suggestions on the new study skills section, "To the Student: Learning Styles—An Important Part of Successful Studying," found on pages xxii–xxvii:

Jeff Bartel, *Kansas State University*
Stan Bursten, *Cameron University*
Sandy Ciccarelli, *Gulf Coast Community College*
Sherry Lantinga, *Dorot College*
Lindette Lent, *Arizona Western College*
Lisa Vogelsang, *University of Minnesota-Duluth*
Brian Schrader, *Emporia State University*
DeAnna L. Timmerman, *Roane State Community College*
H. R. Schiffman, *Rutgers University*

Finally, we would like to express our thanks to the following individuals who reviewed this and prior editions of our text:

Ruth L. Ault, *Davidson College*
Ellen C. Banks, *Daemen College*
William A. Barnard, *University of Northern Colorado*
Joe Bean, *Shorter College*
Angela Becker, *Indiana University–Kokomo*

Barney Beins, *Ithaca College*
Daniel Berch, *University of Cincinnati*
Joy L. Berrenberg, *University of Colorado at Denver*
Amy D. Bertelson, *Washington University*
Deborah L. Best, *Wake Forest University*
Michael Best, *Southern Methodist University*
Jeanine R. Bloyd, *Spoon River College*
Charles Brewer, *Furman University*
Ross Buck, *University of Connecticut*
Joni Caldwell, *Union College*
David M. Carkenord, *Longwood College*
Peter Carswell, *Asheville-Buncombe Technical Community College*
Avi Chaudhuri, *McGill University*
Ronald Comer, *Princeton University*
Gary Coover, *Northern Illinois University*
Catharine L. Cowan, *Southwest State University*
Michael Crabtree, *Washington and Jefferson College*
W.A. Cronin-Hillix, *San Diego State University*
Denys deCatanzaro, *McMaster University*
Patricia Decker, *DeVry Institute of Technology*
William Domhoff, *University of California–Santa Cruz*
Betty Dorr, *Fort Lewis College*
Julie Earles, *Florida Atlantic University*
Robert Emery, *University of Virginia*
Robert Emmons, *University of California–Davis*
Roberta A. Eveslage, *Johnson County Community College*
Sandra R. Fiske, *Onondaga Community College*
Karen E. Ford, *Mesa State College*
Grace Galliano, *Kennesaw State College*
Tracey Geer, *University of Arizona*
Judith Gibbons, *St. Louis University*
Peter J. Giordano, *Belmont University*
Nuria Giralt, *University of Arizona*
John Governale, *Clark College*
Richard A. Griggs, *University of Florida*
Sid Hall, *University of Southern Indiana*
Wayne Hall, *San Jacinto College Central*
Bernice B. Harshberger, *Carteret Community College*
Diane Herbert, *SUNY Farmingdale*
David K. Hogberg, *Albion College*
William D. Hopkins, *Berry College*
Phyllis A. Hornbuckle, *Virginia Commonwealth University*
James Huntermark, *Missouri Western State College*
Ted Jaeger, *Westminster College*
John Jahnke, *Miami University*
George G. Janzen, *Ferris State University*
Laurie L. Jensen, *Northern State University*
James M. Jones, *University of Delaware*
William Kelemen, *University of Missouri–St. Louis*
Mark Kelland, *Lansing Community College*
Allen Keniston, *University of Wisconsin–Eau Claire*
Stephen Klein, *Mississippi State University*
Patricia Lanzon, *Henry Ford Community College*
Randy Larsen, *University of Michigan*
Leslie Joy Larson, *SUNY Farmingdale*

Neil Lutsky, *Carleton College*
Salvador Macias III, *University of South Carolina*
Harold L. Mansfield, *Fort Lewis College*
Janet R. Matthews, *Loyola University*
Ron Mosher, *Rock Valley College*
David Murphy, *Waubonsee College*
David E. Neufeldt, *Hutchinson Community College*
Michele Paludi, *Union College*
Jeffrey Pedroza, *Lansing Community College*
Marites Pinon, *Southwest Texas State*
Tom Marsh, *Pitt Community College*
Retta E. Poe, *Western Kentucky University*
Janet Proctor, *Purdue University*
Neil Salkind, *University of Kansas*
Connie Schick, *Bloomsburg University*
George Schreer, *Plymouth State College*
Alan Schultz, *Prince Georges Community College*
Matthew J. Sharps, *California State University–Fresno*
Craig A. Smith, *Vanderbilt University*
Randolph A. Smith, *Ouachita Baptist University*
Steven M. Smith, *Texas A&M University*
Susan Nash Spooner, *McLennan Community College*
Kimberly Stoker, *Holmes Community College*
Chuck Strong, *Northwest Mississippi Community College*
Michael J. Strube, *Washington University*
Christopher Taylor, *University of Arizona*
Larry R. Vandervert, *Spokane Falls Community College*
Eva D. Vaughan, *University of Pittsburgh*
Wilse Webb, *University of Florida*
Robert A. Wexler, *Nassau Community College*
Gordon Lee Whitman, *Sandhills Community College*
Patrick S. Williams, *University of Houston–Downtown*
Edie Woods, *Madonna University*
Janice Yoder, *University of Akron*
Otto Zinser, *East Tennessee State University*

The editorial team at Prentice Hall deserves special praise. We would like to thank our Editors, Stephanie Johnson and Jayme Heffler. A very special thanks goes to our Development Editor, Susan Moss, whose creativity is in evidence throughout this book. Thanks to all!

Finally, we express our deepest appreciation to our own teachers. Among them we count Anne Anastasi, Virginia Chancey, David Landrigan, Wayne Ludvigson, Alvin North, and Jack R. Strange. Special thanks to "The Teacher of Teachers," Bob Daniel.

S.F.D.

J.J.P.

TO THE STUDENT

LEARNING STYLES—AN IMPORTANT PART OF SUCCESSFUL STUDYING

It happens in nearly every college course: Students listen to lectures throughout the semester. Each student hears the same words at the same time and completes the same assignments. However, after finals, student experiences will range from fulfillment and high grades to complete disconnection and low grades or withdrawals.

Many causes may be involved in this scenario—different levels of interest and effort, for example, or outside stresses. Another major factor is *learning style* (any of many particular ways to receive and process information). Say, for example, that a group of students is taking a freshman composition class that is often broken up into study groups. Students who are comfortable working with words or happy when engaged in discussion may do well in the course. Students who are more mathematical than verbal, or who prefer to work alone, might not do as well. Learning styles and capacities play a role.

There are many different and equally valuable ways to learn. The way each person learns is a unique blend of styles resulting from distinctive abilities, challenges, experiences, and training. In addition, how you learn isn't set in stone; particular styles may develop or recede as your responsibilities and experiences lead you to work on different skills and tasks. The following assessment and study strategies will help you explore how you learn, understand how particular strategies may heighten your strengths and boost your weaknesses, and know when to use them.

MULTIPLE INTELLIGENCES THEORY

There is a saying, "It is not how smart you are, but how you are smart." In 1983, Howard Gardner, a Harvard University professor, changed the way people perceive intelligence and learning with his Multiple Intelligences Theory. This theory holds that there are at least eight distinct *intelligences* possessed by all people, and that every person has developed some intelligences more fully than others. (Gardner defines an "intelligence" as an ability to solve problems or fashion products that are useful in a particular cultural setting or community.) According to the Multiple Intelligences Theory, when you find a task or subject easy, you are probably using a more fully developed intelligence; when you have more trouble, you may be using a less developed intelligence.

Following are descriptions of each of the intelligences, along with characteristic skills. The *Multiple Pathways to Learning* assessment, based on Gardner's work, will help you determine the levels to which your intelligences are developed. You will find the assessment on p. xxiv.

PUTTING ASSESSMENTS IN PERSPECTIVE

Before you complete the *Multiple Pathways to Learning* assessment, remember: No assessment has the final word on who you are and what you can and cannot do. An intriguing but imperfect tool, its results are affected by your ability to answer objectively, your mood that day, and other factors. Here's how to best use what this assessment, or any other, tells you:

Use Assessments for Reference Approach any assessment as a tool with which you can expand your idea of yourself. There are no "right" answers, no "best" set of scores. Think of it in the same way you would a set of eyeglasses for a person with blurred vision. The glasses will not create new paths and possibilities, but will help you see more clearly the ones that already exist.

Use Assessments for Understanding Understanding the level to which your intelligences seem to be developed will help prevent you from boxing yourself into categories that limit your life. Instead of saying "I'm no good in math," someone who is not a natural in math can make the subject easier by using appropriate strategies. For example, a learner who responds to visuals can learn better by drawing diagrams of math problems. The more you know yourself, the more you will be able to assess and adapt to any situation—in school, work, and life.

Face Challenges Realistically Any assessment reveals areas of challenge as well as ability. Rather than dwelling on limitations (which often results in a negative self-image) or ignoring them (which often leads to unproductive choices), use what you know from the assessment to look at where you are and set goals that will help you reach where you want to be.

Following the assessment, you will see information about the typical traits of each intelligence, and more detailed study strategies geared toward the four intelligences most relevant for studying this text. During this course you should make a point to explore a large number of new study techniques, considering all of the different strategies presented, not just the ones that apply to your strengths. Why?

Change Because you have abilities in all areas, though some are more developed than others, you may encounter useful suggestions under any of the headings. Furthermore, your abilities and learning styles change as you learn, so you never know what might work for you.

Strategies Help Weaknesses, Build Strengths Knowing learning styles is not only about guiding your life toward your strongest abilities; it is also about choosing strategies to use when you face challenges. Strategies for your weaker areas may help when what is required of you involves tasks and academic areas that you find difficult. For example, if you are not strong in logical-mathematical intelligence and have to take a math course, the suggestions

Intelligences and Characteristic Skills

Intelligence	Description	Characteristic Skills
Verbal/Linguistic	Ability to communicate through language through listening, reading, writing, speaking.	• Analyzing own use of language • Remembering terms easily • Explaining, teaching, learning, & using humor • Understanding syntax and meaning of words • Convincing someone to do something
Logical/Mathematical	Ability to understand logical reasoning and problem solving, particularly in math and science.	• Recognizing abstract patterns and sequences • Reasoning inductively and deductively • Discerning relationships and connections • Performing complex calculations • Reasoning scientifically
Visual/Spatial	Ability to understand spatial relationships and to perceive and create images.	• Perceiving and forming objects accurately • Manipulating images for visual art or graphic design • Finding one's way in space (using charts and maps) • Representing something graphically • Recognizing relationships between objects
Bodily/Kinesthetic	Ability to use the physical body skillfully and to take in knowledge through bodily sensation.	• Connecting mind and body • Controlling movement • Improving body functions • Working with hands • Expanding body awareness to all senses • Coordinating body movement
Intrapersonal	Ability to understand one's own behavior and feelings.	• Evaluating own thinking • Being aware of and expressing feelings • Taking independent action • Understanding self in relationship to others • Thinking and reasoning on higher levels
Interpersonal	Ability to relate to others, noticing their moods, motivations, and feelings.	• Seeing things from others' perspectives • Cooperating within a group • Achieving goals with a team • Communicating verbally and non-verbally • Creating and maintaining relationships
Musical/Rhythmic	Ability to comprehend and create meaningful sound and recognize patterns.	• Sensing tonal qualities • Creating or enjoying melodies and rhythms • Being sensitive to sounds and rhythms • Using "schemas" to hear music • Understanding the structure of music and other patterns
Naturalistic	Ability to understand features of the environment.	• Deep understanding of nature, environmental balance, ecosystem • Appreciation of the delicate balance in nature • Feeling most comfortable when in nature • Ability to use nature to lower stress

geared toward logical-mathematical learners may help you build what skill you have.

As you complete the assessment, try to answer the questions objectively—in other words, answer the questions to best indicate who you are, not who you want to be (or who your parents or instructors want you to be). Then, enter your scores on p. xxiv. Don't be concerned if some of your scores are low—that is true for almost everyone.

STUDY STRATEGIES FOR DIFFERENT LEARNING STYLES

Finding what study strategies work best for you is almost always a long process of trial and error, often because there is no rhyme or reason to the search. If you explore strategies in the context of learning style, however, you give yourself a head start.

Pathways to Learning

Rate each statement: rarely = 1, sometimes = 2, often = 3, almost always = 4
Write the number of your response on the line next to the statement and total each set of 6 questions.

1. _____ I enjoy physical activities.

2. _____ I am uncomfortable sitting still.

3. _____ I prefer to learn through doing rather than listening.

4. _____ I tend to move my legs or hands when I'm sitting.

5. _____ I enjoy working with my hands.

6. _____ I like to pace when I'm thinking or studying.

_____ **TOTAL for Bodily-Kinesthetic**

7. _____ I use maps easily.

8. _____ I draw pictures or diagrams when explaining ideas.

9. _____ I can assemble items easily from diagrams.

10. _____ I enjoy drawing or taking photographs.

11. _____ I do not like to read long paragraphs.

12. _____ I prefer a drawn map over written directions.

_____ **TOTAL for Visual-Spatial**

13. _____ I enjoy telling stories.

14. _____ I like to write.

15. _____ I like to read.

16. _____ I express myself clearly.

17. _____ I am good at negotiating.

18. _____ I like to discuss topics that interest me.

_____ **TOTAL for Verbal-Linguistic**

19. _____ I like math.

20. _____ I like science.

21. _____ I problem-solve well.

22. _____ I question why things happen or how things work.

23. _____ I enjoy planning or designing something new.

24. _____ I am able to fix things.

_____ **TOTAL for Logical-Mathematical**

25. _____ I listen to music.

26. _____ I move my fingers or feet when I hear music.

27. _____ I have good rhythm.

28. _____ I like to sing along with music.

29. _____ People have said I have musical talent.

30. _____ I like to express my ideas through music.

_____ **TOTAL for Musical**

31. _____ I like doing a project with other people.

32. _____ People come to me to help them settle conflicts.

33. _____ I like to spend time with friends.

34. _____ I am good at understanding people.

35. _____ I am good at making people feel comfortable.

36. _____ I enjoy helping others.

_____ **TOTAL for Interpersonal**

37. _____ I need quiet time to think.

38. _____ When I need to make a decision, I prefer to think about it before I talk about it.

39. _____ I am interested in self-improvement.

40. _____ I understand my thoughts, feelings, and behavior.

41. _____ I know what I want out of life.

42. _____ I prefer to work on projects alone.

_____ **TOTAL for Intrapersonal**

43. _____ I enjoy being in nature whenever possible.

44. _____ I would enjoy a career involving nature.

45. _____ I enjoy studying plants, animals, forests, or oceans.

46. _____ I prefer to be outside whenever possible.

47. _____ When I was a child I liked bugs, ants, and leaves.

48. _____ When I experience stress I want to be out in nature.

_____ **TOTAL for Naturalist**

Write your 8 Multiple Intelligences in the table below according to your scores.

Scores 20–24 = Highly Developed	Scores 14–19 = Moderately Developed	Scores below 14 = Underdeveloped

Now that you have completed the Multiple Pathways to Learning assessment, you will be able to look at the following material with a more informed view of what may help you most.

The strategies presented here are linked to four intelligences, selected because they have the most relevance to your study in this course—Verbal/Linguistic, Logical/Mathematical, Visual/Spatial, and Interpersonal. Although they are written in the context of strength, remember that the strategies can also help you build up an area of weakness. Try strategies from all different areas and evaluate them. Do the ones that match your strengths work best for you? Do the ones that correspond to your weaker areas help you improve? Does a winning strategy come from an unexpected intelligence area? What might that help you learn about yourself?

Note Taking Because it is virtually impossible to take notes on everything you hear or read, the act of note taking encourages you to evaluate what is worth writing down and remembering. Note taking keeps you actively involved with the material and helps organize your thinking. Knowing how you learn will help you decide how to take notes in class and from the textbook.

Learners with Verbal/Linguistic Strength Words are your thing, and notes are words, so you generally take comprehensive notes. In fact you may often overdo it by trying to write down everything that you hear. Your challenge is to be choosy, and organized, with what you write.

- Rewrite notes to cut out unnecessary material and focus on the important ideas.
- Summarize the main ideas and supporting points of chapters.
- Avoid writing out every word—use abbreviations and other "personal shorthand."

Learners with Logical/Mathematical Strength You prefer organized notes that flow logically. Unfortunately, not all classes and instructors make it possible for you to take the kind of notes you prefer. You often need time to convert your notes into a more structured format.

- On your own time, rewrite notes and organize the material logically.
- Write outlines of class notes or text material.
- Leave one or more blank spaces between points, in case making your notes more logical requires filling in missing information later.

Learners with Visual/Spatial Strength You retain best what is presented in some sort of graphic, visual format. Courses that primarily consist of lectures don't make the most of your abilities. Look for materials that tap into your strength—or create them when none exist.

- Take notes in a visual style—for example, use a "mind map" or "think link" that connects ideas and examples using shapes and lines.
- Use different colors—either during class or after—to organize your notes.
- Start a new page for a new topic.

Learners with Interpersonal Strength Material stays with you best when you learn it and review it actively with others. Some classes give you the opportunity to interact—and some don't. Make your notes come alive by making interaction a part of your note taking experience.

- Go over notes with one or more fellow students, helping one another fill in the gaps.
- Solidify your understanding of your notes by teaching concepts to someone else.
- If you tend to talk with classmates and get distracted, try not to sit with your friends.

Reading Research has shown that it is far more effective to break your reading into several steps than to spend the same amount of time going through the material once. SQ3R is a textbook reading technique that will help you grasp ideas quickly, remember more, and review effectively for tests. The symbols S-Q-3-R stand for *survey, question, read, recite,* and *review.* Following is a brief overview of SQ3R:

Survey Surveying refers to the process of previewing, or pre-reading, a book before you actually study it. When you survey, pay attention to frontmatter (table of contents and preface); chapter elements (title, outline or list of objectives, headings, tables and figures, quotes, summary, other features); and backmatter (glossary, index, bibliography).

Question Questioning means reading the chapter headings and/or objectives and, on a separate piece of paper or in the margins, writing questions linked to them. If your reading material has no headings, develop questions as you read. These questions focus your attention and increase your interest, helping you build comprehension and relate new ideas to what you already know.

Read Your questions give you a starting point for *reading,* the first R in SQ3R. Learning from textbooks requires that you read *actively*—engaging with the material through questioning, writing, note taking, and other activities. As you read, focus on your Q-stage questions, look for important concepts, and make notations in your textbook (marginal notes, highlighting, circling key ideas). Read in segments and make sure you understand what you read as you go.

Recite Once you finish reading a topic, stop and answer the questions you raised in the Q stage of SQ3R. You may decide to *recite* each answer aloud, silently speak the answers

Survey	Question	Read	Recite	Review
A **Chapter Outline** begins each chapter	**Questions** appear after each major chapter heading and also in the **Psychological Detective** features	The text is designed to flow, minimizing interruptions to the reader	**Check Your Progress** quizzes appear at the end of each main section of each chapter	**Review Summaries** appear at the end of each main chapter section; **Study Charts** appear in many chapters

to yourself, tell or teach the answers to another person, or write your ideas and answers in brief notes. Writing is often the most effective way to solidify what you have read because writing from memory checks your understanding.

Review   *Review* soon after you finish a chapter. Reviewing, both immediately and periodically in the days and weeks after you read, solidifies your understanding. Reviewing techniques include rereading, answering study questions, summarizing, group discussion, quizzing yourself, and making flash cards. Reviewing in as many different ways as possible increases the likelihood of retention.

This text has features that fit into the SQ3R steps and reinforce your learning. The Table above shows how you can use specific features as you move through the steps of SQ3R. Here are some reading tips geared toward the intelligences:

Learners with Verbal/Linguistic Strength   You tend to function well as a reader. Set yourself up for success by being as critical as you can be when you read.

- As you read the text, highlight no more than 10%.
- Mark up your text with marginal notes while you read.
- Recite information by rewriting important ideas and examples.

Learners with Logical/Mathematical Strength   When reading material is organized and logical, you tend to do well. When it is not, you may run into trouble.

- Look for patterns and systems in your reading material.
- Read material in sequence.
- Think about the logical connections between what you are reading and the world at large.

Learners with Visual/Spatial Strength   Textbooks with tables, figures, and other visuals help you to retain the concepts in your reading. You can make your own when there are few or none.

- As you read, take note of all visuals—photos, tables, figures, other visual aids.
- Reconstruct what you have read using a visual organizer (mind map, timeline, chart).
- Take time out to visualize concepts as you read.

Learners with Interpersonal Strength   Since reading is solitary, not your strongest setting, you need to find group situations that can enhance your understanding of what you read.

- Start a study group that discusses assigned class readings.
- Have a joint reading session with a friend and take turns summarizing sections for each other.
- Teach someone else selected concepts from your reading.

Memory   In one theory, the human memory is compared to a computer, with an encoding stage, a storage stage (with three storage levels—sensory, short-term, and long-term), and a retrieval stage. Taking this view, memory improvement involves rehearsing information in order to move it from short-term to long-term memory. Another theory proposes that there are different levels of processing information that lead to varying degrees of memory. From this perspective, improving your memory requires using increased effort when processing information. You can learn more about some of the following strategies in Chapters 7 and 8 of the text.

Learners with Verbal/Linguistic Strength   Use words to rehearse information.

- Write summaries of your text passages and notes.
- Rewrite notes, working to make them neater, more concise, easier to understand.
- Make up word-based mnemonics, such as acronyms.

Learners with Logical/Mathematical Strength   Organizing your material will help you remember.

- Impose structure on information—write outlines, use grouping or chunking techniques.
- Put dates and events into timelines.
- Review systematically—for example, for 30 minutes at a particular time every day.

Learners with Visual/Spatial Strength   Make your material visual.

- Draw mind maps and fill them in with important information.
- Turn information into charts or graphs.
- Use imagery—visualize items as you learn them.

Learners with Interpersonal Strength   Reviewing with others helps you cement what you learn.

- Discuss material in a group; make quizzes for one another; teach one another.
- Work together to create mnemonic devices.
- Perform songs or poems for others that contain the information you need to remember.

Test Taking   Test taking is about learning. Tests are designed to show what you have learned and to help you figure out where you need to work harder. The best test takers understand that they train not just for the test but to achieve a solid level of competence. Using a learning styles-based approach to studying for and taking tests will boost your ability—if you learn the material in the way that suits you best, you will best be able to retain it and communicate it in a testing situation.

Learners with Verbal/Linguistic Strength   Put your focus on words to good use.

- Think of and write out questions your instructor may ask on a test—and write answers.
- Pay attention to important words—directions that tell you how to answer, for example, or negatives that sway the meaning of a question ("Which of the following is *not* . . .").
- For math and science tests, do word problems first—and translate the words into formulas.

Learners with Logical/Mathematical Strength   Find a sequential system.

- Devise and use a system that you prefer—going through the test in its exact order, for example, or doing all the simple problems first and then coming back to harder ones.
- Outline the key steps involved in topics on which you may be tested.
- If you don't know the right answer to a multiple-choice question, look for patterns that may lead to the right answer. For example, when there are two similar choices, one of them is usually correct.

Learners with Visual/Spatial Strength   Do what you can to make the test appeal to the visual.

- Underline key words and phrases in the test questions.
- Make drawings to illustrate concepts you are being tested on.

- Create mind maps to organize your thoughts before completing an essay question.

Learners with Interpersonal Strength   Testing, usually a solitary enterprise, rarely makes use of your strengths. Do what you can to prepare in settings that provide interaction.

- Study for tests in pairs and groups.
- In your group, write possible test questions and ask each other questions in an oral-exam type format.
- Debrief with others—talk about the test, how you answered questions, what you wish you had done differently, and what you will do differently next time.

SUMMING UP

Now that you have explored some possibilities of how to apply your learning styles knowledge to your study techniques, you can spend some time trying out strategies and finding what works best for you. As you read the text, watch for "Study Tips" in the text margins that offer specific strategies for mastering key concepts in the text. The "Study Tips" are color-coded for each of the four learning styles, and look like this:

- For Verbal/Linguistic
- For Logical/Mathematical
- For Visual/Spatial
- For Interpersonal

Refer to your study guide for additional material to help you review and prepare for exams. Also, if you have online access, check out the Companion Website to this text at **www.prenhall.com/davis**, where you'll find:

- *Live!Psych* animations that enhance the visual learning aspect of key concepts in almost every chapter.
- Interactive lectures that summarize each section and include graphics.
- Interactive quizzes that give you instant feedback.
- Flashcards to boost your memory of key terms.

Be strategic as you read, study, and learn, and you will find that your self-knowledge and your abilities can take you forward to a bright future in college and beyond.

These study tips and the "Pathways to Learning" assessment are from *Keys to Success, Third Edition* (© 2002, Prentice Hall), by Carol Carter, Joyce Bishop, and Sarah Lyman Kravits.

Psychology, Research, and You

CHAPTER OUTLINE

This chapter introduces you to psychology, a field that has grown tremendously over the years. Here we describe the methods psychologists use to gather information about the numerous problems and areas they research, examine the historical development and growth of psychology, and look at the different types of jobs that psychologists currently hold. In addition to introducing you to the broad and exciting field of psychology, we also explain how you can become a knowledgeable consumer of psychological research. The results and claims of psychological research fill our daily lives; we need to know how to evaluate them. Once we have put contemporary psychology in perspective in this chapter, we will be ready to examine its special topics in greater detail in subsequent chapters.

Almost every day we encounter events in our lives or in the mass media that involve what we call "psychology." These events cover a wide variety of topics. Consider the following examples.

EXAMPLE 1. Patty's friends have convinced her to take one of the many tests they have located on the Internet. Patty has always wanted to know her IQ, so she selects an IQ test with a picture of Albert Einstein at the top.

She answers multiple-choice questions such as "What is the color of the sky at night?" and "The color of the sky is caused by." After she completes the test, she is told her score is 48 and is able to view a list of people who had received high scores on this test. Because her score of 48 is toward the top of the list and more than 162,000 persons had visited this Internet site, Patty is convinced she has a high IQ. We will have more to say about Patty's IQ test in Chapter 8.

EXAMPLE 2. At a university on the other side of town, Keith is enrolled in a history class that covers the events leading to World War II. Today's lecture deals with the atrocities committed in the Nazi concentration camps. Keith hears how millions of Jews, gypsies, and members of other devalued groups were forced onto trains and taken to concentration camps as part of Adolf Hitler's "Final Solution." The instructor graphically depicts the conditions endured by prisoners at camps like Dachau and Auschwitz. The examples include unprovoked beatings, separating children from their parents, and using gas chambers to kill hundreds of people at a time. Keith tries to comfort himself with the thought that such unspeakable cruelty could never happen anywhere else. Nevertheless, as he walks to his next class, a psychology course, he cannot stop thinking about the lecture. Will his psychology class help him understand what he heard in his history class?

After Keith takes his seat, the psychology instructor begins the class by asking, "How much electric shock, from 0 to 450 volts, would you administer to someone as part of a psychology experiment?" Keith learns that a social psychologist, Stanley Milgram (1974), conducted a study in which people were asked to administer shocks to others as part of what they believed was an investigation of how people learn. Although no shocks were actually delivered, the participants were unaware of this fact. They continued to administer "shocks" even when they believed the shocks could be harmful. Keith is both surprised and saddened by the results of Milgram's study, which we discuss in more detail in Chapter 15.

BECOMING A PSYCHOLOGICAL DETECTIVE

Social psychologist Stanley Milgram investigated the factors that produced unquestioning obedience. Such factors may have contributed to the deaths of millions of people in Nazi concentration camps during World War II.

Each of these situations poses questions that psychologists might ask and try to answer. Yes, psychologists are very much like detectives; they seek to find the best answers to questions about behavior. A psychologist has earned a doctoral degree and is interested in the behavior of human beings and animals. We define **psychology** as the science of behavior and mental processes. Although this definition emphasizes behavior, it does not exclude the rich inner life that we all experience; it includes dreams, daydreams, and other inner experiences. As a science of behavior and mental processes, psychology provides the tools we need to answer questions about IQ testing, ethics in research, and countless other issues.

To understand each of these situations, you need to be clear about what happened before you can determine why and how each one happened. For example, was Patty's IQ score an accurate indication of her intellectual ability? Will most people administer a 450-volt shock to another person as part of a study of learning? Answering such questions helps you understand similar situations and provides the tools you need to answer questions about other situations.

How can you learn to be a psychological detective when every day you are bombarded by information designed to influence your opinion, persuade you to buy products, entertain you, or inform you about the world (Pratkanis & Aronson, 1991)? The information flows from newspapers, radio, television, family and friends, and advertisements. Often it takes the form of headlines like the following:

> Miracle Happy Pill Banishes the Blues
> You'll Read 200% Faster with Better Comprehension
> Recovered Memories Point to a History of Abuse
> Hidden Messages in Rock Songs Linked to Suicides
> Three-Year-Old Psychic Predicts the Future

To evaluate such information, psychologists have found certain techniques to be helpful in thinking critically. We introduce these techniques in the next section, but first let's consider a common alternative: folk wisdom.

When we try to understand events in the world around us, we sometimes turn to what is known as *folk wisdom*. Table 1-1 contains examples of folk wisdom in the form of proverbs. Read each proverb and decide whether you agree with it.

Such efforts to explain events are usually presented in ways that can never be proved wrong (Smith & Davis, 2004). Look at the list of proverbs again and notice that the proverbs in List B contradict those in List A. Folk wisdom can provide an explanation

psychology
Science of behavior and mental processes

TABLE 1-1

Folk Wisdom

This test of folk wisdom includes general principles of behavior. Which ones do you agree with? Why?

List A	List B
1. Look before you leap.	1. People who hesitate are lost.
2. You can't teach an old dog new tricks.	2. It's never too late to learn.
3. Out of sight, out of mind.	3. Absence makes the heart grow fonder.
4. Two heads are better than one.	4. If you want something done right, do it yourself.
5. A penny saved is a penny earned.	5. Nothing ventured, nothing gained.
6. Opposites attract.	6. Birds of a feather flock together.

for every conceivable event—as well as for its exact opposite (Teigen, 1986). Hence folk wisdom answers all situations but explains none. If folk wisdom does not provide helpful guidance in understanding our world, where can we turn?

The answer is to look for insights and explanations through psychological research methods. Psychologists are trained to ask good questions, to gather useful information, to arrive at appropriate conclusions, and to develop and ask further questions based on the information collected. However, there are right and wrong ways to ask questions and arrive at conclusions. Becoming a good psychological detective requires practice. To understand the need to practice the skills of a psychological detective, let's journey back to England in 1920.

Arthur Conan Doyle's Belief in Fairies

After World War I, *spiritualism* (a belief in the supernatural) sparked interest on both sides of the Atlantic. Almost every city had several *mediums*—people who claim that they can contact the spirit world and communicate with the dead during a séance (Hines, 1988). The participants in a séance hold hands as they sit around a table in a darkened room. Strange things often seem to happen during a séance: Spirits are heard to speak through floating trumpets, cool breezes and touches are felt, and tables tip over even when no one has touched them.

Sir Arthur Conan Doyle, the creator of the master detective Sherlock Holmes, was deeply interested in spiritualism. His interest started as a hobby but later became the focus of his life because he wished to communicate with his son, who had been killed in World War I. In fact, Doyle believed he had spoken with his son on several occasions (Hanson & Hanson, 1989).

In May 1920, Doyle heard reports that fairies had been photographed; he greeted the reports with enthusiasm because they seemed to confirm his belief in the existence of the spirit world. The photographs had been taken by two young girls who said they had observed the fairies in a nearby field. Doyle dismissed the possibility of fraud because the girls were young and did not know how to use photographic equipment (although one of the girls had worked in a photography shop). In 1921, he presented the results of his investigation in a book, *The Coming of the Fairies*. Doyle's authoritative statements led many people to believe the photographs were genuine, and hundreds of people wrote to him describing fairies they had seen in their gardens (Randi, 1987).

Modern technology has shown the fairies to be a hoax. Computer enhancement of the photographs reveals the supposed fairies were actually cardboard cutouts from a children's book suspended by almost invisible threads.

What lessons can we learn from the story of the fairies? First, although prominent public figures may have great credibility, their statements should not keep us from asking our own questions. Second, we should be aware of the potential for **bias,** or beliefs that interfere with objectivity. Such preconceptions can cloud our observations, influence the questions we ask, determine the methods we use, and influence our interpretation of the data we gather. Before Conan Doyle had seen the photographs of the fairies, he was already convinced of the existence of a spiritual realm. Unlike Sherlock Holmes, the fictional detective he had created, Doyle did not require stringent proof of "what I hear with my own ears or see with my own eyes" (Hanson & Hanson, 1989, p. 96). In short, he allowed his beliefs to cloud his thinking, something all of us probably do from time to time. Had Doyle been a good detective, he would have recognized the potential for bias, asked good questions, and arrived at appropriate conclusions.

bias
Beliefs that interfere with objectivity

God, Satan, and the Media

Frances Griffiths is shown with some of the cardboard cutouts she used to convince Sir Arthur Conan Doyle that she had contacted the fairies.

law of parsimony
Principle that simple explanations of phenomena are preferred to complex explanations

The Law of Parsimony.   In studying Doyle's claim that fairies exist, you have applied the **law of parsimony.** Suppose we have two or more explanations for an event or claim. Which one should we accept? Assume for a moment that all the proposed explanations explain the event or claim. The law of parsimony tells us to adopt the simplest explanation—the one that requires the fewest assumptions.

Doyle was faced with two explanations for the apparent sighting of the fairies by the girls. One explanation was that the girls had actually seen the fairies. The second explanation was that the girls had played an elaborate hoax on Doyle. Which explanation is simpler and involves fewer assumptions? Clearly, the belief in the existence of fairies involves many more complex assumptions than does the view that the girls perpetrated a hoax.

One of our goals in writing this book is to help you become a better psychological detective—capable of asking good questions, collecting useful information, arriving at defensible conclusions, and being aware of your own biases and those of others. The process we discuss can be applied to the story of Doyle's fairies, to everyday headlines in news stories and advertisements, to this chapter's opening scenes of IQ testing and 450-volt shocks, and to countless events you experience during the course of a typical day.

Guidelines for the Psychological Detective

How do you know what to believe? How do you separate sense from nonsense? Critical thinking, or the reasoning we do in order to determine whether a claim is true (Gray W. D., 1991, p. 1), is a cornerstone of psychology. In this text you will read about many experiments in which psychologists put critical thinking into action to reach conclusions about behavior and experience. You will be encouraged to assess facts intelligently and improve your own reasoning skills. And, you will learn how to evaluate critically the information you read and hear in the media and elsewhere. Use the following questions as guidelines in evaluating a statement or claim.

What Is the Statement or Claim, and Who Is Making It?   Before accepting a statement or claim, consider the possibility of personal bias. Whenever a person makes what seems like an extraordinary claim, always ask yourself if he or she has anything to gain by making that claim. Salespeople have a personal stake in convincing you to purchase the products they sell. For example, car dealers want new customers to know that past buyers have been satisfied, and to prove their point they often offer the results of surveys. Car manufacturers mail surveys to recent buyers to determine their level of satisfaction. According to *Consumer Reports* ("Selling It," 1991), some car dealers have offered their customers incentives to complete these surveys—but only if they take the survey to a dealer, who is more than happy to help them complete it!

Besides considering the influence of personal bias, we should also evaluate the authority of the person making the claim. Authority figures often provide helpful insights, but we should not be blinded by those insights. Remember, credibility does not automatically transfer from one field of expertise to another.

We have focused on the potential for bias among people who make some claim. We must recognize, however, that the very assumptions we hold can themselves create biases that in turn influence our views of claims, questions, or proposed solutions to a problem. The influence of bias is not limited to the experts; we are all subject to its influence and must strive to recognize its sometimes subtle effects. Table 1-2 contains a series of seemingly simple questions. Try answering them, and then check to see if your answers are correct.

Is the Statement or Claim Based on Scientific Observations?   Many people support conclusions about behavior by citing personal experiences or anecdotes. For example, you may think that you succeeded on an exam because you sat in your "lucky

TABLE 1-2

Simple Questions That May Reveal Some Evidence of Bias

Answer each of the following questions as well as you can. Then compare your answers with those on page 39.

1. Is the sun closer to the Earth or farther from the Earth during the winter months, or is the distance the same in summer and winter?
2. Whose face appears on a penny?
3. Who stole the greatest number of bases in a single season of professional baseball?
4. Can you transform the following figure into a perfect square using just one straight line?

Source: Adapted from Beins, 1993.

seat." Personal experiences are also frequently offered as proof of the quality of particular products, ranging from detergents to cars.

Whenever you come across such a claim, ask whether it is justified. For example, does the fact that one customer is satisfied with a product prove that the product is consistently satisfactory? Critical thinking also requires us to question where the facts came from. Was the information based on scientific research, or was it based on casual observation? Later in this chapter we discuss several research methods that psychologists use to collect data for answering questions. Only one of these methods, the experimental method, can provide the basis for cause-and-effect statements.

Popular sources ranging from such tabloids as the *National Enquirer,* the *Star,* and the *National Examiner* to more respected newspapers such as *The New York Times* and

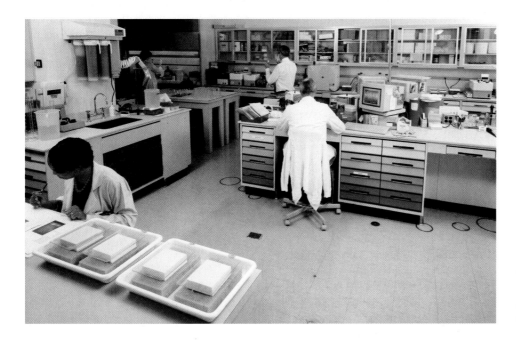

The modern crime lab uses the latest scientific methods in their quest to obtain accurate information and solve cases.

the *Philadelphia Inquirer* often print news related to psychology. However, fewer than 50% of these articles specify the research methods on which the claims in these news stories are based. Thus many sources of the claims we read in the print media pay little attention to the process of scientific inquiry, which makes it difficult for us to evaluate these claims. The same cautions hold true for the Internet. Anyone can create a Web page and post information on the Internet. There is no guarantee that the information you find there is accurate.

What Do Statistics Reveal?   Many students are fearful of statistics in any form, yet we use statistics all the time—although not always wisely. Never hesitate to ask for numbers to support a claim, but be sure you understand them.

Claims are often presented as some type of average (or typical score). An average conveys information about the middle of a distribution, or collection of numbers. There are actually three types of averages, however, and you need to know which type is being presented and whether it is appropriate.

When evaluating claims, we need to know whether the findings could have occurred by chance. Researchers usually report the likelihood that their findings might have resulted from the operation of chance alone. Findings that exceed chance occurrence are said to be *statistically significant*. It is important to remember that you cannot tell if a finding is statistically significant just by looking at the results; a statistical test needs to be performed.

Such tests, and other statistical topics, are covered in Appendix A. We encourage you to read this material at this time; it will improve your ability as a psychological detective.

Are There Plausible Alternative Explanations for the Statement or Claim?
Researchers frequently report that two variables (behaviors or events) are related. When we deal with an association between two variables, called a *correlation* (see p. 13), we must consider the possibility that the relation is actually due to a third variable. The fact that two events are correlated does not *prove* that one of the events caused the other; however, knowing the relationship between two events helps us to make predictions about when events will occur in the future. For example, whenever the moon is full, the police report more crimes and emergency rooms treat more accident victims. Is there a relation between the full moon and these occurrences?

One study actually indicated a relation between the full moon and increases in accident rates and incidents of violence. Closer inspection revealed, however, that the researchers had inadvertently selected periods when the full moon occurred on weekends. Because accident rates are higher on weekends than on weekdays, it is not surprising that these studies found a relation between the full moon and higher accident rates. Researchers who have examined broader periods have consistently failed to find such a relation (Rotton & Kelly, 1985).

Although all the world's events demand an explanation, some are mere coincidences. Consider the statements in Table 1-3. Did one of the factors cause the other, or are there other factors involved?

TABLE 1-3

Cause and Effect

Consider each of the following statements. Does one of the factors in each statement cause the other? If not, what other factors might be involved?

1. The phone always rings when I'm in the shower.
2. I lose my keys only when I'm in a hurry.
3. People always call at the wrong time.
4. It always rains just after I wash the car.
5. An item goes on sale the day after I buy it.
6. The doorbell always rings just as the baby is going to sleep.

Among the many claims we encounter every day are ones about drugs and other remedies. Patients may respond to drug treatment even if the treatment contains no active ingredient. Why? The way you respond to a drug depends on many factors, including your beliefs about the drug's effectiveness. If you expect that a drug will give you relief from some ailment, that belief itself may bring about a reduction in the symptoms. This positive response associated with your belief or attitude is termed the **placebo effect.** The claims made for drugs often sound quite impressive; when judging a drug's effectiveness, however, we need to know how many patients may have improved because of the placebo effect alone. Only when we have obtained this comparative information can we judge the true effectiveness of a drug.

We have presented four guidelines that can be helpful in evaluating a claim:

1. What is the statement or claim, and who is making it?

2. Is the statement or claim based on scientific observations?

3. What do statistics reveal?

4. Are there plausible alternative explanations for the statement or claim?

Using these guidelines does not guarantee that you will always arrive at a complete and accurate understanding of any claim or proposed explanation. Not even a well-conducted scientific experiment can guarantee that you have found the truth. Depending on the specific type of experiment conducted, the culture in which the experiment is conducted, and the personal interpretation of the results, different views of "the truth" may exist. The guidelines do, however, help you avoid certain pitfalls that can easily lead to inaccurate conclusions.

In the next section we examine the methods psychologists use to answer research questions. These techniques truly are the tools of the psychological detective.

placebo effect
In drug research, positive effects associated with a person's beliefs and attitudes about the drug, even when it contains no active ingredients

STUDY TIP

Gather in a group of four. Find, in a current newspaper or magazine, a statement or claim to use for the exercise. Each student should take one of the four "Guidelines for the Psychological Detective." Then, each person should evaluate the claim, using his or her guideline, aloud to the group.

R E V I E W   S U M M A R Y

1. The events of our daily lives pose questions that psychologists can answer. In answering these questions, **psychology** can help us develop the skills needed to evaluate claims critically.

2. The case of Sir Arthur Conan Doyle and the photographs of alleged fairies teaches us the importance of asking good questions and demonstrates the importance of being aware of how **bias** can influence the questions we ask and the conclusions we draw.

3. When there are two (or more) competing explanations for an event or claim, the **law of parsimony** indicates we should select the one requiring the fewest assumptions.

4. By asking good questions, collecting useful data, and arriving at defensible conclusions, we can become good consumers of psychological research.

5. In evaluating causal or research claims, we need to know exactly what the claim is and who is making it. Authority figures

often have great credibility, but their expertise does not transfer from one field to another, and their pronouncements should not be accepted uncritically.

6. Determining whether claims are based on scientific observations is also important. Even though science does not guarantee the researcher will find truth, conclusions based on systematic and empirical (objectively quantifiable) observations of large samples are stronger than those based on a few personal testimonials.

7. Understanding and using statistics is a great aid in evaluating claims. Psychologists usually report the likelihood that their findings might have resulted from chance alone.

8. We need to realize that a relation between two events does not prove that one of the events caused the other. We should consider alternative explanations that might account for a particular event or claim.

✓ CHECK YOUR PROGRESS

1. What is the *best* definition of the discipline of psychology?
   a. the science of behavior
   b. the science of mental processes
   c. the science of behavior and mental processes
   d. the science of human behavior and mental processes

2. What is the major problem in relying on folk wisdom or proverbs to explain behavior?
   a. Folk wisdom and proverbs cannot be refuted because they can account for any event.
   b. Folk wisdom and proverbs are never correct.

    c. Folk wisdom and proverbs are too vague.

    d. Folk wisdom and proverbs provide no insight into behavior.

3. Which of the following is likely to be characteristic of biased scientific investigation?

    a. Researchers remain objective at all costs.

    b. Researchers allow preconceptions to cloud their observations.

    c. Researchers require more stringent proof than what is normally demanded.

    d. Researchers ask their own questions regardless of what other people tell them.

4. Read each of the following claims and assess its validity by using the guidelines for the psychological detective presented on pages 6–9.

    a. Students in an introductory psychology course were intrigued by the topic of dreams; they posed questions about dream recall, the meaning of dreams, and the presence of color in dreams. They decided to conduct a survey to answer their question about color in dreams. The students reported whether color appeared in any dream they had the previous night. Only 2 of the 50 students reported color in their dreams. The class concluded that we rarely dream in color.

    b. A testing firm reported the results of a taste test of two colas under the heading "Fizzy Beats Foamy." The company concluded that "an amazing 60% said Fizzy tastes as good as or better than Foamy."

    c. In the disorder known as *autism,* the affected person tends to avoid human contact and displays little or no ability to speak; many people with this disorder are also mentally retarded. To help autistic persons to communicate, researchers developed a technique in which an assistant guided an autistic person's arm to point to letters on a keyboard and thus spell words. With this assistance, people who were previously unable to communicate reportedly learned how to spell correctly, to construct grammatically correct sentences, to write poetry, and to solve math problems. Critics were skeptical, however. They noticed that the autistic persons rarely looked at the keyboard while the assistant guided their arms.

5. Which guideline for the psychological detective is concerned with the question of cause and effect?

    a. What do statistics reveal?

    b. What is the statement or claim, and who is making it?

    c. Is the statement or claim based on scientific observations?

    d. Are there plausible alternative explanations for the statement or claim?

ANSWERS: 1. c **2.** a **3.** b **4. a.** The claim of rarely dreaming in color is not based on scientific observation. Moreover, this finding also could be explained by other factors, such as poor recall of one's dreams. **b.** There are several problems with the finding that "an amazing 60% said Fizzy tastes as good or better than Foamy." We really do not know who participated in the taste test; perhaps they were paid employees of the Fizzy Company. The 60% figure that seems to support the company's claims is misleading at best. What if 90% of this number feel that both brands taste equally good? That leaves only 10% who like Fizzy better than Foamy, and 40% who like Foamy best. Much more information is needed. **c.** There is no indication that the autistic individuals had anything to do with the movement of their arms. It is likely that the facilitator is responsible for the results we are considering. **5.** d

RESEARCH METHODS IN PSYCHOLOGY

Brandy and Michael spent Saturday afternoon surfing the Internet. They were amazed at the variety of sites they visited. One site described the growing phenomenon known as "road rage" (Davis, Evans, & Farris, 1997). They wondered what causes such aggressive behaviors in motorists. Another site (Davis, S. F., 1997) described a new disorder that involves people becoming hooked on or addicted to the Internet. Again, they wondered about the causes. Later they came across a site where they could order a product being advertised by a well-known celebrity. They wondered if the product was as good as the celebrity claimed. *How would psychologists answer the kinds of questions asked by Brandy and Michael?*

The science of psychology is concerned with events like these and the ones described at the beginning of this chapter. The goals of psychology are to describe such events, to make predictions about the conditions that gave rise to them, and then to use that knowledge to predict and, possibly, to control events in the future.

    As we have noted, psychology is the scientific study of behavior and mental processes. What makes psychology a science? Psychologists share a basic assumption with all other sciences: Physical and psychological events have causes that can be un-covered through scientific investigation. Scientists do not rely on guesswork, hunches, or unsystematic collections of personal experiences. Rather, they use a system of inves-tigation known as the **scientific method.** Like all scientists, psychologists begin their work by making very careful and precise observations of different phenomena or events. They then use the information they have obtained to develop explanations for the phenomena they have observed, which we call **theories.** From these theories psy-chologists develop **hypotheses,** which are predictions about future behaviors. They then test these hypotheses through more research and observation.

How do psychologists collect the data they need to develop theories and test hy-potheses? Psychologists use a number of research methods, including case studies, nat-uralistic observations, and experiments. Each of these methods has strengths and weaknesses, and all of them contribute to our knowledge of claims and events. The choice of the specific method used usually is determined by the type of problem being investigated. Let's look more closely at each of the methods that psychologists use.

The Case Study

The **case study** (sometimes called a *clinical study*) is an in-depth analysis of one person. This method was used in the 1800s by the physician Paul Broca, who discovered the brain area responsible for the language difficulties experienced by one of his patients (see Chapter 2). It was subsequently popularized by Sigmund Freud (see Chapter 11) as he developed his psychoanalytic theory of personality. A major advantage of the case study is that concentrating on one person (or sometimes a few people) allows re-searchers to gather a great deal of detailed information. The goal of a case study is to use the information obtained from one person to understand the behaviors of others. The case study is often an excellent source for suggesting research ideas that can be ex-plored with other methods.

One potential disadvantage of the method is that what we learn by studying one person may not necessarily apply to other people. For example, an intensive study of the interpersonal behaviors and personality attributes of the president of the United States may not tell us much about such behaviors and attributes in other American men or women. The president lives in unique circumstances and leads a life that few people can relate to. Findings that have limited applicability are said not to *generalize*.

Naturalistic Observation

In contrast to the casual, informal observations of behavior that each of us makes every day, scientists make formal, recorded observations of events. The goal of such **naturalistic observation** is to describe the settings, frequency, and characteristics of certain behaviors. For example, psychologists interested in the use of seat belts have stationed themselves at the exits of shopping malls to see how many drivers used them. They have also observed whether children riding in the cars used seat belts. When psy-chologists make naturalistic observations, they observe behaviors as they occur, without intervening or altering the behaviors in any way.

The observers must be careful not to affect the behaviors they observe and record. Observations that interfere with the behavior being studied are termed *reactive*. Have you ever noticed someone in a restaurant watching you while you are eating? If so, you are familiar with a reactive observation. Try to remember if the observer's scrutiny may have changed your behavior in any way. For example, did you check to see if you had food on your clothing or face, or did you make an effort to use your best table manners? Psychologists who make naturalistic observations try to make sure that they themselves are not observed—they try to "blend in with the surroundings" so that they are not no-ticed by the persons being observed. Another method is to find some way to gather data without being physically present. For example, Gibson, Smith, and Torres (2000) were

 1.1

By using a one-way mirror, the researcher is concealed and can make naturalistic observations of the children at this day care center.

interested in whether proximity of a bystander was related to the glancing behavior of a person using an automated teller machine (ATM). From their concealed vantage point, they observed that as bystander distance decreased, glancing behavior by the person using the ATM increased.

Correlational Research

1.2   *Live!* **psych**

Imagine that it is your senior year in high school and you are faced with all the choices and decisions involved in getting ready to go to college. Before applying to the college of your choice, you likely took an entrance examination, such as the Scholastic Aptitude Test (SAT) or the American College Test (ACT). What purpose do tests such as the SAT and ACT serve? Psychologists have found that the scores on these tests are related to (*correlated with*) your performance as a college student. For example, certain researchers (Hopkins, Stanley, & Hopkins, 1990) say that "the College Board's Validity Study Service has conducted more than 2,000 studies in almost 700 colleges; the mean validity coefficient for freshman GPAs [grade-point averages] for the SAT was 0.42" (p. 347). This means that scores on the SAT enabled educators to predict how a student would do during his or her first year in college. Keep in mind, though, that just because two variables are correlated, even highly correlated, one variable does not *cause* the other. In this case, SAT scores are related to—but do not actually cause—grade-point averages.

Figure 1-1 presents two possible **scatterplots**—graphs that illustrate the relation between two variables (in this case, SAT scores and first-year [freshman] grade-point average). In these examples, each dot in the scatterplot represents one student. The location of the dot is determined by both the student's SAT score (along the vertical axis) and his or her freshman grade-point average (along the horizontal axis). If the relation between SAT scores and grades was perfect—that is, if the student with the highest SAT score had the highest grade-point average and so on down the line—the dots would fall on a straight line from the lower left to the upper right, as in Figure 1-1A. The collection of dots in Figure 1-1B looks more like a large oval running from the lower left to the upper right of the diagram; the higher the SAT score, the greater the *tendency* to have higher grade-point averages. Hence there is some predictability here, but it is not perfect.

Scatterplots tell us whether the values of two variables are *correlated*—whether they tend to occur together. We can summarize the information presented in a scatterplot

scatterplot
Graph that illustrates a relation between two variables

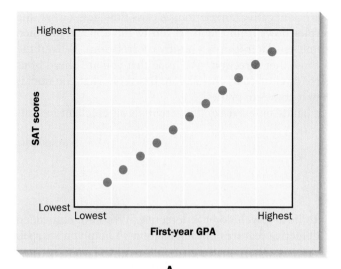

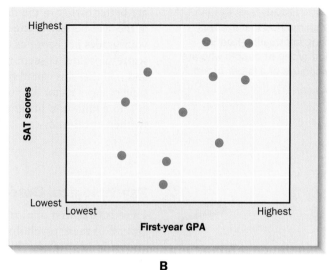

A   **B**

FIGURE 1-1   Scatterplots indicating (A) a perfect positive relation and (B) a moderate positive relation between SAT scores and first-year grade-point average (GPA).

with a single number, a bit of shorthand that is very helpful when you do not have a scatterplot handy. This number, known as a **correlation coefficient,** is symbolized by the letter r (see Appendix A). A correlation coefficient can have a value ranging from -1.00 to $+1.00$—no higher and no lower. The number tells you the strength of the correlation, and the sign tells you the direction of the relation. What do those numbers mean? First, disregard the sign ($-$ or $+$) in front of the numbers for a moment. The higher the r, the stronger the relation. Thus if r is 0.70, the two variables are more strongly associated than they would be if r were 0.30. If r is 0, the two variables are not related at all.

The sign ($-$ or $+$) tells us the *direction* of the relation. A plus sign tells us that as the values of one variable (in our example, SAT scores) increase, so do the values of the other (in our example, grade-point average). Thus values of both variables are headed in the same direction; they are *positively correlated*. Consequently, if SAT scores are high, grade-point averages also tend to be high. Similarly, the number of hours students study for an exam and the grades they earn are positively correlated. By contrast, a minus sign tells us that the values of the two variables travel in opposite directions; they are *negatively correlated*. As the values of one variable increase, the values of the other tend to decrease. For example, students who study a great deal should make fewer errors on an exam. Those who do not study much would probably make more errors. The variables of study time and errors on an exam are negatively correlated.

correlation coefficient
Number ranging between -1.00 and $+1.00$ that represents the degree and direction of relation between two variables

Hands-On

Here's an opportunity for you to heighten your understanding of correlational research by constructing a scatterplot. Use the time of each of your classes as one variable. Plot each of these times on the vertical axis of your graph. Start with your earliest morning class and work toward your latest afternoon class. Be sure to leave some space between each class time (don't crowd them all at the lower end of the axis). Your grades will be the second variable; you will plot them on the horizontal axis. Start with lowest grades and increase in equal units as you move further out on this axis (e.g., 40, 50, 60, 70, 80, 90, 100). It's an easy task to plot your grades as a function of class time. You can plot your grades for each test in all of your classes, or you could plot several tests on the same graph. Now, examine the scatterplot to see if the variables correlate. If the scatterplot flows from the upper left of the graph to the lower right, then your grades

survey method
Research method that involves collecting information from a selected group of people who are representative of a larger group

are better earlier in the day (this is a negative correlation; as class time gets earlier, the grades get better). If the scatterplot flows from the lower left to the upper right, then your grades get better as class time gets later (this is a positive correlation). What if the scatterplot doesn't seem to flow in either direction? We hope that you are ahead of us and said that this would be a zero (or close to it) correlation. Based on what you find, is time of day a factor for you when it comes to grades?

In addition to being a great hands-on exercise, this activity is an excellent logical-mathematical study tip.

Psychological Detective

Here is your first opportunity to be a "psychological detective." We have embedded several of these psychological detective features in each chapter to help you sharpen your critical thinking skills. Please give these sections some thoughtful attention and generate some answers for each question before reading further.

The two variables in our preceding example were SAT scores and grade-point average. Before reading further, make a list of some factors that could be responsible for the association between these two variables.

Surveys are a means of collecting large amounts of information. Face-to-face interviews allow interviewers to ask for clarification of answers.

One factor that could explain the association between SAT scores and grades is the possibility that certain students (especially those with higher SAT scores) were raised by families that stressed enrichment and learning activities. These families provided information and experiences that contributed to better study habits—and, consequently, higher grades—and higher SAT scores. We highlight this possibility because a correlation between two variables does not mean that one variable causes the other. The two variables may be related because of the influence of a third variable. Correlations do allow us to make predictions, however; the larger the correlation, the better the prediction.

Survey Research

Psychologists and other social scientists devised the **survey method** of research to gather data from a sample that represents a larger population. Surveys are often used because they can be efficient ways to collect large amounts of information. They can be conducted in face-to-face interviews, by telephone through written questions, and even by computer.

An interest in understanding violence might lead researchers to ask, "How much violence exists in our society?" We could answer this question by asking every person in the country whether he or she had been the victim of a violent crime (such as robbery or assault) during the past year, but this kind of approach would be extremely expensive and impractical.

Psychological Detective

Suppose that we decided to answer our question about violence by examining the number of violent crimes reported to the police. Can you think of why this approach might not provide an accurate estimate of the amount of violent crime in our society? What are some ways the type of survey might influence the information that is collected? Write down some reasons before reading further.

Gallup Polls

The number of violent crimes reported to the police would not reflect the actual amount of violent crime in society because many crimes are never reported to the

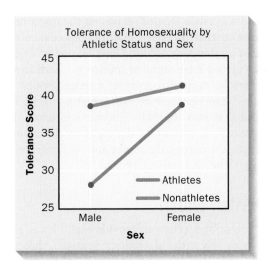

FIGURE 1-2 Tolerance of homosexuality by athletic status and sex.

Source: McKinney BA, McAndrew FT (2000). Sexuality, gender, and sport: Does playing have a price? *Psi Chi Journal of Undergraduate Research* 5, 152–158.

police. In 1988, the U.S. Department of Justice found that only 37% of all crimes were actually reported to the police; that is, for every 37 crimes reported, 63 were not reported (Jamieson & Flanagan, 1988). To counteract the problem of underreported crimes, the Justice Department collects data on crime victimization in its annual National Crime Victimization Survey. The survey depends on victims' reports; therefore, it cannot assess the frequency of murder, a crime that is typically reported to police or discovered by them. How "violent" crimes are defined also will influence the number of crimes that are reported. Is death or hospitalization included in the definition? Is property damage a requirement? These features of the survey will have a direct influence on the number of violent crimes that are reported.

In another example of survey research, McKinney and McAndrew sought to determine the tolerance of homosexuality among male and female collegiate athletes and nonathletes. As you can see in Figure 1-2, their results showed that male athletes were significantly less tolerant of homosexuality than any of the other groups (McKinney & McAndrew, 2000).

When conducting a survey, researchers must obtain a **representative sample**—one that is selected to reflect the characteristics of a larger group (the *population*). The researcher tries to make sure that the sample is a miniature version of the population. You see the survey method applied every November, when news anchors announce election winners based on information from polling researchers, with only 2% of the vote tabulated. How can anyone make a prediction based on 2% (or even less) of the vote? News organizations can make these predictions because their polling experts have identified key areas within the state that represent the entire population from the standpoint of gender, ethnicity, and political preference; thus, a small but representative segment of the population can be used to predict the way the entire population is voting.

Obtaining a representative sample is not the only important consideration when conducting surveys. Questions must be carefully worded to elicit meaningful and useful responses. Consider a survey of the number of headaches reported by respondents. When the question was phrased "Do you get headaches frequently, and, if so, how often?" the average number of reported headaches was 2.2 per week. When the word *occasionally* was substituted for the word *frequently*, the average number of headaches reported was only 0.7 per week (Loftus, 1975). The respondents' answers may also depend on whether researchers include a "Don't know" option (Schuman & Presser, 1981). The absence of a "Don't know" response seems to create subtle pressure to offer opinions, even on fictitious, or imagined, issues (Bishop, Tuchfarber, & Oldendick, 1986).

Survey questions are sometimes slanted in ways that invite biased results. For example, in 1993, H. Ross Perot and his United We Stand organization conducted a nationwide survey. Skeptical of the results, *Time* and CNN asked Yankelovich Partners, a professional survey company, to conduct two surveys of random samples of the U.S.

representative sample
Sample selected so that it reflects the characteristics of a population of interest to the researcher

experimental method
Research method that involves manipulating independent variables to determine how they affect dependent variables

independent variable
Variable manipulated by a researcher to determine its effects on a dependent variable

dependent variable
Variable that shows the outcome of an experiment by revealing the effects of an independent variable

operational definition
A careful and precise definition that allows other researchers to repeat an experiment

experimental group
The group in an experiment that receives the effect of the independent variable being manipulated

control group
A comparison group in an experiment that does not receive the effect of the independent variable being manipulated

1.3

Controlling
an Experiment

population. One sample was given Perot's version of the questions; the second sample was asked similar questions that had been rewritten to reduce the potential for bias. Perot phrased one question this way: "Should laws be passed to eliminate all possibilities of special interests giving huge sums of money to candidates?" The Yankelovich version was "Should laws be passed to prohibit interest groups from contributing to campaigns they support?" The results were eye-opening. To the Perot version, 80% of respondents said yes and 17% said no. In the Yankelovich survey, 40% favored the passing of such laws, whereas 55% supported the right to contribute (Moore & Parker, 1995). As we noted earlier, the nature of a survey and the way a project is conducted can result in different views of the true state of affairs.

The Experimental Method

The research methods described so far can provide useful leads, strong data, and excellent descriptions. Yet, as we saw with correlational research, those methods cannot provide us with cause-and-effect statements. By contrast, the **experimental method** can provide such statements. With this method, researchers manipulate certain *variables*, or factors, to determine how they affect other variables. Therefore it is considered the most powerful research method.

The logic of the experimental method starts with a *hypothesis*, or testable prediction, about which variable or variables cause the behavior under consideration. For example, which variables could conceivably affect violent behavior? Some possibilities are crowding, frustration, and hot weather. Each of these variables could affect the probability that an act of violence might occur. Even though hypotheses guide many experiments, Proctor and Capaldi (2001) caution against relying too heavily on hypotheses to guide psychological research. They believe that research should be guided by observable findings, not just by predictions made by an experimental hypotheses.

In the logic of an experiment, the variables that might cause an effect are called **independent variables.** The psychologist's goal is to manipulate one or more independent variables to determine the effect on a **dependent variable**—a behavior that shows the outcome of an experiment by revealing the effects of an independent variable (see Smith & Davis, 2004). In the study of violence, hitting a person could be a dependent variable; the number of hits might change if we manipulated an independent variable that actually affects the probability of violence, such as observing an aggressive model. Researchers are careful to offer clear and precise definitions for both the independent and dependent variables. Such definitions, known as **operational definitions,** allow other researchers to replicate (repeat) an experiment exactly as it was originally done in order to verify the findings. In a simple case, some participants in the experiment are exposed to the independent variable; they constitute the **experimental group.** Other participants are not exposed to the independent variable; they constitute the **control group** that will be compared with the experimental group on the dependent variable. If our independent variable had an effect on violence, the value of the dependent variable (number of hits) exhibited by the control group and the experimental group would be quite different.

Let's consider a classic experiment. In the 1960s, Albert Bandura and colleagues (Bandura, Ross, & Ross, 1963) conducted an experiment to determine whether children learn aggressive behaviors by observing the actions of others. They hypothesized that children who observed an adult behaving aggressively would be more likely than children who observed an adult not behaving aggressively to exhibit aggressive actions. Nursery school children were assigned to two groups; one group observed an aggressive adult model, and the other group observed a nonaggressive model. The independent variable in this experiment was observing an aggressive or a nonaggressive model. Later, all the children were given an opportunity to hit a Bobo doll (see Figure 1-3A); therefore, the dependent variable was the number of blows directed at the Bobo doll. Bandura and colleagues found that children who observed an aggressive model engaged in more aggressive behavior than those who observed a nonaggressive model. The independent variable (observing an aggressive model) led to a higher rate of aggression

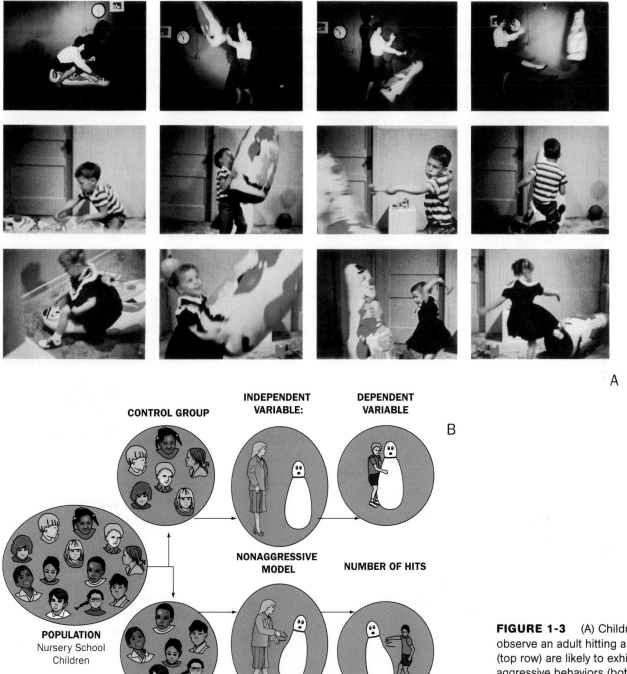

FIGURE 1-3 (A) Children who observe an adult hitting a Bobo doll (top row) are likely to exhibit similar aggressive behaviors (bottom rows). (B) Design of the Bandura, Ross, and Ross (1963) study of the effects of modeling on aggression.

(hitting a Bobo doll)—the dependent variable. Although the research demonstrated that modeling can play a part in causing children to act aggressively, you need to keep some other factors about the experiment in mind. The specific details of the experiment, such as the type of participants, age of the models, sex of the models, measure of aggression, and so forth, may have influenced the results. Possibly other procedures, participants, and measures of aggression would have produced different results. Such considerations clearly point to the need to replicate or repeat research; they also highlight the care that experimenters must take in conducting and interpreting their research.

Psychological Detective

Suppose that Bandura and colleagues had assigned all of the boys to the group that observed the aggressive model and all the girls to the group that observed the nonaggressive model. Could they conclude that boys were more aggressive because they observed an aggressive model? Give this question some thought, and write down your response before reading further.

If all the boys had been assigned to the group that observed an aggressive model, we could not conclude that the aggressive model was responsible for their aggression in the second part of the experiment. Boys might be more aggressive than girls no matter what kind of model they observed. The logic of the experimental method requires that the *only* difference between groups be the independent variable (or variables) manipulated by the experimenter—in this case, the type of model observed. If you hold all other variables that could also influence the results of the experiment—known as **extraneous variables**—constant, you may identify the cause of the behavior under consideration. If all of the boys had been assigned to the aggressive-model group, there would be two possible explanations for any increased aggression: being a boy and observing an aggressive model.

In general—and this was also true for the study by Bandura and colleagues—we need to select two groups that are as much alike as possible before an experiment begins. One way to accomplish this objective is to use the procedure called **random assignment,** or assignment of participants to two or more groups on the basis of chance. Random assignment usually results in two groups that are quite similar in many characteristics. In this case, we would probably have about the same numbers of boys and girls in each group (see Figure 1-3B).

In the coming chapters, you will see these research methods applied to answer questions about a wide range of behaviors. Examining the Study Chart should help you understand the differences among these research methods. Remember that each method can make a contribution to our understanding and that the methods are often used in combination.

In this section, we have seen how, through careful design and execution, experimental research can show cause and effect. Once a research project is completed, however, the results must be analyzed before they can be understood and shared with other professionals.

extraneous variables
Variables, other than the independent variable, that can influence the outcome of an experiment

random assignment
Assignment of experimental participants to two or more groups on the basis of chance

STUDY CHART

Research Methods in Psychology

Method	Description
Case study	Use of information obtained from one person or a few people to illuminate the behaviors of others and to suggest further research.
Naturalistic observation	Observation of behaviors as they occur, without any intervention or alteration.
Correlational research	Research in which data on the incidence of two variables are analyzed to determine the extent to which those variables tend to occur together.
Survey research	Research in which information is gathered from a representative sample of a larger population, using face-to-face or telephone interviews or written questions.
Experimental method	Research technique in which an independent variable (or variables) is manipulated to determine whether it affects a dependent variable—a behavior that is the outcome of an experiment.

Statistics and Psychologists

The practice of doing experiments created the need for methods to summarize experimental results before researchers presented them to the scientific community.

Psychological Detective

Why is it necessary to summarize research data before disseminating them? Jot down some answers to this question before reading further.

If you are conducting an experiment and a classmate simply hands you a sheet of paper with several hundred scientific observations on it, you are no closer to having an answer to your research question than before you started. You need to make sense of the data that have been collected. Psychologists have turned to a branch of mathematics called statistics for assistance. **Statistics** involves the summarization, analysis, and interpretation of data. The two main branches of statistics assist your decisions in different ways. **Descriptive statistics** are procedures used to summarize a set of numbers so that you can understand and talk about them more intelligibly. **Inferential statistics** are procedures used to analyze data after an experiment is conducted to determine if an independent variable had a significant effect. Let's see how these two branches of statistics operate.

Descriptive Statistics.   Your instructor just returned the test you took Tuesday. The score on your paper is 67. What is your reaction? Because you do not have enough information to know whether your score of 67 is good or bad, a reaction of uncertainty and confusion is understandable and predictable.

Psychological Detective

What additional information do you require to judge the quality of your work? Give this question some thought and write down your answers before continuing.

Your first response may have been, "How did the rest of the class do?" You're on the right track, but let's see if we can be a bit more precise. First, we need to know what the typical score was. When we report the typical score in a set of numbers, we are presenting a **measure of central tendency.** Undoubtedly you are already familiar with one measure of central tendency, the arithmetic average or *mean*, which is calculated by dividing the total of the scores by the number of scores. By itself, however, a measure of central tendency does not provide enough information for you to fully understand your test score of 67; you also need to know about the *variability* or spread of the other scores in the class. **Measures of variability** provide information about the variability or spread of the scores in a set of data. If all of the scores are clustered closely around the *mean* or other measure of central tendency, then you will view the score of 67 differently than if the scores are spread out widely. Measures of central tendency and variability are the primary descriptive statistics used by psychologists; they are described in more detail in Appendix A.

Inferential Statistics.   When an experiment is conducted we hope that the manipulation of our independent variable (IV) will have a pronounced effect on the dependent variable. Typically the effect of the IV is evaluated by the difference between the groups in the experiment; the larger the difference, the greater the effect of the IV. Not all differences between groups, however, are attributable to the influence of the IV. Sometimes the differences are due to chance variation among the participants who

statistics
Branch of mathematics that involves the collection, analysis, and interpretation of data

descriptive statistics
Procedures used to summarize any set of data

inferential statistics
Procedures used to analyze data after an experiment is completed; used to determine if the independent variable has a significant effect

measures of central tendency
Descriptive measures of a set of data that tell us about a typical score

measures of variability
Descriptive measures that tell us about the amount of variability or spread in a set of data

are in the groups. Even though we may select our groups randomly, they will never be perfectly identical. So how does the experimenter distinguish between differences among the experimental participants and differences caused by the IV? *Inferential statistics* offer a solution to this dilemma. Conducting an inferential statistical test allows the researcher to mathematically evaluate the difference between the groups in an experiment and decide whether the observed difference occurred frequently or rarely by chance. If the difference occurs *rarely* by chance, then the experimenter concludes that the result is "significant" and that the difference was caused by the IV. Further discussion of inferential statistics and a sample inferential statistical test are found in Appendix A.

Research, however, is not conducted or reported in a vacuum; psychologists are obligated to adhere to a code of ethical behavior.

Research Ethics

Let's return to the Milgram study described at the beginning of this chapter (see p. 3). Imagine being a participant and being asked to administer 450 volts of electric shock to another person. How would you react if you agreed to administer the shock? Later you are told that no shocks were actually delivered, but you realize that if they had been delivered, you might have killed someone. Clearly, there is the potential for long-term, traumatic effects on the research participants in this experiment. This example highlights a major concern for researchers: how to conduct research in an ethical manner.

The American Psychological Association (2002) has adopted ethical guidelines that prescribe standards of conduct for the professional work of psychologists in their roles as researchers, clinicians, and teachers. These guidelines include several general principles. For example, psychologists must maintain high standards of competence in their work, including recognizing the limitations of their expertise. They also must show respect for the rights and dignity of people, such as rights to privacy and confidentiality.

The ethical guidelines for conducting research require that all research proposals be reviewed to ensure compliance with the guidelines. Each proposal must be approved by an institutional review board (IRB) established by a college, university, or other organization where research is conducted (Smith & Davis, 2004).

Protection from Harm.   What's more, the ethical guidelines state that psychologists who conduct research using human participants must ensure they are protected from physical and psychological harm. For this reason, the study conducted by Milgram several decades ago would not be permitted today. Although no shocks were actually given, the study required the participants to obey the experimenter despite the moral imperative that they not hurt another person. This type of conflict is certainly unpleasant and could cause psychological harm to some people.

Psychologists today are very careful to follow the ethical guidelines for research. Consider the work of two psychologists who studied the relationship between handedness (preferred hand) and life expectancy. Diane Halpern and Stanley Coren "did not want to appear to be ghouls or to be insensitive to people's feelings when they were grieving over the death of a loved one" (Coren, 1992, p. 216). First, they consulted a bereavement counselor who suggested that they not contact anyone unless at least 9 months had passed since the loved one's death. The counselor also suggested that they make the contact as gentle as possible and not follow up or press people for responses. The researchers decided that they would not contact next of kin if the death had been a result of murder or suicide or if the deceased was a child age 6 or younger. Their research proposal was evaluated and cleared by a university research ethics committee. Despite their precautions, a few people they contacted did become upset by questions about deceased loved ones (Coren, 1992). Figure 1-4 shows the postcard the researchers used.

Please answer the following questions about the deceased person:

		Circle one	
1) Hand used for writing	Right	Left	Don't know
2) Hand used for drawing	Right	Left	Don't know
3) Hand used for throwing a ball	Right	Left	Don't know

4) Did this person suffer from any allergies? If so, explain: ____________________

____

5) Cause of death (circle one and explain at the bottom
   a) medical
   b) accidental
   c) don't know

____

____

Thank you. Please deposit this card in a mailbox at your earliest convenience.

FIGURE 1-4 Postcard used in Coren and Halpern (1991) study of the relationship between handedness and life expectancy.

Source: Coren & Halpern, 1991.

The results of this study show that being left-handed was associated with reduced longevity (Coren, 1992; Coren & Halpern, 1991). Left-handed people died at an earlier age (mean, 66 years) than right-handed people (mean, 75 years). Other researchers have not found handedness to be associated with earlier death (Harris, 1993; Salive, Guralnik, & Glynn, 1993), although these findings have been disputed (Halpern & Coren, 1993). Study of the possible relation, if any, between handedness and death continues; the research is conducted in accordance with established ethical principles designed to protect participants (in this case, the relatives of deceased persons) from any harm.

Confidentiality. The ethical guidelines also require that any research records associated with a person's name or identity be kept confidential. For example, Halpern and Coren "kept no records as to whom we contacted, and there was no identifying information on any of the materials that we sent" (D. F. Halpern, personal communication, August 3, 1992). In other cases, psychologists may use code names or numbers for their participants so that information cannot be associated with the actual names of people who have taken part in research.

Voluntary Participation. Participants, including college students in introductory courses, must be told that their participation in research is voluntary. They cannot be coerced into participating. College students may be part of a pool from which researchers draw participants for their studies. If a student objects to participating, he or she must be given an opportunity to select other ways to earn the same amount of credit or to complete the course requirement. In other words, no one may be punished for not participating in research. To enable potential participants to make proper judgments about their participation, the researcher must describe the procedures of the experiment and obtain a written agreement to participate, which is called an **informed consent.** This document indicates that the participant knows the nature of the research and what he or she has agreed to do before participating.

informed consent
Written document in which a person who might be involved in a research study agrees to participate after receiving information about the researcher's specific procedures

Deception and Intimidation. Some experiments require the use of deception. For example, researchers would be unable to study the true effectiveness of drug treatments without the use of placebos. Participants who are given placebos are led to believe they are taking the actual drug so that researchers can assess the influence of expectations on

Source: *Psi Chi Newsletter* 22, no. 1 (Winter 1996). Reprinted with the permission of Psi Chi.

debriefing
Procedure during which a complete explanation of research that has involved deception is provided to a participant

STUDY TIP

Come up with visuals—icons, or pictures—to assign to each of the principles of research ethics in order to help you remember them.

Dr. Jesse Purdy studies the behavior and learning abilities of fish in his laboratory at Southwestern University.

the drug's effectiveness. When psychologists use deception in their research, their participants must undergo a **debriefing** session immediately after the study in which they are given a complete explanation of the research that has used deception. During the debriefing participants are allowed to ask questions and the researcher checks for possible negative aftereffects of the deception. In addition, participants in psychological research have the right to end their participation at any time. Researchers cannot use any form of threat or intimidation to force them to complete tasks in a study.

The Ethics of Research with Animals.   As you will see throughout this book, many of psychology's most enduring findings have resulted from research with animals (Domjan & Purdy, 1995). For example, much of our knowledge about the structure and functioning of the brain (Chapter 2), sensation and perception (Chapter 3), motivation and emotion (Chapter 6), basic processes of learning (Chapter 5), developmental processes (Chapter 9), and maladaptive behavior (Chapter 12) is the result of animal research. Yet the use of animals in psychological research has not gone unchallenged (Mukerjee, 1997).

The ongoing debate between advocates of using animals in research and those who deplore such efforts has been heated and emotional at times (Galvin & Herzog, 1992). Animal rights activists view the use of animals in psychological and medical research as cruel and unnecessary. What's more, they note that such research often involves stress, pain, punishment, or social and environmental deprivation (Bowd & Shapiro, 1993; Rollin, 1985). On the other hand, the value of animal research has been defended by arguments that such research has led to improvements in human welfare (Baldwin, 1993; Miller, N. E., 1985). Psychological and medical researchers point out that some types of research could not be conducted without using animals. Ethical Standard 8.09 adopted by the American Psychological Association (2002) lists seven areas of concern in the ethical treatment of animals in psychological research.

1. Psychologists acquire, care for, use, and dispose of animals in compliance with current federal, state, and local laws and regulations, and with professional standards.

2. Psychologists trained in research methods and experienced in the care of laboratory animals supervise all procedures involving animals and are responsible for ensuring appropriate consideration of their comfort, health, and humane treatment.

3. Psychologists ensure that all individuals under their supervision who are using animals have received instruction in research methods and in the care, maintenance, and handling of the species being used, to the extent appropriate to their role.

4. Psychologists make reasonable efforts to minimize the discomfort, infection, illness, and pain of animal subjects.

5. Psychologists use a procedure subjecting animals to pain, stress, or privation only when an alternative procedure is unavailable and the goal is justified by its prospective scientific, educational, or applied value.

6. Psychologists perform surgical procedures under appropriate anesthesia and follow techniques to avoid infection and minimize pain during and after surgery.

7. When it is appropriate that an animal's life be terminated, psychologists proceed rapidly, with an effort to minimize pain and in accordance with accepted procedures.

Researchers who use animals in their research are subject to a long list of regulations, including local, state, and federal laws. These regulations seek to define under what circumstances it is acceptable to sacrifice animals for research. Moreover, the regulations often mandate certain requirements concerning food, cage space, and veterinary care.

A number of factors influence individuals' judgments about the ethics of using animals in research. These factors are complex and include the similarity of the animals to humans, their "cuteness," and the perceived importance of the research to alleviating human suffering (Herzog, 1990).

The influence of the animal rights movement is evident. A decline in the number of studies using certain animal species such as cats, dogs, and rabbits may be due, in part, to the attention that the animal rights movement has focused on this issue (Viney, King, & Berndt, 1990; Vook, 1997). What's more, researchers are now looking for ways to reduce the number of animals used in research. For example, they are investigating alternatives to the use of animals for testing potentially toxic chemicals. The new methods do not involve testing intact higher animals, such as dogs and cats; instead, they rely on bacteria, cultured animal cells, or fertilized chicken eggs (Goldberg & Frazier, 1989). Such methods, however, do not eliminate the need for animals in certain types of research. Opinions on the use of animals in research will no doubt continue to be highly personal, emotional, and strong (Plous, 1996a, b).

Now that we have discussed the need to be a good psychological detective and the methods used by psychologists to conduct and analyze their research, it is time to stand back and get a general overview of the field of psychology before we begin our chapter-by-chapter coverage of specific psychological topics. A brief review of the history of modern psychology and a consideration of the activities of contemporary psychologists should prepare you for this more in-depth coverage.

REVIEW SUMMARY

1. The goals of psychology are to describe, predict, and control behavior. These goals are accomplished by using the **scientific method,** which is systematic and empirical (based on observable events).

2. A **case study** is an in-depth analysis of a single person or event. Although the findings of a case study may apply only to the person who was studied, they may provide direction for further study using other methods.

3. To study behavior in real-life settings, psychologists often use **naturalistic observation.** This technique also may suggest research projects using more controlled approaches. In using naturalistic observation, the onlooker must be unobtrusive and avoid influencing the behavior being studied.

4. **Correlational research** tells whether the values of two variables are related. Although correlational methods do not inform us about causality, they can provide useful insights and help us to make predictions.

5. By asking questions of a **representative sample,** researchers using the **survey method** can provide useful information about a much larger population. The wording of the questions can influence participants' responses.

6. Because it can generate cause-and-effect statements, many psychologists believe that the **experimental method** is the most powerful research approach. By manipulating an **independent variable** (the cause), the researcher determines whether it influences the **dependent variable** (the effect). Despite these strengths, the results and interpretation of a scientific experiment can be influenced by the specific way the research is conducted, the culture in which the research is conducted, and the experimenter's personal biases.

7. **Statistics** involves the collection, analysis, and interpretation of data. **Descriptive statistics** summarize data, whereas **inferential statistics** are used to determine if the results of an experiment are significant.

8. **Measures of central tendency** provide information about the typical score in a set of numbers. **Measures of variability** provide information about the variability or spread in a set of data.

9. The American Psychological Association has established ethical guidelines for making decisions about research with both human and animal participants.

CHECK YOUR PROGRESS

1. Which research method focuses on gathering detailed information about one individual?

   a. a case study
   b. an experiment
   c. a correlational study
   d. a naturalistic study

2. Which aspect of a correlation coefficient tells you the *direction* of the relation between the variables? Why?

3. Which goal of psychology is most closely met through naturalistic observation?

   a. altering behavior
   b. predicting behavior
   c. describing behavior
   d. controlling behavior

4. The variable an experimenter manipulates in order to determine its effects in an experiment is called the

   a. dependent variable.
   b. extraneous variable.
   c. controlled variable.
   d. independent variable.

5. What kind of statistical procedure is used to analyze data after an experiment is conducted to determine whether the independent variable had a significant effect?

   a. descriptive
   b. inferential
   c. summary
   d. biased

6. Discuss one of the strengths and one of the weaknesses of naturalistic observation as a research technique. What is a reactive measure? How can it be avoided?

7. In each of the following sets of correlation coefficients, which one represents the strongest relation?

   a. +0.25 − 0.30 + 0.10
   b. +0.65 − 0.88 − 1.00
   c. −0.20 − 0.05 + 0.33

8. "Correlation does not imply causality." What does this statement mean?

9. How do researchers ensure that their groups of participants are equal before they begin an experiment?

   a. They randomly assign participants to groups.
   b. They measure the dependent variable repeatedly.
   c. They use independent variables that are correlated with extraneous variables.
   d. They assign participants who have identified themselves as having control of extraneous variables.

10. Identify the independent variable and the dependent variable in each of the following situations:

   a. A researcher is interested in how fast college students can turn off a buzzer when it sounds. The participants are tested under two conditions: dim light and bright light.
   b. The Board of Directors of the National Football League has decided that half of its teams will sell beer until the end of the game; the other half will stop sales at the end of the third quarter. The board is conducting a study to determine whether the timing of beer sales influences the number of fights and arrests that occur at games.
   c. An industrial psychologist has developed two possible packages for a new shampoo that will be on the market soon. She is interested in determining which package has the greater sales appeal.

ANSWERS: 1. a **2.** The plus or minus sign in front of the correlation coefficient tells you whether the relationship is positive (plus sign) or negative (minus sign). **3.** c **4.** d **5.** b **6.** The main advantage of naturalistic observation is that behaviors are observed as they occur in the real-life setting; there is no interference with them. A disadvantage is that the researcher has no control over the research and cannot reach any firm conclusions concerning the cause(s) of the behavior in question. A reactive effect occurs when the participants know they are being observed and change their behaviors. Being inconspicuous will help deal with the reactivity problem. **7. a.** −0.30 **b.** −1.00 **c.** +0.33 **8.** Just because the two variables are correlated, we cannot say that one caused the other. The relationship may have been caused by a third factor that we are not aware of. A representative sample reflects the characteristics of the population, so our conclusions are more likely to generalize to that population. **9.** a **10. a.** The independent variable (IV) is the lighting conditions (dim and bright); the dependent variable (DV) is reaction time. **b.** The independent variable is length of beer sales (stop at end of third quarter or sell for entire game); the dependent variable is the number of fights and arrests. **c.** The independent variable is the (two different) shampoo packages; the dependent variable is sales appeal.

THE ORIGINS OF MODERN PSYCHOLOGY

Some friends came over the other day and were talking about the courses they are taking at the university. Several of them are enrolled in a psychology course. They are fascinated by the topics covered and wonder whether psychology has always been part of the university curriculum. *What are the origins of scientific psychology?*

Although people have observed and studied human behavior for millennia, scientific psychology is a relatively new discipline. The origins of modern psychology can be traced to the University of Leipzig in Germany, where the first laboratory devoted to the scientific study of psychology was established in 1879.

Wundt and Structuralism

Wilhelm Wundt (1832–1920) is credited with establishing the first psychology laboratory (Bringmann, Bringmann, & Ungerer, 1980). Because the profession of psychology was not a career choice at that time, Wundt was originally trained as a physician. His mission in establishing the laboratory was to describe the contents of the conscious mind. Wundt and his student Edward B. Titchener (1867–1927), who brought Wundt's type of psychology to the United States, wanted to study psychology in the same way that a person would study physics or chemistry. If researchers could break down the contents of the mind into basic units like the basic elements of matter in chemistry, they could identify the structure of conscious experience and describe its major components (for example, feelings, sensations, and images). This approach to psychology became known as **structuralism.**

Titchener's research depended on a method called **introspection,** in which participants gave verbal reports of their conscious experiences. For example, participants given an orange would not describe it as a fruit but would instead describe its color, shape, and texture and other aspects of their own experience of the orange. Across a variety of tasks, however, the participants had difficulty producing similar reports; this fact raised questions about the existence of any common elements of conscious experience. Structuralism was replaced by other approaches, and at times conscious experience was not even considered a legitimate subject of psychological research.

During the past decade or two, psychologists have rediscovered conscious experience and investigated it using more sophisticated techniques than those available to the structuralists at the end of the nineteenth century (Coon, 1993; Gardner, H., 1985). Today a rapidly growing area of psychology has broadened the early interests of structuralists; it is called **cognitive psychology.** Cognitive psychologists are not interested in the structure of conscious experience; instead, they study higher mental processes such as thinking, knowing, and deciding. Their research is designed to determine how we store and recall information, solve problems, and make decisions (Bourne et al., 1986). We discuss the cognitive perspective in greater detail later in this chapter.

Functionalism

A new approach to psychology developed in the United States in the late 1800s. **Functionalism** was concerned not with the structure of the mind but with the purposes of consciousness—what the mind does and why. One early proponent of functionalism, William James (1842–1910), was especially interested in what he termed the "stream of consciousness" (Simon, 1996). Because consciousness was like a continually flowing stream, it could not be easily broken down into its elements as Wundt had hoped. According to James, if it were broken down into elements, it would lose its reality.

Functionalists wanted to see how people use information to adapt to their environment (Goodwin, 1999). James and his functionalist colleagues were among the first applied psychologists; they were interested in the practical aspects of psychology, such as creating optimal conditions for learning or selecting the right workers for various jobs. Functionalism reached its peak in 1906 with James Rowland Angell's presidential address to the American Psychological Association. During its influential period, functionalism was associated most strongly with James Rowland Angell at the University of Chicago and Robert S. Woodworth at Columbia University.

Wilhelm Wundt is credited with establishing the first psychology laboratory in 1879.

Archives of the History of American Psychology—The University of Akron.

structuralism
Earliest approach in modern psychology, founded by Wilhelm Wundt; its goal was to analyze the basic elements of conscious experience

introspection
Structural psychologists' major method, in which participants reported the contents of their conscious experience

cognitive psychology
Study of higher mental processes, such as thinking, knowing, and deciding

functionalism
Approach to psychology that focused on the purposes of consciousness

FIGURE 1-5 Although a strip of film contains a series of separate images, we perceive those images as continuous when they are projected on a screen. This phenomenon, known as apparent motion, gave rise to the Gestalt school of psychology.

Ivan Pavlov. His studies of digestion in dogs led to important observations about how animals associate events in their environment.

Gestalt Psychology

A group of psychologists who termed their approach **Gestalt psychology,** which was noted for emphasizing that perception of a whole differs from that of the individual stimuli that make up the whole, spearheaded the challenge to the structuralists' notion that conscious experience could be broken down into elements (Ash, 1995). The key members of this group were Max Wertheimer (1880–1943), Wolfgang Köhler (1887–1967), and Kurt Koffka (1886–1941). The Gestalt approach started in Germany in 1912, when Wertheimer (King et al., 1994) described the visual illusion called *apparent motion*, in which a rapid sequence of stationary images creates the illusion of movement, as in a movie (Rock & Palmer, 1990; see Figure 1-5). Soon Gestalt psychologists were describing other phenomena that supported their contention that what we perceive (the whole) is different from the sum of its parts (the individual stimuli). We perceive unified forms, rather than bits and pieces. Because the German word *Gestalt* can be translated as "pattern," "shape," or "configuration," it is not surprising that Gestalt psychologists have made their greatest contributions in the area of perception, as we see in Chapter 3.

The Behavioral Perspective

The **behavioral perspective,** unlike the approaches we have discussed thus far, focuses on observable behaviors; thus it does not speculate about mental processes such as thinking. Moreover, this perspective emphasizes the importance of learning in understanding how various behaviors occur.

In the early 1900s the Russian physiologist Ivan Pavlov (1849–1936) was studying digestion in dogs when he noticed a curious phenomenon. When the dogs were about to be fed, they began salivating at the sight of the food or the jangling of keys used to unlock the rooms where they were kept. The dogs seemed to have learned an association between certain sounds or sights and being fed. As we see in Chapter 5, this simple observation led to the development of our understanding of how organisms learn to associate events in their environments.

The American psychologist John B. Watson (1878–1958) read about Pavlov's work and saw great promise in it. Watson believed psychology should be concerned not with the mind or consciousness but solely with observable behaviors. He asserted that the application of rigorous scientific principles, as used in Pavlov's laboratory, could lead to major advances (Buckley, 1989). Watson developed and applied his principles in the laboratory under strictly controlled conditions. Laboratory animals made excellent subjects for his research, which he later expanded to human participants.

The behavioral tradition started by Pavlov and continued by Watson found many strong proponents. The most notable was B. F. Skinner (1904–1990), who has been called the "greatest contemporary psychologist" (Fowler, 1990). In some ways,

John B. Watson. The founder of behaviorism declared that psychologists should limit their research to observable behaviors.

Gestalt psychology
Approach to psychology most noted for emphasizing that our perception of a whole is different from our perception of the individual stimuli

behavioral perspective
Perspective that focuses on observable behavior and emphasizes the learned nature of behavior

Skinner's approach to psychology was simple: Behavior changes as a result of its consequences (Björk, D. W., 1997). Thus environmental consequences, rather than free will, shape human behavior. The behavioral psychologist's goal is to identify and change the environmental conditions that control behavior (O'Neill, 1995).

Skinner's followers used many of his basic principles to alter human behavior in a variety of settings (Martin & Pear, 1996). Some of Skinner's methods have been used to teach people diagnosed with schizophrenia to speak after years of being mute, to improve safety in manufacturing plants, and to teach basic skills to mentally retarded persons. If you have ever visited an amusement park that features trained dolphins, seals, whales, or other animals, you have seen an application of Skinner's principles (see Chapter 5).

B. F. Skinner. His principles provided the basis for many applications of psychology.

Sigmund Freud and the Psychodynamic Perspective

Historically, Skinner's approach followed the development of Watson's behaviorism. At about the same time Watson was defining psychology as the study of observable behavior, however, Sigmund Freud (1856–1939), across the Atlantic, was delving deeply beneath observable behaviors (Gelfand & Kerr, 1992). Few people have had such a profound impact on the way we think about ourselves as Freud, and few have been—or continue to be—so controversial (Crews, 1996).

Freud was trained as a neurologist, rather than a psychologist. The patients who came to him suffered from a variety of anxieties and other disturbances. Freud and his followers developed the **psychodynamic perspective,** which suggests that both normal and abnormal behaviors are determined primarily by unconscious forces. The term *psychodynamic* is used because these forces are believed to interact with one another. Freud's experiences in treating his patients convinced him that the unconscious mind exerted great control over behavior. Among the observations that led him to this conclusion were "slips of the tongue," in which the patients' true feelings were apparently revealed, and analysis of his patients' dreams. Freud came to believe that the mind often disguises dreams so that the dreamer is not aware of their true meaning (see Chapter 4).

Freud also focused on early childhood experiences as a major influence on personality development. According to Freud, if you want to understand a person's personality, you must examine his or her early experiences, which could have long-lasting effects. Freud gained great fame and notoriety by suggesting that people (even children) are driven by motives that are sexual in nature.

In treating his patients, Freud first turned to hypnosis (see Chapter 4), but he abandoned it when he determined that not everyone could be hypnotized. The treatment approach for maladaptive behavior that he eventually developed, known as **psychoanalytic therapy,** attempts to bring unconscious causes of distress to the conscious level. According to Freud, once the sources of distress are brought to awareness, they can be changed.

Sigmund Freud. His influence can be seen not only in psychology but in many other fields.

The Humanistic Perspective

Over time, the psychodynamic and behavioral approaches were questioned. Many psychologists viewed the behavioral approach as cold and unappealing. To these psychologists, the notion that all behavior is controlled by environmental circumstances left no room for personal freedom, and the suggestion that we are doomed to behave in environmentally determined ways was unattractive. These critics believed that behaviorists seemed to avoid the unique and positive qualities of human behavior, such as creativity and love. What's more, the argument went, their views of human nature were either neutral or negative.

psychodynamic perspective
View taken by Sigmund Freud and his followers suggesting that normal and abnormal behaviors are determined primarily by unconscious forces

psychoanalytic therapy
Treatment for maladaptive behavior developed by Sigmund Freud; its goal is to bring unconscious causes of behavior to the conscious level

Carl Rogers. His system of humanistic psychology focused on free will and being able to control one's own behavior.

Candace Pert. This physiological psychologist discovered the brain receptors for the neurotransmitters called endorphins and enkephalin.

humanistic perspective
Approach to psychology associated with Abraham Maslow and Carl Rogers; emphasizes free will and individuals' control of their own behavior

physiological perspective
View that behaviors and mental processes can be understood and explained by studying the underlying physiology

evolutionary perspective
Interest in the role a physiological structure or behavior plays in helping an organism adapt to its environment

To some, the psychodynamic approach was no more appealing because its proponents viewed behavior as resulting from irrational forces that are not even under conscious control. Psychoanalysts studied people suffering from a variety of pathological problems, whereas behaviorists attempted to identify conditions that influence behavior by studying lower animals under controlled laboratory conditions. Critics argued that neither of these perspectives led to a true understanding of human behavior because neither focused on the creative potential and psychological health of human beings. As a result, a new approach to psychology developed. Emphasizing free will and individuals' control of their own behavior, the **humanistic perspective** was characterized by a distinctly positive view of human nature. Humanistic psychologists viewed themselves as a "third force" because they were an alternative to the behavioral and psychodynamic perspectives in psychology (Goodwin, 1999).

The proponents of this approach, notably Carl Rogers (1902–1987) and Abraham Maslow (1908–1970), focused on the freedom they believed characterizes human behavior. According to the humanists, people have choices in their lives, and we cannot understand their choices by studying animals in laboratories or people experiencing adjustment problems.

Rather than attempting to develop general principles, Rogers and Maslow sought to understand each person as a unique individual. Humanists believe each person experiences the world differently. One of the most important humanistic principles is that all human beings have a basic need to grow to their fullest potential. The humanists' major contributions to psychology have been their dramatically different view of human nature and the development of a variety of psychotherapeutic techniques (Barton, 1992).

The Physiological Perspective

As we discuss in Chapter 2, every behavior of human beings and animals is related to some physiological change within the body. These physiological changes are the focus of psychologists interested in the **physiological perspective.** Physiological psychologists have a special interest in the functioning of the brain and the rest of the nervous system (Kalat, 2001). To assess neurological function they now use sophisticated equipment that can create images of the brain. These imaging techniques reveal differences in the functioning of various areas of the brain depending on the task given to a person.

Physiological psychologists also study how our nerve cells, called *neurons*, communicate with one another through special chemical substances called *neurotransmitters*. Scientists have identified a number of different neurotransmitters; each seems to play a special role in a variety of normal and abnormal behaviors. Most drugs influence our emotions and behaviors by altering levels of these neurotransmitters in the body.

During recent years physiological psychologists have shown a special interest in the influence of heredity on personality characteristics, abilities, and the potential for developing certain abnormal behavior patterns. A number of psychologists are examining the wide range of physiological changes that occur when we are under stress. Their research has determined that illness is not simply a function of the presence of disease-causing viruses or bacteria. More and more, psychologists are investigating how personal factors such as how we deal with stress can influence our health status.

The Evolutionary Perspective

Determining why a behavior or physical structure developed and how that behavior or structure aids in adaptation to the environment characterizes the **evolutionary perspective.** Charles Darwin (1859), who popularized the theory of evolution, maintained that evolution unfolds according to the principle of *natural selection*, which states that the strongest or most fit organisms are those that have adapted best to their environment. These organisms are more likely to survive and pass on their characteristics (genes) to future generations. Organisms with (or that inherit) different characteristics are less likely to survive. Therefore, researchers who work from an evolutionary perspective consistently ask what role a physiological structure or behavior plays in helping the organism survive and adapt to its environment. Researchers have successfully applied the evolutionary explanation to numerous areas, such as mate selection, aggression, kin selection, care of offspring, and parenting.

Let's see what an evolutionary explanation for a common behavior might look like. Consider a pet cat. What happens when the cat is frightened? The cat's hairs "stand on end." An evolutionary researcher would want to understand how this behavior contributed to the survival of the species. The most plausible explanation is that when the hairs are erected, the animal looks larger and more intimidating to potential predators. Hence, millions of years ago cats that were able to erect their hairs when they were frightened were more likely to scare off predators and survive to pass their genes on to future generations. Thus, this once-adaptive behavior persisted and continues to be displayed.

Now, let's consider an evolutionary explanation for a human behavior. Likely, we would receive little disagreement that aggression has the potential to aid in adaptation to the environment; aggressive organisms are able to acquire resources and defend their own territories. Now, would we predict a difference between men and women in the total amount of aggression they would display? No, there doesn't seem to be any reason to make such a distinction. How about the type of aggression they would display? Here's where evolutionary theory makes a distinction between men and women. It is predicted that men will display more direct aggression (hitting, kicking), whereas women will display more indirect aggression (gossiping, ostracizing). Why? The evolutionary explanation centers around maternal involvement on the part of women. According to Hagenah, Heaps, Gilden, and Roberts (2001) "high amounts of maternal care given to offspring require that women minimize their risk of physical injury" (p. 128). Indirect aggression minimizes the chances of retaliatory injury, compared to direct aggression. Research by Buss and Shackelford (1997) and Hagenah et al. (2001) supports these evolutionary predictions.

In addition to behaviors, evolutionary psychologists are also interested in why certain physical structures developed and how they contribute to adaptation. Consider the evolution of the human hand. Why do comparable structures differ among different species? Because such considerations will include an examination and understanding of the functioning of the structure involved, evolutionary psychologists frequently employ a *functional approach* in their research. Often they compare the use of a structure among species; such comparisons use the *comparative approach*.

    1.4

The Cognitive Perspective

Because they focused only on observable behaviors, the behaviorists did not study cognitive processes—processes such as thinking, remembering, and determining how material is organized and stored in the mind—as part of the mainstream of psychological research. Consequently, from the 1920s to the 1960s, psychologists gave little research attention to these processes. Certain psychologists, however, disagreed that observable behavior should be the sole subject matter of psychology. For example, the Gestalt psychologists advocated the study of cognitive processes. Psychologists George Miller and Jerome Bruner established the Center for Cognitive Studies at Harvard University in 1960, and Ulrich Neisser published the book *Cognitive Psychology* in 1967. The appearance of a widely read article supporting the study of cognitive processes (Liebman, 1979), combined with the ability of the computer to simulate human thought processes, generated considerable interest and research. Many psychologists have accepted the **cognitive perspective**—where the focus is on how thought occurs, memory processes, and information storage and utilization—and currently conduct research in the area of cognitive processes.

cognitive perspective
View that focuses on the study of how thought occurs, how our memories work, and how information is organized and stored

Mary Whiton Calkins, the 14th president of the American Psychological Association, was the first woman to be elected to that position.

Christine Ladd-Franklin was a noted researcher who was denied a regular academic position because she was married.

Milicent Shinn was the first woman to receive a Ph.D. from the University of California at Berkeley. She later abandoned her career to care for her aging parents.

The Cultural and Diversity Perspective

Attend a major meeting of psychologists and you are likely to be surrounded by dozens of different types of psychologists. Many are employed by colleges and universities, where they may teach, conduct research, or work in a psychological clinic sponsored by the university. The presence of women and minority psychologists provides a vivid contrast to the Caucasian, male-dominated field of only a few years ago. Psychologists are beginning to realize that the culture in which research is conducted; the gender, ethnicity, and personal biases of the researcher; and the gender and ethnicity of the research participants all influence our research results and contribute to our conception of "truth." Psychology is becoming more diverse, but this has not always been the case.

In the past, numerous barriers limited access to the field, especially for women and ethnic minorities. For example, Mary Whiton Calkins (1863–1930) completed her work at Harvard University, where she was a student of William James, but the university refused to award the doctoral degree she had earned because it did not grant degrees to women (Furumoto, 1979). Despite this setback, Calkins had a distinguished career in teaching, founded one of the first psychology laboratories in the United States, and was the first woman to be elected president of the American Psychological Association (Madigan & O'Hara, 1992).

In some cases, marital status and family ties hindered the careers of the first female psychologists. For example, the noted researcher Christine Ladd-Franklin "was not considered a suitable candidate for any regular academic position" because she was married (Furumoto, 1992, p. 180). Similarly, the tradition of the eldest daughter taking care of her aging parents cut short the budding career of Milicent Shinn, the first woman to receive a Ph.D. from the University of California at Berkeley in 1898. Shinn established herself as a leading expert on the mental and physical growth of infants and seemed poised for an eminent career in psychology until her parents' illness forced her to return to her family farm (Scarborough & Furumoto, 1987). Her career stopped completely at that point and was never resumed.

A century after Harvard refused to award Calkins a doctoral degree, women are entering the field of psychology in great numbers (see Figure 1-6). Women outnumber men two-to-one as undergraduate psychology majors and now earn more doctoral degrees in psychology than do men.

The struggle of racial minorities to become recognized professionals parallels that of the early women psychologists. Robert Guthrie (1998) summarized the struggles of African-American psychologists in his influential book *Even the Rat Was White.* For example, he indicates that professional training was not an option for black Americans during the late 1800s and early 1900s. It wasn't until 1920 that Francis C. Sumner (1895–1954) became the first African American to receive a Ph.D. in psychology. Subsequently, Sumner established the psychology program at Howard University and turned it into the major source for doctoral degrees for African-American students during the first half of the twentieth century. Sumner has been followed by a succession of eminent African-American psychologists such as James Arthur Bayton (1912–1990), who achieved national recognition for his marketing research.

Doctoral degrees in psychology were not granted to African-American women until the 1930s. Two women in this group are noteworthy. Inez Beverly Prosser (1897–1934) was the first African-American woman to receive a doctoral degree in educational psychology; she received this degree from the University of Cincinnati in 1933. Unfortunately, her career was cut short by a tragic automobile accident one year later. Ruth Winifred Howard (b. 1900) received her Ph.D. in psychology in 1934 from the University of Minnesota. She was the first person to publish research on triplets.

Until recently, few members of racial minority groups obtained jobs in psychology. Today the number of minority candidates receiving doctoral degrees and finding employment in psychology is increasing (Howard, A., et al., 1986). In fact, in 1970 the American Psychological Association elected an African American, Kenneth B. Clark

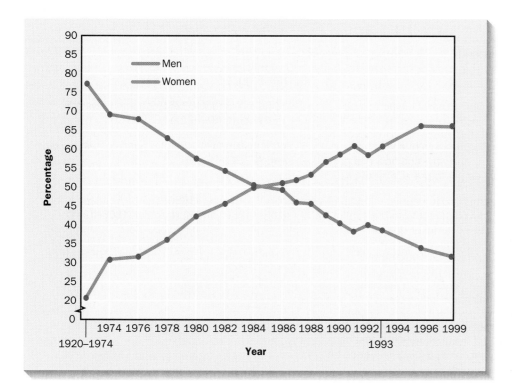

FIGURE 1-6 Percentages of doctoral degrees in psychology awarded to men and women.

Sources: Henderson, Clarke, & Woods, 1998; National Science Foundation, 2001.

Kenneth B. Clark was the first African American to serve as president of the American Psychological Association.

Mamie Phipps Clark conducted important research on consciousness of self and social indentification in African-American preschoolers.

STUDY TIP

Summarize the origins of modern psychology by writing a short "book" called "The Story of Psychology." For each page, create a summary of one of the perspectives of modern psychology. Think of it like a children's book—make your summaries short, straightforward, and written as though the reader were completely uninformed.

(b. 1914), as its president. Clark is noted for his research on the harmful effects of segregation, which was cited by the Supreme Court in the landmark 1954 case, *Brown v. Board of Education*. His wife, Mamie Phipps Clark (1917–1983), received her doctoral degree in psychology from Columbia University in 1944 and achieved considerable recognition through her research and publication on such topics as "The Development of Consciousness of Self and Emergence of Racial Identification in Negro Preschool Children," which appeared in a 1939 issue of the *Journal of Social Psychology*.

An Asian American, Richard Suinn, was elected president of the American Psychological Association in 1997. However, attaining prestigious offices in professional associations is not the only visible sign of the influence of culture and diversity.

The impact of different cultures and diversity on psychology is seen in contemporary psychological literature. Studies on diverse groups and topics—such as gender issues, ethnic groups, national cultures, sexual orientation, and persons with disabilities—abound in the psychological journals. It is arguable (Matsumoto, 1998) that there is a revolution afoot in the field of psychology; there is a move toward a cultural psychology where such topics are the rule rather than the exception. Psychologist David Matsumoto believes that "the psychological principles we derive about people may be consistent or discrepant across cultures. To the extent that differences do exist, it is important for all of us to appreciate how cultural factors moderate our psychological processes. In gaining such appreciation, we can learn how our own viewpoint, developed within our own cultural framework, can distort our interpretation of others' behaviors." For example, in a cross-cultural study of the intensity of facial expressions of emotion in Americans and Japanese, Matsumoto, Kasri, and Kooken (1999) showed that Americans exaggerated their ratings. Previously, it had been assumed that the difference between the two cultures occurred because Japanese participants suppressed their ratings. At the same time, we need to know what kinds of cross-cultural similarities exist in psychological principles and basic processes. Knowledge about these similarities as well should help us in our endeavors to apply these principles to improve our lives (Matsumoto, 1997, p. 2).

These different perspectives are summarized in the Study Chart on the next page.

Major Perspectives in Psychology

Perspective	Description	Key Figures
Structuralism	Attempted to identify the basic elements and structure of conscious experience	Wilhelm Wundt (1832–1920) and Edward B. Titchener (1867–1927)
Functionalism	Concerned with the purposes of consciousness—what the mind does and why—and how that information could be put to practical use	William James (1842–1910) and James Rowland Angell (1869–1949)
Gestalt psychology	Made major contributions to understanding how we perceive the world as different from the sum of its individual elements	Max Wertheimer (1880–1943), Wolfgang Köhler (1887–1967), and Kurt Koffka (1886–1941)
Behavioral	Focuses on observable behaviors without speculating about mental processes such as thinking; a major emphasis is that learning plays a key role in controlling and influencing all behaviors	John B. Watson (1878–1958) and B. F. Skinner (1904–1990)
Psychodynamic	Based on the belief that the unconscious mind exerts great control over behavior and that early childhood experiences are a major influence on personality development	Sigmund Freud (1856–1939)
Humanistic	Focuses on the creative potential and psychological health of human beings while emphasizing the individual's interpretation of events	Carl Rogers (1902–1987) and Abraham Maslow (1908–1970)
Physiological	Focuses on the underlying physiology involved in all forms of behavior and mental processes; uses increasingly sophisticated research tools to investigate brain functioning and conduction of nerve impulses; also investigates the role of heredity in normal and abnormal behavior patterns	Karl S. Lashley (1890–1958)
Evolutionary	Focuses on why a particular behavior or physical structure developed and how that behavior or structure aids in adaptation to the environment	D. M. Buss
Cognitive	Focuses on the processes of thinking, memory, and organizing and storing information	George Miller (b. 1920), Jerome Bruner (b. 1915), and Ulrich Neisser (b. 1928)
Cultural and diversity	Focuses on the influence that different cultures and diverse individuals have on the research process and the results of that process	Janet Hyde and David Matsumoto

PRESENT-DAY PSYCHOLOGY

Psychologists today are interested in a diversity of topics. In fact, there are few endeavors that would not interest at least one of the more than half-million psychologists in the world (Rosenzweig, 1992).

Present-day psychologists do not align themselves strictly with any of the approaches we outlined in our earlier discussion of the origins of psychology. Instead they tend to choose the approach they consider appropriate to each issue under consideration. Because they use several approaches, many psychologists have adopted an **eclectic approach** to psychology.

eclectic approach
View of psychology that combines several different approaches

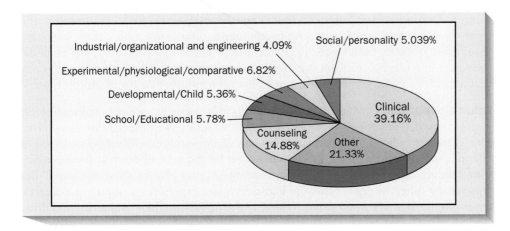

FIGURE 1-7   Specialties in psychology.

Note: Figures are based on a survey of doctoral recipients, 1986–96.

Source: Henderson, Clarke & Woods, 1998.

Most psychologists earn an advanced degree, usually a doctorate. In a number of states a person cannot assume the title of *psychologist* unless he or she meets certain standards of education and training set by a state board. Psychologists all over the world are working to establish legal status for their profession. Their purpose is to protect the public by ensuring that people who represent themselves as psychologists have appropriate training and professional experience.

Although all psychologists share a keen interest in advancing our knowledge of human and animal behavior through research, some psychologists, by choice, engage in little or no research. A rapidly growing number of psychologists have entered what are termed *health service provider* or *direct service specialties* (Howard, A., et al., 1986). These psychologists are interested primarily in the applications of psychology. As you can see from Figure 1-7, the largest specialty in psychology is a direct service one, clinical psychology.

PSYCHOLOGICAL SPECIALTIES

Clinical and Counseling Psychology.   Most students who major in psychology are interested in the work done by clinical psychologists. More and more students want to "work with people." Although most psychologists work with people in one way or another, those involved in **clinical psychology** specialize in helping people with behavioral or emotional problems adjust to the demands of life.

Clinical psychologists are frequently confused with psychiatrists (Murstein & Fontaine, 1993). Members of these two professions share an interest in diagnosing and treating people who are experiencing various behavioral and emotional problems. Clinical psychologists and psychiatrists differ, however, in the advanced degrees they obtain and in other aspects of their training. After completing an undergraduate degree, clinical psychologists earn a doctoral degree (Ph.D. or Psy.D.), which usually takes four or more years. They then complete an internship of at least one year to develop their diagnostic and therapeutic skills; during this time they are supervised by experienced clinical psychologists.

By contrast, **psychiatrists** are medical doctors; they have earned an M.D. degree. After graduating from medical school, they complete a three-year residency, often at a major psychiatric hospital. Although some aspects of the training of clinical psychologists and psychiatrists are similar, there are major differences. For example, psychiatrists are trained in the medical assessment of disorders and hence are more likely to view the disorders as caused by medical conditions. Their treatments reflect this medical orientation—they are likely to prescribe drugs to alleviate their patients' symptoms.

A specialty that has much in common with clinical psychology is **counseling psychology;** counseling psychologists also administer psychological tests and provide

clinical psychology
Specialty of psychology that involves the diagnosis and treatment of psychological disorders

psychiatrist
Medical doctor with specialized training in the medical treatment of mental and emotional disorders

counseling psychology
Specialty of psychology that deals with less serious problems than those treated by clinical psychologists

research psychologist
Psychologist whose primary activity is to conduct and report the results of experiments

ethnocentrism
The view that other cultures are an extension of one's own

cross-cultural psychology
Branch of psychology whose goal is to determine if research results can be applied to other cultures

therapy. One difference between clinical and counseling psychologists involves the types of clients they see. Counseling psychologists often work with clients who have less serious problems than those of patients seen by clinical psychologists. For example, the counseling psychologist is more likely to deal with people who are having difficulty dealing with everyday problems, such as a physical handicap or a vocational decision.

Other Specialties.   Many people believe that psychologists are engaged exclusively in providing diagnostic and therapeutic services to sufferers of mental disorders; however, there is a wide range of specialties beyond clinical and counseling psychology. For example, you may hear the term *experimental psychologist* used to describe psychologists who conduct experiments on learning, motivation, and physiological processes. Because many different types of psychologists conduct experiments, the term **research psychologist** is more appropriate. Table 1-4 summarizes these research specialties. Often you will find research psychologists dividing their duties between conducting research and teaching at a college or university.

Because modern psychology is identified so highly with the United States, we may have a tendency to view our psychological research as applying to all other cultures. The view that other cultures are an extension of your own is called **ethnocentrism** (Smith & Davis, 2004). **Cross-cultural psychology** is a branch of psychology that seeks to determine if research results are universal (that is, if they can be generalized or applied to other cultures [Matsumoto, 1994]). As psychologists recognize the increasingly diverse nature of their field, the importance of cross-cultural research is clearly highlighted. The understanding of "human" behavior requires that we know which of our findings are universal and which are limited to specific cultures. This approach has aided the development and expansion of the culture and diversity perspective we discussed previously.

TABLE 1-4

Research Psychologists and Their Interests

Area or Specialty	Description of Research Interests
Animal behavior	Behavior and basic learning processes; comparative studies using different species
Biopsychology/ neuropsychology	Physiological mechanisms of learning, memory, and behavior
Cognitive processes	Mental processes used to take in, store, and utilize information in thinking, remembering, and making decisions
Cross-cultural	Research conducted to determine whether results are universal or culture-specific
Developmental	Processes of growth, development, and change throughout the entire life span
Educational	Application of psychological findings and principles to the classroom
Motivation	Causes and consequences of motivation in animals and humans
Personality	Factors that make individuals unique, as well as factors that are shared
Psychometrics	Theoretical and practical aspects of psychological testing and measurement
Sensation and perception	Process of sensory input and the use and interpretation of sensory information
Social	Influence of other people on behavior

Psychological Detective

How might cultural differences affect the development and conduct of psychological research? Write down some possibilities before reading further.

The different attitudes, values, and behaviors held by different cultures can influence the choice of research problems, the research hypothesis that is developed, the variables that are studied, and even the type of survey or questionnaire that is used. In short, culture has the potential to influence all aspects of psychological research. Hence we must be very cautious in generalizing results from one culture to another. Finally, keep in mind that there are numerous different cultural groups within the United States; their differences must also be considered. Just because a piece of research was conducted in the United States does not guarantee that its results are applicable to all Americans. Clearly, these cross-cultural issues must be the concern of all research psychologists.

School psychologists are employed by school systems as consultants to other educational personnel. Can you imagine a time when "there were no state or national level organizations to serve the interests of school psychologists, no codes of practice, no training or credentialing guidelines, and no accreditation or credentialing" (Fagan, 2000, p. 756). In the 21st century, with such organizations as the National Association of School Psychologists (NASP) developing standards, accrediting programs, and hosting an annual national convention, and the American Psychological Association having a separate division for school psychologists, such conditions may seem more like a flight into imagination and fancy than based in reality. These conditions were, however, the order of the day in the late 1800s and early 1900s. Currently, a school psychologist may visit several schools in a district during the course of a week to make psychological evaluations, discuss specific students with teachers, and meet with parents.

Industrial and organizational psychologists (also known as **I/O psychologists**; see Chapter 16) are concerned with all aspects of work and the structure and function of organizations. Their responsibilities vary with the employer, but they may be asked to design a system for selecting employees or to implement an employee assistance program to deal with alcoholism, drug abuse, and stress both on and off the job. Once new employees are hired, I/O psychologists may assist in designing and evaluating programs to train them for their new jobs. In addition, they may be asked to design methods to measure worker productivity, increase worker motivation, evaluate work schedule efficiency, or design systems for resolving disputes within organizations (Jewell, 1998).

Some I/O psychologists are involved in the design of equipment and manufacturing plants. When they design equipment, they take into consideration the relation between the worker and the equipment and, also, the capabilities of the worker. These psychologists are also called human factors psychologists, and they work in a specialty that is called *ergonomics.*

Consumer psychology is the scientific study of the behavior of consumers. Although your last purchase of a portable cassette player or a hair dryer may have seemed an unremarkable event, such apparently casual events provide the basis for consumer psychologists' questions. They may want to know how you became aware of the product, how you went about evaluating various brands, or what made you select a particular brand.

A recent addition to the list of psychology's specialties is **health psychology.** This diverse and rapidly growing specialty is concerned with the relations between psychological factors and health. Health psychologists work to promote health and prevent illness; they study the causes and treatments of illness and the ways people cope with their illnesses (see Chapter 14). They also investigate ways to reduce risk for disease by changing unhealthy or harmful behaviors (Friedman, 2002). For example, they may investigate the effects of exercise on cholesterol levels and subsequent heart attacks, or they may evaluate techniques to encourage the practice of safe sex. Because stress is an ever-present part of our lives, health psychologists also try to increase our understanding

school psychologist
Psychologist whose specialty encompasses diagnosing and treating learning disabilities and providing consultation on other problems of school-age children

industrial and organizational (I/O) psychologist
Psychologist who applies psychology to problems of businesses and other organizations

consumer psychology
Specialty of psychology that studies consumers and the choices they make

health psychology
Subfield of psychology that is concerned with how psychological and social variables affect health and illness

TABLE 1-5

Job Titles Held by Psychology Majors with Bachelor's Degrees

A. Job Titles Directly Related to Psychology

Academic advisor	Director of volunteer services	Public information specialist
Alcohol/drug abuse counselor	Eligibility worker	Public relations specialist
Behavior analyst	Employment counselor	Publications researcher
Career counselor	Family services worker	Radio/TV research assistant
Career planning and placement	Gerontology aide	Rehabilitation advisor
Counselor	Group home coordinator	Residential counselor
Case management aide	Housing/student life coordinator	Residential youth counselor
Case worker	Life skill counselor	Secondary school teacher
Child care worker	Mental health technician	Social service assistant
Child protection worker	Mental retardation unit manager	Social services director
Community outreach worker	Parole officer	Social work assistant
Community support worker	Political campaign worker	Urban planning research assistant
Corrections officer	Probation officer	Veteran's advisor
Counselor aide	Program manager	
Day care center supervisor	Public affairs coordinator	

B. Job Titles Not Directly Related to Psychology, but Appropriate for Psychology Majors

Administrative assistant	Fast food restaurant manager	Newspaper reporter
Advertising agent	Film researcher/copywriter	Occupational analyst
Advertising trainee	Financial researchers	Park and recreation director
Affirmative action representative	Historical research assistant	Personnel worker/administrator
Airline reservations clerk	Hospital patient services representative	Public information officer
Claims specialist	Human resources recruiter	Public relations
College admissions officer	Insurance agent	Sales representative
Community recreation worker	Intelligence officer	Small business owner
Congressional aide	Job analyst	Staff training and development
Customer relations	Law enforcement officer	Statistical assistant
Customer service representative	Loan officer	Store manager
Director of alumni relations	Lobbying organizer	Technical writer
Director of fund raising	Management trainee	Vocational rehabilitation counselor
Employee counselor	Marketing representative	Warehouse manager
Employee relations assistant	Marketing researcher	
Energy researcher	Media buyer	

Source: Adapted from Landrum & Davis, 2004.

of the factors related to stress and to discover ways to alleviate its negative consequences. For example, health psychologist Tom Boll is using psychological tests and other measures to select potential heart transplant patients who are best able to handle the stress of the operation (De Angelis, 1992).

Emerging Specialties.   Psychology is not a static science; its proponents continually strive to discover new arenas for research and application. Among the recent additions to the field are forensic (legal) psychology, sport psychology, and neuropsychology.

Forensic psychologists work within the legal system; they may work in a prison to evaluate incoming prisoners or assist in selecting a jury for a trial (Weiner & Hess, 1999; Wrightsman, Nietzel, & Fortune, 1994). Carefully wording the questions asked of prospective jurors can help identify potentially biased jurors, who can then be excused from service (Cutler, Moran, & Narby, 1992; Goodman, Loftus, & Greene, 1990). Forensic psychologists also provide testimony as expert witnesses (see Chapter 7). For example, psychologist Elizabeth Loftus has testified many times about how stress affects the accuracy of recalled events, how observing violent crimes affects eyewitness identifications, or how police lineups can sometimes lead witnesses to an incorrect identification of a suspect (Loftus, 1991).

Sport psychologists apply the theories and knowledge of psychology to enhance athletes' performance (Wann, 1997). They may consult with coaches about the use of specific coaching techniques or provide supportive therapy and encouragement to players recovering from injuries. They also help athletes improve their performance by using techniques such as relaxation and imagery (Green, 1992; Murphy, 1994). Since 1978, sport psychologists have been part of the team of experts who help U.S. athletes prepare for the Olympics.

Given that Congress designated the 1990s as "the decade of the brain," it is not surprising that one of the emerging specialties in psychology is concerned with brain functioning (see Chapter 2). **Neuropsychologists** are trained to diagnose disorders of the brain. Using various tests, they try to identify specific brain areas that may be malfunctioning. They often conduct research to identify early symptoms that predict the development of disorders such as Huntington's disease (Diamond et al., 1992). They also devise rehabilitation programs to help patients regain as much of their abilities as possible after suffering brain damage, strokes, or traumatic brain injury (Diller, 1992).

If you are thinking about a career in psychology after you graduate, there are numerous employment opportunities for psychology majors with a bachelor's degree. In fact, the job possibilities are as diverse as the field of psychology itself. Several job possibilities are shown in Table 1-5.

forensic psychologist
Psychologist who applies psychology to law and legal proceedings

sport psychologist
Psychologist who provides services to athletes and coaches based on psychological principles

neuropsychologist
Psychologist trained in the diagnosis and rehabilitation of brain disorders

R E V I E W   S U M M A R Y

1. The history of modern psychology began in 1879, when Wilhelm Wundt established the first psychology laboratory at the University of Leipzig in Germany. The goal of Wundt's school of psychology, known as **structuralism,** was to identify the elements of conscious experience by using the method of **introspection.**

2. Another perspective, which came to be known as **functionalism,** focused on the purposes of consciousness and was especially concerned with the applications of psychology. **Gestalt psychology** is concerned primarily with our perception of our environment. **Cognitive psychology** studies higher mental processes such as thinking, knowing, and deciding.

3. Influenced by the Russian physiologist Ivan Pavlov, John B. Watson was interested in how the environment affects behavior.

Because consciousness cannot be observed directly, Watson defined psychology as the study of observable behavior. The **behavioral perspective** was continued by B. F. Skinner, probably the best known and most influential psychologist of our time.

4. Sigmund Freud's **psychodynamic perspective** focused on unconscious determinants of behavior. Freud also developed a treatment approach known as **psychoanalytic therapy.**

5. Dissatisfaction with both the behavioral and the psychodynamic perspectives led psychologists Abraham Maslow and Carl Rogers to develop the **humanistic perspective.** Humanists believe that other perspectives pay too little attention to uniquely human characteristics such as free will and individual control.

6. The **physiological perspective** focuses on the underlying biological bases of all forms of behavior.

7. The **evolutionary perspective** focuses on why a particular behavior or physical structure developed and how that behavior or structure aids in adaptation to the environment.

8. The field of psychology has begun to recognize the contributions made by women and ethnic minorities, and additional contributions from these groups can be expected in the future. The **cultural and diversity perspective** focuses on such research contributions.

9. Most psychologists have earned a doctoral degree (Ph.D. or Psy.D.). Although many psychologists teach and engage in research, a growing number provide direct services to clients.

✓ CHECK YOUR PROGRESS

1. Who is credited with establishing the first psychological laboratory?

   a. Ivan Pavlov
   b. William James
   c. Max Wertheimer
   d. Wilhelm Wundt

2. An early proponent of functionalism who was interested in the stream of consciousness was

   a. Ivan Pavlov.
   b. William James.
   c. Wilhelm Wundt.
   d. Max Wertheimer.

3. Gestalt psychology had its greatest impact in the study of

   a. memory.
   b. perception.
   c. nerve conduction.
   d. abnormal behavior.

4. What barrier toward becoming a psychologist did Mary Whiton Calkins face in the late 1880s?

   a. As a woman, she could not complete graduate courses at Harvard.
   b. As a woman, Harvard would not award her the doctoral degree she earned.
   c. Women could not establish psychological laboratories in the United States at that time.
   d. She was not allowed to join the American Psychological Association.

5. What is the current gender representation in psychology?

   a. Men earn more doctoral degrees than do women.
   b. Women and men earn approximately equal numbers of doctoral degrees.
   c. Women earn more doctoral degrees than do men.
   d. Psychology does not categorize doctoral degrees by gender.

6. Each of the following descriptions could apply to one of the historical perspectives on psychology discussed in this chapter. Which perspective best fits the description?

   a. believes unconscious forces are the most significant determinants of behavior
   b. is concerned with the biological processes involved in a behavior
   c. is interested in the elements of consciousness
   d. believes the whole is different from the sum of its parts
   e. is interested in studying decision making and problem solving

7. Identify the person who is most likely to have made each of the following statements.

   a. "I never received my Ph.D., although I earned it."
   b. "The study of my patients convinces me that unconscious forces lie beneath many of their disturbances."
   c. "What impresses me about human behavior is the freedom each of us has to make choices."

8. Name the type of psychologist (or specialty) described in each of the following:

   a. was asked to diagnose and treat a 35-year-old man who hears frightening voices every day
   b. helped an out-of-work auto mechanic decide on a new career
   c. designed a survey to determine whether purchasers of a liquid detergent were satisfied with the product
   d. testified as an expert witness on factors that influence the accuracy of eyewitnesses

ANSWERS: 1. d **2.** b **3.** b **4.** b **5.** c **6. a.** Psychodynamic **b.** Physiological **c.** Structuralism **d.** Gestalt **e.** Cognitive **7. a.** Mary Whiton Calkins **b.** Sigmund Freud **c.** Abraham Maslow or Carl Rogers **8. a.** Clinical psychologist **b.** Counseling psychologist **c.** Consumer psychologist **d.** Forensic psychologist

ANSWERS   ## To Questions in Table 1-2

1. The answer depends on the hemisphere you are in when you answer the question. For people in the Northern Hemisphere, the Earth is closer to the sun from September to May; for people in the Southern Hemisphere, the Earth is closer to the sun from May to September. The degree of warmth is not associated with distance from the sun; the tilt of the earth as it receives the sun's rays determines warmth.

2. It depends. If the country minting the coin is the United States, the answer is Abraham Lincoln (you may be aware of the much older and very valuable "Indianhead" pennies). In Canada, the Queen of England appears on a penny.

3. The answer is Sophie Kurys, who played for the Racine Belles in the Women's Professional Baseball League in 1946; she stole 202 bases.

4. The answer is simple, provided that assmptions do not get in your way. Extend the line on the right side downward and you will produce the number 4 (a perfect square).

Behavioral Neuroscience

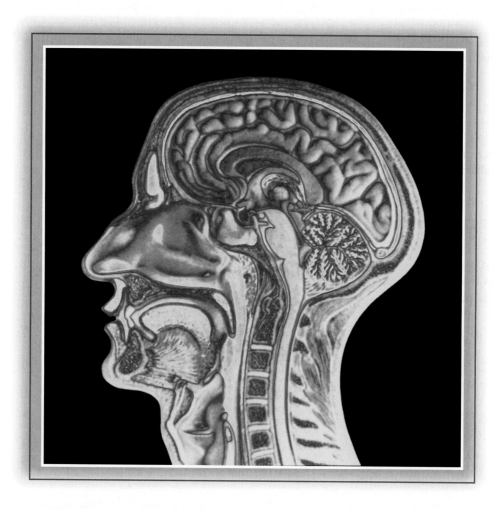

CHAPTER OUTLINE

Этhis chapter begins our in-depth exploration of the various areas of psychology. As you progress through the pages of this book, you will notice that our plan is to move from basic topics to general and broad ones. Notice we did not say that we would progress from the simple to the complex. As you read about the nervous system, the endocrine system, and our basic biological processes in this chapter, we are sure you will agree that these topics are not simple. Sensing, processing, and responding are vital to our ability to adapt to a changing environment. In subsequent chapters we expand our discussion of the biological basis of psychological processes to include such topics as how we receive and process information from the environment (Chapter 3) and the various states of consciousness that we may experience (Chapter 4). From time to time throughout the book we will return to a consideration of the biological basis of behaviors to help explain topics such as human development (Chapter 9), the varieties of abnormal behavior (Chapter 12), and some forms of treatment (Chapter 13).

BIOLOGY AND BEHAVIOR

Thousands of years ago, our ancestors roamed the planet trying as best they could to survive. They faced animals that saw them as prey and they navigated in darkness that frequently made movement dangerous. Some of our ancestors survived and passed on their genes to subsequent generations; others perished. Across thousands of years and numerous generations, the brain and the rest of humans' nervous system was evolving. Those persons who survived left us a legacy of emotional reactions such as fear that had survival value, as well as a broad collection of bodily changes that motivated us to fight or to flee. As new ways of coping with the environment developed, the brain encoded these methods, which enabled us to transmit them to new generations for future use. *What is the significance of biology for understanding animal and human behavior?*

The study of the relationship between biological and psychological functions is rapidly expanding, complex, and fascinating. Knowing how the human body and brain work helps us to understand many areas of psychology: the nature of personality, the causes of certain abnormal behaviors, our reaction to stressful situations, the effectiveness of some types of therapy with certain patients but not with others, and much more. Recognition of the potential importance of the relation of the nervous system to behavior led the U.S. Congress to designate the 1990s as "the decade of the brain."

In their efforts to understand the brain and the rest of the nervous system, many researchers have adopted an *evolutionary perspective* (Gaulin & McBurney, 2001; Gray, 1995), which focuses on the role a particular physical structure or behavior plays in helping an organism adapt to its environment over time. This perspective began with an around-the-world scientific journey taken by Charles Darwin. The large array of animal and plant species Darwin collected was intriguing; he wondered why nature came in so many varieties. His efforts at answering this question led to "what may be the single most important and far-reaching scientific theory that has ever been formulated (Gaulin & McBurney, 2001, p. 19). Darwin (1859) maintained that evolution unfolds

natural selection
According to Charles Darwin, the process by which inherited characteristics that lead to an advantage in adapting to the environment are more likely to be passed on to subsequent generations through genetic material

behavioral neuroscience
A general term encompassing a range of disciplines such as neurology, psychology, psychiatry that focus on the role of the nervous system, especially the brain, in understanding behavior

stimulus
Environmental feature that provokes a response from an organism

receptors
Specialized cells that are sensitive to specific types of stimulus energy

2.1

according to the principle of **natural selection:** the process by which inherited characteristics that lead to an advantage in adapting to the environment are more likely to be passed on (through genetic material) to future generations. Over thousands of years of evolution, mutations have occurred in the grand plan for development contained in an organism's genes. Some of these mutations result in changes that increase the chances of survival. For example, the mutation resulting in an eagle's strong talons and sharp beak gave those organisms an advantage in catching and devouring prey, compared to eagles without these changes. Consequently, these physical characteristics were passed to future generations. Certain species of moths have spots on their wings that resemble the eyes of the predator owl. How would such a characteristic be advantageous? These spots are generally hidden; however, when a bird (such as an owl) approaches, the moth's wings flip open exposing the eyespots. Birds tend to fly away when they see the spots, keeping the moths relatively safe from predators (Carlson, 2001). Accordingly, researchers who work from an evolutionary perspective ask what role a physical structure or behavior plays in helping an organism survive and adapt to its environment.

In addition to studying the process of natural selection, researchers also focus on discovering the actual genetic material responsible for the physical structure or behavior under investigation. We say more about genetics in Chapter 9. Keep the evolutionary perspective in mind as you read this book. See if it helps you understand why a particular behavior or physical structure developed.

The researchers who study the biological basis of animal and human behavior are working in an area called **behavioral neuroscience.** This relatively new term focuses attention on the relation between biological factors and behavior. What's more, the term implies that these scientists represent several disciplines including psychology (especially physiological psychologists), biology, medicine, and others. Why are so many disciplines involved? These researchers are studying the nervous system, which includes the brain—*the* most complex machine ever constructed. In fact, the brain is infinitely more complex than the most sophisticated computer! Our examination of this very complex machine begins with an overview of how humans relate to their environment.

To survive, human beings must be able to perform three interrelated activities: sensing events, or *stimuli*; processing stimuli; and responding to stimuli. A **stimulus** is a feature in the environment—such as a traffic light, a sign, an alarm, or the smell of smoke—that may provoke a response. The specialized cells of the nervous system that sense stimuli are called **receptors.** We discuss several receptors (for example, those

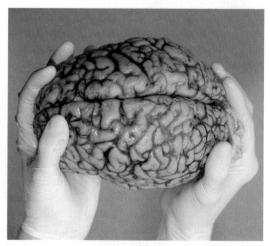

Although the laptop on the left and the human brain on the right are approximately the same size, the computer is the product of the human brain. Despite its size, the human brain has been called the most complex machine ever constructed. Part of its complexity derives from the millions of connections that are possible among its component parts. And unlike the computer, the human brain is capable of creativity and can, in some ways, even repair damage to itself.

A Sensing   **B** Processing   **C** Responding

FIGURE 2-1 An example of the activities of sensing, processing, and responding to stimuli. You are driving down the road and come to a light that is amber, about to turn red. You also notice (Step 1) a sign restricting turns depending on the time of day. You have a lot of information to process and sort out (Step 2). You decide to stop at the light and quickly recognize that you can make the turn on a red after stopping. You stop and then proceed to make the turn (Step 3).

located in the eyes and ears) in Chapter 3. For now, remember that we are concerned with a chain of events that typically begins when a stimulus activates a receptor.

The second activity in the chain is interpreting, or *processing*, the information that reaches the receptors. This processing typically takes place in the brain. Once we've processed and understood the sensory input, we may need to respond to it. Therefore, the third activity occurs when the brain sends messages to the muscles to produce a response. As you can see in Figure 2-1, these three activities are involved in events as common as driving a car.

THE NERVOUS SYSTEM

The activities of sensing, processing, and responding are coordinated and controlled by the nervous system, which has two major divisions (Figure 2-2): the **central nervous system (CNS)** and the **peripheral nervous system (PNS).** The CNS consists of the brain and spinal cord; the PNS connects the outer portions (or periphery) of the body with the CNS.

The brain has two halves (called *hemispheres*), one for the right side of the body and one for the left. The right hemisphere receives input from the left side of the body, and the left hemisphere receives input from the right side of the body. The arrangement whereby each hemisphere receives input from the opposite side of the body is called *contralateral conduction.* The basic cells of the nervous system are **neurons,** and we say more about them shortly. First, we take a closer look at the peripheral and central nervous systems.

The Peripheral Nervous System

The PNS consists of all the parts of the nervous system that are outside the CNS. If we think of the nervous system as a computer, the PNS would consist of the "peripherals," such as the monitor, keyboard, or printer, which transport information in and out of the central portion of the computer. The two major divisions of the PNS are the somatic division and the autonomic division (see Figure 2-2).

The Somatic Division. The **somatic division** of the PNS makes contact with the environment. It consists of nerves that connect receptors to the spinal cord and brain,

central nervous system (CNS)
Division of the nervous system that consists of the brain and spinal cord

peripheral nervous system (PNS)
Division of the nervous system that consists of the neural fibers lying outside the brain and spinal cord

neurons
Basic cells of the nervous system

somatic division
Division of the peripheral nervous system that consists of nerves coming from the receptors to the brain and spinal cord, as well as nerves that go from the brain and spinal cord to the muscles

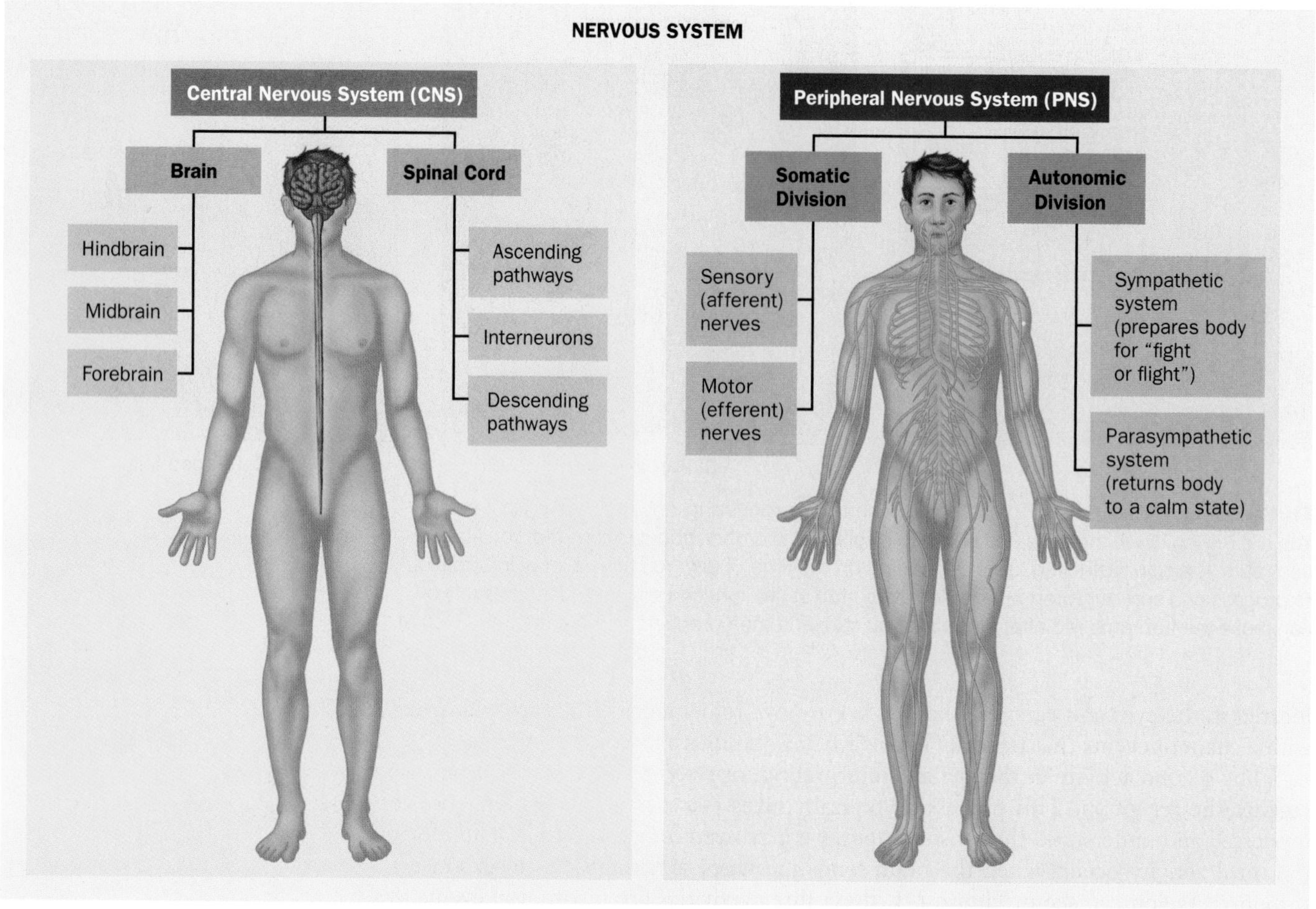

NERVOUS SYSTEM

FIGURE 2-2 Major divisions of the nervous system: the peripheral nervous system (PNS) and the central nervous system (CNS). The CNS consists of the brain and spinal cord. The PNS connects the outer portions of the body with the CNS.

afferent (sensory) nerves
Nerves that carry information from the receptors to the spinal cord and brain

efferent (motor) nerves
Nerves that carry information from the brain and spinal cord to the muscles

autonomic division
Division of the peripheral nervous system involved in the control of bodily functioning through organs and glands

sympathetic system
Subdivision of the autonomic nervous system that is responsible for mobilizing the body in times of stress, preparing organisms for "fight or flight"

as well as nerves that go *to* and *from* the brain and spinal cord to the muscles. The nerves that carry information from the receptors to the brain and spinal cord are called **afferent (sensory) nerves;** those that carry information from the brain and spinal cord to the muscles are called **efferent (motor) nerves.** The somatic division is involved in sensing and responding, Steps 1 and 3 of the chain of events described in Figure 2-1. As you are driving, your eyes are scanning the environment and you pick up the changing traffic light and signs (Step 1). Afferent nerves convey information about the traffic light and signs to the CNS to be processed: Is the light red or is it amber? Do I stop or continue; and, if I continue, may I turn on a red light (Step 2)? Efferent nerves then convey information from the CNS so you can make a response (Step 3). Because the responses we make are often planned and organized, the somatic division is said to be a *voluntary* system—that is, under our conscious control.

The Autonomic Division.   The **autonomic division** of the PNS affects our organs and glands in ways that regulate bodily functioning. Because the autonomic division operates without our conscious awareness, it is described as an *automatic*, or *involuntary*, system. The autonomic division has two main components: the sympathetic system and the parasympathetic system.

The Sympathetic System.   The **sympathetic system** mobilizes the body in times of stress or danger. In ancient times, this mobilization was especially helpful in dealing with dangerous animals. Our ancestors' bodies were prepared for "fight or flight" when their sympathetic system was activated (see Chapters 6 and 14). Have you ever been scared by a loud clap of thunder? How did you react when someone suddenly pulled in front of you as you were driving? Did your heart start to race? Did your skin tingle? Did your muscles tense? These indicators of physiological arousal were produced by the sympathetic nervous system.

Psychological Detective

Suppose that your tire blows out while driving at a high rate of speed. After this happens, the sympathetic nervous system is at work. You become prepared for fight or flight—mostly flight, in this case. Imagine yourself in this situation. Which sympathetic processes are in operation? Write down the processes that you would experience and then read further.

The reactions that you experience when your tire blew out or while giving your first class presentation are evidence that the sympathetic system is operating. During these times the body is prepared for action by a series of coordinated changes, including enlargement (dilation) of the pupils of the eyes, acceleration of the heart rate, inhibition of digestive activities, and release of sugar (glucose) to produce energy.

Look at the left side of Figure 2-3 to see the major sympathetic responses. Are there any that you are not experiencing when you are "scared out of your wits" at a horror movie? Most likely you experience all of them to some degree in this rather stressful

FIGURE 2-3   The sympathetic and parasympathetic systems of the autonomic division and their functions.

Source: Shaver & Terpy, 1993.

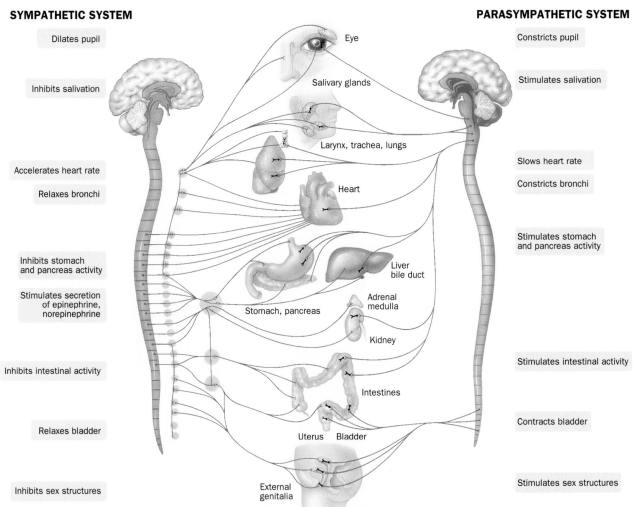

STUDY TIP

Make flash cards for the sympathetic and parasympathetic systems; on one side, write the organ and either "sympathetic" or "parasympathetic," and on the other side, write the organ's function in that particular system. Make sure all organs are accounted for in both systems—in other words, you should have two cards for each organ, one sympathetic and one parasympathetic. Then, do flash card drills with a classmate, seeing if you can both guess the functions correctly.

parasympathetic system
Subdivision of the autonomic nervous system that is responsible for returning the body to a resting or balanced state

homeostasis
The tendency of the body to maintain a balanced state; characterized by the functioning of an optimal range of physiological processes

reflex
Automatic behavior in response to a specific stimulus

situation. Notice that some of these processes involve an increase in a particular bodily function, whereas others involve a decrease in function.

The Parasympathetic System. The **parasympathetic system** slows the processes that have been accelerated by activation of the sympathetic system. For example, when the parasympathetic system is operating, the pupils of the eye constrict (or close) and heart rate slows. These effects, and others shown on the right side of Figure 2-3, return the body to a more normal or balanced state of functioning, characterized by an optimal range of physiological processes, called **homeostasis.**

The Central Nervous System

The other major division of the nervous system, the CNS, consists of the brain and spinal cord (see Figure 2-2). The CNS is analogous to the engine of a car or to the central processing unit (CPU) of a computer. The following section introduces some of the components of the CNS.

The Spinal Cord. The spinal cord is tucked safely into a protective jacket known as the *vertebral column*, which in humans is made up of 24 bones called *vertebrae*. The sensory nerves of the PNS enter the spinal cord and the motor nerves exit the spinal cord between the vertebrae in an orderly manner (see Figure 2-4): Sensory nerves enter the back portion of the spinal cord; motor nerves exit from the front portion. The spinal cord serves as the body's information superhighway. Information that is not processed solely within the spinal cord itself is sent to the brain via ascending pathways; information that is sent back down from the brain follows descending pathways. Within the central nervous system, *interneurons* connect neurons to each other. They send information either directly to a motor nerve so a response can be made or sent up the spinal cord for further processing by the brain. Figure 2-4 shows interneurons in the spinal cord.

When information provided by the sensory nerves does not have to travel all the way to the brain to produce a response, automatic behaviors known as **reflexes** are produced. The message that brings about a reflex typically takes a shorter journey than

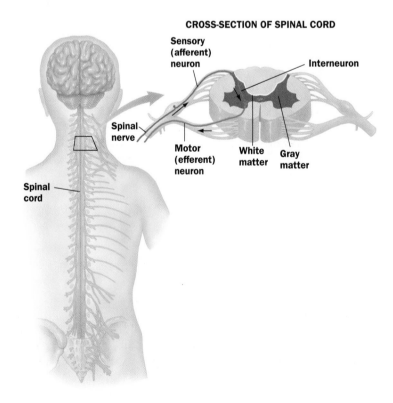

FIGURE 2-4 Cross-section of the spinal cord. Sensory nerves enter and motor nerves exit in an organized manner. In many cases, the sensory and motor nerves are connected by small interneurons.

Source: Benjamin, Hopkins, & Nation, 1989.

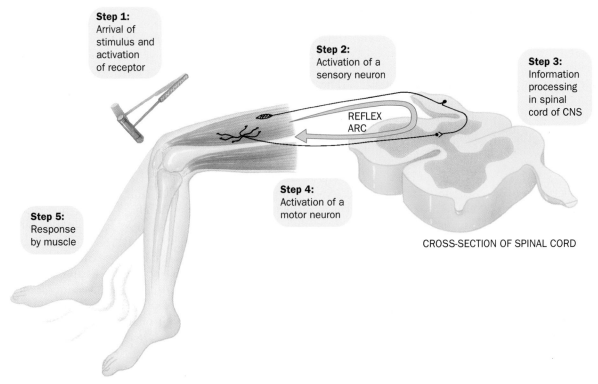

Step 1:
Arrival of stimulus and activation of receptor

Step 2:
Activation of a sensory neuron

Step 3:
Information processing in spinal cord of CNS

REFLEX ARC

Step 4:
Activation of a motor neuron

Step 5:
Response by muscle

CROSS-SECTION OF SPINAL CORD

FIGURE 2-5 The knee-jerk reflex. A light tap on the knee sends information to the spinal cord. Information is then sent from the spinal cord to cause muscular contraction. Note that this reflex arc (stimulus-to-spinal cord response) does not involve processing by the brain.

Source: Martini & Bartholomew, 2000.

it would if it had gone to the brain for further processing. This shortened distance means faster conduction, which has an evolutionary advantage. Touch a hot stove and your hand withdrawal occurs quickly. Why? The sensory message does not have to go all the way to the brain. The sensory nerve is connected by an interneuron in the spinal cord to a motor nerve that leads to withdrawal. If a physician hits your knee lightly with a hammer, your leg would jerk reflexively—that is, quickly, automatically, and involuntarily. As you can see in Figure 2-5, when the knee-jerk reflex occurs, the sensory information produced by hitting your knee enters the spinal cord and contacts the efferent nerve, which returns a signal almost immediately to your leg to produce movement. Similarly, an object placed in an infant's mouth stimulates a sucking reflex. Because reflexes are automatic, we may not even realize that they have occurred. Reflexes occur *very* rapidly: the reaction to a painful stimulus occurs in approximately 0.8 millisecond (a millisecond is 1/1,000 of a second).

THE ENDOCRINE SYSTEM

Besides the nervous system, which is crucial to the activities of sensing, processing, and responding, another system plays a major role in shaping and controlling behavior and mental processes. The **endocrine system** consists of glands that produce and *secrete* (release) chemicals known as **hormones.** When stimulated, the endocrine glands secrete hormones into the bloodstream. The blood flow carries hormones throughout the body and, ultimately, to their target, which may be another gland located some distance away. As we discuss the endocrine system, keep in mind that it can, and does, interact with the nervous system.

endocrine system
System of glands that produce and secrete chemicals called hormones that can have effects some distance from the gland that secreted the hormone

hormones
Chemicals produced by the glands of the endocrine system that are carried by the bloodstream to other organs throughout the body

Major Endocrine Glands

The locations of some of the major endocrine glands are shown in Figure 2-6. A brief description of the function of each gland follows.

The Pineal Gland. The pineal gland, located deep in the brain, produces the hormone *melatonin*, especially at night. This hormone is important in regulating our sleep-wake cycle (see Chapter 4). As night approaches and we get closer to our usual bedtime, melatonin levels increase. As daylight approaches and we awaken, melatonin levels decrease.

The Pancreas. Located near the stomach and small intestine, the **pancreas** secretes one of the best-known hormones, *insulin*. The cells of our body require insulin to use blood sugar (called *glucose*); without insulin, cells do not receive adequate nourishment from the available glucose. Too little sugar in the blood (hypoglycemia) can lead to perspiration, shallow breathing, anxiety, and even unconsciousness. Sixteen million people in the U.S. have a hormonal disease called diabetes, which affects glucose levels (Mader, 2000). If untreated, diabetes can result in blindness, kidney disease, and circulatory disorders. In Type I (juvenile) diabetes, the pancreas does not produce insulin; insulin injections replace the hormone the body is not producing on its own. In Type II (adult-onset) diabetes, insulin is produced but the cells are insensitive to it. Obesity and inactivity are factors that increase the risk of this type of diabetes. This form of diabetes can be controlled, to a degree, by a balanced, low-fat diet and exercise.

The pancreas is a good example of the feedback system of the endocrine glands. When you eat a meal and the food is broken down into glucose, the rise in glucose level in your blood signals (feedback) the pancreas to secrete insulin. Then as the blood

pancreas
An endocrine gland that lies between the stomach and the small intestine; the primary hormone released, insulin, regulates levels of glucose in the body

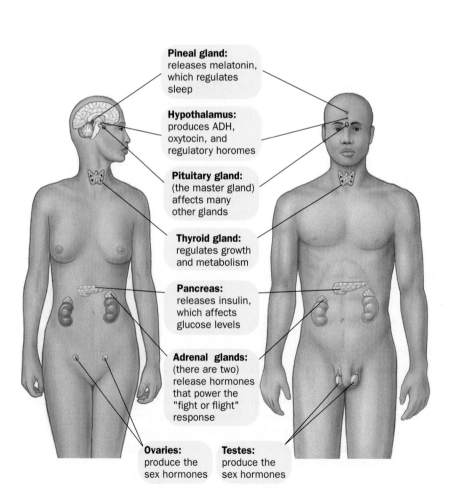

Pineal gland:
releases melatonin, which regulates sleep

Hypothalamus:
produces ADH, oxytocin, and regulatory horomes

Pituitary gland:
(the master gland) affects many other glands

Thyroid gland:
regulates growth and metabolism

Pancreas:
releases insulin, which affects glucose levels

Adrenal glands:
(there are two) release hormones that power the "fight or flight" response

Ovaries:
produce the sex hormones

Testes:
produce the sex hormones

FIGURE 2-6 Locations and functions of the major endocrine glands.

glucose level drops, the amount of insulin secreted by the pancreas decreases. As we have noted, in diabetic patients the body either does not produce the needed insulin or the cells do not respond to the insulin that is present.

Hypothalamus.   Located rather deep in the brain, this small gland actually has multiple roles. It is both an endocrine gland and a key center for a wide variety of behaviors related to survival. The **hypothalamus** signals its close neighbor, the pituitary, to release hormones that have a range of effects. It also contains key centers for controlling aggression (fighting), fleeing, sexual activity, and hunger.

The Pituitary Gland.   The **pituitary gland** is often called the *master gland* because its secretions control many other glands. The *pituitary* is responsible for the release of *somatotropin*, a growth hormone that acts directly on bones and muscles to produce the growth spurt that accompanies puberty. The *thyroid-stimulating hormone* stimulates the thyroid gland to regulate the release of its hormone, *thyroxine*. *Adrenocorticotropic hormone* (*ACTH*), which has been linked to learning and memory, causes the adrenal glands to secrete *cortisol*, resulting in an acceleration of the production of energy-producing glucose during stress. The release of these pituitary hormones reflects the interplay between the nervous system and the endocrine system.

The Thyroid Gland.   This butterfly-shaped gland is located below the *larynx* (voice box). When activated by the pituitary's *thyroid-stimulating hormone*, the **thyroid gland** secretes thyroxine, which regulates growth and metabolic rate throughout the body. Undersecretion of thyroxine (*hypothyroidism*) results in a small, dwarflike person. Administration of thyroid hormone can initiate growth; however, treatment must start within two months of birth or mental retardation will result. If hypothyroidism occurs in adults, the individual will exhibit lethargy, weight gain, hair loss, slower pulse rate, lowered body temperature, and thickening and puffiness of the skin. These conditions can be corrected by administering doses of thyroid hormone (Mader, 2000). Oversecretion of thyroxine results in *hyperthyroidism*. One form of *hyperthyroidism*, Grave's disease, is characterized by insomnia, protruding eyes, nervousness, hyperactivity, irritability, and a wild stare. Untreated hyperthyroidism can lead to death from heart disease.

The Gonads.   The **gonads**—**ovaries** in women and **testes** in men—produce sex hormones (*androgens* in men; *estrogens* in women) that activate reproductive organs and structures at puberty. These hormones also affect the appearance of secondary sex characteristics like facial and body hair, change of voice, and breast development (see Chapters 9 and 10). Testosterone levels are also related to aggressiveness (Dabbs & Morris, 1990; Dabbs, Riad, & Chance, 2001); higher levels of testosterone are associated with greater aggressiveness.

Some athletes take *anabolic steroids*, or artificial versions of testosterone, which occurs in both males and females. Taken in pill form or by injection, anabolic steroids build muscle faster (*anabolic* means growing or building). They also weaken the immune system (thus making people more susceptible to disease), can lead to liver damage, and can permanently stop bone growth in teenagers. Anabolic steroids are associated with shrinkage of the testes in males and cessation of menstruation in women; mood changes including severe depression and irritability may also occur (National Institute on Drug Abuse, 1997).

If a postmenopausal woman is treated with estrogen (estrogen replacement therapy), her brain will behave like the brain of a younger woman in terms of reading and memory (Restak, 2000). Estrogen also seems to increase activation of brain regions responsible for storing the sounds that make up the words we speak. The use of estrogen replacement therapy is quite common and has several medical benefits, including a reduction in the risk of bone loss. Although some researchers believe estrogen reduces the possibility of heart disease, any potential effects on heart disease are still a matter of controversy.

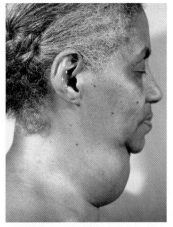

The normal production of thyroid hormones sets the rates of cell metabolism. The body needs iodine (often found in table salt) to manufacture thyroid hormones. In the absence of the needed iodine, the thyroid continues to try to manufacture its hormones but the result is a swollen and enlarged thyroid gland or *goiter* as shown here. Although goiter is an infrequent problem in the United States, it is a problem in many parts of the world.

hypothalamus
Gland and brain structure that sends signals to the pituitary gland and contains key centers for fighting, fleeing, sexual activity and hunger

pituitary gland
An endocrine gland located in the brain below the thalamus and hypothalamus; called the master gland because its secretions control many other glands

thyroid gland
Endocrine gland located just below the larynx that releases hormones including thyroxine, which has widespread effects throughout the body via its effects on metabolic rate

gonads
General term that refers to sex glands in either males (testes) or females (ovaries); releases hormones that affect sexual development

ovaries
Female gonads

testes
Male gonads

adrenal glands

Pair of glands located at the top of each of the kidneys; they release a range of hormones including epinephrine and norepinephrine

STUDY TIP

From memory and in informal outline form, list the endocrine glands and write a summary of the function of each.

The Adrenal Glands.   When you experience stress, the **adrenal glands** secrete *epinephrine* and *norepinephrine* (originally called adrenaline and noradrenaline, respectively), which power sympathetic nervous system activity. When the adrenal cortex is stimulated by the pituitary hormone ACTH, it secretes *glucocorticoids*, steroid hormones that are involved in the production of glucose.

The endocrine system is an important, if sometimes overlooked, part of the human body. Although it is easy and convenient to talk about the endocrine system and the nervous system as if they were completely independent, they are not. For example, when our body prepares for "fight or flight," the nervous system sends the first alarm to activate the sympathetic nervous system, but it is the endocrine system's hormones (especially epinephrine and norepinephrine) that keep the level of arousal up over a longer period of time. When you are under stress, the adrenal glands secrete epinephrine and norepinephrine, preparing you to make a fight-or-flight response. The importance of hormones is also seen in our understanding of various disorders. For example, is a young adult's depression a reaction to recent, disturbing life events, or does it reflect alteration in one or more of the hormones? Is a young child's hyperactivity an indication of youthful exuberance, or a disorder such as attention deficit/hyperactivity disorder? Or, might it be the end result of alterations in the hormones produced by the thyroid gland?

So far, we have provided an overview of the entire nervous system along with a more detailed look at the endocrine system. But what is it that makes the entire nervous system operate? In the next section, we will take a closer look at the smallest units of the nervous system—the tiny, microscopic cells that make up our nervous system.

REVIEW SUMMARY

1. The **evolutionary perspective** stresses the role of physiological structures and behaviors in an organism's adaptation to the environment and ultimate survival. The principle of **natural selection** states that the most fit organisms survive because they adapt best to the environment and thus pass on their genes to future generations. The term **behavioral neuroscience** describes the work of scientists from several disciplines who work to understand how the nervous system is related to behavior.

2. We use the processes of sensing, processing, and responding to interact with the environment. The nervous system, which is divided into the **central nervous system** (CNS—brain and spinal cord) and the **peripheral nervous system** (PNS—all parts of the nervous system outside the CNS), coordinates these three activities.

3. The PNS is composed of the **somatic division** and the **autonomic division.** The somatic division consists of **afferent**

(sensory) nerves that run from the receptors to the brain and **efferent (motor) nerves** that run to the glands and muscles. The autonomic division consists of the **sympathetic system,** which mobilizes the body's resources, and the **parasympathetic system,** which returns the body to a normal state of **homeostasis.**

4. The spinal cord is composed of sensory (afferent or ascending) and motor (efferent or descending) nerves; *interneurons* may connect sensory and motor neurons.

5. The **endocrine system** affects behavior by producing and secreting **hormones,** which are chemicals that regulate body functions. Among the major endocrine glands are the **pineal gland, hypothalamus, pituitary gland,** the **thyroid gland,** the **pancreas,** the **gonads,** and the **adrenal glands.**

✓ CHECK YOUR PROGRESS

1. What is the evolutionary perspective?

2. On your way to class you see a $5 bill in the street. Because you want something more than a soda for lunch, you claim the bill as yours. For this situation, describe each of the steps involved in interacting with the environment—sensing, processing, and responding.

3. For each of the following activities, indicate whether the sympathetic or parasympathetic system of the autonomic division is involved.

   a. A sinking feeling in the pit of your stomach tells you that you are lost in a run-down section of a city at night and have no money to make a phone call or catch a bus.

b. Getting "psyched up" before a football game, you are ready to devastate the opponents.

c. Soothing music helps calm you after a very frustrating test.

4. Which of the following are reflexes? Explain why.

a. deciding to see a movie

b. blinking when a puff of air hits your eye

c. a baby's sucking when a pacifier is placed in her mouth

d. jerking your hand out of very hot water

5. What are the cells that detect stimuli?

a. receptors

b. effectors

c. glands

d. sensory tracts

6. Which endocrine gland produces insulin?

a. pineal

b. thyroid

c. adrenals

d. pancreas

7. Jake caught his hand in a tight space under the seat of his car. The resulting pain signals traveled to the brain via _____ nerves, and the message to pull harder to release his hand was sent from the brain to his hand via _____ nerves.

a. afferent, efferent

b. primary, secondary

c. central, peripheral

d. involuntary, voluntary

8. Which of the following is the result of sympathetic nervous system activity?

a. Digestion ceases.

b. Your heart rate slows.

c. The pupils of your eyes constrict.

d. Rate of release of sugar is decreased.

9. Physicians in training use a computer that presents cases and asks for a diagnosis. The current case is 16-year-old Tim who is very muscular, is depressed, and has testes that have shrunk considerably. Which of these will the future physicians suggest as their course of action?

a. Check for high estrogen levels.

b. Check for possible use of anabolic steroids.

c. Run tests that might reveal use of substances like marijuana.

d. Run tests that might reveal the presence of a malformed spleen.

10. Which endocrine gland controls several other glands?

a. adrenal

b. thyroid

c. pituitary

d. pancreas

ANSWERS: 1. Based on the theory of Charles Darwin, the evolutionary perspective focuses on how and why a particular physical structure developed over time. **2.** *Sensing*—seeing the $5 bill; *Processing*—deciding you need the money for lunch; *Responding*—picking up the $5 bill. **3. a.** Sympathetic **b.** Sympathetic **c.** Parasympathetic **4. a.** Not a reflex—voluntary behavior **b.** Reflex—involuntary behavior **c.** Reflex—involuntary behavior **d.** Reflex—involuntary behavior **5.** a **6.** d **7.** a **8.** a **9.** b **10.** c

NEURONS: BASIC CELLS OF THE NERVOUS SYSTEM

In 1906, an English physiologist, Charles Scott Sherrington (1857–1952), was conducting research on reflexes in dogs. Shortly after he pinched a dog's foot, the foot would rise reflexively. Because he had disconnected the dog's brain from its spinal cord, Sherrington was confident that he was observing reflexive behavior. But he did not understand the delay that occurred between the time he pinched the dog's foot and the time the foot was raised. The length of the neurons that ran from the foot to the spinal cord and from the spinal cord to the muscles that controlled the foot had been carefully measured. Sherrington also knew the speed at which the neural impulse traveled. The reflex simply took too long to occur. *Why was Sherrington's observation important in the history of psychology?*

As we mentioned earlier, the nervous system is composed of cells called *neurons*. Like other cells in the body, neurons have a nucleus, are enclosed in a membrane, and contain an assortment of smaller structures. Unlike other cells, however, neurons send and receive messages to and from one another. Neurons come in a variety of sizes and shapes. Motor neurons usually have longer distances to travel, so they tend to be large.

dendrite
Short, branchlike structure of a neuron that receives information from receptors and other neurons

soma
Cell body of a neuron, which contains the nucleus

axon
Elongated part of a neuron that transmits information to other neurons, muscles, and glands

Interneurons are small, so a large number of them can occupy a given area. The greater the number of neurons in an area, the more complex the interconnections among them.

Components of the Neuron

Most neurons are similar to each other in that each has a cell membrane, dendrites, a cell body (soma), an axon, and terminal buttons (see Figure 2-7). First we look at these common components and what they do; then we consider the part that makes neurons different—the myelin sheath.

The Cell Membrane.   The *cell membrane* is like a fence that surrounds the entire neuron, giving it shape and keeping the cell's internal fluids inside. The cell membrane, however, is *semipermeable*: It allows some—but not all—substances to pass through it.

Dendrites.   The short, branchlike structures of neurons, called **dendrites,** receive signals or information from the receptors (for example, the eyes, ears, skin) or from other neurons. Most neurons have many (even thousands) dendrites. Hence, it is possible for a single neuron to receive signals from many other neurons.

The Cell Body.   Once a signal has been received by the dendrites, it passes through the *cell body*, or **soma.** Like other cells, the soma of the neuron has a nucleus containing genetic material, and is involved in the *metabolic* (energy regulation), processes of the cell. The soma relays the neural signal from the dendrites to the axon.

2.2 *Live!* psych   **The Axon.**   The **axon** is the long part of the neuron that transmits electrical signals to other neurons and to muscles and glands. Only one axon extends from the cell body

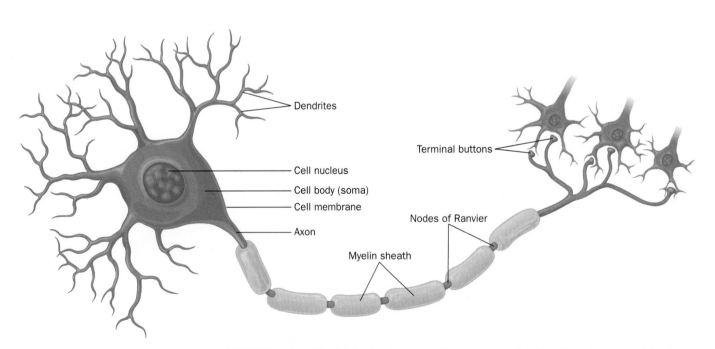

FIGURE 2–7   The basic structures of all neurons are the dendrites, (soma) cell body, axon, and terminal buttons. In some neurons, the axon may be covered by a fatty myelin sheath, which is white in appearance.

Source: Morris & Maisto, 2002.

of each neuron. Whereas most dendrites tend to be rather short, axons can vary greatly in length (but have a constant diameter), depending on the location of the neuron. The axons of some neurons located in the brain are microscopic; others are quite long. For example, the axon of a motor neuron can stretch from your spinal cord all the way to your hand or foot.

Terminal Buttons.   Although only one axon leaves the cell body (soma), it may branch several times before it reaches its target. Because the axon branches, the same signal can be sent to several different neurons. Most axons have several small knobs, called **terminal buttons,** at their ends. The terminal buttons store neurotransmitters prior to their release and are directly involved in transmitting a chemical and electrical signal from one neuron to the next.

The Myelin Sheath.   Now that we know the structures common to all neurons, we can examine how neurons differ. One of the major differences among neurons is found in their axons. The axon in Figure 2-7 is surrounded by a **myelin sheath,** which is a fatty protein substance. The myelin sheath is composed of **glial cells** (from the Greek word for "glue"), another special type of cell found in the nervous system. Glial cells have several functions: removing waste, occupying vacant space when neurons die, guiding the migration of neurons during brain development, and insulation. If neurons are the stars of the show, then glial cells are the supporting cast members. Just as in the movies, there are scores of supporting players with small, but important, parts to play. Glial cells are considerably smaller and more numerous than neurons; there are about 10 glial cells for every neuron.

Consider what happens when you accidentally put your hand on a hot stove. It is imperative that you remove it—immediately! From an evolutionary perspective, speed of reactions like motor responses is important; escaping from a predator often requires speed. Without that speed, there is a reduced chance of passing on one's genes! Even though a signal is transmitted rapidly down the axon, motor axons are often very long (axons in the spinal cord can be 3 feet or longer); therefore, anything that speeds up the transmission will help. Accelerating the transmission of the neural signal is one function of the myelin sheath (Toates, 2001), which acts like insulation on electrical cords. The sheath covers the axon except at small, regularly spaced gaps, called *nodes of Ranvier* (see Figure 2-7). Myelin is whitish in appearance, which accounts for the whitish appearance of the spinal cord with its long myelin-covered axons. On the other hand, there are fewer myelin-covered axons in the brain, which appears grayish, the color of the rest of the neuron as well as that of unmyelinated axons. We say more about the myelin sheath and the nodes of Ranvier on page 62.

Psychological Detective

What happens when the myelin sheath degenerates? Review what you have learned about the myelin sheath and give this question some thought. Write down your answer before reading further.

Although many diseases of the nervous system affect the soma or cell body, some destroy the mylein sheath. Among these *demyelinating* diseases are *amyotrophic lateral sclerosis* (Lou Gehrig's disease) and multiple sclerosis (Andreasen, 2001). **Multiple sclerosis** occurs when the immune system attacks the central nervous system, resulting in degeneration of small patches of myelin called *plaques* (Mohr & Cox, 2001). As the disease progresses, entire myelin sheaths are destroyed. The severity of the disease depends upon where the plaques occur. Plaques in the spinal cord or brain stem are serious because the myelin does not regenerate; such damage can leave the patient wheelchair-bound (Vertosick, 1996). The physical symptoms associated with multiple

terminal buttons
Component of a neuron located at the ends of the axon where neurotransmitters are stored before being released into the synapse

myelin sheath
Whitish, fatty protein substance, composed of glial cells, that covers some axons and increases speed of neural transmission

glial cell
Special type of cell found in the nervous system that forms the myelin sheath, which increases the speed of neural conduction by providing insulation of the axons

multiple sclerosis
Disease caused by degeneration of myelin in the central nervous system. Plaques formed in the myelin sheath interfere with neural transmission resulting in a variety of effects depending on their location in the body, but most often affecting motor movement

ataxia
Loss of motor coordination

synapse
Site where two or more neurons interact but do not touch; neurotransmitters are released into the space in order to continue neural impulses

sclerosis include weakness, tremors, and visual problems; however, the most prominent symptom is **ataxia,** loss of motor coordination.

The Synapse and Neurotransmitters

You now know the components of neurons, but how do these special cells work? In this section we explore how neurons are organized and how information is transmitted from one neuron to another.

The Synapse.   To send messages, neurons must be organized in a particular way. Because a neural signal is sent from one neuron to the next through the terminal buttons of the axons, the most common arrangement is for a neuron's terminal buttons to be near, but not touching, the receptive dendrites of neighboring neurons. This arrangement is diagrammed in Figure 2-8. The membrane on the side that sends the message is the *presynaptic* membrane. The membrane on the receiving side of the synapse, the *postsynaptic* membrane, can be viewed as a docking station.

     The most common arrangement at the end of an axon consists of a terminal button to send the signal, a dendrite to receive the signal, and the gap between the two, which is the synapse. The **synapse** is microscopic—2/100 of a micrometer (a micrometer is 1/1,000 of a millimeter)—yet the neurons never touch each other. To give you a better idea of the size of the synapse, it would take more than 12.5 million of them to fill an inch.

Neurotransmitters.   If there is a gap between the neurons, why doesn't the neural signal simply stop when it arrives at the terminal buttons? The answer involves chemicals called *neurotransmitters*. When Charles Scott Sherrington was studying reflexive foot raising in dogs, he noticed that reflexes occurred more slowly than the speed of the neural impulse in the axon would predict. He reasoned that another process must be involved. Because Santiago Ramón y Cajal (1852–1934) had previously

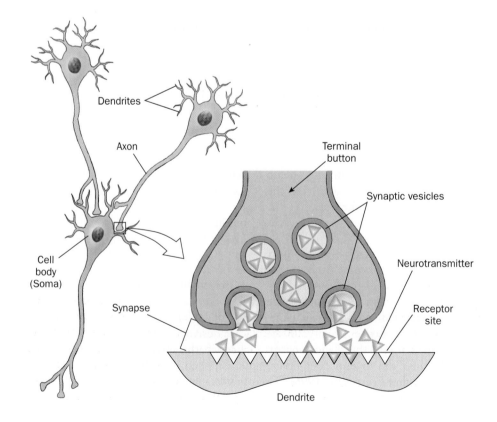

FIGURE 2-8 Neurons communicate with one another as well as with muscles and glands across microscopic spaces called synapses. At the end of the neurons's axon are terminal buttons, where we find synaptic vesicles. The neurotransmitters packaged in these vesicles are released into the synapse where they carry the neural message to dendrites of the receiving neuron.

Dendrites

Axon

Terminal button

Synaptic vesicles

Neurotransmitter

Cell body (Soma)

Receptor site

Synapse

Dendrite

shown that neurons are separate units of the nervous system, Sherrington concluded that the process he inferred must occur in the space separating the neurons—that is, in the synapse.

Sherrington proposed that transmission of impulses across the synapse must involve special chemicals, which today are called **neurotransmitters.** The neurotransmitters are stored in the terminal buttons at the end of axons. When the electrical signal reaches the terminal buttons, it causes the terminal button to release a chemical signal in the form of a neurotransmitter into the synapse. As the neurotransmitter enters the synapse, it contacts the postsynaptic membrane (usually the dendrite) of the next neuron. When the molecules of the neurotransmitter contact specially shaped receptor sites located on the postsynaptic membrane, they attach, or *bind*, to them, thereby allowing the neural signal to be transmitted from one neuron to the next.

When the neurotransmitter occupies the appropriate receptor site, depending on the type of neurotransmitter and the location of the synapse in the nervous system, one of two outcomes are possible. The neuron that is receiving the neurotransmitter may become more likely to transmit the message to subsequent neurons; this process is called *excitation*. In other instances the neuron that receives the neurotransmitter becomes *less* likely to transmit the message to subsequent neurons; this process is called *inhibition*.

The importance of neurotransmitters in even basic behaviors like moving is evident in the case of John, a 65-year-old carpenter. Several years ago, John noticed that his fingers felt stiff and that he was beginning to exhibit slight tremors in both hands. Over the course of several months, his condition became progressively worse until he was unable to work.

After a physical examination and a series of diagnostic tests, a neurologist determined that John suffers from *Parkinson's disease*, a disease that usually occurs in people over age 50. Many people are now aware of this disease because several well-known individuals are counted among the afflicted: boxer Muhammad Ali, Pope John Paul II, actor Michael J. Fox, and former attorney general Janet Reno. They have a disease that results from the death of neurons in the brain that release the neurotransmitter dopamine; the loss of these dopamine-releasing neurons makes it difficult to initiate motor movements (MacPhee & Stewart, 2001; Stone & Darlington, 2000). People with Parkinson's disease would have to bring all their attention to bear on acts as simple as getting out of a chair, holding a coffee cup, or starting to walk. In addition, their muscles become more rigid because they are partially contracted; other symptoms include tremors, slowness of movements, and poor balance.

Although we do not know the specific cause of the loss of these dopamine-releasing neurons, there are several possible explanations: brain infections, injury, strokes, tumors, and toxins.

Former heavyweight boxing champion Muhammad Ali once proclaimed that he could "float like a butterfly, sting like a bee." Millions of fans were drawn to him for his athletic prowess, his intensity in the ring, and his engaging personality. Among his many fans were children he would entertain with magic tricks. Parkinson's disease robbed him of his athletic ability in the ring as well as his ability to perform magic tricks. He testified before the Congress of the U.S. on the need for additional funds to search for a cure for Parkinson's disease.

Psychological Detective

If Parkinson's disease results from low dopamine levels, a likely treatment would seem to be administering dopamine to patients. This logical treatment, however, is not successful. Give this situation some thought and think of reasons why the solution to the problems of Parkinson's disease is not administering dopamine.

The brain is a complex and crucial organ that must be protected. Although the skull offers some protection, the environment contains numerous substances that could have toxic effects on the brain. Through thousands of years of evolution, humans developed a *blood-brain barrier* (Klein, 2000; Toates, 2001), a screenlike element that allows some substances into the brain and keeps out other substances. Sometimes this barrier keeps out potentially helpful substances; for example, dopamine does not cross the blood-brain barrier. As we will see (Chapter 4), this barrier can also let in some potentially harmful substances like alcohol. L-dopa is a chemical *precursor* of dopamine

neurotransmitters
Chemical substances that are stored in terminal buttons and released into the synapse between two neurons to carry signals from one neuron to the next neuron

(a building block that certain brain neurons use to manufacture dopamine), and it crosses the blood-brain barrier. Once L-dopa crosses the blood-brain barrier, neurons in the brain use it to manufacture dopamine. The resulting increase in dopamine levels leads to significant improvement in the motor symptoms of patients suffering from Parkinson's disease. The changes can be dramatic: "Patients who may have been virtually immobile with Parkinson's disease, even for several years, suddenly come alive within an hour or so of taking L-dopa" (Stone & Darlington, 2000, p. 120).

This treatment, however, does not cure Parkinson's disease. After several years, the positive effects of L-dopa wear off, and patients gradually lose sensitivity to the treatment, which begins to work for shorter periods of time (Youdim & Riederer, 1997). L-dopa treatments also produce side effects such as nausea and sleep disorders (Obeso et al., 1989). Although a solution to these side effects has not been found, researchers are on the trail of promising leads. For example, it may be possible to transplant normal dopamine-producing tissue into the damaged brain areas (Björklund, 1992). Surgeons have recently developed an implantable electronic device that provides stimulation of the affected areas of the brain. This treatment, *deep brain stimulation*, has been used for several movement disorders (Tarsy, 2001).

Here is a closer look at some of the major neurotransmitters:

Dopamine.   This neurotransmitter controls arousal levels and, as we have discussed, plays a role in motor movement. What's more, dopamine is involved in brain pathways that are responsible for reward and punishment. As a result, dopamine seems to play a role in producing dependence on (addiction to) drugs such as amphetamines, cocaine, and morphine. All of these drugs increase the release of dopamine from nerve cells in the brain (Stone & Darlington, 2000).

Serotonin.   In the late 1960s, faculty members at a major university were joking with one of their colleagues who had devoted his career to studying serotonin. Why would anyone devote a career to what was then viewed as "sleep juice" and nothing more? How wrong they were! In the 21st century, we now know that serotonin plays a role in weight regulation, sleep, depression, suicide, obsessive-compulsive disorder, aggression, and a wide range of other disorders and behavior problems (Mann, Brent, & Arango, 2001; Dolan, Anderson, & Deakin, 2001). Levels of this neurotransmitter are increased by such well-known antidepressant drugs as Paxil, Prozac, and Zoloft.

Acetylcholine.   This neurotransmitter controls activity in brain areas related to attention, learning, and memory. People with Alzheimer's disease (see Chapter 9) typically have low levels of acetylcholine; drugs that boost its levels *may* improve memory. Alzheimer's disease results in degeneration of neurons in the brain. The disease generally afflicts older people, although some variants of the disease may occur in people in their fifties. In industrial countries, Alzheimer's disease is the third-leading cause of death after heart disease and cancer. Each year, almost 400,000 new cases are reported in the United States (*Harvard Mental Health Letter*, 2001). People afflicted with Alzheimer's exhibit a progressive loss of memory, and eventually they are completely incapable of caring for themselves. The following description gives a glimpse of this disease: "Imagine your brain as a house filled with lights. Now imagine someone turning off the lights one by one. That's what Alzheimer's disease does. It turns off the lights so that the flow of ideas, emotions and memories from one room to the next slows and eventually ceases" (Nash, 2000, p. 51).

Acetylcholine (Ach) also operates at the junction of many of our nerves and skeletal muscles. For hundreds of years, South American Indians have rubbed a poison, *curare*, on the ends of their arrowheads. When the curare enters the victim (animal or human), it takes the place of acetylcholine in synapses. Messages from the brain are carried down the nerves but when they reach the muscles the messages do not get through, resulting in paralysis and death.

Improperly preserved food may contain the botulin bacteria, which prevents the release of Ach. Without Ach, the muscles we use to breathe

Paxil, Prozac, and Zoloft are well-known prescription drugs. All of these drugs are classified as antidepressants and affect the neurotransmitter serotonin. They are currently prescribed for a wide range of psychological and medical problems.

are paralyzed resulting in death from respiratory failure. The venom in a black widow spider's sting stimulates a flood of Ach; the resulting muscle spasms can also cause death.

GABA (gamma-aminobutyric acid) is an inhibitory neurotransmitter that is widely distributed throughout the brain and the spinal cord. What purposes do inhibitory neurotransmitters serve? The neurons in the brain are packed tightly and they are closely interconnected. The general effect of excitatory neurotransmitters on these neurons is to increase the tendency to excite their neighboring neurons, which excite other neurons, and so on down the line. Without the braking action of inhibitory neurotransmitters, neurons could fire uncontrollably, which is what occurs when someone experiences an epileptic seizure. Thus, the damping effect of inhibitory neurotransmitters is necessary to create a balance in the brain.

The importance of inhibitory neurotransmitters is also apparent in the following scenario. Imagine that you have removed a very hot pot from the stove. Although you are using a pot holder, it is not thick enough to provide protection from the searing heat. The pain caused by the heat triggers a withdrawal reflex that would cause you to drop the hot pot, yet you manage to get it to the table without dropping it. How did this happen? In this case, the excitatory neurotransmitter was powering motor neurons to pull away from the pot (and drop it). However, this excitation was counteracted by inhibition from the brain, which recognized the disaster that would occur if you dropped the pot (Carlson, 2001).

Norepinephrine. This primarily excitatory neurotransmitter induces physical and mental arousal and heightens our mood. It is found in the autonomic nervous system and is part of the power behind the fight or flight response. Norepinephrine has also been implicated in anxiety disorders such as panic attacks (see Chapter 12).

Table 2-1 provides a review of the features of the neurotransmitters we just discussed. This table will serve as a helpful review, so refer to it often.

At the age of 83, former President Ronald Reagan was diagnosed as suffering from Alzheimer's disease. Six years after the diagnosis was made, he no longer remembered being president and requires continual care from caregivers, including his wife, Nancy, who he does not recognize.

 2.3

STUDY TIP

Convert Table 2-1 below (Selected Neurotransmitters . . .) into a visual organizer. You can use a mind map or think link format, different color pens, or whatever strategy works best for you.

TABLE 2-1

Selected Neurotransmitters: Their Effects, Locations, and Functions

Neurotransmitters	Effects	Location	Functions
Acetylcholine (Ach)	Excitatory or inhibitory	Brain spinal cord, synapses of the parasympathetic nervous system	Involved in muscle movement and also memory, Alzheimer's disease is associated with low levels
Dopamine	Inhibitory or excitatory	Brain (three major circuits: hypothalamus, pituitary, midbrain)	Involved in movement and reward centers; destruction of dopamine-secreting neurons can lead to Parkinson's disease; implicated in the development of schizophrenia
Gamma-aminobutyric acid (GABA)	Inhibitory	Local transmission in CNS	Involved in levels of excitability; drugs used to treat anxiety increase the ability of GABA to bind to postsynaptic sites, which lead to a reduced arousal
Norepinephrine	Generally excitatory	Brain stem (nerve tracts extend to many areas of the brain and spinal cord) and sympathetic nervous system	Involved in sympathetic nervous system activity; influences arousal, mood, and reward centers; cocaine and amphetamines block reuptake
Serotonin	Inhibitory or excitatory	Brain stem (nerve tracts extend to many areas of the brain and spinal cord)	Involved with mood, appetite, sleep, aggression

Hands On

Orientation, Memory, and Concentration Test

INSTRUCTIONS: Score 1 point for each wrong answer, up to the maximum. Multiply the number of mistakes by the weight. Then add to get the final score.

Questions	Maximum Number of Errors	Errors × Weight = Score
1. What year is it now?	1	× 4 =
2. What month is it now? Repeat this memory phrase after me: John Brown, 42 Market Street, Chicago	1	× 3 =
3. About what time is it? (within 1 hour)	1	× 3 =
4. Count backward 20 to 1.	2	× 2 =
5. Say the months in reverse order.	2	× 2 =
6. Repeat the memory phrase again.	5	× 2 =

Total score can range from 0 (no mistakes) to 28 (all wrong). A score greater than 10 is usually consistent with dementia. Alzheimer's disease is the most common form of dementia.

Source: *Time*, July 17, 2000, p. 56 (from Gerontological Society of America).

Clearing the Synapse.   How does the neurotransmitter get out of the synapse? If you think about this question for a moment, you will understand the importance of clearing synapses. It's like your telephone. If you talk to only one person and never hang up, only one message can be sent and received. You must hang up to receive additional calls. Likewise, synapses must be cleared, and cleared rapidly, before additional signals can be transmitted.

The synapse is cleared in one of two ways, depending on the particular neurotransmitter involved (Toates, 2001). In the first method, *breakdown*, the neurotransmitter (for example, acetylcholine) is broken down and removed from the synapse. After acetylcholine affects the next neuron, an enzyme breaks it down. Once the acetylcholine is broken down and the receptor sites are unoccupied, the postsynaptic membrane can receive another signal. This rapid breakdown is important for producing rapid motor responses required to play the piano, type, or use a calculator.

The second method for clearing the synapse, *reuptake*, involves taking the neurotransmitter back into the terminal button from which it came. Once the neurotransmitter has had its effect on the postsynaptic membrane, it reenters the terminal buttons, where it is ready to be used again. All neurotransmitters, except acetylcholine, are removed from the synapse by reuptake.

Neurotransmitters and Drug Action.   Understanding the way neurotransmitters operate has increased our knowledge of how drugs affect the brain and, consequently, our behavior. Most drugs exert their effects by influencing the operation of a neurotransmitter: Some drugs increase the effectiveness of neurotransmitters, other drugs reduce the effectiveness. Regardless of the specific effect that a drug may have, it is very likely that the key biological action takes place in or near the synapse.

Agonists.   Drugs that promote or enhance the operation of a neurotransmitter are called **agonists.** The effects of neurotransmitters can be enhanced in a number of ways (see Figure 2-9). For example, some agonists eliminate the enzyme that breaks down the neurotransmitter in the synapse. Without the enzyme, the neurotransmitter remains active in the synapse for a longer period, resulting in a more intense response. For example, the drug physostigmine inactivates the enzyme that breaks down acetylcholine. Thus the acetylcholine remains active longer. Drugs such as physostigmine

agonist
Drugs that enhance the effects of a particular neurotransmitter

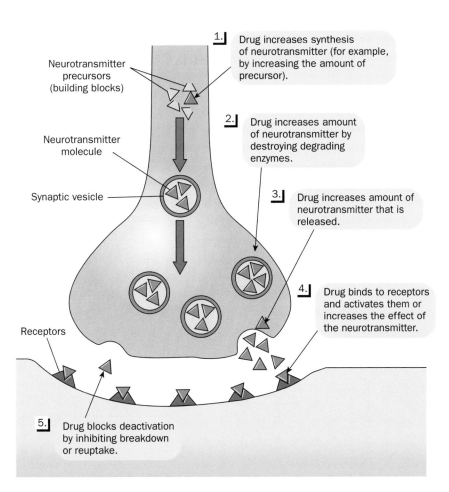

1. Drug increases synthesis of neurotransmitter (for example, by increasing the amount of precursor).

Neurotransmitter precursors (building blocks)

2. Drug increases amount of neurotransmitter by destroying degrading enzymes.

Neurotransmitter molecule

Synaptic vesicle

3. Drug increases amount of neurotransmitter that is released.

4. Drug binds to receptors and activates them or increases the effect of the neurotransmitter.

Receptors

5. Drug blocks deactivation by inhibiting breakdown or reuptake.

FIGURE 2-9 Agonists are drugs that increase the effectiveness of a neurotransmitter. These drugs can work in a variety of ways.

Source: Adapted from Klein, 2000.

produce a range of behavioral effects that may include nightmares and vivid dreaming (see Chapter 4), as well as parasympathetic effects such as decreased heart rate and constriction of the pupils of the eyes.

The class of drugs known as the *benzodiazepines* work by enhancing the ease or tightness of binding of the neurotransmitter *GABA* (Julien, 2001; McKim, 2000). Although the name benzodiazepines may not be familiar, you have probably heard the trade names Librium, Valium, and Xanax. These drugs are most often prescribed to reduce anxiety, but they also promote sleep, relax the muscles, and decrease the likelihood of seizures.

Another class of drugs, *selective serotonin reuptake inhibitors (SSRIs)* is often used to relieve depression (McKim, 2000). Drugs such as Prozac block the reuptake of the neurotransmitter serotonin into the terminal buttons (see Chapter 13). When reuptake is blocked, the neurotransmitter remains active in the synapse for a longer time period than usual. Because depression is alleviated when the effective level of serotonin in the synapse is raised, researchers have proposed that depression may occur when abnormally low levels of this neurotransmitter is present.

Antagonists. Drugs that oppose or inhibit the operation of a neurotransmitter are called **antagonists.** Antagonists can work in a variety of ways to reduce the effectiveness of a given neurotransmitter (see Figure 2-10). For example, they may attach to receptor sites and block the neurotransmitter from attaching there. By stopping the action of the neurotransmitter, they prevent transmission of neural signals. For example, the drug, haloperidol (Haldol), attaches to dopamine receptors and blocks them; as a result, less dopamine binds to the receptors on the postsynaptic membrane. As we shall see in Chapter 12, researchers believe that some psychological disorders (for example, schizophrenia) result from high levels of dopamine. Drugs such as Haloperidol are effective in the treatment of these disorders because it reduces the level of dopamine.

antagonist
Drugs that oppose or inhibit the effects of a particular neurotransmitter

FIGURE 2-10 Antagonists are drugs that decrease the effectiveness of a neurotransmitter. These drugs can work in a variety of ways.

Source: Adapted from Klein, 2000.

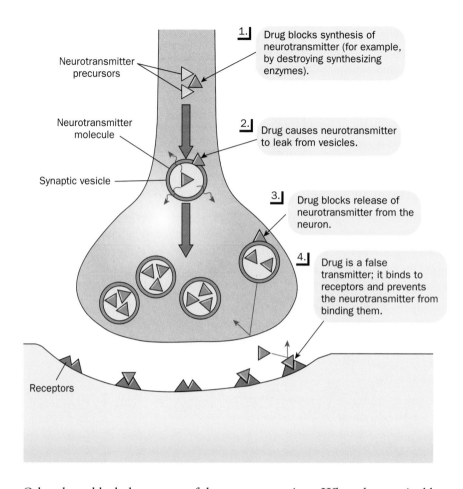

Other drugs block the storage of the neurotransmitter. When the terminal buttons empty their contents into the synapse, a reduced amount of the neurotransmitter is released, and the effect on the postsynaptic membrane is less than normal. The blood pressure drug reserpine operates in this manner. Reserpine destroys the membrane of the terminal buttons that contain dopamine. With no membrane to protect it, the dopamine is destroyed by an enzyme contained inside the terminal button. As a result, less dopamine is released into the synapse.

Neuromodulators.   The search for additional neurotransmitters led to the discovery of other chemicals, **neuromodulators,** that influence the transmission of signals between neurons. The release and action of neurotransmitters is confined to synapses in a specific area; the distribution of neuromodulators is more widespread. For example, neuromodulators can have simultaneous effects on diverse brain regions; their activity may be indirect and longer-lasting. Some neuromodulators produce their effects by facilitating the release of neurotransmitters; others inhibit the release of neurotransmitters.

One of the best-known neuromodulators, morphine, relieves pain. Consider the case of Kevin, who broke his leg while playing football. The injury was so severe that Kevin had to be hospitalized and given morphine injections to reduce the pain. Morphine blocks or inhibits transmission of neural signals that transmit pain signals. Perhaps the body produces a substance that is similar to morphine, otherwise, would it have developed receptors for such substances?

This question led researchers to seek and locate receptors that are sensitive to chemicals like morphine (Pert & Snyder, 1973). These receptors do not exist just to receive external substances like morphine, so researchers set out to identify the endogenous (internal) chemicals that naturally occupy these receptors. Researchers found two of our body's natural painkilling chemicals (Hughes, J. et al., 1975). The best known of

neuromodulators
Chemicals that may have a widespread or general effect on the release of neurotransmitters

these natural painkillers are the **endorphins,** which are released in response to pain or during vigorous exercise. Endorphins are endogenous opioids, which means they are opium-like chemicals produced from within. They reduce the sensation of pain and induce feelings of relaxation, exhilaration, and even euphoria. Even after long runs, some runners experience a "runner's high," which is likely due to the body's production of endorphins. Have you heard of someone who can have dental work (for example, teeth drilled) without injections of a pain killer? One explanation for this phenomenon is that people differ in their levels of endorphins.

Humans have an elaborate and complex system to sense pain and then block it (Fernandez & Turk, 1992). Would it be better if we did not sense pain at all? Consider the case of Miss C., who had been insensitive to pain from birth (Melzack & Wall, 1982):

> The young lady . . . seemed normal in every way except that she had never felt pain. As a child, she had bitten off the tip of her tongue while chewing food and had suffered third-degree burns after kneeling on a radiator to look out of the window. . . . She felt no pain when parts of her body were subjected to strong electric shock, to hot water . . . , or to a prolonged ice-bath. (pp. 16–17)

Miss C. was unusual because she lived into her teens. Most people who cannot sense pain die at an early age. To adapt to and survive in our environment, we must be able to sense occurrences that could lead to injury or illness.

The Nature of the Neural Signal

Earlier in this chapter we mentioned that the basic function of the nervous system is to receive information or signals from specialized cells called receptors. As demonstrated in the example of figuring out traffic signals and how to respond, a great deal of this information is processed by the brain and then translated into action. We turn our attention to the neural signals themselves. To understand the signal, we must consider the inside and outside of the neuron at the same time.

If you examine the chemicals on the outside of the neuron's semipermeable cell membrane and compare them with chemicals on the inside of the cell membrane, you would notice a difference in small electrically charged particles called *ions*. The two types of ions, positive (+) and negative (−), resemble the two poles or ends of a battery. The most important negative ion is chloride (Cl^-); potassium (K^+) and sodium (Na^+) are important positive ions.

When a neuron is not sending or receiving a signal, it is in a **resting state,** with more negative ions on the inside than on the outside. Relative to the outside, the inside of the neuron is about −70 millivolts (a millivolt, mV, is 1/1,000 of a volt) when the neuron is in the resting state. Because of this unequal distribution of ions, the neuron is *polarized*, like a battery. This −70 mV difference in electric charge between the inside and outside of a neuron at rest is the *resting potential* (see Figure 2-11).

What happens when a neurotransmitter enters the synapse? One of two reactions may occur. The presence of the neurotransmitter may result either in **depolarization** (the neuron becomes less negatively charged) or **hyperpolarization** (the neuron becomes more negatively charged). Which reaction occurs is determined by the type of neurotransmitter and the location of the synapse. For example, the presence of acetylcholine at synapses located in skeletal muscles, results in depolarization: its presence at synapses located in other parts of the body, such as the heart, results in hyperpolarization.

When excitatory neurotransmitters occupy appropriate receptor sites, they cause the cell membrane to allow positive ions to pass inside (see Figure 2-12). The increase of positive ions on the inside of the neuron causes the resting potential to drop. This change, which brings the potential closer to zero, is *depolarization*. If enough of the neurotransmitter is present to cause the dendrite and soma to depolarize to between −65 and −60 mV, the neuron generates its own electrical signal. At this threshold (the minimum amount of change required for the neuronal response to occur) the axon membrane suddenly allows large quantities of positive (Na^+) ions to rush inside. In less

Why would the human body contain receptors for a substance similar to morphine? This intriguing question led researchers to discover that nature had prepared us to deal with pain by providing us with our own painkillers–endorphins. Endorphins not only reduce pain, they can also induce relaxation and even euphoria, which is sometimes seen in a "runner's high."

endorphins
Substances produced by the body that block pain; these substances are opium-like chemicals

resting state
Electrical charge (−70 mV) of a neuron when it is not firing

depolarization
Process in which the electrical charge of the neuron becomes less negative

hyperpolarization
Process in which the electrical charge of the neuron becomes more negative

FIGURE 2-11 The change in electrical charge involved in firing a neuron (generating an action potential) and resetting it.

Source: Morris & Maisto, 2002.

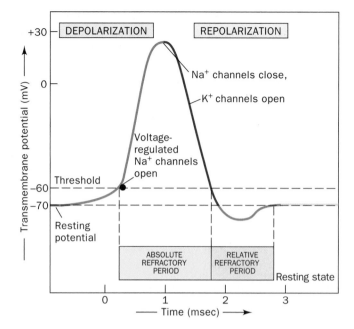

action potential
Reversal in electrical charge of a neuron that occurs when the neuron fires

than a millisecond (1 millisecond is 1/1,000 of a second) the neuron changes from −60 to +30 mV, completely reversing its electrical nature or polarity. This reversal along the axon is the neural signal we have been talking about. We call it an **action potential,** or all-or-none response: When the axon fires, it does not fire more or less than it did last time. An action potential has the same magnitude each time.

Once the dendrite and soma reach the threshold, the action potential spreads rapidly down the axon until it reaches the terminal buttons, where it causes the release of a neurotransmitter. The action potential, or signal, is nothing more than an exchange of ions. For axons that do not have a myelin sheath, the ion exchange takes place along the entire axon. If a myelin sheath is present, the ion exchange occurs only at the nodes of Ranvier. Hence there is less work to be done, and the action potential

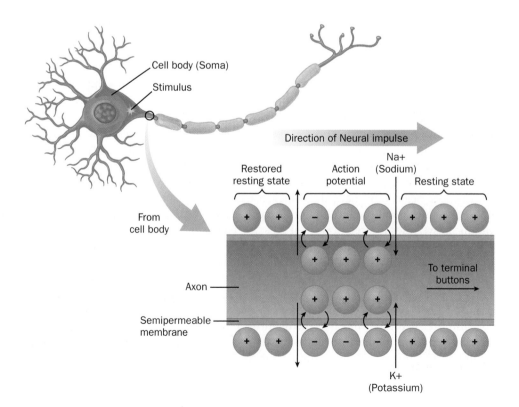

FIGURE 2-12 The sequence of events that occurs within neurons as the neural signal moves along the length of neurons (soma to axon to dendrite).

Source: Adapted from Morris & Maisto, 2002; Worchel & Shebilske, 1995.

arrives at the terminal buttons more rapidly. The large myelinated axons in your legs transmit action potentials as fast as 100 meters per second (224 miles per hour); small, unmyelinated axons (such as the ones in your brain) conduct action potentials as slow as 1 meter per second (2.24 miles per hour).

At the same time that the action potential is being transmitted, the initiating neurotransmitter is being cleared out of the synapse. Removal of the neurotransmitter causes the receiving neuron to return to a resting state and allows it to generate another action potential—that is, to fire again. When the neuron is being reset—called the *refractory period*—the neuron cannot fire again. When the neuron returns to the resting state, it can be fired normally. This process is diagrammed in Figures 2-11 and 2-12.

The action potential and the refractory period occur within 2 milliseconds. Many messages can be transmitted when neurons fire 500 or more times per second! The rate at which neurons fire is important because stimulus magnitude or intensity is indicated in this manner. Strong stimuli produce a high rate of firing, whereas weaker stimuli produce a lower rate of firing. The pressure from a fly landing on your hand results in a low rate of firing compared with the pressure of a 50-lb. weight on your hand.

Not all neurons respond to the presence of a neurotransmitter by depolarizing or generating an action potential; the result may be just the opposite. In these cases the neurotransmitter is inhibitory and causes additional negative ions to cross the cell membrane and enter the neuron. When inhibition occurs, the neuron becomes more negative than it was during the resting state (hyperpolarized) making an action potential harder, if not impossible, to generate. Some acetylcholine synapses in the parasympathetic system reflect this inhibitory nature. When acetylcholine is released, the neurons hyperpolarize, and the result is a decrease in a parasympathetic activity such as heart rate.

Now that we discussed the workings of the basic units of the nervous system (neurons) and the operation of neurotransmitters, we are ready to move on to the bigger picture—the operation of the brain. We will begin our discussion of the brain by looking at the methods neuroscientists have developed to investigate the structure and function of the brain. As you will see, some remarkable advances have occurred, in part, by putting computers to work in studying the brain. Then, we will look at the specific structures and functions of the brain itself.

REVIEW SUMMARY

1. The cells that make up the nervous system, **neurons,** are composed of **dendrites** (receive signals from adjacent neurons), a cell body or **soma,** an **axon** (transmits signals), and **terminal buttons** (contain neurotransmitters).

2. **Neurotransmitters** enable the signal from one neuron to be relayed to other neurons across the **synapse,** a small gap that separates neurons. A **myelin sheath** covers the axons of some neurons to increase the speed of transmission of the neural signal.

3. Among the key neurotransmitters, dopamine has been implicated in the development of Parkinson's disease. Acetycholine seems to play a role in Alzheimer's disease, and serotonin has been implicated in a variety of disorders, including depression and obsessive-compulsive disorder.

4. **Neuromodulators** have more widespread and indirect effects than neurotransmitters, and also influence transmission between cells.

5. **Agonists** are drugs that promote the action of a neurotransmitter; **antagonists** are drugs that oppose or inhibit the action of a neurotransmitter.

6. Neurotransmitters must be removed from the synapse before another signal can be transmitted. Removal is accomplished either by destroying the neurotransmitter (breakdown) or by taking it back into the terminal buttons (reuptake).

7. *Ions* (electrically charged particles) are found on the inside and outside of the neuron's semipermeable cell membrane. When a neuron is in a **resting state,** more negative ions are on the inside of the cell (measured at -70 mV) than on the outside.

8. Neurotransmitters stimulate the cell membrane to allow ions to enter the neuron, resulting in either **depolarization** (positive ions move inside the neuron resulting in excitation) or **hyperpolarization** (additional negative ions move inside resulting in inhibition).

9. If depolarization of the dendrite and soma reaches a threshold level, the axon quickly reverses its electrical charge, and the signal is transmitted to the next neuron. This reversal in electrical charge is known as the **action potential.**

✓ CHECK YOUR PROGRESS

1. What are the basic building blocks of the nervous system?

   a. cones
   b. neurons
   c. agonists
   d. sheaths

2. Send is to receive as _____ is to _____.

   a. axon, soma
   b. myelin, axon
   c. soma, dendrite
   d. axon, dendrite

3. While moving furniture in his apartment, Andy notices the insulation on the wire for a lamp and is reminded of something he learned in class today. If the topic was the structure of the neuron, what part was the focus of Andy's thoughts?

   a. dendrite
   b. synapse
   c. terminal button
   d. myelin sheath

4. A teacher tries to make learning the terminology of neurons a visual exercise. She has two students play the role of neurons. At one point she says one neuron "spits" a chemical at the other to continue neural conduction. What is the name for the chemical that was "spit?"

   a. myelin
   b. hormone
   c. endorphin
   d. neurotransmitter

5. Which individual is most likely to be diagnosed as suffering from Parkinson's disease?

   a. Alice, who is 28 and suffers from nightmares and depression
   b. Barry, who is 45 and suffers from panic attacks and memory loss
   c. Carl, who is 68 and experiences tremors and has difficulty initiating motor movements

   d. Darla, who is 34 and has difficulty remembering what day it is and believes that people do not like her

6. Which of the following is the best description of what happens when a neural signal proceeds down an axon?

   a. ebb and flow of hydraulic pressure
   b. a flood of a neurotransmitter under high pressure
   c. a rapid exchange of charged particles called ions
   d. pulling and pushing of tension within the cell body

7. Once a neurotransmitter has been released, it must be removed from the synapse before the neuron can fire again. What are the two major ways in which this is accomplished?

   a. reduction and retrieval
   b. breakdown and reuptake
   c. condensation and expiration
   d. inactivation and innervation

8. As part of a drug company research project, participants are given a drug described as an *agonist*. Because you are new to your job in the company, you wonder what effect this drug is likely to have. After looking up the term, which of the following will you conclude is the likely effect of the drug?

   a. The drug will cause a genetic mutation.
   b. The drug will self destruct after hitting its target organ.
   c. The drug will increase effectiveness of a particular neurotransmitter.
   d. The drug will multiply rapidly in the body so that its effects will be greater than originally anticipated.

9. What is a neuromodulator? How does it differ from a neurotransmitter?

10. Parkinson's disease occurs when there are reduced levels of which neurotransmitter?

    a. GABA
    b. dopamine
    c. serotonin
    d. acetylcholine

ANSWERS: 1. b **2.** d **3.** d **4.** d **5.** c **6.** c **7.** b **8.** c **9.** Like neurotransmitters, neuromodulators affect the transmission of information between neurons. They are, however, more widespread or generalized than neurotransmitters. **10.** b

THE BRAIN: A CLOSER LOOK

It's a bright, slightly chilly day in the 1800s in a small town in the United States. As Sam walks down the street, his attention is drawn to a sign for a phrenologist. His inquisitiveness gets the better of him and he walks in to inquire, "What is a phrenologist?" The man in the storefront says that phrenology is a way to assess a person's "faculties" by checking the skull for bumps and indentations. Sam slams down a few pennies and says, "What do I have to lose; let's give it a try." After a few minutes of what seems like a head massage, the phrenologist tells Sam about his strengths and weaknesses as evidenced by the bumps and indentations on his skull. *What does phrenology have to do with the study of the brain?*

In the 1800s a German physician and anatomist Franz Joseph Gall (1758–1828) developed the pseudoscience *phrenology* ("science of the mind"). Gall, who has been described as "part scientist, part charlatan, and all show-man" (Restak, 2000, p. 9), argued that the brain was like a muscle; exercise it and it grows larger. Furthermore, he believed that various skills and personality characteristics could be located on the brain. How? Just rub your hand over someone's skull and find the bumps. According to Gall, the bumps on the skull represented especially well developed skills and personality characteristics. In fact, Gall identified a long list of areas in the brain that he believed were responsible for acquisitiveness, secretiveness, mirthfulness, benevolence, firmness, and many others. Although all that is left of phrenology today are Gall's model skulls (see Figure 2-13), this early attempt to understand the brain had a modest element of truth. You see, Gall believed that skills and characteristics could be *localized* in certain areas of the brain. For the last hundred years, neuroscientists have been trying to identify some of these locations. As you will see, they have been trying to locate language, motor movement, and sensory impressions rather than mirthfulness and firmness. In just over a century, the study of the human nervous system has progressed from feeling a person's skull to collecting evidence of the brain in action without interfering with that activity.

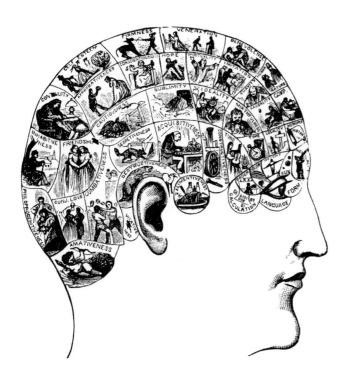

FIGURE 2-13   This model of the human brain represents Franz Joseph Gall's ideas on the locations of various skills and characteristics, which he thought could be discovered by reading bumps on the skull.

Source: Library of Medicine. Boston, MA.

Investigating Brain Functioning

Identifying the parts of the brain does not necessarily tell us the functions of those parts. How have neuroscientists learned about these functions? How do we know, for example, which areas of the brain play key roles in memory? And how do we know which areas of the brain are responsible for speech, motor movement, and emotion?

The Case Study Method. In 1861, the French physician Paul Broca used a technique for understanding the brain—the clinical or case study method. As we saw in Chapter 1, in this method a single patient is studied intensely. Broca treated a patient with a leg infection who was nicknamed "Tan" because this was one of the few sounds he could make. Tan's vocal system was not paralyzed, and he could understand what was said to him. A few days after being treated, Tan died. As we will soon see, today neuroscientists can use sophisticated brain scans to answer the questions that Broca answered by conducting an autopsy (Carter, 1998). The autopsy revealed damage in the left hemisphere of the brain. Based on the study of several other patients, Broca correctly concluded that this area was responsible for our ability to produce speech. In recognition of his discovery, this speech area is called *Broca's area.*

Phineas Gage's story (Harlow, 1868) is one of the most famous cases of survival from massive brain injury (Fleischmann, 2002; Macmillan, 2000a,b). Gage, a railroad foreman, was working with explosives in Cavendish, Vermont, on September 13, 1848, trying to clear a railroad right-of-way through granite bedrock. The procedure was arduous but straightforward. First, drill a hole into the rock by hand and then drop an explosive charge and fuse into the hole. Use a specially designed rod (called a tamping iron) to compact the explosive carefully. After some sand was poured in, the material could be vigorously compacted because the sand provided a shield against premature explosion. Unfortunately, this afternoon, Gage's attention was distracted from the task at hand; when he dropped the iron onto the powder it hit rock causing a spark. With the drilled hole serving as a launching pad, the tamping iron became a 13¼-lb. three feet seven inch rocket that shot through the left side of Gage's face and exited through his head. Gage became the "survivor of one of the most remarkable, if not the most remarkable, injuries to the brain in medical history" (Macmillan, 2000a, p. 11). Figure 2-

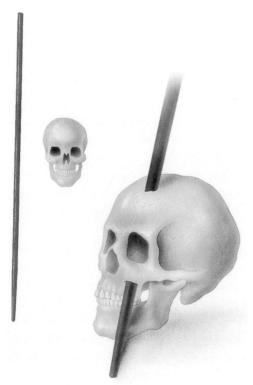

FIGURE 2-14 Phineas Gage had a tamping iron blasted through his head and lived to tell about it! The tamping rod missed sections of the brain that are absolutely crucial to survival. Although the damage was very close to the eyes and their neural pathways, there was no damage to his sense of vision. The damage to the brain occurred almost exclusively to Gage's left frontal lobe. The relative size of the iron bar that passed through his head is shown on the left. The path the bar took is shown on the right. In 1998, the town of Cavendish dedicated a memorial plaque recognizing the 150th anniversary of the accident.

14 shows the relative size of the rod that went through Gage's head and the path it took. Surprisingly, Gage was not killed in the accident; however, several problems were evident after the accident. Before the accident, Gage had been an excellent worker who got along well with others and carried through with his plans. After the accident, he made plans he never carried out, used gross profanity, refused to listen if what others said interfered with what he wanted, and was very moody.

The study of people who have suffered brain damage like Phineas Gage provides an abundance of information about brain functioning. A stroke (*cerebrovascular accident*) or temporary loss of blood flow to the brain is the most common form of brain damage in adults (Ginsberg, 1995). Direct injury produced by a blow to the head or gunshot wound is another common cause. By comparing a person's behavior, thought processes, and intelligence before and after brain damage, *neuropsychologists* (clinical psychologists with specialized training in the diagnosis and treatment of disorders of the central nervous system) can learn a great deal about specific functions of the brain (Sundberg, Winebarger, & Taplin, 2002). These comparisons are made with tests that evaluate sensory abilities (for example, vision and hearing), intelligence, memory, and language. In addition to administering tests to determine which brain areas regulate which processes, neuropsychologists coordinate and direct treatment programs. Not surprisingly, there have been major advances in neuropsychology after wars in which a large number of injuries occurred. Advances in locating key parts of the brain and identifying their functions led to increased attempts to alter those structures when abnormal behaviors were noticed. Various forms of brain surgery (psychosurgery) to alter abnormal behaviors were prominent among these efforts.

Stereotaxic Surgery.   In 1904, brain researchers created a device that made studying certain brain structures possible (Valenstein, 1973). Before the invention of this device, structures that were deep in the brain could be examined only by removing or damaging the tissue that covered them. The *stereotaxic instrument* holds the head in a fixed position and allows an electrode (a fine piece of specially treated wire) to be inserted into a specified area of a patient's brain. The electrode is thin enough that it does not damage tissue as it passes through. The electrode can record electrical brain activity, stimulate brain activity with a mild electric current, or destroy a brain area by lesioning (or destroying) the area by passing a strong electric current through it. These procedures (recording, stimulating, and lesioning) provide information about the functions of various structures and are commonly used to study brain functioning in animals. The stereotaxic instrument is also used to inject chemicals into selected brain areas. These chemicals can be used to stimulate or destroy brain areas (Joyner & Guillemot, 1994), either temporarily or permanently.

Stereotaxic instruments are individually created for each species and have been used on a variety of animals and humans. The stereotaxic instrument depicted in Figure 2-15 is used to study and to treat human brains. The use of this technique raises ethical questions, such as the risk that the operation will cause permanent changes in the patient's abilities or personality. For this reason, stereotaxic surgery (a form of psychosurgery) on humans is a last resort. When it is used, the purpose is to destroy a brain area believed to be malfunctioning and creating serious behavior problems such as excessive, unprovoked violence (Mark & Ervin, 1970). In another procedure, parts of the brain that are thought to cause intractable forms of obsessive-compulsive disorder (see Chapter 13) are destroyed (Jenike, 1998) in an effort to reduce the severity of the symptoms.

The Electroencephalograph.   More recently developed techniques have enabled neuroscientists to examine brain functions and anatomy without resorting to autopsy or invasive stereotaxic surgery. In 1929 Hans Berger developed the **electroencephalograph (EEG),** a device that monitors and records the brain's electrical activity. To make an EEG recording, a technician places several round metal discs, called *electrodes,* on a patient's scalp (see Figure 2-16A). These electrodes sense the brain activity occurring in the region beneath them and transmit this information to the EEG system, which amplifies the signals. These amplified signals activate a pen that records the type of electrical activity (known as *brain waves*) occurring in the region monitored, thus producing an electroencephalogram.

Brain waves (identified by Greek letters) are distinguished by their frequency, which is measured in cycles per second (called *hertz* and abbreviated *Hz*), and their amplitude, which reflects strength. Brain researchers have labeled a number of different types of brain waves; each is generally associated with a particular state of consciousness (see Figure 2-16B). In other words, the presence of a particular type of brain waves tells us something about what is going on in the brain at the time; however, the information is often not specific enough for making diagnoses or for fine-tuned analysis of brain functioning. Here are some of the most commonly identified brain waves:

Alpha Waves.   These are fast brain waves (8 to 12 Hz) that are not high in amplitude. The brain generally produces

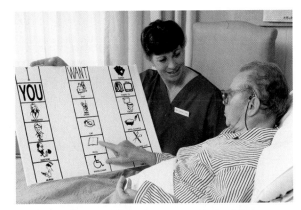

Clinical neuropsychologists have developed an array of measures to assess people who have suffered brain damage. These clinical measures not only help identify the specific form of brain damage, they are also useful in devising approaches for rehabilitation. The patient pictured here has suffered a stroke and his language abilities are being assessed in order to help him communicate better.

electroencephalograph (EEG)
Device that monitors and records electrical activity of the brain in the form of a graphic representation of brain waves

FIGURE 2-15   The stereotaxic instrument allows researchers to insert a fine piece of wire called an electrode into deep brain areas. The electrode can be used to record brain activity, stimulate a brain area, or destroy (lesion) an area. This technique has been used to reduce the symptoms of disorders such as obsessive-compulsive disorder.

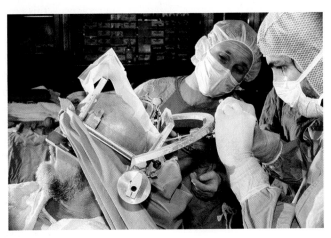

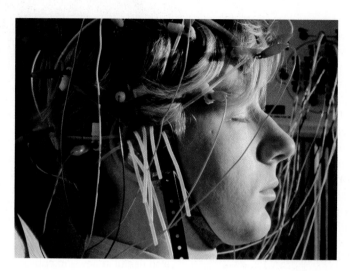

Alpha waves	Alpha waves are characteristic of normal resting adults
Beta waves	Beta waves typically accompany intense concentration
Theta waves	Theta waves are seen in children, in frustrated adults, and in very light sleep
Delta waves	Delta waves occur in deep sleep and in certain pathological states

1 sec

A   B

FIGURE 2-16   (A) EEG participant with scalp electrodes in place. Each small electrode senses the electrical signals generated by millions of neurons under it. (B) The signals that are sensed by electrodes are amplified and recorded. Several commonly observed types of brain waves are illustrated here.

alpha waves when the individual is in a calm, relaxed state and is not concentrating on anything in particular.

Beta Waves.   These are very fast brain waves (13 to 30 Hz), but not high in amplitude. These brain waves are associated with mental activity such as reading this chapter, taking notes in class, or answering test questions.

Theta Waves.   These brain waves (3.5 to 7 Hz) are irregular in frequency and low in amplitude. When we are in a light stage of sleep or daydreaming, our brains are likely to produce this type of wave.

Delta Waves.   These brain waves are quite slow (below 3.5 Hz) and quite high in amplitude. They are associated with the deep stages of sleep.

We will have more to say about brain waves and the different states of consciousness with which they are associated in Chapter 4.

Although the EEG is useful for detecting the abnormal brain waves found in epilepsy and for identifying certain sleep disorders (see the discussion in Chapter 4 of narcolepsy), this record of overall brain activity has limited usefulness. The EEG is not precise enough to monitor localized activity in specific areas of the brain. Because of the general nature of the EEG, more detailed technology has been developed to determine which brain areas are involved with the behavior in question. For example, neuroscientists can now use *magnetoencephalography* (*MEG*) to measure the brain's magnetic fields and thus determine levels of electrical activity. This method is easier to use and more precise than the traditional EEG procedure.

The development of new techniques to investigate the brain and the rest of the nervous system has occurred at a rapid pace. In just a few decades, researchers have developed ever more sophisticated methods that have advanced our knowledge. Our understanding of neural activity "jumped a quantum leap" (Gazzaniga, Ivry, & Mangun, 1998, p. 77) with the development of methods to record the activity of a single neuron in laboratory animals. No longer would researchers have to rely on gross measures such as the EEG, which records and averages the activity of millions of neurons. Using these techniques, researchers have learned that neurons involved in the processing of visual

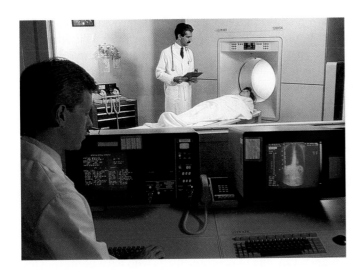

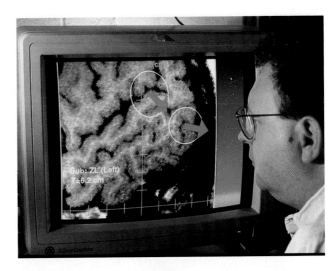

A

B

FIGURE 2-17   (A) A patient preparing for a CT scan is about to be positioned in the gantry. (B) The result of a CT scan showing the structure of an isolated portion of the brain.

information in primates do not all respond to the same elements of the stimulus. In fact, neurons that are adjacent to one another may or may not respond to characteristics such as stimulus shape or movement.

Computerized Brain Imaging.   The advent of computers has led to major advances in the study of the brain. With the newest techniques, a computer uses measures of brain activity to produce a brain image. Some of these brain imaging techniques provide static or single-point-in-time pictures of brain structures that are similar to the way an X-ray provides an image of a bone. These static images are provided by computerized axial tomography (CT or CAT) and magnetic resonance imaging (MRI). In addition, the most recently developed brain imaging techniques provide ongoing or dynamic images of the brain. **Positron emission tomography (PET)** is one example of these dynamic scans; however, these scans tend to be very expensive and therefore are not as widely used as the other brain scans.

If you were to undergo a **CT or CAT (computerized axial tomography)** scan, an imaging technique involving computer interpretation of a large number of X-rays, you would find yourself lying on a table with your head positioned inside a large collar-like structure called a *gantry*. Figure 2-17A shows a patient about to be put into a gantry. An X-ray machine located inside the gantry is completely rotated around the patient's head while numerous X-rays are taken. The patient remains in the CT scanner for approximately 15 to 30 minutes. The X-rays are taken from a variety of angles, and a computer combines the X-rays to produce multiple brain images. Figure 2-17B shows the result of a CT scan.

The **MRI (magnetic resonance imaging)** uses a strong magnetic field and radio waves, rather than X-rays (Warach, 1995). With this process, a patient's head is positioned within a strong magnetic field, which causes the hydrogen atoms in brain cells to become aligned—that is, to spin in the same direction. Radio waves directed at the brain cause the spinning hydrogen atoms to emit a signal. The denser or thicker the tissue, the greater the number of hydrogen atoms and, therefore, the stronger the signal. A computer amplifies and analyzes signals from the hydrogen atoms to construct a picture of the brain tissues. The MRI procedure takes about twice as long as a CT scan, but the results are often worth the extra time. Compare Figure 2-17B with 2-18, and you will see that the details produced by the MRI (Figure 2-18) are superior to those of the CT (Figure 2-17B).

positron emission tomography (PET)
Imaging technique that involves monitoring the metabolic activity of the brain

computerized axial tomography (CT or CAT)
Imaging technique that involves the production of a large number of X-rays interpreted by a computer

magnetic resonance imaging (MRI)
Imaging technique that involves the use of radio waves and a strong magnetic field to produce a signal that can be interpreted by a computer

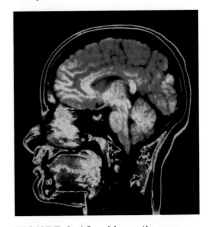

FIGURE 2-18   Magnetic resonance imaging (MRI) provides neuroscientists with a detailed image of the living human brain.

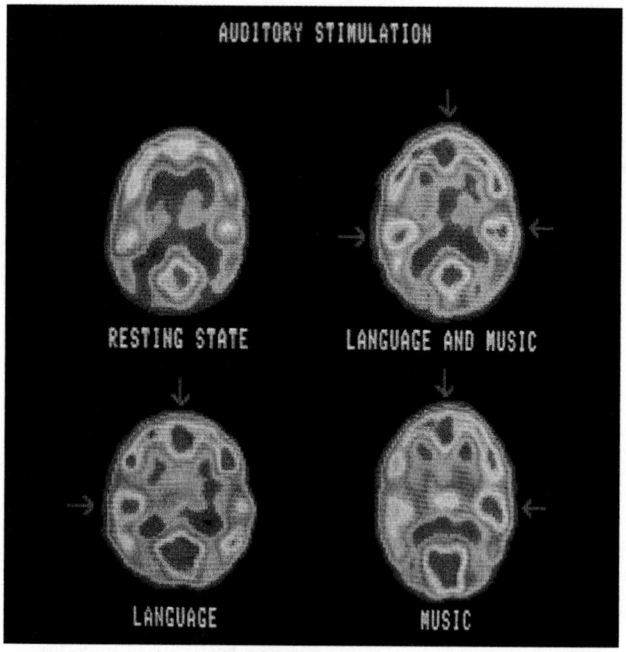

AUDITORY STIMULATION

RESTING STATE   LANGUAGE AND MUSIC

LANGUAGE   MUSIC

FIGURE 2-19 Photographs of PET scans taken while a person is in a resting state, and while listening to music and language, together and separately. The color of the scan reveals the level of activity in various areas of the brain: Red and yellow indicates a high level of brain activity; green indicates an average level of activity, and blue indicates a below-average level of activity.

Positron emission tomography (PET) provides information about the brain's metabolic activity or energy use. With this procedure, the patient is injected with a radioactive form of glucose (blood sugar). Because active neurons require larger amounts of fuel, the radioactive glucose accumulates in the most active areas of the brain. The PET procedure scans the brain and monitors the radioactivity of various brain areas. Figure 2-19 shows patterns of brain activity while a person is resting and listening to language and/or music. The areas of highest glucose utilization (highest activity) are shown in yellow and red. Green areas indicate average activity; blue areas indicate below average activity. As you can see, different areas of the brain are activated. Although the PET scan provides useful information, it is time-consuming and requires the patient to be conscious and able to process the stimuli that are presented. Nevertheless, it has proven quite valuable to neuroscientists who have been studying the relationship between the nervous system and various mental processes.

An MRI will not work well and is potentially dangerous if you have a heart pacemaker or any other metal implant. The magnets in an MRI exert a gravitational pull that is approximately 40,000 times greater than that of the earth (Carter, 1998)! Technicians who forgot to take off watches or jewelry have been dragged across a room by the MRI magnet. In 2001, a 6-year-old boy was undergoing a routine MRI following surgery to remove a brain tumor. When an oxygen tank was wheeled into the room, the powerful magnets of the MRI turned the 6.5-pound metal tank into a projectile. Two days later the boy died of the resulting injuries (Archibold, 2001).

Although the standard MRI produces excellent structural images, it does not depict *ongoing* (temporal) brain activity. **Functional magnetic resonance imaging (fMRI),** a modified version of the standard MRI, provides both excellent structural views and temporal changes in brain activity. Neuroscientists have used the fMRI to determine the role played by various brain structures in a range of behaviors (Pine et al., 2001; Whalen et al., 2001). For example, dyslexics tend to underuse the more efficient word-processing regions of the brain and instead rely on speech production areas. Quick, now, what is 12×11? About how many miles is it from your classroom to the nearest McDonald's? Using fMRI scans, researchers found that college students use different brain areas in answering these types of questions. When doing multiplication tables, students tend to use areas involved with verbal memory; when giving distance estimates, they rely on regions involved with visual and spatial tasks (Murray, 2000). This type of research would not have been possible just a few years ago.

Psychological Detective

A construction worker suffered a head injury that may have resulted in brain damage. If you were on duty in the emergency room when the patient arrived, what technique would you use to diagnose the extent of any possible brain damage? Your choices include the EEG, MEG, a CT scan, a PET scan, and the MRI. Think about the situation, and write down the procedure you would recommend. Why did you make this choice?

functional magnetic resonance imaging (fMRI)
A modification of the standard MRI procedure that allows both structural and temporal images of the brain to be gathered

Because of the time involved, an MRI is not used when quick evaluations are needed. The PET scan and EEG procedure would not be used because they are not designed to detect damaged tissue and the results are not sufficiently precise. Victims of accidents typically require the quicker CT scan. In this section we have discussed the various methods neuroscientists use to study the brain; now we turn our attention to what those methods have revealed about the structures and functioning of the brain.

Major Components of the Brain

What makes us different compared to other organisms on this planet? Is it our height? Surely not, for there are taller organisms. How about our speed? No. Most people would say it is our brain, but they may be surprised by a few facts. You see, humans do not have the largest brain of any creature on the planet. Here are the humbling facts, which indicate that size is not everything (Restak, 2000):

- An average human brain weighs 1,300 grams (about 3 pounds)
- The bottlenose dolphin's brain weighs 1,500 grams
- An elephant's brain weighs 6,000 grams
- A sperm whale has a brain of 7,800 grams

What makes us unique? Consider these facts: Blood flow to the brain accounts for 15 to 20% of the blood leaving the heart. Why? It takes a lot of blood, glucose, and oxygen to run the estimated 100 billion or more neurons in the brain. It takes a lot of energy to keep this machine operating 24 hours a day, seven days a week. Every thought we have, every breath we take, every emotion we experience, every decision we make involves this approximately 3-lb. mass that is "as big as a coconut, the shape of a walnut, the colour of uncooked liver and the consistency of chilled butter" (Carter, 1998, p. 15). Each neuron can make contact with thousands of other neurons, thus creating a network that is not matched anywhere in nature or made by the hands of humans. As noted earlier, the complexity of the human brain cannot be matched by modern computers.

Before we discuss some of the more complicated processes controlled by the brain, let's begin with a review of some behaviors that do not even reach the brain. Recall that some of your behavior consists of reflexes like knee jerks and the attempt to yank your hand out of a car door. As we noted, such behaviors are not processed by the brain; apparently, the time saved by restricting these behaviors to the spinal cord had survival value and thus have been passed on. But we live in an ever-changing environment with new challenges that require more than reflexes. What would you do if your hand were stuck below the seat in your car and you couldn't pull it free? Let's follow that information as it is sent up the spinal cord to the brain. (Bear in mind that although it takes us some time to describe this journey, the entire process happens in milliseconds.)

Initially the information travels upward in a group of nerves called a *tract*; its ultimate destination is the brain, which sits on top of the spinal cord. The three main divisions of the brain are the hindbrain, the midbrain, and the forebrain. A cross-section of the brain is shown in Figure 2-20. Let's take a closer look.

The Hindbrain.　As the information about what has happened to your hand leaves the spinal cord, it passes through structures in the **hindbrain**. The major components of the hindbrain are the medulla, the pons, and the cerebellum. From an evolutionary perspective, these are the oldest parts of the brain, and they have important survival functions. The **medulla** (short for *medulla oblongata*) contains our respiratory center, which keeps us breathing, especially when we are asleep. Obviously, we can breathe voluntarily (take a deep breath now) or involuntarily without thinking about it. If our respiratory center is damaged, however, we cannot breathe automatically because we would have to think about every breath. Thus, if we stopped thinking, we would stop breathing (Vertosick, 1996)! The medulla also controls heart rate, vomiting, swallowing, and blood circulation. When the hand-in-the-door information reaches and activates the medulla, that structure may cause your breathing to increase.

The **pons** (from the Latin for "bridge") connects the two halves of the brain at the hindbrain level; this part of the hindbrain is important for sleep and arousal. The cerebellum coordinates skilled movement sequences that deal with objects in motion. Without the control exerted by the **cerebellum,** we would have great difficulty performing such behaviors as pointing to a moving object. Although it is accurate to say that the cerebellum coordinates motor movements, this description fails to explain how

THE FAR SIDE® BY GARY LARSON

"Whoa! *That* was a good one! Try it, Hobbs—just poke his brain right where my finger is."

Electrical Brain Stimulation

hindbrain
Oldest of the three main divisions of the brain; its major structures are the medulla, pons, and cerebellum

medulla (medulla oblongata)
Structure located in the hindbrain that regulates automatic responses such as breathing, swallowing, and blood circulation

pons
Structure of the hindbrain that connects the two halves of the brain; has nuclei that are important for sleep and arousal

cerebellum
Structure of the hindbrain that coordinates muscular movements

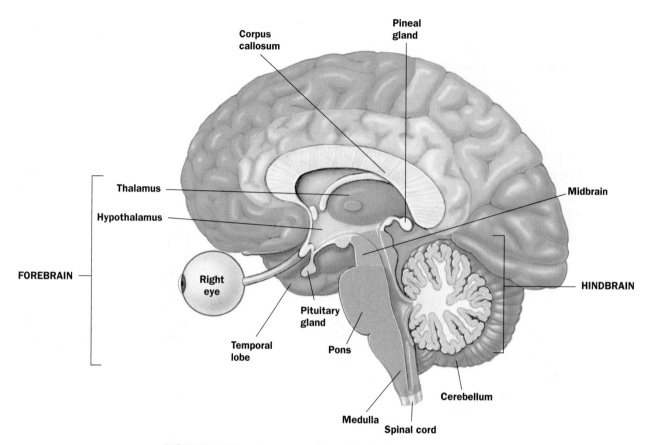

Corpus
callosum

Pineal
gland

Thalamus

Hypothalamus

Midbrain

FOREBRAIN

Right
eye

HINDBRAIN

Pituitary
gland

Temporal
lobe

Pons

Medulla

Spinal cord

Cerebellum

FIGURE 2-20 A cross-section of the brain showing structures at the hindbrain, midbrain, and forebrain levels.

the cerebellum works in conjunction with other brain areas that initiate motor movements (which we will discuss later). The cerebellum "fine tunes" the gross motor signals that come from the upper brain; thus, the cerebellum's output is purely inhibitory. Neurons in the cerebellum dampen the activity of other neurons in the brain (Vertosick, 1996); however, it does not take much to disrupt the work of the cerebellum. Even small amounts of alcohol can affect the cerebellum. Drivers suspected of driving under the influence of alcohol are often asked to complete a series of tests that can indicate if their motor coordination has been affected by alcohol's influence on the cerebellum.

The Midbrain.   Continuing its trip to the higher brain centers, the information about your injured hand passes through the **midbrain.** Together the hindbrain and midbrain are known as the **brain stem** because they form the stem, or stalk, on which the remainder of the brain rests. The midbrain also is composed of nerve pathways that go *to and from* higher brain centers. Psychologists have found that this complex network of fibers, known as the **reticular formation,** is very important in controlling our level of arousal or alertness. Actually, the reticular formation reaches all the way from the hindbrain through the midbrain and into the forebrain.

When you first moved into your new dormitory room or apartment, you probably did not sleep very well for several nights. Every little noise probably sounded like a cannon going off in your bedroom. Now that you are accustomed to your new environment, you can (and do) sleep through everything (except classes). Your reticular formation was involved in this change because it acts like a gatekeeper. When we need to be aware of new and unfamiliar information, such as the sound of an ambulance or a fire engine, the reticular formation allows it to pass on to higher brain centers for

midbrain
Major division of the brain that contains fibers known as the reticular formation

brain stem
The oldest part of the brain, begins at the top of the spinal cord, and contains brain centers responsible for basic survival activities

reticular formation
Nerve fibers passing through the midbrain that control arousal

Police officers use a variety of tests (called field sobriety tests) to determine if a driver has been driving under the influence of alcohol. Among the tests are: walking a straight line heel to toe or closing one's eyes and touching the tip of the nose with a finger. The detrimental effects of alcohol on the cerebellum are likely to be seen in the driver's performance on such tests.

forebrain
Major division of the brain that consists of subcortical structures and the cerebral cortex

corpus callosum
Wide band of neural fibers that connects the two hemispheres of the brain

subcortical structures
Structures of the forebrain, such as the amygdala, hypothalamus, and thalamus, that are located beneath the cerebral cortex

cerebral cortex (cerebrum)
The convoluted (wrinkled) outer layer of the brain

limbic system
System of interconnected subcortical structures that regulates emotions and motivated behaviors, such as hunger, thirst, aggression, and sexual behavior

thalamus
Subcortical structure that relays incoming sensory information to the cerebral cortex and other parts of the brain

processing. Familiar information that is of no immediate consequence, such as the sound of a refrigerator motor or air conditioner, is blocked by the reticular formation, and we do not become aware of it.

The Forebrain. As the injured-hand information leaves the brain stem and moves upward, it enters the **forebrain.** Examination of the forebrain reveals that this part of the brain is divided into two distinct halves with duplicate structures in each half. These two halves or hemispheres are connected by a wide band of fibers known as the **corpus callosum** ("hard body"). The two hemispheres of the forebrain communicate with each other through the corpus callosum. Within the forebrain, the areas that the information about your injured hand encounters first are collectively known as **subcortical structures** because they are located beneath the other main division of the forebrain, the **cerebral cortex** (also known as the *cerebrum*) or outer covering of the brain.

Several of the major subcortical structures are summarized in Table 2-2 and appear in Figure 2-20. Take some time to familiarize yourself with these structures and their functions, and refer to Figure 2-20 so that you know the location of each one.

Deep down in the brain—below the cortex—you will find the basal ganglia, a series of interconnected structures that play a significant role in motor movement. These structures are also connected to other parts of the brain that play a role in motor movement. The motor difficulties that occur in Parkinson's disease are the result of loss of neurons in the basal ganglia that produce dopamine.

The **limbic system** (see Figure 2-21) is a group of interrelated subcortical structures that are involved in the regulation of emotions and motivated behaviors such as hunger, thirst, aggression, and sexual behavior. Table 2-2 describes several components of the limbic system.

The **thalamus** (from the Greek word for "inner room") is important because it sends sensory information to the cerebral cortex and other parts of the brain. Because so much information

2.4

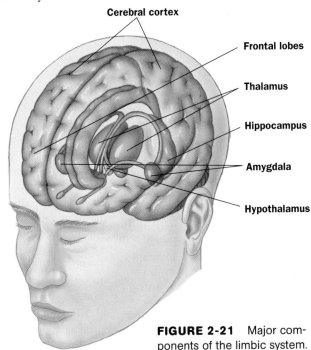

Cerebral cortex

Frontal lobes

Thalamus

Hippocampus

Amygdala

Hypothalamus

FIGURE 2-21 Major components of the limbic system.

TABLE 2-2

Selected Subcortical Structures and Their Functions

Limbic system
A group of structures involved in the control and direction of emotional behavior. The amygdala is involved in emotional reactivity, aggression, and the processing of odors. The hippocampus is involved in emotional reactivity and the storage of memories.

Hypothalamus
Some neurons in the hypothalamus are involved in the control of arousal, emotionality, food and water intake, sexual behavior, and body temperature; considered by some researchers to be part of the limbic system. Other hypothalamic neurons control pituitary hormone production and release.

Thalamus
A structure that integrates incoming sensory information and relays it to appropriate areas of the cerebral cortex.

Basal ganglia
A group of structures located near the thalamus that are involved in the control of slow, voluntary movement, such as standing, sitting, and walking.

FROG

PIGEON

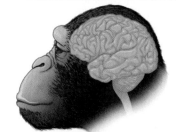

CAT

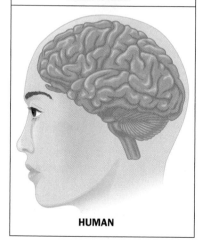

CHIMPANZEE

HUMAN

FIGURE 2-22 Both the size and the surface of the brain (the cortex) differ across species. In general, more sophisticated and developed organisms have a more wrinkled and crumpled cortex. This wrinkling and crumpling is nature's way of stuffing more cortex into the limited space provided by the skull.

comes into and goes out of the thalamus, it is called the brain's great relay station. A large number of nerve fibers radiate from the thalamus and route information to specific areas of the cerebral cortex (Barth & MacDonald, 1996). For example, some fibers go to your sensory cortex, others go to your motor cortex. The major structures of the brain are summarized in the Study Chart on the next page.

You may be wondering how sensory information finds its way to the correct location for further processing. Remember that nerve tracts bring sensory information up the spinal cord and then through the brain stem. When these tracts reach the thalamus, each goes to an area that is appropriate for the information it is carrying. There is an area for vision, one for audition (hearing), one for taste, one for touch, and so on for all the other senses, except the sense of smell, which is processed in the olfactory bulb. Information is then relayed from these areas to appropriate areas of the cortex.

Ultimately, the information about your hand caught in the car door reaches the appropriate areas in the cerebral cortex. As you can see in Figure 2-21, the cerebral cortex covers the subcortical structures we have been discussing. As Figure 2-22 shows, the cortex in lower animals such as cats or frogs is smooth and not very thick. The more complex the brain, the rougher the cortex. The human cortex has a very wrinkled and crumpled appearance that resembles a walnut or cauliflower. In prehistoric times, when the human brain began to develop, a great deal of growth and expansion took place in the cerebral cortex. Because the brain was confined within the bony skull, this growth caused the expanding cortex to wrap around subcortical parts of the brain and take on its characteristic ridges and valleys (called *fissures*). If the cortex for various organisms were unfolded, here is what you would find: A rat's cortex (basically smooth) would be the size of a postage stamp. A monkey's cortex would be the size of an envelope, whereas a chimp's cortex would be approximately the size of one of the pages in this book. The human cortex would take up about four pages of this book. This expansion and development of the cerebral cortex sets the human brain apart from the brains of lower animals. In fact, the human cerebral cortex has been described as "the most intricately organized and densely populated expanse of biological real estate in the world" (Restak, 2000, p. 20).

Because the ridges and valleys are similar from one person to the next, they are used as landmarks to locate specific areas of the cortex, called *lobes*. Figure 2-23 shows

STUDY CHART

Major Structures of the Brain

Location	Structure	Function
Hindbrain	Medulla	Controls autonomic responses such as breathing, swallowing, and blood circulation
	Pons	Serves as a bridge to connect the brain's two halves
	Cerebellum	Coordinates muscular movements
Midbrain	Reticular formation	Controls levels of arousal or alertness
Forebrain	Corpus callosum	Allows the forebrain's two hemispheres to communicate
	Cerebral cortex (cerebrum)	Handles sensory processing, motor control, memory formation and storage
	Limbic system	Regulates emotions and motivated behaviors such as hunger, thirst, aggression, and sexual behavior
	Thalamus	Integrates incoming information and relays it to the cerebral cortex

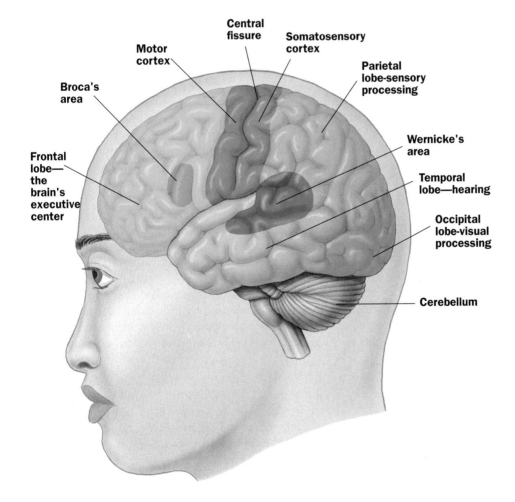

FIGURE 2-23 Locations and functions of the four lobes of the cerebral cortex. *Frontal lobes*: Involved in the control of body movement, decision making, and language. *Temporal lobes*: Serve a variety of functions, including memory and processing of auditory information. *Parietal lobes*: Contain major sensory areas of the cortex. The sensory information, however, is received from the opposite side of the body. Thus, the left parietal lobe receives information from the right side of the body, and vice versa. *Occipital lobes*: Contain the primary visual-processing areas of the cortex.

frontal lobes
The largest lobes of the cortex; they contain a motor strip, Broca's area (speech), and areas responsible for decision making

parietal lobes
Lobes located behind the frontal lobes and containing the sensory cortex

the locations and functions of each of the four lobes—frontal, temporal, parietal, and occipital lobes—in each hemisphere. (Remember, there are two halves, or hemispheres, of the brain. The cortex of each hemisphere has four lobes.) Each of the lobes seems to have some specialized responsibilities. Here is a closer look at each of them.

Frontal Lobes. As a result of their names, the **frontal lobes** are easy to locate. What's more, they are easy to spot because they are quite large (compared to the other lobes), accounting for almost 50% of the volume of each of the cerebral hemispheres (Restak, 2000). The frontal lobes are frequently referred to as the *executive arm* of the brain (Goldberg, 2001). This description is based on the responsibilities of these lobes: language, movement, reasoning, planning, problem solving, and personality. Figure 2-24 illustrates the amount of the frontal lobe's motor cortex devoted to various parts of the body. In general, more cortical area is devoted to motor functions that are most important to our survival. Because the use of our hands is so important to survival, large motor areas are devoted to manual dexterity.

The importance of the frontal lobes is clearly revealed in the case of Phineas Gage. As you will recall from our earlier discussion, a tamping iron was blown through Gage's head, yet he lived to tell about it. Miraculously, the tamping iron (1.25 inches in diameter) created a tunnel from just under his left eye through his skull, yet it did not damage any areas necessary for survival. Gage's vision and motor abilities were not affected. The physical results of the accident were evident in the scars, but the damage to his personality seemed to be even greater and evident to those who knew him best and proclaimed that he was "no longer Gage." His ability to plan, to make good decisions, and his overall judgment were severely impacted. Formerly an efficient, dependable, and responsible worker, he would never again return to the type of work he had enjoyed, and was even relegated to being a side show attraction in the circus. The damage made him susceptible to the kind of whims that the frontal lobe generally holds at bay via its inhibitory functions. Gage died 11½ years after the accident as a result of severe seizures, which were likely a result of the accident.

Parietal Lobes. The **parietal lobes** are located just behind the frontal lobes. Their major responsibility is to process every sensation received except smell, which, as we discuss in Chapter 3, has direct connections to the limbic system of the brain. The parietal lobes can also be thought of as a *sensory integrator* because they are responsible for body position as well as our sensory cortex or somatosensory strip. Figure 2-24 presents a map of the sensory cortex. Notice how the parts of the body that are most important in dealing effectively with the environment have the largest brain areas. For example, information received from your fingers is more important to your survival than information received from the middle of your back. Therefore, more brain area is devoted to the fingers than to the back.

Damage to the parietal lobes can result in a neurological condition called neglect syndrome. If the damage affects the somatosensory strip, the patient will fail to acknowledge objects or events in the space opposite the lesion. For example, damage to the right parietal lobe renders a patient unable to perceive or respond to stimuli on the left side. One consequence of this syndrome is that patients may neglect an entire side of their own body and fail to engage in typical behaviors such as grooming.

Myth or Science

How did neuroscientists map the brain's motor and somatosensory strips? Electrically stimulating parts of the brain provided the information needed to create these maps. Typically, this procedure can occur while patients are fully awake; interestingly, the brain has no pain receptors so patients do not experience any pain from the electrical simulation. Put an electrode on a spot near the top of the brain in the right frontal lobe's motor strip and a person will move his or her left hand. Keep moving that

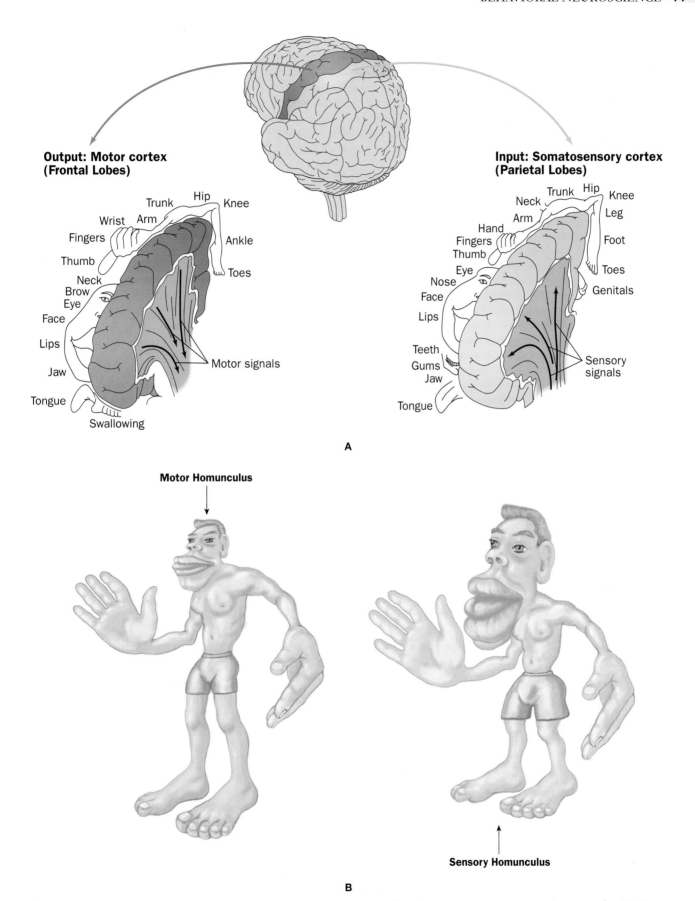

FIGURE 2-24   (A) Map of the motor cortex and somatosensory cortex. More important senses occupy larger areas. (B) These odd-looking figures are called homunculi (singular is homunculus). A homunculus represents how human beings would look if our bodies were in proportion to the amount of brain space devoted to our motor and sensory functions.

electrode just a bit and the whole series of motor movements and brain areas responsible for such movements will be revealed.

One of the interesting findings from efforts to map the brain is that stimulating most areas of the brain do not give rise to a motor response or a particular sensory impression. In fact, much of the brain is composed of what are called association areas that serve to connect other areas with one another. In many ways, these areas are like highways, in this case, they move memories, thoughts, impressions and connect them with other elements such as emotions and future plans. Because most of the brain is composed of association areas, many people believe that we use only 10% of our brain. Psychologist Donald McBurney (2002) has called this belief "one of the hardiest weeds in the garden of psychology." Although this notion is appealing and perhaps we would even want it to be true, it is not true. Although much of the brain is association area, this does not mean these are unused areas. The results of the brain scans discussed earlier indicate that large areas of the brain are used for various cognitive tasks, and these areas are often different depending on the task at hand. So, you certainly should give a task your best effort, but don't be fooled into believing that 90% of your brain is not used.

Temporal Lobes.   The **temporal lobes** contain areas that are responsible for hearing and understanding speech (Wernicke's area). They also contain connections to the hippocampus and amygdala, which are important in learning, memory, and emotion.

Occipital Lobes.   The back of the brain contains the **occipital lobes,** which may be the simplest of the lobes in terms of responsibilities. The occipital lobes' primary responsibility is to process visual information. Although we receive sensory visual information through the eyes, we process and understand it at the very back of the brain.

Each of the occipital lobes processes information received from half of the visual field. This contralateral organization means information from the right visual field is sent to the left occipital lobe and vice versa. Of course, there are numerous connections between the two occipital lobes, so visual information is ultimately processed holistically unless there is some type of damage. Damage to both occipital lobes may cause *cortical blindness*, which means a person has no damage to the eyes but the occipital lobes are unable to process the visual information received. If only one occipital lobe is damaged, the result is blindness in the opposite visual field.

Language and the Brain.   One of the key differences that sets humans apart from lower animals is the existence of a complex and continually developing language. As a result, it is not surprising that neuroscientists have focused on the brain structures responsible for language as well as the problems that develop when these areas are damaged. As we saw earlier, Broca's area (in most people it is in the left frontal lobe) is the key area involved in language production. Wernicke's area (in most people it is located in the left temporal lobe) is the key area involved in understanding language. Damage to either or both areas can have significant effects on a person's language abilities.

The term **aphasia** refers to a loss of the ability to speak or understand written or spoken language. Aphasia is quite common, occurring in approximately 40% of people who have suffered a stroke (Gazzaniga, Ivry, & Mangun, 1998). Damage to Broca's area results in *nonfluent aphasia*. People with this type of aphasia have difficulty producing speech, although they generally understand what others say to them.

The speech of people with Broca's aphasia is often slow, effortful, lacking function words, and thus resembles a telegram. They may struggle to string together the appropriate words or combine words to express their thoughts. Here is an example of the spontaneous speech of a person with Broca's aphasia: "Son ... university ...

Broca's Aphasia

temporal lobes
Lobes responsible for hearing and understanding speech (Wernicke's area)

occipital lobes
The lobes located at the back of the brain, which are responsible for processing visual stimuli

aphasia
General term for problems in understanding or producing spoken or written language

smart . . . boy . . . good . . . good . . . ". They may also experience difficulty understanding reversible sentences such as "The boy was hit by the girl. Who hit whom?" Although you would have no difficulty answering this question, damage to Broca's area is likely to lead the person to answer "Boy hit girl" (Gazzaniga, Ivry, & Mangun, 1998, p. 307).

In 1874, a German neurologist Carl Wernicke (1848–1905) identified a second brain area that plays a significant role in language. Damage to Wernicke's area results in language problems called *fluent aphasia*.

In contrast to the speech of people with damage to Broca's area, damage to Wernicke's area results in fluent-sounding but meaningless speech. Imagine listening to someone who speaks another language (Dutch, for example). Although you may not understand a word of what is being said, what you hear sounds right to your ear. If the speaker has Wernicke's aphasia, however, the following might be a translation of what sounded right to your ear:

> I called my mother on the television and did not understand the door. It was not too breakfast, but they came from far to near. My mother is not too old for me to be young (Gazzaniga, Ivry, & Mangun, 1998, p. 308).

Although the Dutch version of this translation might have flowed smoothly, the translation indicates it is utterly without meaning and also contains several semantic errors.

Although the aphasias revealed by Broca's and Wernicke's patients are the two most common, there are other intriguing types. For example, *optic aphasia* is the inability to read more than one letter at a time (Buxbaum & Coslett, 1996), whereas a person suffering from *word deafness* cannot understand spoken language despite the presence of normal hearing and reading abilities (Davis, 1993).

Apraxias are deficits in nonverbal skills. As you might suspect, apraxias involve damage to the right hemisphere. Depending on the site of the damage, one might observe a *dressing apraxia*, in which a person has trouble putting clothing on one side of the body, or a *constructional apraxia*, in which a person cannot copy a simple drawing.

Oliver Sacks (1985) reported an interesting apraxia that involved the inability to smell odors. After a head injury, a gifted young man suffered complete loss of his sense of smell. This loss was a terrible blow to him: "It was like being struck blind. My whole world was suddenly radically poorer" (Sacks, 1985, p. 159). Some time passed, and he felt he was regaining his ability to smell. Once again he could savor the fine aroma of his favorite pipe. Examination showed that he had not regained any ability to smell, however: His memories of favorite aromas were taking over and making his world more complete. In addition to the scent of his pipe, he could smell a cup of coffee and the aromas of spring.

In addition to apraxias, the right hemisphere controls *prosody*, the ability to express emotion. People suffering from *motor aprosodia* speak in a flat monotone regardless of their real feelings. Such people simply cannot display emotions.

Consider the following case: Dr. P. was a music teacher who had some very peculiar visual problems. He was frequently seen patting parking meters, which he mistook for children (Sacks, 1985). This music teacher's problem is called *visual agnosia*, the inability to identify objects visually. The problem was the result of a tumor in the visual area of his brain. Despite these problems, Dr. P. was able to continue teaching music until the last days of his life. Were Dr. P.'s problems limited to parking meters and children? To determine the extent of his problem, he underwent extensive visual recognition tests. When looking at a rose, for example, he described it as "a convoluted red form with a linear green attachment." The researchers concluded that he was suffering from visual agnosia—he did not recognize or remember anything he saw. Once he mistook his wife's head for his hat—he tried to lift it from her body and put it on his head.

Do you remember your first day at school and the first class you attended? Did you scan the students in the class hoping to recognize a familiar face? Recognizing faces is an important function of the nervous system; it forms the basis of our reactions to

apraxia
Deficits in nonverbal skills

others as well as our predictions about their behavior. For some people, however, recognizing faces become difficult or even impossible. Brain damage, especially to the temporal and/or occipital lobes can disrupt our ability to recognize faces, although recognition via voice is not affected. This inability to recognize faces, called prosopagnosia, is not a result of intellectual deterioration or damage to the eyes. In one particular case a patient who could not recognize his wife noticed a strange person staring at him. The patient had been staring at himself in a mirror!

The Plastic Brain

The word *plastic* is not likely one that you would ever consider using with reference to the brain; yet, it is actually an apt description. Plastic can be molded and changed into many forms. It is a pliable material that can take on different forms and even functions. In some ways, the same can be said of the brain, which can change remarkably over time.

Consider the following case: For the first three years of his life, Matthew developed normally, like other children. Just before he turned 4, however, Matthew began to experience seizures that did not respond to drug treatments. The seizures were severe (life-threatening) and frequent (as often as every 3 minutes). The eventual diagnosis was Rasmussen's encephalitis—a frightening name for a rare and incurable condition that includes epilepsy, cognitive and motor decline, and loss of brain cells (Tran et al., 2000). Neurosurgeons proposed an extreme treatment—removal of half of Matthew's brain. The surgery, a *hemispherectomy*, is performed a few dozen times each year in the United States. Matthew's parents agonized over their difficult choices—a radical surgical procedure or almost certain death. They decided on the surgery, which was performed at Johns Hopkins Hospital in Baltimore (Swerdlow, 1995).

Psychological Detective

Can people live with only half of their brain? What are the likely consequences of such a drastic surgical intervention? Give these questions some thought, and then write your response before you read further.

After the surgery, Matthew was left with a scar that runs along one ear and disappears under his hair; his face has no lopsidedness. He has no right peripheral vision in either eye, a slight limp, and limited use of his right arm and hand. The space left by removal of the left hemisphere quickly filled with cerebrospinal fluid.

After discussing all of the parts of the brain and their associated functions, it would seem impossible to survive if half of the brain were surgically removed (or damaged in an accident). The cerebrospinal fluid that filled the space left by removal of Matthew's left hemisphere does not operate like the brain's neurons. It would seem that functions of the lost parts of the brain would be lost forever. Yet, the brain is remarkably adaptable, especially to a change that occurs early in life, as it did for Matthew. After the surgery, Matthew underwent weekly speech therapy. As part of the therapy, the therapist would place cards in front of him. If the card said "fast things" Matthew had to name as many fast things as he could. He does not offer as many examples as other children his age; however, he made progress in the use of language. Like other children who have undergone this operation, the remaining parts of the brain have taken over some of the tasks of the part that was removed. This ability to change is what neuroscientists mean when they say the brain is *plastic*.

One reason the brain, especially of children, can change in response to experiences (including removal of an entire hemisphere) is humans do not come into this world with a fully developed, hard-wired brain. In contrast to fish and reptiles, young mammals (including humans) are cared for by adults. "Consequently, the evolutionary process did not have to produce a brain with specialized circuits that performed specialized tasks. Instead, it could simply produce a larger brain with an abundance of neural circuits that could be modified by experience" (Carlson, 2001, p. 18).

For as long as we can remember, teachers have taught and students have believed it is impossible to grow new neurons in the human brain. Now, new data is challenging this longstanding notion in ways that suggest the brain is even more plastic than we had imagined (Gibbs, 1998).

Although researchers have known for some time that animals such as the rat, opossum, and tree shrew can grow new neurons as adults, this process, has, until recently, never been demonstrated in humans. Certainly, the invasive procedures, such as sacrificing the organism to prepare brain sections, used to make such determinations in animals are not applicable to humans. Likewise, because "new" and "old" neurons are indistinguishable (Gibbs, 1998), postmortem examination of the brain did not offer researchers a viable tool for addressing this research question.

A group of researchers devised a simple, yet ingenious technique (Eriksson et al., 1998) to investigate the development of new brain cells (*neurogenesis*). They located an oncologist (cancer specialist) who was tracking the progress of tumors by injecting patients with a chemical that labeled cells that had divided. Fortunately, this chemical (bromodeoxyuridine) can be seen under a microscope. The researchers obtained five postmortem brain samples from this group of patients (the patient's ages ranged from 57 to 72). Microscopic examination of these samples located the bromodeoxyuridine and indicated that hundreds of new neurons had developed in an area of the hippocampus. As we are learning, the brain is more plastic (changeable) than we had ever imagined.

The Split Brain

Earlier in this chapter we described the two hemispheres of the cerebral cortex, which are connected by the corpus callosum (about the size of a small banana). For years, psychologists wondered what would happen if the corpus callosum was cut, eliminating communication between the two hemispheres. Would there be two independent minds inside one head? In the early 1960s, two neurosurgeons, Philip Vogel and Joseph Bogen, discovered that cutting the corpus callosum reduced seizures in untreatable epileptic patients (Bogen, Fisher, & Vogel, 1965). Even though we do not know exactly why this operation controls seizures, it is still performed as a last resort in severe cases of epilepsy.

Initially, no other changes were noticed in patients who had this operation; however, research by Nobel Prize winner Roger Sperry (1964) and his colleague Michael Gazzaniga (1967) produced some remarkable findings. They showed that in people with a severed corpus callosum, the two hemispheres appeared to be doing different things. Indeed, it was as if there were two minds in one head! For example, the right hand might unbutton the patient's shirt, while the left hand buttoned it! Such conflicts typically occur shortly after surgery and tend to subside as the separated hemispheres learn to work together (Myers & Sperry, 1985).

Let's look at the logic behind the Sperry and Gazzaniga testing procedure. Figure 2-25 shows the transmission of visual information from the left and right visual fields to the brain. If you trace the pathways, you see that when the corpus callosum is cut and the person focuses on the center of the visual field, information presented to the left visual field of each eye goes only to the right hemisphere, whereas information presented to the right visual field goes only to the left hemisphere. In people with an intact corpus callosum, information presented to only one hemisphere is quickly transmitted to the other. In short, in a person with a severed corpus callosum, the two hemispheres of the brain cannot communicate with each other.

FIGURE 2-25 Transmission of visual information to the brain. All information from the right visual fields goes to the left hemisphere, whereas information from the left visual fields goes to the right hemisphere. In Part A, the image in the right visual field will travel over the corpus callosum to the right hemisphere. In Part B, the corpus callosum is severed, so the image cannot be transferred to the right hemisphere.

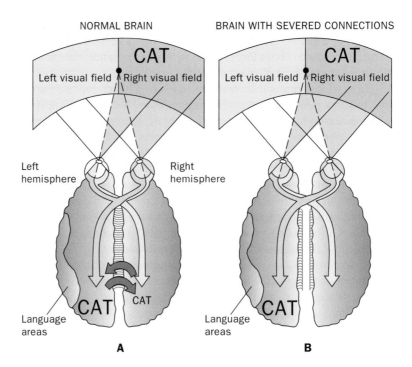

Psychological Detective

Assume that you have undergone this operation. You are seated in the testing apparatus, wearing a special set of glasses that allows a technician to present a visual stimulus separately to either your right or your left visual field. What kind of responses might you be required to make when an object is presented to you? Will the response you are able to make differ depending on which hemisphere receives the information? Write down and explain your answers to these questions before reading further.

Suppose that we flash a picture of a baseball in your right visual field and ask you to name the object. If we trace the visual input, we find it ends in the left hemisphere. Responsibility for naming the object falls on the left hemisphere. If we switched visual fields, the right hemisphere would be involved. Such tasks pose major problems for patients with a severed corpus callosum; they can name an object only when it is presented to the right visual field. If, however, the task is reversed, so that when the patient is shown the word *baseball* in the left visual field and told to select what was seen from a group of objects on a table with the left hand, the left visual field–right hemisphere combination can perform the task, whereas the right visual field–left hemisphere combination cannot (see Figure 2-26). Why?

Studies like those just described support the conclusion that the left hemisphere is involved in speech and language production. Thus you can easily identify a baseball or a cup of coffee when it is presented to your right visual field because this information is processed in the left hemisphere. In addition, the left hemisphere operates in a logical, sequential, and analytical manner (Bradshaw & Nettleton, 1981).

Although the right hemisphere has only limited language functions (Levy, 1983), it is essential for adding emotional content to our speech (Shapiro & Danly, 1985). It is also important for spatial abilities such as recognizing complex geometric patterns (Clarke, Assal, & deTribolet, 1993) and people's faces and selecting objects. The right hemisphere operates in a more holistic or all-encompassing manner.

We do not want to leave you with the impression that the split-brain operation leaves the patient in an unusual or abnormal state. Other than having some trouble maintaining attention, split-brain patients do not suffer deficits in intelligence or motivation (Hoptman & Davidson, 1994).

2.5

In this chapter we have examined the biological foundations of psychology: the nervous system—especially the brain—and the endocrine system. We have seen how these systems are involved in sensing, processing, and responding to stimuli in our environment. In the next chapter, we look more closely at these processes. We explore the ways in which specialized receptors in the nervous system sense stimuli and how the resulting sensations are processed to produce the perceptions that are the raw materials of psychological functioning.

STUDY TIP

Taking the basic outline of the chapter shown on the chapter opener page as a beginning structure, construct a detailed outline of the chapter. Use this outline to help you see the logic of the flow of information through the chapter.

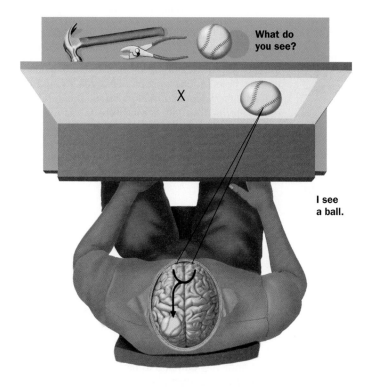

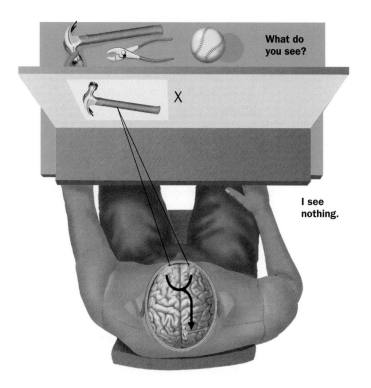

FIGURE 2-26 Testing the split-brain patient. In the top panel, the image of a baseball is projected on the right side of the screen and transmitted to the patient's left hemisphere. The patient is able to select the object by touch from a group and identify it verbally. When the image of a hammer is projected on the left side of the screen and transmitted to the right hemisphere (bottom panel), the patient is able to locate the object by touch but cannot identify it verbally.

REVIEW SUMMARY

1. *Phrenology* is a pseudoscience popularized in the 1800s by Franz Joseph Gall, who believed we could determine a person's skills and characteristics by identifying bumps on the skull.

2. Early studies of brain functioning involved stimulating or removing portions of the cortex. The *stereotaxic instrument* allowed examination of structures that are deep within the brain.

3. The **electroencephalograph (EEG)** provides an investigator with a chart of a person's brain waves. Images of the structures of the brain can be produced by computerized techniques such as the **PET (positron emission tomography),** the **CT** or **CAT (computerized axial tomography),** the **MRI (magnetic resonance imaging),** and the **fMRI (functional magnetic resonance imaging).**

4. The brain is divided into the **hindbrain** (which handles survival functions and motor control), the **midbrain** (where the **reticular formation** is located), and the **forebrain** (two hemispheres joined by the **corpus callosum**).

5. The cerebral cortex covers the forebrain and is divided into four lobes: **frontal, parietal, temporal,** and **occipital.**

6. A group of **subcortical structures** involved in emotion, memory, eating, drinking, and sexual behavior are located beneath the cortex. These structures include the **limbic system, thalamus, and hypothalamus.**

7. The brain has been described as *plastic,* which means it can change over time and recover to some degree even from removal of an entire hemisphere.

8. Studying the human brain yields information about **aphasias** (language deficits) and **apraxias** (nonverbal deficits).

9. The split-brain operation involves cutting the **corpus callosum** to help reduce epileptic seizures. The study of split-brain patients provides information about the functions of the two hemispheres. The left hemisphere is responsible primarily for language abilities and speech production, as well as rational and logical thought; the right hemisphere is better suited to dealing with spatial relations and the perception of more holistic concepts.

✓ CHECK YOUR PROGRESS

1. Suppose you are hooked up to an EEG while reading this question. What brain waves would we find on the EEG record?

   a. beta
   b. alpha
   c. delta
   d. theta

2. As part of a research project you agree to undergo a brain scan. According to the informed consent form, you will be injected with a radioactive form of glucose. Which of the following brain scans is being used?

   a. magnetic resonance imaging (MRI) scan
   b. computerized axial tomography (CT) scan
   c. positron emission tomography (PET) scan
   d. functional magnetic resonance imaging (fMRI) scan

3. Why is Phineas Gage so well known to neuroscientists?

   a. He developed the first EEG.
   b. He suffered a form of epilepsy that was treated with surgery.
   c. The effects of his brain damage helped us understand brain functioning.
   d. The development of brain scans was dependent on his willingness to undergo invasive brain surgery.

4. Damage to Wernicke's area is likely to have an effect on a person's ability to

   a. eat a balanced diet.
   b. maintain fluid balance.
   c. understand spoken language.
   d. anticipate the consequences of aggressive behavior.

5. Explain how the two hemispheres of the brain can be separated. Why has this operation been performed? What are its consequences?

6. If Andy has damage to his occipital lobes, which of the following is most likely to be observed during testing by a neuropsychologist?

   a. Andy will not know his name.
   b. Andy will exhibit visual difficulties.
   c. A slight hand tremor will be noticed.
   d. A series of violent outbursts will occur.

7. A language deficit or difficulty is an

   a. alexia.
   b. apraxia.
   c. aprosodia.
   d. aphasia.

8. Which part of the brain is responsible for breathing, heart rate, swallowing, and blood circulation?

   a. pons
   b. medulla
   c. corpus callosum
   d. reticular formation

9. A series of brain scans reveals that Darrin has slight damage to the left front lobe of his brain. Neurologists suspect that the damage will develop further over time, so they will make careful observations of Darrin. Which of the following will be most helpful in charting the progress of the damage?

   a. levels of hunger and thirst
   b. motor movements on his right side

c. visual acuity in his right eye

d. level of glucose after fasting

10. A neuropsychologist was invited to speak to a class on the issue of whether the brain changes over time. Which of the following would make the best title for this presentation?

a. "More Plastic Than We Ever Thought"

b. "The Brain Is Like a Mountain: Ever Moved a Mountain?"

c. "Resisting the Effects of Experience to Protect the Brain"

d. "Our Genes Are Responsible for the Changes in the Brain Over Time"

Sensation and Perception

In Chapter 2 we discussed the importance of our physiological makeup in adapting to the demands of our constantly changing environment. In Chapter 3 we take this discussion a step further. First, we examine the systems that receive sensory information about vision, hearing, taste, smell, body position, and movement. Then we see how we process or perceive this information to bring meaning to it. Keep in mind that this meaning varies according to experience and culture. For example, many people in the United States report seeing the "man in the moon" when they look at the moon on a clear night. Native Americans, however, report seeing a rabbit, and Chinese people see a woman trying to escape from her husband (Samovar & Porter, 1991).

As you read the remainder of this book, keep in mind that the basic building blocks of sensation and perception are crucial to states of consciousness (Chapter 4), emotional behaviors and reactions to stress (Chapters 6 and 14), learned responses (Chapters 5 and 7), maladaptive responses (Chapter 12), and our interactions with other people (Chapter 15). Without adequate sensory input and perceptual processing, these and other more elaborate systems simply would not perform appropriately.

SENSATION, PERCEPTION, AND PSYCHOPHYSICS

For some time you have been planning to have several friends over for dinner—not carry-out pizza, but something you prepare yourself. The big day is here; you've spent the whole afternoon in the kitchen. The aromas filling your apartment suggest that a superb meal is in the making. To be sure that everything tastes as good as it smells, you sample the offerings frequently. The more you sample, however, the less satisfied you are. The spicy sauce tastes bland, and the potato dish does not seem to have any flavor. Some additional spices will cure this problem, you hope. *Are more spices the solution to your problem?*

The problem just described has to do with how we experience and understand our world—that is, it is concerned with the processes of sensation and perception.

Sensation and Perception

In Chapter 2 we discussed the sensitivity of specialized cells, called *receptors*, to specific types of environmental stimuli. **Sensation** refers to the activation of these receptors, and sensations can be viewed as the basic building blocks of perception. **Perception** is the process of organizing and attempting to understand the sensory stimulation we receive. When the receptors are stimulated, information can be transmitted to the brain. Transmission of neural impulses to the brain is not enough, however, to give us an understanding and awareness of our surroundings.

If the receptors do not receive stimulation from the environment or are unable to process the information they receive, no information is transmitted to the brain and perception does not occur (Dennett & Kinsbourne, 1992). For example, people who are color-blind cannot tell from their perception of color when a traffic light is red or when it is green; because they cannot sense color information, they depend on brightness and position cues to determine the color of the signal.

STUDY TIP

Make flash cards using all of the marginal definitions in this chapter: write the words on one side and the definitions on the other. Test yourself frequently.

sensation
Activation of receptors by stimuli in the environment

perception
The process of organizing and making sense of sensory information

The sights, sounds, and odors of a large city provide ample stimuli to activate the sensory receptors (sensation). The brain will interpret these stimuli (perception).

It sounds simple—activate the receptors (sensation) and then transmit the information to the brain to make sense of it (perception). As you will see, however, the process is more complicated than that.

To activate a particular receptor, a specific type of energy must be present—light waves for vision, movement of air molecules for hearing, molecules in a liquid solution for taste, and so forth. If you shine a flashlight in your ear, do not expect to have a visual response; there are no light-sensitive receptors there.

As we saw in Chapter 2, neurons operate on the basis of changes in electrical charge and the release of chemical substances called *neurotransmitters*. Somehow, the physical energies of light and sound waves and those of odor and taste molecules must be changed into electrochemical forms the nervous system can process. This process of converting the stimulation received by the receptors into electrochemical energy that can be used by the nervous system is called **transduction.** When you hear a sound, for example, sound waves cause a number of very fine hairs located in your inner ear to bend. These hairs are your auditory receptors. If they are bent sufficiently, the first neuron in the auditory pathway will fire (display an all-or-none response). Now auditory information can be transmitted to your brain.

Continued presentation of the same stimulus, however, causes the receptors to become less sensitive to that particular stimulus; hence, a stronger stimulus is required to activate the receptors. This process, known as **adaptation,** occurs very rapidly when odors and tastes are involved. In some cases—for example, when a sewer is clogged—adaptation is highly desirable. In other situations, such as when preparing dinner for your friends, adaptation may be disadvantageous. Think back to the cooking scenario at the beginning of this chapter. Are more spices the solution to your tasting problem? Because your repeated tastings have caused your receptors to adapt, a stronger stimulus (in this case, more spices) is now required to activate them. Therefore adding spices may create a bigger problem than the one you think you have. Your guests, whose receptors have not adapted the way yours have, will find the meal very spicy!

Psychophysics

Before we explore how our sensory systems operate, let's take a look at the methods used by early researchers, known as *psychophysicists*, who studied the relations between the mind and the body. At the same time Wilhelm Wundt was founding psychology (1879), a group of German psychophysicists were studying the relation between stimuli and the participant's experience. Their basic procedures were clear and straightforward. A

transduction
Conversion of stimuli received by the receptors into a form (patterns of neural impulses) that can be used by the nervous system

adaptation
Loss of sensitivity to a stimulus by the receptors as a result of continued presentation of that stimulus

stimulus was presented, and the individual was asked to indicate whether the stimulus was perceived (when only one stimulus was presented) or if the stimulus that was presented differed noticeably from a comparison stimulus that was also presented. In short, they studied the relation between the mind and the body.

Ernst Weber (1795–1878) was interested in determining the smallest detectable difference between two stimuli. For example, can you tell that a 105-watt light bulb is brighter than a 100-watt bulb? Would you notice that a 95-watt light bulb is dimmer than a 100-watt bulb? Weber's research indicated that the amount of change required to perceive such a difference could be described by the formula $K = \Delta I/I$. This formula, known as **Weber's law,** indicates the change in stimulus intensity (ΔI) divided by the comparison intensity (I) is equal to a constant (K). The constant is relatively the same for all tests of the same sense, but it differs from one sense to another. For example, the constant for identifying noticeable changes in auditory intensity is 5 percent, whereas the constant for vision is 8 percent. Thus, you wouldn't reliably be able to differentiate 95 watts and 100 watts, or 100 watts and 105 watts, but you could differentiate 95 watts and 105 watts.

Weber's study of the **just noticeable difference (jnd),** or the smallest difference between two stimuli that is noticeable 50 percent of the time, gave psychology one of its first laws. By showing that the amount of stimulus increase or decrease required to notice a change, divided by the original stimulation, was a constant, Weber showed how the mind (our perceptions) could be related to the body (the physical stimulation we receive).

Thresholds

Absolute and Differential Thresholds.   How intense does a stimulus need to be in order for it to be noticed by a receptor? Through his study of sensory thresholds, Gustav Fechner (1801–1887) refined and expanded the work Weber had begun. Fechner studied both the absolute threshold and the differential threshold. To determine the **absolute threshold,** one asks, "What is the smallest amount of stimulus energy that must be present for perception to occur 50 percent of the time?" As you can see from Table 3-1, the absolute threshold for each of our senses is astonishingly low.

To determine the **differential threshold** or **jnd,** we investigate the amount of stimulus energy that must be added to or subtracted from an existing stimulus for a participant to notice a difference (that is, to produce a *just noticeable difference*) 50 percent of the time. For example, a psychophysicist studying the differential threshold might be interested in how much the intensity of a light or a tone must be increased (or decreased) for a test participant to notice the change. Think back to the cooking vignette that opened this chapter: When you were trying to decide how much spice should be added, you were dealing with a differential threshold problem.

Ernst Weber (1795–1878) studied the smallest detectable difference between two stimuli.

weber's law
The observation that the amount of stimulus increase or decrease required to notice a change, divided by the original stimulation, is a constant

just noticeable difference (jnd)
Smallest difference between two stimuli that is noticeable 50 percent of the time by participants

absolute threshold
Minimum amount of energy required for conscious detection of a stimulus 50 percent of the time by participants

differential threshold
Smallest amount of stimulation that must be added to or subtracted from an existing stimulus for a person to be able to detect a change 50 percent of the time (see **jnd**)

TABLE 3-1	
Examples of Absolute Thresholds	
Sense	**Threshold**
Vision	A candle flame at 30 miles on a clear, dark night
Audition	The tick of a watch 20 feet away in a quiet room
Olfaction	One drop of perfume diffused throughout a small house
Gustation	One gram of the bitter substance denatonium saccharide diffused in one million grams of water
Touch	An insect wing falling on your cheek from a distance of 1 centimeter

Although Fechner's research on the absolute and differential thresholds was important, it failed to take into account two factors: (a) the condition under which the stimulus was perceived and (b) the nature of the perceiver. Both factors are important in determining thresholds. For example, the task of determining either the differential or the absolute threshold for a light is much more difficult in a brightly lit room than in a darkened room. In a brightly lit room, distinguishing changes in the target stimulus (*signal*) from the background illumination (*noise*) is more difficult than in a darkened environment. **Signal detection theory,** or the contention that the threshold varies with the nature of the signal and noise, was developed to explain the difficulties one might encounter in distinguishing a certain stimulus from the background or noise (Swets, Tanner, & Birdsall, 1961). Signal detection problems occur frequently in everyday life. How often have you thought you heard (or later learned that you failed to hear) the ringing of your doorbell or telephone (*signal*) while you were watching television or listening to music (background *noise*)?

The importance (or lack of importance) of detecting the signal also influences our detection of it. If your car is in the repair shop and you are waiting for a call telling you that it is ready, detecting the signal (hearing the phone ring) is very important. You can afford to make a few mistakes (for example, picking up the phone only to hear the dial tone), as long as you answer it when the repair shop calls. Such mistakes are called *false positives* because we mistakenly believe that the awaited signal is present. A radar operator who is monitoring for incoming enemy aircraft cannot afford to make any false positive mistakes; such errors would result in a full-scale alert and the mobilization of many personnel. By the same token, the radar operator cannot afford to overlook any incoming enemy aircraft. Such mistakes are called *false negatives*. Such errors might prove to be costly in terms of loss of life and property. These decisional factors (see Table 3-2) are called *receiver operating characteristics*. Understanding such decisions as indicating that you think a target is there when it isn't, or vice versa, is important to a complete understanding of whether a stimulus is detected.

Subliminal Perception.   The study of thresholds raises an interesting question. Can stimuli that are below the threshold for perception have any effect on us? Such events are called **subliminal stimuli** because, even though they do activate our receptors, we are not consciously aware of them. For example, if a persuasive message (see Chapter 15) could arouse our unconscious motives, it might stand a better chance of succeeding because we would not consciously try to resist it. This is the premise behind the use of subliminal perception in advertising. Because *subliminal* stimuli are below the level of conscious awareness, they should have a direct effect on unconscious motivation. To accomplish this goal, visual stimuli may be presented so rapidly that we do not consciously perceive them, or tape recordings may be played during sleep (Silverman & Lachmann, 1985). Thus, some researchers believe that both subliminal visual and auditory stimuli may have an effect on our behavior.

The most famous apparent demonstration of the effectiveness of subliminal perception occurred in 1956, when ads for popcorn and soft drinks were supposedly shown at 1/3,000-second intervals during a movie. Because this interval is too short for conscious awareness, moviegoers would have been unaware they had seen the ads. Yet popcorn and soft drink sales supposedly rose dramatically (McConnell, Cutler, &

signal detection theory
The contention that the threshold varies with the nature of the stimulus (signal) and background stimulation (noise)

subliminal stimuli
Stimuli that are below the threshold of consciousness

TABLE 3-2

Receiver Operating Characteristics in Signal Detection Theory

	Signal Present	Signal Absent
Respond "present"	True Positive	False Positive
Respond "absent"	False Negative	True Negative

McNeil, 1958). Despite the claim of the success for subliminal perception in that instance, convincing data were never presented. Moreover, more adequately controlled studies have failed to reproduce those results (Trappey, 1996).

Although a limited number of presentations of a subliminal stimulus, as in the popcorn and soft drink example, may not alter our behaviors dramatically and immediately, there is some evidence that repeated subliminal presentations may change our attitudes and opinions (Abrams & Greenwald, 2000). The more frequent our contact with a person, object, or idea is, the more likely we are to be positively attracted to that person, object, or idea. Thus frequent subliminal exposure to a stimulus may influence our attitudes. Perhaps this is why advertisers continue to use subliminal techniques, especially in magazine ads. For example, many liquor ads appear to contain cleverly disguised sexual stimuli (Key, 1989). The advertisers hope that unconscious attraction to these stimuli will persuade the reader to purchase a particular brand of liquor. Similarly, in the 2000 presidential campaign, it was claimed that the word *RATS* was inserted in a Bush television ad when the announcer was describing "the Gore prescription plan" to bias voters against Gore (Berke, 2000). Because the word would have been shown at 1/30th of a second, it would be considered a subliminal stimulus. Even though we will never know whether this technique had any effect, subliminal techniques are being used in a variety of settings.

With this general information about sensation, perception, and the methods of psychophysics in mind, we can now look at several of our sensory systems to see how they operate.

What do you see in the ice cubes above?

SENSORY SYSTEMS

If you spend time watching other people, you will notice that they blink frequently. Although the rate of blinking varies from one person to another, the average rate is about one blink every 4 seconds (Records, 1979). When the air is dry, the blink rate goes up. Why? Because blinking moistens the delicate surface on the front of the eye and keeps it from drying out. *How else is blinking related to our sensory processes?*

Many people would argue that vision is the most important and most highly valued sense. Ask several people which of their senses they would least be willing to lose, and almost all of them would say vision. We fear blindness because we are primarily visual creatures. Why? Our brain has more neurons devoted to vision than to hearing, taste, or smell (Restak, 1994).

What adjustments would you have to make in your lifestyle if you lost your sight? Compare these changes to the adjustments that would be required if you lost your sense of smell. Given the importance of vision and the ease with which the eyes can be studied, it is not surprising that vision is the sense that has been studied most thoroughly.

Vision

To appreciate our visual abilities, we need to know two things: what we see and the components of our visual system.

What We See: The Visual Stimulus.   Vision is a process that involves the reception of electromagnetic waves by visual receptor cells. This kind of energy travels in waves that vary greatly in length. For example, gamma waves are very short, whereas some of the waves involved in broadcasting are miles long (Block & Yuker, 1989). We measure **wavelengths,** or the length of waves, in nanometers (nm), which are billionths of a meter. The only light waves that humans can detect have wavelengths between approximately 380 nm and 760 nm (see Figure 3-1). This

wavelength
Physical length of a light wave measured in nanometers

FIGURE 3-1 The visible spectrum and the three characteristics—wavelength (hue or color), amplitude (intensity or brightness), and saturation (purity)—of the visual stimulus.

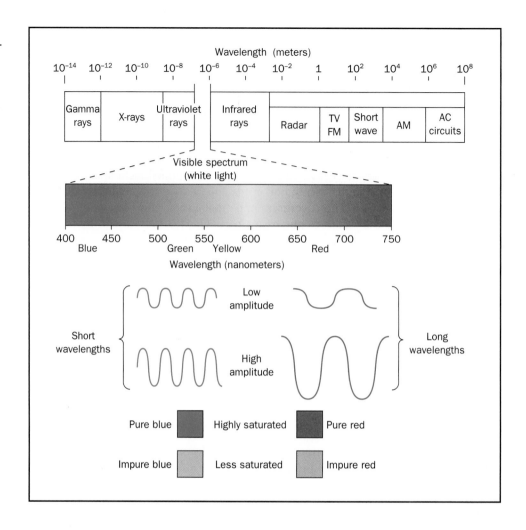

limited range of stimuli (the human eye can see only a small portion of the spectrum) is called the *visible spectrum*. Different light wavelengths are associated with different colors. For example, we see a wavelength of 425 nm as violet and a wavelength of 650 nm as red. Thus the psychological counterpart of wavelength is *hue* or color.

As you can see from Figure 3-1, light waves can differ in two additional ways: amplitude and saturation. **Amplitude** refers to the strength or intensity (brightness) of the light. **Saturation** refers to the "trueness" or purity of the colors we perceive. The more saturated a color seems, the more likely you are to be seeing only one wavelength.

To understand the concept of saturation we need to distinguish between radiant light and reflected light. With **radiant light,** visible energy is emitted (released) directly by an object. There are only a few sources of radiant energy: the sun, light bulbs, and other hot, energy-releasing objects. If you place a piece of red cellophane in front of a light bulb, you will see a red light because red wavelengths are shown through the red cellophane.

What happens when you simultaneously look at red and green lights? As you can see in Figure 3-2A, you will perceive yellow. If you add a blue light to the red and green mixture, you will see white. Why? Because the three primary wavelengths are added together and are being sensed at the same time. *Adding* the three primary wavelengths results in the perception of white (in other words, no specific wavelength is dominant).

With **reflected light,** by contrast, energy is reflected by objects. Most of the light waves we receive are not radiant; they are reflected from objects in our environment. In other words, the light waves strike an object and bounce off it; we receive the waves that have bounced off the object. You perceive the colors of grass, a rose, and your sweater as a direct result of the reflection of light from those objects.

amplitude
Strength or intensity of a stimulus (brightness for visual stimuli; loudness for auditory stimuli)

saturation
Trueness or purity of a color

radiant light
Visible energy emitted by an object

reflected light
Energy that is reflected by objects

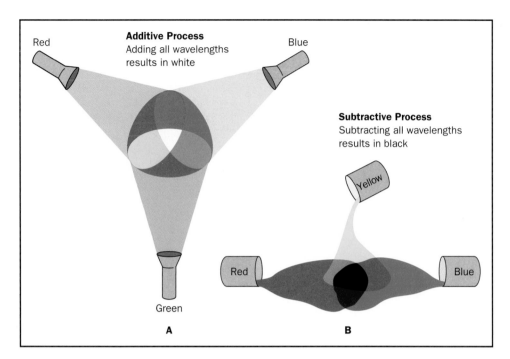

Additive Process
Adding all wavelengths results in white

Red

Blue

Subtractive Process
Subtracting all wavelengths results in black

Yellow

Red

Blue

Green

A

B

FIGURE 3-2 The additive and subtractive processes of color mixing. (A) When lights are mixed, wavelengths are added. For example, red and green lights combine to form yellow. (B) When paints are mixed, wavelengths are subtracted. For example, red, yellow, and blue paints combine to form a dark or blackish color.

Psychological Detective

What is it about reflected light waves that enables us to see different colors (wavelengths)? Spend a few moments thinking about the process that might make the reflection of different wavelengths possible. Here's a hint: When light strikes an object, are all the different wavelengths reflected to your eye? Write down your suggestions before reading further.

Knowing that objects absorb light waves in addition to reflecting them should help you understand the reflection of different colors. If all of the light waves are absorbed, the object or surface appears black; by contrast, if all of the light waves are reflected, the object or surface appears white. We see colors when certain wavelengths are reflected and others are absorbed. As you can see in Figure 3-2B, when red, yellow, and blue

The red car is a source of *reflected light*, whereas the light bulb is a source of *radiant light*.

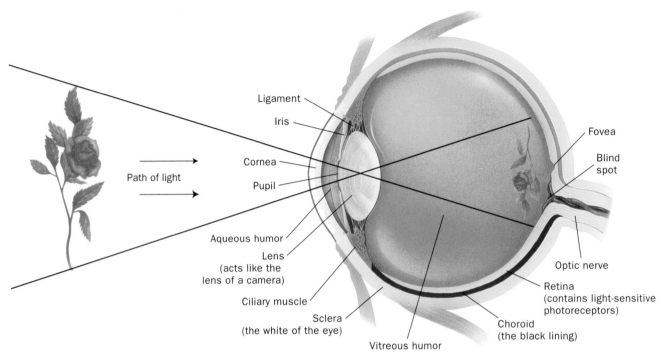

FIGURE 3-3 Structures of the eye.

Source: Pinel, 1993.

3.1 *Live!* psych

paints are mixed, all wavelengths are absorbed or subtracted, and the result is black because no hue is reflected.

If a surface reflects only one wavelength, the color you perceive is pure. The degree of purity decreases as the number of different, *reflected* wavelengths increases.

How We See: The Visual System.   Vision involves a complex chain of events. The structures of the eye are depicted in Figure 3-3. Familiarize yourself with them as we trace how light waves travel through the eye.

Initially, light waves pass through the protective *cornea*. The cornea is transparent but becomes an opaque, whitish covering, known as the *sclera*, over the rest of the eyeball. In addition to its protective function, the cornea helps focus the light waves.

After striking the cornea, light waves enter an open area called the *anterior chamber*. Here they pass through the *aqueous humor*, a clear watery fluid. This fluid, which is continuously recycled, helps supply nourishment to the eye. Then the light waves are funneled through the small opening known as the *pupil*. The pupil is surrounded by a colored membrane, the *iris*, which changes shape (like the diaphragm of a camera) to regulate the size of the pupil and therefore the amount of light taken in.

Next, the light passes through the *lens*. The lens, which is supported by two powerful *ciliary muscles*, is elastic; it can change shape to focus the visual image. Changing the shape of the lens to focus is known as **accommodation.**

After passing through the lens, the light waves enter a second, larger open space called the *posterior chamber*. Another clear, jellylike fluid, the *vitreous humor*, fills the posterior chamber. The vitreous humor also provides nourishment and helps give shape to the eye. Finally, the light waves strike the **retina**, the light-sensitive tissue at the back of the eye that contains the visual receptors (*rods* and *cones*). The basic sequence to remember is

cornea ➔ pupil ➔ lens ➔ retina.

Figure 3-4 shows that the retina is made up of several layers: The three major layers are the ganglion cell layer, the bipolar cell layer, and the photoreceptor layer.

This explanation would be much simpler if we could tell you that when the light waves strike the retina, they first stimulate the receptors and then progressively activate

accommodation
In focusing, action of the ciliary muscles to change the shape of the lens

retina
Tissue that contains the visual receptors, located at the back of the eye

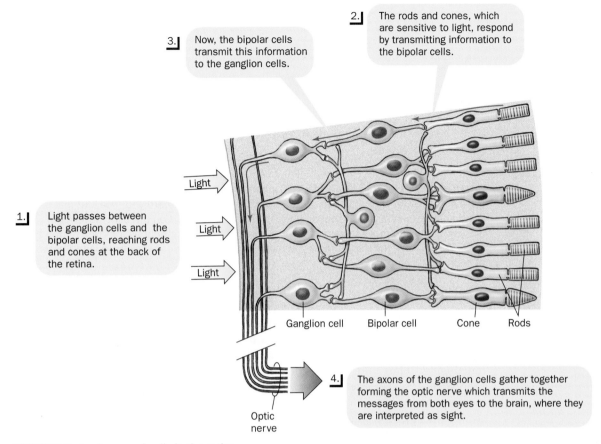

3. Now, the bipolar cells transmit this information to the ganglion cells.

2. The rods and cones, which are sensitive to light, respond by transmitting information to the bipolar cells.

1. Light passes between the ganglion cells and the bipolar cells, reaching rods and cones at the back of the retina.

Ganglion cell   Bipolar cell   Cone   Rods

Optic nerve

4. The axons of the ganglion cells gather together forming the optic nerve which transmits the messages from both eyes to the brain, where they are interpreted as sight.

FIGURE 3-4 Layers of cells in the retina.

Source: Dowling & Boycott, 1966.

layers of cells located toward the back of the retina, with the optic nerve exiting at the very back of the retina and going to the brain. In reality, however, the reverse is true: After light strikes the surface of the retina, it must travel *through* several layers of cells before it activates the visual receptors, which make up the back layer of the retina (see Figure 3-4). Light waves cause the receptors to change their electrical charge. If that change is great enough, the **bipolar cells** fire. If enough bipolar cells fire, the next layer of cells, the **ganglion cells,** fire. The axons of the ganglion cells come together to form the optic nerve, which carries visual information to higher brain centers.

Why are our visual receptors "wired" backwards? The arrangement may seem impractical, but it is the only way the receptors can be positioned close to the blood supply that lies behind the retina to receive the proper nutrients and maintain their correct biochemical status.

At the point where the axons of the ganglion cells come together and leave the eyeball, there are no receptors. This area is known as the **blind spot.** If you follow the directions in Figure 3-5, you will experience your own blind spot.

bipolar cells
Cells in the retina that connect the receptors to ganglion cells

ganglion cells
Cells in the retina whose axons form the optic nerve

blind spot
Location at which the optic nerve leaves the eyeball; contains no receptors

Psychological Detective

As we suggested at the beginning of this section, blinking may have more to do with sensation than just keeping the eyes moist. When you blink, light does not enter your visual system. Because no light is being processed during a blink, you should experience 15 or more brief visual blackouts each minute. Can you explain why we do not experience such blackouts? Write down some possible reasons before reading further.

X

FIGURE 3-5 Hold the book about 20 inches in front of you. Close your left eye and stare at the X with your right eye. Gradually move the book toward you. The bird that is approaching its nest will disappear when its image is focused on the blind spot. As the book continues to move toward your eyes, the image will reappear as it moves off the blind spot. Do you now understand how you may miss things because they were in the blind spot of your eye?

Frances Volkmann, Curnin Riggs, and Robert Moore (1980) proposed that when the brain signals the eyelids to close in a blink, it also stops or inhibits activity in the visual system. When the blink is completed, the visual system returns to its normal functioning. Thus information about visual blackouts simply is not transmitted or processed. Also, because we have a very brief (lasts about one quarter of a second) memory that persists during the blinks—*iconic memory*—for the object we are looking at, we remember the object and do not notice the blinks.

The Visual Pathway.   The pathway taken by the optic nerve is diagrammed in Figure 3-6. The optic nerves from each eye join at the **optic chiasm,** which is located on the underside of the brain just in front of the pituitary gland. The fibers from the nasal half (closest to the nose) of the retina cross to the opposite hemisphere; those from the peripheral (outlying) half of each retina continue to the hemisphere on the same side of the body. The next stop is an area in the *thalamus,* the relay station in the *forebrain* (see Chapter 2). Ultimately, the visual information is received by the occipital lobe of the cortex, where higher-level visual processing begins (Knierim & Van Essen, 1992; Zeki, 1992).

The Visual Receptors.   Because they are so important to what we see, the visual receptors, the rods and cones, deserve special attention. The **rods** (120 to 125 million per eye) are the most prevalent visual receptors. They have a lower threshold and lower acuity (sharpness of perception) than cones and do not detect color. By contrast, the **cones** (6 to 7 million) are less prevalent, have a higher threshold and higher acuity, and are able to detect color. The rods are slender and cylindrical, whereas the cones are much broader (see Figure 3-4). Most of the cones are found in one area, the **fovea,** an indented spot in the center of the retina (see Figure 3-3). Both the rods and cones contain light-sensitive chemicals called *photopigments.* When light strikes the rods and cones it causes a chemical reaction in these photopigments (Wang et al., 1994). This change *hyperpolarizes* (see Chapter 2) the rods and cones and releases their inhibitory influence on the bipolar cells (Lamb & Pugh, 1990). With this inhibition removed, the bipolar cells exhibit excitation, and a message is sent to the brain.

Look again at Figure 3-4. Do you see that the cones have a more direct, or one-to-one, hookup with the bipolar cells? Compare this arrangement with that of the rods: Several rods synapse (come close to but do not actually touch; see Chapter 2) on each bipolar cell. Which receptor do you think provides more detailed and precise information? If you are unsure, consider this analogy: Suppose that you are having a one-on-one

optic chiasm
Point at which the optic nerve fibers from each eye join; fibers from the nasal half of the retina cross to the opposite hemisphere of the brain

rods
Most prevalent visual receptors; have lower threshold and lower acuity than cones and do not detect color

cones
Visual receptors that are less prevalent than rods; have a higher threshold and higher acuity and are able to detect color

fovea
Indented spot in the center of the retina that contains only cones

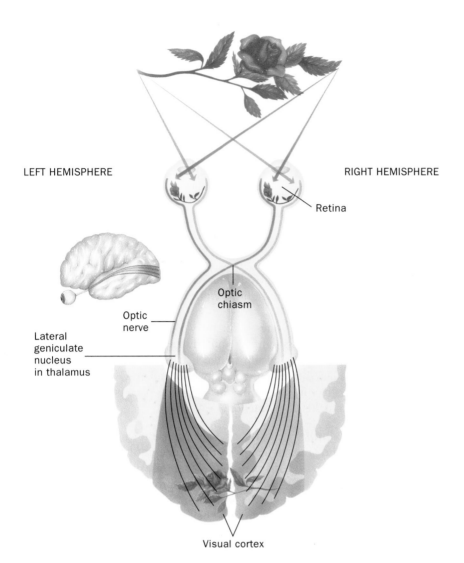

FIGURE 3-6 Pathway taken by a visual stimulus from the eye to the brain.

LEFT HEMISPHERE

RIGHT HEMISPHERE

Retina

Optic chiasm

Optic nerve

Lateral geniculate nucleus in thalamus

Visual cortex

discussion with a classmate about the next psychology test. Each of you knows exactly what the other is saying. This conversation is like the information sent by the cones to the bipolar cells—it is clear and direct. In comparison, information transmission from the rods to the bipolar cells would be like members of a large psychology class heatedly discussing posttraumatic stress disorder. Because of the size of the class, you often cannot tell exactly who is talking at any given moment.

To experience the difference in the acuity (sharpness), of the rods and cones, hold this book about 12 inches from your face and look straight at it. Focus on a letter in the middle of a word in the middle of a paragraph. Now, *without* moving your eyes, see how many letters to the left and right of your target letter you can read clearly.

Psychological Detective

The letters to the left and right of your target letter should appear blurred and more difficult to read. Why? Give the situation some thought, and write down some possibilities before reading further.

The letters you are looking at are not focused on the same areas of the retina. Because you are looking straight at the target letter, it is focused on the cone-rich fovea,

TABLE 3-3

Differences Between Rods and Cones

Rods	Cones
1. Are numerous and found in the peripheral retina	1. Are concentrated primarily in the fovea
2. Have a lower threshold for activation	2. Have a higher threshold for activation
3. Have lower acuity	3. Have higher acuity
4. Do not process color	4. Process color

FIGURE 3-7 Watch the rose turn black! Under high levels of illumination we are using our cones and can see color. As we experience lower levels of illumination, however, we shift to rod vision and cannot see color. To experience this shift, find a room in which the lighting can be decreased gradually with a dimmer switch. Slowly turn the intensity of the lights down, and you will see the rose change from red to black—the point at which you have shifted from cone to rod vision.

trichromatic theory
Color vision theory stating that there are three types of color receptors

opponent-process theory
Color vision theory stressing the pairing of color experiences; activation of one process can inhibit its partner

whereas the letters to the left and right of your target letter will be focused on areas of the retina around the fovea. Rods predominate in these areas. The lowered acuity of the rods causes the image to become blurred. That is why you hold documents with fine print, such as your apartment lease, right in front of your eyes: to focus the print on the cones in the fovea.

We have said that rods and cones differ in two important respects: Rods have a lower threshold than cones, so less light is required to activate them, and cones are used for color vision (Table 3-3). Rod vision is like black-and-white television—you can adjust brightness levels, but you see only black, white, and gray. Therefore if illumination is decreased gradually you should be able to watch objects lose their color. Use Figure 3-7 to demonstrate this phenomenon.

Theories of Color Vision. Researchers have long known that the sensation of color is transmitted to the brain by cones in the retina; until recently, however, they have not known exactly how this happens. Two theories, originally proposed in the 1800s, have guided our progress toward understanding this process. The **trichromatic theory** was originally proposed by Thomas Young in 1802 and modified by Hermann von Helmholtz in 1852. Young and Helmholtz believed there are three types of cones, each maximally responding to one of the three primary colors: red, green, and blue. What about all the different shades of color that we see? According to the trichromatic theory, different shades are created when we receive sensory input in different amounts or proportions from the three types of cones.

There is some support for this theory. In the 1960s, researchers (such as Brown & Wald, 1964) identified three types of cones in the retina, each of which is sensitive to one of the primary colors. These three types of cones are maximally sensitive to wavelengths of either 445, 535, or 570 nm. As you can see by comparing these values with those in Figure 3-1, Young and Helmholtz were a bit off in proposing red, green, and blue wavelengths; blue-violet, green, and yellow-green wavelengths are the maximally sensitive wavelengths (Pick & Reid, 1995).

If the trichromatic theory seems to account for color vision, do we need to discuss the second theory of color vision? For several years after the existence of three types of cones was verified, researchers did not think so. Continued research, however, has provided support for another theory of color vision. When it was originally proposed in 1870 by Ewald Hering, the **opponent-process theory** stated that the cones are arranged in pairs; red is paired with green, whereas blue is paired with yellow. The operation of one member of a pair directly inhibits or opposes the operation of the other member. For example, if a red cone fires, the green cone paired with it is inhibited, and vice versa.

As knowledge of the retina grew, the opponent-process theory was abandoned when the trichromatic theory was verified. By the late 1960s, however, brain researchers (such as De Valois & Jacobs, 1968) who recorded the signals from single neurons discovered that some pairs of cells do respond as Hering had said. These cells are

FIGURE 3-8 Color afterimages. Stare at the dot in the center of the four color patches for 1 minute. Now stare at the dot in the center of the right panel. The color afterimages you see will be the opposites of the first ones you looked at.

not cones, however, and they are not located exclusively in the retina. These *opponent-process cells* are found in the lateral geniculate nucleus (LGN), an area of the thalamus (see Figure 3-6). Opponent-process cells also exist in the bipolar-cell layer of the retina. Therefore the trichromatic theory accounts for color processing by the cones in the retina, whereas the opponent-process theory accounts for color processing by the bipolar cells and the thalamus.

Opponent-process cells may also be responsible for the production of color afterimages. A **color afterimage** is the perception of a color that is not really present; it occurs after viewing the opposite or complementary color. For example, after staring at a red object, you will see a green afterimage when the object is taken away (see Figure 3-8); green is the opposite of, or *complementary* to, red. According to the opponent-process theory, continual viewing of red weakens the ability to inhibit green; adaptation has occurred.

color afterimage
Perception of a color that is not really present; occurs after viewing the opposite or complementary color

Psychological Detective

Having learned some of the basics of color vision, now consider a challenging question. Do other animals, such as dogs, cats, and birds, have color vision? If we were testing a primate (gorilla) for color vision, we could present a colored piece of plastic and require the animal to select the same color from a large group of equally bright plastic pieces to receive a reward. How would you test other animals? Write down some possible testing procedures before reading further.

Psychologists have shown that many primates can match colors successfully, but demonstrating color vision in other animals is more difficult. Consider the case of an Asian elephant named Ruby (Gilbert, B., 1990). Keepers at the Phoenix (Arizona) Zoo noticed that Ruby continually made marks in the sand with a stick. In 1987, one of Ruby's trainers had seen

> an elephant in southern California who had learned to paint. She thought of Ruby and decided to offer her some lessons. Ruby immediately showed interest and within a week had mastered the basic techniques. She has become increasingly adept with brushes, and her present paintings are generally much more intricate than the first, rather crude ones. (Gilbert, B., 1990, p. 50)

A session with Ruby occurs in the following manner. An elephant trainer

> brings out an easel, a stretched canvas, a box of brushes (like those used by human water colorists), and jars of acrylic paints fixed onto a palette. With

FIGURE 3-9   Ruby the elephant admires a painting she has just completed. Ruby painted Fire Truck after seeing a fire engine and its blue-clad rescue squad in action.

monochromat
Person who sees only shades of gray; caused by a rare form of color deficiency

dichromat
Person who has trouble seeing one of the primary colors (red, blue, or green); caused by a form of color deficiency

FIGURE 3-10   A test for color deficiency. All of the dots in this pattern are of the same brightness. Only the difference in wavelength allows one to see a number. Individuals who do not see the number may have trouble with red–green color vision.

the marvelously manipulable tip of her trunk, Ruby taps one of the pigment jars and then picks a brush. The [trainer] dips the brush into this jar and passes it to Ruby, who begins to paint. Sometimes she asks, in her own way, to have the same brush refilled repeatedly with the same color. Or she may change brushes and colors every few strokes. After a time, usually about ten minutes, Ruby puts her brushes aside, backs away from the easel and indicates that she is finished. (Gilbert, B., 1990, p. 40)

Ruby and an example of her artwork are shown in Figure 3-9. How did the trainers discover that Ruby had color vision? They noticed she was matching the colors she painted with those she saw in her environment. If people wore red on a particular day, she painted with red. If yellow vehicles were outside her enclosure, she painted with yellow.

Ruby's artwork has become very popular; her paintings sell for several hundred dollars apiece and have increased in value since her untimely death while she was giving birth. The proceeds go to the Phoenix Zoo Conservation Fund to pay for further research on behalf of Ruby and other endangered species. Although many mammals have only two cones and are red–green colorblind, no one is sure how many animals have color vision (Fischler & Firschein, 1987); it is an exciting challenge to complete the list.

Color Deficiencies.   People who suffer deficits in color vision are said to be *color deficient* (Hsia & Graham, 1997). In rare instances they can see no color; these people are called **monochromats**. Monochromats possess only one type of cone; as a result, in affected people the brain treats all received light waves as the same, and only shades of gray are perceived.

You can experience what it is like to be a monochromat. Because rods are monochromatic receptors, they process only shades of gray. The next time you are in dim light and cannot see color, you will know how true monochromats perceive the world.

Dichromats are another type of color-deficient people. A **dichromat** has trouble seeing one of the primary colors (red, blue, or green). A person with this deficiency lacks one type of cone and therefore has trouble with the opponent-process function. If the deficiency involves a red or green cone, the person sees only blues and yellows and shades of gray. If the deficiency concerns the blue cones, the person sees only reds and greens and shades of gray. Special tests have been developed to evaluate color deficiencies. One of these test patterns is shown in Figure 3-10. If you do not see a number there, you may have trouble with red–green color vision.

Because there more male dichromats than female dichromats, color deficiencies may have a genetic or hereditary basis (Bowmaker, 1998). Factors such as diabetes, a diet lacking in vitamin B_{12}, or a change in the lens of the eye, which filters color, can lead to an acquired color deficiency. For example, as we grow older, the lens becomes yellow and loses some of its ability to filter short wavelengths. This change can lead to color confusion, especially between blues and greens. Color confusion may become a life-threatening problem for elderly people who have to deal with colored medicine pills and capsules.

REVIEW SUMMARY

1. **Sensation** refers to stimulation or activation of the receptors. Sensations are the basic building blocks of **perception,** the process of interpreting or making sense of our sensory input.

2. Receptors for each sensory system respond to only one type of environmental stimulus. **Transduction** is the process by which the receptors change the energy they receive into a form that can be used by the nervous system. **Adaptation** occurs when continued presentation of the same stimulus results in a loss of sensitivity.

3. Psychophysicists, such as Ernst Weber and Gustav Fechner, studied the relationship between the mind and the body. **Weber's law** relates the amount of change in a stimulus and the conscious experience of change in the stimulus. Fechner studied the smallest amount of energy that could be detected 50% of the time (the **absolute threshold**) and the smallest change that could be detected 50% of the time (the **differential threshold** or **just noticeable difference [jnd]**).

4. The visual receptors, the **rods** and **cones,** respond to a limited range of light waves, the visible spectrum. Light waves differ in terms of **wavelength** (hue) or color, **amplitude** (intensity), and **saturation** (purity).

5. The **cones** have greater acuity, respond to color, and have a higher threshold for activation; the **rods** have lower acuity, respond to black and white and shades of gray, and have a lower threshold.

6. The visual receptors are located in the **retina** at the back of the eye. To reach the receptors, light waves pass through several other structures in the eye, as well as several layers of retinal cells.

7. Two theories of color vision have been formulated. The **trichromatic theory** proposes that there are three different types of cones; the **opponent-process theory** argues that color-sensitive cells are arranged in pairs. Both theories are supported by research findings.

8. **Dichromats** lack the ability to see one of the three primary colors. **Monochromats** are unable to see color.

✓ CHECK YOUR PROGRESS

1. Sensation refers to
   a. activation of the receptors.
   b. attempting to understand the stimulation we receive.
   c. reduction in sensitivity of receptors to a particular stimulus.
   d. converting stimulation received by receptors into electrochemical energy.

2. Match each term with its characteristic.

   a. Differential threshold 1. Sensitive to color
   b. Absolute threshold 2. Activation of receptors
   c. Sensation 3. Minimum amount of energy
   d. Rods 4. Less visual acuity
   e. Cones 5. Minimum change in energy
   f. Wavelength 6. Hue

3. You push the volume button on your remote control until you can tell that the television's sound is louder. The number of times you pushed the button represents your
   a. perceptual limit.
   b. absolute threshold.
   c. signal detection phase.
   d. just noticeable difference.

4. The process by which receptors become less sensitive to repetitions of the same stimulus is called
   a. adaptation.
   b. transduction.
   c. sensation.
   d. perception.

5. You are watching TV while expecting an important phone call. Periodically you think you hear the phone and pick up the receiver, only to hear a dial tone. According to signal detection theory, what type of decision have

you made?

a. false negative
b. false positive
c. true negative
d. true positive

6. Erin has learned to create a "truly blue" light by focusing on only one wavelength of the visible spectrum. She is most likely to be concerned with which property of light?

a. amplitude
b. magnitude
c. intensity
d. saturation

7. "We can see only a small portion of the visible spectrum." Explain this statement.

8. What color would you see if a researcher simultaneously passes radiant light through red, yellow, and blue filters?

a. white
b. black

c. dark gray
d. light gray

9. Which sensory receptors receive information related to color?

a. rods
b. cones
c. sclera
d. transducers

10. Alex's hospital chart has the following notation: "Patient is a monochromat." Assuming this notation is accurate, what would you conclude about Alex?

a. He sees only bright colors.
b. He cannot distinguish colors.
c. He prefers one color over others.
d. He can pay attention to only one input at a time.

11. Opponent-process theory accounts for

a. color blindness.
b. why we need rods and cones.
c. our ability to see in the dark and the light.
d. color processing by the bipolar cells and thalamus.

ANSWERS: 1. a **2.** a-5, b-3, c-2, d-4, e-1, f-6 **3.** d **4.** a **5.** b **6.** d **7.** Our visual receptors are sensitive only to wavelengths between 380 and 760 nm. **8.** a **9.** b **10.** b **11.** d

Audition (Hearing)

Next to vision, the sense of hearing, or **audition,** is our most important link to the environment. Just as we see light waves, we hear sound waves. In this section we explore what we hear (the auditory stimulus) and how we hear (the auditory system).

What We Hear: The Auditory Stimulus. Have you ever stopped to ask, "What is a sound wave?" To understand audition, we need to answer that question. A *sound wave* is essentially moving air. Objects that vibrate cause air molecules to move, and the movements of these molecules make up sound waves. Examples of sound waves are shown in Figure 3-11.

Like light waves, sound waves have three distinct characteristics: wavelength (frequency), amplitude (intensity), and purity (also known as *timbre*). Shorter wavelengths occur more frequently; longer wavelengths occur less frequently. Frequency is measured in cycles per second and expressed in **hertz (Hz).** People with longer vocal cords have lower voices (lower frequencies) than people with shorter vocal cords because the longer vocal cords of lower-voiced people do not vibrate as rapidly.

As with light waves, the amplitude, or height, of the sound wave affects its intensity. Greater amplitude results in a more intense sound. The volume control on your CD player adjusts the amplitude or intensity of the sound you hear. The amplitude of sound waves is measured in **decibels (db).** Decibel levels represent the amount of energy producing the pressure of the vibrations we perceive as sound; the greater the pressure, the stronger or more intense the vibration (see Table 3-4).

Just as we seldom see pure colors, we do not hear only one pure tone at a time. Consider the variety of sounds you hear when you listen to the radio. Then add your roommate talking, traffic noise from the street, and a ringing phone. The purity or *timbre* of a sound wave can be measured, but we do not experience many pure tones in our lifetimes.

Like the visual receptors, the auditory receptors are sensitive to a limited range of sound waves. Basically, we hear sounds with wavelengths between 20 and 20,000 Hz. Even within this "normal" range of hearing, we do not hear all sounds equally well. As you can

audition
Sense of hearing

hertz (Hz)
Unit of measure (in cycles per second) of the frequency of a sound wave

decibel (db)
Unit of measure of the amount of energy producing the vibrations we perceive as sound

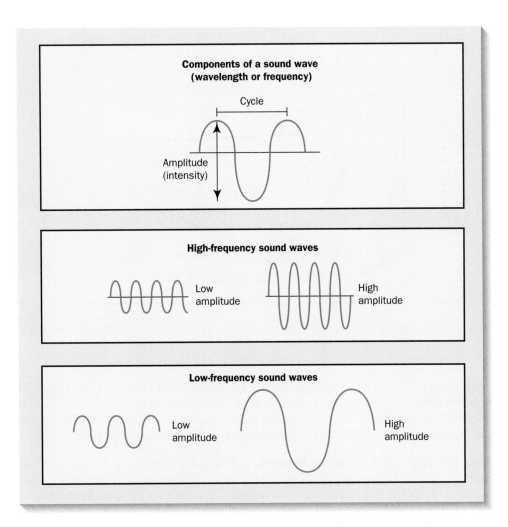

FIGURE 3-11 Sound waves are measured in terms of the number of times the wave repeats itself each second. Each repetition is called a cycle. Cycles per second are also called hertz (Hz). The greater the hertz, the higher the pitch of the sound. Some objects vibrate more strongly than others. This difference in vibration results in varied amplitudes or intensities of the sound waves. The stronger the vibration, the more intense the sound.

TABLE 3-4

Various Sounds, Their Decibel Level, and the Risk of Damage to the Auditory System

Decibel Level		Situation Harmful Exposure Time
180	Rocket launch	Immediate permanent hearing loss
150	Jet plane, shotgun blast	Any exposure dangerous
120	Rock concert (near speakers)	Immediate danger
100	Chain saw	Damage in 2 hours
90	Truck traffic, lawnmower, motorcycle	Damage possible in less than 8 hours
80	Heavy city traffic	Damage possible after 8 hours
70	Constant exposure to a noisy restaurant	Critical level—prolonged exposure can result in damage
60	Normal conversation	No danger

FIGURE 3-12 Threshold at which we hear different frequencies (pitches). Greater intensity is needed to reach threshold for very high and very low tones, whereas tones of around 1,000 Hz require much less intensity.

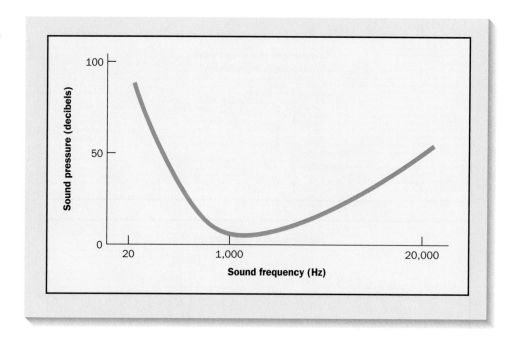

see in Figure 3-12, there is a relation between the frequency of a sound and the threshold at which we hear it. Our hearing is more acute at 1,000 Hz; greater intensity (amplitude) is required if we are to hear tones at lower and higher frequencies. Thus to hear all of the low and high frequencies on a CD, we would need to turn the volume up very high.

How We Hear: The Auditory System. The remarkable range of our auditory ability suggests the presence of an intricate system. A diagram of the auditory system is shown in Figure 3-13. The auditory system is divided into three components: the outer ear, the middle ear, and the inner ear.

The outer ear, especially the *pinna*, gathers sound waves and starts them on their way to the auditory receptors. The sound waves are then funneled down the *auditory canal*. Ultimately they strike the *eardrum* and cause it to move. Movement of the eardrum in turn causes the three bones (hammer, anvil, and stirrup) of the middle ear, collectively called the **ossicles,** to vibrate. The *hammer* (malleus), which is attached to the eardrum, strikes the *anvil* (incus). The anvil in turn strikes the *stirrup* (stapes). The stirrup is connected to the **oval window,** which connects the middle ear to the snail-shaped *cochlea* of the inner ear.

Look at Figure 3-13B as we continue with the chain of events. When the stirrup causes the oval window to vibrate, fluid located in the cochlea is set in motion. The motion of the fluid produces vibration in the **basilar membrane.** This vibration in turn causes the **organ of Corti,** which rests on it, to rise and fall. When the organ of Corti moves upward, the hair cells that project from it brush against the **tectorial membrane** located above it.

The hair cells are the auditory receptors where transduction occurs. Contact with the tectorial membrane causes them to bend; when they bend, they depolarize (Fettiplace, 1990). Sufficient depolarization of the auditory receptors causes the neurons that synapse with them to fire. The axons of these neurons come together before they leave the cochlea to form the *auditory nerve*, which transmits auditory information to higher brain centers. From the cochlea, the auditory nerve travels to the medulla, where some fibers cross to the opposite hemisphere. The remaining fibers do not cross. The next stop is the thalamus. Ultimately the information reaches the temporal lobe of the cortex for processing.

At present there are two theories to explain how we hear different tones or pitches. The older **place theory,** proposed by Hermann von Helmholtz in 1863, says that hair cells located at different places on the organ of Corti transmit information about

ossicles
Three bones (hammer, anvil, and stirrup) located in the middle ear that conduct sound from the outer to the inner ear

oval window
Structure that connects the middle ear with the cochlea of the inner ear; its movement causes fluid in the cochlea to move

basilar membrane
Membrane located in the cochlea of the inner ear; movement of cochlear fluid causes it to vibrate

organ of Corti
Structure located on the basilar membrane of the inner ear that contains the auditory receptors

tectorial membrane
Membrane located above the organ of Corti in the inner ear

place theory
Theory stating that the basilar membrane vibrates at different places to create the perception of different pitches

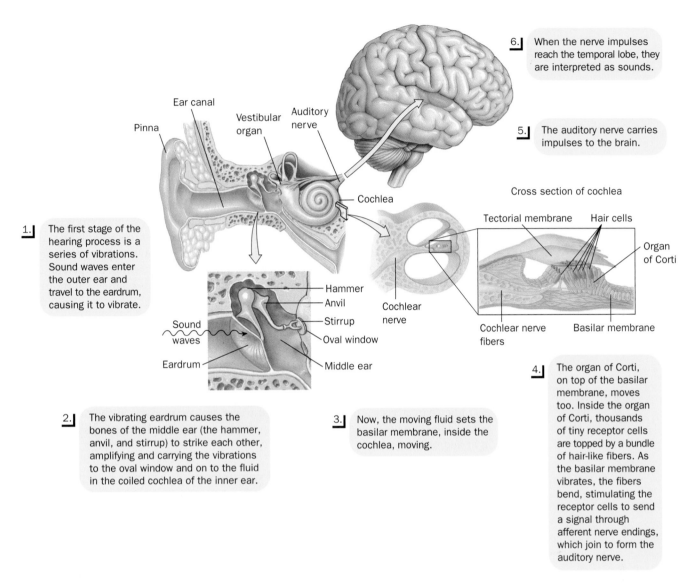

1. The first stage of the hearing process is a series of vibrations. Sound waves enter the outer ear and travel to the eardrum, causing it to vibrate.

2. The vibrating eardrum causes the bones of the middle ear (the hammer, anvil, and stirrup) to strike each other, amplifying and carrying the vibrations to the oval window and on to the fluid in the coiled cochlea of the inner ear.

3. Now, the moving fluid sets the basilar membrane, inside the cochlea, moving.

4. The organ of Corti, on top of the basilar membrane, moves too. Inside the organ of Corti, thousands of tiny receptor cells are topped by a bundle of hair-like fibers. As the basilar membrane vibrates, the fibers bend, stimulating the receptor cells to send a signal through afferent nerve endings, which join to form the auditory nerve.

5. The auditory nerve carries impulses to the brain.

6. When the nerve impulses reach the temporal lobe, they are interpreted as sounds.

FIGURE 3-13 Sound waves enter the outer ear, activate the hammer, anvil, and stirrup in the middle ear, and then cause activation of the auditory receptors in the inner ear.

Source: Shaver & Tarpy, 1993.

different pitches. For example, bending hair cells located near the oval window results in the perception of higher frequencies, whereas bending those located farther away results in the perception of lower frequencies. The place theory says that what you hear depends on which hair cells are activated. For this theory to be correct, the basilar membrane has to vibrate in an uneven manner, which is exactly what happens with frequencies above 1,000 Hz. This uneven vibration, known as a *traveling wave*, is caused by the differential thickness of the basilar membrane. The basilar membrane is thinnest near the oval window and becomes progressively thicker (von Bekesy, 1956).

What about frequencies below 1,000 Hz? Here the **frequency theory** of Ernest Rutherford applies. In 1886, Rutherford suggested that we perceive pitch according to how rapidly the basilar membrane vibrates. The faster the vibration, the higher the pitch, and vice versa. The frequency theory works fine with frequencies up to 100 Hz; typically, however, neurons do not fire more than 100 times per second. How do we get from 100 to 1,000 Hz, where the place theory begins? The *volley principle* (Rose et al., 1967) suggests a likely possibility. According to this view, at frequencies above 100 Hz auditory neurons do not all fire at once; instead they fire in rotation or in volleys. For example, for a 300 Hz tone, one group would fire at 100 Hz, to be followed by a second

3.2

frequency theory
Theory stating that the basilar membrane vibrates at different rates to create the perception of different pitches

group that also fired at the next 100 Hz interval, and then by a third group that fired at the next 100 Hz interval. The activation of these three groups of neurons would tell the nervous system that you had heard a tone of 300 Hz.

Certainly the ability to discriminate among various pitches is an important attribute. Equally important is our ability to locate sound in space. Think of how confusing our world would be if we could not tell where sounds were coming from. Driving would be a nightmare, we could not tell which people were talking to us unless we saw their lips moving, and it would be impossible to find a lost child by hearing a call for help.

Two mechanisms help us locate the source of a sound. The first is blockage of certain sounds by the head. Because the head partially blocks sound waves coming from the opposite side of the body, those sounds are a bit weaker and are perceived as farther away. For example, if someone on your right side is talking to you, the sounds of his or her speech enter your right ear unblocked. Your head, however, partially blocks these sounds before they enter your left ear. In this way the sounds entering your right ear are a bit stronger than those entering your left ear, and you are aware that the person is on your right. Similarly, your pinnas (outer ears) help block sounds coming from directly behind you.

The second mechanism is time delay in neural processing. The brain processes the difference in time when a sound enters one ear and when it enters the other ear to enable you to locate sounds in space. If a sound is presented on your right, it enters your right ear first, then enters the left ear. Even though the time difference may be only a few milliseconds, it is enough time for your brain to process and help you locate objects in space.

The characteristics of light and sound waves are summarized in the Study Chart. Spend a few minutes reviewing facts about the frequency, amplitude, and saturation of light and sound waves.

Hearing Disorders. For a number of years, reports in the media have warned that loud noises such as those from rock concerts, jet planes, sirens, and air hammers can cause hearing damage. If you are like most people, you probably want to know if these claims are true. Some damage-risk comparisons are presented in Table 3-4. Extended exposure to sounds with intensities of 70 db or more can result in hearing loss. As the decibel level increases, the exposure time needed to produce damage decreases. In other words, the louder the sound, the shorter the exposure time before your hearing is damaged. Are you doomed to suffer from hearing loss? Contemporary living involves potentially dangerous sounds; however, the extent of exposure to them is often within your control.

STUDY CHART

Characteristics of Light and Sound Waves

Characteristic	Description	Unit of Measurement	Visible/Audible Range
Wavelength (frequency)	Length of the wave, represented by the distance between the crests of successive waves	Light: nanometers (1 nm = one billionth of a meter) Sound: hertz (Hz; cycles per second)	Light: 380–760 nm Sound: 20–20,000 Hz
Amplitude	Strength or intensity of the wave, represented by its height	Sound: decibels (db; amount of energy producing the wave) Light: foot-candles (ft-c; usually measured with a light meter)	Sound: 0–180 db Light: varies according to reception; rods more sensitive than cones
Saturation	"Trueness" of the color/sound percentage	Presence of wavelengths other than the target wavelength	Depends on percentages of other wavelengths

Many people have hearing problems. Three such problems have been studied extensively: conduction deafness, sensorineural deafness, and central deafness. The first two may be caused by exposure to very loud noises. **Conduction deafness** refers to problems associated with conducting or transmitting sounds through the outer and middle ear. In addition to excessive exposure to loud noises that can cause the eardrum to burst, common causes of conduction deafness are excessive ear wax or damage to the hammer, anvil, or stirrup. **Sensorineural deafness** is caused by damage to the inner ear, especially the hair cells. Noise that is sufficiently loud to cause the hair cells to break can cause this type of deafness. **Central deafness** is caused by disease and tumors in the auditory pathways and auditory cortex of the brain. Although sensorineural and central deafness can be inherited, they can also develop from exposure to measles and other contagious diseases before birth, inadequate oxygen supply during birth, and childhood diseases such as meningitis (Cremers & van Rijn, 1991).

Conduction deafness can be treated; hearing aids are often used to offset hearing loss resulting from damage to the bones of the middle ear. Sensorineural and central deafness are treatable only with cochlear implants, which stimulate the auditory nerve, or surgery of the auditory portion of the central nervous system. However, in many cases, there is no way to restore hearing when there is sensorineural or central deafness.

conduction deafness
Deafness caused by problems associated with transmitting sounds through the outer and middle ear

sensorineural deafness
Deafness caused by damage to the inner ear, especially the hair cells

central deafness
Deafness resulting from disease and tumors in the auditory pathways or auditory cortex of the brain

gustation
Sense of taste

taste buds
Structures that contain the taste receptors

The Chemical Senses: Taste and Smell

Unlike humans, many animal species rely heavily on the chemical senses (taste and smell); hence these are sometimes called *primitive senses*. Taste involves the mixing of molecules in a liquid, and smell involves the mixing of molecules in the air.

Taste (Gustation). Few people would disagree that **gustation** (the technical term for taste) is a meaningful and often enjoyable link with our environment. As one researcher has described it, "The tongue is like a kingdom divided into principalities according to sensory talent. It would be as if all those who could see lived to the east, those who could hear lived to the west, those who could taste lived to the south, and those who could touch lived to the north. A flavor traveling through this kingdom is not recognized in the same way in any two places" (Ackerman, 1990, p. 139). Because taste receptors adapt so quickly and because tasting typically does not occur without smelling, our knowledge of the sense of taste is not as complete or as accurate as it could be.

What We Taste: The Gustatory Stimulus. The stimuli for taste are molecules dissolved in a liquid. But how do we account for the distinctive tastes of dry foods? If you think of the saliva that is produced when you eat dry foods, you know the source of the liquid. Have you ever eaten dry cereal as a snack? The first few bites are likely to be bland and dry, but when your saliva starts flowing the full flavor of the food comes through.

How We Taste: The Gustatory System. Once molecules are in solution, they can come into contact with the taste receptor cells, which are located in structures known as **taste buds** (see Figure 3-14A). Each taste bud contains approximately 20 taste receptors.

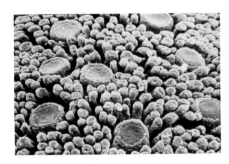

A

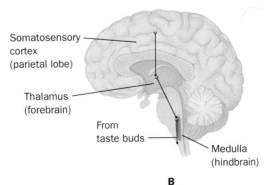

Somatosensory cortex (parietal lobe)

Thalamus (forebrain)

From taste buds

Medulla (hindbrain)

B

FIGURE 3-14 (A) The large, round tastebuds are clearly visible in this photograph. (B) Pathway of the gustatory nerve.

papillae
Bumps or protrusions distributed on the tongue and throat that are lined with taste buds

microvilli
Hairs that project from taste receptors

olfaction
Sense of smell

The taste buds line the walls of small bumps on the tongue and throat called **papillae** (Latin for "bumps"). Although the primary locations of the taste buds are the tip, back, and sides of the tongue, some taste buds are located in the back of your throat, on the roof of your mouth, and inside your cheeks.

Individual taste receptor cells do not last forever; with a life expectancy of only 10 days to 2 weeks, the cells within a taste bud are continually being replaced (McLaughlin & Margolskee, 1994). The number of taste buds increases during childhood to a maximum of about 10,000. At approximately age 40 the trend reverses, and our sense of taste declines (Schiffman, S. S., 1983).

How do the taste receptors work? Although researchers are not absolutely sure, the most credible theory advanced to date suggests that molecules in the solution attach to or fit into receptor sites. The actual taste receptor sites are located on microscopic hairs, known as **microvilli,** that project from the tips of the taste receptor cells. The receptor sites have different geometric shapes, so the shape of the molecule determines whether it fits into a specific receptor site (Tetter & Gold, 1988).

For nearly a century, researchers have agreed with the proposal that we are sensitive to at least four primary tastes: sweet, sour, bitter, and salty (Henning, 1916; Scott & Plata-Salaman, 1991). Hence it is reasonable to suppose that there are at least four different types (shapes) of receptor sites. The arrangement is like a key fitting into a lock. In this case, the key is the molecule and the lock is the receptor site. Once the sites are occupied, depolarization occurs and information is transmitted through the gustatory nerve to the brain (see Figure 3-14B). A number of molecules can occupy a receptor site: The better the fit, the greater the depolarization (McLaughlin & Margolskee, 1994). Keep in mind, however, that the lock-and-key theory is not absolute. Even though a receptor signals a certain taste more than others, it can also contribute to the perception of other tastes (Erickson, DiLorenzo, & Woodbury, 1994).

Psychological Detective

This four-taste, lock-and-key theory sounds reasonable, but has it occurred to you that we experience more than four tastes? With only four proposed types of receptor sites, how do you explain the wide variety of tastes that we are able to experience? Write down some possible answers before reading further.

The explanation of our ability to experience a variety of tastes despite the existence of only four types of receptor sites appears to lie in the *pattern* or *combination* of neural activity the gustatory nerve sends to the brain (Pfaffmann, 1955; Hettinger & Frank, 1992). For example, one taste could be represented by considerable activity from all receptors except the salty ones, whereas a second taste could be represented by high activity levels of only two types of receptors.

As Figure 3-14B shows, the gustatory nerve goes from the taste buds to the medulla in the hindbrain (see Chapter 2), where they synapse. From there the information travels to the thalamus and is then relayed to the somatosensory cortex in the forebrain. At this point you are able to determine the nature of the taste you have experienced.

Throughout the world, humans have learned to like many tastes. Because various food sources are more plentiful in different locations and countries, cultural and ethnic differences in tastes have developed. As Diane Ackerman (1990) points out, "Many people eat rodents, grasshoppers, snakes, flightless birds, kangaroos, lobsters, snails, and bats. Unlike most other animals, which fill a small yet ample niche in the large web of life on earth, humans are omnivorous. Diversity is our delight" (p. 133).

Smell (Olfaction). Unlike animals that rely on their sense of smell for survival (Menco, 1992), humans typically do not pay much attention to odors unless they are unusually bad (like 3-week-old perishable garbage) or unusually pleasant (like a freshly baked pizza). **Olfaction,** the ability to sense odors, is not crucial to our survival, but certain odors—such as those of leaking gas, spoiled food, or smoke—are important. Even if olfaction is not essential for survival, consider how bland our world would seem if we could smell nothing. Humans can recognize approximately 10,000 scents; many animals, such as bloodhounds, can detect and discriminate among many more (Axel, 1995).

What We Smell: The Olfactory Stimulus.   Odors are produced by molecules in the air. The more easily a substance's molecules mix with the air, the easier it is for us to smell it. Gasoline molecules mix with air quite easily and are readily detected; glass molecules do not mix well. Can you describe the smell of glass? Although no one can describe the smell of glass, some people cannot even describe the smell of common odors. More than 2 million Americans have a significant loss in the ability to smell. This condition, called *anosmia*, can result from genetic defects, aging, viruses, allergies, or certain prescription drugs. The most common cause, however, is head trauma, which can shear off axons that run from the olfactory nerves to the brain (Freedman, 1993).

How We Smell: The Olfactory System.   Olfaction is not considered a major sensory system in humans and therefore has not received as much research attention as vision and hearing. What's more, the location of the olfactory receptors makes it difficult to examine them directly. You may be surprised by that statement until you realize that the nose does not contain the olfactory receptors; its function is to collect and filter the air we breathe. As you can see in Figure 3-15, the olfactory receptors are located in an area of tissue of about 2.5 cm (1 in) square in each nasal cavity (Breer & Boekhoff, 1992).

We have about 10 million olfactory receptors, each of which has 6 to 12 hairlike projections called *cilia*. Like taste receptors, olfactory receptors are continually dying and being replaced (Moulton, 1974; Wang, Wysocki, & Gold, 1993). The life span of an olfactory receptor is about 5 to 8 weeks.

In 1991, Linda Buck and Richard Axel identified several specific olfactory receptor sites. Other researchers (Raming et al., 1993) have since identified additional ones. In fact, there may be as many as 1,000 different types of olfactory receptor sites. Although

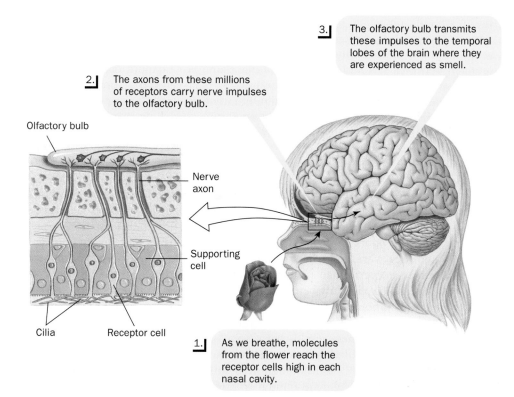

3. The olfactory bulb transmits these impulses to the temporal lobes of the brain where they are experienced as smell.

2. The axons from these millions of receptors carry nerve impulses to the olfactory bulb.

Olfactory bulb

Nerve axon

Supporting cell

Cilia   Receptor cell

1. As we breathe, molecules from the flower reach the receptor cells high in each nasal cavity.

FIGURE 3-15 The location of the olfactory receptors makes them very difficult to study.

researchers do not know a great deal about how they work, the olfactory receptors appear to operate under the same type of lock-and-key/pattern recognition (Malnic, Hirono, & Buck, 1999) principle as the taste receptors (Amoore, 1970). When air molecules of a certain shape fit into a receptor site (Gesteland, 1986), the receptor depolarizes and a message is sent to the brain (Mori, Mataga, & Imamura, 1992). The olfactory nerve takes a somewhat different route to the brain from the other senses we have discussed. The first step is a synapse in the *olfactory bulb*, which is located near the optic chiasm on the underside of the brain. From there some of the olfactory nerve fibers go to the amygdala, which, as noted in Chapter 2, is part of the limbic system. From the amygdala the olfactory nerve travels to the thalamus and hypothalamus and then on to the cerebral cortex for higher-level processing.

The link between odors and memories is familiar to everyone. Charles Dickens claimed that a mere whiff of the type of paste used to fasten labels to bottles would bring back all the anguish of his earliest years, when bankruptcy had driven his father to abandon him in a hellish warehouse where such bottles were made. Do you ever find that the smell of gasoline, pizza, fresh-baked bread, after-shave lotion, sweat, perfume, or pine trees evokes memories? Likewise, many travelers also comment that different countries and cultures have their own unique smells. How old are these memories? How vividly do you recall them? Are there emotions attached to them?

For most people, a number of odors are associated with very emotional memories (Engen, 1987). This relation is a natural consequence of the fact that the *limbic system*, the emotional center of the brain, is involved in the processing of odors and memories. Diane Ackerman (1990) described the memories that are triggered by odors in the following manner: "Smells detonate softly in our memory like poignant land mines, hidden under the weedy mass of many years and experiences. Hit a tripwire of smell and memories explode all at once. A complex vision leaps out of the undergrowth" (p. 5). Manufacturers of cologne and perfume have long taken advantage of their knowledge of the involvement of the limbic system in processing odors.

The Vivid World of Odors

Myth or Science

Sometimes the outlandish claims that characterize much popular psychology actually lead to scientifically sound experiments and meaningful discoveries. For example, in the early 1980s, most people scoffed at the proposal that spraying a fragrance in the air would improve productivity, dismissing it as just another advertising gimmick. Research, however, has actually supported this claim. For example, certain psychologists (Warm, Dember, & Parasuraman, 1991) found that men and women who smelled a pleasant peppermint odor performed significantly better on a boring computer task than comparable participants who breathed only unscented air. Another researcher (Griffin, 1992) reported similar results in a large commercial firm in Tokyo and in New York subway cars.

Do men and women differ in their sense of smell? The olfactory systems in men and women appear to be structurally the same, but there may be sex-based differences in sensitivity and odor memory. William Cain (1982) investigated this question by presenting 80 different odors to men and women. The participants sniffed each odor several times and then were told what the odor was. A series of odor recognition tests followed; women outperformed men on the majority of these tests. Among the 63 odors women learned to identify better than men were those of cigarette butts, leather, pipe tobacco, ginger, honey, and machine oil. Men learned the smells of such things as after-shave, ammonia, bourbon, and bubble gum more readily than women did. We do not know the reason for these results, but it seems that in general women have better odor memory than men. Perhaps these results also mean that women have a better sense of smell in general. It will be interesting to see what answers further research brings and to determine if there are cultural differences as well.

The Interaction of Smell and Taste. So far we have treated smell and taste as if they were independent; however, these two sensations interact quite dramatically to determine flavor—remember how your food tasted the last time you had a head cold? One set of researchers (Mozel et al., 1969) reported the results of an experiment that proved the interdependence of smell and taste in experiencing a flavor. In this study they placed a drop of a certain flavor on a participant's tongue and asked the person to identify the taste. When participants could smell normally, they were correct on most tries; when the experimenter prevented them from smelling, however, they were often unable to identify it. For example, when participants could taste and smell coffee, its flavor was identified correctly nearly 90 percent of the time. When they were permitted only to taste, its flavor was identified correctly less than 5 percent of the time.

You can demonstrate this phenomenon yourself. Cut an apple and a potato into small pieces. Close your eyes, hold your nose, and have a friend put a piece of apple (or potato) into your mouth. Can you tell whether you were given an apple or a potato? When we must rely on taste alone, we often confuse various flavors (Mozel et al., 1969; McBurney, 1986). Thus, odor is an important cue to what food we are eating and how it should taste.

The interaction of taste and smell does not end with the demonstration that odors and odor memories influence our perception of taste. When an odor component is added to a taste, the sensation of taste—not that of odor—is amplified (Murphy, Cain, & Bartoshuk, 1977). Prove it for yourself: Start eating with your fingers pinching your nostrils closed, then add the odor component by releasing your fingers to open your nostrils. The flavor will seem to come alive in your mouth because chewing releases chemicals into the nasal passages.

Somatosensory Processes

Vision, hearing, taste, and smell are important senses; however, they are not our only ones. If you have ever ridden a roller coaster at an amusement park, ridden in a fast-moving subway train that stopped suddenly, worn a piece of clothing that was too small, or put your hand into a pan of scalding water, you are well aware of your other senses. In this section we discuss the somatosensory processes: the vestibular sense, the kinesthetic sense, and the cutaneous senses.

Vestibular Sense. The **vestibular sense**, which originates in the inner ear (see Figure 3-13), provides information about the body's orientation and movement. The vestibular system consists of the three semicircular canals in the inner ear and the utricle. The **semicircular canals** are located at right angles to each other to provide information about movement in all directions. Each semicircular canal is filled with a jelly-like fluid that moves as the head moves. Movement of the fluid in the canal causes hair cells located in the canal to bend. Bending the hair cells sends information about movement to the brain (Gresty et al., 1992).

The **utricle**, a fluid-filled chamber also located in the inner ear, operates on the same principle as the semicircular canals and serves as a gravity detector. To experience the vestibular system, move your head and continue reading. You should have no problem. Now try moving the book while you are reading. The act of reading should be noticeably harder. Why? Because our head movement activates our vestibular system. When we sense movements of our eyes, head, and body, we can make adjustments to keep our world in some perspective. This perspective helps us to orient ourselves to our environment.

Kinesthetic Sense. Have you ever sat on one leg or kept an arm in an awkward position until it tingled or "went to sleep"? Remember how difficult it was to walk or move your arm under those circumstances? The reason for the difficulty is that when this tingling sensation occurs, you no longer have adequate information to determine the location of your leg or arm. Such information about our muscles and joints

vestibular sense
System located in the inner ear that allows us to make adjustments to bodily movements and postures

semicircular canals
Fluid-filled passages in the inner ear that detect movement of the head

utricle
Fluid-filled chamber in the inner ear that detects changes in gravity

The vestibular sense is active during this Olympic skater's performance.

kinesthetic sense
System of receptors located in the muscles and joints that provides information about the location of the extremities

cutaneous senses
System of receptors located in the skin that provides information about touch, pressure, pain, and temperature

constitutes our **kinesthetic sense.** Sense receptors located in the joints and muscles send information to the brain concerning muscle tension and joint position. The brain combines this information with other sensory input, such as vision and audition, to help you determine the location of your limbs. The importance of kinesthetic information is most apparent in the performance of skilled activities, such as gymnastics, swimming, dancing, playing basketball, and driving a car. Such activities require input from a variety of sensory systems, including the kinesthetic sense. As you will see in the next section, sensations from the skin also provide valuable information.

The Cutaneous Senses.   The **cutaneous senses** involve several kinds of information that are sensed by receptors in the skin (Iggo & Andres, 1982). A microscopic view of the skin yields an amazing picture (see Figure 3-16).

Some sections of our skin are packed with a variety of receptors that respond to some form of cutaneous information—touch or pressure, pain, and temperature. The wide variety of skin receptors for touch or pressure are called *mechanoreceptors*; the receptors for temperature are called *thermoreceptors*.

Pain.   The sensation of pain is caused by a harmful stimulus such as extreme heat or cold, toxic chemicals, or breaking or invasion of the skin. The general term for receptors that respond to painful stimuli is *nocioreceptors*. Think of the different types of pain you have experienced. A bright, sharp pain can be caused by pinprick, whereas a dull, chronic pain can result from physical overexertion. Because pain warns us of impending injury, it helps us adapt to the environment.

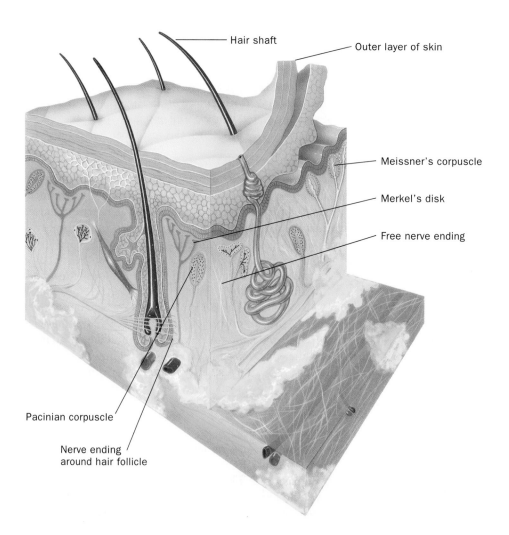

FIGURE 3-16   Cross-section of the skin showing several of the receptors located there.

Source: Shaver & Tarpy, 1993.

One theory of pain, the **gate control theory** (Melzack & Wall, 1965), has greatly influenced our understanding of pain. According to this theory, pain impulses are transmitted from the *receptors* (free nerve endings) to the spinal cord. The axons of the pain neurons release substance P (see Chapter 2) in the spinal cord (Piercey et al., 1981; Levine, Fields, & Basbaum, 1993). In turn, substance P causes neurons in the spinal cord to send information about pain to the brain for processing and perception.

Thus the painful stimulus, in conjunction with substance P, opens the pain gate. How is the gate closed? Neurons that descend from the brain to the spinal cord release opioid peptides (see Chapter 2) called *endorphins*. In turn, the endorphins block the release of substance P (Reichling, Kwait, & Basbaum, 1988), and the pain gate is closed. Pain and stressful or thrilling situations are among the conditions that elicit the release of endorphins.

Is pain perceived similarly by all people? Evidently not. For example, Hall and Davies (1991) found that varsity female athletes had higher pain thresholds than female nonathletes. Likewise, cultural differences in the response to pain have been reported. For example, Nepalese research participants have higher pain thresholds than Western research participants (Clark & Clark, 1980).

The **cutaneous receptors** work together to provide comprehensive information concerning the types of objects we encounter. Once the cutaneous information has been sensed, the sensory nerves travel up the spinal cord and synapse in the thalamus. The sensory information is then relayed to the somatosensory cortex, which is located in the parietal lobe (see Chapter 2), for higher-level processing. As you saw in the map of the sensory cortex (Figure 2-24), the areas of the skin with the most receptors send information to larger areas of the cortex.

The following study chart summarizes the properties and operation of the five major senses.

gate control theory
Theory of pain stating that the release of substance P in the spinal cord produces the sensation of pain

cutaneous receptors
Receptors in the skin that provide sensory information

STUDY TIP

In a group of five, assign each student one of the five senses. Students prepare short oral reports on the basic facts of the senses and deliver them to the group.

STUDY CHART

The Five Senses

Sense	Receptors	Objective Stimulus	Subjective Experience
The ability to detect stimuli	Specialized cells that allow us to experience this sense	Energy or chemicals that cause these receptors to fire	What we experience when these receptors fire
Vision	*Rods and cones* in the retina	Electromagnetic waves between 380 to 760 nm	LIGHT
Hearing (Audition)	*Hair cells* in the basilar membrane	Molecules that vibrate between 20–20,000 Hz	SOUNDS
Taste (Gustation)	*Microvilli* on the tongue	Molecules of substances dissolved in a liquid	TASTES
Smell (Olfaction)	*Olfactory cells* in the walls of the passageway between the nose and the throat	Molecules of substances in the air	ODORS
Touch (Cutaneous)	*Mechanoreceptors* in the skin that respond to skin deformation	Skin indentation, vibrations, and hair movements; changes in temperature; and mechanical or thermal stimuli that begin near levels that can produce tissue damage	PRESSURE
	Thermoreceptors in the skin that respond to changes in temperature		TEMPERATURE
	Nocioreceptors in the skin that respond to painful stimuli		PAIN

REVIEW SUMMARY

1. **Audition,** the sense of hearing, is initiated by the movement of molecules in the air. Vibration of the eardrum starts a chain reaction that results in movement of fluid in the inner ear and the bending of specialized hair cells, which are the receptors for hearing.

2. The pitch or frequency of a sound wave is determined by the location of the hairs that are activated **(place theory)** and the rapidity with which the basilar membrane vibrates **(frequency theory).**

3. Hearing disorders can result from damage to the bones of the middle ear **(conduction deafness),** the inner ear, especially the hair cells **(sensorineural deafness),** or the auditory nerve and auditory cortex **(central deafness).**

4. The chemical senses include the sense of taste **(gustation)** and the sense of smell **(olfaction).**

5. Molecules in solution stimulate taste. Hairs, located on structures known as **taste buds,** serve as the receptors. Although receptors may respond to several tastes, each one is maximally sensitive to one of four tastes: sweet, sour, bitter, or salty.

6. Molecules in the air stimulate the sense of smell. Hairs located in the nasal cavity serve as the receptors. Olfaction has a direct connection to the limbic system; as a result, many of our memories involving odors are highly emotional.

7. The **vestibular sense** enables us to adjust to different bodily movements. The **kinesthetic sense** allows us to determine the position of our extremities. **Cutaneous receptors** for pressure, pain, and temperature are located in the skin.

✓ CHECK YOUR PROGRESS

1. Describe what causes a sound wave. How are sound waves measured?

2. Match each term with a term closely associated with it.

   a. Hertz (Hz)
   b. Pacinian corpuscle
   c. Decibels (db)
   d. Microvilli
   e. Semicircular canals
   f. Substance P
   g. Kinesthesis

   1. Taste receptors
   2. Vestibular sense
   3. Somatosensory processing
   4. Position of arms and legs
   5. Pain
   6. Frequency
   7. Intensity

3. What is the basic function of the outer ear?

   a. to protect the eardrum
   b. to gather and guide sound waves to the eardrum
   c. to amplify low-intensity sounds so they can be heard
   d. to reduce high-intensity sounds to tolerable levels

4. What theory proposes that above 100 Hz auditory neurons do not fire all at once but in rotation?

   a. place theory
   b. volley principle
   c. frequency theory
   d. rotational theory

5. We can locate sounds around us through

   a. volume of sound and timbre of sound.
   b. the volley principle and volume of sound.

   c. timbre of sound and differences in time for sound to reach each ear.
   d. volume of sound and differences in time for sound to reach each ear.

6. What are papillae?

   a. gustatory receptors
   b. protrusions that contain taste buds
   c. the most sensitive portion of the taste bud
   d. taste buds located at the back of the throat

7. Herman has been having a difficult time smelling the baker's hot apple pie. He may be suffering from

   a. anosmia.
   b. anoxic syndrome.
   c. olfactory decline.
   d. gustatory seclusion.

8. Distinguish between the stimuli for taste and smell.

9. Why has research on the olfactory system not progressed at a rapid rate?

10. Feedback about our balance and bodily position is provided by movement of fluid in the

   a. cochlea.
   b. nasal cavities.
   c. semicircular canals.
   d. Meissner corpuscles.

ANSWERS: 1. Movement of air molecules causes a sound wave. Sound waves are measured in decibels. **2.** a-6, b-3, c-7, d-1, e-2, f-5, g-4 **3.** b **4.** b **5.** d **6.** b **7.** a **8.** Gustatory (taste) stimuli are molecules in a liquid solution, whereas olfactory stimuli are molecules in the air. **9.** Research in olfaction has not progressed at a rapid rate because olfaction is not considered one of the major senses *and* because the olfactory receptors are rather inaccessible and difficult to study. **10.** c

PERCEPTION

Spring break is over, and you are driving back to school. Having savored every minute of your leisure time, you get a late start and skip lunch and dinner. Now it's 9 P.M., and you have become painfully aware of every sign on the highway that mentions food. The other signs are a blur; in fact, you aren't even sure that there have been any other signs. At last you reach the exit for the fast-food place you've been reading about for the past 25 miles. You pull off; after a burger, fries, and a shake, you're back on the road. *Why did you fail to perceive the other billboards?*

As we discussed at the beginning of this chapter, perception is the process of organizing and making sense of the stimuli in our environment. Because we rely so heavily on the visual sense, much of our knowledge about perception has been learned through research on vision. Thus to understand perceptual processes, we focus on visual perception. Many of the processes that we discuss also apply to other senses, however; as you read this section, try to use these principles to describe the perception of sounds, tastes, and odors as well as pressure, pain, and temperature.

Like so many areas in psychology, perception is not a simple and straightforward matter. Because our motives (needs, drives, and even prejudices) may distort or determine what we perceive, our discussion of perception begins with a description of how attention is influenced by motivation and attention.

Motivation and Attention

We do not perceive everything in our environment; our motives greatly influence our perceptions. Similarly, certain stimuli are more likely than others to attract our attention.

Motivational Influences.   Think back to our opening vignette—to the part about noticing only those billboards advertising food. In this scenario, why did you fail to perceive the other billboards? Those other billboards certainly activated your receptors (sensation), but you did not perceive them because they were not related to hunger, your dominant motive at the time. Now that your need for food has been satisfied, you begin to notice other things. You glance at your instrument panel and panic—the gas gauge reads "empty"! Now you become aware of an entirely different set of billboards—those advertising gas stations.

Attention.   We cannot possibly attend to and process all of the stimuli received by our sensory systems at any one moment; some of them must be filtered out. Have you ever tried to listen to two friends talk to you at the same time? This is an example of the need to filter information.

Hands On

You can re-create such a situation by conducting a *dichotic listening* exercise (Goodwin, 1988). In dichotic listening experiments, a different message is presented to each of a participant's ears, and the participant is asked to recall both messages. These experiments usually involve the use of a tape recorder and special headphones. However, three people, minus this equipment, can accomplish the same goal. The procedure is as follows: Place three chairs side by side. You, the participant, sit in the middle chair. Have a person seated on your right and a person seated on your left read different passages at the same time. After a fixed amount of time, such as 20 or 30 seconds, try either to repeat verbally or write down whatever you can recall. You can create interesting variations of this basic procedure, such as a male voice in one ear and a female voice in the other ear, or fast reading in one ear and slow reading in the other. When you try to listen to both messages, you will probably find yourself switching back and forth between them and becoming quite confused.

Dichotic listening tasks are designed to study **divided attention,** the ability to attend to more than one message or type of information at the same time. Research in this area has uncovered some intriguing information about human perception. For example, we hear (and understand) much more than the information of which we are consciously aware. This fact is demonstrated by the famous "cocktail-party phenomenon" (Cherry & Bowles, 1960). With this phenomenon, the scene is a typical weekend party—lots of people doing lots of talking. You are having a conversation with five or six friends when suddenly you hear your name mentioned in a conversation on the other side of the room. Your name was not shouted, and you are not aware of anything else that was said—only your name. Clearly, you have been listening to and processing other conversations during your conversation with your friends. Only when the content included something important, like your name, did the conversation enter your consciousness and sharpen your awareness or perception.

The cocktail-party phenomenon. You can hear something that is very important to you, such as your name, even though it is said in a normal voice across a noisy room.

The *cocktail-party phenomenon* demonstrates that attention can be divided to some extent. The ability to listen to two messages at once might be very beneficial. Can you do anything to make this task easier or more effective? The answer is to practice. The more you practice at processing two separate messages simultaneously, the more skilled you will become at it. And, you will find that it is easier to divide your attention when you are processing different *types* of information. For example, most of us have little difficulty listening to a CD while driving. We divide our attention between the visual stimuli involved in driving and the auditory stimuli produced by the CD. This type of divided attention is easy to accomplish on a monotonous interstate highway or in a familiar neighborhood, but what happens when you find yourself in rush-hour traffic in a strange metropolitan area? Many people turn the volume of the music down or turn it off completely. The shift in attention from the music to the demands of the signs and traffic around them shows selective attention at work. We do not want to leave you with the impression that trying to divide your attention is always a good objective. The numerous traffic accidents that have resulted from people trying to talk on cell phones while they are driving is a good example of a potentially hazardous situation.

In addition to needs, motives, and prejudices, certain aspects of stimuli determine which ones get our attention. For example, people generally pay more attention to stimuli that are larger, louder, or more colorful than others. You can watch television commercials any night of the week to see how advertisers exploit this phenomenon. What's more, your attention is attracted to stimuli that stand out from or contrast with the objects around them.

When something happens unexpectedly our attention is attracted very quickly. When contrast and surprise combine, our attention is commanded even more quickly. If your instructor wore pajamas to class, for example, this unusual occurrence would catch your attention immediately.

Although motivation and attention are important aspects of perception, they do not provide the complete picture. Once a stimulus has attracted our attention, there are basic perceptual abilities that we use to respond to it.

divided attention

The ability to process more than one source of stimulation at the same time

Basic Perceptual Abilities: Patterns and Constancies

We perceive objects in our environment as having features such as pattern, constancy, depth, and movement. Our perception of these objects and their features is so automatic that we often take them for granted. However, they are crucial components of perception. In this section we describe them in detail.

Pattern Perception. Among the most basic perceptual abilities is the ability to perceive patterns. To survive in modern society, we must be able to perceive a staggering number of shapes and figures. A few of the patterns we deal with every day are the letters of the alphabet, traffic signs, friends' facial features, food items in the grocery store, the buildings in an apartment complex, and the automobiles in a parking lot. Psychologists refer to the ability to discriminate among different shapes and figures as **pattern perception.** Although some cortical cells appear to function as *feature detectors* that are sensitive to specific shapes, such as lines, bars, or edges, we still need to translate these features into a perception of our environment (Hughes, Nozawa, & Kitterle, 1996). There are several theories concerning the process of pattern perception.

The **feature analysis theory** of pattern perception (Lindsay & Norman, 1977) states that we perceive basic elements of an object and mentally assemble them to create a complete object. As when a house is built, various pieces are put together until the structure is completed. In short, we start from the bottom and work up to a completed and recognizable building. Once the object has been assembled, it is matched against items stored in memory. If there is a match, we are able to identify the item. If there is no match, we probably search for the memory that resembles it most closely.

In terms of perceptual processes, your perceptual experience starts with receptor activity and works toward progressively higher brain centers. This process of starting with basic elements and working toward a more complex perception is known as a *bottom-up model.* If, however, we look at the task of recognizing words, this bottom-up model of feature analysis runs into problems. Several studies (such as those by Johnston & McClelland, 1973, 1974) have shown that we can recognize an entire word better than we recognize individual letters. These results suggest that, at least in some instances, we use a *top-down approach* in which the whole object is recognized before its component parts are identified. But top-down processing results in mistakes when the word is not perceived correctly, such as reading the word *house* for the word *horse.*

Perceptual Constancies. You do not have to treat every perceptual change as if your environment had changed completely. Once you have identified an object, you continue to recognize it even if its location and distance from you change, thereby casting a different image on your retina. A change in the retinal image does not signal a change in the object. This tendency to perceive the size and shape of objects as relatively stable despite retinal changes is called **perceptual constancy.** The importance of perceptual constancies should be obvious; they allow us to deal with our environment as relatively stable and unchanging.

Shape Constancy. **Shape constancy** means that your perception of the shape of an object as viewed from different angles does not change even though the image projected on your retina does so. In other words, the shape of an object is perceived independently of the image it casts on the retina. This phenomenon is easy to demonstrate. Look at this book from a number of angles. You see nothing but a book being held in different positions. The same could be said for the opening and closing of a door or the image of a car making a left turn in front of you. The image on your retina changes dramatically, yet the object you perceive does not. Almost any moving object displays the principle of shape constancy. For the perception of shape

pattern perception
The ability to discriminate among different figures and shapes

feature analysis theory
Theory of pattern perception stating that we perceive basic elements of an object and assemble them mentally to create the complete object

perceptual constancy
The tendency to perceive the size and shape of an object as constant even though its retinal image changes

shape constancy
The tendency to perceive the shape of an object as constant despite changes in its retinal image

Can you tell the size of this object? When we can't rely on cues for distance or the size of other objects, size constancy is not good. See the end of the chapter for another photo that gives you a better idea as to the size of this object.

size constancy
The tendency to perceive the size of an object as constant despite changes in its retinal image

depth perception
The ability to perceive our world three-dimensionally

binocular cues
Cues for depth perception that involve the use of both eyes

monocular cues
Cues for depth perception that involve the use of only one eye

constancy to occur, however, the object must be familiar and must be seen in an identifiable context. If there is no context or background to which the object can be related, it appears to float in space, and you cannot judge its correct orientation; shape constancy disappears.

Size Constancy.   **Size constancy** also helps us to maintain consistency in our perceptual environment. As objects move toward us, their retinal images enlarge; as they move farther away, their retinal images diminish. We do not perceive the size of those objects as changing, however, instead we perceive the objects as moving toward or away from us. Size constancy depends on our familiarity with the object and on our ability to judge distance. When we are dealing with familiar objects and can easily judge distances, we are more likely to perceive the size of the objects as being constant. When we are dealing with unfamiliar objects and our ability to estimate distance is poor, the objects may appear to change size.

To understand this point, consider a classic example. C. M. Turnbull (1961), an anthropologist, was studying the BaMbuti Pygmies in the dense forest of the Belgian Congo. During his studies, Turnbull traveled from one group of Pygmies to another. On one trip, which took him across the plains, he was accompanied by a youngster, Kenge, who had spent his entire life in the dense forest. Having never been on the plains, Kenge was unable to judge distances and determine the size of unfamiliar objects. A distant herd of buffalo presented a major problem; Kenge "tried to liken the distant buffalo to the various beetles and ants with which he was familiar" (Turnbull, 1961, p. 305). Imagine Kenge's surprise when, as they drove closer to the buffalo, he thought he saw the animals grow steadily larger. Clearly, our culture and experiences influence our perceptions of real life and of pictures (Deregowski, 1980).

Because they are automatic processes, size and shape constancy may seem rather simple; however, these constancies involve much processing. We are using familiar background objects for purposes of comparison (size constancy) and to anchor our perceptions (shape constancy). If the background objects are eliminated and we are confronted with an unfamiliar object, however, we have difficulty perceiving its correct size and distance. As in the story of Kenge, without distance cues and other objects with which to make comparisons, we cannot judge size well. Similarly, without a background to anchor our perceptions, moving objects may appear to change shape rather than simply to move in space (see Figure 3-17).

Auditory constancies are another important aspect of perception. We perceive words as the same when they are spoken by many people with very different voices. Likewise, a melody is recognizable even when it is played on different instruments and in different keys.

Depth Perception.   In addition to a world of constancies, we experience a third dimension, **depth perception.** For decades psychologists have been puzzled by the question of how we are able to perceive depth or distance. The surface of the retina is two-dimensional (top to bottom, side to side), yet we are able to judge distances and locate objects in space (three-dimensionally) quite well. Two main types of cues, binocular and monocular, are used to create our perception of depth. **Binocular cues** require the integrated use of both eyes, whereas **monocular cues** are effectively processed using information from only one eye.

Binocular Cues.   Two binocular cues are adjustments of the eye muscles (a weak/nonprecise cue) and binocular disparity. Let's consider eye muscle adjustments first. Our eyes are supported by muscles that move the eyeball to allow us the best possible view. They also provide feedback for judging distance. When objects are near, the eyes rotate toward a center point. You can feel the muscle tension when you look at objects that are very close. To experience this sensation, focus on this

FIGURE 3-17 Examples of size and shape constancy with an indication of the influence of supporting cues. Notice the hand drums that these women are holding. Even though the drums cast very different images on the retina, shape constancy dictates that they will all be seen as drums, and not as three different shapes.

sentence and gradually move the book closer to your eyes. The closer the book gets, the more eye muscle strain you feel; the farther away the book is, the less eye muscle strain you experience. Binocular disparity provides more precise depth cues than eye muscle adjustments.

If you open and close one eye and then the other, it is obvious you do not see exactly the same thing with each eye. The closer the object, the greater the difference between what the two eyes see. This difference occurs because each eye sees from a different angle, a phenomenon known as **binocular disparity.** When the images from both eyes merge in the brain, a sense of depth is created. The random-dot stereogram relies completely on binocular disparity cues (there are no monocular cues present) to create the perception of depth. If you are having difficulty seeing the 3-D image, don't despair; many people have a hard time seeing the image because of the abnormal focusing (focusing *behind* the picture, not on the picture itself) that is required. What's more, at least 2 to 3% of the population cannot see the image because they have weak or slightly misaligned eyes that keep them from detecting binocular disparity cues.

Researchers have identified cortical cells that respond to binocular disparity (Ohzawa, De Angelis, & Freeman, 1990), assuming that the activity of these cells is a primary cue for depth. You can easily demonstrate binocular disparity by closing one eye and aligning your two index fingers. Now switch eyes. Are the fingers still aligned? This misalignment is even greater when the fingers are closer to the face, as compared with when they are at arm's length.

Monocular Cues.   Monocular cues, which can be perceived by either eye alone, also help determine depth (Stoner & Albright, 1993). For example, when the ciliary muscles change the shape of the lens in accommodation, the muscle adjustments are sensed and are used to help determine distance.

Artists use numerous monocular cues—including interposition (near objects partially obscure more distant objects), *texture gradient* (the texture of a surface becomes smoother with increasing distance), *linear perspective* (parallel lines appear to converge as they recede into the distance), and *relative brightness* (brighter objects appear closer than duller-appearing ones)—to create the illusion of depth. These cues also operate in our day-to-day environment, as you can see in Figure 3-18. After you have studied the three photographs, look around the room you are in and identify other examples of these cues.

In addition to demonstrating the importance of binocular and monocular cues for depth perception, psychologists have investigated whether this perceptual ability is innate or learned. For example, Eleanor Gibson (Gibson & Walk, 1960) has successfully used the visual cliff (see Figure 3-19) to test depth-perception ability in human

binocular disparity
The difference between the images seen by the two eyes

 3.3

FIGURE 3-18 Monocular cues for depth perception: interposition and brightness (left); texture gradient and linear perspective (center); and texture, linear perspective, and interposition (right).

FIGURE 3-19 The visual cliff. Will the child perceive depth or move onto the glass that covers the deep side of the visual cliff?

3.4

Visual Cliff

infants and children as well as in a variety of animals. The visual cliff consists of a two-sided chamber; the bottom of one side of the chamber is shallow and within easy reach, whereas the bottom of the other side is deep. Both sides of the chamber are covered by glass. A test participant is placed on a small platform in the center of the visual cliff and must choose between crawling to the shallow or deep sides. Human infants avoid the deep side from the time they are mobile. Although humans perceive depth from about 6 months of age, when placed over the visual cliff, they can perceive that something is different much earlier. Infants as young as 2 to 4 months old had a significantly higher heart rate when placed on the deep side of the visual cliff (Campos, Langer, & Kravitz, 1970). Gibson's research on perception is so significant that she was awarded the National Medal of Science by President George Bush in 1992, the highest honor that can be bestowed on a scientist by the president of the United States.

Gestalt Principles of Perceptual Organization

The founders of Gestalt psychology (see Chapter 1)—Max Wertheimer, Wolfgang Köhler, and Kurt Koffka—proposed we are born with the ability to organize the elements of our perceptual world in very predictable ways (Sharps & Wertheimer, 2000). The goal of these automatic organizing processes is to produce the best or most complete perception of our environment. Among the most familiar of these processes are figure-ground distinctions and the grouping of elements.

Figure and Ground. The Gestalt psychologists emphasized that one of the ways in which we organize our perceptual world is by sorting stimuli into figure and background (or ground) (Humphreys & Mueller, 2000). The figure is the focus of our attention; the ground constitutes the remainder of our perception. An example of a **figure–ground relations** is shown in Figure 3-20. Notice what we focus on—the figure—tends to be smaller, more colorful, or brighter than the background.

Sometimes these automatic processes can trick us. Look at Figure 3-21 and decide what is figure and what is ground in each example. In each instance the figure–ground relation is unclear or ambiguous, and the task is much more difficult than that in Figure 3-20. When we are confronted with ambiguous figures like those in Figure 3-21, we are able to organize the material in at least two ways. Which do you see first? That may depend on top-down influences created by reading the caption (Did it say "young woman" or "old woman" first?) or on the features that first attracted your attention. Once you have seen both figures in an ambiguous drawing, you can easily reverse the figure–ground relation.

How often do you encounter figure–ground problems in your day-to-day activities? For example, while driving have you ever stopped next to a large truck at a traffic light? Suddenly you feel yourself moving backward! Have your brakes failed? Your foot is on the brake, and you push it harder. Nothing happens, however—the backward motion continues. Only then do you realize that the truck—not your car—is moving.

Unconsciously you perceived your car as the figure and the larger truck as the ground. Because figures normally move across a background, you perceived yourself, rather than the truck, as the moving object. Can you think of other examples of how your perceptions have been fooled by unusual figure–ground relations?

Principles of Grouping. In addition to showing that we perceive figure–ground relationships, the Gestalt psychologists demonstrated that we organize our perceptions by grouping elements (King, 2001). The way we group perceptual elements is extremely important. Think of how much trouble you would have if you had to deal with every perceptual element independently. The letters you are reading fall into groups we call words. What would reading be like if you had to think about every single letter? What would it be like to listen to someone speak if you couldn't group the

FIGURE 3-20 Example of figure–ground relations.

figure–ground relation
Organization of perceptual elements into a figure (the focus of attention) and a background

A Letters or objects?

B Vase or faces?

C Young woman or old woman?

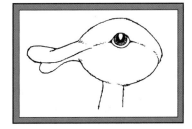

D Rabbit or duck?

FIGURE 3-21 Examples of ambiguous or unclear figure–ground relations. Which object do you see first in each picture? Does it make seeing the other figure more difficult?

proximity
Gestalt principle stating that perceptual elements that are close together are seen as a group

similarity
Gestalt principle stating that perceptual elements that are similar are seen as a group

good continuation
Gestalt principle stating that smooth, flowing lines are more readily perceived than choppy, broken lines

closure
Gestalt principle stating that organizing perceptions into whole objects is easier than perceiving separate parts independently

apparent motion
Illusion of movement in a stationary object

STUDY TIP

Draw your own original pictures for each of the principles of grouping.

sounds into words? We function more effectively and efficiently when we organize perceptual elements into groups.

Several conditions promote the grouping of perceptual elements. Although we discuss these conditions separately, keep in mind that more than one of them can operate at a time. See how many of these conditions you notice in your day-to-day life.

With **proximity,** one of the most elementary Gestalt grouping principles, items that are close to each other are perceived as a group. The words strung together on this page are an example of proximity. According to the Gestalt principle of **similarity,** items that are alike are grouped together: XXXOOO, perceived as three Xs and three Os. These two principles are illustrated in Figure 3-22. Do they operate effectively with senses other than vision? Think about musical melodies or spoken words. What would they be like if you had to pay attention to each separate note or sound?

The Gestalt principle of **good continuation** says that we perceive continuous, flowing lines more easily than choppy or broken lines. What do you see in the fourth panel of Figure 3-22? It should be easier to see a continuous flowing figure rather than two separate lines, as predicted by the Gestalt psychologists.

Now examine the third panel in Figure 3-22. What do you see? It's a bicycle, of course, but is the drawing complete? To complete the picture and identify the object, you had to create the missing pieces perceptually. This process illustrates the Gestalt principle of **closure,** which says that organizing our perceptions into complete objects is easier than perceiving each part separately.

Perception of Movement

Suppose you are on your way to your next class when you notice a message on an electronic sign. It is one of those signs, like a theater marquee, that has letters and words that appear to move across it. Our perception of separate words is created because of the proximity of the letters that make up each group (word) and the spaces between successive groups of letters. Unlike the letters you are reading in this text, the letters on the electronic sign are made up of separate, unconnected points—and we connect them using the principle of closure.

This sign, however, adds another dimension to our consideration of perception. Although the words do not really move across the sign, they appear to do so. **Apparent motion** is the illusion of movement in a stationary object. In the electronic sign, it is created by turning the lights on and off in a particular sequence. How prevalent is apparent motion? Consider movies, television, videocassettes, and DVDs. All of these forms of entertainment rely on the brain's ability to create the perception of motion from a series of still pictures.

When you see "moving" words, such as the ones on this building, you are experiencing *apparent* motion. The words do not actually move.

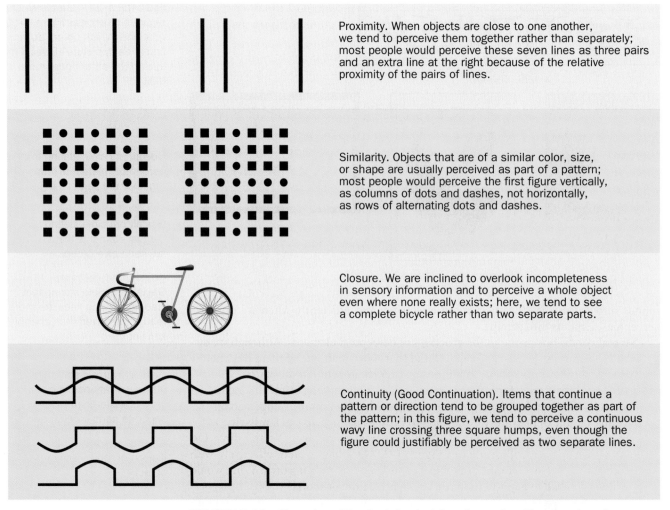

Proximity. When objects are close to one another, we tend to perceive them together rather than separately; most people would perceive these seven lines as three pairs and an extra line at the right because of the relative proximity of the pairs of lines.

Similarity. Objects that are of a similar color, size, or shape are usually perceived as part of a pattern; most people would perceive the first figure vertically, as columns of dots and dashes, not horizontally, as rows of alternating dots and dashes.

Closure. We are inclined to overlook incompleteness in sensory information and to perceive a whole object even where none really exists; here, we tend to see a complete bicycle rather than two separate parts.

Continuity (Good Continuation). Items that continue a pattern or direction tend to be grouped together as part of the pattern; in this figure, we tend to perceive a continuous wavy line crossing three square humps, even though the figure could justifiably be perceived as two separate lines.

FIGURE 3-22 Examples of the Gestalt principles of grouping. The grouping of perceptual elements allows us to deal more effectively with our environment.

Hands On

Motion is so important that your brain creates the illusion of movement even when there is none (Suzuki & Peterson, 2000). This phenomenon, known as the *autokinetic effect*, keeps the visual receptors from adapting. If your receptors adapted, vision would cease. To demonstrate the autokinetic effect, you will need a small flashlight, some string, and a very dark room. Hang the flashlight, pointed down, from a light fixture or ceiling fan. Turn the flashlight on and all the other lights in the room off. Sit on the floor and stare at the flashlight. Within a minute or less the light should appear to move, usually in an elliptical (egg-shaped) pattern. This effect is due to small, involuntary eye movements that the brain doesn't track, so it perceives object motion.

Perceptual Hypotheses and Illusions

We have said that perception involves the brain's attempt to interpret and make sense of the stimuli we receive from our environment. Constancy, figure–ground relations, and grouping processes help us develop educated guesses, or inferences, about the nature of those stimuli. Such inferences are called **perceptual hypotheses,** and they routinely shape our perceptual experience. If you stop and think about it, perceptual hypotheses are examples of *top-down processing* that we discussed previously (see p. 117). Much of the time our perceptual hypotheses are accurate, but sometimes they are wrong. For

perceptual hypothesis
Inference about the nature of stimuli received from the environment

example, how often could you have sworn that your professor said a paper was due next Thursday, rather than next Tuesday? Have you ever been absolutely sure that a traffic light was green, not red?

It is easy to trick our senses into developing an incorrect perceptual hypothesis. Such incorrect perceptual hypotheses form the basis for **perceptual illusions,** which are misperceptions or interpretations of stimuli that do not correspond to the sensations received by the eye or other senses (Block & Yuker, 1989). The case in which grass looks greener on the other side of the fence is an example.

Psychological Detective

How many times have you heard people say, "The grass looks greener on the other side of the fence"? Usually this statement refers to the fact that most of us fail to appreciate what we have and long for what we do not have. Does real grass on the other side of a real fence actually appear greener? Give this question some thought. Write down your answer, and the reasons for it, before reading further.

The answer to the greener-grass question is yes, and there is an explanation. When you look directly down at the grass in your yard, you see both green grass and the dark brown soil in which it is growing. These colors blend together. When you look at the grass across the fence, however, you are not looking straight down, and therefore you do not see the brown soil. Hence you perceive the grass on the other side of the fence as being a purer shade of green. Your senses are tricked into believing that the grass really is greener on the other side of the fence. Figure 3-23 shows how your visual sense may be tricked by the perceptual stimulus.

perceptual illusions
Misperceptions or interpretations of stimuli that do not correspond to the sensations received

  3.5

A

B   **C**

FIGURE 3-23 The type of stimulus and the context in which you view that stimulus can trick your visual sense. (A) The gray in the orange square looks darker than the gray in the blue square even though they are exactly the same. (B) Even though this pattern is regular and uniform, when you look at it your eyes create patterns and movement within the larger pattern. (C) When you do not look directly at the intersections of the white rows and colums, you should see gray spots. If you look directly at these intersections, the spot will disappear.

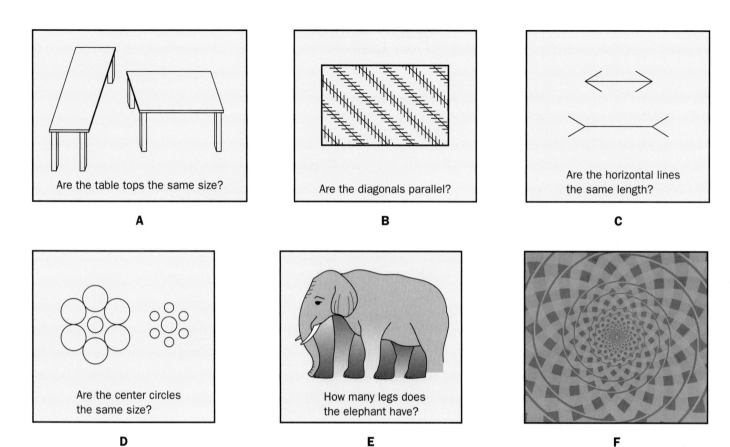

A Are the table tops the same size?

B Are the diagonals parallel?

C Are the horizontal lines the same length?

D Are the center circles the same size?

E How many legs does the elephant have?

F

FIGURE 3-24 Perceptual hypotheses may be the cause of many illusions. (A) Because it is narrow, the table on the left is perceived as being longer than the table on the right is wide; it is not. (B) The short crossing lines (some people call them feathers) help create the perception that the longer lines are not parallel; they are. (C) The <> symbols or "wings" at the ends of the top lines and the >< symbols at the ends of the bottom line create the illusion that the top line is shorter than the bottom line. The amount of error in judging the Muller-Lyer illusion depends on a number of factors (Wraga, Creem, & Proffitt, 2000) such as the angle and length of the wings. (D) Because it is surrounded by several larger circles, the center circle on the left is perceived as smaller than the center circle on the right (Ebbinghaus Illusion). The two circles are exactly the same size. (E) Even though we know that an elephant has only four legs, the additional leg shapes are compelling cues. Are the elephant's real legs dark or light in color? (F) Fraser's spiral creates the illusion of a spiral. If you check carefully, there is no spiral, just a series of concentric circles.

Unconscious Inference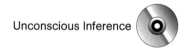

STUDY TIP

Create an outline summary of the basic perceptual abilities (patterns and constancies).

The development of incorrect perceptual hypotheses is at the heart of perceptual illusions. Some of our favorites are shown in Figure 3-24. Look at each and decide what perceptual hypothesis you have developed for it. Figure 3-24D, which depicts the Ebbinghaus illusion (Franz, et al., 2000), suggests that our perceptual hypotheses are influenced by contrast or the tendency to accentuate differences. In this illusion, big circles make a central circle appear small, whereas small circles make a central circle look larger. What aspects of the other drawings trick the visual system causing us to develop incorrect perceptual hypotheses?

One of the most fascinating perceptual illusions is the Ames room. Figure 3-25A shows the view that you would have if you were looking into the Ames room. Notice how much bigger the woman on the right appears. How can this be? People are not supposed to vary this much in height. The explanation is in Figure 3-25B. Although you assume the room is perfectly square, it is not square. The floors you thought were level are not level. The woman is actually closer to you and casts a larger image on your retina. Without information to tell you that one person is closer and on a floor that slants upward, you conclude that this person is abnormally large.

Contemporary Issues and Findings in Perception Research

Parallel Processing, Visual Search, and the Application of Basic Perceptual Research.   During "the decade of the brain" (the 1990s) research on perceptual processes progressed rapidly. According to Woods and Krantz (2001), recent advances in the study of brain functioning promise to change our conception of sensory processes and perception. For example, studies of the human visual cortex (Zeki, 1993) indicate that sensory processing does not occur in a strictly sequential manner where one part of the brain performs an activity and then passes the modified sensation on to another brain area for additional processing. The picture that emerges is of a *parallel processing system* (Friedman-Hill & Wolfe, 1995) in which information simultaneously flows both from lower to higher levels and from higher to lower levels in the brain.

For example, exciting breakthroughs also are occurring in the study of higher-level, more cognitive processes, such as visual search (Geisler & Chou, 1995). **Visual search** is the process of identifying the presence or absence of a target stimulus among a group of distractor items. Research on this topic shows that when stimuli have high *salience* (that is, when they are relevant, meaningful, or distinctive), visual search is done efficiently, rapidly, and in a parallel manner. Indeed, such high-salience stimuli seem to "pop out" from the distractors. Such features as color, motion, brightness (Gilchrist et al., 1997), and prior experience with the target (Lubow & Kaplan, 1997) help create the pop-out effect. The combination of these features (for example, color and form [D'Zmura, Lennie, & Tiana, 1997]), however, can result in a more lengthy and difficult visual search. There are several notable applications of visual search research to real-life situations in which target stimuli must be detected from distractors. These include controlling air traffic (Vortac et al., 1993), driving an automobile (Lajunen, Hakkarainen, & Summala, 1996), and monitoring visual displays (Liu, 1996).

Basic perception research also is playing an important role in our understanding of the family of learning problems known as *dyslexia*. For example, Stein and Walsh (1997) provided data showing that dyslexia is linked to abnormal neural development. Moreover, children with the most common form of dyslexia, *specific reading disability* (Demb, Boynton, & Heeger, 1998) have been shown to have a number of perceptual difficulties. The specific nature of the problem faced by dyslexic people was unveiled by Ballew, Brooks, and Annacelli (2001), who studied the effect of contrast on reading ability. They found that as the contrast between individual letters and the background was reduced, the reading performance of dyslexic children decreased *significantly* more than the reading performance of normal children. Woods and Oross (1998) reported that special stimuli and conditions were not needed to produce these conditions. Clearly, perception research has the potential to offer easily implemented solutions, such as maintaining high letter-background contrast, that can aid the dyslexic individual. What's more, perception researcher Lauren Scharff and her colleagues (Scharff

FIGURE 3-25   If you assume that the Ames room is a regularly shaped room with a normal ceiling height, then the person in the right corner appears much larger than she should be.

Source: Seaman & Kenrick, 1994.

A

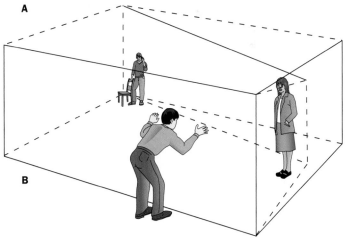

B

visual search

Identifying the presence of a target stimulus among a group of other, distractor items

& Ahumada, 2001; Scharff, Hill, & Ahumada, 2000) have shown that the type of background texture can affect text readability for normal individuals. This area of applied perception research is paying rich dividends for a wide range of individuals.

If you own a flat-screen computer monitor or television, scanner, color printer, or digital camera, contemporary perception research has impacted your life. According to Woods and Krantz (2001), the development of high-tech displays for these applications and "for harsh visual environments such as the airplane cockpit" is one of the prime areas of perception research. For example, someone has to make sure that the colors on these devices are accurate; that's the task of the perception researcher.

Without question, basic perception research has provided important information and promises to yield additional real-life applications in the future. It also has the potential to tell us about social processes.

Perception Is Affected by Social Context.   Because most stimuli have physical properties that can be described precisely, it is easy to get the impression that perception is a rather automatic and mechanical process. In fact, some psychologists have held this view for years. The view is changing rather dramatically, however. Researchers are showing that even basic perceptual phenomena can be influenced by social context. Consider an intriguing research project from the University of Amsterdam, Holland (Stapel & Koomen, 1997).

Do you remember the Ebbinghaus illusion (see Figure 3-24D)? In this illusion, the perceived size of the center circle is influenced by the size of the circles that surround it: When the surrounding circles are large, the center circle is seen as smaller, and vice versa. Stapel and Koomen wondered if this effect could be obtained with stimuli other than geometric figures. If the effect could be obtained with nongeometric figures, they then wondered if other factors influenced it. To answer these questions, they conducted two experiments. In both experiments, college students estimated the size of a human face that was surrounded by faces or other objects.

In the first experiment the target stimulus (a face) was surrounded by (a) identical faces, (b) same-gender faces, (c) different-gender faces, or (d) nonperson objects (trucks or handbags). The magnitude of the illusion was greatest when the target stimulus was surrounded by identical stimuli. Thus the target face was perceived as largest when it was surrounded by small, identical faces. As you can see in Figure 3-26, same-gender

FIGURE 3-26   Results from Stapel and Koomen's Experiment 1, showing the magnitude of the size contrast illusion as a function of physical appearance of context stimuli. *Illusion magnitude* is defined as the difference between the targets in two types of stimulus configurations: the target stimulus surrounded by small context stimuli versus the same target stimulus surrounded by large context stimuli.

Source: Stapel & Koomen, 1997.

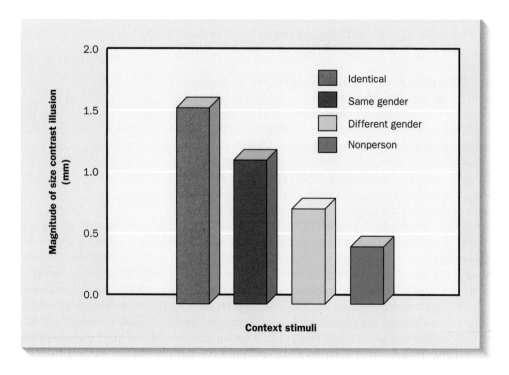

faces produced the next largest contrast, followed by different-gender faces, and nonperson stimuli. Clearly, the type of stimulus that surrounds the target has a significant effect on perception of the target: not all stimuli are perceptually equal.

Psychological Detective

The results of this experiment suggest the operation of a general underlying principle. Spend a few minutes reviewing the results of this study, making sure to consult Figure 3-26. Collect your thoughts and then write down your impression of the general principle.

The results of Experiment 1 indicate that the greater the similarity between the target in the center and the surrounding stimuli, the more pronounced the illusion (the greater the perceived contrast). Stapel and Koomen refer to this effect as "similarity breeds comparability"—that is, the more similar the target and the surrounding objects, the more likely you are to compare them and experience the illusion. This general principle was given an interesting and important twist in Experiment 2.

The stimuli from Experiment 1 were used in Experiment 2. Some participants, however, were given a social description of the target and surrounding faces before they judged the size of the target. For example, one group was told the faces were *all* students. These social descriptions tend to increase perceived similarity of the target and surrounding stimuli. Thus, comparability of the stimuli was greater and the magnitude of the illusion also was increased. For example, even though the target face was female and the surrounding faces were male, when participants were told they were all students (or lawyers), the size of the illusion increased and did not differ from the illusion that occurred when the faces were identical. Thus, nonphysical (social) factors can—and do—influence our basic perception of human and nonhuman objects. We encounter the influence of social context again when we discuss social psychology (Chapter 15).

Now that we have examined both standard and contemporary perceptual phenomena, we turn our attention to an area that always receives considerable media attention—paranormal phenomena.

PARANORMAL PHENOMENA

Thousands of handbills were distributed, posters were displayed, and newspaper advertisements were placed to announce the first public appearance of a famous psychic who had spent years being tested in laboratories around the world. Extra chairs were brought in to accommodate the huge crowd that wanted to see and hear the lecture and demonstration. The psychic began by showing plants perceiving animosity or affection from people. Next he drew some geometric figures that matched those drawn by a member of the audience. Finally, from about 20 feet away and using only the power of his mind, he caused a large heavy rocking chair to move back and forth (Gordon, 1987). *What do people believe is the cause of such phenomena?*

According to a 1990 survey (Gallup & Newport, 1991) of more than 1,000 adult Americans, 93 percent believe in at least one *paranormal* (literally, "beyond normal") or psychic phenomenon, and almost half believe in five or more. Belief in such phenomena is widespread among college students. One-third of them express belief in reincarnation; a similar number believe that communication with the dead is possible. Over half believe that their dreams predict events such as the death of a family member or a natural disaster (Messer & Griggs, 1989).

extrasensory perception (ESP)
Behaviors or experiences that cannot be explained by information received by the senses

Undoubtedly you have heard about **extrasensory perception (ESP),** which refers to experiences or behaviors that occur without sensory contact—in other words, without the use of our sensory receptors. The term *ESP* is reserved for paranormal phenomena that do not involve the senses. The most frequently mentioned examples of ESP are clairvoyance, telepathy, and precognition. *Clairvoyance* (from the French for "clear seeing") is the claimed ability to "see" information from objects or events without direct contact with the senses. If you could tell us what was in a closed box that you had never seen, you might be demonstrating clairvoyance. *Telepathy* is the claimed ability to perceive the thoughts or emotions of others without the use of recognized senses. *Precognition* is knowledge of a future event or circumstance obtained by paranormal means. *Psychokinesis* (once known as *telekinesis*) is the claimed power of the mind to influence matter directly. Because psychokinesis does not involve perception, some researchers do not consider it an example of ESP. The term *parapsychology* is often used to refer to "the study of paranormal phenomena, which are considered to be well outside the bounds of established science" (Hines, 1988, p. 7).

Skeptical Scientists

The study of paranormal phenomena dates from the late 1800s, when there were numerous investigations of *spirit mediums*—people who claimed that they could receive messages from the dead. Modern research on paranormal phenomena began with Joseph Banks Rhine (1895–1980), who coined the term *extrasensory perception* in 1934 and established a laboratory at Duke University.

Many of Rhine's experiments used a deck of Zener cards, which consists of five each of the following designs: circle, cross, rectangle, star, and wavy lines. In a typical study, the participant's task was to guess the design on each card as an experimenter selected it from the deck. Using statistical procedures, Rhine compared each person's success with the success rate expected on the basis of chance—which is 20%, or one in five correct. A number of participants did better than chance and seemed to defy those odds. Unfortunately, some of the best performers may have had an opportunity to cheat. What's more, success rates exceeding chance may also have been due to irregularities in the cards that participants could use as clues. For example, with the right light it was sometimes possible to read the symbol through the back of a worn card.

The claims offered by supporters of ESP are sometimes presented in ways that make designing a definitive test difficult, if not impossible. (Recall the guidelines for evaluating claims presented in Chapter 1.) For example, when participants have done worse than expected on the basis of chance, parapsychologists have taken it as evidence of what has been termed *psi-missing*, or purposely giving the wrong answer. Such claims put critics in the position of playing a game of "heads I win, tails you lose." On the basis of such findings, James Alcock (1989) concluded that parapsychology has failed to produce scientific evidence of its validity. It is not surprising that parapsychology has been termed a "controversial science" (Broughton, 1991).

Most scientists agree that allegedly paranormal phenomena can be explained without resort to nonnormal evidence. Paranormal explanations would require that we rewrite well-established scientific principles to account for them. The law of parsimony

Got Psi?

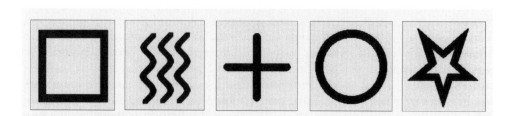

Examples of Zener cards that are use in parapsychological research.

(see Chapter 1) suggests that we look for explanations that require fewer assumptions, provided they can explain the phenomenon in question.

A Believing Public

"Evidence for paranormal claims comes in many guises," one researcher observes. "The overwhelming bulk of the evidence comes from personal experience, anecdotes, and folklore. Although psychologists and other scientists realize that such evidence is unreliable, almost every believer has become convinced because of such evidence" (Hyman, 1989, p. 15). According to Wayne Messer and Richard Griggs (1989), over 40% of college students reported having experienced dreams that predict the future (precognitive dreams). The accuracy of these dreams can be checked by keeping a written dream diary (Alcock, 1981). Even people who claim that their dreams "always come true" find that this is not the case when they use a dream diary to check their accuracy.

The surveys cited earlier indicate that many people believe in psychic phenomena. Why? The answer is simple: Many people have psychic experiences, or at least experiences they interpret as such. Psychologists suggest that paranormal experiences are an inevitable consequence of the way we perceive and remember information (Blackmore, 1992; Hines, 1988). Explanations that rely on some proposed "will to believe" do not enhance our understanding.

We can be fooled by our experiences in much the same way we are fooled by the visual illusions described earlier in the chapter. One illusion that encourages belief in paranormal phenomena such as ESP occurs when we consider coincidences, such as dreams that come true, as evidence of a connection. We have all had an experience similar to this: "He called me today after we hadn't heard from each other in 15 years. I had been thinking about him just a few hours earlier. I know it's not a coincidence—it must be ESP." No doubt the experience is real, but its origins lie in our internal processing, not in the external world. Coincidences do happen!

Imagine sitting in front of a computer designed to generate heads or tails in a coin-tossing game. Your task is to guess whether a head or a tail will appear on the screen. How many correct guesses (called "hits") do you think you will achieve in 20 trials? ESP believers guessed that they would average 7.0 hits; nonbelievers guessed an average of 9.6 hits (Blackmore & Troscianko, 1985). Moreover, the believers were more likely to decide they had influenced the computer, even when the computer was generating a random series of heads and tails. Why? As mentioned earlier, believers underestimate the number of correct guesses achieved by chance alone. People who consistently underestimate chance occurrences may look elsewhere for explanations, and paranormal explanations may look attractive. Underestimating chance underlies the tendency to interpret ordinary coincidence as psychic events and thus strengthens belief in such phenomena.

The media also affect belief in the paranormal, although they may reflect rather than cause the beliefs. Simply stated, paranormal phenomena sell—whether they be ghosts, reincarnation, or spoon bending. Newspaper stories of alleged paranormal phenomena are often reported as facts, with extensive coverage of the proponents' views and less attention to the skeptics' views (Klare, 1990).

A Final Word.   There is a wide variety of paranormal phenomena, and many people report personal experience with some of them. Scientists and believers disagree about what constitutes proof of such phenomena. Believers present anecdotes and point to laboratory research. Skeptics point to flaws in the laboratory research, and psychologists offer explanations for many of these personal experiences. Because psychologists can point to reasons that such phenomena may not occur, they cannot disprove them; the burden of proof for such extraordinary claims rests with the people making the claim.

Although the methods of studying paranormal phenomena have improved, "the goal of a conclusively convincing demonstration or a repeatable experiment has not been achieved" (Blackmore, 1994). At the beginning of this century, the magician

"The Amazing Randi." Magician James Randi has offered $1 million to anyone who can demonstrate paranormal power under satisfying observing conditions.

Harry Houdini challenged mediums to produce phenomena he could not duplicate. No one succeeded. Since 1964, the magician James Randi has offered a substantial reward (currently $1 million) to anyone who could demonstrate paranormal power under satisfactory observing conditions (Randi, 2001; see Randi's Web site for complete details: http://www.randi.com). Again, no one has succeeded. Should we therefore dismiss even the possibility of paranormal phenomena? Before we do, let's consider an important history lesson: Some phenomena that in the past were considered to be paranormal, impossible, or even fraudulent have since been verified to be real.

As late as the 1700s, most people believed that the notion of rocks falling from the sky was ridiculous. Anyone suggesting the possibility was met with jeers that might be similar to the reception often given to present-day reports of unidentified flying objects. Despite these reactions, what was once believed to be impossible is indeed possible: Meteorites do fall from the sky. Perhaps the lesson of history is twofold: First, a certain amount of humility in what we believe becomes us; second, we can be open-minded without neglecting the need for empirical evidence.

REVIEW SUMMARY

1. Perception is the process of organizing and making sense of the stimuli in our environment. Our motives help determine which stimuli we perceive.

2. We engage in *selective attention* because we cannot process all of the stimuli we encounter. Dichotic listening experiments study **divided attention.** With practice we can learn how to divide our attention effectively.

3. To attract our attention, stimuli should be more colorful, larger, and louder than other stimuli in our environment.

4. The ability to discriminate among shapes and figures is known as **pattern perception.** The **feature analysis theory** states that we perceive the elements of an object and then combine them to produce our perception of the object (bottom-up processing). Other research has shown that we perceive the object before we perceive its elements (top-down processing).

5. We experience **perceptual constancies** when our perception of an object does not change, even though the retinal image changes. **Size constancy** and **shape constancy** depend on the presence of a background and our ability to judge distance.

6. The Gestalt psychologists demonstrated that we actively organize our perceptual world into meaningful groups or wholes.

The **figure–ground relation** is one of the most basic perceptual organizations. Additional principles for the grouping of stimulus elements are **proximity, similarity, good continuation,** and **closure.**

7. Perceptual hypotheses are inferences about the nature of the stimuli we sense. **Perceptual illusions** and ambiguous figures may cause us to develop incorrect perceptual hypotheses.

8. Parallel, as opposed to sequential, processing appears to characterize much of our perceptual activity. Parallel processing is seen in **visual search,** in which a target stimulus must be distinguished among a group of distractors.

9. Perception may be influenced by the social context. For example, the Ebbinghaus illusion is influenced by the type of social stimuli used.

10. Extrasensory perception (ESP) refers to the occurrence of experiences or behaviors in the absence of an adequate stimulus. Such occurrences are considered to be paranormal, or beyond our normal sensory abilities. Clairvoyance, telepathy, precognition, and psychokinesis are examples of paranormal phenomena.

✓ CHECK YOUR PROGRESS

1. What is selective attention? Why is it an important feature of the perceptual process?

2. Which of the following illustrates that we hear and understand much more information than actually enters conscious awareness?

   a. focused attention
   b. cocktail-party phenomenon
   c. dichotic listening experiments
   d. motivational effects on perception

3. According to feature analysis theory, how do we identify objects that we perceive?

4. Under what circumstances can divided attention occur most easily?

    a. when you are under stress

    b. when attention to small details is critical

    c. when you are performing two tasks that are highly related

    d. when you are performing tasks that are simple and well-practiced

5. What is meant by perceptual constancy? Give examples of shape and size constancy.

6. Convergence and binocular disparity are important cues for the perception of

    a. depth.

    b. patterns.

    c. constancy.

    d. thresholds.

7. What is a figure–ground relationship? What features characterize figures?

8. Which Gestalt principle helps our perception of WWW XXX?

    a. similarity

    b. figure–ground

    c. inclusiveness

    d. good continuation

9. Your mother claims she was able to read your mind and knew you would try to sneak some food before dinner. What form of ESP might she claim she was using?

    a. telepathy

    b. clairvoyance

    c. precognition

    d. psychokinesis

10. What law argues that we should search for explanations of paranormal phenomena that fit within well-established scientific principles?

    a. law of parsimony

    b. law of simplicity

    c. law of common sense

    d. law of irreproducible results

ANSWERS: 1. Selective attention involves attending to some stimuli and not others. It is important in helping organisms concentrate on the stimuli that are most relevant at the time. **2.** b **3.** We identify the elements or features of the object in question; then we assemble these features to create the complete, identifiable object—i.e., bottom-up processing. **4.** d **5.** Perceptual constancy involves the perception of a stable object, despite a changing retinal image. An example of shape constancy would be the perception that an airplane does not change shape as it rises into the sky and the retinal image of the plane changes. The fact that the same plane is seen as moving farther away, and not physically changing shape, is an example of size constancy. **6.** a **7.** The figure–ground relationship is the organization of the perceptual stimuli we receive into a figure and a background. Figures typically are smaller, brighter or colorful, and display motion. **8.** a **9.** a **10.** a

---

ANSWER | **To Photo on page 118**

With the appropriate cues to distance and size, the object you saw on p. 118 may be much larger than you thought it was.

5

Learning

CHAPTER OUTLINE

Nearly every organism must learn to survive in its environment. Indeed, the ability to adapt to the environment is often the key to determining which organisms survive long enough to pass on their genes to future generations. According to the evolutionary perspective, learning is an adaptive behavior that supports *natural selection*. We have already examined the physical structures (Chapter 2) and sensory and perceptual processes (Chapter 3) that we use to interact with our environment. In some cases our responses to environmental stimuli, such as reflexively blinking in response to a puff of air, are routine, very brief in duration, and do not enter consciousness. In other instances our awareness is critical when it comes to responding to and interacting with our environment. For example, we need to remember how to call 911 to summon the fire department, how to program our VCR to record a television program, and how to stop the bleeding from a severe cut. Similarly, once a field rat has found a way into a farmer's corn crib, it is helpful for the rat to remember how to return to this food source in the future. These longer-lasting effects of interacting with the environment are the focus of this chapter and the next. In short, they are what we mean when we speak of *learning*. In this chapter we discuss several basic forms of learning.

WHAT IS LEARNING?

For a person who has grown up in a small Nebraska town, driving in big-city traffic can be an anxiety-provoking experience. The furious pace and the large number of vehicles on the road can be overwhelming at first; with cars to the left, to the right, and almost in the trunk there is little sanity in sight! After several months of driving to and from work during the height of rush hour in Chicago, however, Linda, who grew up in a small town, has become a "real pro" at driving in big-city traffic. *Why would Linda's improved driving ability be considered an example of learning?*

Most psychologists define **learning** as a relatively permanent change in behavior or the potential to make a response that occurs as a result of some experience (Hergenhahn & Olson, 2001; Mazur, 1998). This definition distinguishes learned behaviors from those that occur automatically in response to external events, like shivering in a cold wind or sweating when it is hot. By including the concept of experience in the definition of learning, we distinguish between learned behaviors and behaviors that become possible as our physical capabilities develop—that is, *maturation*. For example, when you were 6 months old it is unlikely that you were able to walk. Around your first birthday (or shortly after), the ability to walk emerged. Did it occur as a result of learning? As we will see, the answer is no. When you were 2 years old, you did not have the strength to lift a 5-pound weight. By the time you were 10, however, lifting 5 pounds was easy. You did not have to learn anything to be able to walk or to pick up the 5-pound weight. As a result of the process of maturation, your muscles and nerves had developed to the point that you were able to walk and to lift the weight.

To return to our question, why would Linda's improved driving ability in Chicago be considered an example of learning? Unless Linda was very young at the time she

learning
A relatively permanent change in behavior or the potential to make a response that occurs as a result of experience

began big-city driving, we can rule out maturation as a cause for the change in her behavior. Likewise, the change in Linda's driving behavior is not an automatic response, like shivering in a cold wind or blinking when a puff of air is directed toward your eyes. Rather, the repeated experience of rush-hour city driving has brought about a change in her behavior; she has *learned*.

In Chapter 3 we discussed how psychologists study color vision in animals such as Ruby the elephant. Ruby's painting also provides us with a good example of learning. Initially, the sound of the word "paint" had no meaning, and Ruby made no response to it. After the word was associated (paired) with one of her favorite activities, Ruby began to squeal when her trainer said "paint." Ruby had learned that this word signaled the opportunity to engage in an enjoyable activity. The elephant's response is an example of a relatively permanent change in behavior that occurs as a result of experience; she has *learned*.

In this chapter we first discuss two of the three basic types of learning, *classical* (or *respondent*) *conditioning* and *operant* (or *instrumental*) *conditioning*. Later in the chapter we will explore more cognitively oriented perspectives on learning along with the third basic type of learning, *observational* learning or modeling. Keep in mind that the word *conditioning* refers to the fact that the learner forms an association, usually between a stimulus and a response or between two stimuli.

CLASSICAL CONDITIONING

A psychology class is participating in an unusual demonstration. The instructor passes a can of powdered lemonade mix around the room; each student puts a spoonful of the powder on a sheet of paper. Once all students have their own lemonade powder, they are instructed to wet one of their fingers. When the instructor says "now," each student puts a small amount of lemonade powder on his or her tongue with the moistened finger. The effect of putting lemonade powder on the tongue is predictable: The mouth puckers, and saliva begins to flow. The instructor has the students repeat this procedure several times during the class period until all the lemonade powder is gone. Before the class period ends, the instructor says "now" without warning. The students' mouths pucker, and saliva flows. *What is the purpose of this class demonstration?*

This demonstration is an example of *classical conditioning*, which has become so closely associated with the Russian scientist Ivan Pavlov (1849–1936) that it is often called *Pavlovian conditioning*. Pavlov was a physiologist whose work was so well respected that he received a Nobel Prize in Medicine in 1904 for his research on digestion. Although Pavlov conducted much of his research with dogs, examples of classical conditioning can be found in many human behaviors. **Classical conditioning** is a form of learning that occurs when two stimuli—a neutral stimulus and an unconditioned stimulus—that are "paired" (presented together) become associated with each other. For example, the sight of McDonald's golden arches and the smell and taste of a juicy burger have occurred together, and as a result many people associate the golden arches with tasty fast food.

classical conditioning
Learning that occurs when two stimuli—a conditioned stimulus (originally a neutral stimulus) and an unconditioned stimulus—are paired and become associated with each other

Basic Elements of Classical Conditioning

We have said that the procedure for establishing classical conditioning is to present two events—called *stimuli*—so that the pairing of these two events causes a human participant or animal to make an association between them. At the start of conditioning, the first event, which in a laboratory setting may be the presentation of a light or a tone, is neutral—that is, not currently associated with the response to be established.

Ivan Pavlov's research on digestion was so well regarded that he was awarded the Nobel Prize in 1904. In the course of his research, he surgically brought the opening of the salivary gland to the outside of the dog's skin so the secretion of saliva could be seen and measured. Over time, Pavlov and his research team noticed that the dogs began salivating to stimuli other than food. The precision of the laboratory provided Pavlov with the setting in which he could investigate the components of what became known as classical conditioning.

What was the neutral stimulus in the lemonade example at the start of this section? Keep reading and you will find out. When this **neutral stimulus (NS)** is presented, the participant may notice that it is there, but it does not cause any particular reaction. By presenting the second event, called an **unconditioned stimulus (UCS),** after the NS, however, we transform the NS into a **conditioned stimulus (CS).** The NS becomes a CS because it is repeatedly paired with a UCS. This pairing eventually causes the participant to establish an association between the two events; the CS comes to *predict* the occurrence of the UCS. In the lemonade powder example the word "now" was the NS; it became a CS after it was paired with the lemonade powder.

As the term suggests, the UCS automatically produces a reaction; the participant does not have to be trained to react to it. The UCS never fails to produce the same reaction. Food in your mouth causes you to salivate; touching a hot stove causes you to jerk your hand away; a puff of air to your eye causes you to blink. In psychological terms, the UCS elicits, or calls forth, a response. The reaction that is elicited by the UCS is called the **unconditioned response (UCR).** If you have a feeling that we have already discussed this type of response, you are correct. These UCRs are reflexes, like those we described in Chapter 2. You do not have to learn a UCR; all organisms come equipped by nature with a number of built-in responses, which generally have survival value. For example, you do not learn to jerk your hand away when you touch a hot stove; you pull it away automatically. It is a built-in (unconditioned) response. As part of a routine physical examination, a physician may use a small rubber hammer to hit an area just below your knee. When your lower leg kicks up, the physician knows that particular reflex (called knee flexion) is working properly (see Chapter 2). Now, what is the UCR in the lemonade powder example?

When a participant associates the NS (for example, a light or a tone) with the UCS, the NS is transformed into a CS that can elicit a response similar to the UCR (for example, a little less saliva). The response caused by the CS is known as the **conditioned response (CR).** When the CS elicits the CR, we say that classical conditioning has occurred. Ivan Pavlov (1927) used food as the UCS in his pioneering studies. While a metronome was ticking (CS), he placed a small amount of meat powder (UCS) into a hungry dog's mouth. The meat powder caused the dog to begin salivating (UCR). Later, when just the sound of the ticking metronome was presented, the dog salivated (CR).

Let's return to the earlier demonstration in which lemonade powder was associated with the word "now" (Cogan & Cogan, 1984) so that you can experience classical conditioning firsthand. Consider what occurred naturally (UCS–UCR) and what was learned (CS–CR) and complete the blanks in this sentence to see if you can

Classical Conditioning

neutral stimulus (NS)
Stimulus that, before conditioning, does not elicit a particular response

unconditioned stimulus (UCS)
Event that automatically produces a response without any previous training

conditioned stimulus (CS)
Neutral stimulus that acquires the ability to elicit a conditioned response after being paired with an unconditioned stimulus

unconditioned response (UCR)
Reaction that is automatically produced when an unconditioned stimulus is presented

conditioned response (CR)
Response elicited by a conditioned stimulus that has been paired with an unconditioned stimulus; is similar to the unconditioned response

apply the terminology just described to the demonstration. "The CS, _____, paired with the UCS, _____, results in the UCR, _____." The CS is the word "now." The lemonade powder is the UCS; it automatically elicits the unconditioned response (UCR) of puckering and salivating. Initially the word "now" is a neutral stimulus. After it is paired with the lemonade powder several times, however, it becomes a CS and now elicits the conditioned response (CR) of puckering and salivating.

Let's put these elements together in another example. Suppose that your younger brother is just tall enough to reach a hot skillet on the stove. He grabs it and immediately drops it. His pain is obvious and intense, and you try to comfort him. Finally his tears stop, and you put the incident out of your mind. Three days later, however, the same skillet is again on the stove. Your brother enters the kitchen, sees the skillet, and begins to cry. Clearly, the skillet has taken on a new meaning for him, demonstrating that some stimuli are so memorable that they produce learning without the need for repeated pairing.

In classical conditioning terms, initially the skillet was an NS (does not cause any particular response); after conditioning, it became the CS. The intense heat was the UCS, which always elicits pain and an avoidance response. Those responses—the pain and jerking the hand away or dropping the skillet—constitute the UCR. Remember that the classical conditioning sequence involves first presenting the NS and then following it with the UCS. If these two events are associated, the NS becomes a CS that signals that the UCS is on its way.

After a conditioning experience of this type, when the CS is encountered alone, it produces a response—the CR—that is very similar to the UCR. In our example, the sight of the skillet reminds your brother of the pain he experienced. The classical conditioning sequence for this situation is presented in diagrammatic form in Figure 5-1.

The UCS does not have to be a painful event like heat, electric shock, or hitting your finger with a hammer (Capaldi & Sheffer, 1992; Owens, Capaldi, & Sheffer, 1993). A wide variety of stimuli can serve as a UCS; their associated responses are

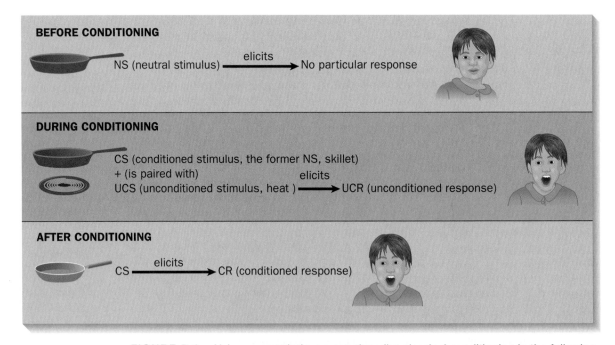

FIGURE 5-1 Using our symbols, we can describe classical conditioning in the following manner: *Before Conditioning*: The NS originally does not elicit a specific response. *During Conditioning*: The NS (now called the CS) is presented just before the UCS. The UCS automatically elicits a UCR. *After Conditioning*: Later, when the CS is presented by itself, a CR, which is similar to the UCR, occurs. In short, a new response, the CR, has been conditioned to the CS because the CS has been paired with the UCS.

TABLE 5-1

Common Unconditioned Stimuli (UCS) and Their Associated Unconditioned Responses (UCR).

The associations between these stimuli and responses are built-in or innate. Each of the responses can be elicited from the organism by using the appropriate stimulus.

UCS	UCR
Voluntary muscles	
sharp or hot stimuli	jerk away and cry
blows, shock, burns	withdrawal
gentle caresses	relaxation and calm
object touches lip	sucking
food in mouth	swallowing
object touches hand	grasping
novel stimulation	reflexive orienting
Circulatory system	
high temperature	sweating, flushing
sudden loud noise	blanching, pounding heart
Digestive system	
good food	salivation
bad food	sickness, nausea, vomiting
Respiratory system	
irritation in nose	sneeze
throat clogged	cough
allergens	asthma attack
Emotional system	
painful blow	fear
sexual stimulation	erotic feeling
Reproductive system	
genital stimulation	vaginal lubrication, penile erection, orgasm
nipple stimulation	milk release (in lactating women)

Source: Baldwin & Baldwin, 2001

reflexes that are often crucial for basic biological functioning, survival, and reproduction (Baldwin & Baldwin, 2001). For example, a bite of your favorite food when you are hungry automatically causes you to salivate. Food in your mouth is the UCS; salivation is the UCR. The positive feelings you experience when you receive a kiss or a hug are also examples of UCS. Table 5-1 contains a list of common UCSs and UCRs; as you will see such stimuli and responses are found throughout our bodily systems. What is important about classical conditioning is that organisms learn to respond not only to the original UCS, they learn to respond to other CSs that become associated with our reflexes (Baldwin & Baldwin, 2001).

Obviously, psychologists do not hide in restaurants waiting to present a tone while you are eating, nor do most instructors take lemonade powder to class with them. Yet people become classically conditioned in much the same way that Pavlov's dogs did. For example, the sights and sounds that accompany meals can become conditioned stimuli.

For many people, the unique decor of a restaurant, an advertisement, or a menu may act as a CS. Have you ever found yourself salivating as you looked at the tempting pictures in an advertisement or browsed up and down the aisles of a grocery store? Numerous examples of classical conditioning of CRs exist in everyday life. Is there a particular song (CS) that prompts you to recall a happy moment (CR)? Do you know someone who purchases cars only of a certain color because that color was associated in the past with a favorite car?

Hands On

Conditioning Your Friends

The ease by which classical conditioning is demonstrated in class can be duplicated in real life. This demonstration rests on the premise that most people have been conditioned to flinch (the startle response) when we see someone stick a balloon with a pin. (The pin is the CS, the bang is the UCS, and the startle response is the UCR.) Use the following procedure to surprise your friends and observe classical conditioning at the same time.

You will need about 20 good-quality balloons and a needle. Any sharp sewing needle will do, but for especially dramatic effect a foot-long needle is best. Blow up 15 to 20 balloons. Then have a friend pop 5 or 6 of them with the needle. Next have your friends watch you use the needle to pop 5 or 6 more balloons. Once you have popped several of them, stick the needle into an area of the balloon where there is less tension (the nipple or around the knot). Because there is less tension at these points, the rubber is relatively thick, and the balloon does not pop when it is stuck. Your friends will still flinch, however. Why? They have been conditioned to expect a loud bang. If you use a foot-long needle, you can make the effect even more dramatic by passing the needle completely through the balloon (enter at the nipple and exit at the knot, see photographs below).

Psychological Detective

Think of your own examples of classical conditioning. You will probably find it easiest to start with the UCS, then decide what the UCR is, and finally determine what CSs might readily occur in the presence of the UCS. Think of a food smell that makes you remember a pleasant childhood memory—perhaps cookies baking or the cinnamon smell of hot apple pie. Do you think of a particular event, and does your mouth water? The food you enjoy is the UCS. What is the UCR? The CS? The CR? (See some possible answers at the end of the chapter.)

Dr. Edie McClellan prepares to demonstrate that a needle can be put through a balloon and not pop it. When the needle approaches the balloon (A), many students flinch—a conditioned response based on past experiences of hearing the noise as a pin was pushed into a balloon. Sticking the needle through the thick part of the balloon allows the needle to be passed entirely through the balloon without popping it (B).

A

B

Classical Conditioning Processes

Pavlov's research revealed several important processes of classical conditioning besides those discussed so far. These findings fall into two general categories: *acquisition*, or how we develop CRs, and *extinction*, or how we eliminate those responses.

Acquisition.   Acquisition is the training stage during which a particular response (for example, salivating or blinking) is learned (occurs after a CS is presented). Several factors influence the acquisition of CRs. Among them are the order in which the CS and UCS are presented, the intensity of the UCS, and the number of times the CS and UCS are paired (Barker, 2001). We now take a closer look at each of these factors.

Sequence of CS-UCS Presentation.   The sequence in which the CS and UCS are presented influences the strength of the conditioning. The optimum sequence is for the CS to precede the UCS and remain until the UCS is presented. This particular sequence is often called *forward conditioning*. Other sequences, such as the UCS preceding the CS (that is, *backward conditioning*), produce weaker conditioning.

Strength of the UCS.   The stronger the UCS, the stronger the conditioning (Holloway & Domjan, 1993). When Pavlov gave his dogs a small amount of meat powder, they did not salivate as much as they did when he gave them a large amount of meat powder. The hot skillet your younger brother grabbed on the stove was a painful and salient stimulus. Stronger UCSs elicit stronger UCRs; weaker UCSs elicit weaker UCRs.

Number of CS-UCS Pairings.   ⌐The more times the CS and UCS are presented together, the stronger the CR becomes. It is easy to conduct research on the relation between the CS and the UCS when we can use a laboratory setup such as Pavlov's. Under such conditions, the number of times the CS and UCS are presented can be determined precisely. The effects of varying numbers of CS-UCS pairings, however, can also be demonstrated in real life. If your little brother grabs the hot skillet more than once, the chances are good that his CR to the skillet will be stronger. If you have eaten at an exceptionally fine restaurant several times, your conditioned responses to the sight of the restaurant and its menu will be stronger than they would be if you had eaten there only once before. Figure 5-2 displays several patterns of classical conditioning acquisition; as you can see, as the percentage of pairings increases, acquisition of the CR becomes stronger.

Extinction.   Once a CR has been acquired, what can be done to extinguish or eliminate that response? The easiest procedure is to present the CS without the UCS and record how strong the CR is and how many times or how long we can present the CS alone before the CR disappears. The number of times the CS is presented without the UCS is a very important factor in eliminating the CR. When Pavlov repeatedly sounded the tone (CS) without giving the dog any meat powder (UCS), the number of drops of saliva produced gradually decreased each time the tone was sounded. Similarly, if your brother grabs the skillet several times when it is cold, his fear will decrease a little each time.

5.1

PAVLOV
KNOCK,
DO NOT
RING BELL,
DOGS
INSIDE

SNIF SNIF...

EVEN **PAVLOV'S** DOG WOULDN'T SALIVATE AT THIS!

FIGURE 5-2 Acquisition patterns in classical conditioning when the UCS is presented at different percentages on trials (a series of presentations of stimuli). Within a given trial, the CS and UCS were paired 25% to 100% of the time. Some participants received the CS and UCS on every presentation during a trial; in other cases, the UCS was presented with the CS only 25% of the time. Across trials, greater pairing of the UCS with the CS led to stronger conditioning, that is, more frequent occurrence of the CR.

Source: Hartman & Grant, 1960.

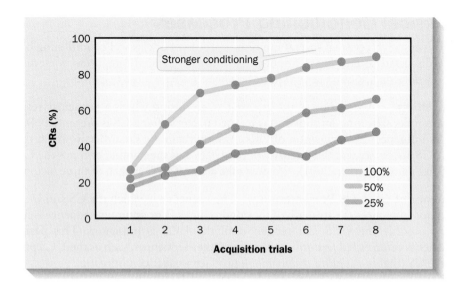

extinction

A general term for the reduction and elimination of behaviors; in classical conditioning extinction occurs when repeated presentation of the CS alone leads to a reduction in the strength of the CR

spontaneous recovery

Reappearance of an extinguished CR after the passage of time

Extinction is a general term for a reduction and disappearance of a behavior; in the case of classical conditioning, extinction occurs when repeated presentation of the CS alone leads to a decrease in the strength of the CR (Schreurs, 1993). The stronger the CR, the longer extinction takes. What takes place during acquisition influences the process of extinction. For example, the stronger the UCS and the more frequently it is presented during acquisition, the longer it will take to extinguish the CR.

Spontaneous Recovery. At times a classical conditioning participant seems to "forget" that extinction has occurred. Consider Pavlov's dog once again. Only the CS (a bell in this case) has been presented to the dog several times during its daily extinction session. The CR (salivation) has decreased until it appears that the dog is not salivating at all. When the dog is returned to its cage, we might conclude that the extinction process is complete. When the CS is presented on the following day, however, the dog begins to salivate once more. Pavlov (1927) called this phenomenon **spontaneous recovery** because the CR recovers some of the strength it lost during the previous extinction session. This process is diagrammed in Figure 5-3. The amount of spontaneous recovery will decrease from day to day until the CR finally does not occur at the start of a session. At this point extinction of the response is probably complete.

Spontaneous recovery is not limited to laboratory experiments; it occurs in real-life situations as well. For example, let's say you went skiing last winter and on the second day you had a very bad fall. After summoning as much courage and

FIGURE 5-3 Extinction occurs when the tone (CS) is presented without meat powder (UCS). By the end of each daily extinction session, the CR is quite weak. It regains some strength, however, by the start of the next session, a phenomenon known as spontaneous recovery. By the end of extinction, the CR is quite low, and the amount of spontaneous recovery may be undetectable.

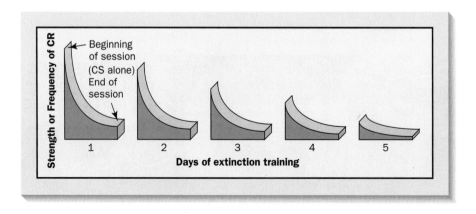

determination as possible, you put your skis on and went back out on the slopes for the next 2 days. Thankfully, there were no additional spills on those days; your fear seemed to be extinguished. Now, a full year later, you have returned to the ski resort. You experience some apprehension as you pull on your ski boots. You thought the fear had disappeared—that it had been extinguished—by the time you were finished skiing last year, but a bit seems to have returned (spontaneous recovery) this year.

Figure 5-4 illustrates the relations among acquisition, extinction, and spontaneous recovery. Consult this figure as you read this section to provide you with the "big picture" of all of the elements and processes involved in classical conditioning.

Generalization and Discrimination.   Suppose that several days after your little brother made the mistake of grabbing the hot skillet, the two of you are walking through the housewares section of a department store when he starts crying and refuses to walk any farther. You note where he is looking and see a display of skillets. Is he afraid of them also? Yes, he is, and the more those skillets resemble the one at home, the greater is his fear.

When a response occurs to stimuli that are similar to a CS, **generalization** has occurred. The effects of classical conditioning may be applied (generalized) to other stimuli that are similar to the original CS; they "spread" from the original stimulus to others. For example, although Pavlov's dogs were conditioned to salivate in response to a specific tone (CS), they also salivated when other tones were presented (see Figure 5-5). Someone who has acquired a fear of snakes, might react with fear when seeing a piece of rope lying on the ground a few feet away. The similarity of the snake to the rope elicits the fear response (CR), which has generalized from the snake. Suppose your favorite color is red and whenever you see it you feel warm all over. You might have a similar, perhaps somewhat muted, reaction to various shades of red.

It is easy to see how generalization occurs. If you have ever been stung by a wasp, you probably have a healthy respect for all flying insects, especially those that resemble

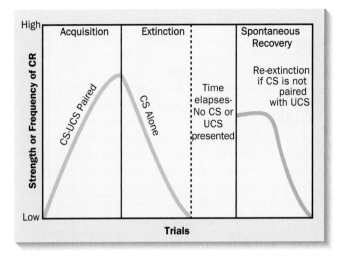

FIGURE 5-4   The basic phases of classical conditioning. In the acquisition or training phase, the CS and UCS are paired together and lead to the UCR. This pairing eventually leads to production of the CR following the CS. Repeated presentation of the CS alone leads to extinction. Following the passage of time, presentation of the CS alone may lead to spontaneous recovery of the CR.

generalization
Occurrence of responses to stimuli that are similar to a CS

A bad fall on a ski slope can result in a classically conditioned fear. Getting up and "hitting the slopes" immediately after such a fall is one of the best ways to extinguish the fear. The extinction may be "forgotten" over the summer, resulting in spontaneous recovery of the fear response when you hit the slopes once again the following year.

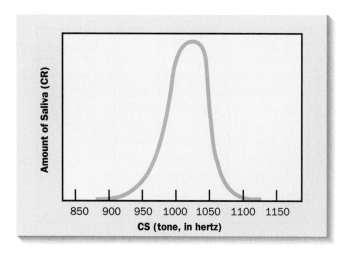

FIGURE 5-5 Generalization occurs when organisms respond to stimuli that are similar to the original CS. As Pavlov discovered, dogs would salivate to tones that are similar to the original CS. Tones that were less similar to the original CS were less likely to lead to the CR of salivation.

wasps. Your response has generalized from one stimulus to many others. But if you are not stung every time you encounter a flying insect, many of these generalized responses will be extinguished. Thus, as children we quickly discover that butterflies and moths do not sting, whereas hornets and bees do. We therefore come to fear the stinging insects but not the others. In other words, we learn to distinguish or discriminate between conditioned stimuli that accurately predict the occurrence of the UCS and those that do not (Bouton & Brooks, 1993; Nakajima, 1993). Through this process of **discrimination,** we have extinguished our fear of insects that do not sting but have retained our fear of insects that do.

Generalization and discrimination work in opposite ways. Whereas generalization makes you more likely to respond to a number of similar stimuli, discrimination narrows your response to the appropriate stimulus and no other. Discrimination thus requires stimuli that are clearly distinguishable. For example, if you could not easily distinguish between insects that sting and those that do not, imagine how apprehensive you would be whenever you went outdoors.

Pavlov (1928) understood this principle and investigated it. First, he trained a group of dogs to discriminate between a circle and an ellipse; the circle was always associated with food. Once this association was made, Pavlov changed the ellipse over a series of presentations until it was indistinguishable from the circle.

Psychological Detective

What behavior(s) did Pavlov's dogs show when confronted by these two indistinguishable stimuli? Write down your answer before reading further.

Because the dogs were unable to discriminate between the two stimuli, they salivated to both of them. They displayed other behaviors that did not occur when they were able to discriminate between the two stimuli. They whined and yelped, became agitated, and tried to escape from their harnesses. To Pavlov's surprise, these behaviors continued outside the experimental room. Pavlov called these inappropriate behaviors *experimental neuroses* and believed that they occurred when an animal or human attempted to solve a discrimination task that could not be solved. This analysis provides a clue concerning a possible origin of some abnormal behaviors in humans (see Chapter 12; Baumrind, 1983). As the next section shows, such agitation and apprehension can influence our motivated behavior.

Applications of Classical Conditioning: Phobias and Beyond

In 1913, John B. Watson proclaimed that psychologists should study only directly observable behaviors. As we saw in Chapter 1, Watson's approach to psychology was called *behaviorism.* According to the behaviorists, the main business of psychology is the study of behaviors such as jogging in the park, running through an airport to catch a flight, and even expressing emotion. Anything having to do with thinking, feeling, or consciousness was not considered an appropriate subject of psychological study because those processes could not be observed directly. The behaviorists' goal was to discover which observable stimuli elicit which responses (observable behaviors). In pursuit of this goal, John Watson and his assistant, Rosalie Rayner, classically conditioned 9-month-old "Little Albert" to fear a white rat (Watson & Rayner, 1920). At first Albert

Little Albert

discrimination
Occurrence of responses only to a specific CS

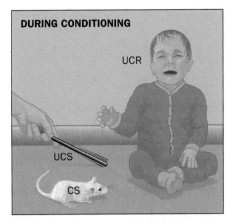

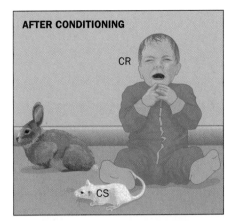

FIGURE 5-6 Conditioning "Little Albert" to fear a white rat. *Before conditioning*: Originally Little Albert had no fear of the white rat (the NS for Little Albert); the rat had no fear of Little Albert (the NS for the rat). *During conditioning*: While Little Albert is playing with the rat, John Watson strikes a steel bar. The loud noise (UCS) elicits a startle and fear response (UCR). The white rat (now the CS) is associated with the loud noise for Little Albert. Little Albert (now the CS) is associated with the loud noise for the rat. *After conditioning*: Later, the white rat elicits fear in Little Albert. Other objects, such as a rabbit, that are similar to the white rat now elicit fear in Little Albert, and the boy, in turn, elicits fear in the rat.

showed no fear of the rat and even allowed it to crawl on him. (You can view a filmed segment of this research on the CD that accompanies this text.) While Little Albert was playing with the rat, Watson hit a steel rod with a hammer, making a sudden, deafening noise. Not surprisingly, Albert was startled and scared. Each time the loud noise was paired with the presence of the rat, Albert cried in fear. After several pairings of the two stimuli, Albert started crying at the sight of the rat, even when there was no noise, and he eventually came to fear any object that resembled a rat, such as a white rabbit and even the white whiskers on a Santa Claus mask. Albert developed a phobia for rats and ratlike objects. Unfortunately, no one followed Albert throughout his life; hence we do not know how long these phobias plagued him.

 Little Albert

Let's analyze the elements of Little Albert's fear. What UCS was used? What was the UCR? What were the CS and the CR? While you think about these questions, remember that the rat was also exposed to a frightening situation. For both Little Albert and the rat, the UCS was the loud noise. The UCR was the state of being startled and scared. For Albert, the CS was the rat; for the rat, the CS was Albert. The CR for both of them was fear of an object that signaled that a loud noise might follow. These relations are diagrammed in Figure 5-6.

Many of the unconditioned responses we make have an emotional component that is either pleasurable or aversive. When a reflex is elicited, it often brings up emotional responses, as was the case with Little Albert. As we have seen, some of these emotional reactions are pleasurable (for example, involving food and sex), whereas others are aversive (for example, painful stimuli). These pleasure and pain components of our reflexes can be traced back to our basic biological survival functions (Keltner & Haidt, 1999; Levenson, 1999).

Psychological Detective

Although the Watson and Rayner study is important because it was one of the first efforts to show that an emotional reaction like fear could be classically conditioned (resulting in a *conditioned fear response*), it raises questions about the ethics of psychological research (see Chapter 1). Was it acceptable for Watson and Rayner purposely to frighten Little Albert so intensely? Would you allow such an experiment to be conducted with your child? Would such a procedure be acceptable if the child's parents authorized it? Write down your responses and the reasons for them before reading further.

John B. Watson (left), his research assistant Rosalie Rayner (right) and Little Albert were part of one of the most well known research efforts in psychology. The findings showed how classical conditioning could be responsible for the development of phobias. This research, however, raised many ethical questions; it could not be conducted under the ethics code in place today.

The Ethical Principles of Psychologists and Code of Conduct, published by the American Psychological Association (2002), would probably say "no" to all of our questions. If Watson and Rayner were to conduct their research with Little Albert in the 21st century, they would have difficulty meeting the ethical standards you read about in Chapter 1.

Despite the questionable ethics exhibited in the Little Albert research, classical conditioning has been a focus of attention in our efforts to understand phobias since the 1920s. Consider the case of Scott, who was 3 years old when he was locked in an abandoned refrigerator by his playmates and nearly died from suffocation. Ever since then, he has avoided closed spaces. Now, 30 years later, he is still deathly afraid of closed spaces and anything that reminds him of them. He cannot stand to ride in an elevator and always takes the stairs, even in tall buildings. Even seeing a picture of a refrigerator makes him break out in a cold sweat. If you were unaware of Scott's background, his intense fear of closed spaces, such as elevators, compact cars, and small rooms might seem strange. Although you may not fear closed spaces to the same degree as Scott, chances are good that you are afraid of certain other objects or situations that most people do not fear. How do we acquire many of these apparently unrealistic, irrational fears?

Many of our fears and anxieties may have been classically conditioned, as in the case of Scott's fear of closed spaces. Because he was locked in an abandoned refrigerator when he was a child and nearly died, Scott now fears anything that remotely resembles a closed space. He has a condition known as a *phobia*; more specifically, he is suffering from *claustrophobia* (*claustrop*, "enclosed place"; *phobos*, "fear"). A **phobia** is an irrational fear of an activity, object, or situation, that is out of proportion to the actual danger it poses. Because phobias create so much anxiety that they interfere with normal functioning, they are classified as *anxiety disorders* (see Chapter 12). Other people with phobias may not be able to recall a specific event that is the cause of the phobia. Thus many phobias exert their influence in a seemingly mysterious and potentially detrimental manner.

As you might expect, phobias can interfere with a person's daily activities. For example, a salesperson suffering from *glossophobia* (fear of speaking) would not do very well in the business world where meeting and greeting clients are the order of the day. A psychiatrist, Joseph Wolpe (1915–1997), developed a treatment, known as *systematic desensitization*, to help eliminate phobias (Rachman, 2000). Basically, systematic desensitization involves classically conditioning a desired response, relaxation, to the phobic stimuli; it has been quite successful in treating a range of phobias (Hoffmann & Odendal, 2001; Schneider & Nevid, 1993; Ventis, Higbee, & Murdock, 2001). For example, using this procedure a person with claustrophobia, like Scott, is conditioned to relax in enclosed spaces. We discuss systematic desensitization in greater detail in Chapter 13.

Classical Conditioning and Our Motives.   As the discussion of Little Albert and the development of phobias reveals, classical conditioning has a lot more to say about human and animal behavior than you might think based on its origins in research on salivation. As a result of his conditioning, Little Albert was motivated to avoid rats and other furry animals. As we will see next, classical conditioning can lead organisms to develop a range of other behaviors that can have long-lasting influences. Even though Jim did not have cats as pets when he was a child, his friends persuaded him to adopt the cute stray kitten he found last week. Jim is now convinced this was a very bad idea. Each evening, when Jim has settled into his favorite chair to watch the evening news,

phobia
Irrational fear of an activity, object, or situation that is out of proportion to the actual danger posed

the kitten launches a sneak attack. After a week of this behavior, Jim becomes tense as soon as he sits in his favorite chair, whether the kitten is in the room or not. The sound of the evening news increases his anxiety. When Jim leaves the room, he immediately feels better.

What is the relation among the kitten's attacks, Jim's tension and anxiety, and motivation? Parts of the story about Jim and his cat may sound familiar. Can we describe the cat's sneak attack in psychological terms that you have already learned? Would certain responses automatically follow such an attack? If you said that pain, fear, or anxiety would follow, we would agree. What kind of stimuli automatically elicit a response? If you are thinking that unconditioned stimuli (UCSs) elicit unconditioned responses (UCRs), you are right again. What about Jim's favorite chair and the evening news program? What role do they serve? After these stimuli have been associated with cat attacks several times, they cause Jim to become tense and anxious. These are conditioned stimuli (CSs), and the tension and anxiety they produce are conditioned responses (CRs).

How is Jim's conditioned anxiety related to motivation? Through the process of classical conditioning, Jim's favorite chair and the evening news have become CSs that elicit tension and anxiety. Jim finds these feelings of tension and anxiety unpleasant and is motivated to reduce them when they occur by leaving the room. Motives that are acquired through the process of classical conditioning are called **learned motives.** Many other motives are acquired in this manner. Phobias are excellent examples of learned motives. Classical conditioning appears to be at the core of many of these unusual fears.

The same procedure and logic can be applied to the learning of goals and incentives. The importance of many of the goals and incentives that motivate our behavior is also learned through classical conditioning; hence they are termed **learned goals (incentives).** Consider money, diamonds, gold, and concert tickets. An infant's response to these objects will quickly convince you that they do not possess intrinsic value; we must learn their value before their acquisition is reinforcing.

Trends in Classical Conditioning: After Pavlov

Our conception of classical conditioning has changed dramatically since Pavlov's time. We now know that conditioning is not an automatic process that simply links conditioned stimuli and unconditioned stimuli. Psychologists now place more emphasis on what information the CS seems to tell or convey to the participant.

Contingency Theory.   One principle that has emerged from this continued research is that the better the CS predicts the occurrence of the UCS, the stronger the conditioning will be (Bolles, 1979; Rescorla, 1968). (Recall that we encountered the importance of predictability when we discussed the sequence of CS-UCS presentation on page 187). A study of classical conditioning in two groups of rats illustrates this point (Rescorla, 1968). For the first group the CS (tone) was always *followed by* the UCS (a shock). The animals in this group were called the *contingent group* because the occurrence of shock always followed (was contingent on) the tone. The animals in the second group heard the tone *before* or *after* the shock was presented. These animals were called the *noncontingent group* because the occurrence of shock did not always follow (was not contingent on) the tone. Because the tone perfectly predicted the UCS for the *contingent* animals, classical conditioning was strong. Classical conditioning was weaker for the *noncontingent* animals because the CS did not always precede the UCS.

This relation should not be surprising. As we have seen, a strong and predictable CS is the goal of the acquisition or training process during which an association between the CS and UCS is formed. A particular CS predicts that a particular UCS is about to occur. For Pavlov's dogs, for example, the sound of the ticking metronome reliably predicted the delivery of meat powder. Conversely, when we undertake extinction, we try to convince the participant that the CS will no longer be followed by—will no longer predict—the UCS (Delemater, 1995). The more reliable the CS is in predicting the UCS, the harder it will be to extinguish the CR. As the next section shows,

learned motives
Motives that are learned or acquired, usually through classical conditioning

learned goals (incentives)
Goals or incentives that are learned, usually through classical conditioning

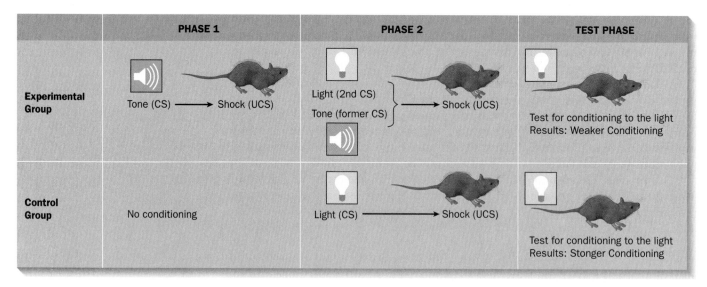

	PHASE 1	PHASE 2	TEST PHASE
Experimental Group	Tone (CS) ⟶ Shock (UCS)	Light (2nd CS) / Tone (former CS) } ⟶ Shock (UCS)	Test for conditioning to the light Results: Weaker Conditioning
Control Group	No conditioning	Light (CS) ⟶ Shock (UCS)	Test for conditioning to the light Results: Stonger Conditioning

FIGURE 5-7   Research on the phenomenon of *blocking* has convincingly demonstrated that the pairing of the CS and UCS is not the only factor involved in classical conditioning. The timing of the pairing can lead to results in which prior pairings can *block* the effect of a particular CS.

Source: Kamin, 1969

however, conditioned stimuli do not automatically become associated with unconditioned stimuli, even if they are predictable.

Blocking.   If classical conditioning simply involves the pairing of a CS and a UCS, the time at which the pairing occurs should not make any difference. But the timing of the pairing does matter. Consider the following research. One group of rats was classically conditioned by presenting a tone (CS) and following it with an electric shock (UCS) (Kamin, 1969). Once a response to the tone was conditioned, a second CS (a light) was also presented before the shock. A second group of animals received only pairings of the light and the shock. The researcher then tested the strength of conditioning to the light. This experimental arrangement is shown in Figure 5-7.

Conditioning was weaker for the animals that received tone–shock pairings before tone and light were paired with shock. The animals that received only the light–shock pairing demonstrated stronger conditioning. The conditioning of the tone before presenting the light had blocked or reduced the conditioning of the light.

If you consider predictability again, this result makes sense. If the tone had already been established as a predictable CS, another predictable CS was not needed (Barnett, Grahame, & Miller, 1993; Williams, 1994). For the animals that had already received tone-and-shock pairings, the result was **blocking** of the light–and–shock association. Because light was the only CS presented to the other group of animals, it was conditioned strongly.

Evolution and Classical Conditioning: Taste-Aversion Learning and Preparedness

Suppose that you have just moved to a large metropolitan area, which is quite different from the small town you left behind. For example, the variety of restaurants is amazing. Last night some friends took you to a seafood restaurant. The décor and atmosphere of the restaurant were intriguing; the taste of the food was delightful and unlike any you had ever had. Unfortunately, however, during the night you came down with the stomach flu that had been going around. For the rest of the night you were nauseated or worse—not a pleasant experience. These events may not seem to involve learning, but

blocking
Situation in which the conditionability of a CS is weakened when it is paired with a UCS that has previously been paired with another CS

classical conditioning took place: You were conditioned to avoid seafood. But why? As it turns out, "The brain is not equally sensitive to all types of stimuli. Some types of stimuli are much more important for survival than others, and evolutionary processes have prepared the brain to locate some types of causal correlations more easily than others" (Baldwin & Baldwin, 2001, p. 24).

Taste Aversion.   Does becoming nauseated after eating a food that is unusual to you have anything to do with learning? The notion of predictability is helpful once again. Whenever a person or animal becomes ill after consuming a food with a novel taste (taste-aversion), that taste (CS) may become a predictor of illness.

Taste-aversion learning involves the development of an aversion to (dislike of) a flavor that has been associated with illness (Batsell & Best, 1992, 1993). In the mid-1960s, John Garcia and his colleagues demonstrated that when a novel flavor was used as the CS and illness or nausea was the UCR, rats developed an intense aversion to the flavor, which has become known as the *Garcia effect*. Classical conditioning of a tone and food occurs best when the tone is sounded one-half second before the food is presented, but strong taste aversions can be conditioned when illness occurs more than an hour after the taste is experienced (Garcia, Ervin, & Koelling, 1966). When Garcia's research was first reported, it was greeted with much skepticism because it did not seem to follow established principles of classical conditioning. The significant amount of time between the presentation of the CS and the UCS was at odds with what researchers had learned from decades of laboratory research. As a result, Garcia's research was refused publication in the major journal devoted to animal behavior. It is credit to his persistence that his work was not only accepted, it is considered classic in demonstrating that "an animal's evolutionary inheritance places limits on what it can learn" (Leahey, 2001, p. 288).

There are two points of interest in these taste-aversion results. First, the flavor had to be novel for it to become associated with the illness. A flavor that has been consumed many times does not predict illness. Second, the time between the onset of the CS (taste) and the onset of the UCS (illness) can be quite lengthy, yet strong conditioning still occurs.

Preparedness.   Certain stimuli, such as flavors, can be associated with certain unconditioned responses, such as illness, more easily than they can be associated with other UCRs, such as electric shock. Animals seem to be biologically ready or *prepared* to associate certain CSs with certain UCSs (Seligman, 1970). Some events seem to go together naturally, whereas others do not. For humans and many animal species, taste and illness form one such natural pairing; presenting a tone or light CS with an electric shock is another natural pair. If instead we try to pair the tone or light CS with illness or the taste CS with an electric shock, we get very weak conditioning (Garcia & Koelling, 1966; see Figure 5-8). Other pairings also are learned quite easily. For example, humans, as well as many household pets, seem prepared to associate the sight of lightning (CS) with the sound of thunder. **Preparedness** occurs when some species are more biologically ready to form certain associations; it may explain why some phobias are learned so easily (see Chapter 12). We do not seem prepared, however, to associate loud noises with nausea or illness.

Psychological Detective

Preparedness may differ according to the species that is being tested. For example, birds use color, rather than taste, as an important cue in food selection. In birds, how would you determine whether color can be conditioned to an illness UCS more easily than a taste? Give this question some thought, and diagram an experiment to test it before proceeding.

taste-aversion learning
Development of a dislike or aversion to a flavor or food that has been paired with illness

preparedness
Theory that organisms are biologically ready or prepared to associate certain conditioned stimuli (CSs) with certain unconditioned stimuli (UCSs)

FIGURE 5-8 Whether rats develop taste aversions depends on the stimuli and the responses involved. *Group 1* was shocked while drinking bright, noisy water: They developed an aversion to water. *Group 2* drank the same water and received radiation that caused nausea: They did not develop an aversion to water. *Group 3* drank a saccharin solution and were shocked: They did not develop an aversion to saccharin. *Group 4* drank a saccharin solution and were irradiated (nausea): They developed an aversion to saccharin. There are natural relations between events and the pain the rats experienced. When pain comes from "out there" rats search for external predictors (light and noise associated with drinking water). Nausea is experienced internally, so rats associate it with an internal stimulus—saccharin. Through evolution, organisms have been *prepared* to make some associations more readily than others.

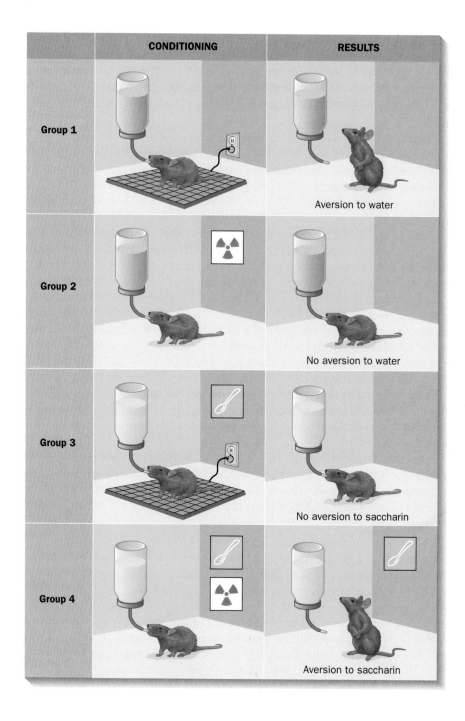

In a study designed to answer this question, investigators first presented blue, sour-tasting water (CS) to quail and then made the birds ill temporarily by giving them a nausea-producing drug (Wilcoxin, Dragoin, & Kral, 1971). After the birds became ill they had a strong aversion to the blue color but not to the sour taste. These findings suggest that the quail were unprepared—or "contraprepared"—to make the taste-illness association. Preparedness theory suggests one important means by which animals adapt to their environments: They learn to avoid potentially dangerous stimuli that have made them ill on a previous occasion. Avoiding such substances increases their chances of survival. With their keen eyesight, birds are more likely to discriminate stimuli on the basis of color, whereas rats and mice, whose eyesight is poor, are likely to discriminate on the basis of taste. Preparedness theory is an excellent example of the evolutionary perspective at work: Animals are prepared to make associations that help them adapt to the environments they inhabit.

As we noted earlier, humans also form taste aversions quite readily. Think of the times you have been nauseated after eating. In most of these cases, had you just consumed a novel food or beverage? Will you ever consume that food or drink again? Chances are pretty good that you are saying "never," and you may be right. Such experiences are surprisingly common. In one survey of undergraduates, 65% of the students reported having at least one food aversion. Most of these food aversions developed several hours after eating food associated with sickness (Logue, Ophir, & Strauss, 1981). What's more, such aversions do not extinguish very easily; they can last for 50 years or more (Garb & Stunkard, 1974).

Sometimes taste aversions have detrimental effects. For example, children undergoing chemotherapy for cancer often develop very strong food aversions that prevent proper eating. Psychologists have applied their knowledge of taste-aversion learning to this problem (Bernstein, 1978; Bernstein & Webster, 1980, 1982). In one study, children were allowed to eat an unusually flavored ice cream (called "Mapletof") shortly before receiving nausea-producing chemotherapy. Later these patients ate less Mapletof ice cream than did a second group of patients whose treatment consisted of surgery rather than drug therapy. Children in the second group had also eaten some Mapletof ice cream before treatment. Because their treatment did not produce nausea, however, these patients did not associate the ice cream flavor with illness. Clearly the taste–illness pairing is crucial for the development of taste aversion.

Subsequent research demonstrated that consumption of the Mapletof ice cream *before* chemotherapy greatly reduced the patients' reluctance to consume their normal diet. After chemotherapy, patients who had previously eaten the Mapletof ice cream and had formed a taste aversion to this flavor were more willing to consume their normal diet than were patients who had not eaten any Mapletof ice cream. The formation of a taste aversion to the Mapletof ice cream tended to block the formation of taste aversions to other foods and thus helped the patients maintain their normal diet without becoming nauseated.

Learning by Various Species.   In 1950, psychologist Frank Beach published an article titled *The Snark Was a Boojum*. Beach's message was straightforward: Comparative psychology should be based on studies of numerous species. He examined 613 research articles and found that 50% of them dealt with the rat, despite the fact that the rat represented only .001% of all living creatures. Failure to heed this caution could result in comparative psychology fading away, just like the hunters in Lewis Carroll's *Alice in Wonderland* who encountered a snark that was a boojum.

Beach's cautions are as relevant today as they were in 1950. In many respects psychology has become the science of the white rat and the American, male, college sophomore. These two types of participants appear far more often in the published research literature than other types of participants (Jones, 1994; Lee & Hall, 1994; Marin, 1994).

Our intent is to alert you to the fact that psychologists should be concerned about looking for such influences in the area of basic learning processes such as classical and operant conditioning. Why is it difficult to point to such influences when basic learning processes are considered?

Part of the answer concerns the nature of the material: basic learning processes. Most researchers and students probably assume that basic processes apply to all animal species and people in all cultures; hence cross-species and cross-cultural studies are not needed. This assumption may be true, but we will never know for sure until such studies are conducted.

A second reason for the lack of comparative and cross-cultural data concerns the orientation of the researchers. This area of psychology traditionally has been very concerned with the methodology that is used in the experiments and in the creation of theories to account for the behaviors and phenomena that are observed. These interests shift attention away to the specifics involved in the conduct of the experiments and away from investigating cross-species and cross-cultural effects. Keep these concerns in mind as you read about basic learning processes. The future, we hope, will see a change in this state of affairs.

STUDY TIP

After reading the section on the elements of classical conditioning, brainstorm in a group of three. Think of five additional examples, not mentioned in the text, of ways in which human behavior is conditioned. Discuss each behavior and how the conditioning occurred.

REVIEW SUMMARY

1. Learning occurs when experience produces a relatively permanent change in behavior.

2. Classical conditioning involves pairing an **unconditioned stimulus (UCS),** which automatically elicits an **unconditioned response (UCR),** with a **conditioned stimulus (CS),** which is neutral at the start of conditioning. Several pairings during an acquisition phase lead to a situation in which the CS presented by itself elicits a **conditioned response (CR).**

3. When the UCS is intense and presented more frequently, stronger classical conditioning is produced.

4. The classically conditioned response is eliminated or extinguished when the UCS is removed or not presented; this process is called **extinction. Spontaneous recovery** of the CR occurs when time is allowed to pass between extinction sessions.

5. Generalization occurs when CRs are elicited by stimuli that are similar to the CS. **Discrimination** is the opposing process; it involves responding only to the appropriate CS.

6. John Watson and Rosalie Rayner demonstrated that emotions can be learned by classically conditioning 9-month-old Little Albert to fear a white rat. This child exhibited a **phobia,** which is a fear for certain activities, objects, or situations. The research conducted by Watson and Rayner would not be considered ethical by present-day standards.

7. Learned motives and **learned goals** (or learned incentives) are acquired through classical conditioning.

8. Our understanding of classical conditioning has been subject to revision since Pavlov introduced the basic processes. For example, although the association of CS with UCS is important in establishing conditioning, the real key is the degree to which the CS predicts occurrence of the UCS. Previous trials of a CS-UCS pairing can serve to **block** the effectiveness of a second CS.

9. For many species, the pairing of a novel taste with the experience of illness results in learning an aversion to that taste. **Taste-aversion learning** occurs readily in humans; birds, however, more readily associate a color with illness. **Preparedness** is evident when some species are more likely to form certain associations than others.

CHECK YOUR PROGRESS

1. Have you ever found yourself salivating while walking through the bakery section of a supermarket? What was the UCS? the CS? the CR?

2. Complete the following:

  a. Before conditioning, the _____ is automatically elicited by the _____.

  b. The CR is strengthened if the _____ and _____ are paired frequently.

  c. Extinction of a classically conditioned response involves presentation of only the _____. In other words, the _____ is removed.

  d. Extinction causes the _____ to grow gradually _____.

3. State which aspect of classical conditioning is illustrated by each of the following situations:

  a. A tone sounds; half a second later, a puff of air is delivered to your eye and you blink. Once the conditioned eye blink has been established, the puff of air is discontinued and the tone is presented by itself a number of times.

  b. As a child you had the misfortune of being stung by a bee. In addition to the pain of the sting, your body reacted strongly. Your breathing became difficult and you were rushed to the hospital for treatment. Twenty years later you have a fear of bees and other flying insects.

  c. Your roommate went to a new pizza restaurant for dinner and developed a severe case of intestinal flu later that night. The pizza restaurant lost a customer.

  d. Children who play with large plastic bags sometimes become trapped inside the bag and nearly suffocate. If they are fortunate enough to be rescued, they will probably have a conditioned fear of closed spaces.

4. What was the conditioned stimulus (CS) in the case of Little Albert?

  a. rat

  b. hammer

  c. small toy

  d. loud noise

5. In classical conditioning, what automatically produces a reaction?

  a. CS

  b. CR

  c. UCS

  d. UCR

6. For the past few months, Sara has been using a perfume called Passion. Her boyfriend, Jim, really likes the perfume. In fact, on several occasions, he has passed women who were wearing Passion and had the same reaction: his heart rate increased. In this example, the perfume is the _____ and Jim's increased heart rate is the _____.

  a. CS, UCS

  b. CS, CR

  c. UCS, UCR

  d. UCS, UR

7. Taste aversions seem to be specific examples of what type of learning?

  a. insight learning
  b. vicarious learning
  c. operant conditioning
  d. classical conditioning

8. Last week Ted saw a movie that vividly depicted a serial killer's gruesome murders. When school began, Ted had an uncomfortable feeling when one of his teachers walked into class. After class, he realized that the teacher had a striking resemblance to the killer. Ted's reaction to the teacher is an example of

  a. extinction.
  b. acquisition.
  c. discrimination.
  d. generalization.

9. Why is Little Albert such a well-known individual in the history of psychology?

  a. He outlined key elements of classical conditioning in his research on dogs.
  b. A serious bout of the flu led him to discover the major principles of taste-aversion learning.
  c. He was the subject of research that illustrated how classical conditioning can explain the development of phobias.
  d. After he developed a strong aversion to needles, pins, and injections he found a way to use hypnosis to overcome such reactions.

10. Which of the following illustrates an unconditioned response?

  a. A large ice cream sundae.
  b. Your favorite ice cream shop.
  c. Salivation when you taste an ice cream sundae.
  d. Salivation when you see your favorite ice cream shop.

OPERANT CONDITIONING

Bob's roommate, Greg, is a complete slob. In Bob's view, the condition of Greg's room is Greg's business, but the condition of the bathroom they share is another matter. Almost every week they have major arguments about cleaning the bathroom, and Bob ends up doing the cleaning. When the unfairness of the situation is more than Bob can stand, he tries a new approach. Whenever Greg does anything to help clean the apartment, Bob praises him: "Good job, Greg; the apartment really looks great." Gradually Greg begins helping on a more regular basis, and one week he even offers to clean the bathroom. *What technique did Bob use to get Greg to help clean the apartment?*

We will now discuss the second basic type of learning, operant conditioning. In **operant conditioning,** also known as *instrumental conditioning*, an organism operates on its environment to produce a change (Leahey & Harris, 2001). In other words, the organism's behavior is *instrumental*—it results in a change in the environment. As you will see, the type of change that is produced is a critical element of this type of learning.

Reinforcers: The Basic Concept of Operant Conditioning

Probably no one has been associated more closely with operant conditioning than the late Harvard psychologist B. F. Skinner (1904–1990), who has been described as the most famous psychologist who has ever lived (Fowler, 1990). Skinner was strongly influenced by John B. Watson's behavioral view of psychology (see page 190). As we have seen, Watson believed that if we could understand how to predict and control behavior, we would know all there was to know about psychology. Skinner therefore

operant conditioning
Learning that occurs when the participant must make a response to produce a change in the environment

FIGURE 5-9 (A) An operant conditioning chamber, or Skinner box. Pecking the circular disk or "key" is the target response that delivers a food reinforcer for the pigeon. (B) The cumulative recorder automatically logs the participant's responses.

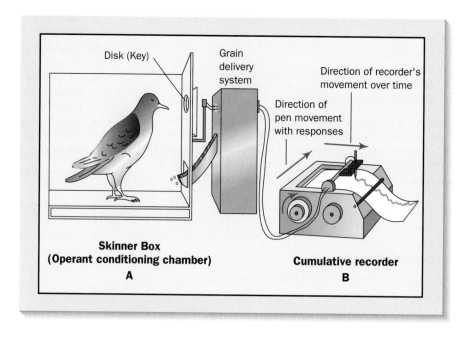

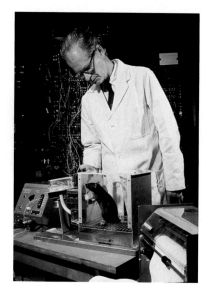

B. F. Skinner training a rat in a Skinner box.

reinforcer
Event or stimulus that increases the frequency of the response that it follows

positive reinforcer
Event or stimulus presented after the target response that increases the likelihood that this response will occur again

began to look for the stimuli that control behavior. To isolate those effects, he developed a special testing environment called an *operant conditioning chamber*, which is usually referred to as a *Skinner box* (see Figure 5-9). Although Skinner relied on the use of animals such as rats and pigeons, his ideas can be applied to human behavior. The advantage of the Skinner box and laboratory studies is that they allow researchers to exert a great deal of control in their research and thus they are in a better position to identify the actual influences on behavior.

Let's take a moment to return to the question we posed earlier: How did Bob convince Greg to help clean their apartment? The answer is that he praised his behavior, thus using what Skinner called a *reinforcer*.

In some cases, operant behavior may result in the delivery of a stimulus or an event. When you insert money into a soda machine, for example, you receive a cold drink. When Greg cleaned the apartment, he received praise. In other instances, the operant behavior may result in the elimination of a stimulus or an event. For example, you have probably learned the quickest way to eliminate the sound your alarm clock makes early in the morning. Such events, or reinforcers, are at the heart of operant conditioning. Thus we can define a **reinforcer** as an event or stimulus that makes the behavior it follows more likely to occur again (Skinner, 1938). For example, obtaining a cold drink from the soda machine and eliminating the annoying sound of your alarm clock are both reinforcers. The behavior that a reinforcer follows can be thought of as the *target response*—it is the behavior that we want to strengthen or increase. Reinforcers can be either positive or negative; in either instance, they can serve to increase the occurrence of the target response.

Positive and Negative Reinforcers. **Positive reinforcers** are events or stimuli such as food, water, money, and praise that are presented after the target response occurs. They are generally considered desirable and pleasant and are therefore sought by people and animals alike. For example, a real estate agent earns a commission for each house she sells; the commissions reinforce her efforts to sell as many houses as possible. Your little brother is allowed to watch cartoons on Saturday mornings after he has cleaned his room; as a result, he cleans his room every Saturday. We hope that you have been praised for receiving good grades on psychology tests; the praise should encourage you to study even harder in the future.

Psychological Detective

Can a positive reinforcer encourage unethical behavior? Consider the problem of cheating. Children are taught that cheating is wrong, but this behavior persists in most segments of our society. Why? Take a few moments to analyze the behavior of cheating in operant conditioning terms. Be sure to write down the target response and the reinforcers.

Suppose a student consults a concealed cheat sheet during a test or passes answers to a friend. The target responses here are the acts of cheating. The reinforcer is receiving a high (or passing) grade. Because the grade is given (presented), it is a positive reinforcer. Do threats of punishment counteract this behavior? The answer appears to be no; the number of students who admit to having cheated on examinations is quite high: As many as 40% to 95% of college students surveyed have reported having cheated at some time (Burnett, Rudolph, & Clifford, 1998; Davis et al., 1992; Davis & Ludvigson, 1995); consequently, cheating is a serious concern on college campuses (McCabe et al., 2001; Whitley & Spiegel, 2002). There is growing concern that current expansion of distance learning formats may make it even easier to cheat (Kennedy et al., 2000). What's more, detection rates are very low—frequently less than 2 percent (Haines et al., 1986). Thus a very small number of cheaters are caught, and even fewer are punished. The prospect of achieving an easy grade, coupled with a relatively low chance of getting caught, can be a powerful reinforcer of cheating on tests. The same analysis also applies to other familiar events. For example, the number of people who receive tickets for speeding on the highway is very low, relative to the number of people who speed.

When students see the word *negative*, they tend to assume that a behavior will decrease. Don't get caught up in this misconception, which has been called one of the major mistakes made by students of psychology (Leahey & Harris, 2001; McConnell, 1990). Both positive and negative reinforcers make the target response more likely to occur again. **Negative reinforcers** are events or stimuli that are removed because a response has occurred. Examples of negative reinforcement include playing music to reduce boredom, cleaning your room so that your roommate will stop complaining that you're a slob, and turning off the alarm clock to stop that annoying sound. In these situations something stopped (boredom) or was removed (criticism) because you performed a target response. What response will occur the next time these unpleasant situations arise? If the negative reinforcer has been effective, the target response that terminated it is likely to occur again. The operation of positive and negative reinforcers is diagrammed in Figure 5-10.

negative reinforcer
Event or stimulus removed after the target response, thereby increasing the likelihood that this response will occur again

When rates of detection and punishment are very low, cheating rates may be very high.

WHICH IS THE BEST WAY TO ANSWER MULTIPLE-CHOICE QUESTIONS?

A
THE DICHOTOMOUS-MONETARY METHOD (COIN TOSSING)

B
THE HYPER-PARAMETRIC AERODYNAMIC MISSILE METHOD (BASED ON RESEARCH BY NASA)

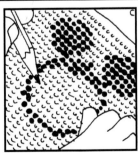
SYMBOLIC PROTEST AGAINST STIFLING OF ARTISTIC EXPRESSION INHERENT IN TESTING KNOWLEDGE WITH MULTIPLE-CHOICE QUESTIONS

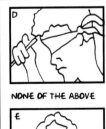
NONE OF THE ABOVE

E
HELP FROM ABOVE

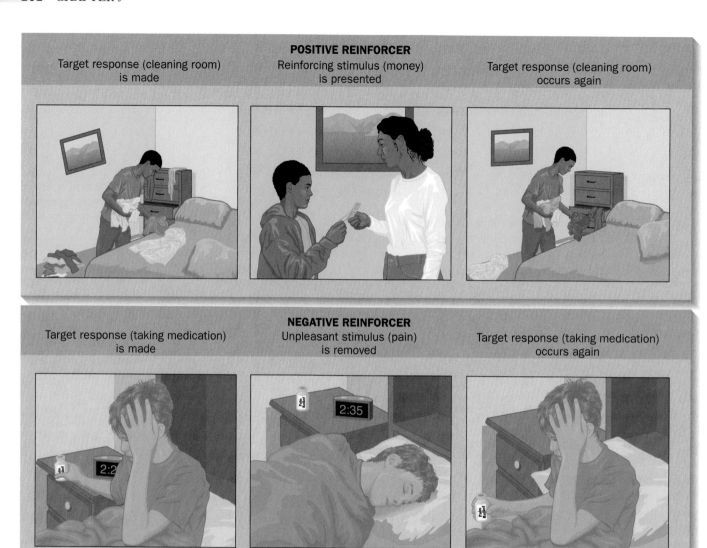

POSITIVE REINFORCER

Target response (cleaning room) is made — Reinforcing stimulus (money) is presented — Target response (cleaning room) occurs again

NEGATIVE REINFORCER

Target response (taking medication) is made — Unpleasant stimulus (pain) is removed — Target response (taking medication) occurs again

FIGURE 5-10 Diagram of the operation of positive and negative reinforcers. In the top panel, the target response of cleaning the room is reinforced with money (a positive reinforcer) resulting in *positive reinforcement* (increase in the target response). In the bottom panel the target response (taking medication for a painful headache) removes the pain (a negative reinforcer) resulting in *negative reinforcement* (an increase in use of the medication). Note that both positive and negative reinforcement lead to increases in the frequency of target responses.

Primary and Secondary (Conditioned) Reinforcers. A **primary reinforcer** is an event or stimulus that has innate (that is, biological) reinforcing properties; you do not have to learn that such stimuli are reinforcers. For a hungry person, food is a primary reinforcer. Water is another primary reinforcer, especially on a very hot day; and the rest provided by sleep, which is welcome, refreshing, and too often insufficient for our needs, is a third example of a primary reinforcer. Needless to say, not all events or stimuli that might follow a behavior will necessarily satisfy some biological need such as hunger, thirst, or sleep. A **secondary reinforcer** is a stimulus that acquires reinforcing properties by being associated with a primary reinforcer. Because you must learn that such stimuli are reinforcers, they are also called conditioned reinforcers. Money may be the best example of a secondary reinforcer. By itself, money has no intrinsic value; children learn that money can be exchanged for primary reinforcers such as ice cream. We also use money to purchase other foods, beverages, and a place to catch up on our sleep, whether it is our apartment, a house, or a hotel room.

primary reinforcer
Stimulus that has innate reinforcing properties

secondary reinforcer
Stimulus that acquires reinforcing properties by being associated with a primary reinforcer

Contingencies and Behavior

Skinner coined the term *operant conditioning* because the behaviors we emit (as opposed to behaviors that are elicited) *operate* on the environment in some way. These changes in the environment determine what happens to a given target behavior. As previously mentioned, if a behavior is followed by a positive reinforcer—as when a student answers a question and the professor says "Excellent!"—the behavior tends to increase in the future. Why? There is a contingency established here: If a student answers a question, then the professor will say "Excellent." Contingencies take the form of "If _____ then _____" relations. Skinner noted that there is a contingency established between the behavior and the outcomes: If a student gives a good answer the professor will say "Excellent." In other cases, such as punishment, the contingency is different: If a child runs into the street, his parents may spank him. Take a moment to think about some of the contingencies that exist in your environment. As you think about these contingencies, you may realize that the final behavior does not always occur right from the start. For example, it is not likely that you learned to drive after just one ride around the block. How does Skinner explain how we develop more complex behaviors, which may not exist before training begins?

When you start training a rat in a Skinner box (see page 200), you should not expect much from the rat. The rat will not begin pressing the lever or bar as soon as it enters this new environment. You may have to help it to learn to press the lever or bar to receive food. The technique you will use is a form of operant conditioning called **shaping.** Shaping involves reinforcing successive responses that more closely resemble the desired target response; in other words, you are using the method of *successive approximations*. When using this method, we generally withhold reinforcement until the animal engages in a behavior that comes closer to the desired target response. Although the concept of shaping is reasonably clear, actually doing the job may be difficult. The timing of reinforcement presentation is crucial; if reinforcers are not presented at exactly the right moment, an inappropriate response may be shaped.

For a rat learning to press a lever for food, the sequence of events might go as follows: When the rat is near the food dish, you drop a piece of food into it. Eating the food reinforces the behavior of approaching the dish. Once the rat has learned where the food is, you begin offering reinforcers only when the rat goes near the response lever. Gradually you make your response requirements more demanding until the rat must actually touch the lever to receive the reinforcement. Once the rat has started touching the lever, you can require that the lever be pressed before the reinforcement is given. In this way you have gradually made the response that produces reinforcement more closely resemble (*successively approximate*) the target response of pressing the lever. In short, you have *shaped* the rat's response.

Perhaps the best known cases of shaping involves a patient who was admitted to a mental hospital at the age of 21 with the diagnosis of schizophrenia; he had been "completely mute almost immediately upon commitment" (Isaacs, Thomas, & Goldiamond, 1960). In fact, he did not say a word for 19 years! No one had been able to coax a single word out of him. He lived day in and day out without uttering a word, staring ahead with a fixed gaze. One day, a psychologist accidentally dropped a pack of chewing gum. The patient's eyes turned to focus on the gum and then returned to their fixed gaze. Finally, there was some small sign of responsiveness. The psychologist decided that gum could be used as a reinforcer. For the first two weeks, the psychologist held up the gum in front of the patient, waiting for some sign of visual contact. Once the response occurred, he was given some gum. Then, the psychologist withheld gum until the patient responded with both visual contact and lip movement. Through a painstaking process of shaping, the patient eventually said "Gum, please"; these were his first words in 19 years. Another case of mutism in a 7th-grade boy who had been selectively mute since kindergarten was treated using a variety of behavioral techniques (Rye & Ullman, 1999).

Shaping has a wide range of applications and is an especially effective tool derived from operant conditioning principles. If teachers find that their students are not able

Psi Chi Newsletter. Reprinted with the permission of Psi Chi.

 psych 5.2

 Operant Conditioning

shaping
A form of operant conditioning in which a desired response is taught by reinforcement of successive responses that more closely resemble the target response

to provide correct answers to questions posed in class, they praise partial answers and even effort. Gradually, they can raise expectations so students have to give more complete responses to earn praise (Eggen & Kauchak, 2001). If you have ever seen bears roller skating, seals catching balls, dolphins "flying" through hoops, or pigeons playing ping pong, you have been entertained by the results of a long series of steps that shaped these behaviors (Coren, 1999). When you stop to think about the range of behaviors we engage in every day, especially the more complex ones, you can see how important shaping can be. Driving a car, playing the piano, and typing are all behaviors that we probably learned through shaping.

Psychological Detective

Whether or not we realize it, shaping techniques have been used to help us acquire many new behaviors. Think about behaviors such as talking, writing, and driving a car. These behaviors were gradually shaped through the appropriate delivery of reinforcers. Remember when you learned to drive? How were your driving skills when you first started driving? How are they now? In which ways were those skills shaped? Recall these behaviors and events and relate them to our discussion of operant conditioning before you read further.

Most of the behaviors of animals we see in shows and theme parks do not occur in their natural habitats. Animal trainers use operant conditioning methods, especially shaping, to train raccoons, seals, whales, dolphins, and other creatures. The key to shaping is to break down complex behaviors into smaller and easier behaviors and then to reinforce successive approximations to the ultimate, more complex behavior.

The first time you sat behind the wheel, you were probably unable to drive around the block or parallel park like an experienced driver. To drive around the block, you had to become accustomed to the rear-view mirrors, use the turn signals, apply the brakes, and perhaps shift gears. Then there was parallel parking, which required much practice. Your instructor reinforced good driving techniques with phrases like "Good job," "Excellent," and "Way to go." Gradually your skills improved until you could maneuver your car into a small space without any difficulty.

Now recall the case of the roommates Bob and Greg, who had trouble keeping their apartment clean. Bob was shaping Greg's behavior. At first he praised anything Greg did to help keep the apartment clean. Gradually he reserved his praise for greater efforts, until finally Greg was cleaning the apartment on a regular basis.

The Premack Principle. Imagine that you are a music teacher in a middle school where your students love to play modern, jazz–rock compositions. Unfortunately, they are less than enthusiastic when it comes to playing the standard works of music that are part of the curriculum (Eggen & Kauchak, 2001). How would you use the principles of operant conditioning to deal effectively with this situation? One clever way of addressing this problem involves use of the *Premack Principle* named after the psychologist David Premack (1965). Premack determined that the opportunity to participate in a preferred activity (playing jazz in this case) could reinforce less preferred activities (playing the standard music pieces). What Premack described in operant conditioning terms has been known for some time as "Grandma's Rule" ("First eat your vegetables, and then you can have dessert"). There are numerous other examples including these:

- completion of homework (less preferred activity) is reinforced by the opportunity to play (preferred activity)
- football players get to run new plays (preferred activity) after they have run their required laps (less preferred activity)
- raking and bagging the leaves on Saturday (less preferred activity) is reinforced by the opportunity to play a video game (preferred activity).

Schedules of Reinforcement

In an operant conditioning chamber, the experimenter can deliver reinforcers, such as a piece of food for a hungry rat or pigeon, according to a preset pattern. Figure 5-9 (p. 200) shows an instrument, known as a *cumulative recorder*, that logs the participant's responses. The results sheet, known as a **cumulative record,** shows the rate of responding in a series of operant conditioning trials; the steeper the line, the higher the rate of responding. Keep in mind that a cumulative recorder keeps track of the accumulation of target responses over time; hence the term *cumulative*.

Psychological Detective

Suppose you are looking at the cumulative record of a rat that is being trained in a Skinner box. As you hold the rat in your hand, you scan the record and note something interesting. Across several days, the record shows a straight, horizontal line. What is likely to have happened to the rat's target response?

This particular rat has stopped responding. The fact that you are holding it, of course, indicates that the animal is still alive. The researcher put this rat on a schedule that led to the reduction and elimination of the behavior (extinction).

The preset pattern or plan for delivering reinforcement is known as a **schedule of reinforcement.** Schedules of reinforcement are important determinants of behavior (Shull & Lawrence, 1998). Once a target response has been shaped, the experimenter can arrange to have the reinforcer delivered according to a specific schedule. A researcher can create many plans or schedules for delivering reinforcers; however, we can describe the most basic schedules or reinforcement as falling into two categories: *continuous* and *intermittent* (partial) reinforcement. What this means is that reinforcement will follow every target behavior or it will follow the target behavior only at times.

Continuous Reinforcement.   As noted earlier, a schedule of reinforcement is a preset pattern or plan for delivering reinforcement. The most basic schedule of reinforcement is **continuous reinforcement,** in which the participant is given a reinforcement after each target response occurs. For example, a rat in a Skinner box receives a food pellet for each bar press; a salesperson receives a commission for each car sold; a soda machine delivers a cold drink each time you put money in it. A continuous schedule of reinforcement produces a reasonably high rate of responding. Once the reinforcer loses its effectiveness, however, the response rate drops quickly. Thus food pellets reinforce responding in a hungry rat, but they are not effective after the rat has eaten a large number of them.

Intermittent (Partial) Reinforcement.   In schedules of reinforcement that do not involve the use of continuous reinforcement, some responses are not reinforced. The term **intermittent (or partial) reinforcement** is used to describe these noncontinuous patterns of delivering reinforcement. There are two main types of intermittent schedules: *ratio* and *interval*.

Ratio Schedules.   When a **ratio schedule** is in effect, the number of responses determines whether the participant receives reinforcement. In some cases the exact number of responses that must be made to receive a reinforcer is specified. For example, a pigeon may be required to peck a key 5 times before grain (a positive reinforcer) is presented. When the number of responses required to produce a reinforcer is specified, the arrangement is

---

cumulative record
Results of a series of operant conditioning trials, shown as rate of responding

schedule of reinforcement
Preset pattern for delivering reinforcement

continuous reinforcement
Reinforcement that follows every target response

intermittent (or partial) reinforcement
Reinforcement that does not follow every target response

ratio schedule
Reinforcement schedule in which reinforcement is based on the number of responses; number may be set (fixed-ratio [FR] schedule) or may vary from one reinforcement to the next (variable-ratio [VR] schedule)

"Actually, he's easy to train, everytime I press the buzzer, he brings me food."

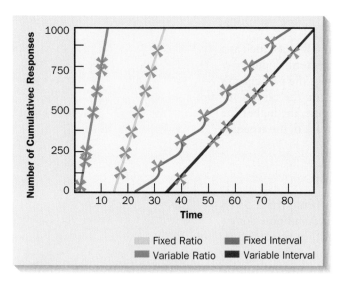

FIGURE 5-11 Examples of fixed-ratio (FR) and variable ratio (VR) response patterns. The steeper the slope of the line, the higher the rate of responding. Note that the responding ceases (flat line) for a brief period after reinforcement has been delivered under the demanding FR schedule. This pause does not occur when the VR schedule is in effect.

interval schedule
Reinforcement schedule based on the passage of time and in which a single response at the end of the designated interval is reinforced; intervals may be set (fixed interval [FI] schedule) or may vary from one reinforcement to the next (variable-interval [VI] schedule)

known as a *fixed-ratio (FR) schedule*. Requiring a pigeon to peck 5 times to receive reinforcement is designated as a "fixed-ratio 5" (FR5) schedule. A continuous reinforcement schedule can be thought of as a "fixed-ratio 1" (FR1) schedule.

On other occasions we may not want to specify the exact number of responses. Sometimes the reinforcer will be delivered after 15 responses, sometimes after 35 responses, sometimes after 10 responses, and so forth. Because the exact number of responses required for a reinforcer is not specified, this arrangement is called a *variable-ratio (VR) schedule*. Typically the average number of responses is used to indicate the type of variable-ratio schedule. In our example, in which the values 15, 35, and 10 were used, the average number of responses would be 20 [(15 + 35 + 10)/3 = 20]. This particular schedule would be designated as a "variable-ratio 20" (VR20) schedule.

Whether we are dealing with a VR or FR schedule, our participants usually make many responses. Frequent responding makes good sense in these situations: The more responses are made, the more frequently participants receive reinforcers. Although both FR and VR schedules produce many responses, VR schedules tend to produce the highest rates of responding. These differences in rates of responding are shown in Figure 5-11.

When an FR schedule is in effect, the participant may pause for a brief period after the reinforcement has been delivered. This *postreinforcement pause* typically does not occur when a VR schedule is used. When an FR schedule is used, the reinforcer seems to serve as a signal to take a short break. If you were responding on an FR schedule, you might be thinking, "Five more responses until I get the reinforcer, then I'll rest for a bit before I start responding again."

Suppose that you have a job stuffing envelopes. For every 200 envelopes you stuff, you receive $10 (a positive reinforcer). To earn as much money as possible, you work very hard and stuff as many envelopes as possible. Every time the 200th envelope is completed, however, you stop for a minute to straighten the stack and count how many piles of 200 envelopes you have completed (Mazur, 1998).

The duration of the postreinforcement pause is not the same for all FR schedules; the higher the schedule (the greater the number of responses required to produce a reinforcer), the longer the pause. In addition, the more time expended in responding, the longer the postreinforcement pause will be.

Now consider a case in which there is no postreinforcement pause. Last year Barbara and some of her friends spent their spring break in Las Vegas. The slot machines proved to be Barbara's downfall. Sometimes the jackpot bell rang and she collected a potful of quarters, which encouraged her to continue playing. Before she knew it, she had been putting quarters into the "one-armed bandit" for 6 hours straight. When she counted her winnings and losses, she had spent $250 just to win $33. Why did Barbara put so much money into the slot machine?

The answer is that slot machines "pay off" on a VR schedule. As Barbara put quarter after quarter into the machine, she was probably thinking, "Next time the bell will ring, and I'll get the jackpot." She knew that she would receive a reward (hitting the jackpot) at some point, but because slot machines operate on a variable schedule, she could not predict when she would be rewarded. If you have ever become "hooked" on playing the lottery, you can understand this process. Keep in mind that VR schedules of reinforcement can lead to high rates of responding in a Skinner box or in front of a one-armed bandit in Las Vegas.

Interval Schedules. The second type of intermittent (partial) schedule of reinforcement, the interval schedule, involves the passage of time. When an **interval schedule**

TABLE 5-2

Reinforcement Schedules and Examples

Continuous	A teacher "walks students through" the steps for solving simultaneous equations. They are liberally praised at each step as they first learn the solution.
Fixed-ratio	The algebra teacher announces, "As soon as you've done two problems in a row correctly, you may start on your homework assignments so that you'll be able to finish by the end of class."
Variable-ratio	Students volunteer to answer questions by raising their hands and are called on at random.
Variable-interval	Students are given unannounced quizzes.
Fixed-interval	Students are given a quiz every Friday.

is in effect, responses are reinforced only after a certain interval of time has passed. As with ratio schedules, there are two basic types of interval schedules, fixed-interval and variable-interval. Table 5-2 lists some common examples of the schedules of reinforcement that we are discussing.

Under a *fixed-interval (FI) schedule*, a constant period of time must pass before a response is reinforced. Responses made before the end of that period are not reinforced. No matter how many times you check your mailbox, you will not receive mail until it is time for the daily mail delivery. Under an FI schedule, participants try to estimate the passage of time and make most of their responses toward the end of the interval, when they will be reinforced. If your mail always is delivered between 3:00 and 3:30 P.M., you won't start looking for it until close to that time. Participants (humans or animals), however, tend to make what are called *anticipatory responses* before the end of the interval. Suppose a turkey for Thanksgiving dinner is scheduled to roast for 4 hours. How many of us can resist opening the oven door before the 4 hours, especially as the end of the 4-hour time period approaches? In general, however, the longer participants stay on an FI schedule, the better they become at timing their responses.

When reinforcement occurs on a *variable-interval (VI) schedule*, the participant never knows the exact length of time that must pass before a response is reinforced; the time interval changes after every reinforcement. Because a response can be reinforced at any time, it makes sense for the participant to maintain a steady—but not especially high—rate of responding. Think of the times you have called a friend on the phone only to get voice mail. You probably did not start redialing at a frantic pace. Most likely you initially called back a few minutes later, and then a few minutes after that if you were not successful, and so on. You could not determine whether your friend was having several short conversations or a lengthy one—that is, you did not know when your dialing would be reinforced by the sound of a ringing telephone. Only time would tell. At some point your friend hung up, and you were able to get through. As time passed, your chances of getting through got better and better.

The average amount of time that must elapse before a response produces reinforcement under a VI schedule influences the rate of responding; the longer the interval, the lower the rate of responding. For example, pigeons reinforced on a VI 2-minute schedule responded between 60 and 100 times per minute, whereas pigeons reinforced on a VI 7-minute schedule responded 20 to 70 times per minute (Catania & Reynolds, 1968). The characteristic response patterns for FI and VI schedules are shown in Figure 5-12.

The Study Chart on the next page compares classical and operant conditioning. Check your understanding of these basic forms of learning before reading further.

FIGURE 5-12 On a fixed-interval (FI) schedule, most responses are made toward the end of the interval when a response will be reinforced. Once the reinforcer has been delivered and the interval begins again, the rate of responding decreases drastically. Under the variable-interval (VI) schedule, the participant cannot predict the end of the interval and therefore cannot judge when to respond. A low, steady rate of responding is maintained.

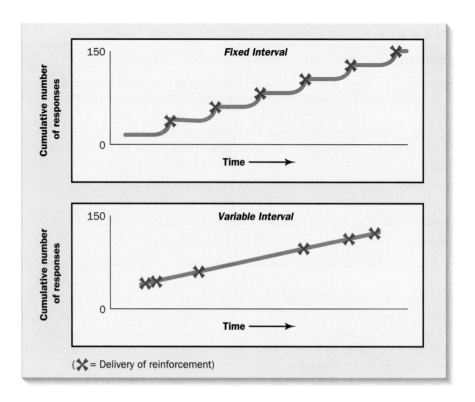

(✖ = Delivery of reinforcement)

The Partial Reinforcement Effect

Every day you look in your mailbox for a letter from a friend. After 3 months of looking, you are finally convinced your friend is not going to write; no letters have come, and there is no reason to expect any. Completely removing the reinforcer—in this case, your friend's letters—from the operant conditioning situation eventually results in *extinction*, or elimination, of the operantly conditioned response. There are some basic similarities between the way extinction is produced in classical conditioning (by omitting the UCS) and the way it is produced in operant conditioning (by removing the reinforcer).

So why is it so difficult to stop playing a slot machine once you have started? As you saw earlier in this chapter, intermittent or partial reinforcement schedules can produce very high rates of responding. This outcome is especially true of ratio schedules, in which the harder the participants work, the more reinforcement they receive. Because partial reinforcement schedules involve making a number of responses that are not reinforced, it may be difficult to tell when reinforcement has been discontinued completely and when it has merely been delayed. Because Barbara cannot tell whether the slot machine is broken or whether it will pay off the next time she puts in a quarter, she continues to play. Many players stop only when all their money is gone. Gambling is not the only behavior occurring on a partial schedule of reinforcement. Do you know a friend who has a lucky seat in class? Do you know someone who carries a rabbit's foot for luck? Do you own a "lucky" hat that you must wear to the big game? These are all examples of behaviors that could be described as superstitious. A critical thinker might collect data to determine that any supposed relation between the lucky seat and grades does not hold up to scrutiny, but few of us check the data. Superstitious behaviors are generally reinforced on partial schedules of reinforcement just like slot machines, and they are difficult to stop (Vyse, 1997).

Do you see a general pattern concerning extinction and operant conditioning? If reinforcement is delivered in a predictable manner, it should be easier to tell when it has been discontinued and when extinction has begun. Hence extinction should occur more rapidly following FR training than following VR training. Likewise, extinction

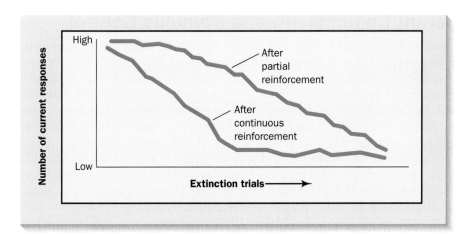

should occur more rapidly following FI training than following VI training. What's more, it should be even easier to extinguish responding that has been conditioned through the use of continuous reinforcement than responding that has been conditioned through any partial or intermittent schedule.

These facts have been verified experimentally. The **partial reinforcement effect** states that extinction of operant behavior is more difficult after partial or intermittent reinforcement than after continuous reinforcement. Have you ever taken pity on a hungry, stray cat and put out some food for it? Sometimes when it comes to your door you feed it, and other times you don't. When you finally decide you are never going to feed the cat again, you find it will not go away. The cat has been reinforced on an intermittent or partial schedule of reinforcement. It will return again and again for quite some time. Figure 5-13 shows differences in extinction after continuous and partial reinforcement training in a Skinner box.

partial reinforcement effect
Phenomenon in which extinction of an operant response following partial or intermittent reinforcement takes longer than extinction following continuous reinforcement

STUDY CHART

Comparison of Classical and Operant Conditioning

Basic Process	Classical Conditioning	Operant Conditioning
	An unconditioned stimulus (UCS) causes an unconditioned response (UCR); after pairing a conditioned stimulus (CS) with the UCS several times, the CS comes to elicit a conditioned response (CR).	Reinforcement (positive and negative) is used to shape a target response; once the response is established, a schedule of reinforcement (fixed or variable, interval or ratio) may be implemented to maintain it.
Training—Acquisition of a new response.	The CS and UCS are paired; after several pairings the CS comes to elicit a CR.	Because the target response is followed by a reinforcer, its probability or rate increases.
Extinction—Probability or frequency of a conditioned response is decreased.	The CS is presented alone, and a decrease in the CR is observed.	Reinforcement is discontinued and the rate of responding gradually decreases.
Generalization—Responses are made to stimuli other than those used in training.	Stimuli similar to the CS elicit the CR.	Responding occurs when stimuli similar to the discriminative stimulus are presented.
Discrimination—Responses are made only to stimuli used in training.	Stimuli that are similar to the CS do not elicit a CR.	Only the discriminative stimulus results in responding.

discriminative stimulus
Stimulus or signal telling the participant that responding will be reinforced

punisher
Stimulus that produces a decrease in responding; may take the form of presentation of a stimulus or termination of a stimulus

law of effect
Thorndike's view that reinforcers promote learning, whereas punishers lead to the unlearning of responses

punishment
The process of using a punisher to decrease response rate

The "open" sign is a discriminative stimulus signaling that the response of pulling the door handle will be reinforced by your being able to enter Mother Myrick's for an afternoon snack.

Operant Conditioning and Stimulus Control

Bringing a behavior under stimulus control means that a particular stimulus or signal tells the participant that its responses will be reinforced (Fetterman, 1993). In an operant conditioning chamber, for example, a green light or a tone can be a signal to a rat that pressing the lever will be reinforced. Such a signal is called a **discriminative stimulus.** When the light or tone is present, lever presses are reinforced under the schedule of reinforcement that the rat has experienced during training. When the discriminative stimulus is absent, the responses are not reinforced, and extinction occurs.

A vast number of discriminative stimuli are found in the real world. The "Open" sign in a store window is a discriminative stimulus signaling that the response of reaching for the door handle will be reinforced by your being able to enter the store and shop. The color of the traffic light at an intersection signals that the response of stopping your car (red) or proceeding through the intersection (green) will be reinforced by safe arrival at your destination. Your friend's mood serves as a signal that a response such as telling a joke or making a sympathetic remark will be appreciated.

Punishment: The Opposite of Reinforcement

We have seen that the effect of a reinforcer (either positive or negative) is to increase the likelihood of a target response. A **punisher** has the opposite effect: to decrease the likelihood or rate of responding of a target response.

Everyone seems to have an opinion about the usefulness and desirability of punishment. In the early 1900s, educator E. L. Thorndike developed an influential theory of learning. One of the main components of that theory was the **law of effect** (Thorndike, 1911), which stated that presenting a "satisfier" (a reinforcer) leads to the strengthening or learning of new responses, whereas presenting an "annoyer" (a punisher) leads to the weakening or unlearning of responses. Thorndike later concluded that punishment might not be effective, but he may have been premature in dismissing the influence of punishment. We now turn our attention to different types of punishers as well as some guidelines for using punishment effectively.

As you can see in Figure 5-14, punishers may be 1) aversive stimuli or events that are presented, or 2) pleasant stimuli or events that are removed. Remember that reinforcement (positive or negative) *increases* the rate of responding, whereas **punishment** *decreases* the rate of responding. For example, if a rat in an operant conditioning chamber receives an electric shock after pressing a lever, its rate of responding decreases. Similarly, if a child is scolded for playing in the street, that behavior is likely to occur less often. These are examples of punishment. Other examples of punishment include taking away a child's allowance, grounding a teenager, or swatting your cat for scratching the furniture. Note that punishment decreases or suppresses behavior, it rarely eliminates behavior as is the case in extinction.

Psychological Detective

We have examined how to present reinforcers to obtain a high rate of responding. How can punishment be administered in order to maximize its effects? Select a behavior that you or society find undesirable that you would like to see decreased and then formulate specific answers to this question and write them down before reading further.

If punishment is to be used effectively, there are several procedures that should be followed (Azrin & Holz, 1966; Axelrod & Apsche, 1983):

1. The punisher should be delivered (positive) or taken away (negative) *immediately after the response that is to be eliminated.* Slapping your cat for digging up your African violets while you were out will have no effect except perhaps to make you

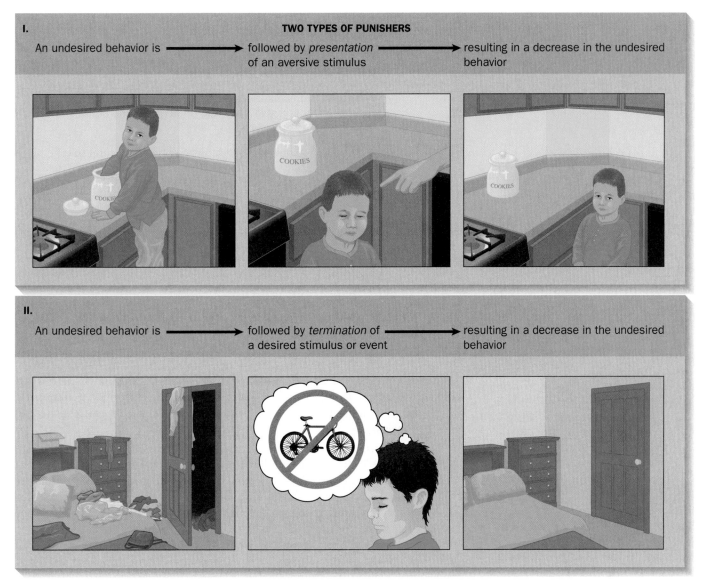

I. **TWO TYPES OF PUNISHERS**

An undesired behavior is ⟶ followed by *presentation* of an aversive stimulus ⟶ resulting in a decrease in the undesired behavior

II.

An undesired behavior is ⟶ followed by *termination* of a desired stimulus or event ⟶ resulting in a decrease in the undesired behavior

FIGURE 5-14 Diagram of the operation of punishers. There are two types of punishers: a) presenting an aversive stimulus (negative reinforcer) such as scolding, b) removing a desired stimulus (positive reinforcer) such as use of the bicycle. In both cases the end result is punishment or a decrease in the response rate of the behavior.

feel better. Why not? The cat will not see any connection between the earlier, undesirable behavior and the current punishment.

2. The punisher should be *strong enough to make a real difference*. Being grounded for two days may not matter very much, but being grounded for two months is a different story. Most people consider the use of extremely strong punishers, particularly those involving physical or violent punishment, unacceptable, if not ethically wrong. We do not want to inflict so much punishment that real damage results.

3. The punishment should be administered *after each and every undesired target response*. Punishment is not as effective when you do not punish all of the undesired responses; it must be administered consistently. Thus if you want to stop a child from using "bad" or offensive language, you should punish the child every time he or she uses it. Permitting even one episode of the undesired behavior to occur after previous punishment greatly decreases the effectiveness of the punishment.

Positive and Negative Reinforcement Compared with Punishment

Reinforcement	Results in an increase in responding
POSITIVE	A stimulus is presented after a target response; an increase in responding occurs (e.g., receiving good grades increases the amount of time one studies).
NEGATIVE	A stimulus is removed after a target response; an increase in responding occurs (e.g., if playing music reduces boredom, the frequency of playing music increases).
Punishment	**Results in a decrease in responding**
POSITIVE	A stimulus is presented after a target response; a decrease in responding occurs (e.g., washing a child's mouth out with soap for cursing reduces the number of curse words the child says).
NEGATIVE	A stimulus is removed after a target response; a decrease in responding occurs (e.g., Saturday morning cartoon privileges are taken away because the child's chores have not been completed).

Studying Modern-Day Pavlov's Dogs

STUDY TIP

Create an outline summarizing the basic points of the material on the Skinner Box, shaping, and schedules of reinforcement.

4. There should be *no unauthorized escape from the punisher*. If the punishment is not applied uniformly, its effects will be weakened. Rats are very clever; frequently they learn how to hang upside down from the top of a cage to avoid an electric shock to their feet.

5. If you use punishment, be prepared for the possibility of *aggressive responding*. Rats do not like to be shocked, children do not like to have their television privileges taken away, and spankings can elicit behaviors other than crying. Children who are spanked may retaliate by kicking and biting. Note that aggressive responding may be directed toward a person, an animal, or an object that cannot retaliate, such as a pet dog or cat; such behavior is called *displaced aggression*. Nor does aggressive behavior always end when the punishment ends. As a child, did you ever try to "get even" with your parents after being punished? In short, punishment can teach a child to use force or other violence against people.

6. Provide an *alternative desired behavior* that can gain a reinforcer for the person. Giving a child a spanking for playing in the street may not be especially effective if there is nowhere else to play. Clearly, it is very difficult to use punishment effectively. Perhaps the best solution is to reinforce an alternate desired behavior. The use of "redirecting" as a disciplinary technique in child-care settings provides an example. When a child engages in an inappropriate behavior, the child is removed from the "scene" and given another, appropriate activity to engage in. Praising the child for success in this appropriate activity is reinforcement of an alternate, desired behavior.

The Study Chart above summarizes the difference between reinforcement and punishment.

REVIEW SUMMARY

1. **Operant conditioning** occurs when an organism performs a target response that is followed by a reinforcer, which increases the probability that the behavior (target response) will occur again.

2. All reinforcers increase the frequency of the response they follow. **Positive reinforcers** are presented after the target response has been made; **negative reinforcers** are withdrawn or taken away after the target response has been made.

Primary reinforcers (for example, food) satisfy basic biological needs; **secondary (conditioned) reinforcers** (for example, money) acquire their power to reinforce behavior by being associated with primary reinforcers.

3. Complex responses may be acquired gradually through the process of **shaping** (*successive approximations*). Psychologists can keep track of the rate of responding by using a *cumulative record*, which keeps track of all target responses made by an organism across time.

4. Once a behavior has been acquired, it may be reinforced according to a particular **schedule of reinforcement.** When a **ratio schedule** is in effect, the number of responses is important. *Fixed-ratio (FR) schedules* require that a set number of responses be made before a reinforcer is delivered; *variable-ratio (VR) schedules* require that the participant perform differing numbers of responses to obtain a reinforcer. With an **interval schedule,** a certain amount of time must pass before a response is reinforced. With a *fixed-interval (FI) schedule*, the time interval is constant; the time interval changes after each reinforcer is delivered when a *variable-interval (VI) schedule* is used. Ratio schedules generally produce higher rates of responding than interval schedules.

5. Operant responses that are not reinforced each time during training take much longer to extinguish than ones that have received continuous reinforcement. This phenomenon is known as the **partial** (intermittent) **reinforcement effect.**

6. A discriminative stimulus signals that responses will be reinforced. Behavior is said to be under stimulus control when responding occurs only when the discriminative stimulus is present.

7. The opposite of reinforcement, **punishment,** involves presentation or withdrawal of stimuli called **punishers,** which results in a suppression of the target behavior.

✓ CHECK YOUR PROGRESS

1. For each of the following situations, find the response that is being reinforced, identify the reinforcer, and determine which schedule of reinforcement is being used.

   a. Playing the lottery has become so popular that people line up to buy lottery tickets. Sometimes they win, and sometimes they lose.
   b. A friend has a part-time job making telephone calls to convince people to sign up for a credit card. For every 25 new customers who sign up, your friend receives a bonus.
   c. Each morning, rain or shine, your dog, McDuff, comes to the back door to wait for his breakfast.
   d. Every time Alan experiences a headache, he takes the medication that his physician prescribed and the pain is relieved enough that he can go about his daily routine without any problems.

2. For each of the following situations, indicate whether a positive or negative reinforcer is being used.

   a. A rat presses a bar to turn off an electric foot shock.
   b. A child digs through a new box of cereal to get a prize.
   c. A teenager pretends to be sick in order to receive extra attention.
   d. A student pretends to be sick in order to avoid having to make a presentation in class.

3. For each of the following, indicate whether partial reinforcement is involved. If it is, indicate the likely schedule of reinforcement.

   a. Receiving praise for each good grade you make.
   b. Sometimes getting caught for speeding.
   c. Having never been caught for cheating in high school.
   d. Occasionally finding money on the ground as you walk to class.
   e. Playing basketball on a team that won 3 out of 15 games last year.

   f. Driving around and around a full parking lot until someone leaves and you can park your car.

4. Explain why learning to play the piano would be an example of shaping. What would the reinforcer or reinforcers be in this situation?

5. In which type of conditioning is the learner's behavior important in bringing about the learning?

   a. backward conditioning
   b. classical conditioning
   c. operant conditioning
   d. Pavlovian conditioning

6. What is an event or stimulus that makes the behavior it follows more likely to occur?

   a. reinforcer
   b. punishment
   c. conditioned stimulus
   d. unconditioned stimulus

7. What is the graph that shows the pattern of a rat's responding in a Skinner box?

   a. shaping record
   b. response pattern
   c. cumulative record
   d. reinforcement pattern

8. The effect of _____ is to decrease the likelihood or rate of a target response.

   a. punishment
   b. positive reinforcement
   c. negative reinforcement
   d. intermittent reinforcement

9. What is the partial reinforcement effect?

a. Extinction after continuous reinforcement is more difficult.

b. Extinction after partial reinforcement is more difficult.

c. Learning under continuous reinforcement is more difficult.

d. Learning under partial reinforcement is more difficult.

10. What two opposing processes are involved in creating discriminative stimuli?

a. shaping and cognition

b. discrimination and generalization

c. positive and negative reinforcement

d. observational learning and modeling

COGNITIVE AND SOCIAL PERSPECTIVES ON LEARNING

The door to the garage was ajar and Mary became frightened; she was afraid that someone might be trying to rob the house. Trembling, she peeked into the garage to discover that her 3-year-old son was in the driver's seat, fiddling with the car key. Suddenly the engine started to run and Mary made a dash to the car to prevent an accident. At a family gathering several weeks after this event, Mary was discussing what had happened; family members seemed quite surprised that a 3-year-old could start the car. One of Mary's cousins, Sally, is a psychology major who had some ideas concerning what happened that day. *How would psychologists explain how this 3-year-old managed to start the car?*

We encountered contingency theory and blocking in our study of classical conditioning (see pages 193–194). These processes suggest that classical conditioning is not a simple mechanical process; rather, mental activity or thought processes (cognition) are in- volved to some degree. The relation of cognition to basic learning processes, such as in- sight learning and latent learning, has been studied for many decades.

The Role of Cognition

Two of the most compelling examples of how cognitive factors are involved in learning are insight learning and latent learning. We will discuss these next.

Insight Learning. The importance of cognition to operant conditioning can be seen in the process known as insight learning. **Insight learning** is a form of operant conditioning in which we restructure our perceptual stimuli (we see things in a different way), make an instrumental (operant) response, and generalize this behavior to other situations. In short, it is not blind, trial-and-error learning that develops gradually but a type of learning that occurs suddenly and relies on cognitive processes. It is the "aha!" experience we have when we suddenly solve a problem.

Research by the Gestalt psychologist (see Chapter 1) Wolfgang Köhler (1927) ex- emplifies insight learning. Using chimpanzees as his test animals, Köhler gave them the

insight learning
sudden grasp of a concept or the solution to a problem that results from perceptual restructuring; typi- cally characterized by an immediate change in behavior

following problem. A bunch of bananas was suspended out of reach of the chimps. To reach the bananas, the chimps had to stack three boxes on top of one another and then put together the pieces of a jointed pole to form a single, longer pole. After several unsuccessful attempts at jumping and trying to reach the bananas, Köhler's star pupil, Sultan, appeared to survey the situation (mentally rearrange the stimulus elements that were present) and solve the problem in the prescribed manner. Köhler believed that Sultan had achieved insight into the correct solution of the problem.

Consider the solution of a particularly difficult math problem. You struggle and struggle to solve the problem, without success. In frustration you set the problem aside and turn to another assignment. All of a sudden you understand what is required to work the math problem successfully; you've had an "aha!" experience. How you perceive the situation has changed; insight has occurred. Once this problem has been solved, you are able to solve others like it. Similarly, one of the authors of this book works on word puzzles; the daily newspaper carries two of them almost every day. Sometimes he struggles to rearrange the mixed up letters to form words, and sometimes the answers appear almost instantly. Quite often (especially after he takes a brief break from the puzzle), the answer seems to occur quickly, as insight has been achieved.

Thus cognitive processes are important in helping us to adapt to our environment. As we shall see, other organisms—even rats—may use cognitive processes as they go about their daily activities.

Latent Learning. Psychologist Edward C. Tolman presented persuasive evidence for the use of cognitive processes in basic learning in his study of maze learning by rats (Tolman & Honzik, 1930). Tolman is associated most often with his study of **latent learning,** which occurs when learning has taken place but is not demonstrated. In one of Tolman's most famous studies, three groups of rats learned a complex maze that had many choices and dead ends. One group of rats was always reinforced with food for successfully completing the maze. These animals gradually made fewer and fewer errors until, after 11 days of training, their performance was nearly perfect. A second group was never reinforced; the rats continued to make numerous errors. The third (latent-learning) group of animals did not receive reinforcement for the first 10 days of training. On the 11th day, reinforcement was provided. The behavior of these animals on the 12th day is of crucial importance. If learning occurs in a gradual, trial-and-error manner, the rats' performance on the 12th day should not have differed much from their performance on the 11th day. If, however, the rats used cognitive processes to learn to navigate the maze, they would exhibit dramatic behavior changes.

In fact, on the 12th day these rats solved the maze as quickly as the rats who had been continually reinforced (see Figure 5-15). How did these rats learn so quickly? Tolman argued that by wandering through the maze for 10 days before the introduction of reinforcement, these animals had formed a cognitive map of the maze. In other words, they had learned to solve the maze, but this knowledge had remained latent (unused) until reinforcement was introduced on the 11th day. Then, on the 12th day, these rats demonstrated that they knew how to get to the location of the reinforcement. Their latent learning had manifested itself. The implications of this finding are clear: It is possible to learn a behavior, yet that learning is not directly observed.

latent learning
Learning that has occurred but is not demonstrated

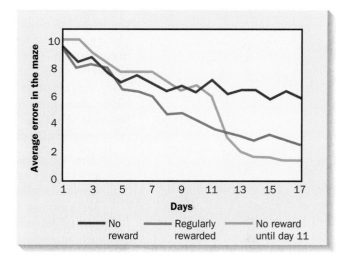

FIGURE 5-15 Results of Tolman and Honzik's maze running experiment are not easily explained by operant conditioning concepts. This research was a significant contributor to the development of more cognitively oriented views of how organisms learn.

Source: Tolman & Honzik, 1930.

STUDY TIP

Create a visual organizer that shows behaviors with cognitive requirements (insight learning, latent learning, and so on) and their most important elements.

Observational Learning

As the previous discussion suggests, our behavior and the behavior of other animals is not just mechanically stamped in or out. There is a degree of cognitive activity or processing of information that is involved when we learn. Consider the following example.

observational learning (modeling)
Learning that occurs through watching and imitating the behaviors of others

Imagine that you have given permission for your 6-year-old son and 8-year-old daughter to participate in a psychological experiment at the local university. During the experiment each child watches an adult play with a large inflatable doll that can double as a punching bag. Because the doll's base contains sand, the doll bounces back when it is punched and then is ready for more punches. The adult gives the doll a merciless beating; then each child is given an opportunity to play with the doll. What can this experiment tell us about learning?

For many years psychologists believed a participant must actually perform an operant response for learning to occur. In the early 1960s, Albert Bandura and his colleagues changed this view (Bandura, Ross, & Ross, 1963). As you will recall from Chapter 1, they found that children who observed an adult hitting and punching an inflatable Bobo doll were likely to repeat those behaviors when they were given a chance to play with the doll. Control participants, who had not observed the adult model, behaved less aggressively. Because the children made no responses while they were watching, the researchers concluded that simply observing the behavior and reinforcement (or punishment) of another participant could result in learning (Bandura, 1977). Such learning is termed **observational learning** or modeling. Because the observation of other people is a central factor in this form of learning, this approach is often called social learning theory.

While a great deal of concern has been raised concerning the possible effects of learning violence from television, a more recent concern focuses on video games, which can be highly violent. Researchers Craig Anderson and Karen Dill (2000) found that playing violent games was positively correlated with aggressive behavior and delinquency in children. The cautions we raised concerning correlational evidence in Chapter 1 should lead you to wonder if there is a causal relationship here. In a second study, the researchers found that exposing a random sample of children to a graphically violent video game had a direct and immediate impact on their aggressive thoughts and behavior. What's more, a review of the literature on the effects of video game violence led researchers (Anderson & Bushman, 2001) to the following conclusion:

> The results clearly support the hypothesis that exposure to violent video games poses a public-health threat to children and youth, including college-age individuals. Exposure is positively associated with heightened levels of aggression in young adults and children, in experimental and nonexperimental designs, and in males and females. Exposure is negatively associated with prosocial behavior (p. 358).

New York Yankee and Hall of Fame baseball player, Yogi Berra, once said "You can learn a lot by watching." There is growing concern that many young people are modeling the violence they see in movies and video games. Today's video games are realistic, attractive, exciting, and captivating. The challenge in the future may be to design games that are as equally attractive and exciting yet provide opportunities to model prosocial and non-violent forms of behavior.

TABLE 5.3

Major Effects of Vicarious Consequences

Vicarious Reinforcement	Vicarious Punishment
• Conveys information about which behaviors are appropriate in which settings	• Conveys information about which behaviors are inappropriate in which settings
• Arousal of the emotional responses of pleasure and satisfaction in the observer	• Tends to exert restraining influence on imitation of modeled behavior
• After repeated reinforcements, incentive-motivational effects are generated; behavior acquires functional value	• Tends to devalue the model's status because the behavior did not lead to a reinforcement

Adapted from Gredler, 2001.

If you stop to think about it, observational learning is the main way we learn about our culture and its customs and traditions. Let's return to the vignette that opened this section. Observational learning is most likely how Mary's 3-year-old son learned to start the car. He has most likely observed his mother and father put the key in the ignition and turn it hundreds if not thousands of times.

One of the keys to observational learning appears to be that the participant identifies with the person being observed. If we put ourselves in the other person's place for a moment, we are better able to imagine the effects of the reinforcer or punisher. This phenomenon is called *vicarious reinforcement* or *vicarious punishment*. Table 5-3 describes the major effects of vicarious (through another) consequences and their implications for learning.

Observational learning is a widespread phenomenon. For example, it is even found among a number of animals. For example, rats that observed the extinction behavior of other rats subsequently stopped responding more rapidly than rats that did not observe extinction performance (Heyes, Jaldow, & Dawson, 1993). In another experiment, monkeys reared in a laboratory didn't fear snakes. After watching another group of monkeys react fearfully to snakes, however, the nonfearful monkeys developed a pronounced fear of snakes (Cook et al., 1985).

Attempts to influence behavior through observational learning occur every day. Turn on the television and you are bombarded with commercials, which are nothing more than a form of observational learning. If you drive this kind of car, wear these clothes, use this brand of perfume, shower with this soap, use this shampoo, and eat this kind of breakfast, you will be rich, famous, powerful, sexy, and so forth, just like the models in the commercials.

According to the social learning theory proposed by Bandura (1986), for observational learning to be effective, the following conditions must be present:

1. You must pay attention to what the other person is doing and what happens to him or her.

2. You probably will not make the modeled response immediately, so you need to store a memory of the situation you have observed. For example, catchy advertising jingles that run through our heads continuously help us remember a particular commercial and its message (see Chapter 6).

3. You must be able to repeat or reproduce the behavior you observed. It might be wonderful to dream of owning a Porsche, but most of us will never be able to reproduce the behaviors needed to obtain one, regardless of how often we watch the commercial.

Observational Learning and Human Aggression

BANDURA
PLEASE WATCH
VIDEOTAPE
ON HOW
TO KNOCK

Palladino, Handelsman, & Butler

Psi Chi Newsletter. Reprinted with the permission of Psi Chi.

4. Your motivational state must be appropriate to the behavior you have learned through observation. Watching numerous commercials of people drinking a particular soft drink will not normally cause you to purchase one if you are not thirsty.

5. You must pay attention to discriminative stimuli. Sometimes we do not choose the best time and place to imitate someone else's behavior. For example, it would not be wise for teenagers to model some of their peers' behaviors at the dinner table.

Observational learning has also been used to reduce or eliminate phobias. For example, adults with an intense fear of snakes were shown live models handling live snakes (Bandura, Blanchard, & Ritter, 1969). These individuals were then encouraged to handle the snakes themselves. A final test indicated that they had less fear of snakes than those people who had watched a film of people handling snakes and a control group who had received no treatment.

We have presented this chapter's various concepts and principles separately to make your learning and understanding easier. In reality, classical conditioning, operant conditioning, observational learning, and punishment are not mutually exclusive. They can, and do, occur simultaneously.

STUDY TIP

Rewrite in your own words, and provide two examples to illustrate, the conditions necessary for effective observational learning.

R E V I E W   S U M M A R Y

1. **Insight learning** involves restructuring our perceptual stimuli to achieve the solution to a problem. Such perceptual restructuring and solutions typically occur rapidly.

2. **Latent learning** occurs when learning has taken place but is not demonstrated until a later time.

3. **Observational learning** takes place when we observe and identify with the behaviors of others. Advertisements and television commercials appeal to this process. Televised violence may result in observational learning and lead to an increase in violent behaviors.

✓ C H E C K   Y O U R   P R O G R E S S

1. Which of the following situations involve(s) observational learning?

   a. Learning to drive by taking a driver education course that emphasizes behind-the-wheel experience
   b. Pushing the remote control to change channels on the television
   c. Using a video to learn how to play golf
   d. Seeing friends go by on their motorcycles, saying to yourself, "I bet I can do that" and trying it
   e. Salivating every time you pass your favorite restaurant

2. Concern has been raised about violence in television and films because of research evidence about

   a. modeling.
   b. classical conditioning.
   c. operant conditioning.
   d. negative reinforcement.

3. Which of the following is the best summary of the evidence on the relation between video game violence and aggression?

   a. To date, only correlational research has been reported.
   b. There is little relation between the two; extreme cases are highlighted in the media.

   c. Although the correlational research finds an association, no laboratory research support any conclusion beyond an association.
   d. Both correlational and laboratory-based research support the existence of a relation between the two.

4. After running rats through mazes, Tolman found evidence for

   a. modeling.
   b. latent learning.
   c. classical conditioning.
   d. vicarious conditioning.

5. Which of the following is another common name for the approach that Bandura described in his famous research involving Bobo dolls?

   a. modeling
   b. latent learning
   c. cognitive imagery
   d. respondent conditioning

6. Evidence offered by Wolfgang Köhler supported the existence of the phenomenon of

   a. insight learning.
   b. operant conditioning.

c. respondent conditioning
d. vicarious conditioning

7. You are given the assignment of writing a paper on the work of Wolfgang Köhler, Edward Tolman, and Albert Bandura. Which of the following would be the best summary of the main points you will make in your paper?

a. Reinforcers are important in all forms of learning.
b. Learning is the result of either operant or classical conditioning.
c. Some cognitive processing of information occurs when we learn.
d. The primary ways in which we learn can be traced to our reflex actions.

ANSWERS: 1. a. Not observational learning **b.** Not observational learning **c.** Observational learning **d.** Observational learning **e.** Not observational learning **2. a 3. d 4. b 5. a 6. a 7. c**

ANSWERS To Psychological Detective on Classical Conditioning

PAGE 186

For the food example, the UCS is the food in your mouth, and the UCR is salivation that occurs when the food is in your mouth. The CS is the name of the food that is spoken to you, and the CR is the salivation that occurs when you hear the name of your favorite food. In the example of Scott's fear of closed spaces, the UCS is being locked in the abandoned refrigerator and the UCR is nearly suffocating. Anything that resembles a closed space is the CS, and the fear he has to closed spaces is the CR.

Memory

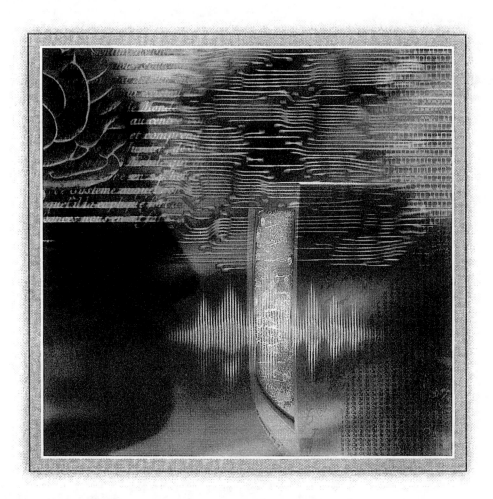

CHAPTER OUTLINE

In Chapter 5 we examined the basic learning processes, especially classical conditioning and operant (instrumental) conditioning, that are characteristic of a wide variety of organisms. In this chapter we highlight some uniquely human aspects of learning and memory. We begin with early studies of memory, giving special attention to the pioneering work of Hermann Ebbinghaus. We then examine the phenomenon of memory in detail and discuss several recent developments in the study of memory. After a look at some techniques for improving your memory, we explore the physiological basis of learning and memory.

In addition to helping us adapt more effectively to our environment, the processes covered in this chapter clear the way for improved communication and the storage of knowledge. As you might have sensed, we are beginning to focus on the processes that define what makes us human and the way we function as individuals and as members of groups.

Before we begin an in-depth examination of memory, let's define our topic. This task may be more difficult than you think; memory is one of those abilities we take for granted. Certainly memory is related to learning. If we did not learn or acquire new knowledge, we would have nothing to store in our memories. In many instances memories last an incredibly long time. Putting these ideas together, we can tentatively define **memory** as a system or process by which the products or results of learning are stored for future use.

INITIAL STUDIES

When Sue graduated from high school, she enrolled in a college several hundred miles from her home. After completing college, she accepted a job as a YMCA program director in a large metropolitan area. Because her trips back home were infrequent, she lost contact with her high school classmates. She has not seen most of them in years. Her 25th high school reunion is now approaching, and Sue wonders how good her memory is. How many of her former classmates will she recognize? *How good is our memory for faces after a long interval of time?*

The scientific study of human memory is almost as old as scientific psychology itself. The pioneer in this area was Hermann Ebbinghaus, a patient and thorough German psychologist who conducted his studies of memory in the late 1800s and early 1900s (Ebbinghaus, 1885). Ebbinghaus asked questions such as, "What conditions are favorable (or unfavorable) for linking or associating the words, sounds, and visual stimuli that make up our store of learned knowledge?"

Because everyday words already have meanings and associations attached to them (that is, some learning already has taken place), Ebbinghaus decided not to use them as stimuli in his experiments. Instead, he invented special stimuli that he called *nonsense syllables*. **Nonsense syllables** are usually composed of three letters arranged in a consonant-vowel-consonant sequence. For example, *gok, taf, ceb,* and *tup* are nonsense syllables. Because nonsense syllables were supposed to have no meaning,

memory
System or process by which the products or results of learning are stored for future use

nonsense syllables
Stimuli used to study memory; typically composed of a consonant-vowel-consonant sequence

Ebbinghaus believed that he would be able to study how associations between these stimuli are formed without any other factors, such as previous learning, complicating the results.

Armed with these new stimuli, Ebbinghaus began his studies with only one research participant: himself. In most instances the task consisted of memorizing lists of nonsense syllables. Before you start questioning the importance of studying how one learns a sequence of nonsense syllables, think about all the lists or sequences that we learn (Curran & Keele, 1993). As grade school children, we learn the alphabet, the names of the presidents, and the multiplication tables. As we grow up, we learn telephone numbers, ZIP codes, addresses, and lock combinations. Ebbinghaus's studies of lists were actually quite relevant.

Psychological Detective

Ebbinghaus's next step was to devise a way to measure memory. Now, if someone says that all you have to do to measure memory is to ask a participant what he or she has learned, you might be skeptical. Measuring memory is more complicated than that. Before you read further, write down some ideas about how you might measure memory when a participant is learning a list of nonsense syllables. Be sure to identify the specific response you are measuring.

Hermann Ebbinghaus (1850–1909) was a pioneer in the study of human memory.

serial learning
Learning procedure in which material that has been learned must be repeated in the order in which it was presented; also known as *ordered recall*

paired-associate learning
Learning procedure in which items to be recalled are learned in pairs. During recall, one member of the pair is presented and the other is to be recalled

free recall
Learning procedure in which material that has been learned may be repeated in any order

Ebbinghaus's method for measuring learning of lists of nonsense syllables was called **serial learning** (also known as *ordered recall*). As a participant, you would be asked to repeat the material in the *order* in which it had been presented. This technique shows whether you have mastered the correct sequence (Baddeley, Papagno, & Andrade, 1993; Watkins & Le Compte, 1991). For example, if you dial or key in 343-7355 on the telephone instead of 343-3755 (the number that was supposed to be learned), serial learning is not perfect.

A second method, **paired-associate learning,** was developed by another early German memory researcher, George Elias Müller, a few years after Ebbinghaus began his work. In this task you associate an unfamiliar word or nonsense syllable with a familiar word. This technique is often used to learn the vocabulary for a foreign language—remember the flash cards you used to learn Spanish or French? The test consists of presenting the familiar word and then producing the foreign word associated with it.

A third method of measuring learning is **free recall.** Here the task is to remember as many items as possible, regardless of their sequence. Naming the major parts of a neuron (see Chapter 2) or the components of classical conditioning (see Chapter 5) are examples of free recall. Free recall is now the preferred method of measuring learning.

The Curve of Forgetting

An important finding of Ebbinghaus's research is the *curve of forgetting*. Ebbinghaus found that our memory for learned material is best right after the learning session. As time passes, we forget more and more. This basic finding has been replicated (reproduced) numerous times since Ebbinghaus discovered it. As you can see from Figure 7-1, Jenkins and Dallenbach (1924) found that participants recalled the most when they were tested immediately after learning. The participants learned a list of 10 nonsense syllables and then were asked to recall the list ½ hour, and 2, 4, and 8 hours later. One-half hour after the initial training session, the participants were able to recall only half of the list; their performance continued to deteriorate with the passage of time. The importance of these results is clear: You can expect your best recall shortly

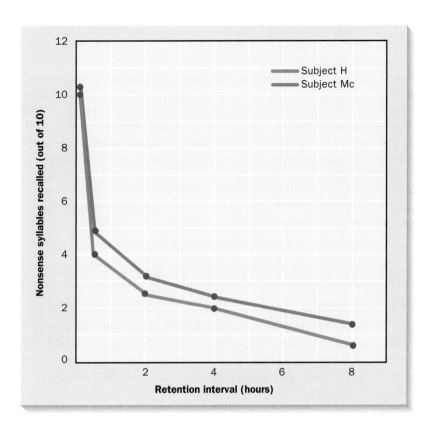

FIGURE 7-1 Number of nonsense syllables recalled at various intervals following learning. In agreement with Ebbinghaus's research, the greatest decrease in recall occurred very shortly after learning had taken place.

Source: Jenkins & Dallenbach, 1924.

after a learning session. This is why students cram for a test as close to the time of the test as possible.

7.1

Recognition and Relearning

Researchers have developed two additional procedures for measuring memory, the recognition test and the relearning test, to supplement the three methods just described. In the **recognition test,** participants pick out the items to which they were previously exposed from a longer list that also contains unfamiliar items (Haist, Shimamura, & Squire, 1992; Yonelinas, Hockley, & Murdock, 1992). This type of memory task is involved in taking a multiple-choice test. Recall Sue from this chapter's opening vignette. When she attends her high school reunion, Sue will be performing a similar task in attempting to recognize her former classmates.

How good is our memory for faces after a long interval of time? The results of a research project indicate that our ability to remember faces for a long time is quite good (Bruck, Cavanagh, & Ceci, 1991). The researchers asked participants to match current photographs of former high school classmates with photos taken approximately 25 years earlier. Those individuals did much better at matching photos than a group of participants who had not gone to high school with the people in the photos.

A **relearning test** is exactly what the term implies. After the passage of a certain amount of time (called a *retention interval*), the original material is learned again. For example, you might study a list of 15 nonsense syllables on Monday afternoon. You study the list until you can repeat it three times without an error; this level of performance, your *performance criterion*, is established by the researcher. One week later you study the same list. The researcher calculates the amount of time, or number of trials, it takes to relearn the material so that you can match your performance criterion; and the two scores are compared. If learning occurred more rapidly the second time you studied the list, this difference is reported as a **savings score** (or *relearning score*). A good

recognition test
Test in which retention is measured by the ability to pick out previously learned items from a list that also contains unfamiliar items

relearning test
Test of retention that compares the time or trials required to learn material a second time with the time or trials required to learn the material the first time

savings score
Difference between the time or trials originally required to learn material and the time or trials required to relearn the material; also known as *relearning score*

encoding
First stage of the memory process; in it information is transformed or coded (a transduction process) into a form that can be processed further and stored

example of relearning is studying for a comprehensive final exam. Chances are good that, with the right concentration, it will take you less time and effort to relearn the material.

Although the work of Ebbinghaus and other early psychologists provided a basic understanding of human learning and memory, much more has been discovered since then. Today few psychologists study how people learn lists of nonsense syllables; they are more interested in examining the processes by which memories are formed, stored, retrieved, and used. This shift in interest occurred because most psychologists abandoned the mechanical, association-based model of memory in which items were simply linked to other items. A new view of the mind began to emerge—one suggesting that the mind is an active agent with many other organizational properties. This developing view prompted different questions. How do we store items in memory? Once memories are stored, how do we retrieve them?

TRADITIONAL MODELS OF MEMORY

Anne is phenomenal! She knows every client by name and can recall the details of particular accounts with ease. She always makes the right decision, often under extreme pressure, and never seems ruffled or disturbed. Business appointments with her are a pleasure. Her friends have frequently commented that her memory is "like a computer." *In what ways might a computer and human memory be alike?*

Human Memory as an Information Processing System

7.2 *Live!* psych

Like the computer, researchers have characterized human memory as an information-processing system that has three separate stages: an *input* or *encoding stage*, a *storage stage*, and a *retrieval stage*, during which an already-stored memory is called into consciousness (see Figure 7-2). Let's take a closer look at each of these stages.

Encoding. In the **encoding** stage, sensory information is received and coded, or transformed into neural impulses that can be processed further or stored for later use.

FIGURE 7-2 Because it has separate encoding, storage, and retrieval stages, human memory is similar to an information processing system.

Just as the computer changes keyboard entries into usable electronic symbols that may be stored on a computer disk, sensory information is *transduced,* or converted, into neural impulses (see Chapter 3), that can be used and stored by the brain. In addition to transduction, a great deal of the encoding process appears to be devoted to rehearsing (practicing or repeating) the input, organizing it into groups, and relating the groups to already stored information. Encoding may even involve giving this information a special name or label.

Suppose that as you drive to school, you listen to a new song on the radio. The sounds are transduced into neural impulses, which are then recognized as making up a song. You remember hearing similar songs and classify the one you are listening to as belonging to that group—for example, "smooth jazz" or "oldie." This procedure is very much like installing a computer program; information is encoded in the central processing unit, and the user gives it a name and file path that helps relate it to similar programs.

What memories does this grade school science class help you retrieve?

Storage. The second stage of memory processing is **storage.** Like the computer program, the encoded information must be stored in the memory system if we plan to retain it for any length of time or use it more than once. Although some bits of information are stored briefly, used only once, and then discarded, others, like certain telephone numbers, are used frequently and are therefore stored on a more permanent basis.

Retrieval. Once a computer program has been named and stored, we can "call it up" by its name and use it again. Human memory works in much the same way. When we recall or bring a memory into consciousness, we have retrieved it. This recall process is known as memory **retrieval.**

We do not store information in memory randomly. The information is organized and related to already stored information in ways that allow us to use certain cues to retrieve it.

Psychological Detective

To see how the retrieval process works, write down the name of your fourth-grade teacher. After you have done so, describe the process that led you to that particular name.

The words *fourth-grade teacher* are the stimuli that activated your memories of the fourth grade. As you retrieve these memories while searching for the name of your teacher, you may recall your school building, your fourth-grade classroom, the ride to school on the bus, and the names of your classmates. In turn, each of these memories could serve as a stimulus to retrieve related memories. There are probably many stimuli that could help you retrieve the name of your fourth-grade teacher.

In some instances, the network of related memories is small and only a few specific cues will successfully retrieve a certain memory. For example, suppose you are in the supermarket trying to choose a brand of detergent when an apparent stranger begins a conversation with you. The "stranger" is talking as if you have known each other for some time, but you have no idea what this person's name is. Why do we find it so difficult to recall some people's names? Knowing about retrieval cues helps answer this question. When the stranger reminds you that you met last Saturday at a party, it is as though a light goes on. Suddenly you remember who this person is and where you met. Because you met under special circumstances, the party, only cues related to that

storage
Second stage of the memory process; in it information is placed in the memory system. This stage may involve either brief or long-term storage of memories

retrieval
Third stage of the memory process; in it stored memories are brought into consciousness

situation will retrieve the memory of the meeting. When those specific cues are presented, the memory returns.

Myth or Science

How often have you heard it said that someone has a "photographic memory"? Although it is likely that nothing more than someone with a very good memory is being described, there are people who appear to have this ability. People with *eidetic imagery* (the technical term for photographic memory) say that they can look at a written page, person, or drawing and then later mentally see that image (Guenther, 1998). It is truly as if these people take photographs and store them in their minds for future use. For example, when you need the information from a page in a book, you simply retrieve that page from memory and read it. Would this ability be great at test time!

Leonardo da Vinci and Napoleon Bonaparte are two of the most famous people with photographic memory. Apparently Leonardo could draw detailed portraits of people after meeting them only once. Likewise, Napoleon could glance at a map briefly and later recall the location of every stream, town, and hill. Clearly, there are some interesting processes of storage and retrieval occurring here.

STUDY TIP

Construct a visual diagram showing the human memory as an information processing system, including the stages from the stages-of-memory model. Include short definitions in your diagram.

The Stages-of-Memory Model

Our encoding-storage-retrieval model of memory would serve our purpose quite well if we had only one type of memory to store. We have, however, at least three well-defined types of memory: sensory memory, short-term memory, and long-term memory. So the information processing model must be modified to read as follows:

$$\text{Encoding} \rightarrow \text{"type" of storage} \rightarrow \text{retrieval}$$

The rest of this section describes the three types of memory and the ways they are used in our daily lives. The stages-of-memory model that we discuss is shown in Figure 7-3. This influential model, developed in 1971 by Richard Atkinson and Richard Shiffrin, is sometimes referred to as the *Atkinson-Shiffrin Model*.

Sensory Memory.   As the name implies, **sensory memory** is a memory or storage of sensory events such as sights, sounds, and tastes, with no further processing or interpretation. Because sensory memory provides us with a fleeting image of the stimuli present at a particular moment, it has the potential to be huge. Because many stimuli are received all the time, sensory memory appears to last only briefly, about 0.5 of a second to 1.0 second, depending on which sensory system is involved.

Sensory information that is not selected for further processing by higher brain centers decays and is replaced by incoming stimuli. As you saw in Chapter 3, we cannot

sensory memory
Very brief (0.5 to 1.0 second) but extensive memory for sensory events

FIGURE 7-3   The stages-of-memory model.
Source: Atkinson & Shiffrin, 1971.

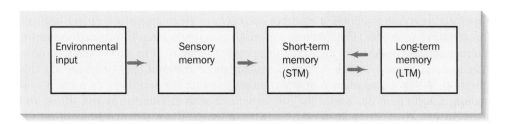

attend to and process all the stimuli we receive; some of them must be filtered out. Stimuli that we attend to are those that are selected from sensory memory for further processing; other stimuli are lost.

After a moment's reflection, you might ask, "If sensory memories last such a short time, how can you demonstrate that they really exist?" In a compelling set of experiments on this topic, researchers presented a display of 12 letters to participants (Sperling, 1960). The pattern might look like this:

D   C   R   M

Y   N   S   V

I   E   G   Z

In the original experiments, the entire pattern was flashed for ¹⁄₂₀ of a second. The participants then recalled and wrote down as many letters as possible. Typically they were able to identify only 4 or 5 of the 12 letters. That does not seem like good evidence for any kind of memory! Some changes made in later experiments, however, produced dramatic improvement. One modification involved assigning a different audible tone to each row of the stimulus pattern: a high tone to the top row, a medium tone to the middle row, and a low tone to the bottom row. As before, the entire pattern was flashed for ¹⁄₂₀ of a second. Immediately afterward, one of the three tones was sounded, and the participants were asked to write down the letters in the row designated by the tone.

Imagine you are a participant in such an experiment. The pattern of letters has just been presented. Now you hear the medium tone, so you write down as many of the letters from the middle row as you can remember. How many letters do you think you will remember?

Sperling found that when tones accompanied the presentation of the letters, participants correctly identified three or four letters in a row, regardless of which row was signaled. Clearly, much more information was potentially available in memory than the original experiments had indicated. Because they did not know in advance which row would be signaled, the participants had to have a memory of all the letters when one of the tones was sounded. Timing is important, however; when the tone was sounded a second after the letters were presented, the participants could remember only one or two letters in the designated row. Thus a significant amount of information is lost from sensory memory very quickly after the stimuli are presented.

The amount of information lost from sensory memory is not a fixed quantity. Rather, it depends on the amount of processing effort that is expended in the next stage of memory. We can either process a few items very thoroughly and lose a great deal from sensory memory, or we can process a larger number of items less thoroughly and retain more from sensory memory.

Because it is important and easy to study, we have been talking exclusively about visual sensory memory. Do we have brief sensory memories for our other senses? Although not much research has been done on this topic, the answer appears to be yes.

Psychologist Ulrich Neisser (1967) proposed the existence of an auditory sensory memory. His proposal was supported by a study in which participants heard simultaneous lists of letters from three loudspeakers in different locations (Darwin, Turvey, & Crowder, 1972). If the students tried to report the letters from all three loudspeakers, they did poorly; if they were asked to repeat the letters from a specific speaker immediately after the list was read, they did much better. If a delay was imposed, their performance decreased noticeably. These results are very similar to those Sperling reported for visual stimuli. You can also experience auditory sensory memory. Hit your hands against the top of your desk. Do you still hear the sound for a brief instant after you have stopped? This sound is an *auditory sensory memory*.

Psychological Detective

Consider the following situation. Jim is sitting in class but is not really paying attention to the lecture. His mind is on the movie he is planning to see that evening. Without realizing it, he is rubbing one hand along the edge of the desk. After rubbing his hand on the desk several times, Jim becomes aware of his behavior. Each time his hand leaves the desk, he is sure he is still feeling the sensation. What causes the sensation that Jim experiences after he rubs his hand along the edge of the desk? Write down some possibilities before reading further.

Sensory memory appears to be involved in the sensation Jim is experiencing. Try it yourself. Rub your hand quickly along the edge of your desk or a table—heel first, fingertips last. For a brief instant after your hand leaves the desk, you will have the sensation that you are still touching it. You have just experienced an example of *tactile* (*touch*) *sensory memory*.

According to the stages-of-memory model, what happens to the information that is selected from sensory memory and not lost? To answer this question we need to continue our exploration of the various types of memory.

Short-Term Memory.   Once information has been attended to or selected from sensory memory, it is transferred to our conscious awareness (Engle, Cantor, & Carullo, 1993; Laming, 1992). According to the stages-of-memory view, information must be processed in **short-term memory (STM)** before it can be transferred to more permanent storage in long-term memory. What is this STM? As the name implies, STM lasts for only a short period—perhaps several seconds. Although researchers have not determined exactly how long such memories endure, it appears that items are lost from STM in 10 to 20 seconds.

For example, research in which participants recalled a three-letter stimulus found that recall fell from 90% correct immediately after presentation of the stimulus to 10% correct after 18 seconds (Brown, J. A., 1958; Peterson & Peterson, 1959). Why? Two processes appear to be at work: (1) Unless memories are practiced or rehearsed, they become weaker and fade away; and (2) to make room for new, incoming information, some of the memories in STM are pushed out or displaced. In the Brown and Peterson and Peterson studies, the participants counted backward by threes to prevent practice after learning the three-letter stimulus. Their results indicated that much of this displaced information is simply lost, but some is transferred to long-term memory.

Psychological Detective

Study the following phone numbers for 15 seconds:

316-343-5800
401-246-4531
912-692-3423

Now write them on a piece of paper without looking at this page. You probably found this task difficult. You would be able to handle two phone numbers better. Why? Write down some possible answers before reading further.

short-term memory (STM)
Memory stage in which information is held in consciousness for 10 to 20 seconds

Exercises like this one, coupled with extensive research, prompted psychologist George Miller (1956) to propose that we can hold approximately seven items (plus or minus two) in STM at any one time. After a moment's reflection you might be sure that this 7 +/− 2 proposal is incorrect. When we remember two telephone numbers, we are

By permission of Johnny Hart and Creators Syndicate, Inc.

Without rehearsal, short-term memory does not last very long.

dealing with more than nine items (7 +/− 2). That would be true if you counted each digit separately. Phone numbers, however, are broken up by dashes. The result is that we are actually dealing with two groups of numbers (343, 5800) rather than with a series of individual numbers (3, 4, 3, 5, 8, 0, 0). When the area code is added (316-343-5800), there still are only three groups of numbers. Say your own phone number aloud. Did you hear the pauses? Those pauses separate the *chunks*, or clusters of information. With two phone numbers, each having an area code, you have only six chunks to remember.

What Miller demonstrated with the principle of grouping or chunking is that although STM may be limited to five to nine items (7 +/− 2), each of those items may consist of a chunk or group of items. In this way the capacity of STM can be increased significantly.

working memory
Second stage of short-term memory; in it attention and conscious effort are brought to bear on material

 Short-Term Memory

Psychological Detective

What would you do if you wanted to remember the following list? Study it for 15 seconds; then close your book and write down as many of the items as possible.

telephone	Ford	pine
poplar	fax	Chevrolet
oak	compact disk	walnut
Buick	Mazda	television
cedar	mail	audiocassette
Saturn	maple	elm

There are 18 items in this list, considerably more than the magic number 7 +/− 2. Hence it will be difficult for you to remember each word by itself. If, however, you set up three categories (trees, automobiles, and communication devices) and put each item into the appropriate category, you should have no trouble remembering all 18 items (see Figure 7-4).

The original concept of STM posed a major problem: It was too short. Although 10 or 20 seconds was sufficient to input and store new information, it did not allow time for the processing of this information (Ashcraft, 1994). It appears that the initial 10- to 20-second STM period often leads to a second phase, **working memory,** during which attention and conscious effort are brought to bear on the material at hand (Baddeley, 1992a, 1992b). For example, let's say you are listening to a lecture in which your instructor makes an interesting but complicated point. While you hold the sentence in STM, you retrieve word meanings from *long-term memory*. Then, in light of what you already know (retrieval from long-term memory), you use working memory to make sense of this new sentence you've just heard. Working memory seems to be an

George Miller, former president of the American Psychological Association, proposed that we can hold 7 +/− 2 items in short-term memory at any one time.

FIGURE 7-4 Chunking helps us create categories that increase the amount of information we can hold in STM.

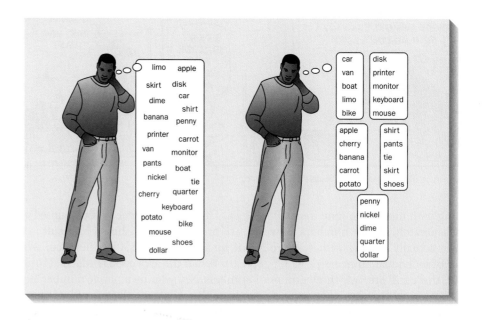

intermediate processing stage between STM and long-term memory. Research, using several of the brain-imaging techniques you learned about in Chapter 2, has begun to isolate the portions of the brain that are active when we are using working memory. For example, Smith (2000) indicates "that human spatial working memory is partly mediated by regions in the parietal and prefrontal cortex" (p. 45). Future research using brain imaging techniques will define these and other brain regions involved in working memory more precisely.

Long-Term Memory. What would your interactions with your environment be like if STM was the only type of memory you had? Because you lacked any capacity for permanent memory storage, you would have to learn the same things over and over again. (We describe a person who has only STM later in this chapter.) It is critical to be able to transfer information from STM to more permanent storage in **long-term memory (LTM).** The stages-of-memory model stresses the importance of rehearsal or practice in this transfer. Items that are rehearsed seem more likely to be transferred than unrehearsed items. For example, you will remember your friend's new telephone number better if you repeat (rehearse) it several times rather than repeating it just once.

There are different types of rehearsal; some types aid in transferring information to LTM, and others do not. One researcher conducted a series of studies of a phenomenon known as *directed forgetting* (Björk, 1975). In these experiments two groups of participants were asked to learn several lists of items, such as nonsense syllables or telephone numbers. Both groups were given the same amount of time to rehearse each list after it was presented. A retention test was given before presentation of the next list. Before beginning the experiment, one group was told to forget all the items from a given list immediately after the retention test. The second group was told to remember all the lists. A typical directed-forgetting experiment (see Fleck, Berch, Shear, & Strakowski, 2001) is diagrammed in Figure 7-5.

Although no differences were found between the groups in retention of individual lists of nonsense syllables, large differences were apparent on a retention test given after all the lists had been presented. The participants who had been directed to forget did much worse than those who had been directed to remember. These differences appear to be caused by different types of rehearsal.

Two types of rehearsal—maintenance and elaborative—have been studied. We use **maintenance rehearsal** when we want to save or maintain a memory for a short

long-term memory
Memory stage that has a very large capacity and the capability to store information relatively permanently

maintenance rehearsal
Rehearsal used when we want to save or maintain a memory for a specified period of time

FIGURE 7-5 Design of a directed-forgetting experiment.

Group 1: Instructed to learn each list of nonsense syllables for a test and then forget the list before learning the next list

Group 2: Instructed to learn and store all lists of nonsense syllables

Learn List 1	Test List 1	Learn List 2	Test List 2	Learn List 3	Test List 3	Test All Lists
	Both groups equal		Both groups equal		Both groups equal	Group 2 superior to Group 1 (evidence of directed forgetting)

period. Examples of maintenance rehearsal include the telephone number for the pizza restaurant you have just looked up or the material you tried to cram for a test. Maintenance rehearsal ensures that the memory remains until it has been used and is then discarded; research participants who are directed to forget a list as soon as they have learned and repeated it use this type of rehearsal. Participants who are instructed to remember a list use **elaborative rehearsal,** which adds meaning to material that we want to remember. For example, you increase your chances of remembering someone's name if meaningful elements are present when you are introduced. Where does the person work or live? What are his or her hobbies? An introduction such as "I would like you to meet my friend Jason Downey. Jason works as the chief parole officer for the state. He is an avid sky diver" provides several elements that are useful to memory. Earlier we saw that the more meaningful material is, the better it is learned. Elaborative rehearsal is an example of this process at work; it results in a more permanent memory and promotes the transfer of information to LTM (Bartlett, 1932; Best, 1999). Unlike STM, LTM has a very large, if not unlimited, capacity.

Forgetting.   Once a memory has been transferred from STM to LTM, it is supposed to be there on a *permanent* basis. If that is true, why do we forget? Some memory loss may be due to the fading or *decay* of memories (Dosher & Ma, 1998), but much loss appears to be caused by *interference.* Old memories that are already stored may be recalled instead of the specific memory we are seeking. This effect is called **proactive interference.** Proactive interference occurs when old information hinders our memory of the new information. When you move to a new house or apartment, you have a new address and telephone number. How often do you find yourself using the old address or phone number? Sometimes this problem lasts for years. Another example of proactive interference can be seen every January, when millions of people continue to write the previous year on their bank checks.

Similarly, information that was learned *after* the material we want to remember may hinder the recall of the earlier learned material. This process is called **retroactive interference.** Sometimes it is important to remember old addresses and phone numbers, but try as we might, new addresses and phone numbers are the only ones that come to mind. The other information may be stored in LTM, but we simply cannot retrieve it. Proactive and retroactive interference are diagrammed in Figure 7-6.

What happens when we retrieve a memory from LTM? As we saw in Figure 7-3, the stages-of-memory model suggests that when a memory is recalled from LTM and enters consciousness, it is placed directly into STM. There it may be combined with new information that has been received, creating a new memory. If this new memory is properly rehearsed, it may be transferred to LTM for more permanent storage.

7.3

elaborative rehearsal
Rehearsal in which meaning is added to the material to be remembered

proactive interference
Situation in which previously learned information hinders the recall of information learned more recently

retroactive interference
Situation in which information learned more recently hinders the recall of information learned previously

FIGURE 7-6 Research designed to test proactive and retroactive interference.

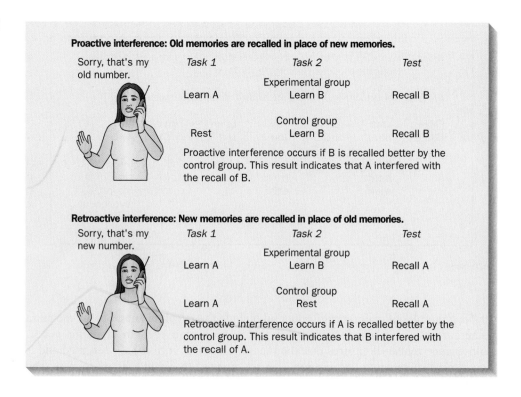

The following study chart summarizes the main components of the stages-of-memory model.

The stages-of-memory approach is not the only model of memory that has been developed. We explore a second influential model, the Craik and Lockhart levels of processing model, in the next section.

STUDY CHART

Types of Memory According to the Stages-of-Memory Model

Type	Description	Example
Sensory	Storage of a large number of sensory events for one-half to one second.	Rubbing your hand across a table top and feeling the sensation for a brief instant after you stop.
Short-Term (STM)	Also called working memory. Lasts for a few seconds unless rehearsal takes place. Conscious awareness is involved.	Remembering the name of a person you just met.
Long-Term (LTM)	More permanent form of memory storage. Rehearsal or practice is important for transferring memories from STM to LTM.	Your telephone number or home address.

R E V I E W   S U M M A R Y

1. Hermann Ebbinghaus conducted the pioneering research on memory in the late 1800s. Ebbinghaus devised **nonsense syllables,** which he believed had no meaning attached to them, to study how associations between stimuli are formed.

2. Through the use of **serial learning,** Ebbinghaus determined that much of what we learn is forgotten very shortly after a learning session. Other methods include **paired-associate learning** and **free recall.**

3. These basic methods were developed and expanded by incorporating additional tasks, such as the **recognition test** and the **relearning test.** The **savings score** is produced by the relearning method.

4. Some investigators have drawn a parallel between the computer and human memory. Computers and human memory have (a) an input or **encoding** stage, (b) a **storage** process, and (c) a **retrieval** process.

5. The stages-of-memory model of memory proposes that memories can be processed in different ways. There are three types of memory: sensory, short-term, and long-term.

6. **Sensory memory** is a very brief (lasting one-half to 1 second) memory for a large array of stimuli.

7. **Short-term memory (STM)** is more limited in capacity than sensory memory but lasts longer (10 to 20 seconds). **Working memory** is the second stage of short-term memory, during which attention and conscious effort are brought to bear on material.

8. With practice or rehearsal, memories may persist even longer and ultimately be transferred to more permanent storage in **long-term memory (LTM).**

9. Memories may not be retrievable from LTM because they have faded or because of interference by other memories.

10. **Proactive interference** occurs when old material interferes with the retrieval of material learned more recently. **Retroactive interference** occurs when recently learned material interferes with the retrieval of material learned earlier.

✓ CHECK YOUR PROGRESS

1. Kevin and Sharon are participants in a memory experiment. Their task is to learn a list of items such as *bok* and *gex*. What are these items called? Why are they used in the study of memory?

2. Once he has learned the list of items, Kevin's task is to reproduce them in the order in which they were presented. What is the procedure for measuring memory called?

3. Explain the statement "human memory is like an information processing system."

4. Indicate whether each of the following statements describes sensory memory, short-term memory, or long-term memory.
   a. very large capacity
   b. capacity of 7 +/− 2 items
   c. permanent storage
   d. lasts only .5 to 1.0 second
   e. lasts 10 to 20 seconds
   f. associated with chunks

5. Describe working memory. How does it differ from short-term memory?

6. You attempt to remember a phone number by repeating it over and over to yourself. What type of rehearsal are you using?
   a. condensed
   b. permanent
   c. elaborative
   d. maintenance

7. Much of our memory loss appears to be due to
   a. fading.
   b. disuse.
   c. interference.
   d. poor encoding.

8. Your final exam was a nightmare. All you could remember was the material you had just learned; the older material seemed to have vanished from your memory. This type of memory failure is an example of what kind of interference?

9. What method of learning are you using when you have to learn a list of items in a particular order?
   a. recognition
   b. free recall
   c. serial learning
   d. paired-associate

10. What psychological phenomenon is evident in the fact that it is more difficult for Heidi to remember her old phone number as time passes since she moved?
    a. memory curve
    b. curve of forgetting
    c. serial position curve
    d. free recall curve

11. Picking a suspect out of a police lineup is an example of
    a. recall.
    b. recognition.
    c. relearning.
    d. paired-associate learning.

ANSWERS: 1. Nonsense syllables. Nonsense syllables are used to avoid the presence of previous associations influencing learning. **2.** Serial learning. **3.** There is an input stage, encoding process, and retrieval process in both the information system and human memory. **4. a.** Sensory memory or Long-term memory **b.** Short-term memory **c.** Long-term memory **d.** Sensory memory **e.** Short-term memory **f.** Short-term memory **5.** Working memory follows the initial 10 to 20 seconds of short-term memory. During working memory, attention and conscious effort are brought to bear on the material. **6.** d **7.** c **8.** Retroactive interference **9.** c **10.** b **11.** b

levels-of-processing theory
Theory stating that deeper processing of information increases the likelihood that the information will be recalled

OTHER APPROACHES TO LEARNING AND MEMORY

Myra volunteered to participate in an experiment involving memory. Her initial task was to read an article in a psychological journal. After reading the article, she was instructed to prepare a brief presentation about the article from the perspective of its author. Finally, Myra took a test that dealt with the content of the article. *What did these procedures have to do with memory?*

Although the stages-of-memory model developed by Atkinson and Shiffrin makes good sense and has generated a large amount of research activity, it is not the only theoretical account of how memory works. In this section we examine several other models of the memory process.

The Levels-of-Processing Model

The **levels-of-processing theory** proposed by Fergus Craik and Robert Lockhart (1972) represents a radical departure from the stages-of-memory model (Challis, 1993; Challis & Brodbeck, 1992). Craik and Lockhart proposed that there is only one type of memory store and that its capacity is enormous, if not unlimited. Once memories have entered this store, they may be retained there for extremely long periods.

You may be thinking, "One large memory store in which memories last for long periods—that seems simple enough. If that's the way our memory is set up, however, why do we forget some things faster than others?" That question gets to the heart of Craik and Lockhart's view of memory: What really matters is the way we process information. Rehearsal is important, but how we rehearse is even more important. As you can see in Figure 7-7, Craik and Lockhart believe that we can engage in several levels of rehearsal or processing. The maintenance and elaborative rehearsal techniques discussed earlier are only two examples.

A very shallow or simple level might involve processing only the physical characteristics of an object. Thus we might characterize the object in Figure 7-7 as red and rectangular. At a deeper or more complex level of processing, we consider additional characteristics such as the fact that the object has pages. This addition is a form of elaborative rehearsal. Now we are dealing with a red, rectangular book. Adding even more

FIGURE 7-7 The Craik-Lockhart (1972) levels-of-processing model of memory.

TABLE 7-1

Instructions Given to Participants in the Hyde and Jenkins (1969) Experiment

Group 1	Count the letters in each word.
Group 2	Mark all the e's in each word.
Group 3	Rate the pleasantness of each word.
Group 4	Memorize the words for a later recall test.

meaning—that is, moving to an even deeper level of processing—we now consider what type of book this is and whether it will help us in any of our courses this semester. This last type of processing requires that we examine the book and compare it with other books and with information already stored in memory. Which courses are we taking? Which books are being used in those courses? Will this book help?

We do not automatically progress from one level to another simply because we spend more time processing. If all our processing time is spent at a very shallow level, our memory will be stored only in terms of shallow cues such as color, shape, or sound. When we want to retrieve this memory, only those shallow cues will be able to access and retrieve it. For example, if we listened only to the sound of a person's name, we might not be able to retrieve it later. The person's physical features, occupation, personality, address, and so forth would be of no help because those cues were not rehearsed when the memory was stored. The sound of the person's name is the only cue that will access the memory of the name. These physical cues are less meaningful; therefore, they do not remain in our memory store as long as more meaningful cues that are rehearsed at deeper levels of processing. In other words, the deeper the level of processing, the greater the likelihood the information will be stored. Time of processing is not as important as depth of processing.

The instructions given to research participants can have a dramatic effect on what is learned. In one classic study (Hyde & Jenkins, 1969), researchers demonstrated the effects that different types of processing can produce. They instructed four groups of participants to study the same list of words. The specific instructions differed for each group, as shown in Table 7-1. A recall test was then given to all four groups. The test was a surprise for Groups 1, 2, and 3, but not for Group 4.

The results (see Figure 7-8) indicated that participants in Groups 1 and 2 remembered significantly *fewer* words than did participants in Groups 3 and 4. Because

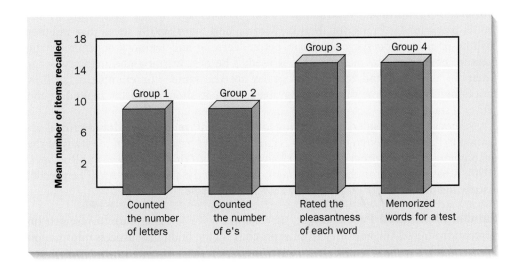

FIGURE 7-8 Mean correct responses on a recall test. Only the participants in Group 4 knew they would be tested. Processing at a deeper level (Group 3) improved memory.

Source: Adapted from Hyde & Jenkins, 1969.

Groups 3 and 4 did not differ, we can conclude that the surprise value of the test did not produce these results. The groups differed in terms of the level of processing in which they engaged. Groups 1 and 2 never dealt with the words themselves—they just counted letters (Group 1) or marked e's (Group 2). Hence Groups 1 and 2 processed the information at a very shallow level. Because they had to take the words into account, the participants in Group 3 (who rated the pleasantness of the words) and Group 4 (who memorized the words for a test) processed the information at deeper levels and therefore remembered it better.

Consider the memory experiment described at the beginning of this section. What did these procedures have to do with memory? The experiment in which Myra participated was concerned with levels of processing. Unknown to Myra, other participants were required only to read the journal article; they were not required to prepare the brief presentation. When researchers designed the study, they hypothesized that preparing the presentation would require a deeper level of processing and result in better comprehension (Kixmiller et al., 1987). This prediction was borne out by the experiment's results.

Although many other studies have produced results indicating that depth or level of processing influences our memories, this theory has not gone unchallenged. Critics assert that the exact meaning of the term "level of processing" has not been specified. Without a clear definition of what a level is or how to measure it objectively (Baddeley, 1998), it is difficult to know how many levels there are. Such criticism has encouraged some researchers to view different levels of processing in terms of the amount of cognitive or mental effort expended. In their view, the greater the effort, the deeper the level of processing.

In support of this proposition, several studies have been interpreted as showing that better retention is linked to greater effort. For example, imagine you are part of an experiment in which the task is to learn words that rhyme. You are presented with a word such as *cat* and asked to generate a word, such as *bat*, that rhymes with it. Your task is to memorize the rhyming words that you have generated. Will you remember your rhyming words better than people who were asked only to memorize rhyming words that were presented to them? Because your effort in generating and memorizing the words was greater than their effort in merely memorizing them, the answer is yes.

Finally, the levels-of-processing model assumes that processing occurs through a succession of independent stages; this assumption has yet to be verified. Because of such issues, other approaches have been developed.

Alternate Approaches

Transfer-Appropriate Processing.   The transfer-appropriate processing (TAP) model proposed by Bransford, Franks, Morris, and Stein (1979) states that whether shallow or deep processing results in better learning and memory depends on the measure of learning or memory that is used. The best learning and memory occur when the encoding and retrieval processes are the same. For example, if shallow processing is applied at the encoding stage, then it should also be applied at the retrieval stage.

Although the considerations prompted by the TAP model have drawn critical attention to the way research in this area is conducted and have facilitated the study of the unconscious memory processing effect known as *implicit* or *priming memory* (Roediger, 1990), it has not fostered the development of a new and elaborate system. The parallel distributed processing (PDP) model has assumed this role.

Parallel Distributed Processing.   In Chapter 3 we saw that current research on perception stresses the notion of parallel processing: the brain may process information in several subsystems simultaneously. Such findings in the area of perception stimulated

STUDY TIP

Describe the stages-of-memory model and the Craik and Lockhart model. Indicate which makes more sense to you as a model of memory, and why. If your ideal model contains elements of both, describe it.

the development of the parallel distributed processing (PDP) model of human cognition and memory by James McClelland and David Rumelhart (1986; McClelland, Rumelhart, & Hinton, 1986). The basic view of this model is that mental processes and activities consist of a system of highly interconnected basic units (possibly composed of single neurons) that communicate with each other. According to Solso (1998), these "units are organized into modules, such as atoms are organized into molecules" (p. 206). When information relevant to learning and memory is received, it is distributed to appropriate units and modules. The processing of information results in a change in the strength of connections between individual units. Thus information is stored in terms of the numerous connections among units. The stronger the connection, the easier it will be to retrieve the memory.

procedural memory
Memory for making responses and performing skilled actions

semantic memory
Memory for general knowledge

tip-of-the-tongue (TOT) phenomenon
Condition of being almost, but not quite, able to remember something; used to investigate the nature of semantic memory

Different Types of Long-Term Memory

Recent research has demonstrated that there is more than one type of long-term memory. We do not just place a memory into LTM (stages-of-memory model) or simply process at a deeper level (Craik-Lockhart model). The type of information being processed influences the nature of the stored memory. Four major categories or types of LTM have been proposed: *procedural, semantic, episodic,* and *priming* (or implicit). In addition, current research has improved our understanding of encoding, processing, and retrieval strategies. We examine some of these current approaches in the following sections.

Procedural Memory. **Procedural memories** are the memories we use in making responses and performing skilled actions (Anderson & Fincham, 1994). Remembering how to rollerblade is an example of procedural memory. Procedural memories are often used at the same time as other types of memory. For example, remembering how to drive a car involves procedural memory. Remembering the traffic laws, however, does not involve the use of motor skills; it involves the memory of general principles. Memory for general principles is known as *semantic memory*.

Semantic Memory. Our fund of general knowledge is stored in **semantic memory.** Because we are dealing with general knowledge, specific dates and times that pertain to people are not included in our semantic memories. You will find these items in episodic memory. Semantic memory includes concepts, the meanings of words, and facts (Lesch & Pollatsek, 1993; Rohrer et al., 1995). The following are some examples of items that might be stored in semantic memory:

1. Texas shares a border with Mexico.

2. $7 - 2 = 5$

3. Big cities tend to be rather impersonal.

Remembering how to rollerblade is an example of procedural memory.

Have you ever been asked a question you could not answer immediately, yet you felt the correct response was "on the tip of your tongue"? Such a question produces what is known as the **tip-of-the-tongue (TOT) phenomenon** (Carpenter, 2000b). You know the answer is there, but you cannot retrieve it.

Psychological Detective

Let's test your semantic memory. Write down the answer to each of the following questions before reading further.

1. Which ocean is adjacent to California?

2. Which tree produces acorns?

3. What type of engine is used to power an automobile?

4. What does a bear do in the winter?

5. Which river separates Kansas from Missouri?

How many of these questions produced a TOT response? Were you able to search your stored memories and find the correct answer? Because most TOT experiences seem to involve semantic memory, they have been studied thoroughly by psychologists who want to learn more about this type of memory and how it is retrieved. Apparently, we are very systematic and organized when we search our semantic memories (Reason & Mycielska, 1982). By observing how people search their stored knowledge, we can learn more about the vast network of semantic memories.

Hands On

TOT Phenomena and Memory

To get a better idea of how the TOT phenomenon is relevant to the study of memory, take the following test. Using strips of cardboard, cover both of the columns of the letters that follow and write down as many state capitals as you can. Then uncover the columns and see if these alphabetical cues aid your recall for those that were on the tip of your tongue. The answers can be found at the end of the chapter.

State	First Letter of Capital	State	First Letter of Capital
Alabama	M	Maryland	A
Connecticut	H	Massachusetts	B
Florida	T	Mississippi	J
Georgia	A	Nebraska	L
Idaho	B	New Jersey	T
Iowa	D	Oregon	S
Kentucky	F	Texas	A
Louisiana	B	Wyoming	C

Episodic Memory. Our personal experiences are stored in **episodic memory.** These memories involve events that occurred at certain times with specific people, places, and things (Goldringer, 1996; Levy et al., 1995; Nyberg & Tulving, 1996). The following are some examples of episodic memories from your authors. What episodic memories do you have?

1. Being in Dallas, Texas, the day President John F. Kennedy was assassinated

2. Watching baseball pitcher Nolan Ryan strike out his 5,000th batter in 1989 and win his 300th major league game in 1990

3. Seeing tornadoes devastate Nashville, Tennessee, in the spring of 1998

4. Graduating from high school

5. Arriving on campus for the first day of college

episodic memory
Memory of one's personal experiences

flashbulb memory
Very detailed memory of an arousing, surprising, or emotional situation

Just as the TOT phenomenon has been studied to help us learn more about semantic memory, flashbulb memories have been examined to provide information about episodic memory. **Flashbulb memories** are detailed memories of situations that are very arousing, surprising, or emotional. Our memories of such events are much more detailed than our memories of more usual, everyday episodes. You might think of flashbulb memories as similar to photos taken with a Polaroid camera. Push the

Where were you on September 11, 2001? These images reflect flashbulb memories for many people, worldwide.

button, and 60 seconds later you have a perfect re-creation of the scene that you can look at whenever you want. In your mind, the situation is illuminated just as it occurred. Because more effort is expended in the formation of flashbulb memories, such highlighting of details might lead to deeper levels of processing as well as provide more cues for retrieval.

Because flashbulb memories are tied to specific dates, places, and times, it is difficult to give examples that everyone can immediately identify. Some people vividly remember where they were when President Kennedy was assassinated in 1963, but others do not. Whereas the explosion of the space shuttle *Challenger* in 1986 and the tearing down of the Berlin Wall in 1989 may be no more than historical facts to some people, to others they are flashbulb memories. The terrorist attacks on the World Trade Center in New York and the Pentagon in Washington, DC, in 2001 are currently flashbulb memories for the majority of people. As new generations grow up, they will not have these flashbulb memories.

Priming or Implicit Memory. The recent addition of **priming or implicit memory** to the list of memory types may be one of the most important advances in the study of memory (Poldrack & Cohen, 1998; Schachter & Badgaiyan, 2001). According to Endel Tulving and Daniel Schachter (1990), "Priming is a nonconscious form of human memory, which is concerned with perceptual identification of words and objects and which has only recently been recognized as separate from other forms of memory or memory systems" (p. 301).

Because priming or implicit memory does not operate on a conscious level, it is difficult to detect and study. The first evidence for priming came from studies of *amnesia*, or memory loss (Warrington & Weiskrantz, 1968). Even though the patients with amnesia had extremely poor memory for recent events, allowing them to study a group of words helped them later when they had to learn those same words. The earlier study period primed or sensitized them to the words they were to learn in the later session. Even though they had no *memory* of the first study session, the *primed* patients with amnesia performed better than other patients with amnesia and normal individuals who had not studied the items earlier. Somehow the earlier study session prepared (primed) the amnesiac patients to recognize the objects they were to learn. Subsequent studies (Schweinberger, 1996) of nonamnesic individuals have examined the timing and

priming or implicit memory
Unconscious memory processing in which prior exposure to stimulus items may aid in subsequent learning

STUDY TIP

In a group of four, each student should briefly study and then describe to the group one of the four types of long-term memory. After a student describes a type, the rest of the group should brainstorm examples of that type.

production of brain waves to study priming. Priming effects are revealed when appropriate brain waves are shown earlier in primed participants.

What is the purpose of priming? Although we still have a great deal to learn, priming apparently facilitates procedural and semantic memory processes by improving our ability to identify perceptual stimuli or objects we encounter (Rajaram & Roediger, 1993). At an unconscious level, priming memory alerts us that we have encountered a particular object previously (Musen & Squire, 1993). This priming effect is better when deeper levels of processing are involved (Hamann & Squire, 1996).

The different types of long-term memory are summarized in the following study chart. Spend a few minutes reviewing it before reading further.

Retrieval

Last year during spring break, Jennifer paid a surprise visit to her former first-grade teacher. Even though the teacher had not seen Jennifer in 10 years, she immediately said, "Well, Jennifer, how are you? Do you still have Buffy, your pet boa constrictor?" At times we are able to retain and retrieve some remarkable memories. Conversely, sometimes things we should remember seem to be gone forever. For example, are you among the large number of people who seem unable to remember their license plate and telephone numbers?

Retrieval from Short-Term Memory. As mentioned earlier, retrieval is the process by which we locate a memory that has been stored and then bring it into consciousness. Because most people have both extremely good and extremely poor memories, psychologists are interested in studying retrieval.

Psychological Detective

When you read the heading "Retrieval from Short-Term Memory," the following question may have occurred to you: "If the information in STM is already in our consciousness, why would we talk about retrieving it?" Give this question some thought, and write down some possible reasons before reading further.

A lengthy series of studies by S. Sternberg (1966, 1975) suggested that retrieval from STM is not instantaneous; we *do* have to scan our STM, locate an item, and process it. Sternberg asked participants to hold a series of letters (such as B, Q, R, D, T, and P) in STM for later recall. But instead of being given the recall test they expected, they were

STUDY CHART

Types of Long-Term Memory

Type	Description	Examples
Procedural	Memories used in making responses and skilled actions.	Remembering how to ride a bicycle, play tennis, or drive a car.
Semantic	Our store of general knowledge.	Water freezes at 32°F; Texas is the largest of the continental states; metabolism decreases when animals hibernate.
Episodic	Memories of personal events.	Your high school graduation, your first day at college, getting your driver's license.
Implicit (priming)	Nonconscious form of LTM that is related to identification of words and objects.	Allowing amnesia patients to study an object and later finding that learning is enhanced even though they do not remember seeing the object.

GEECH. Reprinted by permission of United Features Syndicate, Inc.

presented with a letter, such as B, and were asked whether it was in the list they were holding in STM. If retrieval was not involved, the participants should have responded almost instantaneously. As it turned out, they did not. What's more, as additional letters were added to the list held in STM, the participants took longer to answer. They were scanning the entire list in STM to match the test letter with those they had stored. The longer the list in STM, the longer the search process required to make a match.

Retrieval from Long-Term Memory.   The process of scanning items in STM to retrieve a specific memory is rather straightforward, but retrieval of long-term memories is a different story. Depending on the situation, various processes may be involved. For example, we have to distinguish between retrieval of memories in recognition tasks and retrieval of memories in recall tasks.

Which type of test would you rather take—a short-answer or essay test in which you have to produce all of the answers, or a multiple-choice test in which you have to recognize the correct answer? Most people prefer the multiple-choice test because it is easier; all you have to do is choose the right answer. Consider the following questions on material from Chapter 2. Which question do you think is easier?

1. Which of the following mobilizes the body for fight or flight?
    a. basal ganglia pathway
    b. sympathetic system
    c. cerebellum
    d. limbic system

2. Name the division of the nervous system that mobilizes the body for fight or flight.

If recognition tasks are easier, perhaps they do not require the same amount or type of retrieval processing. It may be simpler to retrieve memories through recognition. Many researchers supported this view until Tulving and his colleagues demonstrated that in some situations, recall memory is actually superior to recognition memory!

Although one type of memory task is not always easier than the other, perhaps the process of retrieval is the same for both. John Anderson and Gordon Bower (1974) have proposed that recognition and recall use the same retrieval process. Both recall and recognition retrieval have an initial stage during which we search stored memories. Our search leads us to a large number of *related* words and phrases. In short, we do not store information as separate bits and pieces; much of it is stored as a semantic network of related items.

Semantic networks are formed by related concepts (called *nodes*) that are linked together (Collins & Loftus, 1975; Collins & Quillian, 1972). For example, mentioning the concept "newspaper" might activate the semantic network shown in Figure 7-9. The process of activating a network constitutes the retrieval process. The length of the lines (called *links*) that connect the various concepts in the newspaper network reflect the strength of the association; shorter links imply stronger associations. For example, the association between "newspaper" and "reporter" is stronger (shorter link) than the association between "newspaper" and "rain" (longer link). Note that in the semantic network every concept is related to the core concept—in this case, "newspaper." In some instances the relation is direct; in others, it is indirect.

semantic network
Network of related concepts that are linked together

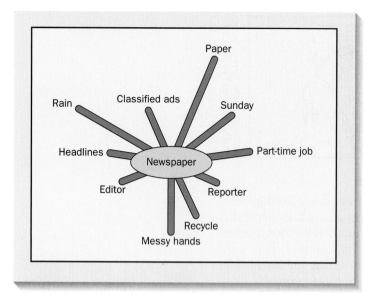

FIGURE 7-9 A semantic network for the concept "newspaper." Longer lines depict weaker associations (links); shorter lines depict stronger links.

Not all of our stored memories are arranged in semantic networks in which one concept triggers a network of related items. There are numerous occasions when we are required to use a grouping or cluster of knowledge about a sequence of events or an object. Such clusters of knowledge or typical ways of thinking about things are called **schemas** (Ahn, Brewer, & Mooney, 1992; Dopkins, Pollatsek, & Nordlie, 1994). For example, suppose that a friend asked you to tell her about the concert you went to last weekend. Because you have been to several concerts during the past year, you have an organized cluster of knowledge (a schema) about going to concerts. Thus your recall of last weekend's concert will be influenced by your schema for concerts and the specific events that occurred at the concert in question. Similarly, you have schemas for grade school, marriage, rude behavior, trendy clothing, and so on.

To get a better idea of the nature of semantic networks and schemas, let's say you have learned a list of words that included the word *horse*. Later in the day you take a recognition test in which you are given a longer list of words and are asked to pick out the ones you have learned. You come to the word *horse*, which serves as a retrieval cue for the semantic network that contains your horse-related memories. Now your job is to determine whether the word *horse* was on the list you learned earlier. Sorting through all of your horse memories could be a rather imposing and confusing task, especially if there are many strong links. On the other hand, the word *aardvark* should be easier to recognize as one of the words you learned because it should activate fewer links than *horse*.

The same process is involved when we retrieve memories under recall conditions. For example, an essay question on your psychology test might ask you to name the four lobes of the cortex. You start scanning your semantic network for items related to the concept "lobes of the cortex." You find a network of related information that includes subcortical structures, stereotaxic surgery, and a group of items that includes the terms *frontal, temporal, parietal,* and *occipital*—the four cortical lobes you've been looking for.

What about the next question on the test: "Explain the contributions of Ivan Pavlov"? In this case, you need to recall more than just names to answer the question; you need to activate an organized cluster of knowledge, a schema. Your schema for Pavlov contains the information the instructor wants. In fact, it contains even more than you need to recall. Could there be some way to retrieve only the desired memory?

schema
Grouping or cluster of knowledge about an object or sequence of events

encoding specificity
Theory stating that the effectiveness of memory retrieval is directly related to the similarity of the cues present when the memory was encoded and when the memory is retrieved

Encoding Specificity. The **encoding specificity** hypothesis states that the effectiveness of memory retrieval is directly related to the similarity of the cues present when the memory was originally encoded to the cues present when the memory is retrieved (Gerrig & McKoon, 2001; Tulving, 1983). In short, specific cues are encoded, and these cues, or very similar ones, should be present when retrieval is attempted.

Have you ever had difficulty recalling material you have studied? Part of the problem may be that the studying took place in one location and the testing occurred in a very different place. Most of the effective retrieval cues (those in the room where you studied) were missing in the classroom where you took the test. Hence it was difficult for them to retrieve the needed information.

Psychological Detective

How can you solve this recall problem? Give this issue some thought and write down some possibilities before reading further.

Eyewitnesses cannot be relied on to provide accurate information.

Try to do some studying in the room where the test will be given. The cues in the room will be among those that can help you retrieve the memory. If you cannot study in the room where the test will be given, try varying the locations where you study. This variety would prevent a single set of cues from becoming associated with the memory of the material you are learning. As a result, retrieval of your memories will be tied less directly to a specific set of environmental cues.

Eyewitness Testimony.   One of the most intriguing applications of the encoding specificity hypothesis has been in the area of eyewitness testimony. Such testimony often plays an important part in jury trials.

The possibility that eyewitness reports may be inaccurate has stimulated a large amount of research. One of the most startling findings concerns what can happen to a memory once it has been retrieved. Earlier we saw that when a memory is retrieved from LTM, it appears to be placed in STM for conscious processing. While this memory is in STM, however, it is possible to add new information to it and then *reencode* the modified memory. The next time you retrieve the new memory, your report may not correspond exactly to what actually happened because the new memory now contains the additional information.

This effect was tested in several ingenious experiments conducted by Elizabeth Loftus and her colleagues (Loftus, Miller, & Burns, 1978; Loftus, 1979). The design of one of those experiments is diagrammed in Figure 7-10. In this experiment, two groups of people watched a series of slides that showed an impending collision between a red sports car and another automobile. One group saw the red sports car approach a stop sign at an intersection. The second group saw the sports car approach a yield sign at the intersection. After the slide presentation was completed, the participants were asked a series of questions about what they had seen. For half of the participants in each group, the questions were consistent with what they had seen. In other words, if they had seen a stop sign, the questions referred to a stop sign, and if they had seen a yield sign, the questions referred to a yield sign. For the remaining participants in each group, the questions were inconsistent—if they had seen a stop sign, the questions referred to a yield sign, and vice versa. Finally, all participants were shown pairs of slides and asked to pick the one they had actually seen (a recognition test).

The results of the Loftus experiment were startling. As you would expect, a large number (75%) of the participants who were asked consistent questions after seeing the slides picked the slide they had seen. When they were asked inconsistent questions, however, only 40% were able to select the slide they had actually seen. The inconsistent questions altered their memory of the incident. Later, when they retrieved this memory,

Eyewitness Testimony

FIGURE 7-10 Diagram of the Loftus (1979) experiment on eyewitness accuracy.

Source: Loftus, 1979.

One group saw the red sports car approaching a *stop* sign.

Experimental Design

Step 1	Step 2	Step 3	Results
See slides of red sports car approaching a *stop* sign.	Answer questions about what they had seen. *Consistent* participants had questions about stop signs. *Inconsistent* participants had questions about yield signs.	View slides and pick those that actually were seen in Step 1.	Participants asked consistent questions in Step 2 were significantly more accurate in picking the slides they had seen than were the inconsistent participants.

The other group saw the red sports car approach a *yield* sign.

Experimental Design

Step 1	Step 2	Step 3	Results
See slides of red sports car approaching a *yield* sign.	Answer questions about what they had seen. *Consistent participants* had questions about yield signs. *Inconsistent participants* had questions about stop signs.	View slides and pick those that actually were seen in Step 1.	Participants asked consistent questions in Step 2 were significantly more accurate in picking the slides they had seen than were the inconsistent participants.

---

many participants reported an incorrect memory because they had encoded inaccurate information in their memory after being asked questions that were inconsistent (Ayers & Reder, 1998; Garry & Polaschek, 2000; Porter, Birt, Yuille, & Lehman, 2000).

In addition to demonstrating the memory-altering effects of inconsistent questions, Loftus (1984) has shown that (1) participants have trouble distinguishing between individuals of other races, (2) violence interferes with memory retrieval, and (3) the degree of confidence of an eyewitness is not related to the accuracy of the memory. Moreover, the false memory effect is exceptionally strong and does not dissipate easily or quickly (Carpenter, 2000a). The problems and concerns that such results create for the credibility of eyewitness testimony are obvious.

State-Dependent Learning. For a number of years psychologists have known that if you learn material under certain special conditions, your retrieval of that material will be successful under the same conditions. For example, Randi drank a lot of coffee while she was studying for her last psychology test. Coffee contains a generous amount of caffeine, a central nervous system stimulant, so Randi was quite alert during her study session. Her physiological state became one of the stimuli that

What you say you saw may not be what actually happened: our memories can be changed.

were present when the memories of the material she was studying were encoded. The implication from the encoding specificity hypothesis should be clear: Randi's retrieval will be best when she is tested after drinking a considerable amount of coffee. In other words, material learned in a particular physiological state is recalled best in the same physiological state, a phenomenon known as **state-dependent learning.**

Gordon Bower (1981) extended this finding to include mood states, such as being happy or sad. His logic was simple. If you learn material while you are happy (or sad), you should retrieve that material more easily when you are happy (or sad). If the mood state that was present during learning differs from the one present during testing, retrieval should be more difficult (Weaver & McNeill, 1992).

As we saw in Chapter 3, odors can be linked to both emotions and memories. The link between odor and memory was tested experimentally by psychologist Frank Schab (1990). In this research Schab tested students who smelled an odor both while they were generating antonyms (opposites) to a set of stimulus words such as *large* and *beautiful* and while they were recalling those antonyms later. These students recalled more antonyms than other students who had smelled an odor only during the learning session or only during the test session. Three very different odors—a chocolate scent, an apple-cinnamon scent, and a mothball scent—were used separately to prove that this memory effect was not limited to one specific odor. The results clearly indicated that regardless of the odor type, participants who smelled the same odor during both training and testing remembered antonyms better than participants who smelled an odor only during training or only during testing.

The phenomenon of state-dependent learning indicates that memories acquired under a specific set of circumstances may be difficult to retrieve at another time or under different circumstances. Perhaps we have memories of events that occurred years ago waiting to be triggered.

If you drink a stimulant, such as coffee, while studying, the state-dependent learning phenomenon predicts that you will be better able to retrieve your memories of the material you studied if you drink a stimulant beforehand.

The Repressed/Recovered Memory Controversy

One of the most dramatic and significant controversies in recent years involves reports of the sudden recall of repressed memories of childhood sexual abuse. For example, a newspaper article carried the headline "Eyewitness Errors Can Doom Innocent" (Associated Press, 2000). Retrieval of such memories has been reported to occur decades after the abuse. The significance of this issue is evident in the fact that the American Psychological Association and the British Psychological Association asked groups of experts to study the issue and write policy statements (Lindsay & Read, 1993). This issue attracts so much professional attention that in 1997 an entire issue of *Current Directions in Psychological Science* was devoted to this topic. The following cases illustrate the basis for the controversy.

Case 1. While Melody was in the hospital for treatment of depression, her therapist repeatedly suggested that her depression resulted from incest during childhood. After a few sessions, Melody reported that her father had raped her when she was 4 years old. When pressed for details, she wrote pages of her emerging repressed memories, including being molested by her father when she was 1 year old. She confronted her parents and consulted a lawyer about filing charges against her father. After leaving the hospital and consulting new therapists, Melody concluded that the abuse never occurred. She now says the memories were "a figment of my imagination encouraged by my therapists and the pop psychology books I was reading" (Wartik, 1993, p. 64).

Case 2. Claudia lost more than 100 pounds in a hospital program for treatment of obesity. While in the hospital, she had flashbacks of sexual abuse committed by her brother. After joining a therapy group for incest survivors, the memories

state-dependent learning
Theory stating that when we learn something while in a specific physiological state, our recall of that information will be better when we are in the same physiological state

George Franklin, Sr., left, appears in a Redwood City, California, courtroom, Wednesday, Jan. 31, 1996. Franklin, 56, who was convicted for a 20-year-old murder based on the repressed-memory testimony from his daughter, was ordered retried and the conviction was overturned.

of abuse flooded back. Her brother had died in combat in the Vietnam War more than 15 years before her memories surfaced. Claudia's parents had left his room untouched since his death. She searched his room and found pornographic materials, handcuffs, and a diary in which he had described sexual "experiments" with his sister. (Bower, 1993)

About half the states in the United States have extended the statute of limitations, allowing people who retrieve memories of abuse to sue alleged perpetrators within 3 to 6 years of the time the memories emerge. A growing number of victims have used these revised laws to file civil and criminal actions.

How are repressed memories retrieved? Psychotherapy (see Chapter 13) is the most common vehicle for the retrieval of memories of childhood abuse (generally incest). Typically a person (usually a 20- to 30-year-old woman) seeks therapy for any of a number of problems. Many therapists believe that childhood sexual abuse is associated with a range of problems. Consistent with this belief, some of them ask about the existence of childhood abuse in the first therapy session, and some even insist such abuse occurred, despite the client's denials.

Many therapists rely on memory recovery techniques they believe help their patients remember repressed memories of abuse. For example, 83% of a sample of therapists agreed with the statement "Hypnosis seems to counteract the defense mechanism of repression, lifting repressed material into conscious awareness" (Yapko, 1994, p. 57). Unfortunately, memory-recovery techniques (like imagery, dream interpretation, and journal writing) can also help people create compelling illusory memories (Ceci & Loftus, 1994; Lindsay & Read, 1993; Yapko, 1994). For example, it has been "known for well over a century that false memories can be implanted in individuals through the use of formal hypnotic procedures or even through simple suggestions, without formal hypnosis" (Yapko, 1994, p. 96).

What is the evidence for repression? The theory that memories can be repressed is a cornerstone of the debate (Arrigo & Pezdek, 1997). Yet after 70 years of looking, researchers have not found evidence that the process actually exists (Holmes, 1994).

In a typical evaluation of repression, participants learn groups of words. Then half of the participants are stressed by being told either that they failed a test or that they have some personality defect. The other participants are either told that they passed the test or they are given neutral personality comments. When asked to recall the words, participants exposed to stress recall fewer words. This result seems consistent with the notion that they had been repressing memories associated with stress. Later, when the stressed individuals are told that they had passed a difficult test or that the earlier test results had been false, they remember the words as well as the control participants did.

Researchers have found that the participants were concentrating on the experience of the stressful event instead of shutting it out, as repression suggests. Thus the participants recalled the words poorly because of the distraction created by concentrating on the stressful event, rather than because of repression. Critics argue, however, that laboratory studies of repression are not relevant to the kinds of real-life traumas that have been associated with repressed memories.

It seems possible that we can lose contact with memories for long periods of time; however, repression is an overused explanation of such memory failures. The more likely explanations are normal forgetting, deliberate avoidance, and *infantile amnesia*, or the inability to form memories before approximately age 3 (Ceci & Loftus, 1994).

There is no evidence that people who report memories of abuse are involved in deliberate deception (Yapko, 1994). On the contrary, Loftus (Loftus & Ketcham, 1994) has shown that it is possible to create false memories of a childhood event (for example, being lost in a shopping mall) that never happened. Not only do participants believe these created memories, but they also expand on them and provide details that were not even hinted at in the initial suggestions.

Perhaps the major problem in evaluating memories of childhood sexual abuse is that there is no way to distinguish true repressed memories from false ones (Lindsay & Read, 1993; Loftus, 1993). Ceci and Loftus (1994) write, "The point is not that suggestive memory work techniques unalterably lead to false memory, but merely that they may do so" (p. 359). There is a tragic risk of uncritical acceptance of allegations made by patients: "These activities are bound to lead to an increased likelihood that society in general will disbelieve the genuine cases of childhood sexual abuse that truly deserve our sustained attention" (Loftus, 1993, p. 534).

A Bad Trip Down Memory Lane

Memory Illusions

Clearly the false-memory research and the repressed-memory controversy have stimulated considerable research. Indeed, a new view of memory may be emerging from this research: "memory is fallible, quirky, and essentially reconstructive in nature" (Lynn & Payne, 1997, p. 55).

Because false memories "occur in many different contexts and can be quite compelling" (Payne et al., 1997, p. 56), several investigators view such occurrences as *memory illusions*. (Do you remember some of the visual illusions on p. 124? With visual illusions, we see things that don't exist.) In the case of memory illusions, we remember things that never happened.

The strength and believability of memory illusions are shown in studies in which lists of words were learned (Payne et al., 1996). In these studies participants claimed they remembered exactly who said the critical but nonexistent words. What's more, some participants refused to believe that the nonexistent words were not part of the original list, even when they heard a playback of the original tape. Other research clearly indicates that memory illusions are created for very complex situations, such as being hospitalized at a young age (see, for example, Loftus, 1997). Memory illusions are very strong and believable, and they seem to operate much in the same manner as other normal memory processes.

Even though memory illusions appear to operate similarly to other normal memory processes, there are some differences between them and true memories. Perhaps the most apparent difference concerns the amount of detail that is recalled: Greater detail is recalled with true memories (Mather, Henkle, & Johnson, 1999; Norman & Schachter, 1999).

What part of the brain is involved in creating memory illusions? Daniel Schachter and his colleagues reported data suggesting that the right frontal lobe plays an important role (Schachter, 1997; Schachter et al., 1996). For example, a patient with damage to the right frontal lobe displayed significantly more memory illusions than did people without frontal lobe damage.

serial position effect
Tendency for items at the beginning and end of a list to be learned better than items in the middle

As we have seen, memory illusions are clearly relevant to eyewitness testimony. However, research has progressed far beyond demonstrating the fallibility of eyewitness testimony to examining specific factors, other than adding misleading questions and planting pieces of misinformation, that can create such memory illusions. For example, Maggie Bruck and Stephen Ceci (1997) demonstrated that interviewer bias is one of the factors leading to memory illusions. Likewise, research on the accuracy of memory recall under hypnosis indicates that such memories are no more accurate than those recalled under nonhypnotized conditions (Erdelyi, 1994). In fact, highly hypnotizable individuals report more memory illusions than do nonhypnotized persons (Lynn et al., 1997; Lynn, Myers, & Malinoski, 2000). Although warning people of the possibility of suggestibility before hypnosis reduces the number of memory illusions, it does not eliminate them (Green, Lynn, & Malinoski, 1999).

Clearly, memory illusions are very real and very prevalent. It will be interesting to see what future research will uncover.

TECHNIQUES FOR IMPROVING MEMORY

Brad is an art major who is having difficulty in his U.S. history course. He cannot remember such facts as the major battles of the Civil War. They have no meaning for him. His friends' advice has not helped. Brad is very frustrated and is thinking of dropping the course. Yet he must pass this required course to complete his degree. *What can Brad do to improve his memory?*

Influential Factors

Psychologists have been trying to answer this question for a long time (Higbee, 1993). As you can see from Table 7-2, they have found several factors that influence learning and memory. Among those factors are number of study sessions, distribution of study sessions, meaningfulness of material, similarity of items, and serial position.

Assuming that Brad really has tried to study, the key to remembering the history assignment is finding some meaning in the material. As long as U.S. history has little meaning or relevance to him, he will have difficulty learning it.

Understanding the factors presented in Table 7-2 also helps us to answer the question "What is the best way to study for a test?" Brad now knows he will do better on his tests if he studies as often as possible (increases the number of sessions) but takes several breaks between study sessions (improves the distribution of sessions). For the best learning to occur, the material he is studying should be meaningful (Moravcsik & Healey, 1995), and he should not try to study several different topics during the same session (maintain similarity of items). Finally, the **serial position effect** (Gershberg & Shimamura, 1994) indicates that he should give a little extra attention to the material he studies during the middle portion of a study session. You might want to try these procedures yourself; they could help raise your grades.

Processing Strategies

Now that you understand how to arrange your study sessions and the type of material that should be studied, you want to know more. Why do some people remember better than others?

TABLE 7-2

Factors That Influence Human Learning and Memory

Factor	Effect
Number of study sessions	The greater the number of study (learning) sessions, the better the learning and memory.
Distribution of study sessions	Study sessions should be spread out. Spaced practice is more effective than massed practice.
Meaningfulness of material	Material that is meaningful will be learned better and remembered longer.
Similarity of items	A group of items of the same general type will be learned better than a group of dissimilar items.
Serial position	Items at the beginning and end of a study session or list will be learned better than items in the middle.

Do they have special secrets or tricks? This section describes some memory techniques that have been shown to work. These techniques, known as **mnemonic devices,** are procedures for associating new information with previously stored memories. Thus they are forms of elaborative rehearsal and result in deeper processing. To remember new material, you first recall previously learned (familiar) information and then recall the new information that has been associated with it. You can decide whether mnemonic devices really work. Like anything else, some practice is required to learn to use them effectively. Among the most common techniques are imagery, grouping, and coding.

 7.4

Imagery.   Researchers have shown that if you create and use mental pictures or images of the items you are studying, you will remember better (Dewhurst & Conway, 1994; Paivio, 1971). Repeating items over and over again does little to help you remember them; however, visualizing them as you are learning can help you recall them. For example, if you are learning the components of classical conditioning (see Chapter 5), you should not simply think "CS," "UCS," and "CR"; rather, visualize a concrete example of each. The CS might be a noisy buzzer, the UCS a delicious apple pie, and so forth. This process of visualizing items as they are being learned is known as **imagery.**

Beyond this general finding, two more specific techniques for mental imagery have been developed. They are known as the *method of loci* and the *pegword technique*.

Method of Loci.   *Loci* is the Latin word for "places"; the already stored cues for the **method of loci** are familiar, specific places. When using this mnemonic device, you start with a set of familiar locations. For example, if you live on campus, you could list (in order) the major landmarks you see every time you go from your dormitory room to the student union. Such landmarks could include the door to your room, the staircase to the first floor, the outside door, a tree, a statue, the science hall, and so forth, until you enter the front door of the student union. Then you would assign to each location an item that you want to learn. So if you were trying to learn the parts of the brain, you could pair the medulla with your door, the cerebellum with the staircase to the first floor, and so on. Some people believe that the more bizarre the image, the better your recall. You could imagine an animated medulla hanging on your door. The cerebellum could become the staircase. To recall the parts of the brain in order, you would call up the mental image of the things you encounter on the way to the student union and remember the part of the brain associated with each location. This procedure may sound a bit complex, but it has been found to be highly effective.

mnemonic devices
Procedures for associating new information with previously stored memories

imagery
Process of visualizing items as they are being learned

method of loci
Use of familiar locations as cues to recall items that have been associated with them

Psychological Detective

Don, the rock-and-roll expert, can name in order all of the songs on each of the most popular "oldies" rock CDs. Tonight Don is studying for a psychology test. During this study session, he listens to some of his favorite songs. Don hopes that rather than interfering with his studying, listening to music will help him to score higher on the test. He plays one type of music for each section of material he is studying. He studies the first section while Beatles music is playing; during the next section he listens to some Billy Joel, and so it goes for the rest of the evening. How will Don's unusual study session assist him when he takes the test? Write down an answer to this question before reading further.

Pegword Technique.   In the **pegword technique,** which is similar to the method of loci, you start with a list of items that you already know quite well. For Don to learn a set of items, all he has to do is assign one item to each song on a particular CD. When he is ready to recall the new information, he simply remembers the song titles and the item associated with each. Don is using the pegword technique to help him remember material for his psychology test. For example, basic learning terms (see Chapter 5) such as *CS, UCS, UCR, CR, reinforcement,* and *extinction* may be associated with the titles on the Beatles CD. Items having to do with states of consciousness (Chapter 4) might be associated with titles on the Billy Joel CD. The main difference between the pegword technique and the method of loci is that in the method of loci you visualize specific *locations,* whereas in the pegword technique you think of an already established list of items.

Grouping (Chunking).   What is your telephone number? You will answer with a group of numbers, such as 316-555-5800. Since the first experiment on grouping (Bousfield, 1953), psychologists such as George Miller, whom you read about earlier, have consistently found that we tend to group or *chunk* items when we recall them. Several clustering strategies can be used. If you must learn material in a certain order, you can group together the first three or four items, the next three or four, and so forth. We use this method of grouping when we learn telephone numbers.

If the material does not have to be remembered in a particular order, the possibilities for grouping increase greatly. You can group items according to their type, their ending, their length, or any other way in which they are similar.

How would you remember the following words?

dolphin, green bean, Mickey Mouse, beet, Goofy, carrot,
minnow, squash, bass, Minnie Mouse, spinach, trout,
Pluto, salmon, celery, perch, Donald Duck

Study this list for 1 minute; then close the book and write down as many of the words as you can. Did you group the items into three familiar categories—fish, vegetables, and Walt Disney characters? If you did not use those three categories, did you use others? If so, how did they differ from the categories we proposed? Chunking seems to be used most frequently and effectively with short-term memory tasks, such as remembering a phone number or a list of words.

Coding.   Items that are not very meaningful or relevant to the learner are not learned as well or as easily as more meaningful or relevant items. Some people create special codes to help them learn material that lacks relevance. They code the less relevant material in a meaningful form and then remember the coded items. It is important, however, to be able to decode the items once they have been learned. For example, the nonsense syllables *cib, xos,* and *gip* would be difficult to remember because they do not have high levels of meaning. What if we were to code each by printing it backward? In that case *cib* becomes *bic, xos* becomes *sox,* and *gip* becomes *pig.* These coded syllables are high in meaning and therefore are much easier to

pegword technique
Use of familiar words or names as cues to recall items that have been associated with them

remember. When we want to recall the coded stimuli, all we have to do is reverse the order of the letters after the familiar words have been recalled.

Acronyms and Acrostics.   The use of acronyms and acrostics are two popular coding techniques. An **acronym** is a word formed by the initial letter(s) of the items to be remembered. To remember the desired information you recall the acronym and then decode it. For example, to help remember the names of the Great Lakes all you need to do is recall the acronym HOMES and then decode it: H (Lake Huron), O (Lake Ontario), M (Lake Michigan), E (Lake Erie), and S (Lake Superior).

An **acrostic** is a verse or saying (often unusual or humorous) where the first letter(s) of each word stands for a bit of information. For example, let's say you are assigned the task of remembering the names of the first seven presidents of the United States in order. One approach would be to use rote memorization. On the other hand, you might do better, spend less time, and have more fun if you made up a little phrase such as this: "**W**ashington **a**nd **J**efferson **m**ade **m**any **a** **j**oke." The first letter of each word in this saying stands for the last name of a president: George **W**ashington, John **A**dams, Thomas **J**efferson, James **M**adison, James **M**onroe, John Quincy **A**dams, and Andrew **J**ackson. Students frequently create acronyms and acrostics when they study for tests.

Evaluating techniques for improving memory naturally led psychologists to look for the physiological basis of memory. We consider their findings next.

acronym
A word formed by the initial letter(s) of the items to be remembered

acrostic
A verse or saying in which the first letter(s) of each word stands for a bit of information

STUDY TIP

Make a set of flash cards naming and describing the different processing strategies. When you are studying material from this or another class, choose a card at random, test yourself on what it means, and then try out that particular strategy with the material you are studying.

R E V I E W   S U M M A R Y

1. Craik and Lockhart proposed only one type of memory. The **level of processing** may determine the permanence of the storage of this memory.

2. Other researchers have proposed that there is more than one type of long-term memory. Four types have been identified: **procedural, semantic, episodic,** and **priming** or **implicit memory.** Each serves to store a different kind of information.

3. The **tip-of-the-tongue (TOT) phenomenon** has been used to study the network of semantic memories, whereas the study of **flashbulb memories** has provided information about episodic memory.

4. Research on the **retrieval** of memories has shown that we scan both STM and LTM to locate an item we wish to recall.

5. **Encoding specificity** has a great deal to do with the ease with which a memory is retrieved. If the cues that were present when a memory was encoded or stored are not present during retrieval, it is difficult to retrieve that memory.

6. Encoding specificity appears to be at work in **state-dependent learning,** which states that we recall information

better when we learn and are tested in the same physiological/psychological state.

7. It has been suggested that memories of childhood sexual abuse may be repressed and recalled during adulthood. Many of these repressed memories appear to have been induced during therapy sessions by suggestions made by the therapist.

8. The number of sessions, distribution of practice, meaningfulness of items, similarity of items, and **serial position** of items influence human learning.

9. Our memory can be improved by using a **mnemonic device** such as **imagery.** The **method of loci** and the **pegword technique** are two popular mnemonic devices.

10. Grouping and coding are two other techniques that can be used as memory aids. **Acronyms,** words formed by the first letter(s) of the items to be remembered, and **acrostics,** a verse or saying in which the first letter(s) of each word stands for a bit of information, are two popular forms of coding.

✓ CHECK YOUR PROGRESS

1. If your strategy in studying for a test is to memorize all the material, you may not do as well as someone else who relates the course material to real-life events. Why?

2. What is the main problem with the levels-of-processing approach to the study of memory?

3. How does the Craik-Lockhart model of memory differ from the Atkinson-Shiffrin model?

a. The second model hypothesizes only one type of long-term memory.

b. The second model assumes retrieval is not an active process in short-term memory.

c. The first model hypothesizes only one type of memory, but different levels of information processing.

d. The first model uses semantic networking as a core concept in determining what is retained in working memory.

4. What is the most important question for Craik and Lockhart's view of memory?

   a. How long do memories last?
   b. How do we process information?
   c. How are visual memories stored?
   d. How much can we store in memory?

5. Which aspect of golf involves procedural memory?

   a. recalling how to swing the golf club
   b. recalling the time you made a hole-in-one
   c. recalling what type of golf ball you're using
   d. recalling that golf was first played in Scotland

6. Explain the relation between priming or implicit memory and improving recall by elderly people.

7. How have psychologists demonstrated the retrieval of memories from STM?

8. The tip-of-the-tongue (TOT) phenomenon is to semantic memory as flashbulb memories are to

   a. implicit memory.
   b. semantic memory.
   c. episodic memory.
   d. procedural memory.

9. Which of the following illustrates a schema?

   a. the definition of the word *mild*
   b. the grocery list you just memorized

   c. your knowledge about "going to a play"
   d. your memory of a time you played basketball

10. What is state-dependent learning? Give an original example of this process.

11. What is the "repressed-memory controversy"? What problem might this controversy be creating?

12. There is an important history exam tomorrow. Amy has been studying a little each day for the past two weeks, whereas you have reserved the two nights before the exam for studying. Who will do better on the exam? Explain your reasoning.

13. Psychologists who speak of working memory are referring to

   a. short-term memory.
   b. long-term memory.
   c. episodic memory.
   d. primary memory.

14. What has occurred when learning one set of items affects the learning of a second set of items?

   a. coding
   b. transfer
   c. relearning
   d. state-dependence

ANSWERS: 1. You are processing at a very shallow level. The person who relates the material to real-life events is processing at a much deeper level. **2.** The term *level of processing* has never been clearly defined. **3.** c **4.** b **5.** a **6.** Priming memory sensitizes persons to the information that is to be retrieved. Thus, an elderly person may find it easier to retrieve memories. **7.** By measuring the time it takes to respond with a *yes* or a *no* to the presence of a letter in STM. As more letters are added to the stimulus, the time required to identify a given letter as one that was present increased. **8.** c **9.** c **10.** State-dependent learning is the storage of a memory under a certain physiological/psychological state. Learning the material for your next psychology test when you are extremely tired would be an example of state-dependent learning. **11.** The repressed/recovered memory controversy refers to the truthfulness of the sudden recall of repressed memories of childhood abuse by teenagers and adults undergoing therapy. Because there is no way to distinguish between true and false repressed memories, this controversy may be leading to false allegations and the likelihood that true instances of repressed memories will not be believed. **12.** Amy will do better on the exam because she has studied more often (increased number of study sessions is superior to one session) and because she has spread her studying out over the 2-week period before the exam (spaced practice is more effective than massed practice). **13.** a **14.** b

THE PHYSIOLOGICAL BASIS OF LEARNING AND MEMORY

When H. M. was 7 years old, he was struck by a bicycle, fell, and injured his head. Although there appeared to be only minimal damage, several years later H. M. began experiencing minor but intense brain seizures. A major seizure occurred when he was 16. By the time he was 27, the frequency and intensity of the seizures warranted surgery to remove large portions of his hippocampus and amygdala (see Chapter 2). The operation took place in 1953. *What can an operation to control seizures tell us about memory?*

In addition to identifying and studying the processes that occur during learning and memory, psychologists have attempted to isolate the physical changes that accompany those processes. In other words, they have attempted to pinpoint and describe the physiological basis of learning and memory. Their research has focused on patients who suffer memory loss as a result of head injuries or operations like the one just described.

Amnesias

After experiencing a physical or psychological trauma, a person can lose his or her memory of people, places, and things. Such memory losses are called **amnesias.** We discuss amnesias caused by psychological traumas in Chapter 12. The study of amnesias resulting from physical trauma provides insight into the nature of memory. Two types of amnesias have been identified: *anterograde* and *retrograde.*

Anterograde Amnesia and the Hippocampus.

The inability to store new information after a traumatic physical event is known as **anterograde amnesia.** The case of H. M. is a well-known example of anterograde amnesia (Scoville & Milner, 1957). What can this case tell us about memory?

As it turned out, H. M.'s operation, in which large portions of the hippocampus and amygdala were removed, provided a great deal of information about the nature of memory. Since the operation, H. M. was unable to form new memories; his entire world consisted of memories that were formed before 1953. He did not remember such things as the names of people he had just met, what he ate for lunch, what was on television last night, or what year it is. In short, his daily experience consisted exclusively of STM, of living from moment to moment, except for his pre-1953 memories.

Psychological Detective

On the basis of this case, you should be able to reach two tentative conclusions. One has to do with the stages-of-memory processing discussed earlier; the second concerns the physiological basis of memory. Spend a few moments reviewing this information; then write down the two conclusions.

If you believe that H. M.'s problem has to do with the memory-storage process, you are correct. For H. M., new information is not reaching long-term storage. Thus we are led to the second conclusion: The hippocampus or amygdala is involved in the process of storing new memories. Notice we said that these structures are *involved in the process* of storing new memories, not that new memories are stored in these structures. If memories were stored in the hippocampus or amygdala, H. M.'s operation would have erased memories stored before 1953.

The conclusion that the hippocampus is involved in the storing of memories is supported by research using animals. When the hippocampus is removed from both hemispheres of the brain in laboratory animals, the animals have difficulty holding information about a learning task they have just mastered in STM (Baddeley, 1988).

Retrograde Amnesia and the Consolidation Hypothesis.

Physical trauma may also result in the loss of memory of events that occurred before the trauma. In such cases we are dealing with **retrograde amnesia.** The fact that the greatest memory loss is for events that occurred just before the trauma suggests an interesting and testable hypothesis. Based on the notion that memories must "set" or "consolidate" to be stored in LTM, the **consolidation hypothesis** predicts that memories that are interfered with before they have consolidated will not be stored. This process is analogous to baking a cake: If the oven door is opened, the cake will fall. The blow on the head that produces retrograde amnesia has interrupted the consolidation process for recent memories.

Both human and animal studies have provided evidence to support the consolidation hypothesis. For example, in some cases of severe depression, *electroconvulsive therapy (ECT)*, also known as *electroshock therapy*, may be used (see Chapter 13). This procedure involves passing an electric current through the patient's brain. In addition

amnesia
Loss of memory that occurs as a result of physical or psychological trauma

anterograde amnesia
Inability to store new memories after a traumatic event

retrograde amnesia
Loss of memories that were stored before a traumatic event

consolidation hypothesis
Hypothesis that memories must be consolidated or "set" before they can be stored

A human patient undergoing electroshock therapy may suffer from retrograde amnesia. According to the consolidation hypothesis, this loss of memory occurs because consolidation and transfer to long-term memory do not take place.

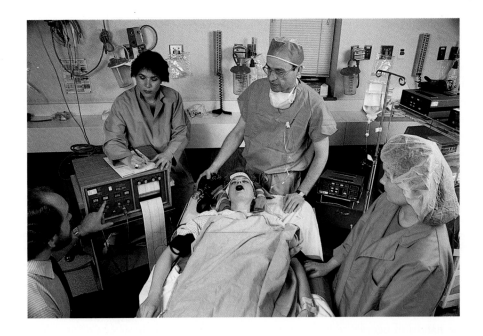

to reducing the depression, ECT produces strong retrograde amnesia. Early studies found that the application of electroconvulsive shock (ECS) to animals shortly after a learning task also produced retrograde amnesia, suggesting that it interferes with the formation of a memory. What's more, the longer the delay between completion of the task and the application of ECS, the less the effect of ECS. In the longer delay conditions, we assumed that the memory had more time to consolidate and therefore ECS did not interfere with it as much.

In one study of the effects of ECS (Chorover & Schiller, 1965), rats were placed on small platforms. The normal response of a rat in this situation is to step down from the platform. When the rats stepped down, however, they received an electric shock to their feet. The rats' task was to learn to stay on the platform to avoid a foot shock. Five groups of rats were tested. These groups received ECS (by passing a mild electric current through the brain) either 3, 5, 7, 10, or 30 seconds after stepping off the platform and receiving a foot shock. Figure 7-11 shows that the longer the interval between the learning task and the delivery of ECS, the greater the percentage of animals staying on the platform on the next trial. Thus it appears that the memory of receiving the foot shock after stepping off the platform was consolidated more strongly when ECS was applied either 10 or 30 seconds after a foot shock. Although not all animal studies have supported the consolidation hypothesis as well (Maki, 1986), there is no doubt that ECS impairs memory storage.

FIGURE 7-11 The longer the delay between original learning and an electroconvulsive shock, the greater the percentage of animals who avoided foot shock by staying on the platform.

Source: Chorover & Schiller, 1965.

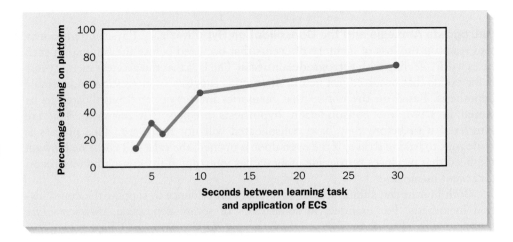

REVIEW SUMMARY

1. Physical trauma may result in a loss of memory known as **amnesia. Anterograde amnesia** occurs when new information cannot be stored, although old memories remain intact. It can result from damage to the hippocampus. **Retrograde amnesia** occurs when memories for events that happened before the traumatic event are lost. It may occur when memories are not allowed to **consolidate** or set.

CHECK YOUR PROGRESS

1. Loss of memory owing to a physical trauma is known as

   a. consolidation.

   b. habituation.

   c. amnesia.

   d. long-term potentiation.

2. After a serious car accident, John cannot remember driving in the rain. Nor can he recall skidding and plowing into a truck. This deficit is an example of

   a. retrograde amnesia.

   b. anterograde amnesia.

   c. encoding specificity.

   d. state-dependent learning.

3. What notion is supported by the fact that electroconvulsive therapy disrupts memories?

   a. neural circuits

   b. consolidation hypothesis

   c. synaptic changes and memory

   d. protein synthesis and memory

4. Which kind of amnesia results from damage to the hippocampus? Why?

5. Laboratory rats prefer to be in dark places; hence they move readily from a brightly lit chamber to a dark one. Assume that a foot shock is administered when the rats enter the dark compartment. What should the rats learn from this experience? What will happen if they receive an ECS three seconds after receiving a foot shock in the dark compartment? What would happen if an ECS was administered one hour after the rats received a foot shock in the dark compartment?

ANSWERS: 1. c **2.** a **3.** b **4.** Anterograde amnesia. Damage to the hippocampus results in the inability to form new memories. **5.** The rats should learn not to enter the dark compartment. If an ECS is administered three seconds after the shock in the dark compartment, there may be considerable disruption of consolidation. If an ECS is administered one hour after the shock in the dark compartment, the memory will have set, and an ECS will have no effect.

ANSWERS   To Psychological Detective

PAGES 287–288

1. Pacific Ocean

2. Oak

3. Internal combustion engine

4. Hibernate

5. Missouri River

ANSWERS   To Hands-On Exercise

PAGE 288

How many capitals were on the tip of your tongue the first time you went through the list of states? Did the first letter help you recall any additional names?

State	Capital
Alabama	Montgomery
Connecticut	Hartford
Florida	Tallahassee
Georgia	Atlanta
Idaho	Boise
Iowa	Des Moines
Kentucky	Frankfort
Louisiana	Baton Rouge
Maryland	Annapolis
Massachusetts	Boston
Mississippi	Jackson
Nebraska	Lincoln
New Jersey	Trenton
Oregon	Salem
Texas	Austin
Wyoming	Cheyenne

CHAPTER 8

Thinking, Language, and Intelligence

CHAPTER OUTLINE

The brain plays a key role in basic processes such as sensing and perceiving the environment, emotional reactions, and states of consciousness. Most of the basic processes we have discussed thus far are also found in lower animals, so we may wonder what separates lower animals from human beings.

The human brain endows us with remarkable abilities to solve problems and to make decisions. In this chapter we explore some of humans' remarkable abilities. As we explore these abilities, we also find that humans can be misled by some of the methods we use to solve problems and make decisions. One of the most remarkable human achievements—the development of complex language—sets us apart from other species. One way to view the intellectual achievements of human beings is to consider this fact: Only human beings are capable of creating methods to measure their intellectual achievements. One of the more contentious issues we discuss is the measurement of intelligence. Our analysis of this topic shows us how the study of a topic changes over time and how new ways of conceptualizing intelligence are offered.

THINKING

After agreeing to take part in an experiment, Sandy was asked to sit in front of a computer screen and view a series of geometric figures that were presented in pairs (see Figure 8-1). Her task was simple: Determine whether the paired figures are the same or different. In some cases she quickly made the determination; in others the process took longer. Although she guessed the experiment was designed to study thinking, she wondered how psychologists could study such an unseen process. *How do psychologists study thinking?*

In Chapter 1 we described how John B. Watson, the founder of behaviorism, redirected psychology to focus on the observation of external events. Because conscious experience could not be observed directly, he concluded that it was not worthy of scientific investigation. Terms such as *thinking* or *thoughts* were not precise, so Watson turned to the study of the muscle movements of subvocal speech as the basis of what we call thinking. Does Watson's proposal to study the muscle movements related to speech seem far-fetched? Ask someone a question (preferably one requiring some deliberation), and watch the person's lips as he or she considers how to respond. Do the person's lips move? As part of his effort to make psychology more objective, Watson claimed that psychologists could study thinking if it consisted of observable muscle movements like those that occur when we speak silently to ourselves.

If thinking consists of barely detectable motor movements, it would be impossible to think if all your motor muscles were paralyzed. To test this notion, Scott Smith injected himself with curare (see Chapter 2), a poison that blocks conduction in motor neurons and therefore causes paralysis (Smith et al., 1947). Had he not been connected to a respirator that could breathe for him, he would have died. While he was paralyzed, his colleagues asked him questions and even gave him problems to solve. After the effects of the curare wore off, Smith told his colleagues what he had been thinking while he was paralyzed. His courageous efforts demonstrated that thinking consists of more than just muscle movements.

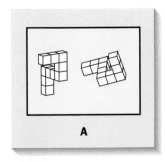

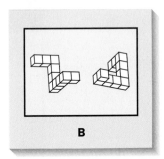

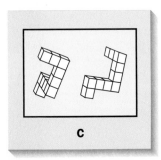

FIGURE 8-1 Pictures of three-dimensional objects shown to participants by Shepard and Metzler (1971). For each, look at the object on the left and determine whether the object on the right is a rotated view of the same object.

Source: Shepard & Metzler, 1971.

Cognitive Psychology

Although the results reported by Smith and his colleagues were striking, behaviorism remained a dominant force in psychology for more than half of the 20th century (Guenther, 1998). Eventually a new perspective, cognitive psychology, gained prominence. **Cognitive psychology** is a branch of psychology that examines thinking: how we know and understand the world, solve problems, make decisions, combine information from memory and current experience, use language, and communicate our thoughts to others. **Thinking** is a mental process involving the manipulation of information in the form of images or concepts that is inferred from our behavior. Thinking is evident, for example, when we solve a problem or make a decision.

Cognitive psychologists infer mental processes from the observable behaviors of the people they study. For example, to uncover problem-solving strategies, they may ask people to think aloud as they solve problems (called a verbal protocol). In the following discussion we consider one way in which cognitive psychologists draw inferences about thinking—through the study of images.

Images. What route do you follow when you walk from the front door of your apartment to your bedroom? What is the shape and color of a highway "yield" sign? Many people report that they visualize events and objects to answer such questions. Visual imagery, the experience of seeing even though the event or object is not actually viewed, can activate brain areas responsible for visual perception, such as the occipital lobes (see Chapter 2). Images do not have to be visual, however; they can be auditory or even olfactory (involving the sense of smell).

Before the development of sophisticated equipment to study brain activation, two researchers, Roger Shepard and Jacqueline Metzler (1971, 1982), investigated how people answer questions about visually presented material. Look again at Figure 8-1, and examine the paired drawings to determine whether the objects on the right are the same as those on the left. If you rotated the objects on the left, would they be the same as those on the right? The pairs of geometric figures used by Shepard and Metzler differed in orientation to each other between 0 and 180 degrees. Half of the pairs were matches that had been rotated; the other half were mirror images that could not be rotated to match. How would you go about answering questions about these pairs of figures? Would you create a visual image of the objects in your mind?

Psychological Detective

The study of visual imagery poses a difficulty for researchers: The process of thinking cannot be directly observed. How could researchers draw inferences about the mental processes involved in answering questions about the paired objects in Figure 8-1? Give this question some thought, and write down your answer before reading further.

Shepard and Metzler found that people were accurate in judging whether the pairs of figures were the same or different. When the object had been rotated a great deal, however, participants took longer to decide whether it was the same or different. Why? The researchers inferred that the increased time was spent mentally rotating the figures. Support for this conclusion is found in data showing that the greater the degree of rotation, the longer people take to rotate the configuration back to the original orientation. To behaviorists, such inferences about unseen mental processes are not a legitimate part of science. In science, however, inference is common: Geologists use the Earth's sediment layers to infer past events, and physicists cannot observe gravity directly, even though they study its effects.

cognitive psychology
The subfield of psychology concerned with the study of higher mental processes such as thinking, knowing, and deciding

thinking
Manipulation of information in the form of mental images or concepts

Visual images allow us to scan information stored in memory and answer questions like the ones we asked earlier; they also help us plan a course of action. For example, Albert Einstein's insight into the theory of relativity occurred when he created a visual image of chasing after and matching the speed of a beam of light. Later he turned this visual image into words. The following examples illustrate the value of imagery in our thinking, as well as its potential application in sports.

Suppose we need to describe the size of an acre. How could we convey this information? If we told you that there are 43,560 square feet in an acre, would that help you understand how large an acre is? Perhaps not. If, however, we used a visual image and told you that an acre is about the size of a football field minus the end zones, we would probably make it more understandable.

Words like *book, house,* and *pencil* readily give rise to visual images and are easier to remember than low-imagery words like *ambition, integrity,* and *responsibility* (Paivio, 1971, 1986). Why? High-imagery words offer two pegs on which to hang our memories: visual images and meaning (see Chapter 7). By contrast, low-imagery words must be remembered from their meaning alone.

Sport psychologists have advocated visual imagery as a practice technique to enhance performance in a number of sports as well as an aid in rehabilitating injuries (Smith et al., 2001; Sordoni et al., 2000). A review of the evidence on effects of imagery on sports performance led to the conclusion that imagery has a positive and significant effect on performance (Driskell, Copper, & Morna, 1994). How does visual imagery enhance performance? Measures of blood flow in the brain show that mental practice can activate brain structures without actual physical movement; this activation appears to improve the control and execution of movement (Decety & Ingvar, 1990; Roure et al., 1999).

Although images play an important role in cognition, not all thinking involves imagery. Much of it involves the formation and use of concepts. Next let's look at the role that concepts play in thinking.

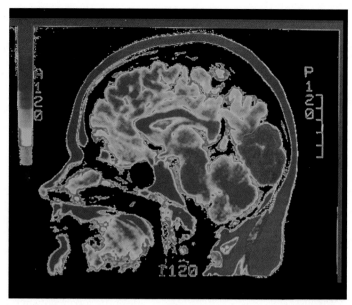

Visual imagery can activate various areas of the brain (indicated in red on this PET scan), especially the occipital lobes, which are responsible for processing visual information.

Visualizing a football field (without the end zones) makes it easier to comprehend the size of an acre.

concepts
Mental categories that share common characteristics

Concepts.   What would life be like if we had to deal separately with each individual animal, object, and person in our environment? How could we learn the names of all of them? We avoid such problems by using **concepts**—mental representations of a class (chairs, dogs, teachers) of things. Cabbage, peppers, and string beans are examples of the concept "vegetables." Concepts reduce the load on memory and enhance our ability to communicate; they also allow us to make predictions about our world.

Imagine sitting behind the wheel of an unfamiliar car. You can predict how the car operates, know the type of fuel needed, understand what happens when you put the key in the ignition, and locate several controls. You can do these things because you understand the concept "car." Much of what we learn in school, especially grade school, involves concepts such as colors, letters, species of living organisms, whole numbers and fractions, time, and distance. The use of such concepts makes communicating a great deal of information possible with relative ease.

One way we classify something as an example of a concept is to use rules that tell us what is and what is not an instance of the concept. Objects that follow the rules and have certain properties are called *positive instances* of the concept; the absence of such properties is the mark of a *negative instance* of the concept. Such rules work well for defining a concept such as "triangles" (closed, two-dimensional figures with three sides and angles that sum to 180 degrees) (Ross & Spalding, 1994).

Psychological Detective

An example of the rules approach to concepts can be found in Figure 8-2, where we have provided positive and negative instances of a concept. Your job is to figure out the rules we used. The first and fourth examples illustrate the concept (positive instances); the second and third examples do not illustrate the concept (negative instances). Write down the rule (or rules) that you believe define the concept before you go on. (The correct answer appears at the end of the chapter.)

One way you might learn this new concept is to use trial-and-error learning: You suggest a preliminary idea of what the concept might be; then you systematically test this idea or hypothesis on new examples. Researchers have used this approach in laboratory studies on concept formation. Were you able to identify the concept illustrated in Figure 8-2? As you thought about this concept, you probably noticed that it is not like those you encounter in everyday life, which usually are more complicated and not defined by neat sets of rules.

Now try to list the properties that could be used to classify an animal as a dog. You might suggest four legs, some fur, a tail, but so far the list of properties still includes cats, foxes, and wolves. You can see that listing a set of properties as the rules for

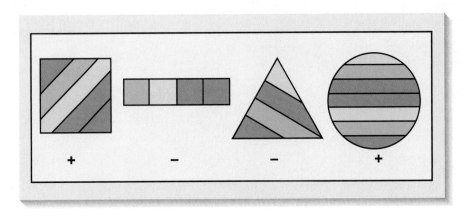

FIGURE 8-2   Sample material used in concept formation experiments.

FIGURE 8-3   All the animals in the photo on the left can be classified under the concept of "dog." Does the fox pictured on the right also belong to this concept? Why or why not?

defining a concept may not work well. Why? As the dog example shows us, many concepts have fuzzy or unclear boundaries (see Figure 8-3). It seems that we do not form concepts the way participants in laboratory research do, by creating a list of properties. Instead we often rely on a **prototype,** or best example, of each concept. When we encounter a new object, we compare it to the prototype.

Think of the concept "fruit." What prototype (image or word) do you have in mind right now? Did you think of an orange, a plum, a date? Think of the concept "sports." Which of the following best fits your prototype of a sport: car racing, chess, or baseball? Now think of a bird. What do you have in mind? When people rated the degree to which various fruits represented the concept "fruit," they rated orange and apple as the best examples; tomato and avocado were least likely to serve as the prototype of a fruit (Rosch, 1975). When we asked you to think of a bird, did you think of a cardinal, a robin, or a sparrow? You probably did not think of a chicken or a penguin.

We classify new objects according to their similarity to our prototypes. Thus membership in a concept category is not an all-or-nothing matter; rather, there are often degrees of similarity to the prototypes. The concepts we encounter and use every day do not have sharp boundaries and are not based on a specific, concrete set of properties.

What's more, our concepts do not exist independently, isolated one from another; rather, they are organized into a hierarchy. Let's take the concept of furniture, for example, where related concepts organized under it become increasingly more specific. At the next-lower level, we might have different types of furniture, including one labeled "chair." Below this heading is yet another level that would include "recliner," "rocking chair," "desk chair," and so forth (Ross & Spalding, 1994).

As we have seen, concepts reduce the load on our memory because we don't have to remember every instance of objects separately. At times, we rely on memory to help us solve problems that are related to similar ones we have seen before. Even when a problem is not similar to past problems, we can turn to some problem-solving methods that have generally stood the test of time.

Problem Solving

Every day we encounter a variety of minor problems; occasionally we face major ones. You may find that the wheels of your car spin on the ice, a zipper on your luggage breaks as you wait to board a flight, or your computer crashes at the most inconvenient time. Some problems are easy to solve, others require great effort, and some may be unsolvable.

The problems we must solve can differ along several dimensions; some are well defined and others are ill defined. Well-defined problems have three specified characteristics: a clearly specified beginning state (the *starting point*), a set of clearly specified

prototype
A specific example of a particular concept that is readily brought to mind; viewed as the most typical or best example of a particular concept

algorithm

A systematic procedure that is guaranteed to furnish the correct answer to a problem if it is followed correctly because the procedure involves evaluating all possible solutions

tools or techniques for finding the solution (the *needed operations*), and a clearly specified solution state (the *final product*) (Guenther, 1998; Medin et al., 2001). A well-defined problem might take the form of "How should I program my word processor to fit a 500-word essay on two pages?"

Here's another example of a well-defined problem. A certain psychologist (with little training in mechanics) took his riding lawnmower to a repair shop for a spring adjustment. The mechanic got the mower running but said the battery might be going bad. The battery was then replaced. When the psychologist tried to start the mower, however, nothing happened (starting point). He reasoned that because it was unlikely that the new battery was bad, the problem must be elsewhere. Because the motor would not turn over at all, the psychologist deduced that the new battery was not properly connected. Once the battery's connecting cables were tightened (needed operations), this well-defined problem was solved and the lawnmower started (final product).

On the other hand, ill-defined problems have a degree of uncertainty about the starting point, needed operations, and final product. An ill-defined question might take the form of "How can I write the type of paper that will earn a grade of A?"

Problem-Solving Methods.   When you recognize that a problem exists, you can search your memory to determine if you have faced a similar problem in the past; if so, you can retrieve the solution from memory and apply it to the current problem (see Chapter 7). If the problem is new and there is no solution in long-term memory, you can use several strategies to attack the problem. High-speed computers have provided scientists with a model that can be used to understand human thinking. To use the computer as a model of human thought, however, researchers need to know what human beings do when they solve problems. Two general approaches to solving problems can be programmed into a computer: algorithms and heuristics.

Algorithms.   One strategy you could use to solve some problems guarantees a correct solution in time (provided that a solution exists). An **algorithm** is a systematic procedure or specified set of steps for solving a problem, which may involve evaluating all possible solutions (Ashcraft, 2002; Medin et al., 2001). This approach guarantees a solution, if there is one. One example of an algorithm is the mathematical formula used to determine the area enclosed by a rectangle: Length multiplied by width gives the answer.

Psychological Detective

Here is an opportunity for you to solve a problem that could involve use of an algorithm. An *anagram* is a collection of letters that can be rearranged to form one or more words. Consider the following anagram:

O E V S L

How would you go about finding the word? As you try to solve this problem, pay attention to exactly what you do.

8.1

Finding the solution to our anagram problem is a bit more complicated than using the formula for the area of a rectangle. Before you start writing all the possible arrangements of the five letters, note that they can be arranged in 120 different ways. Of course, not all such arrangements are words and few of them are even remotely similar to real words.

Algorithms tell us exactly what to do to reach a solution, but they can be time consuming. If you spent 1 second on each combination of five letters, you could spend

2 minutes solving this simple anagram. Because most people solve the anagram in considerably less than 2 minutes, they probably use a method other than an algorithm. (The possible answers to the anagram are *solve*, *loves*, and *voles*.)

Algorithms do not provide answers when the problems are not clearly specified. No procedures can be set up in advance to guarantee a solution for such problems. What's more, some problems are so vast that algorithms are impractical. For example, chess players do not rely on algorithms because it would take centuries to examine all the possible arrangements of the chess pieces!

Heuristics. While you were trying to solve the anagram, you may have decided that the vowels O and E should be separated. It might also be a good idea to separate the V and the S because this combination of letters does not occur frequently in English words; on the other hand, SO is a common combination. These "rules of thumb" are examples of a problem-solving approach known as **heuristics.** Heuristics do not guarantee solutions, but they make more efficient use of time. Using heuristics may lead to quick solutions or to no solution at all.

Obstacles and Aids to Problem Solving. Researchers have compared the problem solving of experts and nonexperts and found that experts know more information to use in solving problems. More important, experts know how to collect and organize information and are better at recognizing patterns in the information they gather. We can use the knowledge researchers have gained to improve our own problem-solving capabilities and avoid obstacles.

Setting Subgoals. As we have noted, one way to study problem solving is to ask people to think aloud. This procedure enables a researcher to follow a person's problem-solving efforts. Using this technique, psychologists have found that expert problem solvers are adept at breaking problems down into subgoals, which can be attacked and solved one at a time. These intermediate subgoals can make problems more manageable and increase the chance of reaching a solution.

Psychological Detective

Try this problem. Nine adults and two children want to cross a river, using a raft that will carry either one adult or two children. The raft must be paddled by a person; it cannot be pulled across the river by a rope. How many times must the raft cross the river to accomplish this goal? (A round trip equals two crossings.) Write down your answer before reading further.

This is not an easy problem. Remember that effective problem solvers break down large problems into smaller subgoals; it is difficult to solve such a massive problem in one swipe. First you need to know how many crossings are required to transport one adult across the river. You find that it takes four crossings to move one adult across the river and return the boat to the original dock. If the two children cross the river, one of the children can return the boat. When the child returns, an adult can cross alone and the other child returns the boat. To move the nine adults across the river you must repeat that sequence of four trips eight more times; it will take 36 trips to move nine adults. One final trip is needed to move the two children across, for a total of 37 trips.

The keys to solving this problem are (1) to identify the sequence needed to transport one adult across the river and (2) to determine that the sequence can be repeated. Finding the solution requires that you break the problem into manageable intermediate subgoals (one person at a time).

---

heuristics
Educated guesses or rules of thumb for solving problems that is not guaranteed to yield the correct answer

Approach to Representing Problems.   Information that is not organized effectively can hinder problem solving. At times we may rely on memory; at other times external representations of a problem are helpful.

Consider the following problem. There are three boxes of equal size. Inside each box are two smaller boxes. Inside each of the smaller boxes are four even smaller boxes. How many boxes are there all together?

The chances of solving this problem improve if it is represented somewhere other than in our heads. Students who were prompted to draw the problem solved it more frequently. (The correct answer is 33 boxes.)

What is 2/3 of 1/2? When you first read this problem, you may become confused and conclude that it is difficult. Now let's represent the problem as $2/3 \times 1/2$. This shows us that we could represent it as "What is 1/2 of 2/3?" This small change in representation converts a moderately difficult problem into a simple one in which the answer almost jumps off the page. Now try to solve a slightly different kind of problem.

Psychological Detective

Connect the nine dots in Figure 8-4 with four straight lines without lifting your pencil from the page. Try to solve this problem before reading further.

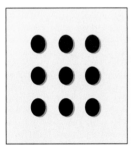

FIGURE 8-4   The nine-dot problem.

What did you see when you looked at the dots? Your perception of the dots probably followed the Gestalt principles of perceptual organization discussed in Chapter 3. One difficulty many people face in solving this problem is the tendency to see the dots as a boundary enclosing a rectangle. Thus our perception can lead us astray; however, nothing in the problem prevents us from taking our pencil outside the imaginary boundary that our mind creates. Try the problem; then turn to the end of the chapter for some solutions.

Here's another problem to solve. How would you put 27 pigs into four pens with an odd number of pigs in each pen? Most problem solvers try to figure a way to divide 27 into four odd numbers. This approach seems reasonable until you realize it is not possible. You tried this approach because you perceived the solution to involve four separate and distinct pens. *Hint*: Try looking at the relationship among the pens again. Consult the end of the chapter for the answer to this problem.

Now try to solve the problems presented in Figure 8-5.

Rigidity.   Using past experience is often helpful in solving problems, but sometimes it can block the path of our problem-solving efforts. *Rigidity* is the tendency to rely too

FIGURE 8-5   Try your hand at solving three more problems. The key to solving them is to break away from obvious ways of looking at things. Consider other perspectives; otherwise you will box yourself in, as you did if you treated the nine dots in Figure 8-4 as a rectangle. The answers appear at the end of the chapter.

Source: Michalko, 1991.

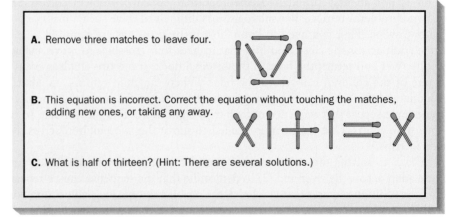

A. Remove three matches to leave four.

B. This equation is incorrect. Correct the equation without touching the matches, adding new ones, or taking any away.

C. What is half of thirteen? (Hint: There are several solutions.)

FIGURE 8-6 The Maier two-string problem. The two strings hanging from the ceiling are to be tied together, using only the chair and the pliers.

Source: Maier, 1931.

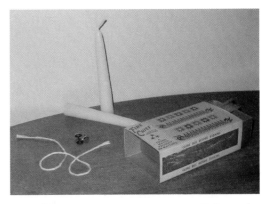

FIGURE 8-7 The candle problem. Using only the materials pictured, find a way to mount the candle on the wall.

Source: Duncker, 1945.

heavily on past experience in solving problems. A specific example of rigidity is the difficulty we experience in using familiar objects in new ways, which is termed **functional fixedness.** One example of functional fixedness, shown in Figure 8-6, is Maier's classic two-string problem (Maier, 1931). The two strings hanging from the ceiling are to be tied together. Among the objects in the room are a chair and a set of pliers.

The strings are too far apart to allow the person to grasp both of them and tie them together. Not surprisingly, most of the solutions tried by participants in Maier's study involved the chair, although unsuccessfully. What is the solution? Think about it for a while.

The solution to this problem is to tie the pliers to the end of one string, set the string in motion like a pendulum, then catch it and tie it to the other string. The solution may seem obvious to you now, but only 39% of participants solved the problem in the 10 minutes allotted. Why did they experience so much trouble with this problem? They displayed functional fixedness: They did not see that the pliers could be used in an unusual way. Now look at Figure 8-7.

functional fixedness
Inability to see new uses for familiar objects

 8.2

Psychological Detective

Your task is to solve the problem presented in Figure 8-7. Imagine that you are in a small, nearly empty room. On the floor are the following objects: a box of wooden kitchen matches, a piece of string, a candle, and several thumbtacks. There is no electricity in the room. The task is to use the materials in the figure to mount the candle on the wall (Duncker, 1945). Write down your solution to the problem before reading further.

The solution is presented at the end of the chapter. Many people fail to solve this problem as a result of functional fixedness. Because the matches are shown in the box,

TABLE 8-1

The Luchins Water Jug Problem

The goal is to obtain the desired quantity of water by using the jugs specified.

		Jugs of Water		Required Water
Problem	A	B	C	D
1	29	3	0	20
2	21	127	3	100
3	14	163	25	99
4	18	43	10	5
5	9	42	6	21
6	20	59	4	31
7	23	49	3	20
8	28	59	3	25

Source: Luchins, 1946.

Experiments on
Ape Intelligence

people attempting to solve this problem often fail to see the box as a possible support for the candle.

Set Effect.   As we have shown, problem solvers can experience difficulty in representing a problem and may also rely only on common uses of objects. Depending on prior experience is another way we restrict ourselves to certain problem-solving approaches even if they are not the most effective. Such a bias is called the **set effect.**

Luchins (1942) presented individuals with the problem outlined in Table 8-1. In this problem, the goal is to obtain the specified amount of water in Column D by using the jugs shown. After the first warm-up problem, the solution takes the form of B minus A minus 2C: Fill Jug B, then pour enough water to fill Jug A, and fill Jug C twice. This solution works for Problems 2 through 6.

Success in solving the first few water jug problems creates a "set" or tendency to use the same approach for the rest of the problems; after all, that approach worked. Nevertheless, there is an easier way to solve Problems 7 and 8. Those problems can be solved with fewer steps by first filling Jug A and then using it to fill Jug C. You may have failed to see this easier solution as you routinely applied the method that had worked so well for the earlier problems. You can continue to develop your problem solving skills by trying the problems in Figure 8-8.

The problems we have described here have solutions. In problem solving we search for solutions; however, our thinking does not involve just solving problems. Sometimes we are asked to weigh advantages and disadvantages of different courses of action. Here there is no problem to be solved, but there is a decision to be made.

STUDY TIP

In a group of three, discuss the material describing problem solving. Together, create a basic problem-solving process. Outline the process, labeling the steps according to the material you have read.

Making Decisions

Each day we make dozens—perhaps hundreds—of decisions. What is the easiest way to get to the family reunion next week? Should I go to the bank today, or wait until tomorrow? Some of these decisions are easy; others are more difficult. How do we make such decisions?

The human brain enables us to process vast amounts of information quickly and accurately. Heuristics are often helpful and economical and can lead to good decisions; at times, however, they may also lead to bad decisions. The same principles that allow us to make judgments easily and often successfully are also responsible for some of our

set effect
Bias toward the use of certain problem-solving approaches because of past experience

Prisoner's Escape

A prisoner was attempting to escape from a tower. He found in his cell a rope which was half long enough to permit him to reach the ground safely. He divided the rope in half and tied the two parts together and escaped. How could he have done this?

Ten Bowling Pins

The ten objects below are pointing toward the top of the page. Move any three of them to make the arrangement point down toward the bottom of the page.

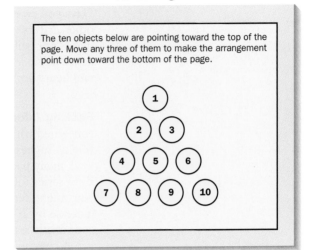

Six Drinking Glasses

By handling and moving only one glass, change the arrangement so that no full glass is next to another full one, and no empty glass is next to another empty one.

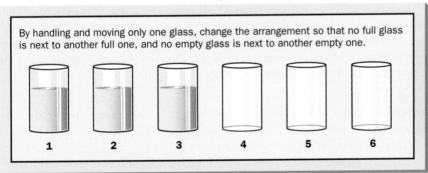

Six Pennies

Move only two pennies in the left diagram to yield the pattern at the right.

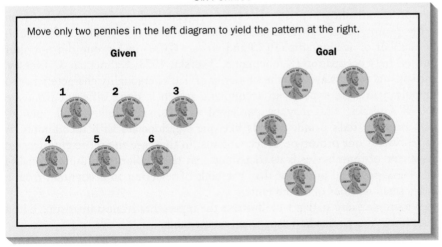

FIGURE 8-8 Here is an opportunity for you to try your problem-solving abilities on several different types of problems. Remember our discussion of the obstacles we face when we try to solve problems. Don't let these obstacles impede your efforts. Try each one of these problems before checking the answers the end of the chapter.

errors. For example, suppose that you see a red car that was involved in an accident. Have you ever decided that people who drive red cars drive faster and less safely than other drivers? If you were asked to estimate the number of crimes in which people plead "not guilty by reason of insanity," it is very likely that you would overestimate the actual number by quite a bit. In this section we look closely at some of the most important heuristics and their usefulness in making decisions.

Seeking Information to Confirm a Solution.   The series *2*, *4*, *6* follows a rule concerned with how the numbers relate to one another. Your task is to discover the rule by suggesting other sets of numbers that follow it. Because the numbers increase by 2, many people suggest a series such as *12*, *14*, *16*, followed by one like *22*, *24*, *26*. Both series follow the rule. Buoyed by these two confirmations of the proposed rule, you might feel confident in announcing that the rule requires that the numbers increase by 2; however, you would be wrong! In fact, 79% of participants in a study confidently stated an incorrect rule when given this problem (Wason, 1960).

A common mistake in testing hypotheses is to commit to one hypothesis without adequately testing other possibilities; this is known as **confirmation bias.** In our example, the correct rule is that the series must consist of three positive numbers that increase. If you tried a series like *1*, *2*, *3*, we would tell you that the series follows the rule and you could modify your initial hypothesis. People who found the correct rule earliest had generated more negative instances, which provided them with information that they could use to modify their hypotheses. This example illustrates an important aspect of our problem-solving and decision-making behavior: the tendency to seek instances that confirm our beliefs, solutions, or hypotheses and to avoid instances that disconfirm them.

The following story illustrates the power of the confirmation bias. A group of children were playing a game of "20 Questions"; the goal in this case was to find a number between 1 and 10,000. They cheered when the teacher said, "Yes, it is between 5,000 and 10,000," and groaned when the answer was "No, it is not between 0 and 5,000." Although both answers conveyed the same amount of information, confirmation was met with jubilation, and lack of confirmation was greeted with disappointment. As adults we do not outgrow the tendency to seek confirmation.

Representativeness.   When we use the **representativeness heuristic**, we determine whether an event, an object, or a person resembles (or represents) a prototype. Suppose that Ted, a college graduate, is very careful and concerned about details. He rarely tells jokes and seems to lack creativity. Give him a task, and he will carry it out according to the rules. Is Ted an accountant or a writer? Your conclusion would most likely be based on the similarity you perceive between Ted's characteristics and those you believe are common among accountants and writers; you would be using the representativeness heuristic. In essence you are looking for a match between Ted and the prototype of either an accountant or a writer. Including information about the number of accountants (30%) and writers (70%) in a group did not alter predictions of Ted's occupation (Kahneman & Tversky, 1973; Kahneman & Tversky, 2000). Participants were swayed by the similarity of Ted's personality characteristics to the commonly held stereotype of an accountant, which is quite different from the stereotype of a writer, who may be perceived as creative, tolerant, and open to experience. Because Ted's profile sounds like one we associate with accountants, it therefore represents our prototype of accountants. In this case the representativeness heuristic—a rule of thumb—leads us to assume that the similarity in the personality profile is a more powerful predictor than the odds of selecting an accountant from a group with a small number of accountants.

Here is a simple exercise that will illustrate the representativeness heuristic. Take a few pennies from your pocket and drop them on the table.

confirmation bias
Committing to one hypothesis without adequately testing other possibilities

representativeness heuristic
Heuristic in which one determines whether a particular instance represents a certain class or category

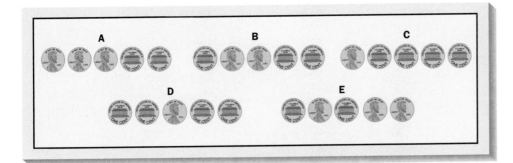

FIGURE 8-9 Look at each series of coin tosses. In observing these series many people conclude that some of them are more representative of true randomness than others. In fact, all of these series were generated by a computer.

Psychological Detective

Suppose that you and a friend are tossing coins. Your friend tosses five heads in a row. It is your turn to bet on the next coin toss. Will it be heads or tails? Write down your choice and your reason for making the choice before reading further.

We expect the numbers of heads and tails to be approximately equal in the long run. Research findings and our own experience tell us that fair coins behave this way across many tosses. Although we also expect to find this approximate equality in the short run, chance does not operate that way. Betting that the next toss will be tails after your friend has tossed five heads in a row is like saying the coin "knows" what happened on the previous five tosses and therefore heads is "due." Although a run of five heads does not seem to be representative of a random distribution of heads and tails, the odds on the next coin toss are *still* 50:50. Those prior tosses do not affect the odds. This faulty assumption is called the *gambler's fallacy*—another example of the representativeness heuristic. A series of heads and tails that does not look like chance is taken as evidence that some nonchance process is operating. Surprisingly, consecutive runs of heads and tails in random sequences can appear to be quite ordered. Some of the computer-generated sequences in Figure 8-9 look more random than the others. Some gamblers may misread the series of heads and tails and assume they have a better chance of predicting the next toss than is actually the case.

Availability. The **availability heuristic** involves making judgments or evaluations based on what comes to mind first. Consider the following: Are there more words with *r* as the first letter than as the third letter? A quick word inventory leads you to conclude that there are more words that begin with *r*, but you are wrong. Why? Words that begin with *r*—rich, reward, right—come to mind more easily than words such as *fare*, *street*, and *word*.

We assume that easily recalled items occur more frequently than ones that do not come to mind readily. What's more, we assume that what comes to mind easily is also more likely to occur in the future (Dawes, 1998; Kahneman & Tversky, 2000). Ease of recall often—but not always—is correlated with actual data. Who is most likely to be killed in a drunk-driving accident? Most people believe the answer is an innocent victim. According to the National Highway Traffic Safety Administration (2001), however, the person most likely to die in a drunk-driving accident is a drunk driver. Why do we give the wrong answer? It is easier to recall incidents in which an innocent person was the victim of a drunk-driving accident because such events are considered newsworthy. Drunk drivers die on the nation's highways every day, yet few of those accidents receive media attention.

Although the events covered by the media may not affect us directly, they play a role in how we assess our risk of accidents, catastrophes, or diseases. Imagine two of

The bets placed by gamblers are sometimes influenced by their observations of runs of numbers or colors. They often assume that a run that does not appear to be random (i.e., a repeated sequence) will reverse itself in the short run.

availability heuristic
Heuristic in which the probability of an event is determined by how readily it comes to mind

In July 2002, a Bashkirian Airlines TU–154 and a DHL (Delivery Service) Boeing 757 collided at 36,000 feet over southern Germany. All 71 on board the two planes were killed. Many of the dead were children on the Bashkirian airliner; they were traveling to summer camp. The extensive coverage given to such accidents leads many of us to overestimate the frequency of airline accidents because examples are easy to recall.

your friends discussing the relative safety of traveling to a vacation destination by either plane or automobile. News coverage of a recent plane crash leads them to decide in favor of travel by car, which they believe is safer. We may be misled because examples of airline accidents are dramatic and thus easy to recall. Yet more people are killed in cars and trucks during a single week than in plane crashes over the course of an entire year. For example, in 1998 there were 41,471 deaths in motor vehicle accidents (an average of almost 800 a week), whereas aviation-related accidents caused 667 deaths (U.S. Bureau of the Census, 2000). Almost all of the aviation deaths occurred in charter operations or general aviation, not the major carriers.

Comparison. We often make decisions by comparing the information we have obtained to some standard. Your standards are constantly changing, and these changes can affect your judgments. For example, a temperature of 68°F seems pleasant in the winter but cool in the summer.

Would you drive 20 minutes to save $5? Your answer may depend on the basis of comparison. If a toaster costs $45 at one store and the same toaster is available for $40 at another, are you likely to drive to the store with the lower price? Would you make the drive to buy a suit priced at $295 instead of $300 (Tversky & Kahneman, 1981; Kahneman & Tversky, 2000)? Most people say they would make the drive for the toaster but not for the suit, yet the amount of money saved would be the same. These choices are examples of the just noticeable difference (see Chapter 3). In short, we tend to see the benefits or gains of a comparison in relative rather than absolute terms.

Framing. When we make decisions we are also influenced by whether our attention is drawn to positive or negative outcomes; psychologists refer to this presentation of an issue as **framing** (Guenther, 1998; Kahneman & Teversky, 2000). When we make decisions we are generally risk averse; that means we want to stay away from negative outcomes. Unfortunately, this tendency has the potential to mislead us at times, causing us to fail to see that the way identical information is presented (framed) can make a dramatic difference in decision making. Consider an example. Imagine that you have lung cancer, and the treatment options are surgery or radiation. To help you make an informed decision, your physician tells you the results for lung cancer patients who selected surgery: 68% are alive after 1 year, and 34% are alive after 5 years. For lung cancer patients who selected radiation, 77% are alive after

framing

The tendency for decision making to be influenced by presentation of negative or positive outcomes; decision making tends to be risk averse

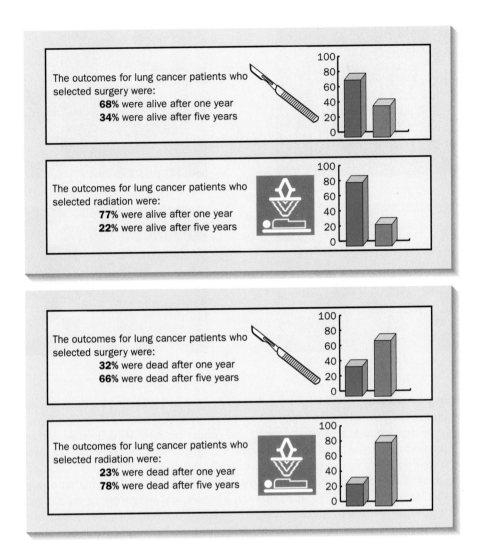

FIGURE 8-10 The way an issue is framed can influence our decision-making even on such important issues as medical treatment. In this case, people were presented with survival rates for one of two types of treatment (surgery represented by the scalpel or radiation represented by the patient receiving this treatment). When survival rates for one and five years were presented, most people selected surgery. When the same information was presented in terms of death rates, only a slight majority opted for the surgery. These differences in selecting treatment options occurred despite the fact that the presented information was the same; it simply had been framed differently.

1 year, and 22% are alive after 5 years. Given this information, which treatment do you select? The vast majority of people would select surgery.

Now let's change the framing a bit and see what happens. Suppose you are given the following information: Among patients who selected surgery, 32% are dead after 1 year and 66% are dead after 5 years. Among patients who selected radiation, 23% are dead after 1 year and 78% are dead after 5 years. Which treatment do you select now? Only a slight majority would select surgery. Note that the choices framed in terms of living or dying are identical (see Figure 8-10), yet the framing affects the option selected.

Keep in mind that the scenarios we have just described did not result from stupidity or a malfunctioning brain: "They illustrate how the mind actually works. Put in evolutionary terms, the mind has evolved to be effective in situations that are most likely to arise" (Restak, 1988, p. 238). We have developed some tried-and-true methods of making decisions that work most—but not all—of the time.

creativity
The ability to produce work that is both novel and appropriate

STUDY TIP

Create icons or pictures to help you remember each of the decision-making heuristics.

Creativity

Although we often face difficulties when trying to solve problems or in making decisions, we are capable of impressive and creative solutions and judgments. Yet **creativity,** or the ability to produce work that is both novel and appropriate, is a difficult concept to actually explain.

FIGURE 8-11 Judging creativity. These mosaics were constructed by individuals with different levels of creativity. Which would you judge to be creative?

Source: Barron, 1958.

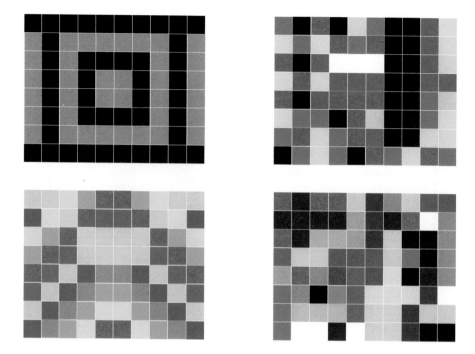

Defining Creativity. Which of the mosaic designs in Figure 8-11 would you judge to be creative? Show these drawings to several friends, and ask for their opinions. Do they agree that some of them are creative and others are not? Which ones? Although you may find consensus, you and your friends might be unable to report the precise criteria that you used in deciding what constitutes creativity.

If there is no absolute standard for creativity, how can we judge whether a work is creative? Teresa Amabile (1982) has proposed a consensual assessment of creativity. She asked a group of judges to make global ratings based on their own definitions of creativity. The judges' ratings of both verbal and artistic products were consistent and reliable. People seem to agree on what is and is not creative.

Measuring Creativity. Intelligence tests were not designed to measure creativity, so it is not surprising that the correlation between measures of creativity and intelligence is not strong (it is generally positive but low to moderate at best). High intelligence does not guarantee high creativity; low intelligence does not halt creativity. In many cases, "The creative solution is not known beforehand, and there is an immense range of possibility for new developments once we get into a problem. Not only are there no 'right or wrong' answers, there really are no 'answers' at all, until they have been tested in someone else's perception, or by external reality." (Barron, 1988, p. 85). This analysis suggests that many examples of creativity may begin as ill-defined problems.

Imagine that thinking is like a line. When all lines of thought converge on one correct answer, we have an example of *convergent thinking*. By contrast, *divergent thinking* takes our thinking in different directions in search of multiple answers to a question. Of the two, divergent thinking is related more closely to creativity.

Creativity typically involves seeing nontypical yet plausible ways of associating items or seeing aspects of an item that are real and useful but not usually the primary focus of our attention. You can gain insight into this process by completing items from the Remote Associates Test in Table 8-2. This test was designed to measure the process of making new associations. Success on the test calls for flexibility in making associations, fluency in the use of language, and originality.

Psychologists have devised other ways to measure creativity. In the Unusual Uses Test, for example, you would be asked to think of unusual uses for common objects such

TABLE 8-2

Sample Items from the Remote Associates Test

In this test you are presented with three words and asked to find a fourth word that is related to the other three. For example, what word do you think is related to these three?

cookies   sixteen   heart

The answer in this case is sweet. Cookies are sweet; sweet is part of the phrase "sweet sixteen" and part of the word "sweetheart." Here is another example:

poke   go   molasses

The answer is slow: slow poke, go slow, slow as molasses. As you can see, the fourth word may be related to the other three for various reasons. Now try these.

1. flap	tire	beanstalk
2. mountain	up	school
3. package	cardboard	fist
4. surprise	line	birthday
5. madman	acorn	bolt

Source: Mednick & Mednick, 1967.

---

as a brick, a ball, or a paper clip. In another measure of creativity, the Consequences Test, you would offer responses to questions such as "What would happen if people could become invisible at will?" "What would happen if all electrical generating plants closed at noon each day?" "What would happen if everyone could read everyone else's mind?" The responses are judged on the basis of novelty and appropriateness. For example, in response to the first item, you could say, "It would rain for 40 days and 40 nights." Although this response is novel (statistically rare), it is not appropriate in the context of the question. Conversely, if someone replied, "We couldn't see other people," the response would be appropriate but not novel. Thus there are two key elements in the definition of creativity as the ability to produce work that is both novel and appropriate.

Personal Factors in Creativity. Are there other keys to understanding creativity? Several personal characteristics distinguish creative people from less creative people. Creative people are not afraid of hard work; they give it their undivided attention and often persevere in the face of obstacles: "Almost every major creative thinker has surmounted obstacles at one time or another, and the willingness not to be derailed is a crucial element of success" (Sternberg & Lubart, 1991, p. 13). For example, Thomas Edison conducted more than 2,000 experiments with different possible filaments for a light bulb before finding one that would not burn out quickly.

Another mark of a creative person is a willingness to take risks and make mistakes. Such people can put their self-esteem on the line for the prospects of rewards greater than others might ever dream about. For example, experts declared Fred Smith's concept for Federal Express to be unworkable. Today Federal Express is the world leader in delivering packages (from letters to jet engines) anywhere in the world overnight. Creative people seem able to tolerate ambiguity, complexity, or a lack of symmetry. According to one expert, "It is clear that creative persons are especially disposed to admit complexity and even disorder into their perceptions without being made anxious by the resulting chaos. It is not so much that they like disorder per se, but that they prefer the richness of the disordered to the stark barrenness of the simple" (MacKinnon, 1978, p. 62).

Situational Factors in Creativity. Creativity often emerges when we rearrange what is known in new and unusual ways that can yield creative ideas, goods, and services. Humor and playfulness provide fertile ground for forming new associations and arrangements. Mozart recognized this possibility when he wrote, "When I feel well and in a good humor, or when I am taking a drive or walking after a good meal, . . . thoughts crowd into my mind as easily as you could wish" (Ghiselin, 1952, p. 44).

Alice Isen and colleagues asked college students to solve the candle problem presented in Figure 8-7 (Isen, Daubman, & Nowicki, 1987). Before trying to solve the problem, some students watched a comedy film; 75% of them found the solution. By contrast, only 13% of students who did not watch a comedy film solved the problem. In another experiment, Isen and her colleagues placed students into three groups. The students in the first group watched a comedy film; those in the second group exercised for 2 minutes; and the third group, the control group, had no special preparation. All the students then tried to solve items similar to those in the Remote Associates Test in Table 8-2. The first group solved more items than the other two; Isen and her colleagues concluded that induced positive feelings can facilitate creativity.

In one study, participants were asked to tell a story or make a collage. Some of them completed the work in exchange for a reward; others were not rewarded (Amabile, Hennessey, & Grossman, 1986). Judgments of the creativity exhibited in the stories or collages were lower when the participants had received a reward. This result was consistent with other studies that have found that extrinsic rewards (as opposed to intrinsic rewards) can change the perceptions of activities and also lower interest in them.

Another perspective on the motivation underlying creativity focuses on how the motivator actually affects the person: Does it direct attention toward the task rather than the goal? A *task-focusing* motivator energizes a person to work and keeps the person's attention on the task. By contrast, a *goal-focusing* motivator leads a person to focus attention on rewards such as money to the detriment of the task. Intrinsic motivators tend to be task-focusing because a goal such as personal fulfillment is integrated with the task. Extrinsic motivators tend to be goal-focusing because the rewards are noticeable and distinct from the task. People vary, however, as to how they focus. Some people focus on the goals, which may distract them from the task; others focus on the task. Thus extrinsic motivators may have either benefits or negative effects, depending on how they influence the person's focus (Lubart, 1994).

Creativity often flourishes under the right mix of intrinsic and extrinsic motivation. Thomas Edison's first invention was an automatic vote recorder for Congress. When he presented it to a member of Congress, he was told that efficiency in lawmaking was the last thing Congress wanted. From that point on, Edison stated that the only reason he invented was to make money; he didn't have the time or interest to modify the world to fit his inventions.

Enhancing Creativity at Work.   Businesses grow and prosper by adapting and creating new products and developing markets. Consequently, the business community has an interest in developing their employees' creativity. Such companies as Frito-Lay and Texas Instruments have introduced creativity-enhancing methods into their training with outstanding results. There is no magic in enhancing creativity; it takes the right attitude and technology in a work climate that is receptive to creative thinking and new ideas (Van Gundy, 1995). Individual and organizational creativity are closely interlocked. For example, environmental conditions at work—including freedom over one's work and sufficient time to think—facilitate creativity (Amabile, 1988).

One key to developing creativity is to be alert to potential problems that might be solved with creative solutions. For example, a track coach paid attention when his runners complained their running shoes were causing blisters. The coach, Bill Browerman, was confident he could improve the design of existing shoes. He cut patterns for the shoes out of grocery bags and found lightweight materials that improved cushion and traction. Browerman's shoes are known today by the brand name *Nike*.

We could also learn from the story of Swiss inventor George de Mestral. The name may be unfamiliar, but his invention is well known. One day he went hunting with his dog; they accidentally brushed against a bush that left both of them covered with burrs.

When he tried to remove them, they clung stubbornly to his clothes. To most of us this would be a minor annoyance, but not to de Mestral. After he got home, he looked at the burrs under a microscope and discovered that hundreds of tiny hooks on each burr had snagged the threads of his pants. The result of this accident was the invention of Velcro fasteners.

We may not all brush up against new ideas like de Mestral did, but we can set the table for creativity. Unfortunately, most people believe the world is divided into two types of people: the creative ones and the rest of us. Yet if you spend some time watching children play, you'll see a great deal of creativity. What happens to diminish creativity as we become adults? Children's imaginations roam freely and are not limited by reality because they are not constrained by adult rules of thinking: "They don't know that they have to color inside the lines" (Wujec, 1995, p. 20). Adults are expected to be serious, yet playfulness and humor can help develop flexible thinking. We need to be open to "fooling around" with ideas to explore new mental connections (Morreall, 1997). Injecting a bit of humor and playfulness into the work situation can stimulate a creative mind-set, including using games and puzzles designed to enhance creativity (Epstein, 2000; see Figure 8-12).

Quite often people fail to develop creative ideas because they do not believe they can be creative (Michalko, 1991). The first step in developing one's creativity is to acknowledge and confront these negative thoughts and replace them with positive thoughts. For example, many workers say to themselves, "I'll never be able to do it." This thought can be altered to the following: "I'll do a little bit at a time to get started. There's no reason that I have to do it all on a crash schedule."

Creativity consultants also aim to inject change into the lives of employees. They encourage employees to break habits by taking a different route to work, listening to a different radio station, or reading a different newspaper. These minor changes are designed to help employees break out of a rut, expose them to new ideas, and get them thinking rather than operating on automatic pilot. Employees are encouraged to look around, to make notes, and to collect lots of ideas.

We also need to recognize that creativity can take many forms. Henry Ford said he invented nothing new; he combined the inventions of others into a car. Ivory soap was run through an ice cream machine to add air that increased the sudsing and allowed the bar to float. Sometimes the creativity is remarkably simple: The key to the initial success of Domino's pizza was promising home delivery in 30 minutes or less.

Creative people can look at the same thing as everyone else but see something different (Wujec, 1995). For example, Arthur Fry, a chemist, was working with a glue that was to be used on fixed surfaces like bulletin boards. Unfortunately, it did not work well. One day while singing he had a creative insight: The adhesive could be used on a bookmark that would replace the little pieces of paper he used to mark his hymn book. Fry used the glue to develop Post-It notes.

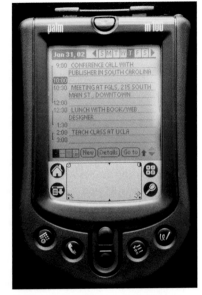

Although we often associate the word creativity with works of art, creativity flourishes in a wide variety of venues including business environments. Many of the new technological gadgets available today reflect creative efforts to develop and apply technology. The Palm Pilot pictured here is one of many creative technological advances that probably could not have been imagined even 5 years ago.

	A	B	C	D	E
1	WIRE JUST	Budget △	O V A T I O N	SHOT	VA DERS
2	NINTH	sitting world	hand hand hand deck	dipping	sight love sight sight sight
3	cancelled	H-O-P-E-S	head ache	ME AL ME AL DAY ME AL	SESAME

FIGURE 8-12 Creativity consultants often suggest that their clients do some puzzle-solving exercises to prepare them to be more creative. In this example, each box is a kind of puzzle for familiar words or phrases. For example, Box 1a can be read "Just under the wire." Try to decipher the other boxes. The solutions can be found at the end of the chapter.

Source: Wujec, 1995.

REVIEW SUMMARY

1. Behavioral psychologists believed thinking could be equated with muscle movements of the vocal apparatus; however, research has shown that this is not correct.

2. **Cognitive psychology** is the study of thinking. Thinking involves manipulation of information that can take the form of images or concepts. Visual imagery is the experience of seeing without the object or event actually being viewed.

3. **Concepts** are mental representations that facilitate thinking and reduce the number of elements we must consider. Concepts may be defined by their properties; however, we usually identify specific examples as members of a concept by judging their degree of similarity to a **prototype,** or best example, of the concept.

4. An **algorithm** is a method of solving problems that involves systematically exploring all possible solutions until the correct one is reached. Algorithms can be time-consuming and do not work for problems that are not clearly defined.

5. **Heuristics** are educated guesses or rules of thumb that are used to solve problems. Although the use of heuristics does not guarantee a solution, it is more time-efficient than using algorithms.

6. Rigidity is the tendency to rely on past experiences to solve problems. One form of rigidity, **functional fixedness,** is

the inability to use familiar objects in new ways. Likewise, set effect predicts that we will attempt to use solutions that have been successful in the past, even when they are not the most effective.

7. The **representativeness heuristic** predicts that we will base decisions on the similarity of characteristics of the situation to previously established concepts. The **availability heuristic** involves judging the probability of events by the readiness with which they come to mind. The way in which information is presented can dramatically alter our decision making; this effect is called **framing.** We also make decisions by comparing the information we have received to some standard. Heuristics facilitate good decisions but may sometimes result in bad ones.

8. **Creativity** depends on divergent thinking, rather than the convergent thinking assessed in tests of intelligence. Creative people have a high capacity for hard work, a willingness to take risks, and a high tolerance for ambiguity and disorder. The business community is interested in enhancing creativity to develop and market products and services. The methods used to enhance creativity include engaging in humorous and playful activities.

✓ CHECK YOUR PROGRESS

1. Identify each of the following:
   a. An educated guess based on some rule of thumb to solve a problem.
   b. Using a mechanical method to generate all possible solutions to a problem.
   c. Relying too heavily on past experience in solving current problems.

2. What is the advantage of creating an external representation when you are solving a problem?

3. You are engaged in a thought game in which your task is to discover the rule by which a series of numbers has been constructed. You are presented with the series 2, 5, 8. What is the next number? You answer 11. Which approach to problem solving does your guess illustrate? Why might this approach not be effective?

4. Eve decides to investigate the relation between intelligence and creativity. Through consultation with her teacher, she selects measures of intelligence and creativity. When the data are collected, she correlates the scores for all the participants in her sample. What is the likely outcome of her research?
   a. It is impossible to correlate creativity, so her research will not reveal any results.

   b. The tests of creativity and intelligence will reveal a low, positive correlation.
   c. The tests of creativity and intelligence will reveal a high, negative correlation.
   d. The tests of creativity and intelligence will reveal a moderate, negative correlation.

5. Which of the following has been found to facilitate creativity?
   a. remarkable rote memory
   b. a history of childhood rebellion
   c. positive feelings induced by humor
   d. the presence of the mental disorder schizophrenia

6. Teresa Amabile has developed a method of identifying creative works. Which of the following statements could summarize her work?
   a. Creativity occurs under conditions that focus on extrinsic motivation.
   b. Only experts in a given field can offer legitimate opinions on creativity.
   c. People reliably identify what they think is creative even if they fail to describe a precise definition.
   d. There is no way to identify creative works; we must rely on the artist to make such judgments lest we inhibit freedom of expression.

7. When asked to name a sports car, Hank says "Mustang" and Sally says "Corvette." A psychologist who is studying thinking might describe these two cars as examples of the _____ used by Hank and Sally.

   a. heuristics
   b. prototypes
   c. representatives
   d. confirmations

8. Which of the following is the best example of functional fixedness?

   a. Sally is unable to use a saw.
   b. Darla uses a comb to fix her hair before an interview.
   c. Dan fails to realize he could use his shoe to pound a nail into the wall.
   d. Sam decides that he is not going to use a steak knife on a hamburger.

9. Researchers called 1,000 people and asked them to estimate the number of people who would be found not guilty by reason of insanity out of 100. The respondents consistently overestimate the actual number. Which concept is a psychologist most likely to use in explaining the survey results?

   a. algorithm
   b. availability
   c. representativeness
   d. functional fixedness

10. Which of the following have psychologists used to explain the greater ease we have in remembering words like *car* and *book* compared to *integrity* and *responsibility*?

   a. framing
   b. imagery
   c. creativity
   d. availability

ANSWERS: 1. a. heuristic **b.** algorithm **c.** rigidity **2.** Reduces the burden on memory **3.** You have generated a solution to the problem without considering that the sequence does not increase by three. Although you have found a solution that confirms your hypothesis, you have failed to generate other possibilities. **4.** b **5.** c **6.** c **7.** b **8.** c **9.** b **10.** b

LANGUAGE

You have agreed to take care of your 30-month-old niece while her parents go out for dinner and a movie. You are intrigued by some of the words she uses. For example, she says the word *mouses*, although you are fairly sure that no one has taught her that word. While she is eating dinner she asks for more "chicken on the cob." When you realize that she delights in eating corn on the cob, you conclude that to her a chicken leg looks like a cob! *How do children's speech errors help us understand the way they acquire language?*

The use of language to communicate is basic to the human ability to develop, refine, and exchange ideas; in fact, language is a universal feature of human society (Ashcraft, 2002). Language acquisition is therefore a critical component of the child's developing cognitive abilities. Both children and adults use language and images to create concepts and solve problems. This section examines the way language develops and how it both reflects and determines our thinking.

Language Development

Between birth and the beginning of formal schooling, children accomplish a monumental feat: They learn to speak and understand language (Collins & Kuczaj, 1991). *Speech* is what people actually say; *language* is the understanding of the rules of what they say. To understand the magnitude of this task, consider this: Apart from stock phrases and remarks such as "Thank you" or "How are you?", almost every sentence we speak or write has never before been spoken or written. Every day we read sentences that we have never encountered before, yet we understand almost every one of them (Ashcraft, 2002; Lederer, 1991).

Acquiring any of the approximately 4,000 languages is a remarkable accomplishment because there is so much to learn. First, a child uses **phonemes** (from the Greek

phoneme
The smallest units of sound understood as part of a language; there are approximately 200 phonemes in all of the languages around the world, but each language uses about 20 to 60

morpheme
In a language, the smallest unit of sound that conveys meaning

syntax
The organization of words into phrases and sentences; thus, an understanding of word order to convey ideas.

word for "sound"), which are the building blocks of language. Phonemes are unique sounds that can be joined to create words. They include consonant sounds like the sound of "d" in *dog* and *did* as well as vowel sounds like the "a" in *at* and *ant* (Vail & Cavanaugh, 2000). Although there are approximately 200 different phonemes in all of the spoken languages, most languages use only 20 to 60 phonemes. English has 26 letters but 40 to 46 phonemes because the same letter, alone or in combination, can represent more than one sound. (Experts disagree on whether some sounds are separate phonemes or blends, hence, there is a range of the estimated number of phonemes.) Perhaps you remember feeling confused when you first learned that the same symbol on the printed page—say *c* or *gh*—could be pronounced in more than one way. A similar experience occurs when we learn a foreign language.

Although it is often convenient to think of words as the basic units of meaning in language, many words have more than one part that has meaning. A **morpheme** is the smallest unit of language that has meaning. For example, the word constructed has three morphemes: *con*, *struct*, and *ed*, the last of which indicates past tense; *unhappiness* has three. When we learn to organize words into phrases and sentences, we are acquiring what is called **syntax.**

The Acquisition of Language.   The baby's early cries and other sounds are probably responses both to the environment and to internal needs such as hunger. No matter what language their parents speak (and even if the parents are deaf), babies make the same sounds at about the same time. At about 2 months of age, an infant begins *cooing*—making squeals, gurgles, or vowel sounds of relatively short duration, such as "*ooooooo*" and "*ahhhhhhh.*" At about 6 months of age, infants begin *babbling*, making one-syllable utterances that usually contain both vowels and consonants (Rice, 1995). As children move from babbling to pronouncing words, they vocalize more of the sounds used in their language community. Toddlers utter their first word that conveys meaning at about 1 year. Because parents are usually the child's primary caregivers, it is not surprising that the child's first words are usually *mama* or *dada*.

By the age of 18 months, the average toddler uses as many as 50 words. Most of these words are used for naming objects, such as *doggie*, but some are action words such as *bye-bye*. At about this age, toddlers combine two or more words to express a single idea, which results in the child's first sentence. Vocabulary development continues at a rapid pace during the preschool years.

Psychologists are especially interested in three characteristics of the infant's language. First, young children often use *telegraphic speech*—they leave words out of sentences as in a telegraph message (Kail & Cavanaugh, 2000). Despite the missing words, the intent of the sentence is usually clear, especially if the nonverbal context helps listeners decipher the child's meaning. For example, Dad knows what his daughter wants when he hears "Daddy juice." Second, children seem to know how to string words together to convey the intended meaning in the correct sequence for their language. If a child sees a car run over a ball, the child might say, "Car hit ball." (The child would not say "Ball hit car.") Third, children often overgeneralize grammatical rules, so the plural of *mouse* should be *mouses*! Children also add *ed* at the end of verbs to indicate past tense. For example, young children will say, "Doggie runned away."

According to behaviorists, including B. F. Skinner (1957), language is learned like other behaviors: through imitation, association, and reinforcement (Leahey & Harris, 2001). Children hear others talk and imitate the sounds they hear. For example, parents will point to an object and name it, and children repeat the words. What's more, sounds that resemble words are reinforced; sounds that do not resemble words may be extinguished. For instance, the baby's babbling of *mama* produces such reinforcers as food, a smile, or a hug. The more often this

Although children appear to learn many elements of language from adults (as well as from other children), they also abstract rules of language that enable them to generate words that they have never heard spoken by adults.

sequence of behaviors and reinforcers is repeated, the more strongly *mama* is associated with the presence of the child's mother. Likewise, the correct sequencing of words to form sentences is reinforced, whereas incorrect sequences may be extinguished. The following is an example of the acquisition of sounds and words as a result of reinforcement (Eggen & Kauchak, 2001):

> A 2-year-old picked up a ball and said, "Baa."
>
> Mom smiled broadly and said, "Good boy! Ball."
>
> The little boy repeated, "Baa."
>
> Mom responded, "Very good."

Although this behavioral theory of language acquisition explains how children can learn words from adults, it fails to explain how they create new and unique words and sentences. Cognitive scientist Steven Pinker (1994) considers it folklore that parents teach children language; parents do not provide explicit grammar lessons. The credit for the acquisition of language should go to the children.

The remarkable ability of children to master the complex rules of language and to use an extensive vocabulary within about 5 years suggests the existence of a built-in brain mechanism that makes this development possible. Except in situations in which access to language samples is denied, the acquisition of language is virtually guaranteed for children up to about age 5 or 6 and becomes more difficult thereafter. There is a critical period during which language develops quite easily, as most college students in foreign language classes know quite well. According to this *nativist* theory of language, children are innately predisposed to acquire language. The major advocate of this position, Noam Chomsky (1972), has called this innate ability our *language acquisition device* (*LAD*). When children hear speech, the LAD programs their brain to analyze what they hear and to extract the rules of grammar. The LAD is responsible for the emergence of babbling and the imitation of speech sounds. Because of these experiences, children are able to apply those rules to their own sentences. Children are not taught grammar explicitly; rather, they construct the rules from the examples they hear. Although parents and others help this process along by providing models of appropriate language use, children are also exposed to inappropriate uses. Consider the following exchange over breakfast between 6-year-old John and his 3-three-old brother Mike as they discussed the relative dangers of forgetting to feed the goldfish versus overfeeding the goldfish:

> *John*: It's worse to forget to feed them.
>
> *Mike*: No, it's badder to feed them too much.
>
> *John*: You don't say badder, you say worser.
>
> *Mike*: But it's baddest to give them too much food.
>
> *John*: No, it's not. It's worsest to forget to feed them.
>
> (Adapted from Bee, 1989, p. 276)

The LAD explains why children in different cultures follow the same (presumably innate) stages of language acquisition (see Table 8-3); it also explains why deaf children pass through stages of language development that are analogous to those exhibited by hearing children. Although the LAD explains how children learn the complex rules of language; it does not explain why children who are raised by their parents at home show better language development than children raised in institutions. Learning theorists point to the greater availability of reinforcements at home than in institutions. As predicted by learning theory, much of the variety in children's language abilities can be attributed to differences in their environments.

Most psychologists currently favor a combination of learning and nativist theories (Eggen & Kauchak, 2001). That is, some of our linguistic abilities seem to be innately determined, and others are acquired through learning. Researchers disagree, however, as to which behaviors belong in which category.

TABLE 8-3

The Sequence of Language Development in a Child

Age (Months)	Language Development
2	Begins making vowel-like cooing sounds
4	Makes vowel-like sounds interspersed with consonant sounds
6	Engages in babbling (one-syllable utterances)
8	Uses two-syllable utterances such as *mama* and *dada*; imitates sounds
10	Understands some words and gestures (may say "no," shakes head)
12	Understands some simple commands; uses single words such as *baby*, has some control over intonation
18	Has a vocabulary of as many as 50 words; may use two-word utterances; still babbles, uses words of several syllables with intricate intonation patterns
24	Has a vocabulary of over 50 words; uses two-word phrases
30	Acquires vocabulary rapidly; uses three- to five-word phrases
36	Has a vocabulary of 1,000 words, of which 80% are intelligible; makes fewer syntactic errors

Sources: Caplan, 1973; Lenneberg, 1973; Rice, 1995

FIGURE 8-13 Examples of hand symbols that indicate words in American Sign Language. In the past sign language was thought to be a form of pantomime that relied on the similarity of its symbols to the ideas they represent. Some signs, called iconic, seem to reflect the object they represent; however, most signs are complex, abstract symbols.

Source: Meier, 1991.

American Sign Language.   When we think of a language, we often think of an oral-auditory one—that is, one that is heavily dependent on audition. Not all languages fit this category, however. A prominent example is *American Sign Language (ASL)* or *Ameslan*, a manual-visual language developed within the American deaf community that is distinct from oral-auditory languages. People who use ASL communicate rapidly via thousands of manual signs and gestures. Words are assembled from hand shapes, hand motions, and the positions of the hands in front of the body (see Figure 8-13). Contrary to common belief, there is no universal sign language. A person who uses American Sign Language could not communicate with someone who uses British Sign Language. What's more, a deaf signer who learns a second sign language as an adult will sign with a foreign accent (Hickok et al., 2001)!

Facial expression and pantomimes of emotions such as lifted eyebrows punctuate and place emphasis in sentences. They may also serve as adverbs; for example, a slight display of the tongue as if in distaste during the sentence "I slept" turns the meaning into "I slept badly." ASL also intensifies meaning by making the sign more rapidly, so "quickly" becomes "more quickly." Emphasis is also added by making the signs faster than other signs.

Although they do not involve spoken words, sign languages are highly structured linguistic systems with all of the grammatical complexity (rules and syntax) found in spoken languages (Hickok et al., 2001; Pinker, 1994). In fact, they are produced and processed by the same parts of the brain involved in spoken language (Hickok et al., 2001; Meier, 1991). What's more, deaf children reared in an environment in which they have no access to spoken language and were not taught sign language sometimes invent their own language.

Until recently, the education of the deaf population emphasized lip reading and speech training to the exclusion of sign language. Approximately 90% of deaf children are born to hearing parents who were discouraged from signing to their deaf children because the use of sign language might impede progress in learning English. Consider the case of Joseph:

> At the age of 11 and with no language at all, Joseph just entered a school for the deaf. Apparently he was born deaf, but this was not realized until he was four years old. Up to that time his failure to understand speech at the normal age was attributed to retardation and then to autism. Although he had never been exposed to sign language, he was deriving great joy from what he was picking up. In fact, he wanted to stay at school all the time because going home meant returning to a communicational vacuum. (Sacks, 1989, pp. 38–39)

In recent years, however, such policies have begun to change as result of pressure from the deaf community. Today ASL is recognized as a legitimate language, and many deaf people emphasize learning sign language over speech therapy.

 Teaching Sign Language to the Chimpanzee Washoe

Thinking and Language

As we have seen, thinking can involve visual images as well as concepts, which are elements of our language. In addition, language can have even more dramatic influences on our thinking. The *linguistic relativity hypothesis* advanced by Benjamin Lee Whorf (1897–1941) suggests that syntax (word order) and vocabulary can mold our thinking. There is little doubt that elements of language can influence how we perceive and remember our world. For example, in one study, people were shown drawings that could represent either of two objects; the experimenters gave the objects either of two names. As you see in Figure 8-14, the original language labels used by the experimenters influenced the participants' memory for and subsequent drawings of the objects (Carmichael, Hogan, & Walter, 1932).

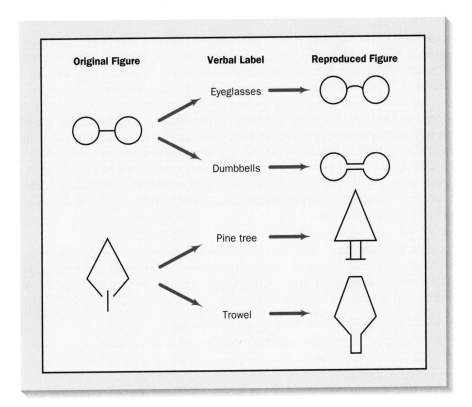

FIGURE 8-14 Effects of verbal labels on reproduction of drawings. The figures on the left were shown to participants along with one of the two verbal labels. The figures that these individuals drew later were influenced by the verbal labels they had been given.

Source: Carmichael, Hogan & Walter, 1932.

TABLE 8-4

Examples of Doublespeak

Term in Ordinary English	Term in Doublespeak
Desks	Pupil stations
Dead	Nonviable condition
New taxes	Revenue enhancement
Bar bouncer	Entertainment coordinator
Invasion	Predawn vertical insertion
Farm animals	Grain-consuming animal units
Fired	Nonpositively terminated or reclassified
Lying	Massaging the truth

Sources: Lutz, 1990; Lederer, 1991.

Using Language to Limit Thought.   Author George Orwell considered language to be a potential weapon that could be used to exploit, oppress, or manipulate people. Published in 1949, Orwell's novel *Nineteen Eighty-four* describes how a totalitarian state created an official state language called *Newspeak* to reduce the range of thought among its citizens. Although Orwell's account of language as a tool for political control was fictional, there are many current examples of the use of language to influence and control thinking.

The use of language by business, educational, and governmental organizations can mislead or control perception and thinking. The term *doublespeak* describes language that is purposely designed to make the bad seem good, to turn a negative into a positive, or to avoid or shift responsibility (see Table 8-4). "Doublespeak is not a slip of the tongue, or language used out of ignorance, but is instead a very conscious use of language as a weapon or tool by those in power to achieve their ends at our expense" (Lutz, 1990, p. xii).

One form of doublespeak is the *euphemism*, an acceptable or inoffensive word or phrase used in place of an unacceptable or offensive one. We frequently use "passed away" when talking to a bereaved person to demonstrate our sensitivity for that person's feelings. When you excuse yourself from the table at a restaurant, you are likely to say you are headed to the "restroom" rather than the "bathroom." No one is misled by these uses of language. But when a Pentagon spokesperson announces that a military unit was "servicing the target," few of us realize that the unit was killing the enemy. Politicians may report that their cities have "pavement deficiencies" rather than potholes. Perhaps some of you work as "part-time scanning professionals," otherwise known as grocery checkout clerks. In sum, although words may not actually determine our thoughts, examples like these indicate that careful selection of words can steer our thoughts in certain directions.

Language and Gender.   Consider the following sentence: "A skilled doctor makes an accurate diagnosis, and then he communicates the information to the patient." What images came to mind when you read this sentence? Now read the following sentences, and pay attention to the images that come to mind:

- A teacher must be careful when he grades exams.
- After a patient takes the prescribed medicine, he needs to rest.
- A business executive must consider all aspects of an issue before he decides on a course of action.

The word *he* may not be intended to convey whether the person is a man or a woman, but most people assume the speaker meant the person was a man. If the images that came to your mind were primarily men, you are not alone. Most people call up such images when they read sentences like these (Gastil, 1990; Hamilton, 1991). Girls and women make up almost 52% of the human race, yet they are systematically left out in daily speech (Paludi, 2002). The words *he*, *his*, and *man* refer to men, but they are often also used to encompass both men and women. These examples demonstrate how the words we use can guide our thinking, perhaps in ways we had not intended or recognized.

Janet Hyde (1984a) asked grade school children to create a story about an individual whose job was that of a "wudge-maker." Groups of children listened to descriptions of a wudge-maker that differed only in the pronouns used: *he, she, they, his,* or *her.* After hearing the story, the children created their own stories. Children who had heard stories with the pronoun *he* put women in their stories only 17% of the time. Apparently, the children understood *he* to refer exclusively to men. What's more, children who heard *he* stories rated women as less competent than men in the job of wudgemaker. Thus the use of a single word can have a significant influence on children's ideas.

When you read a sentence such as "A skilled doctor makes an accurate diagnosis, and then he communicates the information to the patient," you may not consider the possibility that the doctor is female.

Psychological Detective

Read the following sentences:

- The department *chairman* decided to schedule the course in the later afternoon.
- The chemical company *spokesman* will not answer questions concerning the spill in the river.
- Language separates *mankind* from other creatures.

Rewrite these sentences to avoid the suggestion that the person or people in them must be male. Write down your answers before reading further.

Using the word *he* or words like *chairman* when gender is not relevant to the intended meaning conveys the inaccurate notion that gender is a relevant dimension. Some minor wording changes may reduce the stereotyping that occurs when the words are associated with being male. For example, when the title of *chairman* is changed to *chairperson,* college students report fewer male images in describing this occupation; there was little difference in the images associated with *chairman* and *chair* (McConnell & Gavanski, 1994). Thus we could substitute *chairperson, spokesperson,* and *human beings* (or *humankind*) for the italicized words in the Psychological Detective exercise. Professional organizations such as the American Psychological Association, commercial publishers, and many newspapers and magazines have developed guidelines for unbiased (gender inclusive) language. For example, using plural forms and the pronoun *they* and using gender-neutral job titles (*police officer, firefighters*) lets us include all people, and thus avoids stereotypes that can perpetuate prejudice.

Next, we turn our attention to a topic that has a long history in psychology and has proven to be one of the most controversial: intelligence. This broad term is often used to encompass several of the abilities that we have focused on so far in this chapter, such as skills in language and in problem solving.

REVIEW SUMMARY

1. Between birth and the beginning of formal schooling, children learn to speak and understand language. **Phonemes** are the individual sounds of a language; **morphemes** are its smallest meaning-bearing elements. An understanding of the proper order of words in phrases and sentences demonstrates an understanding of **syntax.**

2. There are two major theories of language acquisition: the notion that language is a learned response acquired like any other behavior and the view that children are innately predisposed to acquire language through a built-in *language acquisition device* (*LAD*).

3. American Sign Language (ASL) relies on hand shapes, hand motions, and the positions of the hand in front of the body.

4. The *linguistic relativity* hypothesis suggests that our use of words (and syntax) can influence and even guide thought processes. Although using the male pronoun *he* to refer to both men and women may be convenient, it can lead people to think that only men are being considered. Several organizations have developed guidelines for using language in a gender-neutral manner.

✓ CHECK YOUR PROGRESS

1. The basic sounds of a language are called _____; the smallest meaning-bearing elements of a language are _____.

  a. heuristics; syntax
  b. syntax; heuristics
  c. morphemes; phonemes
  d. phonemes; morphemes

2. You are writing a paper on Noam Chomsky's views on language. Which of the following would be the best title to capture main points the paper should convey?

  a. "Language: Like any other behavior"
  b. "Language is learned via modeling"
  c. "The brain extracts the rules of grammar"
  d. "The genetic coding of different languages around the world"

3. Which of the following is the best summary of the linguistic relativity hypothesis?

  a. Each language has a limited number of sounds with which to convey ideas.
  b. Languages differ in their degree of complexity as a result of the needs of the society.
  c. The order of words and syntax can influence how we perceive and remember our world.
  d. The human brain is limited in the number of concepts it can handle, thus the same ideas are expressed across the planet.

4. How are people who use ASL able to convey ideas such as "badly" or "poorly?"

  a. They rely on their eyes and eyebrows in expressing such ideas.
  b. The signs are made at different speeds to express such ideas.
  c. ASL does not use adverbs so it is not as expressive as spoken languages.
  d. ASL uses a limited number of simple gestures involving both hands that express such ideas.

5. At about what age do most children speak their first understandable word?

  a. 6 months
  b. 8 months
  c. 12 months
  d. 15 months

6. What is the first stage in the developing of language?

  a. cooing
  b. babbling
  c. repetition
  d. generalization

7. Developmental milestones are helpful in determining if infants have problems that need attention. Which of these children does not seem to be reaching language milestones at the expected age?

  a. At eight months of age Don started cooing.
  b. Diane has been babbling since age five months.
  c. Carlos said his first clearly understandable words at 11 months.
  d. At the age of 18 months, Carol has used two-word sentences but still babbles on occasion.

8. What process is occurring when infants form strings of sound containing both vowel and consonant sounds?

  a. cooing
  b. babbling
  c. gurgling
  d. sounding

9. A young child says "Mommy go," signifying that her mother is going to the store. What does this example illustrate about language development?

  a. babbling speech
  b. overgeneralization
  c. telegraphic speech
  d. autonomous grammar

10. Behavioral neuroscientists are using brain scans to identify the parts of the brain involved when people use an oral-auditory language and when they use sign language. What are the brain scans likely to reveal?

    a. The same brain areas are involved in both languages.

    b. Sign language depends primarily on the right hemisphere.

    c. Both languages rely primarily on subcortical areas of the brain.

    d. The primary parts of the brain involved in both languages are the occipital lobes.

ANSWERS: 1. d **2.** c **3.** c **4.** b **5.** c **6.** a **7.** a **8.** a **9.** b **10.** a

INTELLIGENCE

Alex's second-grade teacher gave him a letter to take to his parents. Because Alex is experiencing difficulty in class, the teacher consulted with the school psychologist. They agreed that it would be potentially beneficial to administer an intelligence test and other measures to Alex. They expect that the information obtained from the testing session will help them plan a better educational program to meet Alex's needs. *Why were psychological tests first developed?*

You are familiar with psychological tests because you have taken such tests in school. A psychological test is an objective measure of a *sample* of behavior that is collected according to well-established procedures. Thus psychological tests are like the tests used in other sciences: They are composed of observations made on a small but carefully chosen sample of a person's behavior (Anastasi & Urbina, 1997). Such tests are used for a range of purposes, including measuring differences among people in characteristics such as intelligence and personality (Domino, 2000). The primary purpose of one of the first psychological tests was to identify children with below-average intellectual ability so that they could be given schooling designed to improve that ability.

Psychological Detective

Think about what makes a person intelligent. What behaviors or characteristics do you expect to observe in someone who is judged to be intelligent? Write down your answer before reading further.

To answer this question, Robert Sternberg and his colleagues (1981) asked people in supermarkets, train stations, and a college library to record behaviors and characteristics related to the concept of intelligence. The researchers then gave the resulting list of behaviors and characteristics to other people, who rated the importance of each as an element of intelligence. The laypersons' descriptions of intelligence emphasized practical problem solving ("identifies connections among ideas"), verbal ability ("speaks clearly and articulately"), and social competence ("displays understanding of the world at large"). Experts who were asked similar questions viewed intelligence in a comparable fashion, with some differences of emphasis (Snyderman & Rothman, 1987).

Cultural Views of Intelligence

The descriptions of intelligence offered by people in supermarkets or college libraries were obtained in the United States. How a person defines intelligence depends on whom we ask, and the answers differ across time and place (Sternberg & Kaufman, 1998). Thus what behaviors are perceived as examples of intelligent behavior is influenced in part by culture. Furthermore, culture can influence the processes that underlie intelligent behavior as well as the direction that intellectual development takes (Miller, 1997).

The Japanese place greater emphasis on the process of thinking than people in the United States (Tajima et al., 1991). Japanese people listed several characteristics of intelligence that deal with the process of thinking, such as "good judgment" and "good memory." Americans placed greater importance on external appearances and outcomes when listing characteristics that describe intelligence. The conceptions of intelligence among Taiwanese Chinese included interpersonal intelligence, intrapersonal intelligence, and self-assertion (Sternberg & Kaufman, 1998). Differences such as these suggest that there may be significant differences between Eastern and Western conceptions of intelligence differences that may be due, in part, to the kinds of skills that cultures value (Srivastava & Misra, 1996).

In Africa, conceptions of intelligence focus on skills that facilitate and maintain harmonious group relations (Ruzgis & Grigorenko, 1994). For example, parents in Kenya emphasize responsible participation in family and social life as important aspects of intelligence (Super & Harkness, 1982). What's more, Kenyan children from a rural village perform better on tests of indigenous intelligence that require them to perform a task that is adaptive for them (recognizing how to use natural herbal medicines to fight illness) than they do on Western-style vocabulary tests (Sternberg, 1998; Sternberg et al., 2000). In Zimbabwe the word for "intelligence," *ngware*, means to be prudent and cautious, particularly in social relationships (Sternberg & Kaufman, 1998).

As we continue our exploration of the concept of intelligence, it is important to be aware that the definition used in Western cultures, especially the United States, does not necessarily match definitions used in other parts of the world. What's more, efforts to develop tests to quantify intelligence are primarily a Western phenomenon. Those tests may not be appropriate when translated and used in other cultures because the underlying definition of intelligence may not fit the culture's view.

We can define **intelligence** as the overall ability to excel at a variety of tasks, especially those related to success in schoolwork. Judging from the level of agreement in the United States on the characteristics of an intelligent person, the measurement and understanding of intelligence would not seem controversial. Nevertheless, this topic is one of the most contentious in psychology. The next section explores how psychologists measure intelligence, why these measures were developed, and why the concept of intelligence is controversial.

The History of Intelligence Testing

We can trace the study of differences in intelligence to an Englishman, Francis Galton (1822–1911), an inventor and explorer. This wealthy man had a passion for measurement and shared an interest in heredity with his half cousin, Charles Darwin. Galton suggested that differences in levels of intellectual ability are due to hereditary factors. To check this notion, he traced the family trees of approximately 1,000 distinguished artists, judges, military commanders, poets, scientists, and statesmen and found that a large proportion of these eminent people had eminent family members. On the basis of such findings, Galton contended in his book *Hereditary Genius: An Inquiry into Its Laws and Consequences* (1869) that eminence and creativity run in families because they are inherited characteristics.

Galton set out to measure differences in degree of eminence and, presumably, in the level of intelligence in his anthropometric ("human measurement") laboratory in London. Beginning in 1884, visitors stopped in to have their keenness of eyesight and reaction time to stimuli measured. Galton believed that highly successful people perceive the world more accurately than less successful people. Thus their eyesight should be keener and their reactions quicker than those of less eminent people. Contrary to Galton's beliefs, the results showed that eminent people did *not* perceive the world any better than others.

intelligence
The ability to excel at a variety of tasks, especially those related to academic success

Alfred Binet (1857–1911), a French psychologist, spent years considering ways to measure intelligence. Eventually he decided to assess more complex intellectual functions than sensory discrimination, including memory and reasoning.

In 1881, the French Ministry of Education decided that all children must attend school. Before that time the schools were not obligated to teach children with widely varying ability levels because slow learners usually did not attend school. Consequently, the curriculum was geared to average and above-average students. After the decision, teachers had to adapt their methods to teach children with a wider range of abilities. In 1904, a French commission studying the education of children with below-average ability decided that placing slower learners in special classes would be more effective than keeping them with learners performing at grade level or higher. Although teachers could offer judgments concerning their students' abilities, the commission recognized that such judgments might be tainted by factors (such as discipline problems) that were not related to ability. Their search for an objective measure as the basis for class placement decisions concerning the children led them to Binet.

Binet and his colleague, Theophile Simon (1873–1961) collected simple problems that required higher mental processes such as reasoning, memory, and spatial thinking. In 1905, they developed the Binet-Simon scale. Typical items required children to define common words ("What is a pencil?"), name objects seen in pictures, tell how two objects are alike ("How are a cow and a dog alike?"), draw designs from memory, and repeat a string of spoken digits. Completion of some items seemed to represent an ability level that was typical of children of a certain age, whereas completion of other items was associated with those of a different age. On the basis of this observation, Binet and Simon proposed the concept of **mental age**. To determine a child's mental age, they compared the child's performance to that of the average child at each age. For example, a mental age of 6 indicated that a child's performance was similar to the performance of other 6-year-olds. A 6-year-old child with a mental age of 8 performed much better than the average 6-year-old. Binet believed the use of his scale would increase the likelihood that all children would receive an appropriate education. In fact, he expected that attention, memory, and judgment could be improved with practice and appropriate methods.

The Stanford-Binet Intelligence Scale.   In the United States, Lewis Terman (1877–1957), a Stanford University psychologist, revised the Binet-Simon scale and extended it for use with adults. His Stanford-Binet Intelligence Scale was first published in 1916 and has been modified several times since then; the current version is the Stanford-Binet V.

In 1912, the German psychologist William Stern (1871–1938) devised an index of intelligence by dividing a child's mental age (MA) by his or her chronological age (CA). Terman adopted this idea in the Stanford-Binet test and added one more feature; he multiplied the index by 100 to eliminate decimals. The resulting statistic is the **intelligence quotient (IQ),** calculated, as just explained, as MA/CA $\times$ 100. Thus one's IQ is a ratio of mental age divided by chronological age, multiplied by 100. For example, a 9-year-old child with a mental age of 9 would have an IQ of 100 ($9/9 \times 100 = 100$). If the same child had a mental age of 6, the calculation of the IQ would be $6/9 \times 100 = 67$. Finally, if the child's mental age was 12, the IQ would be $12/9 \times 100 = 133$. The intelligence quotient made it possible to express a child's intellectual ability relative to that of children of the same age.

The Wechsler Scales.   When David Wechsler (1896–1981) was chief psychologist at Bellevue Hospital in New York City, he found it difficult to test adults with the Stanford-Binet Intelligence Scale. Although the Stanford-Binet had been adapted for testing adults by adding more difficult items, time limits on some of the items handicapped a number of adults. Furthermore, even though the concept of mental age

The French psychologist Alfred Binet (1857–1911) was responsible for the development of the first intelligence test. The creation of the test was the result of a specific task given to Binet and his colleague, Simon—create a method to identify students who were learning at a slower rate than the majority of students. As a result most subsequent intelligence tests have been tied to academic achievement.

 Mental Age Testing

 Capacity to Learn

mental age
Measure of intelligence derived by comparing an individual's score on an intelligence test with the average performance of individuals of the same age

intelligence quotient (IQ)
Score that indicates how an individual compares with others on an intelligence test

SUBTEST (VERBAL)	DESCRIPTION	SAMPLE ITEMS
Information	Orally presented questions that tap knowledge of common events, objects, places, and people.	How many wings does a bird have? How many nickels make a dime?
Similarities	Examinee is asked to explain the similarity in pairs of words that are presented orally.	In what way are a lion and tiger alike? In what way are a saw and a hammer alike?
Arithmetic	A series of arithmetic questions are to be solved without use of pencil and paper or calculator.	Three women divided eighteen golf balls equally among themselves. How may golf balls did each person receive?
Vocabulary	Examinee must provide definitions for a series of orally presented words.	What does **near** mean? What does **slander** mean?
Comprehension	A series of orally presented questions that require the examinee to give solutions to everyday problems or to demonstrate understanding of social rules and concepts.	What should you do if you see someone forgot his book when he leaves a restaurant? What is the advantage of keeping money in the bank?
Digit Span	Number sequences are presented orally, and the examinee is asked to repeat them verbatim or in reverse order.	I am going to say some numbers. Listen carefully, and when I am through you say them right after me: 2, 4, 7. Repeat these numbers backward: 4, 6, 1, 7, 5.
SUBTEST (PERFORMANCE) Picture Completion	The examinee is asked to identify the important part that is missing in each of a set of colorful pictures of common objects and themes.	Look at this picture. What important part is missing?
Digit Symbol-Coding	Each of a series of shapes or numbers is paired with a simple symbol; based on a key, the examinee draws the symbol under the corresponding number.	Look carefully at the key that matches numbers with symbols. Then write the number that goes with each symbol in the space below it. 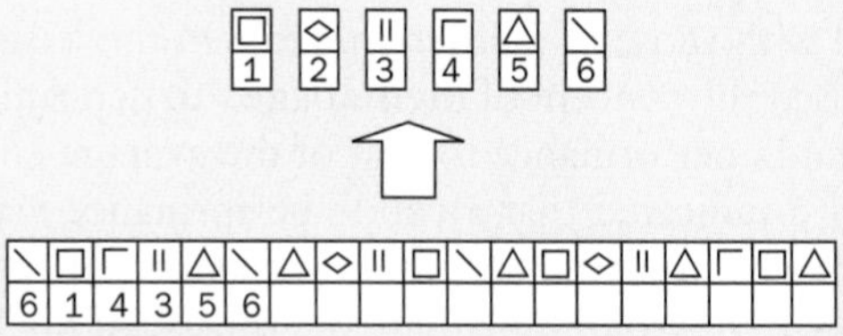
Picture Arrangement	A set of colorful pictures is presented out of order, and the examinee rearranges them into a logical story sequence.	Arrange the pictures on these cards so they tell a story that makes sense. 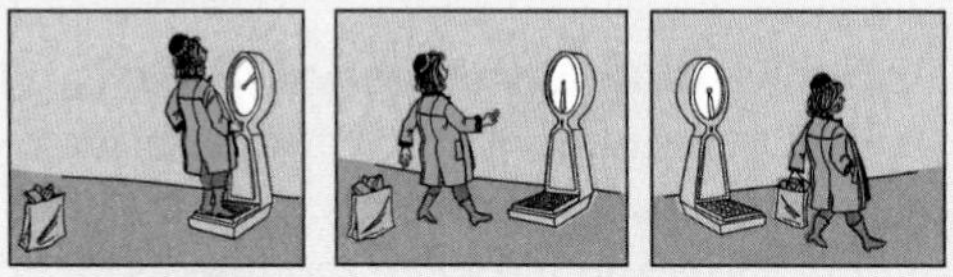
Block Design	The examinee uses two-color blocks to replicate a design from a model or a picture.	Arrange the blocks so they look like the design in the picture. 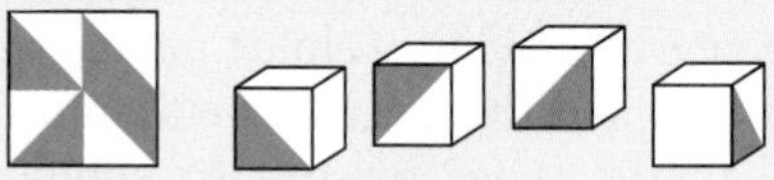
Symbol Search	The examinee scans two groups of symbols (a target composed of two symbols) and a search group of 5 symbols and indicates whether either target symbol matches any symbols in the search group.	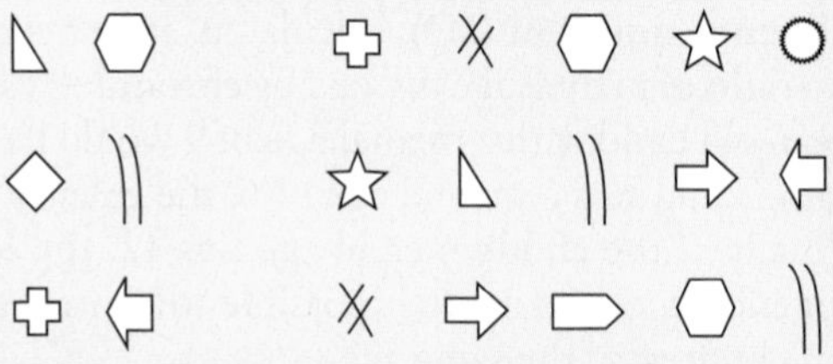

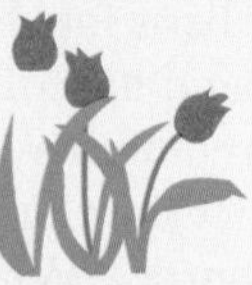

FIGURE 8-15 The Wechsler Adult Intelligence Test (WAIS-III) is an individually administered intelligence test; its subtests consist of verbal and performance items.

The information from an intelligence test can reveal learning disabilities as well as identify a child's areas of strength.

could be applied to children, whose intellectual ability changes from year to year, it could not be applied to adults. The pace of change in intelligence slows considerably in the adult years, so the mental ages of the average 28- and 29-year-old are not likely to differ. For these reasons, Wechsler developed a new intelligence test for adults. Scores on this test are calculated by comparing a person's score with scores obtained by people of a range of ages rather than a single age. The current version of this test, known as the Wechsler Adult Intelligence Scale-III (WAIS-III), is used to assess people between the ages of 16 and 74 (Wechsler, 1997).

Wechsler's scales have also been adapted to assess intelligence at earlier ages. The Wechsler Intelligence Scale for Children-III (WISC-III) tests children aged 6 to 16, and the Wechsler Preschool and Primary Scales of Intelligence-Revised (WPPSI-R) is used to assess children aged 4 to 6½ (Wechsler, 1992, 1994). The multiple scores of the Wechsler subtests provide valuable information about individual strengths and weaknesses and can be helpful in identifying learning disabilities in children.

The Stanford-Binet Intelligence Scale and the Wechsler intelligence tests are individual tests (meaning that one person is tested at a time) that must be administered by a qualified examiner. Administering one of these tests takes between 1 and 2 hours. Individual intelligence tests offer several advantages as compared with group tests. The examiner can directly observe the examinee's reactions, put him or her at ease before the test, and determine whether the examinee understands the instructions. When large numbers of people must be tested, however, these measures of intelligence are time consuming.

Principles of Psychological Tests

A psychological test is like a three-legged stool: If one leg is missing or broken, the stool collapses. Like that stool, psychological tests have three legs representing the essential elements for their effective and appropriate use: reliability, validity, and standardization. These principles apply to all psychological tests, whether they are designed to measure intelligence or personality (see Chapter 11).

Reliability.   To stand up to scrutiny, a psychological test must demonstrate **reliability;** that is, it must yield relatively consistent or repeatable results (Linn & Gronlund, 2000). Like other measuring devices, a psychological test is of little value if it provides inconsistent results. For example, you might be delighted to find that your

STUDY TIP

Create a timeline illustrating the history of intelligence testing.

reliability
Degree to which repeated administrations of a psychological test yield consistent scores

"You can't build a hut. You don't know how to find edible roots and you know nothing about predicting the weather. In other words, you do terribly on our I.Q. test."

bathroom scale reads 138 pounds, indicating that you lost the 12 pounds you wanted to shed. But when you step on the scale again to double-check the weight, the digits flash 154! Your scale is of little value because it is not reliable; it is time to buy a new one. If the scale were a psychological test, it would be time to look for a new measure.

Psychologists use several approaches to determine whether a test is reliable. They can administer a test twice to a group of people, separating the two administrations by a short time period (a few days or a week). Using a correlation coefficient, they can measure the similarity in the scores obtained on the two occasions (see Chapter 1). If the scores are similar, they have established *test-retest reliability*. In another approach, known as the *alternate-forms method*, two different but equivalent forms of a test are administered to the same group of people. If the individuals' scores on the two forms are comparable, the test is reliable.

A psychological test has good reliability if the correlation coefficient that describes the similarity in pairs of scores is .80 or higher. The reliability of the Stanford-Binet and Wechsler intelligence tests is generally .90 or higher (Domino, 2000). Even if a test provides reliable scores, however, we need to know whether the test is valid before we are ready to use it.

Validity.   A psychological test can be reliable, but it is of little value unless it is valid as well. On the other hand, an unreliable test cannot be valid (Linn & Gronlund, 2000). **Validity** tells us whether the test actually measures what its developers intended it to measure. Suppose that we decide to measure anxiety levels by asking people to write down the names of the Seven Dwarfs. The written reports might be very reliable, yet those reports would have nothing to do with anxiety. Thus, reliability does not guarantee validity.

How do psychologists establish test validity? The information they use varies with the type of test and the purpose for which it was designed. For example, for most of the tests you take in college, validity can be established by demonstrating that the test reflects the course content. Students who complain to professors that tests cover only a small part of the material or do not reflect the course material at all are questioning the *content validity* of the test. When a test is used to predict whether examinees will succeed in a particular task or job, the test should have high *predictive validity*.

Another way psychologists establish test validity is by demonstrating relations between test scores and other measures or behaviors that should in theory be related to the test. For example, we would expect a valid test of anxiety while delivering a speech in front of a class to be related to physiological responses (for example, how much you perspire), amount of uncertainty in a speech (for example, the number of "ums" and "ahs" during the speech), ability to maintain eye contact with the audience, and several other behaviors. The relations between the test and these various responses is an indication of the test's *construct validity*.

For a number of reasons, establishing the validity of measures of intelligence is not a straightforward task. Traditionally, psychologists have correlated measures of intelligence with grades, especially in elementary school and high school. They have generally found that the two are, indeed, correlated. Correlations between intelligence and grades in college and graduate school are much lower than those for elementary school and high school. What's more, everyday problems often have little relation to the knowledge or skills acquired in school. For this reason, intelligence tests are often controversial. As we will see later, this controversy has spurred psychologists to look at the concept of intelligence in new and expanded ways that take the concept beyond its traditional connection with grades in school.

Standardization.   The third crucial element of a well-developed psychological test is **standardization,** meaning that the test is administered the same way every time it is used. The instructions, time limits (if any), and scoring procedures must remain identical from one use to the next.

The development of norms is another important aspect of test standardization. At the beginning of Chapter 1 we met Patty, who completed an IQ test on the Internet. She wondered what her obtained score meant; perhaps she asked a friend, "What did

validity
Degree to which a psychological test measures what its developers intended it to measure

standardization
The development of procedures for administering psychological tests and the collection of norms that provide a frame of reference for interpreting test scores

Principles of Psychological Tests

Reliability: Does the test yield consistent results?

- If a test is administered on Monday to a group of fourth through eighth graders, will they obtain similar scores when the same test is readministered the following week?
- There are two forms of a test designed to measure test anxiety in college students; they are designated Form A and B. Will students' scores on Form A be similar to their scores on Form B?

Validity: Does the test measure what it was intended to measure?

- If a test is designed to measure spatial ability needed in the job of an airplane pilot, will the scores on the test predict which persons will make the best pilots?
- Are scores on tests of intelligence related to the grades students receive in various elementary and high school classes?
- Are persons who receive high scores on a test that seeks to identify characteristics related to depression likely to be diagnosed as depressed when they are interviewed by clinical psychologists and psychiatrists?

Standardization and Norms: Does the test have guidelines that specify the instructions, time limits, and scoring procedures? Are there norms to use in interpreting the scores?

- Does the test administrator know when to stop administering items on a particular subscale of an intelligence test depending on the number of items failed in a row?
- Are the scores obtained on a test of general knowledge of public events different depending on the age of the people who take the test?

you get?" If so, she was searching for information to help her interpret her score by comparing it to those obtained by others. **Norms** are scores obtained by a relatively large sample of similar people on the same test. They provide the frame of reference we need to interpret our own scores on a given test.

The scores that describe many physical and psychological characteristics, including height, weight, anxiety, and intelligence, are distributed in the population in a certain way. Most people obtain scores near the middle of the distribution of test scores or physical measurements. The number of people obtaining a given score decreases as we move from the middle to the tails of the distribution (see Figure 8-16). For example,

norms
Distribution of scores obtained by a large sample of people who have taken a particular psychological test

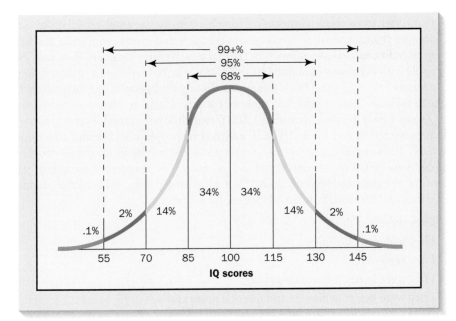

FIGURE 8-16 Normal curve (distribution) of intelligence test scores. This curve has been very useful to psychologists as well as to researchers in other disciplines. Although the curve is derived from theoretical mathematics, researchers found that many psychological and biological variables are distributed in the general population in a manner that fits the curve. As you can see, the majority of the population obtains IQ scores that are close to the mean of 100; scores further away from the mean occur less often.

the height of an average adult American is about 68 inches. The heights of most adults tend to be close to this average; few adults are 38 inches or 88 inches tall. This commonly encountered distribution of scores is called the **normal curve** (or distribution; see Appendix A). Measures of intelligence fit this distribution with the average (mean and median) score set at 100. This bell-shaped curve is widely used because many biological and psychological variables are distributed in the population as described by this curve. About two-thirds of Americans have IQs between 85 and 115, in the large middle section of the bell-shaped curve.

Extremes of Intelligence

Intelligence test scores below 70 or above 130 occur in less than 5% of the population (see Figure 8-16); people with such statistically rare scores are designated as *exceptional*. Those with scores below 70 *may* be diagnosed as mentally retarded if they also exhibit significant deficits in everyday adaptive behaviors, such as self-care, social skills, or communication (American Psychiatric Association, 2000). The diagnosis of mental retardation requires that the condition begin before age 18. In many cases, deficits that occur after age 18 are the result of brain damage from automobile accidents or other forms of trauma to the head and brain.

Exceptional Children. Public Law 94-142 (Individuals With Disabilities Education Act), includes provisions for educating all children with handicaps. This law brought the nature and needs of handicapped children to the attention of educators and the general public. Because the education of all children was affected, the term *handicapped* was changed to *exceptional*. Exceptional children may be classified into five major categories: learning disabilities, behavior and emotional disorders, sensory disabilities, communication disorders, and intellectual deviations (gifted, talented, and mental retardation). Table 8-5 lists some of the major categories of exceptional individuals.

Standard intelligence tests such as the WISC-III are frequently used in the evaluation of children who are perceived as exceptional. Because there are many forms of exceptionality, however, psychologists have developed other assessment instruments in addition to direct observation of behavior. For example, observation of classroom behaviors by teachers is an important component of the assessment of children with behavior disorders.

Exceptional children often require special attention and services, but there is no standard approach to dealing with their needs. For example, the verbal and physical aggression that may characterize children with emotional disturbances requires interventions that differ from those appropriate for children with mental retardation. School psychologists typically work with classroom teachers and special education teachers to develop an *individualized educational plan* (IEP) for each child (Eggen & Kauchak, 2001).

People with IQ scores of about 140 and above may be identified as *gifted*. There are quite a number of myths and misconceptions about gifted people, but fortunately there is data to address these myths and misconceptions. Using teacher recommendations and IQ tests, Lewis Terman identified 1,500 gifted children to track over a lifetime (the study is projected to run until 2010). This study of people who became affectionately known as "Termites" enabled him to put to rest some myths about gifted people. For example, these gifted individuals equaled or surpassed an unselected sample of people in terms of physique and athletic ability. Not surprisingly, they did better academically, and Terman and his team found evidence of the following:

- They were healthier.
- They had more hobbies.
- They read more books.
- They were better adjusted as adults.
- They were better achievers and learned more easily.

TABLE 8-5

Categories and Characteristics of Exceptional Individuals

These categories represent deviations from the average in some aspect of intellectual functioning; both impaired intellectual functioning and superior abilities are represented. Many children who are identified as falling into one of these categories of exceptionality receive some form of special education. Traditional intelligence tests or tests specially developed for use with certain populations, such as the deaf, are often used to collect information that is helpful in identifying cases of exceptionality.

Mental Retardation

Level of Mental Retardation	IQ	Percentage of Total Group	Characteristics
Mild	50–55 to approximately 70	85%	• Often not distinguishable from other children until they begin school • Able to develop social and language skills and can acquire academic skills up to about the sixth-grade level • Usually live in the community or in a supervised group home
Moderate	30–40 to 50–55	10%	• Can learn to communicate during preschool years but are not likely to proceed past second-grade-level academic skills • Usually go through vocational training and may work in sheltered workshops
Severe	20–25 to 35–40	3–4%	• Poor motor development and poor communication skills • May learn to read "survival" words like men, women, and stop • Need a protective living situation such as a group home
Profound	IQ below 20	1–2%	• Language and comprehension limited to simple requests and commands • Majority have some brain abnormality • Need constant supervision

Learning Disability

Group of disorders manifested by significant difficulties in the acquisition and use of listening, speaking, reading, writing, reasoning, or mathematical abilities. About 4 percent of individuals between the ages of 6 and 21 have learning disabilities.

Gifted and Talented

The term *gifted* was first used to describe children whose scores on intelligence tests were well above average. The definition has been expanded to include *talented* individuals who display superlative skills in a specific area as evidenced by outstanding performance or products. These talents are typically not assessed by intelligence tests. The prevalence of the gifted and talented is difficult to determine because the definitions vary greatly.

Savant Syndrome

Designation for mentally retarded individuals who manifest at least one remarkable ability such as handling mathematical calculations quickly and without paper and pencil or calculators. This rare syndrome tends to occur more often among males and those diagnosed as autistic.

Sources: American Psychiatric Association, 2000; Haring, McCormick, & Haring, 1994.

Richard Wawro (1952–   ) is a remarkable Scottish artist who has earned widespread acclaim for his drawings (see right). Although he experienced visual difficulties from birth (he is legally blind) and is autistic, he has used wax oil crayons to create detailed, dramatic images of intense depth and color. He has had exhibitions of his work throughout the U.S. and around the world. Among the owners of his work are Lady Margaret Thatcher (former Prime Minister of Great Britain) and Pope John Paul II. A documentary film about him, *With Eyes Wide Open*, won several international awards. The film was viewed by Dustin Hoffman during his preparation for playing an autistic man in the film *Rainman*. You can view some of Richard's works of art at www.wawro.net.

Savant Syndrome.   In an 1887 lecture, J. Langdon Down (1828–1896) described a group of mentally retarded children who exhibited special abilities (Treffert, 1989). Down eventually became known for his description of Down syndrome, but in the 1887 lecture he offered a description of the savant syndrome.

Savant syndrome occurs in people who are severely handicapped in overall intelligence yet demonstrate exceptional ability in a specific area such as art, calculation, memory, or music (Hou et al., 2000; Miller, 1999). For example, despite very low scores on tests of intelligence (usually between 40 and 70), some savants can report calendar dates from hundreds of years ago (calendrical calculation; O'Connor et al., 2000). Most cases of savant syndrome involve remarkable memory with little understanding of what is being described (Treffert & Wallace, 2002). The essence of the savant syndrome is captured in the following case (Treffert, 1989):

> Tom, a blind boy, had a vocabulary of less than 100 words. Yet he could play over 5,000 musical pieces from memory, including Bach, Beethoven, Chopin, and Rossini. At age 11, he played for the president of the United States. Some musicians felt that Tom had tricked the president and the public. They tested him: Tom was asked to listen to two unfamiliar musical pieces, of 13 and 20 pages each; he then played them perfectly from memory.

Most savants are male, and there is a higher frequency of this syndrome in the autistic population. Savant syndrome occurs in about 1 in 10 people with autism (Treffert & Wallace, 2002). Autism is a rare mental disorder characterized by failure to respond to people in socially appropriate ways and by serious deficits in language. Accumulating evidence suggests that people with this syndrome have suffered damage to the left hemisphere, which apparently results in some form of compensation by the right hemisphere. In fact, all of the abilities exhibited by people with this syndrome are associated with the right hemisphere. Savant syndrome proves a fascinating puzzle for psychologists and other scientists who study the brain and intelligence. What's more, "No model of brain function will be complete until it can explain this rare condition" (Treffert & Wallace, 2002, p. 85). Although the cause of savant syndrome is largely a mystery, its existence prompts us to reconsider the concept of general intelligence.

Kinds of Intelligence

savant syndrome
Case of a mentally retarded person who displays exceptional ability in a specific area

We can divide theorists who study intelligence into two groups: "lumpers" and "splitters." Lumpers view intelligence as an overall ability to acquire knowledge, to reason, and to solve problems. As noted earlier, Sir Francis Galton is credited with originating the concept of intelligence. He could be considered a lumper. Most of the intelligence tests that were developed after his pioneering work yield a single number. A single number, however, may lead us to oversimplify the nature of intelligence. Splitters view intelligence as a collection of abilities that give rise to a diversity of individual strengths and weaknesses. They have developed several theories suggesting that there is more than one kind of intelligence.

Spearman's Model. Charles Spearman (1863–1945), a British psychologist, believed that there are two types of intelligence, one called *g* for *general intelligence* and the other, representing a number of specific abilities, called *s*. Spearman observed that people who perform well on one type of intelligence task tend to do well on most other tasks, although their scores on these tasks are seldom the same. He proposed that any given task reflects both types of intelligence. General intelligence cuts across specific kinds of items and accounts for similar levels of performance on a variety of items. By contrast, specific intelligence is related to the particular task and thus is responsible for the fact that each person does better on some tasks than on others.

In part because there is no universal agreement on the precise definition of intelligence and the way in which it should be measured, theorists differ in how they conceptualize intelligence. Let's say that you view intelligence not as a single overall ability (the kind represented by Spearman's *g*) but as a collection of abilities. It follows, then, that any single number on an intelligence test will provide, at best, an inadequate account of a person's ability (Sternberg, Grigorenko, & Bundy, 2001). "Intelligence is plural, not singular," according to Stephen Ceci (2001, p. 49).

Sternberg's Model. The kinds of intelligence that are rewarded in school may have little to do with success in life outside of school. Robert Sternberg (1988, 1997) believes that there are several ways to be adaptive or effective. He therefore proposed a new model of intelligence called the *triarchic theory of intelligence*. This model comprises (1) *analytical intelligence*, or the ability to break down a problem or situation into its components (the type of intelligence assessed by most current intelligence tests); (2) *creative intelligence*, or the ability to cope with novelty and to solve problems in new and unusual ways; and (3) *practical intelligence*, which is also known as common sense or "street smarts." The third type of intelligence is one that the public understands and values, yet it is missing in standard intelligence tests (Sternberg et al., 1995).

Sternberg believes that most intelligence tests place a premium on speed, which is not relevant in most decisions we must make. This hurried approach to testing can discriminate against children who are not used to it—especially poor, minority, or immigrant children.

The triarchic theory of intelligence is the basis of efforts to match instruction to the strengths students exhibit in analytical, creative, or practical intelligence. Although these efforts are still in the early stage of development, they hold promise for increasing students' success. Students' strengths in one of the three components of the model are assessed; then students receive instruction that emphasizes their strength. At the end of the course, the students are evaluated; however, the focus of the evaluation is consistent with the component of the model that had been emphasized (Sternberg et al., 1996). See Table 8-6 for examples of the type of questions that different disciplines might use to assess each of the triarchic components. The early results demonstrate some "interesting trends; for example, students who were identified as creative, and were subsequently taught in a section emphasizing creative performance, outperformed the other two groups when assessed for creativity related to the course work" (Sternberg, 1997).

The triarchic theory on intelligence emphasizes the *processes* of intelligence. Next we turn to a theory of intelligence that focuses on what could be called the *domains* of intelligence.

Gardner's Multiple Intelligences. Tests of intelligence predict academic achievement because that is what they were designed to do. Had they been developed by artists, salespeople, or politicians, they might be different. To account for the broad

Howard Gardner suggests that there is more to intelligence than scores on current intelligence tests. People can manifest intelligence in many ways that are not tapped by such tests. Oprah Winfrey's high level of interpersonal intelligence is evident to anyone who has seen her show. The Dallas Brass exhibit their musical intelligence in the many concerts they perform across the country. The college basketball players shown here are demonstrating their movement or bodily kinesthetic intelligence.

Intelligence

range of achievements in modern society, Howard Gardner (1993, 1999) originally proposed the existence of seven multiple intelligences. According to Gardner, there is more to intelligence than the verbal and mathematical abilities measured by current intelligence tests. Each person may have different strengths and weaknesses and thus manifest intelligence in various ways. Gardner (1998) has added one additional form of intelligence to the previous seven kinds of intelligence:

1. *Verbal/Linguistic*: Mastery, love, and ability to use language and words; found in poets, speakers, writers, and rap singers
2. *Musical*: High level of competence in composing and performing; sensitivity to pitch and tone; evident in composers, singers, and musicians

TABLE 8-6

Questions Based on Sternberg's Triarchic Theory of Intelligence

The triarchic theory can be applied to teaching and the evaluation of students. These sample questions are based on the three components of the model.

Discipline	Analytic	Creative	Practical
Psychology	Compare Sigmund Freud's theory of dreaming to Calvin Hall's.	Design an experiment to test a theory of dreaming.	How does Sigmund Freud's theory of dreaming apply to your life?
Biology	Evaluate the validity of the bacterial theory of ulcers.	Design an experiment to test the bacterial theory of ulcers.	How would the bacterial theory of ulcers change conventional treatment approaches?
History	How did events in post-World War I Germany lead to the rise of Nazism?	How might President Truman have encouraged the surrender of Japan without dropping nuclear bombs on Hiroshima and Nagasaki?	What lessons does Nazism hold for events in the Middle East today?

Source: Adapted from Sternberg, 1997.

MULTIPLE INTELLIGENCES FOR THE 21ST CENTURY

PROGRAMMING A VCR SO IT DOES NOT FLASH 12-12-12

RECALLING THE LOCATION OF THE REMOTE CONTROL

DRIVING AND SPEAKING ON A CELLULAR PHONE

Source: Reprinted with the permission of Psi Chi, The National Honor Society in Psychology.

3. *Logical/Mathematical*: Used in solving mathematics problems and in logical thinking—for instance, in science and mathematics, especially highly advanced mathematics

4. *Visual/Spatial*: Ability to grasp how objects orient in space, which can be very useful in art and navigation; therefore observed in artists, pilots, and astronauts

5. *Movement or Bodily Kinesthetic*: Ability to control body motions and to handle objects skillfully; found in dancers and athletes

6. *Interpersonal Intelligence*: Sensitivity to people and an ability to understand what motivates them, how to work effectively with them, and how to lead and to follow

7. *Intrapersonal Intelligence*: Understanding one's emotions and being able to draw on them to guide one's behavior

8. *Naturalist*: Ability to recognize patterns in nature; to identify and classify plants, animals, and minerals; and to use this information in activities such as farming or landscaping.

Although Sternberg's and Gardner's perspectives seem to be alternatives to traditional views of intelligence, they are in many ways complementary in their emphasis on different aspects of intelligence. For example, you can think analytically, creatively, or practically in a particular domain (linguistic, for example). You can analyze a work of literature (analytic), write a poem (creative), or discuss the relevance of the travails of a literary character for one's own life (practical).

Sternberg and Gardner both suggest that people should be evaluated on the basis of factors other than their scores on tests of verbal and mathematical ability. Relying exclusively on these scores may cause us to overlook a person's other strengths, such as musical or athletic ability.

Lack Direction?

STUDY TIP

Describe the theories of intelligence. When appropriate, such as with the eight aspects of Howard Gardner's multiple intelligences, give examples.

Misuse of Intelligence Tests

Although current intelligence tests provide reliable scores, those tests and scores have been at the center of controversy. What do intelligence scores mean? The high reliability coefficients that characterize most intelligence tests should not lead to the incorrect conclusion that assessments based on such tests are always accurate (valid). Psychological testing has the potential for abuse when the scores are applied without a full understanding of their meaning. The following examples show the misuse of psychological testing.

Earlier in this chapter we learned that Galton believed that intelligence was determined by heredity. Based on this belief, he proposed that the general intelligence of an entire nation could be increased if only the more intelligent citizens were allowed to have children. This movement, known as *eugenics*, was popularized by Galton and brought to the United States, where sterilization laws in more than 30 states soon barred people of low intelligence from having children (Colman, 1988). Between 1924

Earlier in the 20th century, intelligence tests were used to restrict U.S. immigration. This was done without a proper understanding of the influence of environmental conditions on test scores.

and 1972 more than 7,500 people in Virginia were sterilized, including one woman who was told that she was going to have her appendix removed (Gould, 1981). She did not discover the truth until after she had tried for years to bear a child.

In what has been called "one of the saddest chapters in the history of the testing of intelligence" (Sternberg, 1988, p. 7), intelligence test scores were used to prevent many European immigrants from entering the United States. The tests were usually administered in crowded conditions, and the items required a knowledge of U.S. culture that the foreign arrivals lacked. For example, one item asked examinees to look at a geometric figure and then use a pencil to copy it onto a piece of paper. This item seems easy to us, but many of the immigrants had never seen, let alone used, a pencil. Nevertheless, the results were used to classify many immigrants as feebleminded (Gould, 1981).

Hereditary and Environmental Determinants of Intelligence

The people responsible for testing immigrants' intelligence earlier in this century believed that the test scores reflected the operation of heredity rather than environmental influences. The question of how heredity (nature) and environment (nurture) determine intelligence has sometimes mistakenly been posed as if one factor or the other alone accounted for intelligence. A more appropriate way to ask the question is, "To what degree is intelligence influenced by heredity, environment, and a combination of the two?"

Hereditary Determinants.   One way researchers estimate the influence of heredity on intelligence is to use a mathematical measure called **heritability,** which can range from 0% to 100%. A characteristic that has a heritability of 0% is not influenced by inherited factors at all. When the heritability is 100%, inherited factors are completely responsible for that characteristic. Height has a heritability of 90%, which means that 90% of the differences in height among people are accounted for by variation in genetics; only 10% are due to environmental factors such as diet (Horgan, 1993). Although some estimates of the heritability of intelligence are as high as 80% (Jensen, 1969), most are in the range of 50% to 60% (Plomin et al., 1997; Snyderman & Rothman, 1987). Robert Plomin and his colleagues (Plomin et al., 1997) state, "The evidence for a strong genetic contribution to general cognitive ability (*g*) is clearer than for any other area of psychology" (p. 153). What's more, research identifying the specific genes responsible for a number of forms of mental retardation, reading disability, and late-onset Alzheimer's disease raise the possibility that in the near future breakthroughs will occur in the identification of genes responsible for general cognitive ability (Plomin et al., 1997; Plomin & DeFries, 1998; Plomin & Petrill, 1997).

Although we know the most about the heritability of intelligence at younger ages, evidence suggests that genetic factors can affect intelligence in older age populations. What's more, researchers have found that heritability estimates are not constant across the life span; rather, they change with different age ranges (McClearn et al., 1997; Petrill et al., 1998). Researchers located a sample of twins from the Swedish Twin Registry; they were especially interested in twins who were 80 years of age or older and able to take part in a 1.5-hour testing period. The estimate of the heritability of general cognitive ability—based on an overall intelligence test—was quite high. As you can see from Figure 8-17, the estimates of heritability of intelligence actually tend to increase with age.

Even highly heritable characteristics can be influenced by environmental factors. For example, about 1 of every 10,000 American children is born with the genetic abnormality *phenylketonuria* (*PKU*) (Plomin et al., 1997). Their bodies are unable to produce the enzyme that breaks down phenylalanine, an amino acid found in many foods.

heritability
Percentage of differences among a group of people in a characteristic, such as intelligence, that is believed to be due to inherited factors.

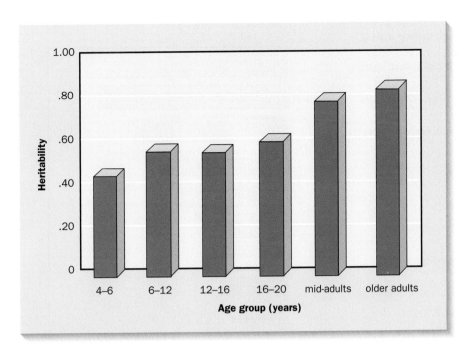

FIGURE 8-17 Influence of genetic factors across the life span. The heritability of intelligence tends to increase with age. In other words, the older we are, the greater the effect of genetic factors.

Source: Plomin & Petrill, 1997.

Undigested phenylalanine accumulates in the body, causes damage to the nervous system (including the brain), and leads to retardation (Dyer, 1999; Luciana et al., 2001). The IQ scores of people with PKU who are left untreated is often below 50 (Plomin et al., 1997).

A diagnostic test performed shortly after birth can determine whether a baby has PKU. Babies found to have PKU are put on a low-phenylalanine diet (some phenylalanine is essential for the body). The general recommendation is to continue the special diet at least through the adolescent years (Plomin et al., 1997). In fact, the majority of treatment centers in the United States and Canada recommend that people with PKU continue their restricted diet throughout life (Fisch et al., 1997). Continued treatment seems to be associated with higher levels of sustained attention as well as greater ability to inhibit cognitive interference (Huijbregts et al., 2002). Although PKU has a heritability of 100%, it can be modified by changing the environment (in this case, diets). In short, heredity is not necessarily destiny.

Psychological Detective

PKU occurs relatively rarely, so it does not tell us a great deal about how heredity influences intelligence in most people. What other evidence could shed light on the way heredity influences intelligence? Give this question some thought, and write down your answer before reading further.

Another way in which researchers estimate the degree to which intelligence is affected by inherited factors is by examining correlations between the intelligence test scores of family members (Bouchard & McGue, 1981). If intelligence runs in families, the intelligence scores of family members should be correlated. The study of twins also plays a key role in investigating the influence of heredity and environment on characteristics such as intelligence. **Identical twins** (also known as monozygotic twins) have exactly the same genes and therefore are always of the same sex. **Fraternal twins** (also known as dizygotic twins) are no more similar than two siblings in the same family. They were born together but have only 50% of their genes in common. As you can see in Figure 8-18, the correlation between the intelligence scores of twins is quite high; the scores of less closely related people exhibit lower correlations. These statistics seem to provide evidence for inherited influences on intelligence. In fact, the correlations between identical twins reared apart provides some of the most compelling evidence for a genetic component to intelligence (Bouchard, 1997).

identical twins
Twins who develop from one ovum fertilized by one sperm; genetically identical to each other

fraternal twins
Twins who develop from two ova fertilized by two different sperm; genetically related as siblings

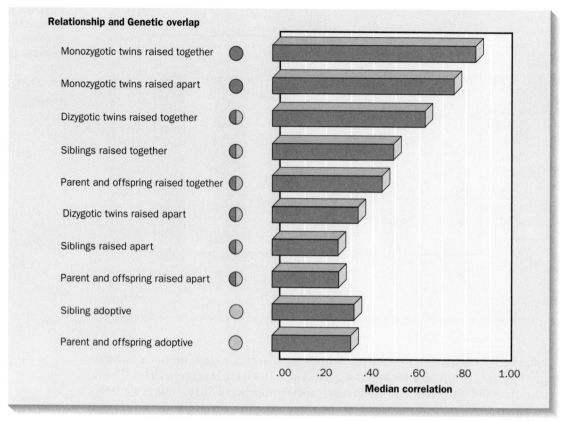

Relationship and Genetic overlap

Monozygotic twins raised together

Monozygotic twins raised apart

Dizygotic twins raised together

Siblings raised together

Parent and offspring raised together

Dizygotic twins raised apart

Siblings raised apart

Parent and offspring raised apart

Sibling adoptive

Parent and offspring adoptive

.00   .20   .40   .60   .80   1.00
Median correlation

FIGURE 8-18   Median correlations between intelligence scores of family members. The degree of genetic overlap ranges from 100% for monozygotic (identical) twins whether they are raised together or apart to 0% for adopted siblings—unrelated children adopted by the same family. The correlations in this table provide evidence for the effects of *both* heredity and the environment.

Source: Plomin & Petrill, 1997.

Family members also share very similar environments, however, making it possible that the correlations among their test scores are due to environmental factors. Yet when twins are raised in separate environments, the correlation between their intelligence scores is still high. So it is unclear whether heredity or environment has a stronger influence on intelligence.

To disentangle the effects of similar environments and heredity, researchers have studied the intelligence test scores of adopted children. Figure 8-18 shows that the correlation between the scores of adoptive parents and their adopted children is approximately .30. What's more, the intelligence scores of adopted children tend to correlate more highly with those of their biological parents than with those of their adoptive parents. In fact, the biological parent's IQ is a better predictor of a child's IQ than is the IQ of the adopting parent, even when the adoption occurs virtually at birth (Hunt, 1995).

What do these results tell us? Do they make a strong case for the influence of heredity on intelligence? Are there any problems with the conduct of such studies that could influence the results?

Several lines of evidence point to a significant influence of the environment on intelligence (Scarr, 1998). Typically, research that investigates the intelligence of adopted children does not tell us whether the environments in which the children were raised were similar to those that their biological parents would or could provide. Sandra Scarr and Richard Weinberg (1986) reported a study of several hundred children in Minnesota who had been placed in adoptive homes. In this case the children were either African American or of mixed racial background. Some of the adoptive parents were African American, but many were white, and most were college graduates with professional occupations. The intelligence scores of these adopted children were similar to those of other children brought up in the same homes. A follow-up of these children in their adolescent years indicated that being reared in a middle- or upper-middle-class environment that represents the culture of the test and schools has a significant effect on adoptees' IQ scores (Weinberg, Scarr, & Waldman, 1992). These findings suggest that the social environment plays a dominant role in determining the IQ of African American and interracial children and that both social and genetic variables contribute to individual variations among them (Weinberg, Scarr, & Waldman, 1992). Thus studies of adopted children suggest that the environment plays a role in intelligence. We next discuss a number of these environmental influences.

Environmental Determinants of Intelligence.   A variety of environmental factors can affect intelligence. For example, exposure to lead is strongly linked to intellectual deficits (Needleman & Gatsonis, 1990). In Taiwan, children who had been exposed prenatally to PCBs (chemicals used to insulate electrical equipment) had small but detectable intellectual deficits that did not decrease with age (Chen et al., 1992).

In the 1930s, Howard Skeels decided that tender loving care and stimulation could be beneficial for two children in an Iowa orphanage (Skeels & Dye, 1939). Skeels placed these quiet, slow, unresponsive sisters in a home for mentally retarded adolescents. On his return several months later, he was surprised to find that the sisters' intelligence test scores had increased and that they appeared alert and active. The attention and stimulation provided by the mentally retarded adolescents and the staff of the institution had made a difference. This finding encouraged Skeels to provide a similar level of stimulation with a larger group of children; again the procedure was successful (Skeels, 1966). Skeels's success provided evidence that early stimulation could influence intelligence.

Since the 1930s there has been a slow but steady rise in performance on IQ tests. The average number of correct responses in samples from 20 countries has risen by about 3 points per decade, or 15 points in 50 years. This effect may be due to environmental factors, such as improved education, or perhaps it is the result of some glitch in the tests (Flynn, 1998; Holloway, 1998). Although performance has improved, the average test score has remained essentially the same. Why is this true? The answer is that IQ scores are a relative rather than an absolute measure; your score is compared with everyone else's. In other words, as the raw scores improve, the standard on which the IQ scores are based also rises. If everyone else is improving, your relative score will not change much (Hunt, 1995). Put another way, a raw score that yielded an IQ of 100 in the 1930s would be equal to an 85 today.

What do you think happens if some children start school with weaker skills than other children? Can anything be done to increase their chances of success? One purpose of preschool programs such as Head Start is to provide these children with educational skills, social skills, and health care before they begin their formal schooling. Head Start is aimed at children around 4 years of age, especially those in low-income and minority populations.

Early evaluations of Head Start were not encouraging; the improvements reported in verbal abilities, emotional maturity, and motivation generally lasted only 3 to 4 years into elementary school—a fairly common phenomenon known as fadeout. On the other hand, some research on various forms of early childhood education, including Head Start, indicated that after participation in these programs, fewer of the children were placed in special education classes and fewer were held back in school (Consortium for Longitudinal Studies, 1983).

In retrospect, it seems that initial expectations for Head Start were too optimistic. Efforts to influence intellectual ability cannot overcome all other environmental influences (Lee et al., 1990), and early intervention does not guarantee success in life: "Early intervention simply cannot overpower the effects of poor living conditions, inadequate nutrition and health care, negative role models, and substandard schools" (Zigler & Styfco, 1994, p. 129). What's more, many Head Start teachers did not have adequate training, and parents were not as involved as they should have been. In addition, the quality of programs varied quite a bit. In the better programs, whose purpose was in part to enhance school readiness, the children often become better achievers by the time they left the program.

Despite its shortcomings, Head Start has widespread public and political support (Takanishi & De Leon, 1994; Zigler & Styfco, 1994). Programs such as the Carolina Abecedarian Project, however, have had greater success. In this project infants from low-income families were placed into intellectually enriched environments until they began school. Compared with controls, the enriched children scored higher on tests of intelligence, even seven years after the end of the intervention (Campbell & Ramey, 1994).

Myth or Science

For almost 30 years the idea that birth order is related to intelligence scores has been the subject of articles and advice from professionals and nonprofessionals. Some articles had provocative (and in retrospect, distressing) titles like "Dumber by the dozen" (Zajonc, 1975). Here is advice from columnist Dr. Joyce Brothers (in answer to a question from a mother of four who asked if she should consider having another baby): "Studies have shown that children reared in small families are brighter, more creative, and more vigorous that those from large families" (Brothers, 1981). But was the advice based on solid evidence? Let's take a look.

One explanation offered to explain the apparent relationship between birth order and intelligence was Robert Zajonc's *confluence model*. This model says that family structure (birth order, family size, and child spacing) influences intellectual development in children. The model was used to explain evidence that average IQ declines with birth order. In other words, the average fifth-born had a lower IQ than the average third-born child. The pattern was clear, but patterns can deceive us.

Joseph Lee Rodgers and his colleagues (Rodgers et al., 2000) reported on the relationship between birth order and intelligence. They note that the decline in intelligence with birth order is based on what psychologists call cross-sectional research. In other words, researchers take all first borns, then all second-born children, all third-born children, and so on in their sample and average the intelligence scores in each group. The observed pattern is indeed one of declining intelligence scores with birth order and recommendations to keep the family small followed. But is it an accurate picture?

Using data from the National Longitudinal Survey of Youth, Rodgers and his colleagues looked at the data within families of a given size (all two-children families, then all three-child families, etc.). The results indicate that low-IQ parents tend to have larger families and thus are inconsistent with the belief that large families make low IQ children. "Parents with lower IQs in the modern United States on average have larger families and have been having larger families for some time (Rodgers et al., 2000, p. 610)." When we use birth order to compare across families as in cross-sectional designs it confounds socioeconomic status, educational level, nutritional quality, maternal age, and other variables. Thus, the apparent decline is due primarily to the fact that lower IQ parents have larger families and these families differ from the rest of the population in variables that are correlated with intelligence.

"There are many good reasons why parents might consider limiting their family sizes. However, the belief that, for a particular set of parents in a modern country like the United States, a larger family will lead to children with lower IQs appears to be, simply, wrong" (Rodgers et al., 2000, p. 611). Simply put, there is no causal role for family size in IQ (Ceci, 2001).

Psychological Detective

Look at the correlations in Figure 8-18. What evidence in those correlations points to the effects of the environment on intelligence? Why? Give this question some thought, and write down your answer before reading further.

A close look at the correlations in Figure 8-18 led some researchers to conclude that both heredity and environment strongly influence the development of intelligence (Plomin, 1989). Where is the support for the influence of the environment among those correlations? If two unrelated children are raised together, will their intelligence scores be similar? If heredity controls intelligence, the correlation between the intelligence scores of unrelated children should reflect their lack of family relationships—that is, it should be 0. Yet the correlation between the intelligence test scores of unrelated children raised together is greater than .30. Now look at the correlations for identical twins raised apart and raised together. The difference between those correlations also indicates that environmental factors have an effect on intelligence.

In most studies of intelligence (and other characteristics) of twins, researchers often assume that the twins (especially identical twins) are treated quite similarly. Researchers are increasingly finding, however, that twins and siblings in general are not treated as similarly as was once assumed. In fact, researchers have begun to use the terms *shared environment* and *nonshared environment* to describe the common and unique elements of the environment. They have found—sometimes to their surprise—that siblings tend to grow up in environments that are more different than similar. These differences in the environment—called nonshared environment—play a major role in accounting for differences among siblings in intelligence and in personality (Chapter 11). Earlier we described a study of the similarity of intelligence scores in twins age 80 years and older. The major finding of that study was a high estimated heritability. From an environmental perspective, however, what is important is that the nonshared environment accounted for 27% of the differences in intelligence among older people. Thus even in old age differences in environment can play a role in shaping intelligence.

Explaining Differences in Intelligence Scores.   The controversy surrounding intelligence testing continues today. Much of it concerns differences in the average intelligence scores attained by members of various racial and ethnic groups. For example, the average intelligence scores obtained by African Americans are lower than those for white Americans (MacKenzie, 1984). These group differences should not obscure the fact that there is a high degree of overlap in the distribution of intelligence scores for all groups.

Although individual differences in intelligence are due in part to heredity, the existence of group differences in IQ scores does not necessarily suggest that there are innate differences in intelligence among groups. Even characteristics that are affected by heredity can vary in response to environmental factors. Consider the analogy proposed by Richard Lewontin (1976): If we take a bag of seeds and sow half in fertile soil and the other half in barren soil, the plants that grow in barren soil will be shorter on average than the plants that grow in fertile soil. Even seeds with the genetic code for tallness are not likely to grow to their full potential if they are planted in barren soil. The differences among the plants within each group may be due to heredity, but the average difference between the two groups reflects environmental factors—in this case, the quality of the soil. In the same way, differences in IQ scores among groups can reflect such environmental factors as academic background, quality of education, and the availability of resources such as books and educational toys.

For this reason, critics of intelligence tests argue that we must take a closer look at the tests themselves. These tests are designed to measure a quality known as "intelligence," but this quality can be difficult to define, let alone measure. Intelligence tests have good predictive validity; that is, they effectively predict the performance of children in school. Success in school, however, can reflect many influences besides innate intelligence. Therefore critics warn against drawing conclusions concerning students' mental abilities based on their test performance.

In fact, some experts have charged that group differences in test scores might reflect certain characteristics of the tests themselves. For example, Janet Helms (1992) suggests that intelligence tests reflect white, middle-class values and therefore are innately biased against members of other cultural groups. Tests assume that standard (white) English is best, so they are written in standard English. Similarly, some of the test questions are based on the assumption that the basic social unit is the nuclear family, which consists of a mother, a father, and their children. Thus children from groups that have a high rate of nonnuclear families are placed at a disadvantage in answering those questions.

Claude Steele of Stanford University has proposed that students' attitudes and approach toward standardized tests can also affect their performance (Steele & Aronson, 1995). According to Steele, African-American students face additional pressures in that a poor performance can be interpreted as confirming negative stereotypes about African Americans as a group. Thus African-American students carry an extra burden that Steele calls *stereotype vulnerability*. To test this hypothesis, Steele and Joshua Aronson gave African-American and white students a test composed of difficult verbal items from the Graduate Record Examination (GRE). Half of the students were told that the purpose of the exercise was to study "psychological factors involved in solving verbal problems." The remaining students were told that the exam was "a genuine test of your verbal abilities and limitations."

The results revealed that African-American students who thought they were simply solving problems performed as well as white students (who performed equally well in both situations). By contrast, the African-American students who had been told that the test measures their intellectual potential performed worse than all the other students. Significantly, all students had been asked to write down their race before taking the test. Thus African-American students who felt they were being evaluated as a group tried to deal with stereotype vulnerability by increasing their efforts, which led them to work inefficiently and inaccurately. Steele and Aronson (1995) concluded that they have uncovered "an underappreciated source of classic deficits in standardized test performance" (p. 810). Although Steele and Aronson's hypothesis has not been applied directly to IQ tests, it suggests an intriguing explanation for group differences in test scores.

The debate over differences in test scores is not merely an intellectual exercise, it has scientific, political, and social implications. Consider, for example, the controversy surrounding the publication of *The Bell Curve* (1994) by Richard Herrnstein and Charles Murray. Herrnstein and Murray assert that there are genetically based differences in intelligence among socioeconomic, racial, and ethnic groups. They further argue that intelligence as measured by IQ scores determines such attributes and behaviors as employment, income, welfare dependence, and quality of parental behavior. Thus low IQ is the best explanation of why some people never get off welfare, why crime is rampant in the inner cities, and why so many teenage girls get pregnant. This argument has profound implications for political and social policy: It suggests that educational and social welfare programs will have limited effectiveness because heredity, rather than environment, is primarily responsible for the problems of low-income groups.

A number of researchers (for example, Ceci, 2001; Gottfredson, 1997) have in fact pointed out that intelligence does matter; for example, intelligence scores are related to job training and performance. Critics note, however, that Herrnstein and Murray fail to distinguish between correlation and causation (see Chapter 1) and thus draw inappropriate conclusions (Hunt, 1995; Kamin, 1995). It is true that people living below the poverty line are likely to have lower IQs and poorer health and to come from families of lower socioeconomic status. Although all of these behaviors are correlated, we do not know whether any cause-and-effect relationships exist among them (Hunt, 1995). For example, these behaviors could result from such environmental factors as inadequate schooling and lack of financial resources.

The controversy over how to interpret IQ scores will likely be with us for a long time. Although the issue is complex, the evidence suggests that performance on standardized tests reflects the interaction of genetic and environmental factors. Drawing conclusions about group differences based solely on test scores can be misleading and counterproductive. What's more, as we have seen, there is a great deal of overlap among all groups in test scores.

REVIEW SUMMARY

1. Francis Galton initiated the intelligence testing movement by developing tests based on the assumption that level of intelligence is related to sensory abilities.

2. Alfred Binet and Theodore Simon developed an intelligence test to evaluate French schoolchildren. They proposed the concept of **mental age,** which compared a child's performance with the average performance of children at a particular age. The **intelligence quotient (IQ)** is the ratio of mental age divided by chronological age and multiplied by 100.

3. Binet's tests became the widely used Stanford-Binet test. Another set of tests, the Wechsler Scales, yield verbal and performance appraisals of intelligence.

4. The three characteristics of a good psychological test are reliability, validity, and standardization. **Reliability** refers to the consistency of scores obtained on repeated administrations of the test. **Validity** refers to a test's ability to measure what it was designed to measure. **Standardization** refers to uniformity in testing procedures and test scoring. **Norms** provide the distribution of scores of a large sample of people who have previously taken a test.

5. Intelligence test scores are distributed in the shape of a **normal curve.** The majority of the scores are clustered around the middle, with fewer scores found at either extreme.

6. According to Charles Spearman, we all possess general intelligence (*g*) along with specific abilities (*s*). Robert Sternberg and Howard Gardner propose that we have several types of intelligence, most of which are not measured by current intelligence tests.

7. Intelligence tests have been used to deny entry into the United States. The *eugenics* movement proposed that the intelligence of an entire nation could be increased if only the more intelligent citizens had children.

8. The **heritability** of intelligence is an estimate of the influence of heredity in accounting for differences among people. Yet, even clearly inherited conditions, such as PKU, can be modified by altering a person's environment.

9. Correlations between the IQ scores of identical twins suggest that intelligence is strongly influenced by heredity. The closer the family relationship, the higher the correlation between the intelligence scores of family members. Studies of adopted children suggest that environmental factors also have an effect on intelligence.

10. Claude Steele has offered evidence that when taking standardized tests, African Americans may experience *stereotype vulnerability.* This notion suggests that something as simple as a question about one's race may have more significant meaning to African Americans than to other people.

✓ CHECK YOUR PROGRESS

1. Imagine that you are taken back in time to visit Galton's Anthropometric Laboratory. Which of the following measurements would be of greatest interest to Galton?
  a. visual imagery
  b. short-term memory
  c. ability to distinguish two objects by weight
  d. speed with which you could run 100 yards

2. Distinguish between mental age and chronological age.

3. You have just completed your sophomore year in college, and you have no idea what you want to do when you graduate. Last week you took a test that was supposed to identify the things you enjoy doing. The results of the test strongly suggested that you should pursue a career in journalism. But you absolutely despise writing! What does the test apparently lack?

4. What do we mean when we say that intelligence scores are distributed like a normal curve? What does this interpretation tell us about extreme scores?

5. An expert on genetic influences on physical and psychological characteristics has been invited to campus to give a presentation. This expert has just finished a review of the evidence on genetics, heritability, and the public's knowledge of such concepts. Which of the following would be the best title for the presentation?
  a. "Heritability Does Not Equal Destiny"
  b. "Genetic Factors: How We Have Overstated Their Influence"
  c. "All in the Genes: Location of the Genes Responsible for Various Facets of Intelligence"
  d. "Genes Don't Influence Environmental Factors, and Environmental Factors Don't Influence Genes"

6. Your professor has given you an assignment to determine the estimates of the heritability of PKU, height, and intelligence. You are to turn in a list of these characteristics ranked from the one with the highest heritability to the one with the lowest. Of the following lists, which will you hand in?
  a. PKU, height, intelligence
  b. height, PKU, intelligence
  c. intelligence, PKU, height
  d. intelligence, height, PKU

7. What evidence supports the idea that intelligence is determined by heredity? What evidence supports the idea that intelligence results from environmental influences?

8. What is Claude Steele's stereotype vulnerability hypothesis?

9. What has happened to measures of intelligence over the past several decades?

   a. Absolute intelligence has declined dramatically from generation to generation.
   b. IQ scores adjusted for changes in level of education have not changed significantly.
   c. It now takes more correct items to obtain an average intelligence score than it did in the past.

   d. The range of acceptable responses has been expanded, so such comparisons cannot be made.

10. Which of these people is part of the age group that has the highest heritability for intelligence?

   a. Alice, a newborn
   b. Ted, a 14-year-old
   c. Rob, a 22-year-old
   d. Sonia, a 75-year-old

ANSWERS: 1. c **2.** Chronological age is simply how old a person is; mental age is how a child's intellectual development compares to other children's intellectual development. **3.** validity **4.** A normal curve tells us that most people obtain scores in the middle of a distribution, with fewer scores as we move away from the middle of the distribution. **5.** a **6.** a **7.** The high correlation between intelligence scores of close relatives and especially the high correlation between identical twins separated at birth support the idea that intelligence is determined by heredity. Research on environmental factors, and programs such as Head Start, suggests that intelligence is influenced by environmental factors. **8.** Claude Steele has proposed that when African-American students take standardized tests, they are subject to the effects of stereotype vulnerability. In addition to the pressures that occur for many students who take such tests, African-American students may feel pressure related to the possibility that poor performance on the test might be interpreted as confirming negative stereotypes about their race. **9.** c **10.** d

---

ANSWERS To Problems in Figures

FIGURE 8-2, PAGE 310
The attribute that defines the concept is an odd number of segments within the geometric figure.

Pigs in Pen Problem, PAGE 314
Place nine pigs into each of three pens. Then place all three pens inside one large pen.

FIGURE 8-4, PAGE 314

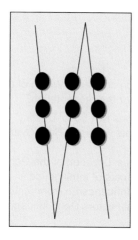  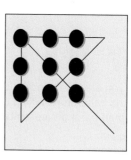

FIGURE 8-5, PAGE 314

A. Remove the matches at the top, bottom, and right.

B. Turn the book upside down.

C. The obvious answer is six and a half. Less obvious answers are:
- halving 13 gives 1 and 3 (1/3)
- halving the word thirteen gives 4 letters on each side
- converting 13 to roman numerals and halving it gives 11 and 2 (XI/II)
- halving it a different way gives 8 (X̶I̶I̶I̶)

FIGURE 8-7,
PAGE 315

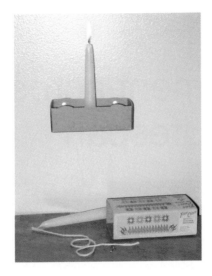

FIGURE 8-8,
PAGE 317

Prisoner's Escape: Divide the rope in half by cutting with the length rather than across the length, similar to unbraiding the rope. Tie the two thinner pieces together and lower yourself to the ground.

Six Drinking Glasses: Numbering the glasses from left to right, pour the contents of glass 2 into glass 5.

Six Pennies: Coins 1, 2, 4, and 6 are already in place, so move coins 3 and 5.

Ten Bowling Pins:

FIGURE 8-12,
PAGE 325

Row 1
a. Just under the wire
b. Balanced budget
c. Standing ovation
d. Shot in the dark
e. Space invaders

Row 2
a. Bottom of the ninth
b. Sitting on top of the world
c. All hands on deck
d. Skinny-dipping
e. Love at first sight

Row 3
a. Canceled check
b. Dashed hopes
c. Splitting headache
d. Three square meals a day
e. Open sesame7

Development across the Lifespan

CHAPTER OUTLINE

So far we have established a biological basis for psychology, examined our sensory and perceptual processes, looked at emotions and states of consciousness, seen how learning takes place and how memories are stored, and considered cognitive processes. Keep in mind that all of these processes take place in the context of a developing organism. In this chapter we discuss the physical, intellectual, social, and psychological changes that occur throughout the lifespan (from conception through old age). As we bring the developmental cycle to its inevitable conclusion, we examine the area of death and dying and our reactions to such losses. As telecommunications and improved travel capabilities increase our knowledge of other cultures, it is important that we understand and appreciate that differences in birthing, child-rearing, and parenting practices—and in attitudes toward the elderly and death—can differ dramatically from one culture to another. Such differences can occur within large segments of the culture in the United States.

From the moment of conception until the moment of death, we change physically, cognitively, and psychosocially. **Developmental psychology** is concerned with the systematic physical, cognitive, and psychosocial processes that lead to these changes that occur throughout life. The various periods of growth across the life span are shown in Table 9-1.

When we think of human development, we probably think first about physical changes that can be *quantified*, or measured. Many of us have watched our younger brothers and sisters or our own children "grow like weeds." We also develop in *qualitative* ways that are not as easily measured as height, weight, and strength. Some of these qualitative changes involve cognitive processes and social interactions. As we grow older and add more information to long-term memory, our views on diverse topics such as pollution, love, and religion may change. We think in different and more complex ways about ourselves, our friends, and our environment.

developmental psychology
Study of physical, cognitive, and psychosocial changes throughout the life span, from conception until death

TABLE 9-1

Approximate Periods of Growth and Development across the Life Span

Zygote	Conception to 2 weeks
Embryo	2 to 9 weeks
Fetus	9 weeks to birth
Infancy	Birth to age 1 year
Toddler	1 to 3 years
Preschool period	3 to 6 years
Middle childhood	6 to 12 years
Adolescence	12 to 20 years
Young adulthood	20 to 40 years
Middle adulthood	40 to 65 years
Late adulthood	65 years to death

nature
Theory that holds that physical and cognitive development is genetically determined

nurture
Theory that holds that physical and cognitive development is determined by environmental factors

behavior genetics
A new field, combining psychology and biology, that studies the influences of heredity and environment on behavior

BASIC ISSUES IN DEVELOPMENTAL PSYCHOLOGY

John B. Watson (1924) proclaimed that "there is no such thing as an inheritance of capacity, talent, temperament, mental constitution, and characteristics. These things depend on training that goes on mainly in the cradle" (pp. 74–75). Watson was so convinced of the impact of the environment on development that he boldly declared that he could train any child to be a doctor, lawyer, artist, merchant, or even beggar or thief if he could control the child's environment (Watson, 1928). *Was Watson correct? Do all of our abilities develop as a result of environmental influences?*

Nature and Nurture

Watson held strong views about the power of the environment to influence development, but many parents, as well as most present-day psychologists, would disagree. According to Robert Plomin (1990a), "Parents are environmentalists [that is, they stress nurture] until they have more than one child. With one child, it seems possible to explain anything that happens. However, when their second child turns out to be different in many ways from the first child, parents realize that they did not treat the two children differently enough to account for the behavioral differences that are so apparent between them" (p. 8). The contrast between these two views illustrates a significant issue in developmental psychology: To what degree does development result from **nature** (heredity) and to what extent is it a product of **nurture** (environmental factors)? In **behavior genetics,** a relatively new field that combines psychology and biology, researchers seek to provide answers to the nature-or-nurture question.

Psychological Detective

To grasp how behavior geneticists examine how people behave, take a moment to consider some of the differences you see in such characteristics as musical ability, athletic ability, shyness, or activity level in your friends and relatives. To what extent are these characteristics genetically determined, and to what extent are they environmentally determined? Write down some of your observations before reading further.

Some of the people you describe may have exceptional musical talent, whereas others may describe themselves as tone-deaf. A few of your friends and relatives are outgoing; others are painfully shy. Why do these people differ in these ways? Environmental factors probably play a critical role in enabling people to develop their individual capabilities. But are some of the differences we observe the result of factors other than environmental influences?

Behavioral geneticists have found that heredity plays a significant role in intelligence, personality, and several patterns of abnormal behavior (Plomin et al., 1997). Yet "the same data that point to significant genetic influences provide the best available evidence for the importance of nongenetic factors" (Plomin, 1990a, p. 179). One of the most significant discoveries of behavior genetics is that environmental factors are experienced differently by children in the same family (see Chapter 11). Consider, for example, identical twins, who share the exact same genetic makeup. The fact that they do not have identical personalities points to the influence of environmental factors. Both nature and nurture play significant roles in development. If we are to understand the development of human thoughts, behaviors, motives, and emotions, we must learn to distinguish the influences of nature from those of nurture. Hence developmental psychologists are careful to use certain special research methods.

Research Methods

Psychologists conducting research on developmental processes face some unique challenges. First, psychologists cannot isolate their human participants in cages like laboratory animals, allowing them to emerge only when it is time for their daily experimental sessions. What's more, ethical considerations prevent researchers from investigating some developmental processes. What is permissible? Is it acceptable to expose children to violent television programs to determine whether they will become violent or aggressive as a result? How does a researcher teach these children that their newly acquired aggressive behavior is wrong?

Longitudinal Versus Cross-Sectional Studies.   Research in human development may take longer than research in other areas of psychology. Developmental research may take months, years, or even decades. Long-term research projects in which the same participants are observed or tested repeatedly are called **longitudinal studies.** Studies that involve observing or testing participants of different ages at *one moment in time* are called **cross-sectional studies.** In other words, longitudinal projects study the same people over a period of time; cross-sectional studies cut across a section of the ages and types of people available at one moment in time (see Figure 9-1). Longitudinal studies allow the researcher to see behavioral trends that develop over time, whereas cross-sectional studies allow the researcher to answer a specific question at a particular point in time. However, longitudinal studies can be very time-consuming and costly. Even though they are less time-consuming and costly, cross-sectional studies do not tell the researcher about behavioral trends over time.

Groups composed of participants born in the same year are called **cohorts** or cohort groups. In a *cohort design,* we compare the responses of different cohorts. For example, by looking at differences among cohorts, we determine the effects on shyness of being born in different decades from 1950 to 1990. The cohort design is also used in cross-cultural research in which same-age groups from different countries can be

longitudinal study
Research technique in which the same partcipants are tested or observed repeatedly over a period of time

cross-sectional study
Research technique in which participants, often of different ages, are tested or observed during a limited time span or only once

cohort
Group of individuals born in the same period

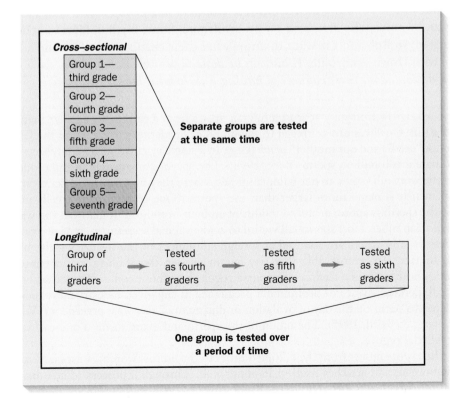

FIGURE 9-1   Comparison of cross-sectional and longitudinal research designs.

Because they are the same age, the children in this grade school class constitute a cohort.

zygote
One-celled organism formed by the union of a sperm and an ovum

mitosis
Process of cell division in which each cell contains the same genetic information as other cells

compared. The validity of a research finding is increased if it is verified across cultural groups as well as across age groups.

DEVELOPMENT FROM CONCEPTION TO BIRTH

Bob and Liz are thinking about having a baby, but they are concerned about the possibility that their child will have chromosomal abnormalities. Bob's brother, who is 22, has Down syndrome and lives in a group home with six men and women who also have Down syndrome. Some birth defects may be inherited, so Bob and Liz want to know what their chances are of having a baby with Down syndrome. *What can be done to provide Bob and Liz with information about their chances of having a child with Down syndrome?*

Great oaks grow from tiny acorns; a human grows from a cell that is smaller than the tip of a pin. Our lives can be traced to the union of our father's *sperm* (from the Greek word for "seed") and our mother's *ovum* (egg). In a single ejaculation, a man releases approximately 360 million sperm (Berk, 1998). The sperm immediately begin a journey from the woman's vagina to her fallopian tubes, where they may meet and penetrate an ovum, which is many times larger than the sperm. (One of the smallest cells in the body, the sperm is approximately 1/600th of an inch from head to tail.) On the way to the fallopian tubes, most sperm fall victim to acidic vaginal secretions; some are caught in recesses, and others are attacked as foreign substances by the woman's white blood cells. In fact, it is remarkable that any sperm survive the journey to penetrate an ovum. A healthy couple having intercourse regularly without contraception has only a 25 to 30 percent chance of beginning a pregnancy in any given menstrual cycle. Most conceptions occur on the day of ovulation or during the 2 days that precede it (Wilcox, Weinberg, & Baird, 1995). The union of the sperm and ovum forms a one-cell structure called a **zygote.**

The zygote moves from the fallopian tubes to the uterus (womb), a fist-sized, pear-shaped organ, and attaches itself to its inner wall. Through a process of cell division called **mitosis,** the zygote reproduces itself: One cell divides to become 2, then 4, and

Fertilization occurs when the sperm penetrates the much larger ovum.

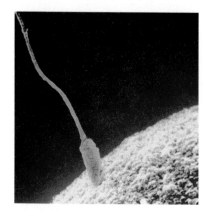

so on; after just 5 days, the zygote contains about 100 cells. During the next 9 months, cell division continues at a furious pace, eventually producing an individual with billions of cells, all of which contain identical genetic information.

From the 2nd to 9th weeks after fertilization, when the major organ systems are formed, the developing human is called an **embryo.** Not all zygotes become embryos, however; nearly one-third of implanted zygotes are rejected from the uterus through miscarriage (spontaneous abortion). The zygotes of most of these early miscarriages are defective in some way.

Heredity

As noted earlier, fertilization occurs when the sperm and ovum fuse, providing the zygote with the inherited (genetic) material that will influence its development. This material is arranged in structures called **chromosomes** located in the cell nuclei. All human cells except the sperm and ovum contain 46 chromosomes, arranged in 23 pairs, with one member of each pair contributed by each parent. The chromosomes carry **genes,** which are the basic units of inheritance and the genetic blueprints for development.

The general chemical name for genetic material is **deoxyribonucleic acid,** or **DNA.** Chromosomes are actually large segments of DNA. The unique genetic blueprint for your development is contained in the chromosomes located in the nucleus of each cell (see Figure 9-2).

Our understanding of the mechanisms of heredity can be traced to the work of a monk, Gregor Mendel (1822–1884), who conducted a series of experiments using garden peas. Through these studies he unraveled the key principles of hereditary transmission; those principles are still relevant today.

During Mendel's time, people believed that a child's traits were a blend of the parents' traits; thus the child would have some intermediate or average value of a trait such as eye color. When Mendel bred peas having white flowers with peas having purple flowers, however, the offspring had purple flowers, rather than pink ones. This surprising finding led him to conclude that the offspring plant's traits were not merely blends of the parent plants' traits.

Mendel also concluded that each adult plant carries hereditary factors that govern the inheritance of a trait. As you just saw, we call these factors *genes,* and they are carried on *chromosomes.* The hereditary factors of the mother and father separate before the formation of their offspring. Thus each parent contributes only *half* of the genetic material to the trait in question.

Finally, Mendel suggested that hereditary factors could be either dominant or recessive. When a *dominant gene* and a recessive gene are present in a pea plant, the dominant gene expresses itself. A *recessive gene* can express itself only in the absence of a dominant gene.

An example of this phenomenon in humans is the inheritance of sickle-cell anemia, which occurs when a person's blood contains too many abnormal hemoglobin molecules. Normal hemoglobin gives blood its red color and carries oxygen to body tissues. Too much abnormal hemoglobin causes the amount of oxygen in the blood to drop. The resulting low oxygen level causes cells to become crescent- or sickle-shaped. An attack of sickle-cell anemia is accompanied by high fever, severe pain, and potential injury to body parts and tissue (Sullivan, 1987).

Sickle-cell anemia occurs in people who have two recessive genes for that trait. People who have one dominant gene and one recessive gene for sickle-cell anemia are called *carriers* (see Figure 9-3) because they can pass the recessive gene on to their children, even though they do not have symptoms of the disease themselves. The children of two carriers have a 1-in-4 chance of having normal hemoglobin, a 1-in-2 chance of being a carrier, and a 1-in-4 chance of having sickle-cell anemia. Because of a relatively low rate of interracial marriage and because they are more likely to carry the recessive gene, African Americans have a higher incidence of sickle-cell anemia than people of other races. Likewise, persons from families of Eastern European Jewish origin are

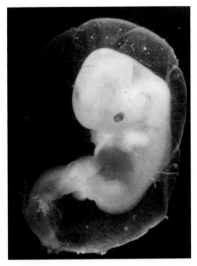
Between 2 weeks and 9 weeks following conception, the developing child is known as an embryo.

9.1

embryo
A developing organism during the stage when the major organ systems are formed

chromosomes
Segments of genetic material located in the nucleus of each cell; human cells have 23 pairs of chromosomes (numbered according to size), one of each pair being inherited from each parent

genes
Units of hereditary material that line the chromosomes and provide information concerning the form and function of each cell

deoxyribonucleic acid (DNA)
Chemical name for the genetic material located in the nucleus of each cell

FIGURE 9-2

Cells–chromosomes–genes–DNA. Genetic material is contained in chromosomes. The chromosomes carry the genes, which are the basic units of heredity. The genes are composed of DNA.

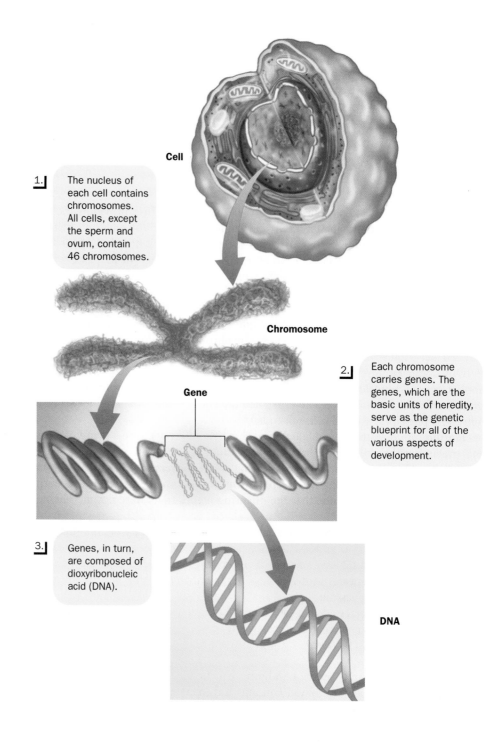

Cell

1. The nucleus of each cell contains chromosomes. All cells, except the sperm and ovum, contain 46 chromosomes.

Chromosome

2. Each chromosome carries genes. The genes, which are the basic units of heredity, serve as the genetic blueprint for all of the various aspects of development.

Gene

3. Genes, in turn, are composed of dioxyribonucleic acid (DNA).

DNA

more likely to be carriers of Tay-Sachs disease (Berkow, 1997). Tay-Sachs disease is caused by an enzyme deficiency that progressively leads to retarded development, paralysis, blindness, and death by age 5.

Polygenic Heredity.   Most human traits are controlled by a number of different genes, a phenomenon termed **polygenic inheritance.** For example, skin color, intelligence, and temperament are examples of polygenic inheritance.

Fraternal (dizygotic) twins develop from two ova fertilized by two different sperm. These children have no more resemblance to each other than other children of the same parents. Identical (monozygotic) twins develop from one ovum fertilized by one

polygenic inheritance

Principle of heredity whereby complex traits, such as intelligence and personality, are determined by many genes

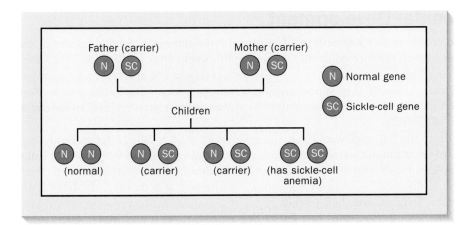

FIGURE 9-3 Parents who have a recessive gene for sickle-cell anemia are carriers for this disease. One-fourth of their children will be normal, one-half will be carriers, and one-fourth will have the disease.

sperm. The resulting cell immediately divides into two zygotes, each containing identical genetic material. Identical twins raised apart offer researchers the unique ability to study the relation of heredity and environment. Because the twins share the same genetic material, shared traits would reflect genetic influences whereas differences would reflect environmental causes.

Determination of Sex. Although many societies have deemed a woman's failure to produce male offspring to be a basis for divorce, the sex of a child is actually determined by the father, not the mother. To understand this process, we need to examine the 23rd pair of chromosomes, the sex chromosomes.

In females, both sex chromosomes are the same; they are labeled XX. After *meiosis* (a type of cell division that results in a reduced amount of genetic material in the cells), the ovum *always* contributes an X chromosome toward determining the child's sex. In males, the pair of sex chromosomes consists of a large chromosome and a smaller chromosome, which are labeled X and Y, respectively (the labels reflect the shapes of these chromosomes). The sperm may carry either an X or a Y sex chromosome. When the sperm contributes an X chromosome, the pair of sex chromosomes will be XX, and the baby will be female. If the sperm contributes a Y chromosome, the pair of sex chromosomes will be XY, and the baby will be male.

Sex-Linked Traits. A gene located on a sex chromosome (X or Y) is called a *sex-linked gene*. The X chromosome is much larger than the Y chromosome and carries more genes. As a result, males are more vulnerable than females to some inherited disorders. In females, a recessive gene carrying a defect can be dominated by a gene on the other X chromosome; in males, however, the Y chromosome may not have the dominant gene, and the trait may appear. Such traits are called *sex-linked traits*.

Red–green color-blindness (see Chapter 3) is a sex-linked trait that occurs in about 8 of every 100 males in the United States. This most common form of color-blindness is controlled by genes on the X chromosome. A female may carry a gene for color-blindness on one X chromosome and a gene for normal vision, which is dominant, on the other X chromosome; she will have normal color vision. A male with a recessive gene for color-blindness, however, has no dominant gene for normal color vision on the Y chromosome, so he will be color-blind. Other sex-linked disorders include hemophilia (the inability of the blood to clot), baldness, and some allergies.

Because they developed from a single ovum that was fertilized by one sperm, these sisters are identical (monozygotic) twins.

Prenatal Development

Let's return to our exploration of embryonic development. As we discussed, major organ systems are formed during the 2nd to 9th weeks after fertilization, when the developing human is called an embryo. Testes develop in the embryo six to eight weeks after conception. If they start secreting testosterone (see Chapter 2), the developing baby will have male external genitals. The absence of testosterone leads to the development of a female.

From the 9th week until birth, the developing child is called a **fetus.** By the end of the 3rd month in the womb, the fetus is about 3 inches long and weighs about 1 ounce. Arms, legs, hands, and feet are visible and move in response to stimulation; the respiratory and digestive systems are functional. At the end of 6 months, the fetus is about 14 inches long and weighs 2 pounds.

The fetus is suspended in a fluid-filled *amniotic sac* that cushions it against sudden movements or blows to the mother. Although it is immersed in amniotic fluid (which is 98 to 99 percent water), the fetus begins to move as early as the end of the 3rd month of pregnancy (Moore & Persaud, 1993). The mother begins to feel movement toward the middle of her pregnancy, when the fetus is large enough to be felt through the abdominal wall (Maurer & Maurer, 1988).

The **placenta** (a Latin word meaning "flat cake") is an organ that develops even more rapidly than the fetus during the early months of pregnancy. The placenta allows an exchange of nutrients from the mother to the developing child and an exchange of waste products from the developing child to the mother. The mother's blood vessels intertwine with those that lead to the child through the umbilical cord (see Figure 9-4). Because the blood vessels of the mother are separated by a membrane from those that lead to the child, however, not all substances pass from one to the other. Nutrients in the mother's blood are released into the placenta (Rixxo et al., 1997), where the fetus's blood takes them up and carries them, via the umbilical cord, to the fetus's body. Waste from the fetus goes in the opposite direction.

fetus
The developing baby from about the 9th week after conception until birth

placenta
Organ that develops in the uterus during pregnancy; it produces hormones that maintain pregnancy, transmits nourishment to the fetus, and filters out certain harmful substances

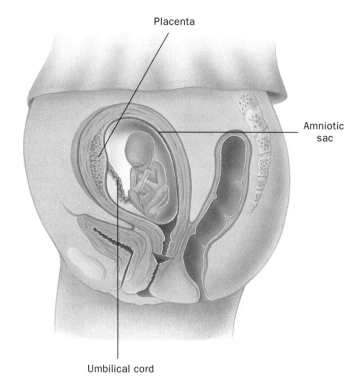

FIGURE 9-4 During gestation, the developing baby (fetus) is suspended in the fluid-filled amniotic sac. The fetus is connected to the placenta by the umbilical cord.

Barriers to Prenatal Development.   If a pregnant woman's diet is inadequate, the baby is more likely to be born prematurely (at or before 37 weeks) or to have a low birth weight (less than 5.5 pounds). Low-birth-weight infants are 40 times more likely than normal-weight babies to die before their first birthday. Countries that have high numbers of low-birth-weight infants include Canada, Germany, Iran, Japan, China, and Norway. Compared with other industrialized countries, the United States has a relatively high infant mortality rate; in fact, 23 countries rank higher than the United States in the rate of infants who survive to their first birthday (Central Intelligence Agency, 1996). The most important factor in causing this high rate of infant mortality is the lack of adequate prenatal care due to lack of adequate financial resources (Rice, 2001).

Teratogens.   A wide variety of factors, including drugs, alcohol, and viruses, can affect the developing fetus. A **teratogen** (from the Greek word for "monster") is any biological, chemical, or physical agent that can lead to birth defects. For example, the virus that causes *rubella* (German measles) can cross the placenta to the fetus. If a pregnant woman contracts rubella before the eleventh week of pregnancy, the baby is almost certain to have birth defects such as deafness or heart problems (Eberhart-Phillips, Frederick, & Baron, 1993). If the mother contracts rubella after 16 weeks, the chances of birth defects are near zero (Miller, Cradock-Watson, & Pollock, 1982).

We draw attention to the period during which rubella exerts its effects to introduce the concept of the critical period. A **critical period** is a specific time during development when certain processes should occur or when damage to normal development can take place. For example, most teratogens exert their most damaging effects during the first 8 weeks of development. A baby may also contract AIDS (acquired immunodeficiency syndrome) if the mother has the disease (Grant, 1995). The virus that causes AIDS may pass through the placenta, or the baby may be exposed to the mother's infected blood during delivery (Weber, Redfield, & Lemon, 1986). Most infants live for only a short time (5 to 8 months) after AIDS symptoms appear (Chamberlain, Nichols, & Chase, 1991).

Drugs.   Almost all drugs cross the placenta freely (Berk, 1998); among those that are harmful to the fetus are antibiotics (such as tetracycline), barbiturates, large doses of vitamins A and B_6, and an acne preparation (Accutane). Even aspirin and caffeine are suspected of causing harm to the fetus. Babies born to mothers who are addicted to heroin are also addicted to those drugs and undergo a painful withdrawal process. For example, babies born to cocaine-addicted mothers may exhibit such behaviors as tremors, irritability, hypertension, rigidity, and poor sleep–wake schedules (Rice, 2001).

Smoking.   *Fetal tobacco syndrome*, a condition characterized by retarded fetal growth resulting in lower birth weight and hyperactivity (Cotton, 1994; Fried, 1993), can occur if a mother smokes as few as five cigarettes per day during pregnancy (Nieburg et al., 1985). Maternal smoking (of cigarettes and marijuana, Iverson, 2000) increases the level of carbon dioxide in the blood of the fetus and is also related to higher rates of infant death (U.S. Department of Health and Human Services, 1989). The number of fetal and infant deaths in the United States could be reduced by about 5,600 each year if all pregnant women stopped smoking (Drews et al., 1996).

Alcohol.   Scientists have been aware for many years that children of alcoholic parents exhibit learning and developmental problems like low birth weight, small head size, and mental retardation. Until the early 1970s, many health professionals attributed these conditions to a disruptive home life and poor caretaking. Then physicians discovered that the mother's drinking behaviors could significantly affect her newborn's health. The identification of the **fetal alcohol syndrome (FAS)** awakened the scientific

teratogen
Any biological, chemical, or physical agent capable of causing birth defects

critical period
A specific time during development when damage may occur or certain processes should take place

fetal alcohol syndrome (FAS)
Condition found in some children born to mothers who drank during pregnancy, characterized by lower birth weight, small head circumference, and mental retardation

Smoking and Cognitive Development

As few as five cigarettes a day can retard fetal growth.

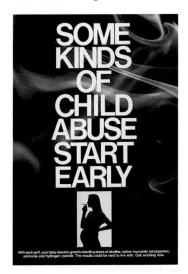

ultrasound procedure
Projection of sound waves onto the fetus, uterus, and placenta to construct a sonogram

sonogram
Outline picture constructed through use of the ultrasound procedure

amniocentesis
Withdrawal and analysis of amniotic fluid to detect genetic abnormalities in the fetus

community to the dangers of alcohol use during pregnancy (Jones & Smith, 1973). The signs of FAS include small head, flat midface, hearing loss, heart defects, and low intelligence (Aase, 1994; Day, 1992). Maternal alcohol use is also associated with adolescent and adult handicaps such as intellectual deficiencies, poor concentration, motor difficulties, and learning problems (Streissguth, Sampson, & Barr, 1989).

Checking the Health of the Fetus. Technological advances have greatly enhanced our ability to detect defects in the developing fetus (Moore & Persuad, 1993). Among the techniques available for this purpose are ultrasound and amniocentesis.

Ultrasound. The **ultrasound procedure** involves directing high-pitched sound waves (more than 20,000 cycles per second) toward the fetus. The sounds pass through the body and bounce back like the sonar waves used by submarines. A computer converts these echoed sound waves into a **sonogram,** an outline image of the fetus, uterus, and placenta. The sonogram determines if growth is normal or if there are any malformations.

Amniocentesis. The mother's age (especially if she is over 35), a family history of genetic defects, or detection of gross abnormalities by ultrasound may suggest the need for more precise testing by amniocentesis. **Amniocentesis** involves inserting a needle into the amniotic sac to withdraw about an ounce of amniotic fluid. The procedure can be done about 14 to 16 weeks after conception, when a sufficient amount of amniotic fluid is present. Amniocentesis tests done earlier may result in an increase in fetal loss and foot deformity (Schreck, 1998). Fetal cells floating in the amniotic fluid are then analyzed. Amniocentesis is not risk-free. There is a small risk of a miscarriage and the possibility of introducing an infection into the uterus (Robinson & Henry, 1985).

Analysis of chromosomes can reveal the sex of the fetus as well as the presence of chromosomal abnormalities such as Down syndrome, which occurs in about 1 in 800 births. In 95% of Down syndrome cases, the individual has three rather than two chromosomes in pair number 21 (Tingey, 1988). Children with Down syndrome are often in the mild-to-moderate range of mental retardation (see Chapter 8) (Plomin, De Fries, & McClearn, 1997). They have distinctive physical characteristics such as small skull, slanted eyes, protruding tongue, short neck, and enlarged abdomen. Heart defects and malformations of the digestive tract put them at risk for premature death (relative to normal children), unless these malformations are recognized and corrected. Depending on the number and type of chromosomes that are present, several other sex-linked chromosomal abnormalities may occur. Among these abnormalities are Kleinfelter's syndrome, Fragile X, and Turner's syndrome. These abnormalities may result in physical abnormalities and mental retardation.

Returning to Bob and Liz, who are worried about having a Down syndrome baby because Bob's brother has the syndrome, amniocentesis will provide the answers they seek. However, the fact that Bob's brother has Down syndrome does not by itself mean that Bob and Liz are at risk. Liz's age is the most important risk factor. If she is well under the age of 40, her chances of having a Down syndrome child are greatly reduced.

Birth

Unless the baby is premature, birth occurs approximately 266 days after fertilization, or 280 days after the last menstrual period. Birth may occur several days or even weeks before or after the "due date."

The first stage of the birth process, *labor*, begins when the pituitary gland and uterus release a hormone, oxytocin, that stimulates contractions of the uterus (Mittendorf et al., 1990). Often the mother becomes aware of the onset of labor when her "water breaks," which refers to a sudden release of amniotic fluid through the widening *cervix* (the narrow constricted portion of the uterus). Labor may last from a few hours to days; it is usually longer for a first birth than for later births. The second stage of the process is *delivery*, the actual birth of the baby. At birth, the average newborn in the United States weighs 7.5 pounds and is approximately 20 inches long. Delivery places tremendous force on the child's body, especially the head. Fortunately, the baby's skull is pliable enough that it can squeeze through the birth canal.

Most of the drugs used to reduce the pain of labor and delivery cross the placenta and are associated with a number of adverse short- and long-term effects on infants. As a result, "the use of medication in labor and delivery is a complicated and sensitive issue, because fetal risk, maternal pain, and physician need are at constant odds" (Bornstein & Lamb, 1992, p. 124). Concern about the effects of pain-reducing drugs has led some physicians to use drugs more cautiously and in lower dosages than they did a few decades ago. Because it takes some time for drugs to cross the placenta, the longer the administration of drugs can be delayed, the better it is for the unborn child.

During the birth process, some babies experience **anoxia,** or lack of oxygen. Anoxia occurs for several reasons: The contractions may compress the umbilical cord, the baby may squeeze the cord, or the cord may be wrapped around the baby. Medication given to the mother usually crosses the placenta and may interfere with the baby's breathing, thus depriving the baby of even more oxygen. Severe anoxia can cause cerebral palsy, a motor disability affecting the arms, head, and legs.

STUDY TIP

With a partner, create flash cards for all of the terms defined in the margins of the section on development from conception to birth. Test each other.

DEVELOPMENT IN INFANCY

You are at the hospital visiting a friend who has just had a baby. You have visited her several times and have seen her baby sleeping, crying, and just lying quietly in the crib. How utterly helpless and unable to interact with her environment she seems to be. *To what degree can newborns perceive and interact with their environment?*

Newborn infants (called *neonates*) may be quite different from those depicted in advertisements for baby products, which often use 3- or 4-month-old babies. The narrowness of the birth canal causes most newborns to emerge red and with facial bruises. The head is misshapen, and the baby is covered with a substance resembling cheese. This "bundle of joy" is apparently capable of little more than crying, sleeping, and excreting.

Just after birth, a baby's motor behavior appears to be uncoordinated and purposeless; however, newborns enter the world equipped with several reflexes (see Chapter 2). The precise functions of some reflexes remain a mystery, but others, such as blinking or sucking, clearly offer protection or promote survival. Lightly stroke a baby's cheek and the baby turns toward the touch; this is the **rooting reflex,** which aids the newborn in finding the mother's nipple to obtain nourishment. Place a nipple in a baby's mouth and it begins sucking. Lightly press a finger in a baby's palm and it grasps with more force than you might imagine. In fact, the **palmar or grasp reflex** is so strong that you can lift an infant by its hands. Sudden noise or the sensation of being dropped elicits the **Moro reflex:** The startled infant flings out its arms and then brings them toward its body as if to hug something. When the bottom of a newborn's foot is stroked, the toes fan upward. This response, the **Babinski reflex,** is routinely used to test the functioning of the central nervous system.

Sensory Abilities

Unable to do more than move reflexively, a baby may look like the picture of psychological incompetence. A closer look at newborns, however, reveals that they are remarkably competent.

anoxia
Reduction or lack of oxygen

rooting reflex
Reflex in which the infant turns its head in the direction of a touch on its face

palmar or grasp reflex
Reflex consisting of a very strong hold on any object placed in the palm

moro reflex
Startle reflex in response to a loud noise or the sensation of being dropped

babinski reflex
Reflex in which the infant's toes fan upward when the bottom of the foot is stroked

Voice Recognition.   Very young infants can recognize their mother's voice just hours after birth. That recognition ability may actually develop before birth, while the baby is in the uterus. Psychologists Anthony De Casper and Melanie Spence (1986) asked 12 women to read a Dr. Seuss story aloud twice a day during the last 5 to 6 weeks of pregnancy. Three days after birth, their babies varied the way they sucked on a pacifier according to whether they heard that story or another one through a loudspeaker. The babies sucked more actively in response to the story they had heard while in the womb, compared with a new story.

Vision.   Estimates of the newborn's visual acuity range from 20/300 to 20/800 (Cole & Cole, 1993). Visual acuity improves to about 20/20 by 6 to 12 months (Cohen, De Loache, & Strauss, 1979). Despite less than perfect vision, newborns can focus on objects that are about 8 to 10 inches away—the distance between the baby and the face of its caregiver during nursing or bottle feeding or when being held. Infants are attracted to and fascinated by faces, whether they are presented in two or three dimensions, in the flesh, or on film. Six-month-old babies prefer to look at attractive faces, even though they lack prior experience with cultural standards of beauty (Langlois et al., 1991) and can also recognize their mother's face (DeHann & Nelson, 1997).

Taste and Smell.   Taste and smell receptors are present and probably functioning by the 4th month of prenatal development. Premature infants are capable of smell, suggesting that the fetus is capable of smell (Hughes & Noppe, 1991). Infant smell sensitivity seems to be present at birth for gross odor differences and rapidly increases in sensitivity during the first few weeks after birth (Porter et al., 1992). Likewise, newborns can discriminate between bitter and sour tastes and between sweet and nonsweet tastes.

How Newborns Learn

As we have seen, newborns are quite adept at perceiving the world around them. Moreover, research on newborns in the United States has shown that they are also quite capable of learning (Adolph, 2000; Adolph, Vereijken, & Denney, 1998; Marcus, 2000) through classical conditioning, operant conditioning, and imitation.

Classical Conditioning.   We saw in Chapter 5 that John Watson and Rosalie Rayner were able to classically condition fear in an older infant, Albert. Carolyn Rovee-Collier and Lewis Lipsitt (1982) demonstrated that newborn infants can also be classically conditioned.

Psychological Detective

How might you demonstrate classical conditioning in a newborn? First you must select a behavior that occurs frequently and automatically when appropriate stimulation is presented. What is such a behavior called? Then there are other components to be considered. Try to recall the name of each element. A review of Chapter 5 will assist you. Write down your answers before reading further.

Sucking is a frequent and automatic response that can serve as the unconditioned response (UCR). A nipple placed in a baby's mouth elicits the sucking reflex, so the presence of the nipple in the mouth is an unconditioned stimulus (UCS). The sound of a particular phrase, such as "Are you hungry, baby?," spoken by the mother just before the baby begins to suck, could be the conditioned stimulus (CS). Each time the baby loses the nipple and stops sucking, the mother could repeat the question. Then one day, when the baby has just been put down for a nap but is a little fussy, the mother says, "Are you hungry, baby?," and the baby starts sucking (conditioned response, CR), leading her mistakenly to think the baby really is still hungry. Try diagramming this arrangement of CS, UCS, UCR, and CR as we did in Chapter 5.

Operant Conditioning. Carolyn Rovee-Collier (1993) demonstrated that as early as two months after birth, an infant can learn to make a kick response when it is reinforced by movement of a mobile suspended over the crib. Moreover, this research has shown that the memory of this learning session may be retained for several days after the conditioning session.

FIGURE 9-5 A young infant is capable of imitating the behavior of an adult.

Imitating Others. Andrew Meltzoff and M. Keith Moore (1989, 1992) studied 40 babies less than 72 hours old to determine whether the newborns could imitate two behaviors modeled by an adult: protruding the tongue and moving the head. According to the authors, "The results show that infants systematically matched the adult display shown to them" (p. 966) (Figure 9-5). Sticking your tongue out and moving your head to imitate another person may not seem like much of an accomplishment, but think about the elements of the task that must be performed by a 3-day-old baby. First, the baby must be able to see the model's behavior well enough to discriminate between tongue protrusion and head movement. Then the baby must transform the perception of these behaviors into a behavioral imitation and store this sequence of perceptual discrimination and responding in memory in anticipation of the next occurrence of the situation.

Maturation

Maturation is the biological unfolding of an organism according to the plan stored in its genes. In humans it refers primarily to the development of the motor and nervous systems. In the nervous system, myelin sheaths (see Chapter 2) begin to cover more axons after birth (Lipsitt, 1986), but myelination may not be complete until young adulthood. The sequence of myelination parallels the maturation of the entire nervous system. The lack of myelin explains why a child cannot jump or stand on one leg at a young age. As myelin sheaths cover more motor axons, children gain voluntary control over their behavior; at the same time, reflexes like rooting drop out of their repertoire.

Development of the Brain. Before birth, the brain develops at an amazing rate, adding up to 250,000 new nerve cells each minute (Bornstein & Lamb, 1992). A spurt in cell development just before birth gives the newborn most, but not all, of its brain cells. The lower brain centers responsible for reflexes, breathing, digestion, and heartbeat are almost fully developed; cells in the cortex are numerous but not yet fully connected. The connections among these cells develop rapidly but are susceptible to environmental influences that include exposure to pollutants (such as dioxin, the industrial chemical PCB, and lead), toxoplasmosis (a parasite found in the fecal matter of cats), and heat (15 minutes in a hot tub containing 102° water can damage the central nervous system of the fetus).

Physical Development. The rate of physical development immediately after birth is not equaled during the rest of a person's life. By the first birthday, height has increased from 20 to 30 inches and weight has tripled, from an average of 7.5 to over 22 pounds (Watson & Lowney, 1967). Figure 9-6 shows different body proportions at different ages.

maturation
Biological unfolding of the genetic plan for an individual's development

FIGURE 9-6 Body proportions at various ages.

Source: Adapted from Bayley, 1969.

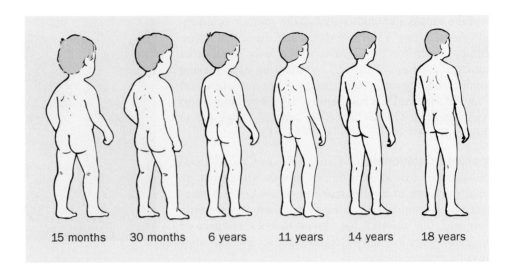

precocious

Developing motor and cognitive abilities at an early age

Sinjin is an active 3-year-old whose physical development owes a lot to his backyard swing set.

As you might expect from our discussion of nature and nurture, inherited characteristics and the environment interact to determine the course of growth (Mott, 1991; Scarr, 1992). Whether you will stand 42 inches tall and weigh 38 pounds by age 3 is determined by your genetic potential to attain this height and weight and the availability of a diet that allows you to realize that potential.

Table 9-2 lists several physical skills that develop during the first 2 years of life and the approximate age at which they are mastered by children in the United States. Some babies and toddlers perform motor behaviors at younger ages than those shown in Table 9-2. Such individuals are **precocious;** that is, they develop motor and cognitive abilities at an early age. Other children take longer than average to develop. Precocious development is frequently a source of pleasure and pride for parents, but slower motor development is not necessarily a cause for concern or alarm. Children develop motor behaviors at widely varying ages.

When a baby's development is seriously delayed, remedial steps can be taken. To determine whether such steps are required, a psychologist or pediatrician may administer the Bayley Scales of Infant Development (Bayley, 1969; Kaplan-Estrin, Jacobson, & Jacobson, 1994). These scales provide indications of average, below-average, and

TABLE 9-2	
Physical Skills Acquired during the First 2 Years of Life	
Approximate Age at Which Skill Is Mastered by Most Children	
Rolling over	5.5 months
Sitting without support	7 months
Standing while holding on	8.5 months
Grasping with thumb and fingers	10.5 months
Standing alone	14 months
Walking well	15 months
Walking up steps	22 months
Kicking ball forward	23.5 months

Source: Adapted from Frankenburg et al., 1992.

above-average responses for a range of behaviors and stages of intellectual development for children between the ages of 2 months and 2.5 years.

Maturation is not an automatic process; cultural practices in infant rearing also can play an important role in physical development. For example, during the 1970s, "more than 75 percent of American infants were bottle fed" (Berk, 1998, p. 124). Recently, along with an increase in the number of natural births, there has been renewed interest in breast-feeding. In addition to being emotionally satisfying for both mother and infant, breast-feeding offers some proven health advantages, especially in poverty-stricken countries.

First, mother's milk transfers antibodies from the mother to the infant; hence, breast-fed infants have fewer respiratory and intestinal illnesses (Ford & Labbok, 1993). Second, mother's milk is more nutritious and appropriate for the infant's developing nervous system than milk from other animals (Raiha & Axelsson, 1995). This comparison is more pronounced when breast-feeding is compared with the poor-quality formulas that infants in economically depressed countries may be fed. The nutrition from breast-feeding increases the chances these infants will survive. There are two potential problems with this conclusion, however. First, it assumes that the breast-feeding mother is in good health; if she isn't, then the quality of her milk may be inferior to even poor-quality formula, and the infant will suffer. Second, the 1990s brought another problem to breast-feeding. Because HIV can be transmitted through breast milk, confused new mothers in impoverished countries with high HIV rates—women who were previously indoctrinated as to the benefits of breast milk—are now being told to return to infant formula, which is nutritionally inferior and very expensive.

The physical development that occurs during infancy and childhood is impressive. As we see in the next sections, psychosocial and cognitive development also occur at an impressive rate.

REVIEW SUMMARY

1. **Developmental psychologists** are interested in the quantitative and qualitative changes that take place from conception until death. Both kinds of changes result from the interaction of hereditary **(nature)** and environmental **(nurture)** influences.

2. **Longitudinal studies** are conducted to evaluate changes over a period of time. **Cross-sectional studies** are used to obtain information at a particular point in time. A **cohort** study involves comparing individuals of the same age who were born in different generations.

3. Conception occurs when a sperm and an ovum unite. The child inherits half of its genetic makeup from each parent. A **zygote** is produced by the union of a sperm and an egg. The zygote embeds itself in the wall of the uterus and develops into an **embryo,** which at nine weeks is considered a **fetus.** At birth, which occurs approximately 266 days after fertilization, the average baby weighs 7.5 pounds and is 20 inches long.

4. Despite the protection of the mother's body, the baby's development may be influenced by the mother's diet, her physical condition, and any drugs she may use, including tobacco and alcohol.

5. Both the **ultrasound procedure,** in which a sound-generated picture of the fetus (a **sonogram**) is produced, and **amniocentesis,** in which the genetic nature of fetal cells is

analyzed, are used to determine the sex of the unborn child and whether any genetic defects are present.

6. Newborn infants are able to recognize voices (audition) and faces (vision), to make appropriate facial reactions to taste and smell, and even to learn.

7. When a particular spoken phrase (CS) is paired with the presence of a nipple in the mouth (UCS), the infant can be classically conditioned to elicit a sucking response (CR) when just the phrase is spoken. Infants have also been operantly conditioned to change their rate of sucking in response to a stimulus they like (positive reinforcer), such as their mother's voice.

8. The biological development of a person according to his or her genetic makeup is termed **maturation.** The rate of physical development right after birth is the highest it will be at any point.

9. The interaction of genetic makeup and environmental factors determines the specific growth pattern for each individual. Some **precocious** babies develop physical and cognitive abilities at an early age; others are slower to develop.

10. Psychologists may use the Bayley Scales of Infant Development to determine whether an infant is average, above average, or below average in behavioral and intellectual development.

✓ CHECK YOUR PROGRESS

1. Explain the concept of polygenic inheritance.

2. The one-celled structure formed when a sperm and an ovum unite is known as a(n)

   a. fetus.
   b. blastula.
   c. zygote.
   d. embryo.

3. The process by which a cell transmits its genetic information to other cells is

   a. mitosis.
   b. development.
   c. differentiation.
   d. RNA fragmentation.

4. Which chemical secreted by the testes causes a developing organism to become a male?

   a. dopamine
   b. estrogen
   c. estradiol
   d. testosterone

5. In the classical conditioning study of infants, identify the role played by the nipple, the spoken phrase, and sucking, respectively.

6. What types of responses did researchers find babies can learn to make through imitation?

   a. uttering sounds
   b. waving their arms
   c. kicking their legs
   d. sticking out their tongue

7. The biological unfolding of an individual according to a genetic plan is known as

   a. maturation.
   b. development.
   c. genetic inheritance.
   d. biological determinism.

8. What term describes babies who develop motor or cognitive activities at an early age?

   a. gifted
   b. precocious
   c. developmentally advanced
   d. motor capable

9. Where are the least-developed brain cells located at birth?

   a. in the cortex
   b. in the hypothalamus
   c. in the breathing control center
   d. in the heart rate control center

ANSWERS: 1. Human traits are controlled by a number of different genes. **2.** c **3.** a **4.** d **5.** The UCS, CS, and UCR, respectively. **6.** d **7.** a **8.** b **9.** a

PSYCHOSOCIAL DEVELOPMENT IN CHILDHOOD

Christiana is a single parent who works to support her 2-year-old daughter, Jerrie. The growing numbers of dual-career and single-parent families are increasingly relying on nonparental care for their children. Waiting lists at day-care centers are growing. Parents who cannot afford private day care may have to wait as long as 2 years for an opening at a subsidized day-care center. Despite the great demand for day care, little is known about the impact it may have on the development of young children. *What are the effects of day care on a child's development?*

The effects of day care are just one of the many topics studied by psychologists interested in the psychosocial development of young children. If you break the word *psychosocial* down into its two components, *psycho* and *social*, you have a good idea of what this section covers. We consider the development of the individual's unique personality (psycho) as well as factors that influence the ability to interact with other people (social). Such abilities may be present at birth; for example, newborns prefer human faces to other visual stimuli. Social behaviors clearly begin to emerge by the time a child is a year old (Moore & Corkum, 1994).

Temperament

Physicians Alexander Thomas and Stella Chess (1980) were struck by the differences they observed in their own children; those differences were apparent even during the first weeks of life. They were also impressed by the low correlations between environmental influences, such as parental attitudes and practices, and the child's psychological development. They decided to study the causes and consequences of differences in temperament. *Temperament* is the "how" of behavior: its quickness, ease of approach to new situations, intensity, and mood. A child's temperament is revealed in measures of activity level, regularity of biological functions, approach to or withdrawal from new situations, adaptability to new or altered situations, intensity of reaction, quality of mood, distractibility, and attention span and persistence. Thomas and Chess examined a cohort of children and identified three types of temperament:

1. *Easy children* (40 percent) behaved in consistent ways, had a positive approach to new situations, and were highly adaptable to change. Their mood was mild to moderate and predominantly positive.

2. *Slow-to-warm-up children* (15 percent) displayed a combination of intense, negative responses to new stimuli with slow adaptability even after repeated contact.

3. *Difficult children* (10 percent) did not behave in consistent ways, were nonadaptable, and usually characterized by an intense negative mood.

As you can see from the percentages, not all children fit easily into one of these three groups. Although heredity seems to play an appreciable role in determining temperament (DiLalla, Kagan, & Reznick, 1994; Emde et al., 1992), the mother's child-rearing attitudes also can influence adolescent temperament (Katainen, Raikkonen, & Keltikanjas-Jarbinen, 1998).

Personality Development

Both Sigmund Freud and Erik Erikson proposed theories of personality development based on the idea that childhood experiences leave lasting marks on the individual's personality. Whereas both theorists believed that personality develops in a series of orderly stages and that childhood experiences are important, they differed in their emphasis. Freud stressed the individual's biological makeup, whereas Erikson stressed social interactions.

Sigmund Freud.   During the late 1800s and early 1900s, Sigmund Freud radically influenced the way psychologists viewed the development of personality. Freud was the first person to propose that the early years of life are crucial to personality development. His theory was concerned with the manner in which children resolve conflicts between their biological urges (primarily sexual) and the demands of society, particularly those of the parents. Freud viewed these conflicts as a series of developmental stages determined largely by the child's age. These developmental stages, along with their unique characteristics and demands, are described more fully in Chapter 11. Freud, the first person to propose a stage theory of personality development, believed that each stage had the potential to affect the personality of the developing child.

Erik Erikson.   Erik Erikson (1902–1994) also proposed a stage theory of personality development. Unlike Freud, however, Erikson did not stress the need to resolve conflicts created by biological needs. According to Erikson, our personality is molded by the way we deal with a series of psychosocial crises that occur as we grow older. A **psychosocial crisis** occurs when a psychological need conflicts with societal pressures and demands. Different cultures present different obstacles to the resolution of these psychosocial crises. Hence certain developmental paths will be more

psychosocial crisis
Developmental problem or obstacle that is created when a psychological need conflicts with the demands of society

Erik Erikson (right) proposed a stage theory of development that stresses the importance of psychosocial crises.

basic trust versus basic mistrust
Erikson's first psychosocial crisis (birth to 1.5 years), in which children learn through contact with their primary caregiver whether their environment can be trusted

autonomy versus shame and doubt
Erikson's second psychosocial crisis (1.5 to 3 years), in which children develop a sense of whether their behavior is under their own control or under the control of external forces

autonomy
The feeling of being able to act independently and having personal control over one's actions

initiative versus guilt
Erikson's third psychosocial crisis (3 to 7 years), in which children begin to evaluate the consequences of their behavior

industry versus inferiority
Erikson's fourth psychosocial crisis (7 to 10 years), in which children begin to acquire the knowledge and skills that will enable them to become productive members of society

appropriate in one culture than in others. For example, the child may have a psychological need to achieve independence. If this child grows up in a Western society that values independence, everything is fine. However, if this child grows up in a collectivist society that does not value independence, the child will develop more group-related activities and behaviors.

Babies experience two psychosocial crises. The first occurs from birth until about 1.5 years of age, when the infant is establishing a pattern of **basic trust versus basic mistrust.** Put another way, can infants trust their environment? Will food be there when they are hungry? Will their diapers be changed? Will other sources of pain and discomfort be alleviated? The person who usually attends to the child's needs, the primary caregiver, plays a major role in the development of basic trust or mistrust. Consistent, loving caregivers facilitate the development of a sense of trust. Having trust in one's caregivers and one's environment is important for developing trust in oneself.

Between the ages of about 1.5 and 3, children deal with a second psychosocial crisis, **autonomy versus shame and doubt.** *Autonomy* is the feeling that we can act independently and that we are in control of our own actions. Children start on the road to either autonomy or shame and doubt by developing a sense of how their behavior is controlled or determined. If children feel their behavior is not under their control but is determined by other people or external forces, they develop an external sense of control. Doubt and shame concerning one's ability to function frequently accompany an external sense of control. For example, if the parents always insist on feeding a child, the child may begin to doubt his or her ability to perform this important activity.

If children develop a sense of being in charge of what happens to them, they have developed an *internal* sense of control, or **autonomy.** The relation between sense of control and autonomy is straightforward: The greater a child's internal sense of control, the greater the independence he or she will feel and exhibit.

The developing sense of independence allows children to begin doing things on their own. They decide what, when, and with whom they will play. This developing independence is the hallmark of the "terrible twos" and often brings children into conflict with their parents over such issues as what to eat and when to go to bed.

The child's growing sense of morality forms the basis for Erikson's third psychosocial crisis, **initiative versus guilt** (approximately ages 3 to 7). A developing sense of right and wrong leads children to evaluate the consequences of the behaviors in which they might engage. Some behaviors, such as playing by the rules and obeying one's parents, can produce desirable consequences; others, such as cheating or not obeying one's parents, produce undesired consequences. To resolve this conflict, children must take the initiative to adopt behaviors and goals that they enjoy *and* that society values. To do otherwise leaves the child (and later the adult) feeling guilty and fearful because his or her behaviors may not be appropriate or valued.

The importance of developing a sense of competence also underlies Erikson's fourth psychosocial crisis, **industry versus inferiority** (approximately ages 7 to 10). Once children have developed basic trust, autonomy, and initiative, it is time to learn the skills and acquire the knowledge that will allow them to become productive members of society. The acquisition of such skills and knowledge reflects the development of industry. If a child is to become a productive member of society, the lessons taught in school must be learned well.

Although critics point out that Erikson's theory lacks precision, supporters note that it captures the reality of the changes that occur as we grow and develop throughout the life span. In addition, it is generally conceded that Erikson's theory is far more optimistic than Freud's. For a summary of all of Erikson's stages, see the summary chart on page 407 later in this chapter.

If you read the sections about Freud and Erikson carefully, you noticed that personality develops in the context of significant other people, usually the parents. The attachments children form to their parents play a major role in shaping their developing personality.

FIGURE 9-7 The wire and terrycloth surrogate mothers used by Harry and Marguerite Harlow in their research on the development of attachment in infant monkeys.

Attachment

Attachment refers to an intense, reciprocal relationship occurring between two people, usually a child and an adult (Hays, 1998; Insel, 2000; Pietromonaco & Barrett, 2000). The first experimental studies on the effects of attachment were reported by psychologists Harry and Marguerite Harlow (Harlow & Harlow, 1962). Approximately 8 hours after birth, baby monkeys were separated from their mothers. The baby monkeys were raised in experimental chambers, where they were exposed to an inanimate object that served as a surrogate (substitute) mother. Some of the surrogate mothers were plain wire cylinders; others were covered with soft terrycloth (see Figure 9-7). Some of the infant monkeys were allowed to come into contact with both types of objects. When a bottle was attached, the baby monkey could be "fed" by the wire or cloth-covered "mother."

The Harlows found that the infant monkeys showed a definite preference for the soft, cloth-covered mother. For example, when confronted by a strange and frightening situation, they ran to the cloth-covered mother for safety and security. The monkeys showed this preference even when they were fed by the plain wire mother; apparently, the **contact comfort,** or warmth provided by the soft terrycloth, was a more important determinant of attachment than the provision of nourishment.

In addition to demonstrating the importance of contact comfort, the Harlows also found that raising baby monkeys in isolation in the laboratory had a detrimental effect on the animals' social behavior (Suomi & Harlow, 1972; Suomi & Ripp, 1983). When the laboratory testing was complete, the juvenile monkeys were returned to a colony with other monkeys. The experimental monkeys, however, did not adapt well in the colony. They avoided contact, fled from touch, curled up and rocked, or tried to attack the biggest, most dominant monkey in the group (often getting seriously injured in the process). Thus a major conclusion of the Harlows' research was that even though attachment was important, it did not ensure normal social development. Environmental contact (nurture) with members of one's own species is needed for this kind of development.

Ethological Theory. John Bowlby's **ethological theory of attachment** (1969; Ainsworth & Bowlby, 1991) stresses the adaptiveness of attachment. Bowlby believes attachment evolved because of its adaptive value; infants are protected when parents or caregivers are near.

For Bowlby, attachment progresses through four stages:

Stage 1. Preattachment (birth to 6 weeks). Babies emit behaviors, such as smiling and crying, that bring them into close contact with humans. Attachment has not occurred because infants do not mind being left with unfamiliar adults.

Nature and Development of Affection

attachment
Intense, reciprocal relationship formed by two people, usually a child and an adult

contact comfort
Preference for holding or clinging to objects, such as blankets or teddy bears, that yield physical comfort and warmth

ethological theory of attachment
Theory stating that attachment evolved because of its adaptive value to the infant

Stage 2. Beginnings of Attachment (6 weeks to approximately 7 months). Infants begin to respond differentially to familiar adults but do not protest when separated.

Stage 3. Attachment (approximately 7 months to approximately 21 months). Attachment to the familiar caregiver is evident. Babies show distress when the primary caregiver leaves. Such separation anxiety appears to begin at approximately 6 to 7 months and increases until 15 months in cultures around the world (Kagan, Kearsley, & Zelazo, 1978).

Stage 4. Reciprocal Relationships (approximately 21 months). As language develops, separation anxiety decreases, and the child understands that the caregiver will return. Language allows the child to make requests of and bargain with the caregiver.

Bowlby (1980) believes that the experiences of these four stages result in the child's unique understanding of the parent–child bond. This understanding sets the stage for future close relationships (Pederson et al., 1998; Van den Bloom, 1997).

The Strange Situation Test. At birth, infants are equipped with behaviors such as crying that promote closeness to a caregiver and operate to activate caregiving behaviors. "At first," Ainsworth (1989) notes, "these attachment behaviors are simply emitted, rather than directed toward any specific person, but gradually the baby begins to discriminate one person from another and to direct attachment behavior differentially" (p. 710).

Once attachment occurs, it can take several forms. One way to determine the kind of attachment a baby has developed is to observe the baby's reaction to being put in a *strange situation*, such as an unfamiliar playroom and the departure of the familiar caregiver. When Ainsworth and her colleagues (Ainsworth et al., 1978) did just that, they found that most babies (66 percent) were *securely attached*. When their mother was present to provide attention and support, securely attached babies explored their environment. A smaller group (20 percent) of babies did not want to be held; they also did not want to be put down. They ignored their mother or greeted her casually on her return. In fact, they seemed to interact with a stranger the same way they did with their mother. Such babies are termed *avoidant*. A third group, the *resistant* babies, sought closeness with the mother before she left. When she returned, these babies displayed angry, resistive behaviors. A fourth group, *anxious-ambivalent* babies, became almost panic-stricken when their mother left. This panic reaction actually began before the mother left. When the mother returned, the baby actively sought, but at the same time actively resisted, contact and comfort.

The percentages of different types of attachment may vary from culture to culture (Van Ijzendoorn & Kroonenberg, 1988). For example, more German infants than infants in the United States, Israel, or Japan are anxiously attached. Cultural practices such as German parents' stressing autonomy at an earlier age may produce such differences; they are not interpreted as deficiencies. However, sleeping out of the home in communal arrangements, such as those found in Israeli kibbutzim, may lead to an increase in anxious-ambivalent attachments (Sagi et al., 1994).

Infants' attachment styles are well documented, but not much is known about how these styles may influence individuals' behaviors as adults. Psychologists found a relation between the attachment style reported by the parents of college students and the students' preferred type of interpersonal relationship as adults (Feeney & Noller, 1990). For both men and women, there was a link between reported infant attachment style and preferred type of adult relationship (Cassidy, 2000; Fraley & Shaver, 2000). For example, securely attached babies grew into adults who had trusting attitudes toward others. A longitudinal study of German children (Wartner et al., 1994) indicates that the lasting effects of attachment style occur in other cultures (Rothbaum et al., 2000).

The Father's Role

We have repeatedly described the attachment established between an infant and its mother. What about the father (Berry & Rao, 1997; Van Ijzendoorn & De Wolfe,

Children in an Israeli kibbutz eat and sleep in a communal arrangement.

Both mothers and fathers form attachments with their children.

1997)? Do fathers form attachments with their children? There is some basis for the emphasis placed on the mother–infant attachment. As David Lynn (1974) pointed out, "One of the factors eroding the father's position in the family is the nature of work today in urban-industrial societies. Fathers now work away from the home, so that a degree of father absence is taken for granted. . . . In our society the absence of the father through death or divorce can be considered simply an extreme on the prevailing continuum of father absence" (p. 6). Despite this father-absent pattern, infants do establish attachments with their fathers at about the same age they form attachments with their mothers (Fox, Kimmerly, & Schafer, 1991). The types of interactions displayed by fathers with their infants may differ from those shown by the mother. Fathers are more likely to invest their time playing with their children than in cleaning or feeding them (Hossain & Roopnarine, 1994). It appears, however, that delaying having children until the father is older (that is, age 35 and over) results in the father's spending more time with the child, having higher expectations for the child, and being more nurturant (Heath, 1994).

The father-absent pattern does not occur in all cultures. For example, in the Chinese patriarchal (father-dominated) family, the most important relationship is between a father and his sons. Other cross-cultural research has found that infants in all cultures become attached to their parents despite widely varying child-rearing practices (Sagi, 1990).

Day Care

In contemporary American society, "maternal employment is a reality. The issue today, therefore, is not whether infants should be in day care but how to make their experiences there and at home supportive of their development and of their parents' peace of mind" (Clarke-Stewart, 1989, p. 271). For example, some parents might be concerned that day care could weaken or change their child's attachment (Belsky, 1986). Comparisons of the attachment of infants who attended day-care centers with that of infants who were cared for at home by their mothers in the United States reveal that infants who attended day-care centers did not differ from infants who were raised at home. Thus concern that full-time day care results in more anxious and more insecure children still continues, but seems unfounded (Azar, 2000; Roggman et al., 1994).

Children may derive some benefits from good day care (Vernon-Feagans, Emanuel, & Blood, 1997), which may be more important for children from disadvantaged homes. "Good quality child care can enhance development of children from disadvantaged, stressed, and dysfunctional homes" (Scarr & Eisenberg, 1993, p. 618). What constitutes a good day-care center? The Committee on Children, Youth and Families (1994) of the

peer group
Group of neighborhood children, classmates, or selected friends of the same age

American Psychological Association proposed the following criteria for good day care:

- Is the number of providers sufficient? A ratio of three or four infants for each provider is desirable.
- Are activities done in small groups? A maximum of eight infants in a group is recommended.
- Do the providers genuinely like their job and enjoy caring for the infants during the day? They should not see this job as simply a way to earn money.
- Are the facilities safe and clean? Is the equipment in good repair?
- Do the providers have appropriate training and knowledge of infant care and development?
- Is the day care center happy and cheerful?

In short, a good day-care center should function as much like a good parent as possible. The social and cognitive foundations established in a high-quality day-care center carry over to the kindergarten and preschool experiences that mark the end of early childhood (Feagans & Farran, 1994). These experiences set the stage for the beginning of formal education in middle childhood.

The Peer Group

Typically composed of classmates, selected friends, or other children in the neighborhood, the **peer group** offers children many opportunities for feedback concerning their abilities, intelligence, and values as they grow into young adults. Lessons about how to get along in a group may also be learned. Social skills are initially learned from parents; then, as interactions with other children become more frequent, newly acquired behaviors may be tested on the parents. Thus the peer group can foster the development of self-esteem and a sense of autonomy. Peer group influences can be negative, however. A youth may start to shoplift, smoke, and drink alcoholic beverages because of pressure from peer group members. For children with low prestige in the peer group, it will be nearly impossible to say no; to do so would surely mean the loss of what little status and popularity they might have and likely encourage hostility and aggressive retribution (Schwartz, Dodge, & Coie, 1993).

Television

Does television really exert as great an influence on children as researchers and the media have led us to believe? The first step toward answering this question is to determine how much television children actually watch. According to Action for Children's Television (Nielsen Media Research, 1998), the rate of television viewing in the United States is extremely high. By the time the average child graduates from high school, he or she will have watched more than 25,000 hours of television, including more than 356,000 commercials. In the typical U.S. household the television is turned on 7.1 hours a day (Berk, 1998). In fact, children "spend more time watching television than engaging in any other activity (including playing and eating) except sleeping" (Rice, 2001, p. 264).

Although there is continuing debate over whether television viewing has intellectual benefits or leads to violence (see Chapter 15), one influence of television is firmly established. The stark reality of adult life portrayed on television has, to a great extent, removed the innocence from childhood. So strong is the impact of television that some observers believe that television role models have undermined parents' ability to act effectively in this capacity (Friedrich-Cofer & Huston, 1986).

Psychological Detective

Are the critics right? Has television assumed a major portion of the parenting role? Do you want the television set to be a surrogate parent for your children in the same way that the wire and cloth forms were surrogate parents for the Harlows' monkeys? What could (or should) be done to correct the situation? Give these questions some thought, and write down your views before reading further.

You could restrict the amount of television that your children watch. This option is effective, and many parents impose such restrictions. What about the quality of the television programs viewed by children? It needs to be improved. Calls for television reform have led legislators to introduce several bills in Congress that are designed to regulate the amount of time allocated for commercials during children's programming and require that stations provide educational programming for children. Although such legislation would be helpful, parents are still ultimately responsible for the type and amount of television their children watch (American Academy of Pediatrics, 1986). Too much television can take away from other desired activities, such as reading and interacting with others (Singer & Singer, 1990).

COGNITIVE DEVELOPMENT IN CHILDHOOD

In 1992, the American Psychological Association celebrated its 100th anniversary. As part of this celebration, a traveling psychology exhibit made stops in major cities. Many aspects of psychology were put on public display. Joe took his two daughters to see the exhibit. The children were fascinated by one of the exhibits, which consisted of two partially filled flasks. The flasks were very wide at the bottom and narrow at the top. They were mounted on a wall in such a way that they could be turned with the top up or down. When the flasks were turned bottom up, the children thought they were fuller than when they were turned bottom down. *What can this unusual display tell us about cognitive development in children?*

Cognitive development refers to the changes that occur in our thought processes as we pass through life. Cognitive development and intelligence go hand in hand. As we saw in Chapter 8, psychologists have measured intelligence since 1905, when Alfred Binet developed a test to measure the intelligence of French schoolchildren. However, measuring the intelligence of babies and young children has been particularly difficult. Babies will not sit still for very long; and their ability to answer questions is limited. Despite such obstacles, the Swiss scientist Jean Piaget (1896–1980) spent his professional career studying the cognitive development of young children.

Piaget's Theory

Early in his career, Piaget worked in Binet's laboratory, translating tests. As Piaget tried out test items on French children, he grew curious about the children's incorrect answers. Children of the same age tended to give the same wrong answers, suggesting that they shared a common way of thinking. Piaget interviewed and observed numerous children (including his own) over the course of many years, concluding that a child's mind is not a miniature version of an adult's mind. Rather, children proceed through a series of *qualitative stages* of cognitive development.

Through his research Piaget identified the processes by which children gain new knowledge. Suppose a child has never seen a cow. The child tries to understand this new element or stimulus by using existing thought patterns or *schemas* (see Chapter 7). Being familiar with dogs, the child tries to understand the cow by using the schema for a dog. To use Piaget's terminology, the child assimilates the cow into the dog schema. **Assimilation** is the process by which we incorporate new information into our accustomed way of thinking. **Accommodation** is the process of altering our ways of thinking (schemas) so we can include new information that does not fit into existing ways of

Jean Piaget spent much of his professional career studying cognitive development in young children.

cognitive development
Changes that occur in our thought processes throughout life

assimilation
Piaget's term for the process of incorporating information into existing schemas

accommodation
Alteration of existing schemas to understand new information

sensorimotor stage
Piaget's first stage of cognitive development, in which children learn about their environment through direct sensory contact and motor activities

object permanence
Recognition that objects continue to exist even though they cannot be directly sensed

mental representation
An internal representation of an object or event that is not present

preoperational stage
Piaget's second stage of cognitive development, in which the child begins to think about objects that are not physically present

symbolic representation
Using a mental thought or activity as a substitute for an actual object

Sensorimotor Development

Because this young child does not look for the toy when it is hidden, object permanence has not been attained.

thinking. For example, you probably found it difficult to include penguins in your schema for birds. Your schema had to be changed to include the fact that some birds do not fly. The processes of assimilation and accommodation operate throughout life.

Piaget proposed that all human beings proceed through a series of orderly and predictable stages of cognitive development at about the same ages. What's more, he claimed that a prior stage must be completed before progression to the next stage. Children proceed from concrete to more abstract thoughts as they grow older.

The Sensorimotor Stage. During the **sensorimotor stage** (birth to age 2), infants learn to coordinate their senses and their motor behavior. For example, infants learn about a rattle by seeing and hearing it; they also learn about the rattle by grasping, shaking, and sucking it. They experience the world in a direct manner and learn basic lessons before proceeding to more complex thoughts. They do not yet use symbols or images to represent objects in the external world, so their world revolves around what they experience directly—the noise of a rattle, the sound of their mother's voice, the movement of a mobile hung over the crib.

Before symbolic communication is possible, infants must learn the principle of object permanence. **Object permanence** refers to the fact that a person or object does not cease to exist when it is not directly perceived. If a 4-month-old reaches for a small toy and you cover it with a cloth, the baby stops reaching and starts looking at something else. Lift the cloth, and the baby will be surprised to see the toy.

Contrast this response with the reaction of a 1-year-old. At this age, the child continues to reach for the cloth-covered toy and is not surprised to find it still there, but would be surprised or upset if you had secretly removed it. At this age cognitive development centers on the ability to use **mental representation.** In other words, once the child begins to think about objects that are not physically present, the principle of object permanence has been established.

The Preoperational Stage. According to Piaget, the child is in the **preoperational stage** of cognitive development from ages 2 to 7. During this stage, children become better able to represent events mentally; therefore they are less dependent on physical stimuli and physical reactions to guide their behavior. They begin to engage in pretend play, letting a doll represent a real baby or a toy car represent a real car. They use language (a symbol system) to ask for a drink rather than walking to the sink and pointing. In other words, the preoperational child is able to use **symbolic representation,** which occurs when a symbol is used to represent an actual object. If a toddler in the sensorimotor stage accidentally pushed a baby buggy against the wall, she might take a step back and thrust the buggy forward again and again, failing to reason out why her forward progress had been halted and what she could do to fix it. By contrast, a child in the preoperational stage would step back, look around, and think. Then she would aim the buggy toward an open doorway.

Children of this age should not, however, be given more credit than they are due. Their abilities have definite limitations. For example, the preoperational child's thought

is characterized by **egocentrism,** or inability to see a situation or event from another person's point of view. Suppose a 3-year-old is talking on the phone to his grandfather. Grandpa asks, "Did you go to the circus yesterday?" The child nods his head silently. The child has failed to consider that Grandpa cannot see his head move. That is, he has failed to take Grandpa's point of view into account. Because preoperational children are not capable of reversible thinking, they frequently explain things by linking events together. This linking of often disconnected facts is called *transductive reasoning*. For example, when asked "Why does it rain?" a preoperational child might reply "Because we have an umbrella." Preoperational thinkers are often defined by their inability to reason logically. The concrete operations stage focuses on the child's changing abilities in this area.

The Concrete Operational Stage.

Children in the **concrete operational stage** are able to represent objects mentally and engage in logical reasoning about the world around them through the use of these mental representations, but they are not yet able to think abstractly. During this stage, thought becomes more logical. For example, at this stage, a child would be able to arrive at the conclusion that if she traded five baseball cards for one card, she would have fewer cards after the trade than before it. Baseball cards are things she is familiar with. Mental representations of such objects can be manipulated; objects can be added or subtracted. Likewise, the same child would deal with a question such as "What can be done to end world hunger?" by saying, "Drop food from parachutes" or "Grow more food."

Recall our description of the traveling psychology exhibit at the beginning of this section. What can the partially filled flasks tell us about the cognitive development of children? Piaget demonstrated that preoperational children do not grasp the principle of **conservation,** the understanding that a change in the size or shape of a substance does not change the amount of that substance. Consider Stacey, a 4-year-old who does not like carrots. Stacey's mother cuts the two carrots on Stacey's plate into several smaller pieces. Stacey bursts into tears and complains bitterly, "Before I only had two carrots; now I've got lots!"

Look at Figure 9-8. The two glasses contain exactly the same amount of water. To a 4-year-old boy who has not acquired the principle of conservation, however, the tall

"Hi, Grandma! Betcha can't guess who this is!"

egocentrism
Inability to see a situation or event from another person's point of view

concrete operational stage
Piaget's third stage of cognitive development, in which the child is able to use mental representations to think about current objects and events but is not yet capable of abstract thought

conservation
Recognition that a physical change in a substance does not change the amount of that substance

9.2

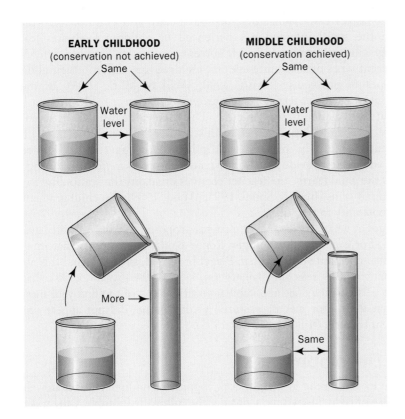

FIGURE 9-8 An example of the acquisition of conservation. During early childhood, children are typically unable to tell that the tall glass and the short glass contain the same amount of water. By middle childhood, the child has acquired the principle of conservation and will be able to tell that the two glasses contain the same amount of water.

Stages of Cognitive Development, According to Jean Piaget

Stage	Age	Characteristics
Sensorimotor	Birth to 2 years	Child explores the environment through sensory and motor behavior. Develops the concept of object permanence.
Preoperational	2 to 7 years	Child becomes able to think about people and objects that are not physically present. Even though mental representations are used, they cannot be manipulated logically. Child's thought reflects egocentrism.
Concrete operational	7 to 11 years	Even though thoughts are still limited to the immediate situation, the child is able to engage in logical reasoning through the use of mental representations. Principle of conservation is understood.
Formal operational	Adolescence and adulthood	The individual is able to use symbolic representations in abstract thought. Can create and logically think through hypothetical situations.

STUDY TIP

Write a summary of Piaget's stages of cognitive development in children. Underline or highlight important terms.

glass has more water than the short one. He will say this even after seeing the water being poured from the short glass into the tall glass. Now think of the flasks at the psychology exhibit. When the flasks are turned base down, the fluid does not rise as high in the container. When the flasks are turned base up, the same fluid rises higher in the container, and the young child will say that there is more fluid. Until a child reaches the concrete operational stage and understands conservation, he or she will believe that changes in the shapes and sizes of objects indicate changes in quantity. Piaget's stages of cognitive development are summarized in the Study Chart above.

Challenges to Piaget's Theory. Despite its impact and importance, Piaget's theory has not gone unchallenged. For example, the Russian psychologist Lev Vygotsky (1930, 1933, 1935/1978) stressed the social context in which a child learns (Berk, 2000). Whereas Piaget's theory deals with internal development, Vygotsky's theory emphasizes external factors such as society and culture. According to this researcher, the social interaction experienced by children facilitates learning and performing skills that are beyond their current capabilities. Because different cultures stress different types of social interactions, children may differ in their ability to solve various types of problems (Rogoff, 1990; Wahi & Johri, 1994). In this context, Vygotsky introduced the term *zone of proximal development* to describe tasks that are too difficult for the child to master alone. The zone is the distance between the actual ability level the child has reached on his or her own and the level of potential development that can be reached with guidance or supervision. The role of the teacher or adult is to provide help or assistance (known as *scaffolding*) during a teaching session. As the child learns, the teacher changes or adapts the scaffolding to reflect the newly acquired skills (Berk & Spuhl, 1995; Wood, 1989); the child gradually assumes more responsibility for the task.

The ages at which the cognitive changes proposed by Piaget occur have also been challenged. For example, psychologist Renee Baillargeon reports that infants display object permanence much earlier than Piaget proposed; she has found this ability in infants as young as 10 weeks old (Baillargeon, 1993, 1994; Overby, 1999). Piaget's belief that object permanence does not stabilize until the end of the first year may be due to the fact that the motor task he required of the infants did not appear until later in development (Flavell, Miller, & Miller, 1993).

Moral Development

In addition to developing in the physical, cognitive, and linguistic realms, children develop a sense of right and wrong. Consider the following example. Billy was told not to go into the dining room, but he wanted to help his mother set the table, so he entered the room, accidentally bumping into a tray of cups and breaking eight of them. Tommy had been told he could not go to the movies, so he was mad at his mother. He went into the dining room and deliberately broke a cup. Who is naughtier?

Lawrence Kohlberg (1973) proposed that there are three primary levels of moral development: the preconventional level, the level of conventional role conformity, and the level of autonomous moral principles. Each of these levels has two stages associated with it; thus the individual progresses through a total of six stages of morality as the three major levels are mastered.

At the **preconventional level** (ages 4 to 10), the child observes external conventions or standards set by others in order to avoid punishment (Stage 1) or receive reinforcement (Stage 2). If a road sign says STOP, the child expects you to stop immediately. Parents frequently hear their 5- or 6-year-old children reprimanding them for not stopping completely at a stop sign or for driving faster than the speed limit. Consider our example of Billy and Tommy in the dining room. To a preconventional child, Billy is naughtier because he broke eight cups, whereas Tommy broke only one. At this level of moral development, intentionality is not as relevant as level of damage.

Level 2, **conventional role conformity** (ages 10 to 13), involves greater internalization of standards and values. *Internalization* occurs when we make external standards and values part of our own set of values and standards. Children at this level are still controlled by external rules, but they now want to behave well to please important people in their lives. Charlie wants to "be good" to please his grandfather because that is what his grandfather expects (Stage 3). At Stage 4 we find children adhering to the rules of their peer group because they have promised to do so. The commitment is still to an external rule, but the promise to obey such rules has become even more internalized.

Kohlberg's third major level of moral development, **autonomous moral principles,** involves true morality. At the earliest, this level may be reached by age 13. Some people reach it in young adulthood; others never achieve it. The attainment of true morality involves complete internalization of control over moral conduct. At Stage 5 we find the adolescent or young adult following, say, the rules of her sorority because it benefits the group. Although these rules may not apply in all situations, in the long run it is better to follow them. At Stage 6 the person decides whether a particular behavior is good or bad, regardless of what others think or of any legal restrictions that exist. For example, one may adopt the belief that life is sacred and may feel that killing is to be avoided at any cost.

Despite its popularity, Kohlberg's theory of moral development has had its share of problems and critics. Prominent among the critics is Carol Gilligan (1982; Gilligan, Lyons, & Hanmer, 1990), who argues that Kohlberg's theory was developed only with male participants but has been applied to women as well. The assumption is that men and women view moral situations in the same manner; Gilligan argues that they do not. According to Gilligan, men tend to have a more absolute view of morality and are more concerned about not interfering with the rights of others. By contrast, women are more concerned with the context in which a behavior occurs and the relationships involved.

Gilligan is not arguing that there are absolute differences between men and women in moral behavior; there is some degree of overlap. She believes, however, that a complete theory of moral development should stress both viewpoints. What's more, as men and women enter adulthood, their patterns of moral reasoning may become more similar (Gilligan, Murphy, & Tappan, 1990). The complexity of life's experiences causes adults to view morality in a more relative and changeable manner than children do.

Cross-cultural research presents another challenge to Kohlberg's stage theory of moral development. For example, Fuchs and colleagues (1986) reported that more Israeli children raised in kibbutzim, in which they received training in the governmental structure and laws of the kibbutz, reached Stages 4 and 5 sooner than did American children. Hence training in cultural laws influences the level of moral development that a person reaches. In a study of moral development in India, Vasudev and Hummel

preconventional level
Kohlberg's first stage of moral development (ages 4 to 10), in which standards set by others are observed in order to receive reinforcement or avoid punishment

conventional role conformity
Kohlberg's second stage of moral development (ages 10 to 13), in which rules and standards are internalized and behaviors are performed in order to please others

autonomous moral principles
Kohlberg's third stage of moral development (age 13 or later, if at all), in which control over moral conduct is completely internalized

(1987) found that even though children may pass through the stages proposed by Kohlberg, their culture may dictate how they choose to deal with moral issues. For example, the resolution of moral dilemmas may be seen as a problem for the entire society (a collectivist view), not as an individual problem.

REVIEW SUMMARY

1. Three types of temperament in young children—easy, slow-to-warm-up, and difficult—have been identified.

2. Sigmund Freud believed that the personality develops as a child deals with conflicts between biological urges and the demands of society.

3. **Psychosocial crises,** or conflicts between psychological needs and societal demands, were proposed as the main determinants of personality by Erik Erikson. Erikson's psychosocial crises include **basic trust versus basic mistrust** (birth to age 1.5 years), **autonomy versus shame and doubt** (1.5 to 3 years), **initiative versus guilt** (3 to 7 years), and **industry versus inferiority** (7 to 10 years).

4. Studies of young monkeys conducted by Harry and Marguerite Harlow indicated that **attachment** was determined by contact comfort, rather than by the presence of food. Attachment to an inanimate object, however, is not sufficient for normal social development.

5. Infants form attachments with their caregivers. Mary Salter Ainsworth reports four main types of attachment: securely attached, avoidant, resistant, and anxious-ambivalent. The baby's style of attachment can influence relationships established during adulthood and may even persist through several generations. Infants form attachments with both the mother and the father. The characteristics of the caregiver may also influence the type of attachment that develops.

6. Day-care centers have become more accepted as the demand for their services has grown. Good day care that is sensitive and responsive to each child's needs may be beneficial to the child's emotional development.

7. **Peer groups,** television, and growing up in troubled areas all influence psychosocial development during middle childhood (ages 6 to 12).

8. Jean Piaget proposed that cognitive development progresses through a series of qualitative stages. During the **sensorimotor stage,** infants and young children learn about their world through their senses and acquire the principle of **object permanence,** the recognition that objects do not cease to exist when we no longer have direct contact with them. The acquisition of object permanence is related to the nature of the object that is tested and the method of testing. During the **preoperational stage,** the child gains the ability to use **symbolic representations** for objects and events that are not physically present. This stage is also characterized by **egocentrism,** the inability to see situations from another person's point of view.

9. Children continue to use mental representations but are not yet able to think abstractly during the **concrete operational stage.** The principle of **conservation**—the recognition that changes in size or shape do not change the amount of a substance—is acquired during this stage.

10. Piaget's theory has been challenged on the basis of lack of supportive cross-cultural data and major deviations from the proposed time lines.

11. A stage theory of moral development was proposed by Lawrence Kohlberg. The three major levels of morality are preconventional (adherence to standards to avoid punishment or receive reinforcement), conventional role conformity (internalization of standards and values), and autonomous moral principles (complete internalization of control over moral conduct).

✓ CHECK YOUR PROGRESS

1. Freud believed that personality is formed by resolving conflicts that occur as a series of _____ determined largely by the child's age.
   a. evolutionary goals
   b. developmental paths
   c. psychosocial crises
   d. developmental stages

2. According to Erikson, children who can choose behaviors and goals they enjoy and societal values have achieved
   a. trust.
   b. industry.
   c. autonomy.
   d. initiative.

3. What were the major findings of the Harlows' studies of attachment behavior in infant monkeys?

4. When Harlow and his colleagues completed their research with baby monkeys raised in isolation, they returned them to the monkey colony. What did they find?
   a. The monkeys immediately fit in socially.
   b. After some initial isolation, the monkeys adapted socially.
   c. The monkeys did not fit in socially at all.
   d. The monkeys eventually became social leaders.

5. Identify four main types of human attachment.

6. Your little sister picks up objects, feels every part of them, and then puts them in her mouth. What stage of Piaget's

model of cognitive development does this behavior suggest?

- **a.** sensorimotor
- **b.** preoperational
- **c.** formal operational
- **d.** concrete operational

7. A child's inability to see a situation from another person's point of view is known as

- **a.** self-view.
- **b.** narcissism.

- **c.** egocentrism.
- **d.** perceptual reversal.

8. Lev Vygotsky believed children's cognitive development depends on their

- **a.** age.
- **b.** heredity.
- **c.** memory ability.
- **d.** social interactions.

ANSWERS: 1. d **2.** c **3.** Warmth and contact comfort were important determinants of attachment. Social ability was harmed by raising the monkeys in isolation in the laboratory. **4.** c **5.** Securely attached, avoidant, anxious-ambivalent, and resistant. **6.** a **7.** c **8.** d

ADOLESCENCE

You climb a ladder to the top of a crane that is nearly three stories tall. Once you reach the top, large rubber straps are attached to your ankles. Then you jump off. Luckily, the crane is suspended over water! Depending on how the straps have been adjusted, you may go completely below the surface of the water or just come close to it. In any event, you bounce back and forth several times before this daredevil feat is complete. Some people engage in this unusual behavior by jumping from hot-air balloons or bridges with the rubber straps attached to a waist harness. Known as bungee jumping, the practice is popular among teenagers around the world (see Figure 9-9). *What can a phenomenon like bungee jumping tell us about developmental psychology?*

To answer this question, imagine that people are not jumping from a crane or a hot-air balloon. Instead, they are jumping from a tall platform. Vines, rather than rubber straps, are attached to their ankles (see Figure 9-10). This event is dangerous and scary; some of the boys will not survive the jump—the vines may break or be too long. The survivors will be honored by their village. You can think of these events as graduation ceremonies that mark the start of adulthood. Although bungee jumping also offers teenagers and young adults in urban societies a chance to display their independence and demonstrate their "adult" status, it does not carry the same meaning.

In most modern societies, no single event or ceremony marks the passage from childhood to adulthood. Rather, we experience an extended transition period that links childhood and adulthood. That period is known as adolescence.

Physical Changes

Many adults remember **adolescence**—the years between approximately ages 12 and 20—as a period filled with trouble and turmoil. Whether these perceptions of troubles and turmoil are accurate, adolescence is characterized by major physical, intellectual, psychological, and social changes.

The period (approximately two years long) that ends in the achievement of full sexual maturity, or **puberty,** is known as **pubescence.** During pubescence the sex organs mature and secondary sex characteristics appear. The dramatic physical maturation observed during pubescence, called the *growth spurt,* is second only to the one that

FIGURE 9-9 Bungee jumping. What does this practice have to do with developmental psychology? Why has it become so popular in modern societies?

adolescence
The years between approximately age 12 and age 20

puberty
The time at which an individual achieves full sexual maturity

pubescence
Period of rapid growth, maturation of sexual organs, and appearance of secondary sex characteristics that precedes puberty

FIGURE 9-10 These boys are not jumping for the thrill of it. This is a rite of passage into adulthood. If the boys survive this jump, they will have become men.

secular trend
Tendency of members of one generation to begin puberty at an earlier age than their parents

primary sex characteristics
Characteristics directly related to reproduction

menarche
Beginning of menstruation

secondary sex characteristics
Sex-related characteristics that develop during adolescence and are not directly related to reproduction

occurs during infancy. Look at the picture of fifth-graders in Figure 9-11. One feature of the growth spurt is apparent: Not all children enter pubescence at the same time.

Sex is among the most important factors determining the onset of pubescence. Girls begin pubescence, and therefore achieve sexual maturity, earlier than boys. The age range for girls entering pubesence is from 8 to 14; the typical girl begins at age 10 or 11. The age range for boys entering pubesence is from 10 to 16, with the typical boy beginning at 12 or 13. Thus a person who has reached puberty is still considered an adolescent. Interestingly, the higher a family's standard of living, the earlier children in succeeding generations reach puberty. This effect, referred to as a **secular trend,** is due to better nutrition and health care. This trend appears to have leveled off in Europe and North America (Hopwood et al., 1990).

Although both boys and girls experience a growth spurt during pubescence, there are differences in the nature of that growth. In boys the shoulders broaden; in girls the hips broaden. Boys experience more large-muscle growth, giving them a strength advantage over girls for the first time in their lives. In other respects, growth is similar: Adolescents of both sexes may look gangly when their hands and feet grow more rapidly than their arms and legs. In addition, the lips, nose, and ears grow more quickly than the head. Complex hormonal changes underlie the development seen during pubescence. For example, increased secretion of *growth hormone* and *thyroxine* produce the growth spurt. Sexual development is controlled by the secretion of the male and female sex hormones, *androgens* and *estrogen,* respectively.

Primary and secondary sex characteristics and capabilities develop to full maturity during pubescence. **Primary sex characteristics** are directly related to reproduction. The maturation of these characteristics in girls includes development of the ovaries, uterus, and vagina. The occurrence of **menarche** (the first menstrual period) signals that puberty has been reached. The maturation of primary sex characteristics in boys includes development of the testes, penis, seminal vesicles, and prostate gland. The ability to ejaculate semen, often in *nocturnal emissions,* or "wet dreams," signals that a boy has reached puberty.

You can think of **secondary sex characteristics** as signals or signs not directly related to reproduction that sexual maturity has been achieved. The secondary sex characteristics found in both girls and boys include the growth of axillary

FIGURE 9-11 The differences between these fifth graders indicate that children enter pubescence at different times.

(underarm) hair and pubic hair and changes in the skin, which becomes coarser and oilier, sometimes resulting in complexion problems.

The maturational differences we have mentioned can lead to adjustment problems (Brooks-Gunn et al., 1994). Early-maturing girls and late-maturing boys face the most difficult adjustments. Early-maturing girls are taller and show the developmental aspects of pubescence more obviously than their classmates. For example, their large feet and developing breasts often provoke teasing. In the United States, early-maturing girls may also feel social pressure to begin dating and associating with older adolescents. In countries such as India, where many marriages are arranged, early maturation does not create such problems.

The late-maturing boy presents a different picture. First he sees himself physically outdistanced by the girls in his class, and then he is passed by most of the other boys. His lack of physical development becomes a source of scorn and shame. As a result, late-developing boys are sometimes less poised and less relaxed than their peers. One study (Wadsworth, 1979) found that a higher percentage of late-developing than normally developing boys became juvenile delinquents.

Adolescence ends when the individual becomes an adult; however, the exact point at which a person enters adulthood varies considerably from society to society. As we saw in the opening vignette, a ritual, such as jumping off a platform, may mark the passage to adulthood. In some countries, such as the United States, the definition is arbitrary and based on age. Despite such variability, almost all countries have a developmental period that intervenes between childhood and adulthood (Schlegel & Barry, 1991).

Cognitive and Intellectual Changes

By the time they reach adolescence, many individuals have entered Piaget's final stage of intellectual development, the **formal operational stage.** This stage is characterized by abstract thinking—the ability to think in terms of possibilities as opposed to concrete reality. At this stage of cognitive development, the individual is able to think about an issue in general terms and then deduce specific outcomes from these general considerations (Inhelder & Piaget, 1958). For example, a high school student may read about the problem of noise pollution and then design and conduct an experiment to determine the effects of exposure to loud noises.

Although age may have something to do with entering this stage of development, merely having reached a certain age does not guarantee that a person will be capable of formal operations. Many adults remain at the level of concrete operations unless they are provided with appropriate educational opportunities and stimulation (Piaget, 1972; Neimark, 1982). What's more, our reasoning performance is higher when we are dealing with problems or issues that are relevant to our own lives (Sebby & Papini, 1994).

Adolescent Thought Patterns.   Although many adolescents can think and solve problems in an adult manner, much of their thought and behavior continues to be somewhat childish and contradictory. In his book *All Grown Up and No Place to Go,* David Elkind (1984) describes some of the thought patterns that characterize the adolescent years. Adolescent egocentric thought also leads to the belief that "I am invulnerable; it will never happen to me." This view of not being subject to the same rules as others is called the **personal fable** (Elkind, 1984; Quadrel, Fischoff, & Davis, 1993). For example, although adolescents may think about death in the abstract, they frequently engage in high-risk behaviors, like bungee jumping, taking drugs, driving fast, or being members of gangs.

According to Elkind, adolescents can envision ideal people, situations, and societies. Once such ideals are envisioned, the real world, with all its flaws and problems, becomes a target for criticism. Thus criticizing and finding fault are characteristic of adolescent thought. For example, Elkind (1984) indicates that "a boy who never washed, changed his shirt, or used a fork without a battle becomes a connoisseur of

formal operational stage
Piaget's final stage of intellectual development, characterized by abstract thinking; achieved during adolescence or adulthood

personal fable
Feeling shared by many adolescents that one is not subject to the same rules as other people

This Custer Middle School Odyssey of the Mind team, shows off their pneumatic shoe invention on May 1, 1996, in Custer, S.D. They took the invention to the Abilities Festival of the Paralympic Games in Atlanta. They were inspired in their project by fellow student Natalie Molitor, center, who uses a wheelchair. Clockwise around Molitor are, from front right, Chris Kehr and Jenny Phillipe (holding the shoe), and Matt Noble, Bradley Kehr, Dustin Kirk, and Brandon Haug. These students are likely at the stage of cognitive development that Piaget termed formal operations.

imaginary audience
The adolescent's assumption that everyone else is concerned with his or her appearance and behavior

identity versus identity confusion
Erikson's fifth psychosocial crisis, in which the adolescent faces the task of determining his or her identity and role in society

manners, dress, and behavior. Out of the blue, as it were, parents are told that they do not know how to walk, how to talk, how to dress, how to eat" (p. 30). If a better world can be envisioned, why has it not been created? When adolescents discuss such issues with adults, arguments may develop. Parents can turn this *argumentativeness* into a growth experience for the adolescent. Rather than seeing them as a time for combat, parents should view these arguments as opportunities to help adolescents develop and extend their reasoning powers.

In contrast to such lofty ideals, adults often find a great deal of *apparent hypocrisy* among adolescents. For example, adolescents may join a peace movement during a war. Their vocal demonstrations may lead to violent confrontations with people who support the war. How can the adolescent espouse peace and engage in violent behavior at the same time? Just as an answer to that question is formulated, another aspect of adolescent thought becomes apparent.

Adolescent thought also becomes *self-centered* and *self-conscious*. Adolescents tend to create an **imaginary audience** that is constantly observing each and every one of their behaviors. David Elkind (1984) describes the imaginary audience in the following manner:

> Because teenagers are caught up with the transformations they are undergoing—in their bodies, in their facial structure, in their feelings and emotions, and in their thinking powers—they become self-centered. They assume that everyone around them is concerned about the same thing they are concerned with, namely, themselves. I call this assumption the imaginary audience. It is the imaginary audience that accounts for the teenager's extreme self-consciousness. Teenagers feel that they are always on stage and that everyone around them is as aware and concerned about their appearance and behavior as they themselves are. (p. 33)

Through continuing interactions in which they become aware that other people have different, equally valid views and that their self-consciousness is greatly exaggerated, adolescents begin to establish the kind of understanding and empathy that form the basis for mature, adult relationships. An increase in self-disclosure to others (Windle, 1994; see Chapter 15) and the keeping of a diary in which adolescents express their thoughts, feelings, and emotions (Burt, 1994) may be important components of this maturing process.

Personality and Social Changes

Throughout the lifespan, social change appears to be the rule rather than the exception. How we react to such changes and challenges may affect our personality.

Erikson's fifth psychosocial crisis deals with **identity versus identity confusion.** For the adolescent who is experiencing a major growth spurt and developing signs of adulthood, the search for an identity and a place in society is most important (Erikson, 1975). This search can also be extremely frustrating. For some individuals, the search for an identity may not end for years; for others, it never ends.

The development of a strong sense of personal identity and intimacy may, however, take different courses for boys and girls. Susan Basow (1992) observes that, according to Erikson's life span perspective, "the sexes diverge during adolescence: boys generally establish a strong autonomous identity before establishing an intimate relationship, whereas girls frequently establish an intimate relationship first and may never establish a strong autonomous identity" (p. 120).

The new roles open to the adolescent also are influenced by ethnic and racial background, geographic locale, family values, and societal values. It is quite unlikely that a 15-year-old girl from rural Nebraska will see her place in society in the same way as a 15-year-old girl from Los Angeles. Being raised on a farm in a small town in the Midwest gives one a different view of possible societal roles than does being raised in a major metropolitan area (Holland & Andre, 1994). Although both adolescents search for a place in society, their perceived options are quite different. The same could be said for the comparison of adolescents in the United States with adolescents in other countries. For example, in the United States, young people tend to choose an occupation, whereas many adolescents in other cultures do not have a say in what their occupation will be. In some countries, such as Italy, the parents' occupation will likely become that of their children.

Possible Outcomes of Identity Formation. In individualistic cultures such as the United States, adolescents who have explored the alternatives and adopted a well-chosen set of values and goals have reached **identity achievement** (Marcia, 1980). These adolescents have a good sense of psychological well-being (Tevendale et al., 1997). They know where they are headed and what it takes to get there.

In other instances, the frustrations of this stage of development may cause adolescents to accept uncritically the values and desires of their parents. In this situation, called **foreclosure,** the adolescent's unique identity is not allowed to develop. Consider Willard, a successful but frustrated surgeon. Willard grew up in a small town in southwestern Oklahoma. As a boy, he enjoyed electronics and building radios. He could easily have become an electronics engineer. However, he became a doctor because that was the occupation his family chose for him; nobody asked him what he wanted to do with his life. Remember, however, that in many societies, lack of choice may be the norm with regard to occupation, family, and role according to birth order; it does not have the same stigma that it does in the United States.

Some adolescents find the identity expected of them unacceptable but are unable to replace it with an acceptable alternative. In such situations, the adolescent may develop a **negative identity** by adopting behaviors opposite to those that are expected. For example, Ken's family always expected that he would become a lawyer. After a rebellious college career and a frustrating semester of law school, Ken dropped out of school; he now drives a cab to support his real passion, building computers. **Identity diffusion** occurs when the adolescent has few goals and is generally apathetic about schoolwork, friends, and the future (Archer & Waterman, 1990). The individual lacks an identity and is not motivated to find one.

Finally, some adolescents may go through a period in which they try out several identities without intending to settle on a specific one. It is as if a **moratorium** had been called on actually selecting an identity. The years spent in college may be viewed as a moratorium. A student may sample several different subject areas before settling on a major and choosing a career.

Adolescent Peer Groups. During adolescence the peer group promotes a sense of identity and defends against identity confusion. The peer group can have a pronounced influence on an adolescent's attitudes, values, and behaviors. Belonging to groups such as the French club, the hiking club, or an athletic team may have a positive influence. Not all adolescent groups, however, help develop a strong and productive sense of identity and an appropriate adjustment to society. For example, the prevalence of teenage gangs has added to the crime and violence in the nation's cities (Williams, Singh, & Singh, 1994). John Coleman (1980) highlighted three functions that make peer groups so important to the adolescent:

1. Through the process of experimentation, adolescents find out which behaviors and personality characteristics will be accepted and praised and which ones will be rejected. Peer groups provide the all-important feedback.

2. The peer group serves as a support group of contemporaries who are also experiencing the same social and physical changes.

3. Because adolescence is a period of questioning the behavior, standards, and authority of adults, it is hard for adolescents to seek help and advice from their parents. The peer group serves this important function.

identity achievement
Adoption of a set of well-chosen values and goals

foreclosure
Uncritical acceptance of parental values and desires; hampers the development of a unique identity

negative identity
Adoption of behaviors that are the opposite of what is expected

identity diffusion
Failure to develop an identity because of lack of goals and general apathy

moratorium
Period during which an adolescent may try several identities without intending to settle on a specific one

The adolescent peer group promotes a sense of identity.

Any peer group can serve these three functions. Hence it is important for adolescents to be associated with a positive peer group if they are to become contributing members of society.

Family Influences.   The importance of the adolescent's peer groups should not lead you to believe that the family has ceased to have an influence (Andrews, Hops, & Duncan, 1997). For example, Kenneth Felkers and Cathie Stivers (1994) found that family attitudes play a major role in determining whether adolescents, especially girls, develop eating problems such as anorexia nervosa and bulimia. Family relations are also an important variable in predicting juvenile delinquency (Hoge, Andrews, & Leschied, 1994) and other instances of adolescent distress (Harold & Conger, 1997). A study of Norweigan adolescents indicated that good family relations were important in producing good mental health and reducing depression in adolescents (Pedersen, 1994); a study of Canadian adolescents has also shown the importance of family perceptions of adolescents in protecting them against depression (McFarlane et al., 1994).

Making a Commitment.   Adolescence is the stage of life in which most individuals begin to make sustained personal commitments. Such commitments may be to another person, a religious cause, career preparation, or a social program. Commitments help the adolescent develop a sense of identity and accomplishment.

The decision to become sexually active represents a major personal commitment that has important consequences. Nowhere is the importance of this decision more clearly seen than in the case of teenage pregnancy in the United States (Henshaw, 1998). The teenage pregnancy rate in the United States is more than 90 pregnancies per 1,000 girls, and that rate is over double the rate for Great Britain, Canada, France, Australia, and Sweden (United Nations, 1991). Additionally, a high teenage abortion rate (approximately 40%) and a high percentage of births to unwed teenage mothers (approximately 70%; Children's Defense Fund, 1997) are associated issues that must be addressed. When careers and educational opportunities seem out of reach, many teenagers appear to turn to parenthood as a way of entering adulthood (Caldas, 1993; Murray, 1992).

Effective procedures for encouraging teenagers not to be sexually active include teaching teenagers to understand the problems of sexual activity (Hutchinson & Cooney, 1998; Raffelli, Bogenschneider, & Flood, 1998) and the importance of using contraceptives (Piccinino & Mosher, 1998). For example, the adolescent role-plays various situations involving pressure to be sexually active and learns to say no. Role-playing helps adolescents find it easier to say no when the actual situation presents itself.

EARLY ADULTHOOD

Sam and Ann were married less than a year ago. They want to have children, but they are not sure that they want to start their family right away. *What are some of the advantages of having children when you are in your mid- to late twenties? Are there any advantages to becoming a parent at an earlier age?*

Early adulthood lasts roughly 20 years, from approximately age 20 until age 40. During this period most people embark on careers, marry and have children, and become established members of society.

Physical Changes

Early adulthood is usually characterized by good health. It is also the time at which we reach the peak of physical and sensory fitness. In our early twenties we possess our maximum strength and our greatest sensitivity in both vision and hearing.

Unhappy in Class, More are Learning at Home

early adulthood

Period from approximately age 20 to age 40

The physical abilities of young adults are seen in their sports and leisure activities.

Nowhere are the physical and sensory abilities of young adults more evident than in professional athletes. By the time athletes are in their mid-thirties or early forties, most are considered old-timers on the threshold of retiring. At about age 30, there is a *gradual* decline in muscular strength, vision, and hearing. The decline in visual and auditory sensitivity may not be noticeable until middle adulthood; it may be of some comfort to know that your sensitivity to tastes, odors, and temperatures does not begin to decline until your late forties or early fifties.

As we will see in Chapter 14, good health, a good diet, and exercise help us cope with stress. Engaging in these healthy practices during early adulthood has a major impact on health later in life. The way you treat your body during early adulthood directly affects your health during middle adulthood and old age. If you don't smoke, your lungs will be less susceptible to cancer; if you exercise, your risk of heart disease is decreased.

Cognitive and Intellectual Changes

If our physical abilities begin to decline during early adulthood, it seems likely that our intellectual abilities may also decline as we grow older. But whether intellectual abilities decline during adulthood is a subject of debate.

Psychological Detective

How would you investigate the prediction that intellectual abilities decline with age? What type of research would you conduct? Give this question some thought and write down some answers before reading further.

One possibility is to administer an intelligence test to a number of people in several age groups and compare the scores obtained by those groups (a cross-sectional approach). Will this procedure give us a valid answer to our question? No. The cohort effect that we discussed earlier has not been taken into account. For example, people who are currently 80 to 90 years old are fairly unlikely to have finished high school, but today's 40-year-olds are likely to have received at least that much education. Therefore, when we compare present-day 40- and 80-year-olds, they differ in terms of both aging and educational experience. Consequently we cannot be sure whether any differences we observe are due to the different ages of our participants or to differences in their past experiences. We should be looking at changes in intelligence in the same individuals (a cohort) over a specified period.

fluid intelligence
Intelligence involving the ability to see new relationships, solve new problems, form new concepts, and use new information

crystallized intelligence
Intelligence that involves the ability to retrieve and use information that has been learned and stored

K. Warner Schaie (1983, 1990) recognized the problems involved in conducting cross-sectional studies and conducted his own cohort studies to determine whether intelligence actually declines with age. His results indicated that most people actually improve in basic mental ability during adulthood. To avoid the possibilities that the improvement he observed was due to familiarity with the test and testing procedure and that only the most physically and mentally fit individuals returned for repeated testing, Schaie also tested a new group of individuals in each age category whenever he tested his original cohorts. After taking these possible problems into account, Schaie (1990) concluded that intelligence increases until the late thirties or early forties, remains stable until the mid-fifties or early sixties, and may not show any significant decline until the early seventies.

Types of Intelligence.　Even though Schaie does not believe that a decline begins until late adulthood, others disagree and suggest that intellectual abilities continually decline as a person grows older. John Horn and his colleagues (Horn & Donaldson, 1976; Horn & Hofer, 1992) believe that the answer to the question of whether intelligence declines with age is yes and no; it depends on the type of intelligence that is measured. There may well be a decline in **fluid intelligence,** which involves the ability to see new relations, solve new problems, form new concepts, and use new information. Putting together a jigsaw puzzle falls into this category of intelligence. The best puzzle solvers can visualize what a particular piece must look like if it is going to fit into a certain spot in the puzzle. Likewise, creative solutions are required to solve environmental problems, such as the need to recycle (see Chapter 8). The ability to see new relations reflects fluid intelligence in action. The decline in fluid intelligence appears to begin during young adulthood (approximately age 30) and continues gradually throughout the remainder of the individual's life.

A second type of intelligence, crystallized intelligence, appears to increase throughout life. **Crystallized intelligence** involves the ability to retrieve and use information that has been learned and stored. Solving a crossword puzzle is an example of the use of crystallized intelligence. Here are some examples from a crossword puzzle (the answers are given at the end of the chapter):

Fluid and Crystallized Intelligence

1. Acid found in apples (5 letters)
2. Chinese temple (6 letters)
3. Egg-shaped (5 letters)
4. Hambletonian gait (4 letters)

The best crossword puzzle solvers are those with the greatest usable store of knowledge. This type of intelligence favors older individuals who have been using their store of knowledge for years. The ability to remember words and meanings that most people have never heard of reflects crystallized intelligence. Figure 9-12 depicts the relation between changes in fluid and crystallized intelligence over the life span

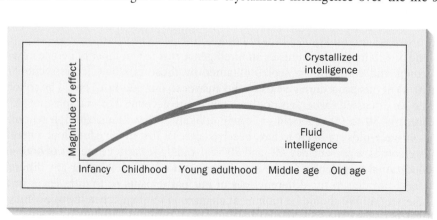

FIGURE 9-12　As we grow older, fluid intelligence gradually declines, but crystallized intelligence continues to increase gradually.

Source: Horn & Donaldson, 1980.

(Horn & Donaldson, 1980). The large number of politicians and judges who are over 65 demonstrates the importance of crystallized intelligence.

Personality and Social Changes

Along with the physical and intellectual changes that characterize adulthood come important personality and social changes. In the United States and other individualistic cultures, the world is the adults' oyster; they can make of it what they want. For many persons, career and lifestyle choices are almost unlimited; diversity is a key word for the adult. Remember, however, that in collectivist cultures family responsibilities, group membership, and obligations to others may be the norm.

Intimacy versus Isolation.   It may be difficult to believe that one can experience a psychosocial crisis when one is in the best of health and at the height of one's physical and intellectual powers. Yet this is exactly what Erikson suggests. He believes that young adults experience the crisis of **intimacy versus isolation.** *Intimacy* refers to the ability to make a strong commitment to other people. An individual who cannot establish intimate relationships becomes isolated. Adolescents who have developed a strong sense of personal identity and worth are better prepared to make the compromises and sacrifices required in a successful relationship. When they become young adults, such adolescents are more likely to establish close and satisfying relationships in the workplace when a career takes precedence over marriage and family (Weiland, 1993). Those who lack a strong personal identity are likely to feel insecure and to avoid close relationships.

Marriage.   A young adult who is able to establish intimate relationships faces a number of important decisions. Among those decisions are whether to marry or cohabit. Research on such topics as cohabitation has yielded some interesting results (Horwitz & White, 1998). Data from a sample of 180 college students indicated that the willingness to cohabit was shown by older students who had lower levels of religiosity, more liberal attitudes toward sexual behavior, and less traditional views of marriage and sex roles (Huffman et al., 1994).

Both marriage and cohabitation have benefits and costs. For example, married people are healthier and tend to be happier than unmarried people. With nearly a million divorces granted each year in the United States, however, it is clear that marriage is difficult (Wallerstein, 1994). According to Feldman (2000), "A look back at the television shows of the 1950s (such as *Ozzie and Harriet* and *Leave It To Beaver*) finds a world of families portrayed in a way that today seems oddly old-fashioned and quaint: mothers and fathers, married for years, and their good-looking children making their way in a world that seems to have few, if any, serious problems" (p. 205). Currently, we live in an era during which the number of single-parent families has grown dramatically, a large number of people live in nonfamily housing, and an adolescent gives birth every minute (Feldman, 2000). The divorce rate in the United States is the highest in the world. It is almost double that of Sweden, the country that ranks second (Berk, 1998). Although people who have divorced are likely to remarry, the rate of redivorce also has increased.

Children.   As you saw with the discussion between Sam and Ann (p. 392), whether and when to have children is another major issue of young adulthood that has both costs and benefits (Garrison et al., 1997). Statistics show that the average age at which women have their first child has been rising since the 1960s (Rice, 2001).

If you wait until you are in your mid- to late twenties or older to have children, you will have greater earning power, and you will be able to provide a better lifestyle and education for your children. Your career goals will be more fully developed. Your role and responsibilities as a parent will be clearer, and you are likely to have more time to enjoy your children.

intimacy versus isolation
Erikson's sixth psychosocial crisis, in which the young adult faces the task of establishing a strong commitment to others (intimacy) or having to deal with isolation

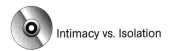
Intimacy vs. Isolation

Most of the advantages of having children when one is younger are related to the effects of aging. Younger parents are likely to be more active and energetic than older parents; hence, they may be able to deal with the demands of caring for a baby more effectively than older parents. Health is another age-related factor. As the age of child-bearing during young adulthood increases, the health risks to both mother and child increase (Fryns, 1987). Recall that the risk of having a child with Down syndrome increases as the age of the mother increases. Age is not the only factor that affects the decision to have children, however; career aspirations may also play a major role.

Consider the case of Nancy and Charles. Nancy aspires to become an electrical engineer, and Charles is planning a career in advertising. As partners in a dual-career marriage, they have been forced to make compromises; sometimes their schedules conflict and create tension between them.

But there are also several potential benefits. The sharing of child-care responsibilities can result in a closer relationship between a father and his children. Compared with wives who do not work outside the home, the wife in a dual-career couple has additional opportunities to develop her skills and build identity and self-esteem outside of her parenting role. Because neither partner dominates the family in terms of responsibility and earning power, dual careers can lead to a more egalitarian relationship. Dual careers can also result in a variety of problems, however, such as rivalry between husband and wife, conflicts between family and work roles, insufficient time to meet children's needs, and changes in family decision-making processes (Hoffman & Youngblade, 1998).

Parenting Styles. Whether to place their children in a day-care center is only one of the many decisions parents face. How much television will the children be allowed to watch? Should children be spanked when they misbehave? How important to a child's diet are vitamins, vegetables, and milk? Such decisions reflect prevailing child-rearing practices and parenting styles (Darling & Steinberg, 1993) as well as the personalities and preferences of individual parents.

On the basis of extensive observations and interviews, Diana Baumrind (1971) concluded that 77% of the families studied would fit into one of three parenting styles (see also Steinberg et al., 1994):

1. *Authoritarian.* Parents shape and control their children's behavior according to a set standard; they emphasize the importance of obedience and use punitive measures to reduce misbehavior.

2. *Authoritative.* Parents know that they have more knowledge, skill, control, resources, and physical power than their children, yet they believe the rights of parents and children are reciprocal. They explain rules and decisions and are willing to listen to the child's point of view, although they do not always accept it. They are less likely to use physical punishment and less likely to stress obedience.

3. *Permissive.* Parents demonstrate less control than either authoritarian or authoritative parents because they believe children must learn how to behave through their own experience or because they do not take the time to discipline their children. They give children considerable leeway to set schedules and choose activities. They demand less achievement and are more willing to tolerate immature behavior.

Each parenting style is associated with a different set of habits and behaviors. Children of authoritarian parents tend to be less sociable and friendly and more withdrawn than other children. Children of permissive parents are more likely to be immature, moody, and dependent. Children of authoritative parents have good social skills and are well liked, independent, and cooperative.

Different cultures may emphasize different parenting styles (Bornstein, Tal, & Tamis-Lemonda, 1991). For example, the parenting styles of the Chinese are demanding and emphasize strict discipline and respect for elders (Chao, 1994). In turn, having been raised with a particular parenting style may assist one's adaptation to a particular culture. For example, children raised by authoritarian parents function well in a more regimented, authoritarian culture, whereas children raised in an individualistic culture would not function well in an authoritarian culture.

The Feminization of Poverty.   If someone asks you to think about poverty, what image comes to mind? We asked a number of people, and the typical response was "minority people." That view is far from accurate. Because women, regardless of age, make up the majority of poverty-status adults, the term *feminization of poverty* is appropriate (Goldberg & Kremen, 1990). What's more, this situation is not limited to any specific ethnic group(s). The poverty differential between men and women becomes even greater in cases of divorce or separation in families with children. Because children typically remain with the mother, she is faced with significant added responsibilities and demands. Given the high rate of divorce in the United States, it should not surprise you that the feminization of poverty in the United States is ahead of that in other industrialized societies.

This sex difference in poverty is not limited to the United States and other industrialized nations; it is a global problem (63% of the world's illiterate are women). According to a United Nations (1995) report, fewer than 50% of women in South Asia, Sub-Saharan Africa, the Middle East, and North Africa are literate. The same situation does not exist for men. Illiteracy sets a vicious cycle into motion: Illiterate women marry at an early age, take poor-paying jobs, have large families, are likely to experience divorce, and are faced with severe poverty. The cycle repeats itself for the daughters of these women.

One step toward solving these problems is simple: Decrease illiteracy among women. In addition to benefiting individuals, such education has a positive impact on the entire country.

Career Development.   As this discussion suggests, career development is one of the major tasks young adults face. Until fairly recently, a discussion of career development would have dealt exclusively with men. The dramatic increase of women entering previously male-dominated professions has changed this situation, however. For example, in 1997, 62% of all married women over the age of 16 and 64% of all married women whose youngest child was under 6 years of age were in the workforce (U.S. Bureau of the Census, 1997). Despite the dramatic increase in the number of women in the workforce, however, women continue to encounter barriers, such as equity in salaries. Even though they perform the same job as men, women are paid less in virtually all occupations (U.S. Bureau of Labor Statistics, 1998).

During young adulthood the main focus is on developing a well-paying, satisfying career.

MIDDLE ADULTHOOD

Consider the case of John, a successful business executive. For years, his daily routine never varied, and most people saw him as dull. Then, at age 46, he made a dramatic change in his lifestyle. His gray and blue business suits and white dress shirts were replaced with brightly colored, trendy clothes. He traded the family sedan for a small sports car. John's new car and flashy clothes suggest he is undergoing a midlife crisis. *Is it possible that he is trying to deny his advancing age by adopting symbols of youth? How satisfying and productive has his life really been?*

Middle adulthood encompasses the period from approximately age 40 to age 65. Many of the changes of middle adulthood are in the form of a decline; hence adjustments are made, and coping strategies are adopted.

middle adulthood
Period from approximately age 40 to age 65

Physical Changes

The physical changes that began during early adulthood become more noticeable during middle adulthood. Changing sensory abilities may require new ways of adapting to the environment. Many people now need reading glasses to adjust to **presbyopia,** the farsightedness that often accompanies aging (Whitbourne, 1985). Presbyopia occurs because of a stiffening of the lens of the eye, resulting in difficulty in focusing on near objects (Lemme, 1995). The most pronounced hearing deficit, **presbycusis,** is reduced ability to hear sounds at higher frequencies (see Chapter 3). Because these frequencies are not crucial to everyday behavior, such losses are often not noticed until they begin to interfere with speech perception. A detectable loss of sensitivity in other senses, such as taste and smell, does not occur until at least age 50.

The gradual decline that began in early adulthood eventually results in a reduction of more than 10% in physical strength. For individuals who rarely exert themselves fully, this decline in strength may not be detected. As we grow older, reaction time slows (Birren, Woods, & Williams, 1980) and may be more noticeable than the decline in strength; for example, it may take longer to step on the brakes when driving.

Middle adulthood also brings with it a change in reproductive ability. During the late forties or early fifties, a woman's body undergoes a series of hormonal changes, known as **menopause,** that lead to the cessation of ovulation and menstrual periods. Menopause may result in important psychological reactions. Some women mourn the loss of their reproductive capacity (even if they have not given birth in many years); others rejoice in their freedom from worry about pregnancy and the discomfort of monthly periods. The physical changes during menopause include a decrease in estrogen levels, a hormone that plays a central role in the development of primary and secondary sex characteristics and the sexual drive. Unless preventive measures are begun before menopause, the decrease in estrogen can lead to **osteoporosis,** a condition in which the bones become thinner and are prone to fractures (Culliton, 1987; Prince et al., 1991).

Osteoporosis occurs in approximately 25% of American women after menopause. It can be prevented if calcium intake is high enough so that the bones do not lose strength. Calcium supplements and weight-bearing exercise are the most popular treatments.

The reproductive changes of middle adulthood are not as dramatic or obvious in men as they are in women. Men in their late fifties may experience fluctuations in hormone production (Kimmel, 1980; Whitbourne, 1985), as well as impotence and depression. The symptoms associated with this period, often called the *male climacteric,* vary considerably from one person to another. For example, there is a decrease in the amount of semen and sperm (Murray & Meacham, 1993), and an increasing number of men 60 and older suffer episodes of impotence (Whitbourne, 1996).

This woman's posture suggests that she may be suffering from osteoporosis. This condition, in which the bones become thinner and are prone to fractures, occurs in 25% of American women after menopause.

presbyopia
Farsightedness that normally develops during middle adulthood; stiffening of the lens results in difficulty in focusing on near objects

presbycusis
Middle adulthood hearing disorder involving reduced ability to distinguish sounds at higher frequencies

menopause
Cessation of ovulation and menstruation; these changes mark the end of the childbearing years

osteoporosis
Condition in which the bones become thinner and more prone to fractures and breaks; typically appears in postmenopausal women

Cognitive and Intellectual Changes

If changes in intelligence are inevitable with aging, then we might expect the gradual decline in fluid intelligence and the gradual increase in crystallized intelligence that began in early adulthood to continue during middle adulthood. During this period, a person may not be able to answer as many questions concerning new facts and knowledge as a younger person, yet people in their forties and fifties are better at solving problems that require the use of a store of practical knowledge. When middle adulthood is reached, considerable information concerning everyday problems and ways to solve them has been accumulated. For example, a seasoned politician can draw on years of experience to help resolve a political issue.

Personality and Social Changes

During middle adulthood, one's occupation takes on added significance. Because prestige, productivity, and earning power may never be greater, these are the "golden years" for many people. The importance of one's job during this stage has been revealed in two different types of research. One set of studies of middle adulthood investigates what people feel they would do if they suddenly became millionaires. In one study, 80% of participants said they would keep working (Harpaz, 1985). The other type of research related to this stage of life deals with the effects of unemployment. Workers who have been laid off report feelings of depression, emptiness, and being lost (Kelvin & Jarrett, 1985).

Midlife Crisis. Recall the description of John that opened this section. For some men in Western countries such as the United States, middle adulthood brings with it the well-known midlife crisis (Levinson, 1986, 1996). The **midlife crisis** is a potentially stressful period that typically occurs during the mid-forties and is brought on when a person comes to grips with mortality issues and begins to review his or her life and accomplishments. Dissatisfaction with one's life may be accompanied by the feeling that rapid action is needed to correct the situation or regain one's youth. It is therefore not uncommon for persons who experience such a crisis to make radical changes in their jobs or lifestyles.

Although some experts feel that few men can avoid the midlife crisis (for example, Levinson, 1986), other research does not paint as bleak a picture. The percentage who experience the classic midlife crisis may be quite low (less than 15%), and a sizable proportion (over 30%) report a satisfying adjustment to midlife (Farrell & Rosenberg, 1981). Thus only a small percentage of people change their lifestyle drastically (Wrightsman, 1994).

Research on midlife changes in women has revealed a different pattern (Reinke et al., 1985). For women, age-related stress tends to occur later, in the late forties and early fifties, when parenting responsibilities have decreased and there is time to cope with other issues (Helson & Roberts, 1994). As more women return to college and enter the labor force, however, the likelihood of a midlife crisis appears to be decreasing. College training and job satisfaction, in conjunction with women's family roles, provide important buffers against midlife difficulties (Baruch, 1984).

Erikson was not directly addressing the midlife crisis when he described the psychosocial crisis of middle adulthood, yet many of the same issues are involved. Erikson believes that during our early forties we face the crisis of **generativity versus stagnation.** To be generative is to have concern for the next generation and for the perpetuation of life. Because teaching, coaching, and parenting reflect an obvious desire to share one's talents and knowledge, this concern is frequently expressed through such activities.

Other Stresses during Middle Adulthood. As their children grow older and leave home to begin their own careers, middle-aged American parents must confront another challenge (Cherlin, Scabini, & Rossi, 1997). During the hustle and bustle of the child-rearing years, communication between the parents may have diminished and in some cases faded entirely. Now that there are no children at home, the parents must become reacquainted. This adjustment is called the **empty nest syndrome.**

midlife crisis
Potentially stressful period that occurs during the mid-forties and is triggered by reevaluation of one's accomplishments

generativity versus stagnation
Erikson's seventh psychosocial crisis, which occurs during middle adulthood and reflects concern, or lack thereof, for the next generation

empty nest syndrome
Period of adjustment for parents after all children have left home

Teaching reflects a concern for the next generation and helps to resolve the crisis of generativity versus stagnation.

Psychological Detective

Many individuals report an improvement in marital satisfaction after their children have left home. What are some possible reasons for this increased satisfaction? Write down your answers before reading further.

Several factors appear to be responsible for the increase in marital satisfaction after the departure of children. First, the family's financial situation usually improves, and there are fewer worries about financial matters (Berry & Williams, 1987). Second, the goal of raising a family has been achieved. Once the children have left home, many of the anxieties associated with this goal are reduced. Finally, there is more time for the husband and wife to do things together.

Despite the benefits of having raised independent children, aging parents of middle-aged Americans may require additional care and attention, thus adding another source of stress (Ganong et al., 1998). The stress of attending to the needs of elderly parents is heightened when the parents live with their children. Such strains can, and do, lead to violence. As many as 1.5 million cases of elder abuse may occur in the United States each year (Baron & Welty, 1996). The magnitude of this problem and the stress it creates have led to the development of counseling and support groups for people who care for the elderly (Cantor, 1983).

Another source of stress that may be reintroduced after the empty nest adjustment period is the return of the birds to the nest. In times of economic hardship, many young couples are forced to return home to live with their parents. Similarly, a daughter and her young children may return to live with her parents after a divorce. These returning offspring are known as *boomerang children* (Mogelonsky, 1996). For middle-aged parents who have adjusted to the empty nest, the interactions and demands of this newly *refilled* nest may be stressful. Routines must be changed, and the needs and desires of additional family members must be addressed.

REVIEW SUMMARY

1. In contemporary U.S. society, no single event marks the passage from childhood to adulthood. Children experience an extended period of **adolescence,** which lasts roughly from age 12 to age 20.

2. During **pubescence,** which takes approximately two years, adolescents experience a major growth spurt and the development of **primary** and **secondary sex characteristics. Puberty,** the achievement of full sexual maturity, marks the end of pubescence.

3. According to Piaget, if adolescents are given appropriate educational opportunities and stimulation, they will enter the **formal operational stage** of cognitive development and be capable of abstract thought.

4. Adolescents experience major psychological and social changes. Erik Erikson proposes that as adolescents struggle to determine what their roles in society will be, they experience the psychosocial crisis of **identity versus identity confusion.** The adolescent peer group provides feedback and helps adolescents achieve a sense of identity and belonging. Some peer groups, however, may interfere with satisfactory adaptation to society.

5. The establishment of a sustained personal commitment may provide adolescents with feedback concerning their identities and potential roles. Such commitments may involve major decisions, such as whether to be sexually active or use drugs.

6. According to Erikson, early adulthood is characterized by the psychosocial crisis of **intimacy versus isolation.** If individuals are not able to make the sacrifices and compromises needed to establish strong commitments, they will be isolated from others.

7. Diana Baumrind has found that over 77% of parents use one of three basic parenting styles: authoritarian, authoritative, or permissive. The particular parenting style has a major impact on the child's development of self-esteem and behavior.

8. Physical changes during **middle adulthood** are characterized by a gradual decline. Visual and auditory sensitivity declines, muscle strength decreases about 10%, and reaction time is noticeably slower. Women undergo a series of hormonal changes, known as **menopause,** that mark the end of childbearing. The decrease in estrogen production that accompanies menopause may result in **osteoporosis,** a condition in which the bones become thinner and prone to fractures.

9. Fluid intelligence (the ability to solve new problems and form new concepts) may begin a gradual decline at about age 30. **Crystallized intelligence,** the ability to retrieve and use stored information, shows a gradual increase throughout adulthood.

10. As people review their lives and achievements, they may experience a **midlife crisis,** which leads them to engage in radical behavior changes aimed at regaining youth.

11. The psychosocial crisis of middle adulthood, **generativity versus stagnation,** centers on concern for the well-being of future generations.

12. When their last child leaves home, parents may need to learn how to communicate and live as a couple once again. This adjustment is known as the **empty nest syndrome.** Other adjustments of middle adulthood include having to provide care for elderly parents.

✓ CHECK YOUR PROGRESS

1. What is the effect of the secular trend on puberty?

   a. The higher the family's standard of living, the earlier children reach puberty.
   b. The lower the family's standard of living, the earlier children reach puberty.
   c. Girls reach puberty before boys.
   d. Boys reach puberty before girls.

2. Identify each of the following as a primary or secondary sex characteristic.

   a. growth of axillary hair
   b. development of the uterus
   c. development of seminal vesicles
   d. coarser and oilier skin
   e. growth of pubic hair

3. Who has the most difficult adjustments to puberty?

   a. late-maturing girls and late-maturing boys
   b. early-maturing girls and late-maturing boys
   c. late-maturing girls and early-maturing boys
   d. early-maturing girls and early-maturing boys

4. All of the following are true of menopause except:

   a. Estrogen levels increase.
   b. It occurs during one's late forties and early fifties.
   c. Women may react favorably or unfavorably to it.
   d. Osteoporosis may result from changing estrogen levels.

5. Anita is in her late fifties. Recently she suffered from several fractures in her arms and legs. The cause of these fractures is unknown. What condition may Anita be suffering from? How could she have avoided developing this condition?

6. Katie declares an art major, then decides this is impractical and switches to accounting. She does not enjoy accounting, so she transfers to psychology. According to one theory, she is experiencing

   a. moratorium.
   b. foreclosure.
   c. fragmentation.
   d. identity diffusion.

7. The uncritical acceptance of parental values and desires is termed

   a. moratorium.
   b. foreclosure.

   c. negative identity.
   d. identity diffusion.

8. An adolescent is likely to be in which of Piaget's stages of cognitive development?

   a. sensorimotor
   b. preoperational
   c. formal operational
   d. concrete operational

9. What type of intelligence is characterized by the ability to see new relationships, solve new problems, form new concepts, and use new information?

   a. fluid
   b. native
   c. intuitive
   d. crystallized

10. You observe a parent who emphasizes obedience through guidelines and punishment. According to Baumrind, such a parent would be termed

   a. permissive.
   b. rigid.
   c. authoritative.
   d. authoritarian.

11. Garland, a man in his forties, changed his appearance and image overnight! He now has a new hairstyle (and hair color), a new wardrobe, a new sports car with a sensational sound system, and new friends who are much younger than he is. What may Garland be experiencing?

12. At what point do most individuals begin to make sustained personal commitments?

   a. adolescence
   b. late adulthood
   c. early childhood
   d. middle adulthood

13. In Erikson's view, the sense that a person is making significant contributions to the next generation is known as achieving

   a. moratorium.
   b. stagnation.
   c. significance.
   d. generativity.

ANSWERS: 1. a **2. a.** Growth of axillary hair—secondary sex characteristic   **b.** Development of uterus—primary sex characteristic   **c.** Development of seminal vesicles—primary sex characteristic   **d.** Coarser and oilier skin—secondary sex characteristic   **e.** Growth of pubic hair—secondary sex characteristic   **3.** b   **4.** a   **5.** Osteoporosis. She could have maintained a sufficiently high level of calcium intake over time.   **6.** a   **7.** b   **8.** c   **9.** a   **10.** d   **11.** Midlife crisis.   **12.** a   **13.** d

late adulthood
Period from approximately age 65 until death

cataracts
Clouding of the lens of the eye

LATE ADULTHOOD

Rex and Samantha have been retired for several years. Their friends frequently comment on how mentally sharp they are. Rex and Samantha just laugh and say that it's due to their enjoyment of playing games such as Scrabble several times each week. *Can playing games such as Scrabble really have an impact on a person's intellectual ability?*

Whether you agree with the theory that we grow old because of wear and tear on the body or the theory that we are genetically programmed to grow old, aging is an inevitable part of the developmental cycle. At approximately age 65 we enter the final period of adulthood—**late adulthood,** or old age.

Physical Changes

Psychological Detective

The following statements will help you think about old age and put it in perspective. Mark each one as true or false before reading further.

- All five senses decline in old age.
- Physical strength tends to decline with age.
- Older workers cannot perform as effectively as younger workers.
- At least 25% of elderly citizens are living in institutions such as nursing homes, mental hospitals, and extended-care facilities.
- Medical practitioners tend to give low priority to senior citizens.

We will respond to these statements throughout the rest of this chapter, but let's focus first on those that are related to physical changes. Despite the physical changes that occur in late adulthood, keep in mind that chronological age may not be a good predictor of ability or performance in elderly people. Hence researchers (such as Neugarten & Neugarten, 1987) distinguish between the *young-old* and the *old-old*. The young-old appear physically young for their advanced years, whereas the old-old show definite signs of decline. A person who is 85 or older could be classified as young-old, whereas a person in his late 60s might be classified as old-old.

Despite the young-old and old-old distinction, predictable physical changes come with advancing age. For example, many older people must contend with impaired vision and hearing. For many, the middle-adulthood problem of farsightedness is replaced by the development of more serious problems, such as **cataracts** (clouding of the lens of the eye), that may require corrective surgery (Segerberg, 1982). The need for hearing aids increases as hearing ability decreases; however, many people refuse to use them because they are a visible sign of advancing age (Olsho, Harkins, & Lenhardt, 1985).

The *gradual* decline in sensitivity to taste and smell that began in middle adulthood continues until the late seventies; after that, the majority of people experience a very sharp drop in olfactory ability (Doty, 1984). Many older people do not enjoy eating as much as they once did because their food does not taste as good as it used to. Why? In Chapter 3 we saw that taste and olfaction influence each other. If we cannot smell our food, it does not taste as good, or as we expect it to taste, and so we may not eat as much as we should. Consequently, malnourishment may become a problem for some elderly people.

The ability to regulate body temperature also declines noticeably during old age. When you visit your older relatives or friends in the winter, you may find their homes very hot. Remember that it is hot for you but comfortable for them.

Although older people do not possess the physical strength that characterizes young adulthood, this decline does not render them unable to perform such activities as taking care of their houses, doing yard work, and playing tennis (Marsiske, Klumb, & Baltes, 1997). Most of these tasks and activities can still be carried out effectively and enjoyably, although they may take longer than previously. Such activities, even aerobic dancing (Hopkins et al., 1990), are important in helping elderly people stay physically fit (Rosengren, McAuley, & Mihalko, 1998).

The slowness of old age is reflected in longer reaction times and an increase in the time required to process information. Thus older people are increasingly likely to be involved in traffic accidents (Sterns, Barrett, & Alexander, 1985). This increase occurs because older individuals are unable to process information from traffic signals, such as stop signs and turn signals, as quickly or as well as they did when they were younger.

Physical appearance also changes with advancing age. People actually shrink as they grow older (Whitbourne, 1985). The shrinking results from compression of the disks between the vertebrae of the spinal column (see Chapter 2). What's more, older people tend to stoop when they stand, which increases the perception of shortness.

Elderly people also experience changes in their sleep patterns. As noted in Chapter 4, their sleep becomes less efficient; that is, they spend less of their time in bed actually sleeping. Their sleep is punctuated by more frequent awakenings, which results from a reduction of Stage 4 sleep and an increase in the light sleep of Stage 1. Older individuals may counteract the loss of deep sleep during the night by napping during the day.

Most of the systems of the body become more susceptible to disease during old age. For example, heart disease is the most frequent cause of death for people over 65. Other prominent causes include cancer, stroke, diabetes, and kidney disease.

Increasing susceptibility to disease is frequently accompanied by an increase in the amount or number of medications taken. In some cases these drugs may combine or interact with one another in unintended, and potentially deadly, ways. Drugs may be prescribed in larger doses than necessary or may be prescribed by different physicians who are not aware that any other drugs have been prescribed.

Most medical practitioners give low priority to the aged population. Forgetfulness and declining abilities make many elderly people difficult to work with. Limited resources make them potential financial risks. Hence many elderly people receive less than adequate attention and care.

Snow skiing is only one of many ways that older people can be active. Continued activity is important to maintaining physical fitness.

Hands On

Experiencing Old Age

Have you ever wondered what it's like to be old? Here's an easy and quick exercise that simulates some of the problems old age may bring that you and one or more friends can do just about anywhere. You will need the following supplies: plastic wrap, cotton, and masking tape. To simulate blurred vision owing to cataracts, cover your eyes (but not your nose or mouth!) with several layers of plastic wrap. Tape the wrap in place so that it will not fall off. Place cotton in your ears to simulate hearing loss, and put masking tape around your knuckles to simulate arthritis. Now try navigating around your dorm room, house, or apartment (try outdoors if you are really daring). Be sure someone is around to monitor your behavior. Once you have experienced this simulated old age, trade places with your friends. Once your entire group has had the "old-age experience," here are some questions you should try to answer (group collaboration is encouraged). What did it feel like to be old? Of all your senses, which would be worst to lose? Which is the second worst? Can you now relate better to old people? If so, how?

Alzheimer's Disease.   **Dementia** is a condition of general intellectual decline involving loss of memory and disorientation (Erkinjuntti et al., 1997; Reisberg et al., 1985). Sometimes dementia is caused by a blood clot that prevents an adequate supply of blood from reaching the brain. This problem can be corrected, and many people who have experienced dementia are able to resume normal functioning. Others are not as fortunate.

dementia
General intellectual decline associated with old age; may be reversible when caused by medication or blood clots

alzheimer's disease
Degenerative brain disorder that results in progressive loss of intelligence and awareness

One form of dementia, **Alzheimer's disease,** is irreversible and there is no long-term treatment at present. (Some drugs, such as Tacrine and Aricept, *inhibit* an enzyme that breaks down the neurotransmitter acetylcholine, thus allowing acetylcholine to be active longer. Such drug treatment shows promise, as these drugs alleviate symptoms in some patients.) Alzheimer's disease is a degenerative brain condition, which means that victims of this disorder show progressive loss of intelligence, memory, and general awareness (Nash, 2000). Because Alzheimer's disease may affect nearly one-third of all people who live to be 85 or older (Heston & White, 1991), it is receiving considerable attention from caregivers and researchers.

Autopsies show that the brains of Alzheimer's victims have changed or deteriorated. For example, many of the axons of neurons in the brain (see Chapter 2) are abnormally twisted and tangled; there may even be loss of complete cells (Roth et al., 1985). Under such conditions, the brain could hardly be expected to function well.

What causes Alzheimer's disease? To answer this question, we need to consider two variants of the disease. One type, which occurs at a somewhat earlier age (during middle adulthood), is thought to be caused by a genetic defect (Hendrie, 2001). If the gene responsible for the disorder could be identified and isolated, we might be able to find a cure for this form of the disease. A second type of Alzheimer's disease (the more common form) usually occurs after age 65. It may be caused by immune system deficiency, concentrations of aluminum in the brain (Cohen, 1987), or infection.

Only continued research will provide a clear picture of this disease and how to combat it. An interesting research project conducted by University of Kentucky researcher David Snowdon has provided some intriguing possibilities. Snowdon has studied 678 School Sisters of Notre Dame in an attempt to determine the factors that led some of the nuns to develop Alzheimer's disease, whereas other nuns did not develop the disease (Lemonick & Park, 2001). Several of these nuns have lived into their nineties without any sign of Alzheimer's disease; others have not fared nearly as well. Why the difference? Among the factors that may help prevent Alzheimer's disease are avoiding head trauma, including folic acid in your diet, expressing positive emotions (for example, love, hope, gratitude, and happiness) instead of negative emotions (for example, sadness, fear, and shame), and staying mentally active.

Culture and Life Expectancy. Even with the physical problems associated with old age, the average life expectancy in the United States has increased at a steady rate (Aaron, 2000; Ervin, 2000). Better medical care and improved nutrition have extended the number of active years before illness or disability really begins. This increase in life expectancy has resulted in rapid growth of the elderly population. As Figure 9-13

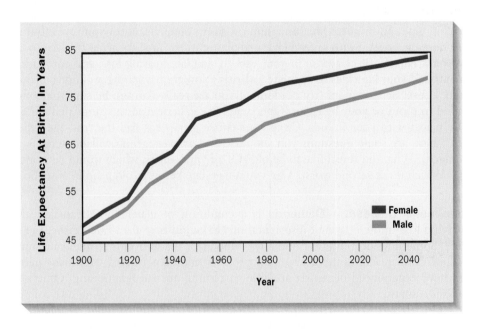

FIGURE 9-13 If increases in life expectancy continue, people may commonly live to be 100 by the next century.

Source: U.S. Bureau of the Census, 1997.

shows, the number of elderly persons is projected to continue through the year 2040 (U.S. Bureau of the Census, 1997). What's more, women have longer life expectancies than men. The disparity, which was small at the start of the 1900s, has grown over the years.

Although longer life expectancies are a relatively new phenomenon in the United States, some areas of the world—Peru, Pakistan, the former Soviet Union, Japan, and Iceland—are famous for the longevity of their inhabitants. Among the very old people found living in the Abkhasia region of Russia was a woman who claimed to be 148 years old and whose daily routine included drinking vodka and smoking cigarettes (Beet, 1974). What is it about the cultural groups in which these people live that has produced longer average life expectancies? These people seem to share four characteristics: (1) Their diets are high in fruits and vegetables and low in meat and fat, (2) both relaxation and exercise are part of their daily routine, (3) they work throughout their lives, and (4) family and community activities are important to them (Pitskhelauri, 1982).

"Look you're 103 years old, you've got to start taking better care of yourself."

Cognitive and Intellectual Changes

The increase in the proportion of older people (see Figure 9-14) has been accompanied by an increase in research on the intelligence and personality of senior citizens and the social aspects of old age. As we have seen, fluid intelligence begins a gradual decline toward the end of young adulthood, whereas crystallized intelligence continues to increase gradually. Why does the decline in fluid intelligence occur? Does the brain simply wear out? If there is some general deterioration, it seems reasonable to predict a decrease in both types of intelligence. As this decrease does not occur for both, we must look for another explanation.

Recall our discussion of the encoding, storage, and retrieval of memory in Chapter 7. The decline in fluid intelligence may be related to a problem with one of these memory processes. Consider the alternatives. The excellent crystallized memory shown during late adulthood indicates that storage problems can be ruled out. Obviously, already stored memories are not being lost. What about encoding? It may be that, as we grow older, we begin to experience difficulties in successfully encoding new material. If encoding problems are the cause of the decline in fluid intelligence, it might be possible to increase memory abilities in the elderly by teaching them techniques that aid encoding. Providing elderly individuals with encoding strategies such as arranging names alphabetically resulted in a level of retention similar to that shown by much younger persons (Poon, 1985).

What about retrieval? Do the elderly have difficulty with this process also? The results of a study in which elderly individuals were provided with memory prompts

This villager in Kirgiz in the former Soviet Union typifies the longevity of the region's inhabitants.

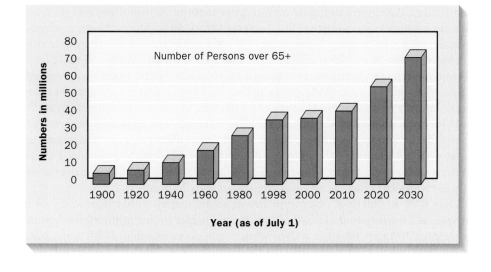

FIGURE 9-14 Population of the United States aged 65 and older, 1900–2030.

Source: American Association of Retired Persons, 1992; based on data from U.S. Bureau of the Census.

Continuing to be intellectually active may help prevent a decline in mental activities in old age.

(Craik, Byrd, & Swanson, 1987) indicate that the answer is yes. When cues or prompts were presented, recall for words from a list improved significantly, as did performance on other verbal tasks. These results suggest that the memories had been encoded and stored but the participants had trouble retrieving them. This study also led to another interesting discovery: Not all of the elderly participants showed a loss in fluid intelligence. In fact, the memory abilities of elderly individuals who had been intellectually active and resourceful throughout their lives were comparable to those of undergraduate students. Results like these point to the advantage of continuing to be intellectually active throughout life. It is possible for older people to learn new things! Because they play board games such as Scrabble, Rex and Samantha, whom we met at the beginning of this section, have continued to be intellectually active and mentally sharp.

Unfortunately, many people do not hold this view. What images flash through your mind when you see or hear such terms as *senior citizens, older Americans,* or *elderly persons*? Do these phrases bring to mind positive or negative scenes? Perhaps you responded with images of feeble individuals hobbling with canes and not understanding what is said to them. The tendency to view the elderly in a negative manner is termed **ageism**. It seems to be triggered by common words, such as *old* (Perdue & Gurtman, 1990). Although the use of such adjectives may be unintentional, it can lead to discrimination.

In many instances, ageism leads to isolation of elderly citizens and keeps them from making valuable contributions to society. A person who sits in a retirement apartment watching television contributes less than someone who has a part-time job or is active in other ways. As the number of elderly people in our society increases and research findings help psychologists and others view them more realistically and positively, perhaps we will see a decrease in ageism (Perdue & Gurtman, 1990). Such isolation may be the product of our more affluent society; in less developed countries, where there are no pension plans or Social Security, older adults do not officially retire. Therefore they do not become as isolated and are afforded greater social status as "wise elders."

Personality and Social Changes

Erikson's final personality crisis, **integrity versus despair,** occurs during late adulthood. To accept one's impending death, one must be able to put one's life in perspective and attach meaning to it. Achieving this goal results in a sense of wholeness or integrity. People who are unable to find meaning in their lives may develop a sense of despair and anguish and wish they could have lived their lives differently. Erikson's stages throughout the lifespan are summarized in the Study Chart on the next page.

Retirement. The crisis of integrity versus despair is reflected in the way people adapt to retirement. According to the American Association of Retired People (1992), more older Americans are choosing to retire than ever before. In addition, the age at which individuals retire is decreasing. Retirement may call forth visions of elderly people enjoying a vacation-like life in ideal climates like Florida or Arizona. Although these images sell condominiums and retirement houses, they are not accurate. Retirement represents a major adjustment (Glick, 1980). Some people look forward to retirement and enjoy it greatly. For others, retirement is a time of frustration, anger, and possibly depression.

Why do people react so differently to retirement? A number of factors are involved. The keys to successful retirement include good planning and preparation, satisfaction with one's accomplishments, good health, and freedom from financial worries. Individuals who begin to attend to these issues during middle adulthood make the transition to retirement much more easily than those who do not.

Over 90% of elderly U.S. citizens live in a community, rather than in an institution such as a nursing home. Most elderly people prefer to live in their own homes or apartments and maintain their independence as long as possible. With some careful

STUDY TIP ◈◈

Create a timeline showing Erik Erikson's stage theory of personality development. Use different colors, or draw icons, to represent the different stages.

ageism
Viewing elderly people in a negative manner

integrity versus despair
Erikson's eighth psychosocial crisis, which occurs during late adulthood; integrity reflects a feeling that one's life has been worthwhile; despair reflects a desire to relive one's life

Crises of Psychosocial Development, as Proposed by Erik Erikson

Crisis	Approximate Age	Characteristics
Basic trust versus basic mistrust	Birth to 1.5 years	Child learns whether to trust the environment. Ability to trust the environment is important for the development of trust in oneself.
Autonomy versus shame and doubt	1.5 to 3 years	Child develops a sense of control. The sense that control is internal (autonomy) helps the child develop independence. The sense that control is external fosters shame and doubt and hinders the growth of independence.
Initiative versus guilt	3 to 7 years	Child experiences conflict between the behaviors he or she wants to engage in and a growing sense of morality and begins to question whether certain behavior is right or good.
Industry versus inferiority	7 to 10 years	To become a productive member of society, the child must master certain skills and acquire a basic amount of knowledge. Successful learning and skill acquisition lead to the development of a sense of competence.
Identity versus identity confusion	Adolescence	The individual asks, "Who am I?" Adolescents seek to establish their sexual, career, and ethnic identities during this period. If these identities are not established, the individual will be confused about the roles he or she plays in the future.
Intimacy versus isolation	Early adulthood	Patterns of intimacy, companionship, and love are established during this period. Failure to develop such patterns results in an individual who lives in isolation from others.
Generativity versus stagnation	Middle adulthood	The individual's career and productivity reach a peak during this period. Families are formed, and children are raised. Failure to accomplish these objectives results in inactivity and stagnation.
Integrity versus despair	Late adulthood	One's life and its meaning are put in perspective. Individuals who feel that their lives lack meaning experience despair over unattained goals and unresolved problems.

Source: Erikson, 1963.

planning, it is often possible to achieve this objective. Consider the case of Peggy, now 91, whose husband died 10 years ago. She continues to live in her own house, as she has for over 40 years. During the day a nurse assists her with meals and provides companionship, but Peggy is as independent as possible.

Owing to physical or financial limitations, however, not all elderly people are able to live in their own homes in this style. In many cultures such responsibilities are handled by the extended family. In the United States, assisted living or extended care facilities, retirement villages, and cooperative housing arrangements, in which elderly people share a house, enable them to live in residential neighborhoods. As the average life span increases, we can expect to see additional arrangements of this nature.

Aging. The form of prejudice known as ageism suggests that all elderly individuals are feeble and crotchety. As noted earlier in the chapter, this view is inaccurate; the majority of elderly people are active and productive. Likewise, the notion that aging occurs in a similar manner across all segments of society is inaccurate. Unfortunately, aging may pose additional problems for members of minority groups.

Whereas the likelihood of illness among elderly minorities is high, the chance of receiving treatment is low. Many elderly members of minority groups have incomes below the poverty level (American Association of Retired Persons, 1992). What's more,

STUDY TIP

After reading the section on late adulthood, write down each of the statistical and/or scientific facts that are part of the picture of late adulthood today. Briefly describe each fact's effects.

many elderly minorities, especially first-generation immigrants, are unaware of or reluctant to take advantage of the social services available to them, such as legal counseling and low-cost health services at the local public health department (Gelfand, 1982).

In some cases these additional problems may be somewhat offset by the extended-family pattern that characterizes many minority groups. For example, Hispanic and African-American families tend to have active extended-kinship networks. These extended families can be counted on to provide emotional and financial support to their elder members (Gibson, 1986).

To be effective, psychologists, social workers, and other health care professionals who provide services to children, families, and elderly people from other cultures must be aware of differences like the ones we have described. As members of a multicultural society, we need to recognize and appreciate these differences. Only when such differences are appreciated will our society be able to function harmoniously.

DEATH, DYING, AND BEREAVEMENT

Galen and Shandra lost their daughter in a car accident over a year ago. You saw them at the funeral. Your studies have kept you busy however, and you haven't seen them since then. When you had dinner with them last week, all they could talk about was their daughter. After dinner, the conversation continued as you spent the rest of the evening watching home videos featuring their daughter. Their inability to take their minds off their loss struck you as morbid. *Is it typical for bereaved parents to dwell on the memory of their child for such a long time?*

For some people, death is seen as the final event in a person's life span. Although it marks the conclusion of a particular individual's developmental history, other people continue to be influenced by their memories of that person. In this section we examine attitudes toward death and the process of bereavement. We see that different attitudes toward death are associated with different stages of development.

Attitudes toward Death

Childhood.   Children do not have an accurate conception of death until they attain the ability to perform concrete operations. They believe that death is reversible—that a dead friend or pet can return to life. Before about age 6, children do not realize that all living things ultimately die and that all functions cease at the time of death. They believe death can be avoided.

Adolescence.   Although adolescents understand the nature of death, they do not have a healthy respect for its implications (Corr, 1995). They focus on how one lives, not on how long. Death may be glamorized and associated with daring deeds and heroic individuals. For example, James Bond, the international spy created by Ian Fleming, is depicted as an individual whose daring deeds repeatedly bring him to the brink of death; Bond, however, never seems concerned. Adolescents frequently idolize individuals who express such feelings; hence death may not be regarded as an event to be feared.

For some adolescents, death may seem the only way out of an intolerable situation (Lennings, 1994). Their self-centered and self-conscious thoughts place a premium on how they lead their lives and who their friends are. Inability to lead one's life in a desired manner may be a major cause of teenage suicide. Having the right car, dating the right people, and being popular in school are important to adolescents. Perhaps as a result of the increased pressures of our complex society, the number of teenage suicides has risen during recent years. Approximately 1 in every 10,000 adolescents commits suicide each year. Warning signs such as a sudden decrease in school attendance, social

Adolescents who idolize a seemingly indestructible hero, such as Batman, may not see death as a feared event.

withdrawal, a breakup in a romantic relationship, previous suicide attempts, and publicized suicides by other adolescents should be taken seriously (King et al., 1990).

Recall the egocentric thoughts and *personal fable* that we discussed earlier. Because they believe they are invulnerable, death is not considered a possibility by many adolescents.

Young Adulthood.   Young adults are at the peak of their physical and sensory abilities and believe that the future has much to offer them. They rarely think of their own death. Consequently, the occurrence of a life-threatening illness usually provokes extreme anger and rage. Young adults with a terminal illness are typically poor hospital patients; they feel death is unfair and they are being robbed of their future.

Middle Adulthood.   During middle adulthood noticeable physical changes, coupled with the death of one's own parents, bring the realization that death is inevitable. This realization often results in changes in lifestyle. These changes may take one of two forms: The individual may adopt behaviors that are characteristic of an earlier developmental period, as in the reaction to a midlife crisis; or the individual may improve dietary and exercise habits to become more physically fit and live as long as possible.

Late Adulthood.   Although death may be imminent, the elderly are more understanding and accepting of this eventuality than younger adults (Reker, Peacock, & Wong, 1987). Elderly people have put their lives in perspective and understand that death is a normal component of the developmental cycle. They have reached the developmental stage of integrity (Veroff & Veroff, 1980).

Confronting Death

Ultimately, we must all face our impending death. How will we react? According to Elisabeth Kübler-Ross, terminally ill patients typically go through five stages in dealing with and understanding death (Kübler-Ross, 1969, 1975): denial, anger, bargaining for extra time, depression, and acceptance (see Table 9-3). Although a person is likely to

TABLE 9-3

Stages of Confronting Death

Stage	Description
Denial	The typical reaction is "This can't happen to me." Because friends and family members may also deny the reality of death, the patient feels isolated and has no one with whom to talk.
Anger	Once the reality has been confronted, the "Not me" attitude changes to an angry "Why me?" complaint. Young and healthy individuals are envied. To move beyond this stage, patients must express their anger and rage.
Bargaining	Once rage and anger have been expressed, the terminally ill person bargains for additional time. Such bargains often take the form of prayers, such as "I will lead a better life if I can only live until...."
Depression	Depression often follows the bargaining stage. As with anger, depression should not be hidden. Only by directly confronting and experiencing the normal feelings of sadness and grief will the person be able to progress to the stage of acceptance.
Acceptance	This stage is characterized by a feeling of being at peace with oneself. Unfinished business, such as setting one's finances in order and seeing old friends for a final time, has been taken care of, and the person accepts the fact that "the time is near."

Research on terminally ill patients conducted by Elisabeth Kübler-Ross indicates that people may go through five stages in dealing with the approach of death.

bereavement
Emotional and role changes that follow death

grief
The emotional changes associated with bereavement

mourning
The behavioral changes associated with bereavement

hospice
Institution where terminally ill patients and their families are given warm, friendly, personalized care

experience each of these stages at one time or another, he or she will not necessarily proceed through them in an orderly manner (Kastenbaum, 1995). Individuals may experience these stages in different orders, and it is not uncommon to alternate between stages or to experience the emotions of two stages simultaneously. The nature of the disease leading to death also influences those emotions and the times when they are experienced. For example, a person suffering from a disease characterized by periods of remission may experience denial several times rather than once.

Cultural attitudes toward death differ significantly and influence the reactions toward it. For example, in several Native American cultures death is met with stoic self-control and a belief in the circular relation between life and death (Lewis, 1990). Buddhism also fosters acceptance of death (Truitner & Truitner, 1993).

Bereavement, Grief, and Support

Death brings numerous changes and adjustments for those who are left behind. Roles change—a wife becomes a widow, a husband a widower, a child an orphan. In addition to adjusting to living alone, widows and widowers must assume the responsibilities of the deceased spouse. Orphans must adjust to a totally new living environment. The emotional and role changes that follow a death are called **bereavement,** and the people whose emotions and roles change are known as the *bereaved*.

Grief, encompassing the emotional changes associated with bereavement, is a normal part of this process and seems to progress through four stages (Kalish, 1985): shock and denial, intense concern, despair and depression, and recovery. First, the bereaved person expresses *shock and denial*. These reactions serve to protect the individual from pain. This stage may last as long as two or three months.

But what about Galen and Shandra, who were still grieving over the death of their daughter a year later? Is it typical to continue to dwell on the memory of a dead child for such a long time? The second phase of grief, which may last for 6 months to a year, is characterized by *intense concern* for perpetuating the memory of the dead person. The majority of the bereaved person's thoughts concern the person who has died. Thus the behaviors Galen and Shandra are displaying are entirely normal.

The third stage, *despair and depression*, is often characterized by confused thinking and anger. Irrational behaviors, such as suddenly selling one's house and moving to an area where one has no friends, may also occur during this phase. **Mourning** involves the behavioral changes associated with bereavement. Untimely deaths, such as the death of Galen and Shandra's daughter, may prolong or intensify the second and third phases, as compared with the natural death of an elderly parent who had been ill for a long time. When the bereaved person shows renewed interest in normal daily activities, he or she has reached the final stage—*recovery*—and the grief is resolved.

Social support is a key ingredient in successful coping with death and bereavement. In Western nations the hospice movement has taken the lead in the delivery of such support services. The **hospice** is more a philosophy of treatment than a set of buildings and equipment. In addition to providing normal medical services for the terminally ill, hospice physicians and staff are trained to give more personalized care and more time to terminally ill patients and their families (Armstrong-Daily, 1991). This philosophy of warm, personal concern and care is not confined to hospitals; it can be implemented just as effectively in the home (National Hospice Organization, 1992). The attitudes and adjustments of hospice patients and their families are superior to those of comparable patients receiving traditional hospital care.

The emotional and role changes that follow a death are called bereavement. People whose emotions and roles change are the bereaved.

REVIEW SUMMARY

1. The physical decline experienced during early and middle adulthood continues during **late adulthood.** Vision and hearing are affected most adversely.

2. Late adulthood is accompanied by an increase in susceptibility to disease. Nearly one-third of individuals age 85 or older may suffer from **Alzheimer's disease,** a degenerative brain disease.

3. If the elderly are taught strategies to enhance encoding and are provided with retrieval cues, their memory capability may not differ from that of young adults. If people remain intellectually active, fluid intelligence may not decline.

4. Ageism occurs when people in a particular age group, such as the elderly, are viewed in a negative light.

5. The psychosocial crisis of **integrity versus despair** occurs during late adulthood. People who are unable to put their life in perspective may experience anger, bitterness, and despair.

6. Death brings the individual's developmental history to its conclusion. Attitudes toward death change with age. Young children believe that death is reversible; adolescents emphasize how one lives, not how long. The threat of death angers young adults and may cause substantial changes in the lifestyle of middle-aged individuals. The elderly are generally more understanding and accepting of the inevitability of death.

7. Elisabeth Kübler-Ross has identified five stages that an individual may go through in confronting death: denial, anger, bargaining for extra time, depression, and acceptance.

8. Role and status changes following a death constitute the process of **bereavement. Grief,** which is a normal part of bereavement, progresses through four stages: shock and denial, efforts to perpetuate the memory of the deceased, despair, and recovery.

✓ CHECK YOUR PROGRESS

1. A degenerative and irreversible brain disease that results in loss of intelligence, memory, and general awareness is

   a. dementia.
   b. dyslexia.
   c. narcolepsy.
   d. cerebral palsy.

2. Which of these individuals is part of the fastest-growing age group in our society?

   a. Jim, who is 65 and recently retired
   b. Dan, who is 33 and works in a factory
   c. Juan, a 14-year-old who lives on a farm
   d. Andrea, who is 22 and just graduated from college

3. Children do not have an accurate conception of death before they attain the cognitive stage Piaget labeled

   a. sensorimotor.
   b. preoperational.
   c. formal operations.
   d. concrete operations.

4. Describe the stages of confronting death outlined by Kübler-Ross.

5. The emotional and role changes that follow a death are called

   a. sorrow.
   b. despair.
   c. burnout.
   d. bereavement.

6. Allowing a person to die with dignity, away from a cold and impersonal institution, is the goal of

   a. hospices.
   b. nursing homes.
   c. moral hospitals.
   d. holistic hospitals.

ANSWERS **To Crossword Puzzle Clues**

PAGE 394

1. Malic

2. Pagoda

3. Ovoid

4. Trot

CHAPTER 11

Personality

CHAPTER OUTLINE

To this point we have covered several basic processes, starting with how our nerves transmit information, how we sense and then understand information from our environment, and how we learn and remember information. We have also looked at how we develop physically and socially, and we briefly considered how personality develops. In this chapter we present an overview of the major theories of personality. The concept of personality is familiar because our language contains many words that describe how our friends, relatives, and strangers differ from one another in the ways they act and react to events. Psychologists have devised a number of methods to quantify such personality differences. How these differences occur is one of the key questions posed by psychologists. In previous chapters we have seen how biological factors such as heredity influence many basic processes. In this chapter we will see that heredity has important influences on personality. Next, we will look more closely at Freud's model for personality development. We will also consider the perspective of psychologists who have proposed that the basic processes of learning can account for some personality differences. Finally, we will see how social and cognitive factors influence what and how we learn and how these differences create what we call *personality*.

ANALYZING PERSONALITY

Karin and her friends were in a shopping mall when they noticed a booth advertising "Personality Analysis by Computer." She completed a test called the GPA, which was a series of true-or-false questions (see Table 11-1). Although she thought some of the items were unusual, she was pleased with the analysis she received. After reviewing the analysis with her friends, however, Karin began wondering whether it was really accurate. *How could a computer generate a personality description based on a series of true-or-false questions?*

How would you describe a friend or relative without referring to his or her physical attributes? You might begin by saying that your friend has "a good personality." This statement usually means a person has made a positive impression on you and exhibits characteristics that you find desirable. In contrast, when we say that someone has "no personality," we usually mean we consider his or her characteristics bland or disagreeable.

Think of another friend who is quite different from the first one you considered, and write a description of him or her. Now examine the words you used to describe these two individuals. You may have used words such as *ambitious*, *happy*, and *sociable*. If your friends are indeed different, the words on the two lists should not overlap.

Defining Personality

The word *personality* is derived from the Latin word *persona*, which means "mask." In ancient Greece and Rome, actors wore masks to convey the personality characteristics of the roles they were playing. The masks made it easier for the small number of actors who played all the parts to portray their diverse roles.

To psychologists, **personality** refers to a relatively stable pattern of thinking, feeling, and behaving that distinguishes one person from another. This definition has two

personality
A relatively stable pattern of behaving, feeling, and thinking that distinguishes one person from another

self-report inventory
Psychological tests in which individuals answer questions about themselves, usually by responding yes or no or true or false

---

TABLE 11-1

The Generalized Personality Analysis (GPA) Questionnaire

This personality questionnaire contains a series of statements. Read each one, decide how you feel about it, and mark your answer to the item. If you agree with the statement or feel it is true about you, answer true. If you disagree with the statement or feel it is not true about you, answer false.

1. Cats are antisocial.
2. Some roads never end.
3. Fast walkers are slow thinkers.
4. I get into the tub with my right foot first.
5. A circle is a square that has rounded edges.
6. Oak trees seem friendlier than pine trees.
7. The majority of right-thinking people are wrong.
8. There is more air in a loaf of bread than in a balloon.
9. Snow can turn to rain faster than rain can turn to snow.
10. Being able to flick a light switch gives me a feeling of power and strength.

Source: Palladino & Schell, 1980.

*"I don't know why everyone says
I don't have a personality."*

---

important components. First, each person's pattern of thinking, feeling, and behaving makes him or her distinctive. Thus each of us wears a mask that is different from those worn by others. The second defining component is the notion that an individual's personality is relatively consistent. We are not completely consistent from one situation to the next; behavior varies across situations. The definition, however, proposes a certain degree of consistency in personality; people display levels of personality characteristics that are relatively stable over time. Psychologists have long debated and studied the issues of consistency across situations and stability over time, as we will see later in the chapter.

Assessing Personality

The methods psychologists use to examine personality include case studies, interviews, naturalistic observations, laboratory investigations, and psychological tests. To be useful, a psychological test must have three characteristics: reliability, validity, and standardization (see Chapter 8). Many of the tests published in popular magazines and newspapers lack all three characteristics; therefore, you should be skeptical of the supposed meaning attached to such tests.

Self-Report Inventories. Some of the best-known and most widely used personality measures are **self-report inventories** that require individuals to respond to statements about themselves (for example, "I am nervous when I speak to a large group of people") in the form of yes-no or true-false answers. This limited range of possible answers means that little, if any, judgment is required to score these tests. Two of the most frequently used self-report personality inventories are the Minnesota Multiphasic Personality Inventory (MMPI) and the California Psychological Inventory (CPI).

The Minnesota Multiphasic Personality Inventory. The most widely used self-report personality inventory, the MMPI (Butcher, Lim, & Nezami, 1998), was developed and first published in 1943 by Starke Hathaway and J. C. McKinley, both of the

Your friend has a "good personality" when she has made a positive impression on you and displays characteristics you like.

University of Minnesota. The test's long history of application is supported by evidence from thousands of studies, and its users have accumulated a great deal of experience (Helmes & Reddon, 1993). The purpose of the MMPI is to help diagnose psychological disorders such as depression and schizophrenia (see Chapter 12). Hathaway and McKinley began by collecting a large pool of items (for example, "I wish I could be as happy as other people") that could be answered "true" or "false." They retained items that were answered differently by normal people and those suffering from any of several psychological disorders. Most of the items deal with a range of psychological and physical symptoms (Groth-Marnat, 1990).

A revision of the MMPI, the MMPI-2, has 567 items and 10 clinical dimensions or scales (see Figure 11-1) that were designed to assess characteristic symptoms associated with several of the major psychological disorders. Four validity scales were designed to detect tendencies for test takers to present themselves in a favorable light (such as answering "false" to "I do not read every editorial in the newspaper every day") or to assess other unusual ways of responding (Graham, 1990).

The MMPI has been adapted for use in at least 22 languages and in many nations and cultures. Test developers follow a series of procedures when adapting the test for use outside of the United States. The elimination of objectionable items during the MMPI-2 revision enhanced acceptability of the test by people in other cultures. The issue of item content, however, still must be addressed each time the test is adapted. For example, items referring to sex might be considered inappropriate by people taking the test in Arabic (Soliman, 1996). In addition to issues related to content, the items themselves must be translated; this process consists of several steps. First, items are translated from English. During this step, translators must take special care with words such as *frequently*, *sometimes*, and *usually* as well as slang or colloquial expressions such as "muscle twitching and jumping." To ensure that the translation retains the original meaning, the translated version is translated back into English (a *back translation*). Any failures to convey the original meaning of the items are identified in this back-and-forth process. Once the translation is completed, the test adapters recheck to ensure that the test maintains its reliability and validity; the researchers check to determine if local norms must be used in place of norms based on a U.S. population (Butcher, Lim, & Nezami, 1998).

"Might I point out, sir, that that one goes particularly well with your tie?"

FIGURE 11-1 MMPI profile of a 40-year-old male. This profile reveals a mild to moderate level of depression and anxiety that suggests ambivalence, indecisiveness, and low self-confidence. Energy and activity levels are likely to be below average. Getting started on new tasks presents difficulty; after tasks are started, there is often self-blame over minor deficiencies in performance.

Sources: Friedman, Webb, & Lewak, 1989; Graham, 1990; Greene, 1991.

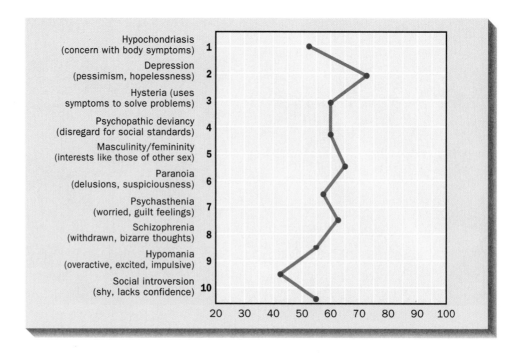

The California Psychological Inventory.

The MMPI has served as the basis for the development of other personality inventories, including the California Psychological Inventory (CPI), which was designed for use with normal adolescents and adults. The 20 CPI scales, such as dominance, responsibility, and sociability (Gough & Bradley, 1996), have been used to predict academic achievement, to understand leadership (Day, Bedeian, & Conte, 1998), and to study individuals in various occupations. The CPI is widely used, and has been translated into 29 languages (Paunonen & Ashton, 1998).

Limitations of Self-Report Inventories.

The MMPI was originally developed in the late 1940s. When the MMPI-2 was developed in the 1980s, the authors used the same clinical scales from the MMPI (Oltmanns & Emery, 2001). Thus, critics have argued that the MMPI-2 is based on outdated concepts that may not be applicable. What's more, the time required to administer and score a lengthy, all-encompassing personality inventory, such as the MMPI, is another limitation. This limitation has led to the development of shorter, more focused inventories, such as the Beck Depression Inventory (BDI), which measures severity of depression. Finally, self-report inventories offer the opportunity for less-than-honest responses. To evaluate the possibility of the patient being less than honest and open, the MMPI and MMPI-2 have incorporated a number of validity scales, such as the L (lie) Scale. If scores on scales such as the L Scale are valid, then the examiner can proceed to the clinical scales.

Projective Tests.

Have you ever stared at the sky and noticed a collection of clouds that reminded you of a crown? When you told a friend what you saw, she said it looked like a dog. Those clouds are similar to the stimuli used in projective tests to evaluate personality. **Projective tests** are assessment techniques that require individuals to respond to *unstructured* or *ambiguous* stimuli. In some projective tests, individuals respond to inkblots, make up stories about pictures, express themselves by drawing, or complete sentences such as "I think other people . . ."

Because there are no correct or best answers, proponents of projective tests believe test takers will find it difficult to fake their responses. The assumption underlying projective tests is that people project their personality characteristics onto the ambiguous stimuli. These responses are thought to reflect unconscious aspects of personality that are not likely to be revealed in answers to more obvious self-report inventory items.

projective test
Psychological test that involves the use of unstructured or ambiguous stimuli in an effort to assess personality

One projective test, the *Thematic Apperception Test* (TAT), has been used to measure achievement motivation (see Chapter 6) and to make predictions of future achievement-related behaviors (McClelland, Koestner, & Weinberger, 1989). The 20 TAT cards contain vague black and white pictures (one card is blank). When administering the test, the psychologist asks the participant to make up a story to fit what is happening in the card and what the character is thinking and feeling, and to give the outcome.

One of the most widely used projective tests is the Rorschach inkblot test (Lubin et al., 1985), which was published in 1921 by a Swiss psychiatrist, Hermann Rorschach. Rorschach dropped ink onto a piece of paper and then folded the paper in half, thus creating a symmetrical pattern (see Figure 11-2). Five of the cards in the test are black, white, and gray; the remaining five cards include various colors.

There are several steps in the administration of the Rorschach. First, the examiner displays the cards one at a time and asks the client to report what he or she sees in each card. The psychologist writes down the client's description of each card and then asks for the aspects of each card that influenced the responses. Finally, the psychologist may code the responses on the basis of characteristics such as the part of the card used (for example, whole blot or small details), the use of color, and the content of responses (for example, humans or sex). Users of the Rorschach believe that these aspects of the responses yield information about an individual's personality. For example, heavy reliance on color might indicate impulsive behavior, and depressed people may use few, if any, colors in their responses.

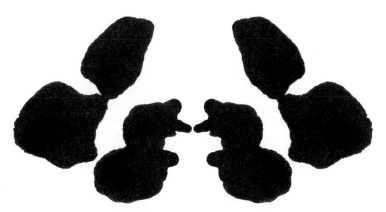

FIGURE 11-2 A card similar to those presented in the Rorschach inkblot test. Projective tests use unstructured or ambiguous stimuli (without obvious meaning or interpretation) like this inkblot, which require test takers to make sense of stimuli that do not have any specific meaning.

Limitations of Projective Tests. Administering and interpreting projective tests requires extensive training. The degree of subjective judgment required to interpret them has led some psychologists to conclude that projective tests do not meet the same objective standards as many self-report inventories (Groth-Marnat, 1990). To address these concerns, more recent approaches to the interpretation of the Rorschach place greater emphasis on the quantification of Rorschach responses and comparisons to norms describing the responses (Exner, 1986, 1991). Although greater quantification and standardization of testing conditions are steps forward, critics still have concerns about validity and reliability (Wood, Nezworski, & Stejskal, 1996) and the possibility that the behavior of the examiner may influence the client's responses.

The Barnum Effect. The assortment of methods used to analyze personality is fascinating. Consider Karin's computer-generated personality analysis (Table 11-2). She believed that a computer had analyzed her answers to the GPA to produce an analysis just for her. She was not aware, however, that the items on the GPA are not typical of self-report inventories; they were selected by researchers who wanted to determine if people would accept general personality feedback they thought was based on unusual items. Thus her responses to those items revealed little about her personality.

The computer-generated personality description that Karin received has much in common with those produced by several nonscientific methods of analyzing personality, such as handwriting analyses and horoscopes (Glick, Gottesman, & Jolton, 1989; McKelvie, 1990). Horoscopes contain statements that are similar to those found in Karin's personality analysis; the statements in Table 11-2 were collected

Fortune-tellers rely on the Barnum effect; they often use favorable descriptions that apply to most people. They frequently phrase their statements as questions in order to elicit additional information from their clients.

TABLE 11-2

Karin's Computer-Generated Personality Analysis

You have a great need for other people to like and admire you. You have a tendency to be critical of yourself. You have a great deal of unused capacity that you have not turned to your advantage. Although you have some personality weaknesses, you are generally able to compensate for them. Your sexual adjustment has presented problems for you. Disciplined and self-controlled outside, you tend to be worrisome and insecure inside. At times you have serious doubts as to whether you have made the right decision or done the right thing. You prefer a certain amount of change and variety and become dissatisfied when hemmed in by restrictions and limitations. You pride yourself as an independent thinker and do not accept others' statements without satisfactory proof. You have found it unwise to be too frank in revealing yourself to others. At times you are extroverted, affable, sociable, while at other times you are introverted, wary, reserved. Some of your aspirations tend to be pretty unrealistic. Security is one of your major goals in life.

Source: Forer, 1949, p. 120.

from an astrology book (Forer, 1949). Although repeated evaluations have demonstrated that astrology has no scientific basis (Crowe, 1990), many people consult their horoscopes every day.

Psychological Detective

Can you provide reasons for people's acceptance of feedback from sources such as horoscopes or the GPA? Why would the statements in Table 11-2 lead an individual to report that his or her personality had been assessed accurately? Think about this question, and write down your answers before reading further.

In study after study, most people rate the personality statements in Table 11-2 as "good" or "excellent" descriptions of themselves (Forer, 1949; Snyder & Larson, 1972). Why? Let's examine the first statement in the personality analysis: "You have a great need for other people to like and admire you." Does this statement describe any of your friends? How many? Read the other statements and ask yourself the same questions. How many friends does each statement describe? In almost every case, the answer is "quite a few." These statements describe a considerable percentage of the population, and they are quite favorable (Furnham & Schofield, 1987; Glick, Gottesman, & Jolton, 1989). According to Paul Meehl (1956), these personality descriptions have something for everyone. He coined the term **Barnum effect** to describe them (after P. T. Barnum, the showman who said a good circus has a "little something for everybody").

The statements in Karin's personality analysis are similar to those found in analyses offered by fortune-tellers. How do fortune-tellers succeed in providing personality analyses their clients accept? In addition to relying on the Barnum effect, they use a method called *cold reading* to collect information from strangers. Fortune-tellers do not ask for information directly (Hyman, 1989; Randi, 1995) but use clues such as clothing, physical features, speech, gestures, and eye contact.

Other Measures. As we noted at the beginning of this section, there are numerous ways to evaluate personality; self-report inventories and projective techniques are only two of these procedures. Other procedures include direct interviews, often conducted by a trained clinical psychologist, and direct observation of behavior. Developmental psychologists, who believe that childhood experiences are important

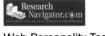

Web Personality Tests

barnum effect
The tendency to accept generalized personality descriptions as accurate descriptions of oneself

One reason we believe that personality is stable is that we observe stability in a variety of characteristics, including physical appearance, over time. These two pictures show the same people.

in shaping personality, frequently use direct observations. For example, they may want to observe the interactions of children at a childcare center or family interactions.

Is Behavior Consistent?

As we have seen, one of the elements of the definition of personality is consistency in behavior. Are you consistent from day to day? Is the behavior of your family members and friends consistent from day to day? Consider these observations of some well-known people and imagine how psychologists interested in personality would evaluate such information.

> Albert Einstein was brilliantly intelligent and humorous. John F. Kennedy was ambitious and charming. Frank Sinatra was aggressive and emotional. Or so their biographers tell us. But perhaps they are wrong. Perhaps Einstein, Sinatra, Kennedy, you, and me [sic] and your cousin Frederick are equally intelligent, humorous, aggressive, emotional, ambitious, and moralistic. Perhaps personality traits . . . are mere fictions. (Kenrick & Funder, 1991, p. 150)

Challenges to the Idea of Consistency. Walter Mischel had the job of predicting how successful Peace Corps volunteers would be. After analyzing reports, Mischel (1968) concluded that "highly generalized behavioral consistencies have not been demonstrated" (p. 140). He therefore advised psychologists to turn their attention from the search for traits to the study of *how situations influence behaviors* (Wright & Mischel, 1987). For example, when you are out with your friends, your behavior with them may be quite different from your behavior during a dinner with relatives. An observer might find it hard to believe you are the same person in the two situations. That is Mischel's point: Behavior is a function of situations, not traits.

In Defense of Consistency. Although the idea of consistency of behavior was dealt some devastating blows by Mischel (1968), belief in this idea persisted. Darryl Bem and Andrea Allen (1974) offered several reasons for believing there is consistency in behavior. One reason is that we rely on preconceived notions of how behaviors are related and may jump to conclusions that are consistent with those preconceived notions. For example, if you expect "friendly" people to be "honest," you may conclude that a friendly person is honest even when you have no evidence to support such a conclusion.

Some characteristics, such as intelligence, emotional reactions, and physical appearance, are consistent over time. For example, Carroll Izard and colleagues (1993) found that tendencies to exhibit certain emotional reactions (for example, anger or enjoyment) are stable across several years. What's more, after early childhood, scores on intelligence tests are quite stable into adulthood.

Another reason for the belief in consistency is that your presence may elicit particular behaviors in your friends or relatives. We often see other people in limited circumstances that can restrict the variety of behaviors that are likely to occur. For example, some parents may be shocked to learn that their child is disruptive in school. If a specific behavior is especially mischievous, their response may be, "Our child never does anything like that at home"—and they would be correct.

Although a number of studies have failed to demonstrate consistency of behavior across situations, there may be limitations in the methods used to study consistency (Bem & Allen, 1974; Small, Zeldin, & Savin-Williams, 1983). One problem can be illustrated by the following situation. Suppose your instructor decides that final grades for a course will be based on a single multiple-choice item. What do you think of this idea? We can hear the moans and groans. Let's examine the reasons for your objections. Your logic probably goes like this: "One multiple-choice item is not a good indicator of how much I have learned. What if I was sick the day the material in that item was covered in class? What if the item covers a topic that I found difficult?" Thus you have concluded that a single multiple-choice item is not a good indicator of your knowledge of the course material. Following the same logic, Lewis Goldberg (1992) notes that arguments against the consistency of behaviors are often based on the false premise that "scientists in the field of personality seek to predict a single response of a particular individual in a completely novel situation" (p. 93).

Psychological Detective

Suppose we have developed a self-report inventory to measure altruism. We could find out how many people volunteered to work for charity last year and then see whether volunteer work was related to scores on our altruism measure. There may be problems with this indicator of altruism, however. How could we provide more convincing evidence that this inventory measured altruism? Does volunteering to work for charity provide evidence of the consistency of altruism over time? Give these questions some thought, and write down your answer before reading further.

We begin by separating a large group of individuals into two smaller groups on the basis of their altruism scores (a group of high scorers and a group of low scorers). When we ask the individuals in each group if they volunteered to help a charity last year, we find few differences between the two groups. We can also ask, however, how many of them donated money to the poor, how many gave clothing to charitable organizations, and how many signed petitions requesting funds to build homeless shelters.

There may be few differences between the two groups of individuals on any one of the behaviors just mentioned. When we look at several behaviors together, however, a pattern emerges. A single behavior is a weak indicator of altruism, just as a single test item is a weak indicator of your knowledge of course material. When the behaviors are added together (like the items on that test), patterns become discernible.

Because a single example of any behavior is a weak indicator, Seymour Epstein (1979, 1980) suggests that researchers use the method of *aggregation*, in which they collect evidence of several behaviors, as we did in the example of altruism. The concept of aggregation is not new (Zuckerman, 1991). For example, psychologists who study operant conditioning do not study a single bar-press in a Skinner box; instead they examine cumulative curves that are aggregations of a series of behaviors over time (see Chapter 5). Similarly, when we aggregate behaviors across situations, we can determine whether those behaviors are consistent over time.

Evidence of Consistency Based on Multiple Measures.   Epstein (1983) notes that both views in this debate believe they are correct and that consequently the other side must be wrong. Each side offers evidence to support its position, but a paradox exists here. Consider the following statements:

1. Behavior is specific to a situation.
2. People exhibit broad, stable tendencies to respond in certain ways across situations.

Behavior depends on the situation, but there are consistent behavioral tendencies across situations. Can we resolve this paradox? The situation also influences the likelihood that a person will exhibit a specific behavior. For example, because there are clear norms for acceptable behavior at a funeral, few people laugh at those events. If we were interested in studying sense of humor and limited our observations to funerals, we might conclude that people with a high sense of humor were inconsistent. We need, however, to acknowledge the role of the situation. If we expanded our observations to other situations, it is likely that a pattern of consistency would emerge.

Stephen Small and his colleagues (1983) studied the behaviors of altruism and dominance in adolescents on a wilderness travel program. Counselors made observations of the campers' behaviors related to altruism (such as sharing possessions) and dominance (such as giving orders). A high degree of consistency was found for both altruistic and dominance behaviors when the behaviors were aggregated. The researchers concluded that revising the methods used by personality researchers can provide evidence in support of personality consistency. This debate has revealed the existence of important regularities in individual behavior (Kenrick & Funder, 1990). At the same time, researchers have come to realize that situations exert important influences on behavior.

Having discussed the various techniques used to analyze or measure personality and whether personality is consistent, we now turn our attention to the various theoretical views of personality that psychologists have developed.

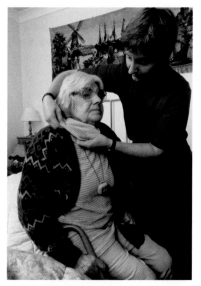

Psychologists are interested in the kind of helping behavior illustrated in this photograph. They avoid, however, relying on only one incident as an indicator of an individual's level of altruism.

TRAIT APPROACHES

We begin this section with a hands-on activity. Complete the following survey. We will have more to say about the "Big Five" shortly.

Hands On

The "Big Five" Test

Using the numbers on the scale from 1 to 5, indicate how true each of the following terms is in describing you.

1 = Not at all true of me: I am never this way.

2 = Mostly not true of me: I am rarely this way.

3 = Neither true nor untrue of me, or I can't decide.

4 = Somewhat true of me: I am sometimes this way.

5 = Very true of me: I am very often this way.

trait
A summary term that describes the tendency to behave, feel, and think in ways that are consistent across different situations

1. _____ imaginative
2. _____ organized
3. _____ talkative
4. _____ sympathetic
5. _____ tense
6. _____ intelligent
7. _____ thorough
8. _____ assertive
9. _____ kind
10. _____ anxious
11. _____ original
12. _____ efficient
13. _____ active
14. _____ soft-hearted
15. _____ nervous
16. _____ insightful
17. _____ responsible
18. _____ energetic
19. _____ warm
20. _____ worrying
21. _____ clever
22. _____ practical
23. _____ outgoing
24. _____ generous
25. _____ self-pitying

Instructions for scoring your answers to the "Big Five" Test can be found at the end of the chapter.

Source: Brody & Ehrlichman, 1998.

We begin our discussion of theoretical perspectives on personality with a look at traits. We chose to start with traits because you use them, probably every day, to describe yourself as well as your friends and relatives. Also, from a historical perspective the concept of traits "may be as old as human language itself" (Matthews & Deary, 1998, p. 3). What's more, most approaches to personality make use of the concept of traits; where they differ is primarily in how they explain the development of individual differences. Indeed, trait theory has become very popular (Winter et al., 1998).

When we asked you to describe a friend or relative, you probably used a number of words expressive of traits, such as *shy* or *friendly*, in your description. **Traits** are summary terms that describe tendencies to respond in particular ways that account for differences among people.

Some people exhibit high levels of a given trait; others exhibit low levels of the same trait. Most people, however, exhibit a moderate degree of a given trait, which is distributed according to the normal curve (see Chapter 8). Keep in mind that Barnum-type statements do not provide information about how much of a trait is exhibited (review the statements in Table 11-2). By contrast, most self-report inventories designed to measure a trait provide norms that allow us to determine the level of the trait that was assessed.

Psychologist Gordon Allport (1897–1967) set out to compose a list of traits, which he described as the building blocks of personality (1961). To do this he examined everyday language because it seems likely we would encode the most important individual differences in human transactions as single terms in our language (John, 1990; McCrae & John, 1992). Trait words are pervasive in our language; we use them to describe people and read them in advertisements that extol the virtues of various products (*dependable, exciting*).

After eliminating words that referred to temporary moods (*frantic*), social evaluations (*worthy*), or physical attributes (*lean*), Allport found that 4,500 words remained (Allport & Odbert, 1936). The key question raised by these results is, Which trait terms are the most important? The large number of terms seemed to be more than were needed to describe a person's personality.

Traits are summary terms that describe tendencies to respond in particular ways that account for differences among people. What traits do you associate with this person?

Factors of Personality: Raymond B. Cattell

For some time, personality psychologists have been searching for a table of the key personality traits. Raymond B. Cattell (1990) decided that he would identify and measure

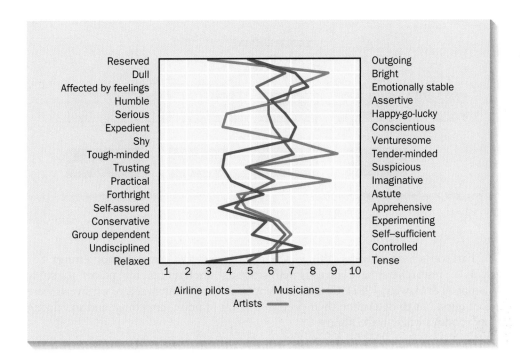

FIGURE 11-3 16PF profiles of airline pilots, artists, and musicians.

Source: Cattell, Eber, & Tatsuoka, 1970.

the most important traits. Cattell's approach is to administer a wide variety of personality measures to many people and to use the results to identify the key personality traits. Cattell used data from a number of sources, including objective tests, records of his participants' lives (for example, school and work records), and observations of their behaviors when placed in contrived situations. He then used a computer program to correlate the data. These correlations indicated that certain bits of information tended to cluster together. Cattell called these clusters *surface traits* because they were easy to identify from the correlations. What's more, Cattell assumed that these surface traits were in turn directed by a smaller number of traits called *source traits*.

Cattell's *Sixteen Personality Factors Questionnaire* (16PF) (Cattell, Eber, & Tatsuoka, 1970) provides an assessment of the levels of a person's source traits (see Figure 11-3); the latest version of this questionnaire is the 16PF5 (Conn & Rieke, 1994). According to Cattell, the same 16 traits can be used to describe each of us; the levels of those traits, however, vary from person to person, which accounts for our distinctiveness as individuals.

Categorization of Traits: Hans Eysenck

Psychologist Hans Eysenck was always interested in how traits are organized. He concluded that one way to deal with the large number of traits is to organize them first into narrowly defined categories, which are in turn placed into broader categories (Eysenck & Eysenck, 1985; see Figure 11-4).

At the broadest level of abstraction, Eysenck said, we can describe personality as consisting of three basic traits: extraversion, neuroticism, and psychoticism. Neuroticism, or emotional instability, consists of traits such as anxiety, guilt feelings, low self-esteem, and shyness. Psychoticism consists of traits such as aggressiveness, impulsivity, and a lack of empathy. We will focus our attention on the trait of extraversion, which can be represented as a continuum from extreme extravert to extreme introvert. People we label as *extraverts* are more outgoing than *introverts*, who are oriented toward internal stimuli such as their own thoughts and moods. Because this trait is a continuum, however, many people have scores that would put them in the middle of the distribution.

FIGURE 11-4 Eysenck's research focused on three major traits. A trait such as extraversion encompasses several other traits, as illustrated here.

Source: Eysenck & Eysenck, 1985.

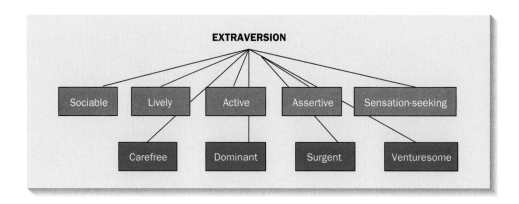

Extraverts and introverts differ in a number of ways and in a variety of settings. For example, researchers have investigated students' preferences for places to study (Campbell & Hawley, 1982). College students identified as introverts or extraverts were asked questions to determine their preferred levels of noise, crowding, and socializing opportunities while in the library.

Psychological Detective

Take a moment to think about what conditions extraverts and introverts would prefer. Write down some possibilities and see how close your answers are.

Introverts reported that they studied in quiet areas and used individual study carrels, which minimize noise and opportunities for socializing. Extraverts chose areas that provided opportunities for socializing as well as auditory and visual stimulation, such as large reading areas with sofas and lounge chairs.

The "Big Five" Traits

Despite the work of Cattell and Eysenck, there is a growing consensus that personality traits can be reduced to five basic ones, although there is some disagreement about the precise labels for the five (Goldberg, 1995). The most common names for the "Big Five" are (1) *openness to experience*, (2) *conscientiousness*, (3) *extraversion*, (4) *agreeableness*, and (5) *neuroticism* (Costa & McCrae, 1992a; Goldberg, 1995; McCrae & John, 1992). Table 11-3 lists and describes these five traits. Note that the names of the Big Five form the acronym OCEAN. Although not all psychologists are enamored with the Big Five approach, many other psychologists (for example, Fleeson & Baltes, 1998; Hall, Lindzey, & Campbell, 1998; Loehlin, McCrae, Costa, & John, 1998) consider it one of the most important developments in recent personality research.

There are several reasons for concluding that these five traits represent basic dimensions of personality (Costa & McCrae, 1992c). These traits appear when peers provided ratings of Air Force officers, fraternity brothers, Peace Corps trainees, and spouses (McRae & Costa, 1987). They also appear in studies of individuals of different ages, in both men and women, in different races, in different language groups, and across cultures (Benet-Martínez & John, 1998; Paunonen et al., 1992; Trull & Geary, 1997). On the other hand, not all researchers agree on the specific names for the Big Five traits, and there is some disagreement on the meaning of the traits, especially the one called *openness to experience* (Matthews & Deary, 1998).

Advances in the technology of genetics and neuroscience have led to an increase in the ability to detect genetic and neurological bases of complex behavior (Turkheimer,

TABLE 11-3

Names and Descriptions of the "Big Five" Traits

Major Trait	Description of Personality
Extraversion	People who score high are described as talkative and expressive as indicated by facial expressions and gestures. They are also assertive, gregarious, highly active, and have good skills in using humor. They like excitement and stimulation and tend to be energetic, optimistic, and upbeat. People with low scores tend to be described as solitary, quiet, having low energy, and reserved.
Agreeableness	People who score high are described as fundamentally altruistic. They are likely to yield in interactions with others. Others view them as sympathetic, straightforward, warm, and considerate. People who score low are described as antagonistic, unkind, suspicious, and unsympathetic.
Conscientiousness	People who score high are described as well organized, dependable, competent, and responsible. They are likely to get things done, able to delay gratification, exhibit highly ethical behavior, and have a high level of aspiration. People who score low are described as disorganized, careless, inefficient, and undependable.
Neuroticism	People who score high are described as self-defeating, basically anxious, and concerned about personal adequacy. They are subject to mood fluctuations and negative emotions, such as anger, guilt, and disgust. They are also prone to irrational ideas, are not always able to control impulses, and are less effective than others at coping with stress. People who score low are described as unemotional, calm, even-tempered, self-satisfied, and comfortable with themselves.
Openness to Experience	People who score high exhibit a preference for new and unfamiliar experiences reflected in appreciation of knowledge, various art forms, and nontraditional values as opposed to tradition and the status quo. They are considered highly introspective, attentive to inner feelings and fantasies, intellectual, and creative. People who score low are described as down-to-earth, conventional, preferring routine, and not intellectually oriented.

Sources: Adapted from Formy-Duval et al., 1995; McCrae & John, 1992; Costa & McCrae, 1992b; Matthews & Deary, 1998.

1998). This ability, combined with the interest in the Big Five, has led to the exploration of trait heritabilities. According to Loehlin et al. (1998), recent assessments of the heritability of the Big Five have concluded that all five traits are moderately and equally heritable. Using three alternative models of genetic and environmental influences, Loehlin et al. found that "51% to 58% of individual difference variation among the Big Five dimensions is genetic in origin" (p. 447). Other researchers, such as Turkheimer (1998) caution that discovering heritability is not necessarily a guarantee of finding specific genetic causes. At this point in time scientists should use such discoveries as useful cues for continued research.

One aspect of research on the five major traits, namely an investigation of their stability, is especially relevant to the definition of personality. Do the levels of these traits in an individual change over time, or do they remain similar through the adult years?

STUDY TIP

Make a think link, or mind map, depicting the "Big Five" traits of personality. Develop five icons, or pictures, to associate with the five traits; incorporate those icons into your think link.

Scores on a self-report inventory and personality ratings completed by spouses tended to remain stable into adulthood (Costa & McCrae, 1988). In fact, a growing body of research suggests that personality traits have considerable long-term stability (McCrae & Costa, 1990). Another area of research has involved the use of the Big Five traits in personnel selection.

The Big Five and Job Performance. The Big Five factors (traits) have been around for some time now, so it is not surprising that they have been used in research on personnel selection. The possibility that personality measures are related to job performance and might, therefore, be useful in personnel selection motivates this research. But which factors of personality are related to job performance? Some of the past research involving the Big Five dimensions used measures that were not derived from the Big Five, yet tried to draw conclusions about the Big Five.

Gregory Hurtz and John Donovan (2000) completed an extensive search for research that investigated the relation between measures of the Big Five factors and job or training performance. Their search yielded 26 studies, with most of them describing a number of correlations for each of the Big Five dimensions.

Their results showed that *conscientiousness* had the highest correlation across occupations with job performance criteria ($r = 0.14$), which was low to moderate but stable across studies. In addition, they noted that:

> Emotional Stability [Neuroticism] showed a rather stable influence on performance throughout nearly all of our analyses. It appears that being calm, secure, and well adjusted and low in anxiety has a small but consistent impact on job performance. Agreeableness also gains importance for those jobs that require interpersonal interactions, so that being likeable, cooperative, and good-natured has a small but consistent impact on performance. Finally, being Extraverted appears to influence sales and managerial jobs, and Openness to Experience appears to affect performance in customer service jobs. (p. 876)

Thus it appears that several of the Big Five dimensions of personality are related to job performance. The strongest predictor of job performance across occupations was conscientiousness.

Alternatives to the Big Five

A great deal of attention has focused on the development of the five-factor model of personality (Bower, 1999). However, not everyone views the five factors as capturing the essence of personality. Drew Westen and Jonathan Shedler (1999) are psychotherapists and research psychologists who don't think questionnaire items address the deeper organizing principles of personality. What's more, the use of complex mathematical procedures, such as factor analysis, to identify the supposed key traits rests on the assumption that everyone has the same interpretation when reading the adjectives in such questionnaires. For example, is a disagreeable person someone who is hostile or someone who tends to pry into others' business? According to these psychologists, if we use questionnaires to provide a glimpse of personality, what we get is a description on a selection of traits that are just statistical entities and only skim the personality's surface.

Westen and Shedler believe that clinicians can use their expertise to get at underlying personality dynamics, especially those dynamics of significance in understanding personality disorders. Experienced clinicians listen to clients tell stories about their lives and watch their actual interactions, which provide rich sources of information for assessing personality.

Their method relies on clinical judgment: Clinicians rate personality-related statements as describing a patient on a scale of 0 to 7. Among the sample statements are

TABLE 11-4

Dimensions of Personality Produced by Clinical Judgment and Clinical Sorting

Dimension	Description
Psychological health	Ability to love others, find meaning in life, and gain personal insights
Psychopathy	Lack of remorse, presence of impulsiveness, and tendency to abuse drugs
Hostility	Deep-seated ill-will
Narcissism	Self-importance, grandiose assumptions about oneself, and tendency to treat others as an audience to provide admiration
Emotional dysregulation	Intense and uncontrolled emotional reactions
Dysphoria	Depression, shame, humiliation, and lack of any pleasurable experiences
Schizoid orientation	Constricted emotions, inability to understand abstract concepts such as metaphors, and few or no friends
Obsessionality	Absorption in details, stinginess, and fear of dirt and contamination
Thought disorder	Believing that one has magical powers over others or can directly read their minds, for example
Oedipal conflict	Adult pursuit of romantic partners who are already involved with others, inappropriate seductiveness, and intense sexual jealousy
Dissociated consciousness	Fragmenting of thought and perception often related to past sexual abuse
Sexual conflict	Anxieties and fears regarding sexual intimacy

Source: Westen and Shedler, 1999.

"tends to feel empty or bored" or "tries to manipulate others' emotions to get what he/she wants." Then they use a statistical sorting technique, which has identified the dimensions of personality. These proposed dimensions are shown in Table 11-4. Note that these dimensions involve characteristics not tapped by the Big Five factors, and they have direct relevance to understanding personality disorders. Westen and Shedler believe that using their assessment system will help psychotherapists develop better treatment plans for clients (especially clients with personality disorders) in the future.

REVIEW SUMMARY

1. Psychologists define **personality** as a stable pattern of thinking, feeling, and behaving that distinguishes one person from another. Two important components of this definition are distinctiveness and relative consistency.

2. Among the widely used **self-report inventories** of personality are the Minnesota Multiphasic Personality Inventory (MMPI) and the California Psychological Inventory (CPI). The MMPI was designed to help diagnose psychological disorders; the CPI is used to assess personality in the normal population.

3. **Projective tests** use ambiguous stimuli and require a great deal of interpretation by the test administrator. The most frequently used projective test is the Rorschach inkblot test.

4. The **Barnum effect** is the acceptance of generalized personality descriptions; it results from the use of favorable personality descriptions that apply to many people.

5. Critics of the concept of consistency in behavior argue that behavior is controlled by situations. In defense of the idea of

consistency, some researchers note that there are some problems with the methods used and the assumptions made in this research. Seymour Epstein proposes that both sides of the consistency issue are correct: Situations control behavior in a given instance, and broad consistencies do exist. Consistencies become visible when we add behaviors together, an approach termed aggregation.

6. Traits are summary terms that describe tendencies to act and interact in particular ways that are consistent across situations. Gordon Allport developed a list of trait terms.

7. Raymond Cattell proposed 16 source traits to describe personality and make predictions of future behaviors.

8. Hans Eysenck proposed the existence of three major traits. Extraversion has been associated with a number of differences in everyday behavior.

9. Current research offers a model of five major traits that seem to be relatively stable across the life span and across cultures.

✓ CHECK YOUR PROGRESS

1. Which psychological test might be used in each of the following circumstances?

  a. A hospital needs to determine the most likely diagnosis of mental patients.

  b. A company wants to use a self-report inventory to select new salespeople.

  c. A psychologist is interested in assessing a person's unconscious thought processes but has no direct access to those processes.

2. What term do psychologists use to describe a stable pattern of thinking, feeling, and behaving that distinguishes one person from another?

  a. ego

  b. psyche

  c. self-image

  d. personality

3. Fortune-tellers use cues about people such as their clothing, speech, and gestures to persuade clients that they know a great deal about them. This process is known as

  a. cold reading.

  b. aggregation.

  c. standardization.

  d. projective testing.

4. Which assessment technique requires individuals to respond to unstructured or ambiguous stimuli?

  a. dynamic

  b. objective

  c. projective

  d. predictive

5. Which of the following Big Five traits has been shown to be related to measures of job performance for several occupations?

  a. neuroticism

  b. agreeableness

  c. conscientiousness

  d. openness to experience

6. Personality descriptions that have something for everyone fit the

  a. Barnum effect.

  b. base-rate fallacy.

  c. self-fulfilling prophesy.

  d. social-desirability bias.

ANSWERS: 1. a. MMPI **b.** CPI **c.** Rorschach inkblot test or TAT **2.** d **3.** a **4.** c **5.** c **6.** a

BIOLOGICAL FACTORS IN PERSONALITY

The identical twins who live down the street—Kelly and Sharin—often dress alike. Family members, neighbors, and friends are amazed at how similar they are in their everyday behaviors. They both are on the high school basketball team, love to swim, and play in the school orchestra. Both sisters are outgoing and make friends easily. You wonder whether their similarities are due to the way they were raised ("nurture") or to hereditary influences ("nature"). *To what extent are our personalities influenced by nurture (factors in our environment) or nature (hereditary factors)?*

There is little doubt that people differ in the personality traits they exhibit. But why? Are differences a result of early child-rearing experiences? Does heredity influence differences in personality? If heredity plays a role in personality traits, can those traits change over time?

Early Biological Approaches

As you can see from the Myth or Science feature below, the idea that physical and biological factors hold a key to personality has a long history. From the perspective of modern science, however, some of the earliest attempts to relate personality to biological factors appear primitive. The research tools were too crude and the hypotheses too broad; nevertheless, those efforts started a search that continues to this day.

Myth or Science

Trephining (see Chapter 13), involves the opening of a hole in the skull, leaving the membranes surrounding the brain intact (Feilding, 1978). Trepanation, which involves operating on the skull, but not on the brain, is one of the oldest medical procedures (Kabillo, 1998). Stone-age cave paintings suggest that primitive people used trepanation as a cure for seizures caused by epilepsy (McGrew, 1985) and as a treatment for mental disorders.

Trepanation did not cease as civilization progressed. It still has some advocates today. The main concept of the modern trepanation movement lies in the word *brainbloodvolume* (the amount of blood supplied to the brain; Kabillo, 1998). Trepanation supposedly allows greater flow of blood in the capillaries of the brain. The increased amount of blood in the capillaries results in the brain cells having a larger source of energy and, therefore, they function at a higher level accelerating brain metabolism and expanding consciousness. In short, trepanation may have a pronounced effect on a person's personality.

Most researchers and physicians do not have a high opinion of the supposed benefits of trepanation. Trepanation is illegal in the United States and Europe. Among the risks it produces are blood clots, brain injuries, and infections leading to meningitis or death (Colton, 1998). Obviously, a great deal more research is needed before we can distinguish between myth and science with regard to trepanation. You can learn more about it, admittedly from the proponents' point of view, at http://www.trepan.com.

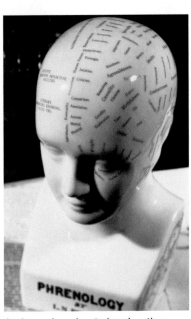

A phrenology bust showing the numerous brain areas that the phrenologists thought they had identified by studying the bumps on the head.

Humors and Bumps. Hippocrates (460–377 B.C.E.), a Greek philosopher and physician, believed the human body contained four bodily "humors" or fluids: black bile, blood, phlegm, and yellow bile. The humor that predominated in a person was believed to determine that person's characteristics. For example, a predominance of black bile was thought to make a person depressed. Although we now know the body is not filled with humors, interest in the role of biological factors in personality has continued.

In the 1800s, phrenologists (*phrenology* was an attempt to study a person by analyzing bumps and indentations on the skull, see Chapter 2) attempted to link personality with features of the brain. Franz Joseph Gall (1758–1828) compared the brain to a muscle and tried to locate various characteristics by looking for well-developed parts of the brain. Bumps on the skull might signify the development of underlying brain tissue, which in turn should reflect higher levels of characteristics such as benevolence. Eventually it became clear that any bumps on the skull had no connection to personal characteristics, and interest in phrenology faded. Still, phrenology played an important role in encouraging the study of brain functions.

Body Types.   William Sheldon (1899–1977), a psychologist with medical training, suggested that the shape of one's body determines one's personality (Sheldon & Stevens, 1942; Sheldon, Stevens, & Tucker, 1940). He developed a scheme consisting of three body types: *Endomorphs* are round, *mesomorphs* are rectangular, and *ectomorphs* are thin. Sheldon also collected information about the personalities of people representing each of the body types and reported high correlations between body type and personality characteristics. According to Sheldon, endomorphs love comfort and are outgoing, mesomorphs are assertive and energetic, and ectomorphs are restrained and lonely. When other researchers could not replicate these correlations, they suspected that preconceptions about the relationship of body type to personality (for example, the stereotype of fat people as outgoing) had influenced Sheldon's results.

Although there is little convincing evidence that body type is related to personality, researchers are investigating the role of other biological factors in personality. Among those factors is the person's general level of neural arousal.

Drag-race champion Eddie Hill was the first person to go 1/4-mile from a standing start in less than 5 seconds. Drag racing is a high-risk occupation that probably attracts people with high scores on the Sensation-Seeking Scale.

Sensation Seeking.   Organisms appear to seek an optimal level of arousal or stimulation that varies by individual. Stimulation that is too far above or below that level is perceived as unpleasant. Is it possible to measure a person's need for stimulation? Psychologist Marvin Zuckerman has developed a self-report inventory to measure what he calls *sensation seeking* (see Chapter 6), defined as a general tendency to seek stimulation from a variety of sources. Sensation seeking is related to the broad trait of extraversion (review Figure 11-4) as well as to conscientiousness (Zuckerman, 1994).

Sensation seeking can be divided into several related components. *Disinhibition* is the tendency to seek sensation through social activities such as parties; *thrill seeking* is the desire to engage in physically risky activities; *experience seeking* is the tendency to seek novel experiences through the mind and the senses; and *boredom susceptibility* is an intolerance for repetitive experience.

Hands On

Sensation Seeking Scale

You will be able to estimate where your score falls on the Sensation Seeking Scale by completing the following items. The full scale consists of 40 items; we have reproduced 13 of them here so that you can get a feel for the types of items used to measure sensation seeking.

The Sensation Seeking Scale was designed to measure differences among individuals seeking stimulation from a variety of sources. For each of the following items, select the alternative that best indicates your preference. Then check your choices against the scoring key at the end of the chapter.

1. a. I would like a job that requires a lot of travel.
   b. I would prefer a job in one location.
2. a. I am invigorated by a brisk, cold day.
   b. I can't wait to get indoors on a cold day.
3. a. I get bored seeing the same old faces.
   b. I like the comfortable familiarity of everyday friends.
4. a. I would prefer living in an ideal society in which everyone is safe, secure, and happy.
   b. I would have preferred living in the unsettled days of our history.
5. a. I sometimes like to do things that are a little frightening.
   b. A sensible person avoids activities that are dangerous.

6. a. I would not like to be hypnotized.
   b. I would like to have the experience of being hypnotized.

7. a. The most important goal in life is to live it to the fullest and experience as much as possible.
   b. The most important goal in life is to find peace and happiness.

8. a. I would like to try parachute-jumping.
   b. I would never want to try jumping out of a plane, with or without a parachute.

9. a. I enter cold water gradually, giving myself time to get used to it.
   b. I like to dive or jump right into the ocean or a cold pool.

10. a. When I go on vacation, I prefer the comfort of a good room and bed.
    b. When I go on a vacation, I prefer the change of camping out.

11. a. I prefer people who are emotionally expressive even if they are a bit unstable.
    b. I prefer people who are calm and even-tempered.

12. a. A good painting should shock or jolt the senses.
    b. A good painting should give one a feeling of peace and security.

13. a. People who ride motorcycles must have some kind of unconscious need to hurt themselves.
    b. I would like to drive or ride a motorcycle.

Source: Zuckerman, 1994.

STUDY TIP

Take the "Big Five" test on pp. 467–468 and the "Sensation Seeking Scale" test on pp. 476–477. Write a paragraph describing what you have learned about yourself, using the terminology to which you have been introduced in this chapter.

Research on sensation seeking reveals that high sensation seekers enjoy spicy, sour, and crunchy foods more than low sensation seekers. This preference is probably due to the varied experiences such foods can provide. High sensation seekers tend to use more drugs and alcohol than low sensation seekers (Simon et al., 1994; Stacy, Newcomb, & Bentler, 1991). Predictably, people in certain high-risk occupations—such as firefighters, race-car drivers, riot-squad police officers, and emergency-room nurses—tend to score rather high on this scale. Sports and recreation reveal similar expected differences: Scores of skydivers soar above those of golfers and aerobics participants (Jack & Ronan, 1998; Wagner & Houlihan, 1994).

Biological differences may be at the root of differences in behavior related to sensation seeking, and these difference may have a genetic basis (Fulker, Eysenck, & Zuckerman, 1980; Tellegen et al., 1988). The enzyme MAO breaks down the neurotransmitter norepinephrine (see Chapter 2). Drugs that inhibit MAO increase levels of norepinephrine and cause individuals to be euphoric, impulsive, and aggressive. A negative correlation between MAO levels and sensation-seeking behavior (Zuckerman, Buchsbaum, & Murphy, 1980; Zuckerman, 1987) indicates that low levels of MAO (and hence high levels of norepinephrine) are associated with high sensation-seeking scores. For example, gamblers who are well known for their impulsiveness and risk taking exhibit low levels of MAO (Carrasco et al., 1994). Lest we forget, a correlation between a biological variable and a personality variable does not prove causation; nevertheless, the findings are intriguing.

A growing body of research points to the importance of biological factors in several personality characteristics. Is it possible that some of these personality characteristics are inherited? The study of twins can shed light on questions concerning the heritability of personality characteristics.

Twin Studies

One day in the 1980s, Oskar Stohr and Jack Yufe arrived in Minneapolis to participate in a study of identical twins reared apart. The twins had been separated shortly after birth, about 40 years earlier. Oskar was raised in Germany as a Nazi and a Catholic;

The twins shown here are among those studied at the University of Minnesota. Many of those twins reported remarkable similarities across a range of experiences and behaviors.

Jack was reared by his Jewish father in Trinidad. The two men proved to have a great deal in common. Consider the following:

They both had mustaches.

Both wore wire-rimmed glasses.

They stored rubber bands on their wrists.

They read magazines from back to front.

They dipped buttered toast into their coffee.

Jim Springer and Jim Lewis had been adopted into separate working-class Ohio families in infancy. While in school, they both liked math but not spelling. Both had law enforcement training and worked part time as deputy sheriffs. They both vacationed in Florida, drove Chevrolets, and had dogs named Toy. Both had married and divorced women named Linda; their second marriages were to women named Betty. Both of them chew their fingernails and suffer late-afternoon headaches (Holden, 1980, 1987a).

These two stories depict remarkable similarities in twins who were separated at birth. Since 1979, the University of Minnesota Study of Twins Reared Apart has been recruiting twin pairs like those just described. Friends, relatives, or the twins themselves bring separated twin pairs to the attention of the researchers. Almost 1,000 twin pairs have agreed to participate in the research (Mann, 1994); most of them complete many hours of medical and psychological assessments.

Psychological Detective

How can we explain the similarities in the behavior of twins who were separated early in life? Do these similarities convince you that they are due to inherited factors? What other evidence could be gathered from these twins that would help us understand genetic influences on personality? Give these questions some thought, and write down your answers before reading further.

The stories of Oskar and Jack and the Jim twins are dramatic, but we should ask whether the remarkable similarities might be coincidences. The participants had many opportunities during the lengthy testing they underwent to discover similarities in their

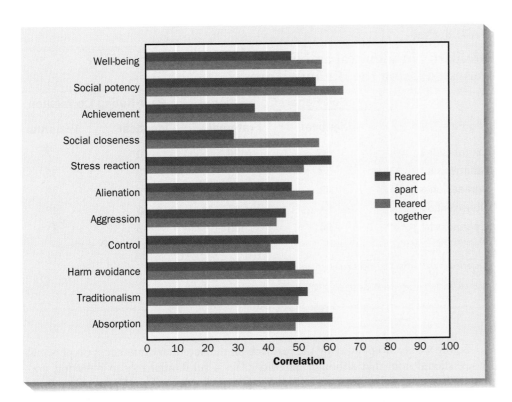

FIGURE 11-5 Correlations of personality characteristics for identical twins reared apart and identical twins reared together. The small differences suggest that environmental factors play a small role in determining these personality characteristics.

Source: Tellegen et al., 1988.

11.1

behaviors. Is there other evidence of similar personalities in identical twins who were separated early in life that cannot be explained as a series of coincidences?

Recall from Chapter 9 that fraternal twins are no more similar to each other than you are to your brother or sister; in contrast, identical twins have the same genes. Because identical twins share the same genes, we would expect their personalities to be similar. A problem often arises, however, in conducting research on twins: Identical twins may be treated more similarly than fraternal twins. Thus we cannot be sure whether similarities between identical twins are due to their identical heredity or to the similarity of their environments. The study of twins who were separated early in life allows researchers to isolate the effects of nature (heredity) from those of nurture (environment).

The University of Minnesota research team reported the results of a study of 44 pairs of identical twins who were separated early in life (Tellegen et al., 1988). The twins completed the Multidimensional Personality Questionnaire, a self-report inventory that yields 11 scales. As you can see from Figure 11-5, the difference between the correlations for identical twins reared apart and for those reared together are very small. The correlations are similar whether the identical twins were reared apart or together.

Let's turn to research focused on possible genetic influences on the Big Five traits we discussed earlier. Almost 1,000 twins took part in a study conducted in Germany and Poland. Each twin's personality was assessed by two different raters using the Big Five traits. A correlation of .63 between the raters demonstrated strong agreement in the assessments of the personalities by peers. The averaged peer ratings correlated .55 with the twins' self-report ratings. The correlations across identical twins were consistently higher than the correlations for fraternal twins, suggesting a genetic influence on personality (see Table 11-5). The researchers concluded that personality measured either by self-ratings or peer ratings shows a genetic influence, with no evidence for a shared environmental influence (Angleitner, Riemann, & Strelau, 1995). Similar results were obtained in a study of twins in Canada and Germany, which the researchers interpreted as support for genetic influences in personality traits across cultures (Jang et al., 1998).

TABLE 11-5

Similarity in Identical and Fraternal Twins in Personality Assessed Using the Big Five Traits

Big Five Trait	Self-Report Correlation		Peer-Rating Correlation	
	Identical	Fraternal	Identical	Fraternal
Extraversion	.56	.28	.40	.17
Neuroticism	.53	.13	.43	.03
Agreeableness	.42	.19	.32	.18
Conscientiousness	.54	.18	.43	.18
Openness to experience*	.54	.35	.48	.31

*Referred to as "Culture" by these researchers.

Source: Angleitner, Riemann, & Strelau, 1997.

Before we are swept away by the research on the hereditary influences on personality, we should note that although heredity plays a substantial role in behavior, nongenetic factors are also important (Plomin, Owen, & McGuffin, 1994). Although the size of the genetic effect—estimated by what is called *heritability* (see Chapter 8)—can be 51–58%, most cases are between 20 and 50%. Therefore differences among people in most personality characteristics are due at least as much to environmental factors as to heredity (Plomin, 1990b; Plomin & Rende, 1991). Even in the case of identical twins, about half of the differences in personality traits are not shared and hence are not due to hereditary factors. What's more, researchers have also found that siblings who grow up in the same family can be very different (Dunn & Plomin, 1990).

In trying to explain differences among siblings, researchers focused on differences across families. It now seems that what is important is not the environment shared by siblings but the nonshared environment. That is, each child experiences the environment differently, and these nonshared environmental factors appear to be more important than shared experiences (Plomin, Owen, & McGuffin, 1994; Plomin & Rende, 1991). For example, surveys of parents and children as well as naturalistic observations in the home suggest that parents may not treat each child alike, despite social pressure to do so.

Personality and the Evolutionary Perspective

We have seen, through the twin studies, that a considerable amount of our personality may be determined genetically. The evolutionary perspective would predict that those aspects of our personality that help us adapt to environmental demands are passed along to subsequent generations. However, although it is one thing to *suggest* that personality characteristics might be transmitted genetically, it is a much more demanding task to offer scientifically acceptable evidence. (Remember that determining if a knowledge claim is based on scientific evidence is one of the guidelines for the psychological detective that we discussed in Chapter 1.)

Researchers have generated considerable data in support of the theory of psychologist David Buss (1987, 1989) that evolution has had an impact on the type of people that men and women choose as dates and mates. Specifically, Buss predicts that women will choose men who have good resources (food, shelter, and protection). He indicates that, "In humans, resources can take many forms . . . income, occupational and social status, possessions, networks of alliance, and family background. Personality characteristics such as hard-working, ambitious, energetic, industrious, and persevering also appear to be correlated with achievement potential" (Buss, 1987, p. 340). Buss believes that women will reject dates and sexual overtures from men who do not satisfy most or all of these criteria. What about men? Buss indicates that, "According to this evolutionary argument, males should come to value and view as attractive those physical and behavioral cues in potential mates that correlate with female reproductive capacity" (p. 341).

To understand these differing predictions, remember that perpetuation of a person's genes via his or her offspring is a key underlying principle. Because women produce only a limited number of offspring, it is important that each offspring receive optimal care in order to increase chances of survival; hence, women seek men who have resources. Men, on the other hand, perpetuate their genes by: (1) seeking a number of temporary mates or (2) seeking a single long-term mate. In either case, reproductive ability is the dominant characteristic that men seek and Buss believes that age and health are two important indicators of this characteristic.

In a study that exemplifies the research support for Buss's theory, Driggers and Helms (2000) tested "the role of salary in date selection by men and women" (p. 76). They predicted that willingness to date would increase as salary increased and that salary would be more important to women because it was an indicator of greater resources. Male and female participants in three groups rated opposite-sex pictures in terms of willingness to date (1 = not willing, 7 = extremely willing). Scores were smallest (least willingness to date) in the lowest salary group and increased significantly at the next two salary levels. At the highest salary level, the women showed significantly more willingness to date; salary was indeed more important for them.

Clearly, genetic factors present at birth can have important influences on the development of our personality. Next we turn to a very different approach to understanding personality. Sigmund Freud thought that our early experiences set the stage for personality throughout life; his focus, however, was on how unconscious factors could determine our personality.

REVIEW SUMMARY

1. Efforts to connect personality to biological factors can be traced to Hippocrates' theory of "humors" and later to phrenology.

2. William Sheldon suggested a relationship between body type and personality. Subsequent research demonstrated that his findings were influenced by his preconceptions.

3. Additional support for the belief that biological factors influence personality is found in the negative correlation between sensation-seeking scores and levels of the enzyme MAO.

4. The study of identical twins reared apart allows researchers to identify the effects of heredity independently of the influence of environmental factors. Evidence from such studies indicates that heredity plays a role in a wide range of personality characteristics as evidenced by heritability estimates between 20 and 50%.

5. Recent evidence suggests that nonshared experiences exert a major influence on the personality of siblings.

✓ CHECK YOUR PROGRESS

1. Who was the Greek philosopher who proposed that body fluids influenced personality? What name did he give those fluids?

2. Sheldon believed that personality was related to
   a. body type.
   b. bodily humors.
   c. facial features.
   d. bumps on the skull.

3. Why are identical twins reared apart so important in research designed to determine the influence of nature and nurture on personality?

4. The strongest evidence for a genetic role in personality is found in similar personality characteristics between

   a. identical twins reared apart.
   b. fraternal twins reared apart.
   c. identical twins reared together.
   d. fratenal twins reared together.

5. Researchers find that Ted's body has low levels of the enzyme MAO. Based on this finding, you conclude that Ted is likely to obtain a high score on a test designed to measure

   a. openness.
   b. achievement.
   c. sensation seeking.
   d. emotional stability.

6. What factor has been found to explain both differences in personality among siblings and personality change?

   a. shared heredity
   b. shared environment
   c. nonshared heredity
   d. nonshared environment

THE PSYCHODYNAMIC PERSPECTIVE

One morning, in Sally's philosophy class, the professor referred to the ideas of Sigmund Freud. Later in the day the professor in a literature class used Freud's ideas to explain hidden meanings in a poem about dreams. Then a sociology professor used Freud's ideas to explain aggressive behavior in some members of society. *Why have Freud's ideas been influential in so many disciplines?*

Sigmund Freud (1856–1939), a neurologist, developed both a theory of personality (psychodynamic theory) that emphasized unconscious factors and a therapy (psycho-analytic therapy) for patients exhibiting abnormal behaviors (see Chapter 13). Today almost everyone knows the name Sigmund Freud. Have you ever heard or used the terms *Freudian slip, unconscious,* or *repression?* If you have, you should recognize Freud's impact. As we saw in the case of Sally's classes, Freud's views and theories have found their way into several academic disciplines as well as into everyday speech. One reason for the pervasiveness of Freud's thinking is that he suggested that our behaviors may be determined by irrational forces outside of conscious awareness.

To understand Freud, it is important to understand the times in which he lived. Freud was born to Jewish parents in Austria in 1856 and grew up in Vienna. He lived during the Victorian era, a time notorious for its repressive views of sexuality. The prevailing social norms prohibited the discussion of sex. The time was also marked by extreme anti-Semitism (prejudice against Jews), which blocked Freud from pursuing a career as a scientist. His future looked bleak, and he needed money to get married, so he reluctantly went into private practice as a neurologist.

Most of Freud's patients were women who suffered from hysterical disorders. (As described in Chapter 12, these disorders involve physical symptoms such as blindness or paralysis that have no known physical cause.) Freud proposed that these disorders resulted from psychological conflicts, especially sexual ones. During therapy sessions, his patients related stories of sexual contact with an older male. At first Freud believed that these events had actually occurred, but later he changed his mind and concluded that they were fantasies. He believed his patients could not differentiate their sexual desires from what had actually happened earlier in their lives. Some critics believe Freud had uncovered evidence of sexual abuse of children, which he was either unwilling to report or unable to accept as true (Masson, 1985).

Freud believed that his patients were not consciously aware of these sexual conflicts. If these conflicts were not brought to conscious awareness, they would continue

Sigmund Freud, a neurologist, developed both a theory of personality that emphasized unconscious factors and a therapy for patients exhibiting abnormal behaviors.

to exert an influence in the form of physical and psychological symptoms. To deal with these symptoms and to bring the conflicts to the conscious level, Freud developed a therapeutic approach called *psychoanalysis* or *psychoanalytic therapy* (see Chapter 13).

Basic Concepts

Three concepts form the backbone of Freud's theory: psychic determinism, instincts, and levels of consciousness. Let's look at each of these concepts.

Psychic Determinism.   **Psychic determinism** refers to the influence of the past on the present. Freud believed that much of our behavior, feeling, and thinking is determined by events that occurred earlier in our lives. For example, sexual conflicts occurring in childhood can bring on physical symptoms in adulthood.

Psychological Detective

What does the term *Freudian slip* mean to you? What, if anything, do you think a Freudian slip reveals about a person? Give these questions some thought, and write down your answer before reading further.

A Freudian slip is one example of the concept of psychic determinism. According to Freud, these errors in reading, speaking, or writing reveal something about our "inner" thoughts or "real" intent. Imagine attending an extremely boring party, which drags on for more hours than you can count. After several hours, you decide to leave and typically intend to say something like, "I'm sorry I have to leave now." Your true feelings, however, may be revealed in words such as "I'm glad I have to leave now."

Instincts.   What inner forces might lead to these Freudian slips? Freud believed we are driven by the energy of certain instincts in much the same way that a car is propelled by the energy contained in gasoline. He described two key instincts: *eros* for life-giving and pleasure-producing activities, including sex, and *thanatos* for aggression or destruction.

The Unconscious.   The third major concept in psychodynamic theory is Freud's proposal that there are various levels of consciousness. In Chapter 4 we defined *consciousness* as personal awareness of internal and external events. Freud described three levels of consciousness (see Figure 11-6). The *conscious* level refers to the thoughts, wishes, and emotions you are aware of at this moment. The level just below consciousness is called the *preconscious*; its contents are waiting to be pulled into consciousness like fish from a pond.

The third—and in Freud's theory the most important—level of consciousness (or awareness) is below the preconscious and is called the **unconscious.** The unconscious consists of thoughts, wishes, and feelings that exist beyond our awareness; we can gain access to them only with great effort. The techniques of psychodynamic therapy are designed to gain access to the contents of the unconscious (see Chapter 13). Freud believed that much of our behavior is caused by unconscious forces, that the contents of conscious thought are only a small portion of our inner life.

The Structure of the Mind

According to Freud's comprehensive theory, the mind consists of three separate but interacting elements: the id, the ego, and the superego. (Note he was not describing actual parts of the brain but hypothetical concepts.) This model compares the mind to an

psychic determinism
The psychodynamic assumption that all behaviors result from early childhood experiences, especially conflicts related to sexual instincts

unconscious
Part of the personality that lies outside of awareness yet is believed to be a crucial determinant of behavior

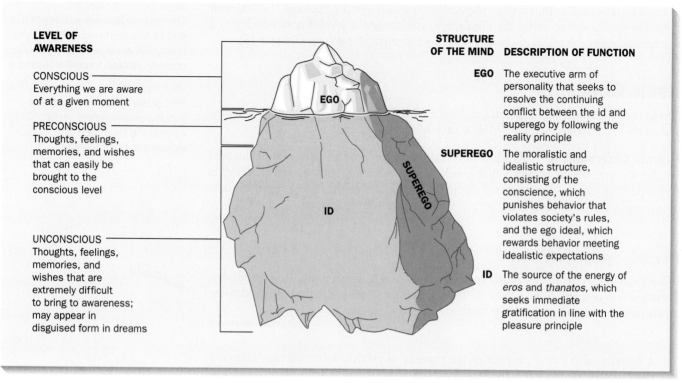

LEVEL OF AWARENESS

CONSCIOUS
Everything we are aware of at a given moment

PRECONSCIOUS
Thoughts, feelings, memories, and wishes that can easily be brought to the conscious level

UNCONSCIOUS
Thoughts, feelings, memories, and wishes that are extremely difficult to bring to awareness; may appear in disguised form in dreams

STRUCTURE OF THE MIND

EGO

SUPEREGO

ID

DESCRIPTION OF FUNCTION

EGO The executive arm of personality that seeks to resolve the continuing conflict between the id and superego by following the reality principle

SUPEREGO The moralistic and idealistic structure, consisting of the conscience, which punishes behavior that violates society's rules, and the ego ideal, which rewards behavior meeting idealistic expectations

ID The source of the energy of *eros* and *thanatos*, which seeks immediate gratification in line with the pleasure principle

FIGURE 11-6 Relation of conscious, preconscious, and unconscious thought in Freudian theory. In this iceberg model most of the contents of the mind are below the consciousness threshold and therefore are unavailable to our conscious thoughts.

iceberg (see Figure 11-6). Just as most of an iceberg lies beneath the surface of the water, much of what is truly significant in psychodynamic theory lies below conscious awareness. Figure 11-6 also depicts the relation of the three components of the mind to the levels of consciousness discussed earlier. The next sections examine that relationship.

The Id. The **id** represents the primitive, biological side of our personality. This reservoir of pleasure-seeking and aggressive instinctual energy aims to reduce tension that builds up when our wishes are thwarted. Moreover, the id is extremely selfish and has no concern for the needs or desires of others or for what society may want. As you can see in Figure 11-6, the id is entirely unconscious. Operating on the pleasure principle, it impulsively seeks immediate gratification of wishes through the ego.

The Ego. As time passes, the id's relentless demands for instant gratification are reined in by a new structure, the ego. The **ego** is sometimes called the executive of the personality because it has a realistic plan for obtaining what the id wants; therefore it is said to operate on the reality principle. Seldom, however, do our surroundings provide immediate gratification of our needs, so the ego must tolerate some delay and occasional frustration.

The Superego. The third element of the mind, the **superego,** has two components: the *conscience* and the *ego ideal*. Imagine yourself slightly exceeding the speed limit while driving down a highway. Suddenly the red lights of a state police cruiser are reflected in your rear-view mirror. An anxious feeling spreads throughout your body, your heart beats rapidly, and you start to sweat as you wonder if the trooper is after you. When the cruiser zips by on its way to apprehend a "real" speeder, your

id
In psychodynamic theory, the most basic element of the personality; it is the source of the instincts and operates on the pleasure principle

ego
In psychodynamic theory, the element of the mind that operates according to the reality principle and serves to satisfy the id and the superego

superego
In psychodynamic theory, the element of the mind that incorporates parental and societal standards in what is commonly referred to as the conscience as well as the idealistic ego ideal

heartbeat returns to normal. You reacted the way you did because you felt you had done something wrong and were about to be punished. This feeling stemmed from your conscience. This moral part of the superego is like a little voice that tells us when we have violated our parents' and society's rules. For many (but not all) of us, the conscience exacts punishment for even the possibility of violating those rules.

The second component of the superego, the ego ideal, represents the superego's positive side—the things that make us proud. Achieve excellent grades in school and the ego ideal "pats you on the back" in recognition of your accomplishment. The ego ideal aims for what is right, correct, and ideal; it motivates us to strive for perfection.

Interaction of Id, Ego, and Superego. The relation among the id, ego, and superego is like a car with some special features. Suppose that this car—call it IES (for id, ego, superego)—is designed to pull both to the left and to the right sides of the road, often at the same time. The left and right wheels represent the id and the superego, and they often try to turn in opposite directions. The id tries to satisfy basic biological drives; the superego strives to impose highly perfectionistic and moralistic goals in their place. Thus the id and the superego are unrealistic and irrational in separate but competing ways. The driver represents the ego and is responsible for making adjustments as the id and superego struggle against each other. The ego tries to find an acceptable middle road between these two divergent forces.

Defense Mechanisms

The ego is engaged in an ongoing battle to deal with the competing demands of the id and the superego. If you recall the iceberg model of the mind (Figure 11-6), you will realize that much of this conflict lies beneath the surface, in the unconscious.

Psychological Detective

Imagine that the id, ego, and superego are in conflict. How does a person know that this battle is happening? What does a person do when this conflict develops? Give these questions some thought, and write down your answers before reading further.

Freud proposes that there is a never-ending battle between two irrational forces (the id and the superego) with a mediator (the ego) in the middle. Much of this conflict is unconscious, but when it becomes serious, an alarm goes off. In psychodynamic theory, anxiety or guilt is a warning to the ego that conflict is occurring.

When the anxiety or guilt alarm rings, the ego defends itself through unconscious efforts referred to as **defense mechanisms** (Freud, 1958) that tend to deny or distort reality (see Table 11-6). The effect of defense mechanisms is to reduce anxiety or guilt. The use of defense mechanisms, however, can be helpful or harmful, depending on how much a person relies on them.

Stages of Psychosexual Development

Freud proposed that an individual's personality develops through a series of five stages stretching from infancy to adulthood. These stages are called *psychosexual stages* because each is characterized by efforts to obtain pleasure centered on one of several parts of the body called *erogenous zones*. (The term *psychosexual stages* might remind you of Erikson's stages of *psychosocial* development that we covered in Chapter 9. Although they sound similar, Freud's psychosexual stages were developed first; it is likely that Erikson used Freud's theory as a pattern for his own stage theory.) According to Freud, the five stages of psychosexual development are the oral, anal, phallic, latency, and genital stages.

defense mechanism
Psychodynamic term used to describe primarily unconscious methods of reducing anxiety or guilt that results from conflicts among the id, ego, and superego

Scheherazade in the Consulting Room

TABLE 11–6

Defense Mechanisms

Defense mechanisms protect the ego from anxiety by distorting or otherwise altering reality. Although everyone uses defense mechanisms, excessive use of them is considered a sign of abnormality.

Defense Mechanism	Descriptions	Examples
Denial	Refusing to acknowledge an undesirable experience, memory, or internal need that is anxiety-arousing and behaving as if it did not exist.	A physician tells a parent that her son has terminal cancer. Despite overwhelming evidence that the cancer is not treatable, the parent remains convinced that the child will recover.
Displacement	Shifting feelings from one object to a substitute that is not as gratifying but is less anxiety-arousing.	You want to retaliate against your boss for something she said to you during a performance evaluation. The ego, being relatively wise and in contact with reality, recognizes that such a course of action would be ill-advised. Later in the day, you find yourself yelling at the grocery clerk, cutting off other drivers on the way home, and hanging up on callers soliciting funds for a local charity. Each of these innocent bystanders is a safer outlet for aggression than your boss and hence is less threatening to the ego.
Projection	Attributing to others unwanted feelings, thoughts, or behaviors.	A person who is having difficulty making it to work on time because of procrastination and failure to meet deadlines says, "It's not my fault. My bosses are just too demanding, and my co-workers are uncooperative."
Rationalization	Proposing socially acceptable feelings or reasons in place of actual, unacceptable feelings or reasons for a behavior.	You did not do well on an exam in your economics course. You could admit that you found the material impossible to comprehend, but perhaps this admission would lead to additional anxiety. So you may tell yourself, and anyone else who is listening, that you "don't want to be an economist anyway."
Reaction formation	Defending against unacceptable feelings and behavior by exhibiting the opposite of one's true wishes or impulses.	A person may be attracted to pornographic material (id) yet be repulsed by the thought of such material (superego). Such a person may become involved in a censorship campaign that places him or her in the position of having to review pornographic material.
Regression	Returning to forms of behavior that are indicative of an earlier level of development such as childhood (usually in response to an overwhelming stressor).	An adult has a temper tantrum (a common behavior of 3- or 4-year-olds).
Sublimation	A form of displacement in which a sexual or aggressive impulse is moved from an unacceptable object to one that is acceptable and ultimately has value to society.	A typical example of sublimation involves the direction of sexual energy toward the creation of works of art. Another example involves turning aggressive energy toward socially desirable goals such as surgery to save lives, rather than harming others.

oral stage

The first stage of psychosexual development in which the mouth is the focus of pleasure-seeking activity

The Oral Stage.   Pleasure-seeking behavior in the **oral stage** focuses on the baby's mouth. Infants and toddlers can often be seen biting, sucking, or placing objects in their mouths. Freud hypothesized that if oral needs such as the need for food are delayed, the child's personality may become arrested or fixated. A person whose development is arrested will display behaviors as an adult that are associated with the time of life during which the **fixation** occurred. For example, fixation at the oral stage may be manifest in behaviors such as chewing on pencils or overeating and in personality characteristics such as excessive dependency, optimism, and gullibility.

The Anal Stage.   From about 18 months until about 3 years of age, the child is in the **anal stage.** As the child gains muscular control, the erogenous zone shifts to the anus, and the child derives pleasure from the expulsion and retention of feces. The key to this stage is toilet training. The way parents approach toilet training can have lasting effects on their children. Early in the anal stage the child gains pleasure from the expulsion of feces. A person who is fixated at this stage is referred to as *anal-expulsive.* As adults these people are overly generous. If the parents are strict and demanding, the child may rebel, and the result will be fixation at this stage. Individuals who are fixated at this stage may be overly rigid and orderly as adults and are referred to as *anal-retentive.*

The Phallic Stage.   The **phallic stage,** which begins at about age 4 to 5, is ushered in by another shift in the erogenous zone and the child's pleasure-seeking behavior. During this stage, children derive pleasure from fondling their genitals. The phallic stage is also the time when the **Oedipal complex** (in boys) or the **Electra complex** (in girls) occurs.

Freud believed that young boys develop a sexual interest in their mothers, see their fathers as competitors for the mothers' affection, and therefore wish to get rid of their fathers. The name of this complex is derived from Oedipus, a character in an ancient Greek tragedy who had unwittingly killed his father and married his mother; when he discovered the truth, he gouged out his eyes and spent the rest of his life as a homeless wanderer.

The young boy fears his father's retaliation for these forbidden sexual and aggressive impulses. He fantasizes that the father's retaliation would involve injury to his genitals; as a result, he experiences what is called *castration anxiety.* To reduce the fear, the boy represses his sexual desire for his mother and begins to identify with his father, which means that he tries to be like dad in his behavior, values, attitudes, and sexual orientation. Successful resolution of the Oedipal complex, according to Freud, leads to acquisition of the male sex role (see Chapter 10).

The Electra complex is named for a character in another Greek tragedy who conspired to kill her mother to avenge her father's death. Young girls become aware that they do not have penises, which Freud believed they both value and desire. Thus girls experience *penis envy,* which leads to anger directed at their mothers and sexual attraction toward their fathers. A girl's attraction to her father is rooted in a fantasy that seducing him will provide her with a penis. She also fantasizes about having a baby as another means of gaining the valued organ. Resolution of this complex occurs when the girl represses her sexual desires and begins to identify with her mother.

Freud believed that the male superego receives an intense unconscious push from Oedipal castration fears and that the female superego ends up weaker than that of the male. This belief, however, like a number of Freudian ideas, has not been supported by research (Bower, 1991).

The Latency and Genital Stages   At about age 6, children enter a period when their sexual interests are suppressed. This period, which lasts until the beginning of adolescence, is called the **latency stage.** Sexual interests are reawakened at puberty and become stronger during the **genital stage.** In this stage sexual pleasure is derived from heterosexual relationships. At the beginning of the genital stage, most adolescents have difficulty developing true affection and caring for others; they still experience the selfish qualities of earlier stages of development. As they mature, they develop greater ability to establish such relationships, thus setting the foundation for adult relationships. Freud's stages of psychosexual development are summarized in the Study Chart on the next page.

The first stage of Freud's psychosexual stages—the oral stage—consists of attaining pleasure via the mouth.

fixation
Cessation of further development, resulting in behaviors that are characteristic of the stage of development in which the fixation occurred

anal stage
Second stage of psychosexual development, during which the focus of pleasure is the anus and conflict often occurs as efforts are made to toilet-train the child

phallic stage
The third stage of psychosexual development, in which the genital organs become the focus of pleasure-seeking behavior

oedipal complex
Process that occurs during the phallic stage in which a boy wishes to possess his mother sexually and fears retaliation by his father

electra complex
Process that occurs during the phallic stage in which a girl wishes to possess her father sexually

latency stage
Stage of psychosexual development that extends from about age 6 until the onset of puberty and is characterized by low levels of sexual interest

genital stage
Stage of psychosexual development that begins at puberty and usually leads to normal adult sexual development

STUDY CHART

Freud's Stages of Psychosexual Development

Stage	Approximate Ages	Erogenous Zones	Major Characteristics
Oral	Birth to about 18 months	Mouth	Focus on oral gratification from sucking, chewing, eating, and biting
Anal	End of oral stage to 3 years	Anus	Gratification from holding and expelling feces at the time when these desires for gratification must meet societal demands to control the bladder and bowels (toilet training)
Phallic	End of anal stage to about 6 years	Genitals	Gratification focused on manipulation of genitals; development of sexual interest in the parent of opposite biological sex
Latency	End of phallic stage to onset of puberty	None	Sexual desires not of paramount importance
Genital	Adolescence to adulthood	Genitals	Resurgence of sexual interests; focus on mature sexual adulthood relationships

STUDY TIP

Write an outline on the topic of Sigmund Freud—basic facts, his theories, and their influence on modern psychology.

The Unconscious

Freud in Perspective

Freud attracted both supporters and critics. Some of his most outspoken critics were formerly his greatest admirers who once espoused his views, but for a variety of reasons they developed new perspectives that nonetheless fit the psychodynamic mold. For example, they did not accept Freud's emphasis on the id and the role of sexual motives; instead they emphasized the ego and its role in the development of personality, as well as the social aspects of personality. These individuals are frequently referred to as neo-Freudians.

The Neo-Freudians

One of the best-known neo-Freudians, Carl Jung (1875–1961), split from Freud on more than one issue and developed his own psychodynamic viewpoint. For example, Jung did not want to place as much emphasis on sexuality as did Freud. Jung stressed a more generalized life force, emphasized the future, and placed even more emphasis on the unconscious than did Freud.

Jung suggested that a *collective unconscious* contains images shared by *all* people. Jung's name for these images is *archetypes*. These archetypes are passed along genetically and cause us to respond to events in our environment in particular ways. Among the archetypes that Jung proposed are: *Persona* (a mask of our true personality), *anima* and *animus* (exhibition of both feminine and masculine characteristics, respectively), *shadow* (the animal instinct or "dark" side of our personality), and *self* (the part of our personality that provides unity and stability—attempts to integrate the different aspects of the personality).

Jung proposed the concepts of *introversion* and *extraversion* to reflect the direction of the person's life force. The life force of an introvert is turned inward, whereas the life force of an extravert is turned outward.

He also developed the word association test for use as a personality assessment device. The longer a person took to respond to a word, or if a word produced changes in breathing rate, then Jung believed that an unconscious emotional problem might exist.

Karen Horney (1885–1952), an early disciple of Freudian thinking, rejected several Freudian notions and added several of her own. She viewed personality disturbances not as resulting from instinctual strivings to satisfy sexual and aggressive urges but as stemming from the basic anxiety that all people share. We all feel anxiety because we find ourselves isolated and sometimes helpless in an unfriendly world. Anxiety is an unpleasant state that we seek to reduce.

In order to reduce anxiety, Horney believes that all people use three basic adjustment patterns: *moving toward people* (a person seeks affection and approval), *moving against people* (uses power to control and exploit other people), and *moving away from people* (withdraws from a situation). The choice of which behavior pattern a person uses should depend on the type of situation that is producing the anxiety. A person's behavior becomes "abnormal" (see Chapter 12) when he or she uses only one adjustment pattern in all situations.

Alfred Adler (1870–1937) was a Freudian disciple who was ejected from the Vienna Psychoanalytic Society in 1911 because of his disagreements with Freud. Adler believed that Freud overemphasized the sexual drive in explaining personality. He argued that the primary drive is social rather than sexual.

According to Adler, the young child is inevitably weak when compared to adults. This comparison has the effect that, throughout the rest of the child's life he/she strives to overcome the inferiority feelings that these early experiences create. This striving for superiority is innate; people develop different life styles to achieve it; they are motivated to develop new skills and abilities that lead to a sense of superiority. Thus Adler shifted the emphasis in personality theory from the id to the ego, which strives to gain control over others. He noted that we spend much of our lives striving to compensate for our perceived shortcomings. For example, the Greek philosopher Demosthenes was embarrassed by his stuttering as a child, so he spent years practicing speaking clearly and eventually became a great orator.

Adler can be considered the first "self" theorist due to the emphasis he placed on this concept. For him the self was the most important part of the personality. It is constantly striving for unity. In this context, Adler postulated the "creative power of the self"—the notion that we are able to mold our own destinies (that is, we possess free will). Also, Adler was the first theorist to stress the importance of birth order as a determinant of personality. Although he had a great impact on psychoanalysis and personality theory, his system lacks hard data and replicability; it is largely based on anecdotes.

Evaluation of Freudian Theory. When Freud first published his ideas in the early 1900s, they met with strong negative reactions, especially his notions of sexuality in children. Most people were repulsed by the idea of viewing children as sexual beings. When Freud published his classic book on dreams, about 300 copies were sold.

Eventually Freud's ideas caught on, and they have had a lasting impact. Some researchers report that many of Freud's proposals, such as unconscious influences on emotional responses, social behavior, and habitual behavior, are supported by research (Westen, 1998); nevertheless, there are a great number of critics who note that it is difficult to conduct research on psychodynamic concepts (Bower, 1998; Hergenhahn & Olson, 1999). For example, it is almost impossible to examine the effect of parenting practices on fixations because Freud did not specify the conditions that might lead to fixations. Even when such concepts can be tested, the tests have had mixed results.

Significantly, Freud's theory is based on the study of a small number of disturbed people, who may not provide the basis for generalizations applicable to most people. What's more, many of the patients that Freud treated were women, yet he developed a theory that dealt primarily with male sexuality; this inconsistency makes generalizations quite difficult. His method of data collection was a source of dismay for researchers. During his treatment sessions, Freud sat behind the patient, who was comfortably relaxing on a couch. Freud listened attentively to what the patient was saying. Only after the session was over did Freud write down anything pertaining to what the patient had said. How much information did he forget? How many changes did he make in trying to recall what was said? This subjectivity did not ensure confidence in many critics. Additionally, the validity of Freud's entire system is questionable because he never verified the information that his patients revealed to him during psychoanalysis. This information was used to construct his theory. Finally, Sundberg, Winebarger, and Taplin (2002) indicate that "Many psychologists have criticized Freud for his views of women, especially the notion that they suffer from 'penis envy'" (p. 205).

On the other side of the coin, Freud drew attention to the potential importance of early childhood experiences; he was the first to outline a stage theory of development and to identify key influences operating at each stage. Freud is also credited with drawing attention to the impact of sexuality on human behavior. It undoubtedly took courage for him to offer his ideas at a time when the public wanted to keep sexuality hidden and repressed. He noted the importance of unconscious factors in determining behavior. We are often unaware of the motivations and rationales that underlie our behavior. Some observers therefore view the concept of the unconscious as one of the enduring contributions of psychodynamic theory (Westen, 1998).

Freud's work also popularized counseling and psychotherapy in the United States and around the world. His ideas have been applied to the development of the form of psychotherapy called *psychoanalysis*, which strives to bring unconscious conflicts to the surface so that an individual can deal with them more effectively.

Still, critics note that Freud developed a theory that focused on concern for one's own desires, irresponsibility, and the denigration of women. For example, Freud saw women as more vain than men and having little sense of justice, along with a perpetual sense of inferiority owing to the lack of a penis. What's more, Freud's belief in unconscious instinctual drives may well have overstated the case for such influences.

Historically, a number of psychological perspectives developed, in part, in opposition to psychodynamic theory. Compared with Freud and his followers, the proponents of these perspectives had very different views on the development of personality. We next turn our attention to personality as viewed from the cognitive-learning and humanistic perspectives.

R E V I E W   S U M M A R Y

1. Freud suggested that behaviors, feelings, and thoughts result from past events. Because this **psychic determinism** occurs at an unconscious level, we are often unaware of the true reasons for our behavior.

2. Freud compared the mind to an iceberg, with three levels of consciousness (*conscious, preconscious,* and *unconscious*) and three structures (**id, ego,** and **superego**). Conflicts among the structures of the mind occur beneath the level of conscious awareness.

3. Severe unconscious conflict produces anxiety or guilt that warn the ego. The ego uses **defense mechanisms** to protect itself from being overwhelmed by anxiety or guilt.

4. According to Freud, at different stages of development the id centers its pleasure-seeking behavior on different parts of the body, called *erogenous zones*. The resulting psychosexual stages begin with the **oral stage** and continue through the **anal** and **phallic stages**. The **Oedipal** and **Electra complexes** occur

during the phallic stage. This stage is followed by the **latency stage** and then by the **genital stage** and the emergence of adult sexual desires.

5. The neo-Freudians—including Jung, Horney, and Adler—disagreed with a number of Freud's views (for example, those emphasizing the sexual and unconscious roots of behavior).

6. Freud is credited with pointing out the influence of early childhood experiences and with developing a stage theory of development. In addition, he noted the potential importance of unconscious experiences and the influence of sexuality on human behavior.

7. Critics of psychodynamic theory note that Freud based his ideas on small, unrepresentative samples of disturbed individuals. Additionally, many of his concepts and principles are not directly testable; hence, there is little scientific evidence to support his theory. His subjective method of data collection and views about women also have attracted criticism.

✓ CHECK YOUR PROGRESS

1. Consider each of the following situations, and determine whether the conflict involves the id, ego, and/or superego.

    a. You have not studied for an exam and are afraid that you will fail it. Your neighbor's paper is within sight, and you begin to think about "borrowing" some of her answers.

    b. You are late for an appointment on the other side of town. You are afraid that you will miss an important opportunity if you don't get there soon. While driving to your appointment, you spot a police cruiser just ahead of you.

2. Identify the stage of psychosexual development (oral, anal, phallic, latency, genital) described in each of the following statements:

    a. The Oedipus and Electra complexes occur during this stage.

    b. A child enjoys biting and chewing on almost any object.

    c. This period is relatively calm as far as sexual interests are concerned.

3. Which term describes the influence of the past on the present?

    a. instincts

    b. unconscious

    c. psychoanalysis

    d. psychic determinism

4. An individual operating on the reality principle seeks

    a. immediate gratification.

    b. the perfect accomplishment.

    c. to reveal their unconscious motivations.

    d. rational means for obtaining gratification.

5. What is the warning that signals when there is conflict involving the id and superego?

    a. fear

    b. stress

    c. anxiety

    d. delusion

6. The neo-Freudian, Carl Jung, suggested the existence of a collective unconscious that contained images shared by all people called

    a. schemas.

    b. paradigms.

    c. archetypes.

    d. prototypes.

ANSWERS: 1. a. Id and superego **b.** Id, ego, and superego **2. a.** Phallic **b.** Oral **c.** Latency **3.** d **4.** d **5.** c **6.** c

THE SOCIAL-COGNITIVE PERSPECTIVE

A major exam is scheduled for next week. Alice and Gil overhear several students predicting they will fail; others say they expect to "ace" the test. These differing expectations seem puzzling because everyone will take the same exam. Later that day, Alice and Gil talk about trying to stop smoking. Alice is certain she will succeed, but Gil doubts he will be able to quit. After realizing they sound like the students who talked about the exam, they begin wondering why some people are sure they will "ace" an exam or quit smoking, whereas others are unsure. *What role do beliefs have in our understanding of personality?*

Learning and Cognitive Perspectives

As we noted in Chapter 1, John B. Watson tried to rid psychology of terms like *thinking* and urged psychologists to avoid speculating about inner, unobservable processes. This behavioral or learning perspective was taken up by B. F. Skinner, who emphasized environmental contingencies in explaining human behavior. Skinner suggested the same principles that applied to rats and pigeons in his laboratory could be applied to humans (see Chapter 5). Hence, he believed that personality developed in the same manner as did any other learned behavior; it was influenced by reinforcers and punishers (see Chapter 5).

social learning theory
Theory that learning occurs through watching and imitating the behaviors of others

locus of control
Whether the person sees his or her behavior as controlled by external factors (external locus) or internal forces (internal locus)

According to Skinner, we can explain the distinctiveness of individual personalities without using terms such as *traits*. Each person's behavior is distinctive because each one experiences different histories of reinforcement and punishment. Skinner focused attention on the environmental factors that initiate and maintain behaviors that ultimately distinguish one person from another. For example, John acts aggressively because he was probably reinforced for past aggressive behaviors. If Natasha's friends describe her as having a great sense of humor, her past joke telling probably resulted in reinforcement. According to behavioral or learning psychologists, there is no need to use a concept such as traits in explaining John's aggressiveness or Natasha's sense of humor.

Few psychologists would dismiss the importance of environmental influences like reinforcement. Even studies of the heritability of personality tell us that the environment plays a role; learning can influence personality. Some psychologists such as Julian Rotter, however, say there is more to understanding personality than a person's learning experiences might suggest. Although they do not deny the importance of reinforcement and punishment, these psychologists draw our attention to the effects these processes may have on our thoughts and cognitive processes. Because of our unique histories of reinforcement and punishment, each person comes to see his or her environment differently.

Rotter's Social Learning Theory.   Learning is a powerful tool for understanding animal and human behavior; however, classical and operant conditioning do not explain all the learning that takes place. For example, research on modeling tells us that people can learn without direct experience (see Chapter 5).

Julian Rotter notes that reinforcement does not automatically stamp in a behavior. Rotter continued Skinner's emphasis on the importance of learning; he carried it further, however, by recognizing that past learning affects not just behaviors but also *expectancies* about whether certain behaviors lead to desired outcomes. Most of the reinforcers we strive to obtain are social (for example, hugs, attention, praise), and most learning occurs in social situations (Rotter, 1990). Rotter combined these observations in his **social learning theory** of personality, which incorporated cognitive factors. He acknowledges the role of cognitive factors in understanding human behavior, noting that behavior is often a function of *expectancies*.

The concept of *expectancy* is one of the most important elements of Rotter's theory. When you take an exam, apply for a job, or ask someone out on a date, you have some notion of the likelihood of success or failure. Generalized expectancies operate across a wide variety of situations; specific expectancies are limited to particular situations. What's more, people differ in their tendencies to view themselves as capable of influencing reinforcers or being subject to fate (Strickland, 1989). Some people, called *internals*, believe that they can influence their reinforcers via their skill and ability. Others, called *externals*, believe that whether they attain a desired outcome is due primarily to chance or fate (Rotter, 1990).

Rotter (1966) devised the Internal-External (I-E) Scale to measure individuals' *locus of control* (internal or external); since then, **locus of control** has become one of the most studied concepts in psychology. Each of the 23 items on the I-E Scale offers a choice between an external alternative and an internal one (see Table 11-7).

Why does one person score in the external direction whereas another obtains a score indicating an internal locus of control? One factor that accounts for differences in locus of control is the individual's learning history. Cultural factors also seem to influence locus-of-control scores. For example, people in Western countries tend to have more internal scores than people in Far Eastern countries, especially Japan (Berry et al., 1992). Low socioeconomic status tends to be linked with external locus of control. These cultural differences influence our sense of self.

Suppose we asked you to "describe yourself briefly." What would you write? American responses to this simple question tend to be more confident and elaborated. Japanese responses tend to be more tentative, and more concerned with the responses

TABLE 11-7

Sample Items from Rotter's Internal-External Control Scale

The total score is tabulated by adding 1 point for each item in which an individual selects the externally worded alternative. Thus high scores indicate an external locus of control, and low scores indicate an internal locus of control.

1. a. Becoming a success is a matter of hard work; luck has little or nothing to do with it.
   b. Getting a good job depends mainly on being in the right place at the right time.*

2. a. When I make plans, I am almost certain that I can make them work.
   b. It is not always wise to plan too far ahead because many things turn out to be a matter of good or bad fortune anyway.*

3. a. Most people don't realize the extent to which their lives are controlled by accidental happenings.*
   b. There really is no such thing as "luck."

4. a. What happens to me is my own doing.
   b. Sometimes I feel that I don't have enough control over the direction my life is taking.*

5. a. Many times I feel that I have little influence over the things that happen to me.*
   b. It is impossible for me to believe that chance or luck plays an important role in my life.

*External alternative.

Source: Rotter, 1966.

---

of others (Markus & Kitayama, 1998). What's more, most American respondents focus on ways that make them unique in comparisons to others. This way of responding is characteristic of what has been called an *individualist* (independent) conception of the self (Markus & Kitayama, 1991). In contrast, people in Asian cultures emphasize what has been called a *collectivist* (or interdependent) conception of the self.

How do such differences in the evaluation of self develop? They reflect differences in socialization. Asian cultures tend to emphasize modesty and self-restraint, whereas American children are taught that "the squeaky wheel gets the oil." Conversely, Japanese children are taught, "The nail that stands out gets pounded down." These differences in socialization and their effects on behavior should serve as a reminder that when we speak of personality, we need to keep in mind the cultural context in which we ask questions concerning personality.

The concept of locus of control has a wide range of uses and applications (Strickland, 1989). For example, during the 1960s, researchers discovered that internals were more likely than externals to attend civil rights rallies, sign petitions, or participate in a "freedom ride" to challenge racial segregation in the South. Locus of control is related to measures of school achievement: Internals tend to outperform externals on standardized measures of achievement (Findley & Cooper, 1983).

Locus of control is also related to health behaviors. Internals are more likely to interpret threatening events as challenges. They are more likely to reduce their stress by solving problems that are threatening; by contrast, externals focus on their own emotional responses rather than on the threats. Consequently, internals' reactions to stress are less negative, and externals experience greater anxiety (Lefcourt & Davidson-Katz, 1991).

Bandura's Social Cognitive Theory. Albert Bandura is well known for his research on observational learning or modeling of aggressive behavior and for using modeling to overcome phobias (see Chapter 5). A fundamental question that personality

Albert Bandura added a concern for cognitive factors to the learning theorists' emphasis on external causes.

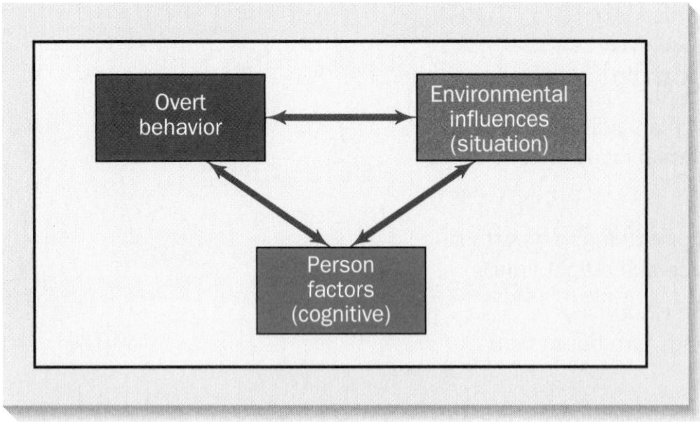

FIGURE 11-7 Bandura's model of reciprocal determinism.

Source: Bandura, 1986.

psychologists ask is, Why do people act as they do? According to Bandura (1986), the answer is that a combination of factors, including an individual's cognitions and the environment, interact to produce a particular behavior. These factors are not independent; they work together and influence one another (Bandura, 1986). This notion, known as **reciprocal determinism,** tells us that the person, environment, and behavior influence one another (see Figure 11-7). The behavioral/learning approaches focus on how environments (situations) influence behaviors (libraries are conducive to studying). An individual's personality also influences behavior, however, as the trait perspective has emphasized. Reciprocal determinism goes beyond these simple explanations of behavior as the result of either situations or personality by suggesting that our behavior can change the environment (studying instead of spending time with friends reduces social pressures or invitations to go out). Thus the environment is not only a cause of behavior, but it is also an effect of behavior. For example, one way personality influences situations is that we select situations differently, depending on our personalities. Achievement-oriented students are likely to spend their time in the library; extraverted people are likely to attend parties and other social gatherings. A complete understanding of personality requires recognition of the mutual influences among the person, the situation (environment), and behavior (Cloninger, 1996).

Another key concept in Bandura's theory is **self-efficacy,** a person's beliefs about his or her skills and ability to perform certain behaviors. The greater a person's sense of self-efficacy, the more confidence that person has in his or her ability to deal with life's challenges. A person's sense of self-efficacy has a powerful effect on his or her behavior, yet self-efficacy is not considered a trait. Why? Self-efficacy can be understood only in relation to specific behaviors and in specific situations. Unlike locus of control, it is not generalized across situations.

Four sources of information can influence self-efficacy. The first is past performance (successes or failures). The second is watching others in similar situations and noting the consequences they experience. The effect of observing others depends on factors such as one's similarity to the observed person. Third, verbal persuasion can also affect levels of self-efficacy; its effect depends on the persuader's trustworthiness and level of expertise. Finally, self-efficacy can be related to physiological arousal. For example, we may associate aversive emotional states with poor performance, perceived incompetence, or perceived failure (Maddux, 1991).

The concept of self-efficacy has been applied to a range of outcomes. For example, measures of self-efficacy predict final course grades among high school and college students (Hackett et al., 1992; Zimmerman, Bandura, & Martinez-Pons, 1992). Self-efficacy also predicts the ability to resist relapse after treatment for alcohol problems (Rchtarik et al., 1992). It is also related to a career outcome such as career exploration (Solberg, 1998) and to how people attempt computer-related tasks (Brosnan, 1998).

STUDY TIP

Pair up with another student. One student should "play" Julian Rotter; the other, Albert Bandura. Each student, as that particular person, should explain his theory (for Rotter, Social Learning; for Bandura, Social Cognitive) to the other and invite questions and discussion.

reciprocal determinism
Contention that person variables, situation variables, and behavior constantly interact

self-efficacy
A person's expectancy concerning his or her ability to engage in effective behaviors; such expectancies differ from one behavior to another

THE HUMANISTIC PERSPECTIVE

One of Randy's favorite quotes from his introductory psychology course is

> I have little sympathy with the rather prevalent concept that man is basically irrational, and that his impulses, if not controlled, will lead to the destruction of others and self. Man's behavior is exquisitely rational, moving with subtle and ordered complexity towards the goals his organism is endeavoring to achieve. (Rogers, 1961, pp. 194–195)

Certainly this view of human personality and behavior differs drastically from the learning-theory model and Freud's stages of psychosexual development. *What type of psychologist proposed this different viewpoint?*

As Randy found out in his introductory psychology course, not all psychologists believe that our behavior is determined by early childhood experiences, biological drives, or even learning histories. Some psychologists believe that to understand human behavior, we must look at unique human aspects and qualities. What sets us apart from lower animals is not objective reality but rather our ability to make choices and our individual perspectives on the world.

A group of theorists called **humanistic psychologists** oppose the basic beliefs of both psychodynamic theory and behaviorism. Rather than concentrate on unconscious motivation and past experience, they focus on the present and the healthy personality. What's more, they view the individual's perceptions of events as more significant than the learning theorist's or therapist's perceptions. For these reasons, they are often called *phenomenological psychologists.* (Phenomenology is the study of experience just as it occurs.) The two most notable representatives of this humanistic or phenomenological perspective are Abraham Maslow and Carl Rogers.

Abraham Maslow. Abraham Maslow (1908–1970) described humanistic psychology as the "third force" in American psychology because it offered an alternative to psychodynamic theory and behaviorism. He viewed those perspectives as incomplete because they emphasized early childhood experience or viewed people as captives of their environments. In addition, he did not believe the study of laboratory animals or individuals suffering from psychological disorders provided a proper foundation for understanding human behavior.

Basic Needs. According to Maslow, human beings have a set of needs that are organized in a hierarchy (see Chapter 6). These needs begin with physiological needs and move on to needs for safety, love and belongingness, and self-esteem. These basic needs exert a powerful pull on our behavior. Once you satisfy physiological needs, you can turn to needs for safety or to be loved by others. The basic biological needs exert a great deal of influence on our behavior, so much so that most people never reach the top level of the hierarchy.

Self-Actualization. **Self-actualization** involves making "the full use and exploitation of talents, capacities, potentialities" (Maslow, 1970, p. 150). In other words, it is the need to develop one's full potential. Maslow believed that this need exists in everyone but is often thwarted by the environment. When our basic needs are met, energy is available for use in striving for greater understanding of ourselves and our surroundings. To illustrate these concepts, Maslow looked for healthy, self-actualized individuals who were doing the best that they were capable of doing.

Maslow's list of self-actualized people included Abraham Lincoln, Thomas Jefferson, Eleanor Roosevelt, and Albert Einstein. Because a number of them were deceased, he relied on historical documents to study them. The details of his analysis of these self-actualized individuals are sketchy, but he arrived at several general conclusions about their characteristics (see Table 11-8). For example, he found that these individuals tended to have accurate perceptions of their environments and were comfortable with those perceptions. Keep in mind that Maslow's selection process is subject to the same criticism that was directed at Freud's psychodynamic theory: The list of self-actualized individuals is not representative of the general population.

Maslow tried to move the study of personality away from the concern with pathology that was evident in Freud's work. He held a distinctly positive view of human nature. Many of his concepts, however, such as self-actualization, are difficult to test empirically.

humanistic psychology
General approach to psychology, associated with Abraham Maslow and Carl Rogers, that emphasizes individuals' control of their behavior

self-actualization
Need to develop one's full potential

A number of the people Maslow identified as self-actualized were historical figures who he analyzed by studying historical documents. Although she is now dead, there is a great deal of evidence to suggest that Mother Teresa would fit Maslow's description of self-actualization.

TABLE 11-8

Characteristics of Maslow's Sample of Self-Actualized Individuals

Accept their own natures

Are spontaneous and natural

Are deeply democratic in nature

Like privacy and tend to be detached

Focus on problems outside themselves

Exhibit a strong ethical and moral sense

Have close but limited number of friendships

Are independent of their cultural and social environment

Prefer a philosophical rather than a hostile type of humor

Have efficient perceptions of reality and are comfortable with those perceptions

Source: Maslow, 1970.

Carl Rogers.   Carl Rogers (1902–1987) shared Maslow's belief that people are innately good and are directed toward growth, development, and personal fulfillment. What's more, he believed there is an "inherent tendency of the organism to develop all its capabilities in ways which serve to maintain or enhance the person" (Rogers, 1959, p. 196). Unfortunately, his clinical experience told him that people are frequently derailed from their quests for fulfillment.

As we develop, our concept of self emerges. The self is our sense of "I" or "me"; it is generally conscious and accessible and is a central concept in Rogers's theory. The self-concept is our perception of our abilities, behaviors, and characteristics. Rogers believed that we act in accordance with our self-concept. If we have a positive self-concept, we tend to act in positive ways; if we have a negative self-concept, we often act in negative ways.

Maslow and Rogers agreed that people have a strong need to be loved, to experience affection. Sometimes, however, people experience affection that is *conditional*—given only if they engage in behaviors that are approved by others. Rogers contrasted this conditional regard with what he called *unconditional positive regard*, in which a person is accepted for what he or she is, not for what others would like the person to be. According to Rogers, if you grow up believing affection is conditional, you will distort your own experiences in order to feel worthy of acceptance from a wider range of people. For example, children may be told they are incapable of doing something or that they are stupid, nasty, or disobedient. This may lead them to understand that conditions are placed on their self-worth; as a result, they may begin to question themselves. This conditional positive regard, in which love and praise are not given unless the child conforms to the expectations of others, can have negative effects on the child's self-concept.

Think of the self as two sides of a coin. One side is the self as it really is, a product of our experiences; this is called the *real self*. The other side is the *ideal self*, the self we would like to be. Maladjustment results when there is a discrepancy between the real self and the ideal self—when the two sides of the coin do not match up.

Conditional positive regard can have a negative impact on a child's developing self-concept.

Rogers used a technique called the *Q-sort* to measure the degree to which the real self-concept matched the ideal self-concept. To complete a Q-sort, the client is given a stack of cards with statements about the self such as "I am generally a happy person," "I am confident," or "I am upset much of the time." The client reads each card and then responds along a continuum that ranges from "Very characteristic of me" to "Not at all characteristic of me." In this way the client provides a picture of his or her real self-concept. The cards are then reshuffled and the client is given a new task—to place the cards on the same continuum in such a way as to indicate his or her ideal self-concept.

Psychological Detective

The Q-sort provides a great deal of information about a person. How could we analyze this information to determine the degree of congruence between a person's real and ideal selves? Remember that there are two sets of cards—one representing the real self and the other representing the ideal self. We are interested in determining the relationship between these two sets of cards. Give this question some thought, and write down your answer before reading further.

Correlations (see Chapter 1) between the two sets of card arrangements provide insight into the discrepancy or similarity between a person's real and ideal self-concepts. Higher correlations are found in well-adjusted individuals, lower correlations in disturbed individuals. This technique has also been used to demonstrate progress resulting from psychotherapy. As clients improve, their real and ideal self-concepts become more congruent; that is, the correlations become higher.

The major theoretical perspectives on personality we have covered in this chapter are summarized for you in the Study Chart below. You should review it now.

STUDY CHART

Overview of the Major Perspectives on Personality

Perspective	Key Figures	Strengths	Weaknesses
Trait	Gordon Allport, Raymond Cattell, Hans Eysenck	Describes the major dimensions on which individuals differ from one another	Sometimes emphasizes different traits as key ones; may not provide an explanation of the development of traits
Biological	William Sheldon, University of Minnesota Twins Reared Apart Project	Focuses on biological aspects of individuals' differences with a special emphasis on genetic influences	May misinterpret research to conclude that environmental factors are not important or that personality cannot change
Psychodynamic	Sigmund Freud, neo-Freudians	Uses case studies to provide in-depth assessment of individuals; focuses on the importance of unconscious processes and conflict as key factors in the development of personality	Uses concepts that are difficult to define and to study; overemphasizes the importance of early development
Social-cognitive	Julian Rotter, Albert Bandura	Adds a cognitive focus to learning-theory explanations of personality	Does not appear to account for broad consistencies in behavior; does not account for genetic influences on personality
Humanistic	Carl Rogers, Abraham Maslow	Focuses on conscious influences on behavior and on the more positive aspects of human nature	Uses concepts, such as self-actualization, that are difficult to define and to measure; takes an overly optimistic view of human nature

REVIEW SUMMARY

1. Behavioral and learning psychologists avoid commonly used terms such as *traits*. They explain the distinctiveness of a person's behavior as resulting from unique learning histories.

2. While acknowledging the importance of learning, Julian Rotter and Albert Bandura incorporated cognitive factors into their theories of personality.

3. Rotter's **social learning theory** recognizes that most reinforcers are social and that most learning takes place in social situations. Expectancy about obtaining a reinforcer in a given situation is an important cognitive variable. Individuals differ in the degree to which they see themselves or chance ("fate") as responsible for their successes and failures.

4. Measures of generalized expectancy, known as **locus of control,** are related to a variety of outcomes, including academic and health behaviors.

5. According to Albert Bandura, individuals not only are affected by the environment but also can influence it. What's more, cognitive factors can influence the person's behavior and his or her environment. This combination of cognitive, behavioral, and environmental effects is called **reciprocal determinism.**

6. **Self-efficacy** is a person's judgment about his or her ability to succeed in a given situation. Unlike a trait, self-efficacy is specific to the situation and can change over time.

7. Humanistic approaches evolved in opposition to the behavioral and psychodynamic perspectives. They propose that human beings are basically good and are directed toward development and growth.

8. Abraham Maslow's hierarchy of needs begins with deficiency needs and leads to **self-actualization** at the top. The power of deficiency needs keeps most people from reaching the level of self-actualization, which Maslow defines as doing the best that an individual is capable of doing.

9. On the basis of his work with disturbed people, Carl Rogers concluded that efforts to achieve personal fulfillment were being stifled. He proposed that people's self-concepts had become distorted by conditions of worth imposed from the outside. In his theory, healthy individuals have a real self-concept that is consistent with their ideal self-concept.

✓ CHECK YOUR PROGRESS

1. B. F. Skinner explained the distinctiveness of individual personalities through different
   a. genetic patterns.
   b. thinking patterns.
   c. individual traits.
   d. histories of reinforcement and punishment.

2. Identify each of the following terms:
   a. Rotter's term for generalized expectancies
   b. In Rotter's social learning theory, a person who believes he or she can influence events
   c. Bandura's term for the relation among person, behavior, and environment
   d. In Bandura's theory, a person's belief that he or she has the skills to succeed in a given situation

3. If Woody believes he must have gotten his latest speeding ticket because the police have it out for him, he may be exhibiting
   a. optimism.
   b. pessimism.
   c. an internal locus of control.
   d. an external locus of control.

4. How did Carl Rogers use correlation coefficients to assess the similarity between real and ideal self-concepts? What type of correlation coefficient would suggest a high degree of similarity?

5. In Carl Rogers's theory, our perception of our abilities, behaviors, and characteristics is known as
   a. personality.
   b. self-regard.
   c. self-esteem.
   d. self-concept.

6. According to Carl Rogers, maladjustment occurs when
   a. the individual has low self-esteem.
   b. there is congruence between the real self and ideal self.
   c. there is a discrepancy between the real self and ideal self.
   d. the individual receives too much unconditional positive regard.

SCORING The "Big Five" Test

PAGES 467–468

To compute your score for each of the five scales, simply add your scores for the items that contribute to each of the scales.

Openness to Experience: 1, 6, 11, 16, 21
Conscientiousness: 2, 7, 12, 17, 22
Extraversion: 3, 8, 13, 18, 23
Agreeableness: 4, 9, 14, 19, 24
Neuroticism: 5, 10, 15, 20, 25

Mean scores for men and women on each of the scales are listed below:

	Men	Women
Openness to Experience	20.3	19.4
Conscientiousness	18.8	20.2
Extraversion	18.8	19.0
Agreeableness	18.8	22.2
Neuroticism	16.3	18.5

Source: Brody & Erlichman, 1998.

SCORING Keys

PAGES 476–477

Add one point to your score for each of the following answers.

1. a

2. a

3. a

4. b

5. a

6. b

7. a

8. a

9. b

10. b

11. a

12. a

13. b

Use the following guidelines to compare your scores with others who have taken this questionnaire.

Score	
0–3	Very low
4–5	Low
6–9	Average
10–11	High
12–13	Very high

Source: Zuckerman, 1978.

Psychological Disorders

For many students, the most intriguing behaviors are those labeled *abnormal*. Perhaps they see symptoms in themselves and wonder what causes such abnormal behaviors. We begin our discussion by describing how we decide which behaviors are labeled abnormal. The disorders we will describe span a wide range, including those that seem close to home—who has not felt anxiety at some time? Mood disorders are extreme examples of feelings and behaviors we have experienced and observed in others. Disorders like *schizophrenia*, involving symptoms such as delusions and hallucinations, are more difficult to understand because they are so unlike anything many of us have encountered.

Our discussion of biological processes will help us understand some unusual forms of behavior. We will also see that learning plays a role in the development of some forms of abnormal behavior. The types of abnormal behavior we describe, however, often have no simple explanations; they result from a combination of factors within and outside the person.

ABNORMAL BEHAVIOR

Above the din of traffic on a downtown Chicago street, a voice filled with rage screams. A disheveled woman paces furiously back and forth, her shopping bag swinging as if to punctuate every angry word. When a passerby approaches, offering to help, the woman stops, stares, and then yells, "Get away. Leave me alone." Later she is taken to a mental hospital because city officials claim she was exhibiting abnormal behavior. *What criteria are used to distinguish between "normal" and "abnormal" behaviors?*

What do we mean when we label a behavior "abnormal"? This is an important question. As we will see, the criteria we use to define abnormal behaviors influence the way we perceive and respond to other people. Thus the way we define abnormality is an important issue with serious consequences.

Criteria of Abnormality

Over time, several criteria have been used to distinguish between normal and abnormal behaviors. Sometimes one criterion will do; at other times we rely on more than one. The most commonly used criteria for distinguishing between normal and abnormal behaviors are statistical rarity, interference with normal functioning, personal distress, and deviance from social norms.

Statistical Rarity. A common way to define abnormal behavior is to determine how often the behavior occurs in the population. Abnormal literally means "away from the norm." Thus a behavior that is abnormal does not occur very often. A neighbor who checks the stove 26 times to be sure it has been turned off would be viewed as abnormal because such behavior is rare. Typing 125 words per minute is also rare and hence, by definition, is also abnormal. Some rare (and therefore statistically

dysfunctional
Term used to describe behaviors that adversely affect an individual's day-to-day functioning

abnormal
Term used to describe behavior that is rare or dysfunctional, causes personal distress, or deviates from social norms

abnormal) behaviors, however, such as earning straight A's or writing a best-selling novel, are acceptable and desirable. By itself, statistical rarity is clearly not a consistently useful indicator of what we should label abnormal.

Interference with Normal Functioning.   Behavior is said to be **dysfunctional** when it interferes with a person's ability to function on a daily basis. Everyone probably experiences some degree of anxiety every day, but imagine a level of anxiety that renders you unable to speak in the presence of others or unable to leave your home. That degree of anxiety is dysfunctional because it interferes with daily activities and affects others who depend on you. Behavior that is dysfunctional is generally considered abnormal.

Distress.   People may be diagnosed as suffering from a psychological disorder if their behavior is upsetting, distracting, or confusing to themselves. The distress criterion is useful in cases in which the psychological disorder is accompanied by discomfort. Imagine the distress felt by someone who believes other people are "out to get" him or by a depressed person who sees suicide as "the only solution." Personal distress does not always accompany abnormal behavior, however. The woman screaming at unseen adversaries on a Chicago street was not distressed by her behavior; she simply wanted to be left alone. Her behavior would not be considered abnormal according to the criterion of personal distress; however, applying the criterion of statistical rarity would lead us to judge the behavior as abnormal.

Deviance from Social Norms.   All social groups, ranging from your neighborhood to an entire society, decide which behaviors are acceptable for group members. The resulting guidelines, called *social norms*, distinguish acceptable behaviors from unacceptable or deviant ones. Norms may be recorded as laws, like those that prohibit writing bad checks. Many social norms do not exist in written form, however, they still guide our behavior and influence opinions about the behavior of others. For example, there are no written laws dictating that people should use polite language such as "Excuse me" or "Thank you," but many people consider these phrases an essential part of interacting with others.

How do social norms relate to the definition of abnormal behavior? Depending on the context—that is, when and where they occur—certain behaviors are considered unacceptable. In other words, they are "against the norm," or abnormal. Norms differ from group to group and also change over time. For example, some groups of people view body piercing as self-mutilation; other groups see it as a valued expression of group solidarity or rebellion against conformity imposed from outside the group.

A Working Definition

Each of the criteria of abnormality we have discussed has advantages and disadvantages. We often use several criteria simultaneously in making judgments about particular behaviors; therefore we can define behaviors as **abnormal** when they are statistically unusual, are not socially approved, and cause distress to the person or interfere with his or her ability to function. Because different cultural groups have different social norms, definitions of abnormality using this criterion are culturally variable.

Keep the following points in mind when making such judgments. First, normality and abnormality are degrees of difference on a continuum; the point at which normal behavior becomes abnormal depends on how you define normality. When we perceive a behavior as abnormal, we are making a value judgment about the appropriateness of that behavior. Second, the person whose behavior is judged may not accept your perspective. (Recall the woman on the streets of Chicago described at the beginning of this section.) Finally, these judgments vary with social or cultural standards, which may change over time.

We use several criteria to judge whether people are exhibiting abnormal behavior. By some standards the dress and behavior of these football fans would be judged abnormal. Many of the people in the stands, however, would judge these enthusiastic fans to be normal and perhaps even models to be imitated.

On March 30, 1981, radio and television stations flashed a news bulletin: John Hinckley Jr. had shot and wounded President Ronald Reagan and three other people. On June 20, 2001, Andrea Yates drowned all five of her young children, and then called her husband at work, asking him to come home. For several years, Yates had been under the care of a psychiatrist. She suffered from postpartum depression—a serious disorder that sometimes follows childbirth.

At the time when Hinckley came to trial, federal law required prosecutors to prove that a defendant was sane. Hinckley's lawyers argued their client had tried to kill the president to attract the attention of an actress. Experts testified that Hinckley suffered from a psychological disorder, but they disagreed about its severity. After deliberating the conflicting testimony, the jury returned a verdict of not guilty by reason of **insanity,** the legal ruling that a person accused of a crime is not responsible for it. In the Yates trial, there was testimony concerning her mental illness, but disagreement concerning whether she was insane under the law of the state of Texas. The jury decided that she was sane at the time she committed the crime. Although the prosecution had asked for the death penalty, the jury recommended a sentence of life in prison.

insanity
Legal ruling that a person accused of a crime is not held responsible for that act; defined in most states as the inability to tell the difference between right and wrong at the time the crime is committed

The jury's determination that John Hinckley Jr. was not guilty by reason of insanity led to changes in the application of the insanity plea across the country.

The Concept of Insanity

The key to understanding the Hinckley and the Yates decisions is the distinction between describing actions (Hinckley fired the shots, Yates drowned her children) and holding someone responsible for those actions (Hinckley was responsible for firing the shots and should be punished, Yates was responsible for the drowning and should be punished). Suppose a 4-year-old child found the keys to the family car, managed to start and drive it, and hit and seriously injured a neighbor. Everyone agrees on the description, but would we hold the child responsible for the consequences? Because we believe a 4-year-old child is not capable of understanding a wrongful and deliberate act, our legal system would not punish the child.

Psychological Detective

Even before the Hinckley trial focused attention on the insanity plea, many people held strong opinions about the plea. What do you think most people believe about the frequency of use and success of the insanity plea? What are the primary sources of the information that lead to these opinions?

In March, 2002 a jury found Andrea Yates guilty of killing her five children (ages 6 months to 7 years) and sentenced her to life in prison. When a police officer arrived at her home, Yates said she had "just killed my children." At trial, the defense argued that she suffered from postpartum depression and that her treatment had been inadequate.

Both the Hinckley and Yates cases showed the media to be a powerful source of information about the insanity defense. Millions of Americans saw newspaper and television pictures of the attempted assassination, which seemed to suggest that people with psychological disorders are dangerous. They saw extensive coverage of the Yates trial, including actual scenes from the courtroom. As many as 86% of newspaper stories that deal with former mental patients focus on a violent crime, usually murder (Shain & Phillips, 1991). Relying on such portrayals, many of us believe that defendants use the insanity plea as a loophole to escape punishment for their illegal acts: The public thinks that 37% of felony indictments involve an insanity plea and 44% of those pleas result in acquittal (Silver, Cirincione, & Steadman, 1994). By stark contrast, an analysis of approximately 1 million felony indictments found insanity pleas were used in less than 1% of the cases, and only 25% of those pleas were successful (Callahan et al., 1991).

How did the concept of an insanity plea develop? In 1843, an Englishman, Daniel M'Naughton, attempted to assassinate the British prime minister but killed the minister's secretary instead. Convincing testimony supported the defense's contention that M'Naughton believed the prime minister and others were conspiring against him. When the prosecution could not refute that testimony, the judge directed the jury to find M'Naughton "not guilty by reason of insanity."

In most states, the basis for determining insanity is the M'Naughton or "right-wrong" rule (Steadman et al., 1993): An accused person is not held legally responsible if he or she was unable to tell the difference between right and wrong at the time of the crime. M'Naughton fired the gun in the belief that he was defending himself against people who were plotting to kill him. The determination of insanity is a legal decision (decided by a judge or a jury), rather than a psychological or psychiatric one, although psychologists and psychiatrists often offer testimony to the court in insanity cases.

Only 15% of insanity verdicts occur in murder cases; assault is the most frequent crime for which defendants plead not guilty by reason of insanity (Callahan et al., 1991). Most defendants who are ruled insane have a history of serious psychological disorders with prior hospitalizations. Release procedures are quite strict, so defendants who are judged insane spend as much or more time in confinement as people convicted of similar crimes. Thus these data contradict the widespread belief that the insanity plea is a legal loophole used by defendants to escape punishment.

Models of Abnormal Behavior

Hundreds of years ago, many people believed that abnormal behaviors occurred when a person was "possessed" by demons. People who behaved in a bizarre fashion were often subjected to brutal treatments designed to drive the demons out. The belief in supernatural phenomena provided one way to understand disorders and also suggested possible treatments.

In their efforts to identify and explain abnormal behaviors, psychologists often adopt models, or general views of what causes those behaviors. Models help by pointing out which symptoms are most important, directing attention to their likely causes and suggesting possible treatments. We can organize the models under two general headings: the medical model and psychological models.

The Medical Model. Near the end of the 18th century, physicians began to document their patients' symptoms and to note which ones occurred together. The occurrence of groups of symptoms, called *syndromes*, helped physicians identify underlying diseases and develop treatments. Approaching abnormal behaviors just as one would approach medical illnesses is known as the **medical model.**

Psychiatrist Thomas Szasz (1993) argues for limiting the medical model to conditions resulting from actual brain dysfunctions. In his opinion, this model has been expanded to cover behaviors that are perhaps annoying or inappropriate but do not constitute diseases of the brain. For example, the list of proposed or recognized diseases includes shoplifting, pathological gambling, and nicotine dependence. According to Szasz, applying the medical model to such behaviors does not advance our understanding of the causes of the problems and allows people to avoid taking responsibility for their problems by attributing them to a disease.

Accumulating evidence shows that a number of psychological disorders are related to elevated or reduced levels of certain neurotransmitters or structural abnormalities in the brain. What's more, evidence is increasing that heredity plays a significant role in the development of a number of psychological disorders.

The Psychological Models. In contrast to the medical model, various *psychological models* emphasize the importance of mental functioning, social experiences, and learning histories in trying to explain the causes of abnormal behaviors. Sigmund Freud's **psychodynamic model** focuses on unconscious conflicts involving the id, ego, and superego or fixations at an early stage of psychosexual development. For example, anxiety is seen as a warning that the ego is about to be overwhelmed by conflict. The **behavioral model,** by contrast, focuses on environmental factors that mold human and animal behaviors. Behavioral theorists such as John B. Watson and B. F. Skinner propose that we learn both normal and abnormal behaviors through the principles of classical conditioning, operant conditioning, and modeling (see Chapter 5). In contrast to the behavioral model, the **cognitive model** focuses on understanding the content and processes of human thought. Cognitive psychologists claim that to understand human behavior, we must look beyond actual events to understand how people interpret those events.

Culture and Disorders. The **sociocultural model** emphasizes the role of social and cultural influences on the frequency, diagnosis, and conception of psychological disorders. Factors such as poverty and discrimination may promote a climate that increases the likelihood that psychological disorders will develop. Poverty is related to the prevalence of psychological disorders, and rates of psychological disorders are influenced by socioeconomic status (Bruce, Takeuchi, & Leaf, 1991; Dohrenwend et al., 1992).

The influence of culture is also seen in the fact that *anorexia nervosa* (a fear of being overweight associated with a failure to maintain appropriate weight; see Chapter 6) occurs primarily in the United States and other Western countries where thinness is considered a sign of female beauty.

Some sets of symptoms, called *culture-bound syndromes,* tend to be limited to specific cultures. In Japan the syndrome called *taijin kyofusho* involves the intense fear that one's body or its functions are offensive to other people (American Psychiatric Association, 2000). This syndrome shares similarities with social phobias, which are concerns related to public scrutiny or possible embarrassment (Kleinknecht et al., 1997). The focus of *taijin kyofusho,* however, is on offending others rather than on the self; the difference in the focus of these related disorders is consistent with conceptions of the self as independent or interdependent in the two cultures (see Chapter 11).

In some Native American cultures, individuals may believe they can hear the voice of a dead person calling them as the spirit travels to the afterworld (Lu, Lim, & Mezzich, 1995). *Ataque de nervios* (attacks of nerves) is particularly prominent among Spanish-speaking people from the Caribbean but also occurs among other Hispanic groups, most frequently women (Guarnaccia et al., 1993; Oquendo, Horwath, & Martinez, 1992; Oquendo, 1995). This brief-duration syndrome involves a variety of symptoms: shouting, crying, trembling, heat in the chest rising into the head, verbal or physical aggression, and seizurelike or fainting episodes. The symptoms typically

medical model
The view that mental disorders are like physical illnesses and have underlying organic causes

psychodynamic model
The view that psychological disorders result from unconscious conflicts related to sex or aggression

behavioral model
The view that psychological disorders are learned behaviors that follow the principles of classical and operant conditioning or modeling

cognitive model
A view that emphasizes thinking as the key element in causing psychological disorders

sociocultural model
A view that emphasizes the importance of society and culture in causing psychological disorders

diagnosis
The process of deciding whether a person has symptoms that meet established criteria of an existing classification system

follow family-related stressful events, such as news of the death of a close relative or witnessing an accident involving a family member (American Psychiatric Association, 2000). Although this "culturally condoned expression of distress" shares symptoms with several disorders (Guarnaccia et al., 1993; Oquendo, 1995), someone unfamiliar with the cultures in which it developed would find it difficult to understand.

Do these various models of abnormal behavior appear to conflict with one another? There is a growing recognition that many disorders have multiple causes; thus the simultaneous use of several models is likely to advance our understanding. This emphasis on multiple causation is evident in the *biopsychosocial* model, which incorporates *biological* (medical-model) factors along with psychological and sociocultural (social) factors. Some people may have inherited a tendency to exhibit strong autonomic reactions, which may predispose them to develop a number of disorders. But will they actually develop any of them? Whether a disorder develops may depend on an interaction of psychological and social factors with an inherited predisposition. For example, exposure to repeated stressful experiences that bring out strong autonomic reactions may lead certain people to begin questioning their ability to cope. Growing up in a family that typically reacts to stressful situations by presenting physical symptoms can lead an individual to report similar symptoms. Thus any one model of abnormal behavior may be an oversimplification.

CLASSIFYING AND COUNTING PSYCHOLOGICAL DISORDERS

You walk into a mental hospital and report that you heard a voice say "empty," "hollow," and "thud." You have no history of any psychological disorder, and except for giving the false report about hearing voices, you answer all questions truthfully. Will you be recognized as a fraud, or will you be diagnosed with a psychological disorder and treated for hearing voices in your head? *Can we tell the difference between normal and disturbed people?*

Suppose someone tells you that your cousin has suffered a "nervous breakdown." You know something is wrong, but you also have a number of unanswered questions. What are the symptoms? How serious are they? Are any treatments available? When you ask these questions, you are asking whether there is a **diagnosis**—the process of recognizing the presence of a disorder and naming it by using an existing classification system.

A major purpose of diagnosis is to make predictions. Given a particular diagnosis, what is the likely course of the disorder? Will the disorder respond to treatment? Which treatment? Success in making such predictions depends on the availability of a diagnostic system that can be used to classify disorders in a reliable fashion.

DSM-IV

One reason for revising the DSM is that diagnoses based on the categories listed in earlier editions were not sufficiently reliable. At times, different mental health professionals who interviewed the same patient failed to agree on the diagnosis. To remedy this problem, the developers of the DSM added rules for making diagnoses. The DSM spells out the number, severity, and duration of symptoms that define each diagnosis. These detailed rules have had the desired effect: The reliability of diagnoses has improved. This improved reliability of the DSM, however, has not silenced critics who question the very act of making a diagnosis.

The most frequently used system for classifying psychological disorders is the American Psychiatric Association's *Diagnostic and Statistical Manual of Mental Disorders*, known as the DSM. More than 200 psychological disorders are listed in the fourth edition of the DSM, called DSM-IV (2000). The major DSM-IV categories and examples of each category are listed in Table 12-1.

STUDY TIP

In a group of three, quiz one another on the major categories of disorders listed in the DSM-IV. Make a set of flash cards that list the disorder type on one side and an example of the disorder on the other. Alternate the sides you use at random. If one student calls out a disorder type, the second student should describe it and the third should give at least one example. If the student calls out a disorder example, the second student should name the disorder type and the third should describe the type.

TABLE 12-1

Descriptions and Examples of Major Categories of Disorders Listed in the DSM-IV

Disorder Type	Descriptions and Examples
Disorders usually first diagnosed in infancy, childhood, or adolescence	These disorders begin before adulthood and include mental retardation, attention-deficit hyperactivity disorder (ADHD), autistic disorder, and separation anxiety.
Delirium, dementia, and amnestic disorders	Disorders characterized by a significant deficit in cognition resulting from a medical condition or substance use. Delirium is a confused state of consciousness; dementia is characterized by multiple deficits in intellectual functioning, including memory deficits. Amnestic disorders affect memory but not other functioning.
Substance-related disorders	Disorders resulting from excessive and persistent use of mind-altering substances such as alcohol, amphetamines, or cocaine.
Schizophrenia and other psychotic disorders	Schizophrenia involves symptoms such as delusions, hallucinations, and deterioration from a previous level of functioning that last for at least six months (examples include catatonic schizophrenia and paranoid schizophrenia).
Mood disorders	Disorders that involve extremes in mood that cause people to feel inappropriately sad or highly elated or to swing between these extremes; category includes major depressive episode and bipolar disorder (formerly called manic depression).
Anxiety disorders	Anxiety is manifested in phobias, generalized anxiety disorder, panic disorder, obsessive–compulsive disorder, or posttraumatic stress disorder.
Somatoform disorders	Physical symptoms such as paralysis cause significant distress or impairment but do not have a medical explanation; examples include somatization disorder and hypochondriasis.
Dissociative disorders	Disorders characterized by a sudden change in the usually integrated functions of consciousness, memory, identity, or perception; they include dissociative amnesia, dissociative fugue, and dissociative identity disorder (multiple personality).
Sexual and gender identity disorders	Disorders include the paraphilias, characterized by arousal involving unusual objects, activities, or situations, and sexual dysfunctions such as inhibition of orgasms; category also includes gender identity disorder.
Personality disorders	Pervasive, inflexible patterns of inner experience and behavior beginning in adolescence or early adulthood that are stable over time, resistant to treatment, and lead to distress or impairment; category includes antisocial personality disorder and paranoid personality disorder.

Source: Reprinted with permission from the *Diagnostic and Statistical Manual of Mental Disorders,* Fourth Edition. © 2000 American Psychiatric Association.

The Labeling Issue

Recall the vignette at the beginning of this section, in which we put you in the position of someone who walked into a mental hospital and reported hearing a voice say "empty," "hollow," and "thud." Do you believe the hospital staff could tell the difference between a normal person and a disturbed one?

Psychologist David Rosenhan (1973) and seven colleagues actually carried out this research. They entered mental hospitals and reported hearing voices. Except for giving false names, they answered all questions truthfully. Most of these "pseudopatients" were admitted to the hospital with the diagnosis of *schizophrenia,* a serious psychological disorder. Although they stopped reporting the symptom immediately after admission, they were hospitalized for an average of 19 days and were given a combined total of more than 2,000 pills (which they did not swallow).

The setting and the labels we use influence our perceptions. Some of the people in this photograph are staff members and others are patients in a mental health treatment setting. Can you tell which people are staff members and which are patients? Would your perceptions of these people be affected if we identified the individuals who had the diagnosis of schizophrenia?

Not surprisingly, Rosenhan's research generated controversy. Critics pointed out that patients do not walk into hospitals and fake symptoms, and hence the study was invalid on its face. Nevertheless, the pseudopatients' experiences reveal how labels such as "schizophrenia" can influence our perceptions of behavior. Once the label "schizophrenic" had been applied to the pseudopatients, it influenced the staff's perceptions of them. Some normal behaviors were perceived as abnormal when filtered through that diagnostic label. For example, while in the hospital, the pseudopatients wrote notes describing their experiences. The hospital staff viewed the writing as a symptom of schizophrenia. Several "real" patients, however, recognized the pseudopatients as normal people who were collecting information about life in a mental hospital. The reactions of staff members were quite different. For example, a pseudopatient might say, "Pardon me, Dr. X. Could you tell me when I am eligible for grounds privileges?" The response would be, "Good morning, Dave. How are you today?" Then the staff member would simply walk off (Rosenhan, 1973). Ironically, a recent attempt at replicating Rosenhan's study involving 7 people with active symptoms of schizophrenia had a very different result. Six of the 7 people were denied treatment, perhaps as a result of limitations on mental health treatment due to budget reductions and managed care (Scribner, 2001).

Rosenhan's pseudopatients could not escape the label, even when they were released from the hospital; they were given the diagnosis of "schizophrenia in remission." These results suggest that the use of diagnostic labels can be a double-edged sword. Diagnosis can help advance our knowledge about the causes of disorders and aid in making treatment decisions, but diagnostic labels may also create a stigma that can be difficult to overcome when looking for housing or a job or simply interacting with other people. Labels inevitably affect how we perceive and respond to others; our responses to those persons labeled as having a psychological disorder are often different from our responses to other people.

The Prevalence of Psychological Disorders

Epidemiologists study the distribution and factors associated with accidents, diseases, and psychological disorders. The data they collect are our best estimates of the numbers of people who suffer from various ailments and disorders. The information is also used to identify subgroups (such as adolescents and the elderly) that are susceptible to particular disorders, to plan and evaluate treatments, and to determine the need for additional health care services. Just as it is problematic to define abnormal behavior, it is also difficult to collect accurate information about the number of people who experience psychological disorders. Many people who suffer from these disorders do not seek treatment; others seek help from family physicians rather than mental health professionals and thus are not readily identified and counted among those who have psychological disorders. Nevertheless, several major surveys provide estimates of the frequency of these disorders in the general population.

Epidemiologists are interested in the **prevalence** of disorders—the percentage or number of a population experiencing a given disorder during some specified period. For example, if 500 people in a population of 10,000 had the flu during the past 6 months, the 6-month prevalence for flu would be 5% (500/10,000). Questions like "Did you have the flu at any time during your life?" yield lifetime prevalence figures.

The **incidence** of a disorder is the rate (or number) of new cases reported during a given period. If there were 100 newly diagnosed cases this year, the incidence of flu in our population of 10,000 would be 1%.

One very useful method for estimating the number of people who have psychological disorders is the face-to-face survey (see Chapter 1). This method was used in two surveys of more than 27,000 respondents: the Epidemiologic Catchment Area Study (Robins & Regier, 1991) and the National Comorbidity Survey (Kessler et al., 1994). In both surveys, trained interviewers asked a series of questions designed to elicit information that would establish the presence of various psychological disorders. A recent re-analysis of the data from these two surveys reported one-year prevalence estimates of several of the disorders listed in the DSM for those cases in which the symptoms reached a level of clinical significance. In other words, these estimates represent the percentage of the population (18 years or older) whose symptoms interfere with their functioning (Narrow et al., 2002). Twenty percent of respondents reported having had clinically significant psychological disorders within the 12 months before the interview. The most frequent diagnoses were phobias, alcohol and drug abuse or dependence (see Chapter 4), and major depressive disorder. One-year prevalence estimates for some of the disorders are presented in Figure 12-1.

These and other psychological disorders, however, often occur with other disorders. Figure 12-2 illustrates the frequency of these concurrent or *comorbid* diagnoses in the same people (Kessler et al., 1994). Approximately 50% of all people with psychological disorders have more than one disorder; comorbidity is even higher in samples of people drawn from those who seek treatment (Clark, Watson, & Reynolds, 1995). The existence of several disorders in a person has important implications in treatment

prevalence
Number or percentage of people in a population that ever had a particular disorder during a specified time period

incidence
Number or percentage of newly diagnosed cases of a particular disorder in a given population

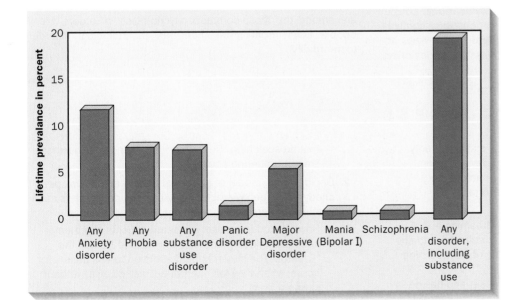

FIGURE 12-1 One-year prevalence estimates for selected psychological disorders based on a combination of data from the Epidemiologic Catchment Area Study and the National Comorbidity Survey. These estimates represent the percentage of the population (aged 18 or older) whose symptoms were associated with a clinically significant effect on their lives. In most cases, the estimates are the average of estimates from the two surveys; in other cases they represent only one survey because the surveys did not include the same set of disorders.

Source: Narrow, Rae, Robins, & Regier, 2002.

FIGURE 12-2 Comorbid psychological disorders. Many people who have one psychological disorder experience other disorders at the same time. The simultaneous occurrence of disorders, or comorbidity, increases the difficulty associated with making appropriate diagnoses and developing effective treatment plans.

Source: Kessler et al., 1994.

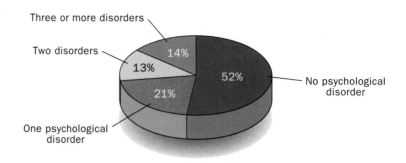

planning. Compared to those with a single diagnosis, individuals with comorbid diagnoses have a more chronic history of disorders, report more physical health problems, and experience greater overall impairment (Newman et al., 1998; Moffitt, 1998).

Most people with psychological disorders do not seek treatment. Yet psychological disorders are associated with significant disability as measured by the number of days individuals are unable to carry out their usual activities or experience restrictions in their social or occupational roles (Ormel et al., 1994).

REVIEW SUMMARY

1. By the standard of statistical rarity, behavior is abnormal when it is infrequent. **Dysfunctional** behavior interferes with a person's ability to function in day-to-day life. The criterion of personal distress is frequently used in identifying the presence of a psychological disorder. Departures from *social norms* are used to define deviant, and therefore **abnormal,** behaviors; social norms, however, can change over time and vary across cultures.

2. **Insanity** is a legal ruling that an accused individual is not responsible for a crime. Contrary to the public's understanding of the insanity plea, such pleas are infrequently used and rarely successful.

3. The **medical model** views abnormal behaviors as no different from illnesses and seeks to identify symptoms and prescribe medical treatments. The **psychodynamic model** considers abnormal behavior as the result of unconscious conflicts, often dating from childhood. The **behavioral model** views abnormal behaviors as learned through classical conditioning,

operant conditioning, and modeling. The **cognitive model** suggests that our interpretation of events and our beliefs influence our behavior. The **sociocultural** model emphasizes the importance of social and cultural factors in the frequency, diagnosis, and conception of disorders.

4. The American Psychiatric Association's *Diagnostic and Statistical Manual of Mental Disorders* (*DSM*) provides rules for diagnosing psychological disorders that have increased reliability.

5. Rosenhan's pseudopatient study raises questions about our ability to distinguish normal and abnormal behaviors and shows how labels affect the perception of behavior.

6. *Epidemiologists* study the **prevalence** and **incidence** of accidents, diseases, and psychological disorders. Phobias, alcohol and drug abuse or dependence, and major depressive disorder are among the most common psychological disorders. Many people suffer from more than one psychological disorder (comorbidity).

✓ CHECK YOUR PROGRESS

1. Decide which criterion of abnormality—statistical rarity, dysfunction, personal distress, and/or deviance from social norms—could be used to judge each of the following cases. (More than one criterion may be applicable.)

   a. Sally spends much of her time daydreaming about "nothing in particular." Her work has suffered, and she has been put on probation because of her declining productivity.

   b. Tim spends most of his money on beer and has been neglecting his appearance. When a friend suggested

   that he seek help, Tim responded, "Mind your business. I'm not bothering anyone."

2. Decide which model of abnormal behavior—medical, psychodynamic, behavioral, cognitive, or sociocultural—is most useful in understanding each of the following cases.

   a. Several students observed some patients at a mental hospital, including one who announced he was the "Creator." The students paid attention to this patient for hours; when they left, the patient walked away without saying a word.

b. After Cara got a D on an exam, she concluded that the low grade "proves that I'm stupid." She ignored the fact that a bout of flu had prevented her from studying.

3. What is the most commonly used legal definition of insanity?

4. Which disorder seems to occur primarily in the United States and other Western countries?

  a. depression
  b. schizophrenia
  c. bipolar disorder
  d. anorexia nervosa

5. Of 1,000 felony cases in a nearby county, how many are likely to involve a plea of "not guilty by reason of insanity?"

  a. 1
  b. 10
  c. 25
  d. 50

6. Your roommate, a psychology major, is completing an internship at the mental health center. Today he told you of a client who was described during a case conference as comorbid. You do not want to reveal your ignorance, so you look up the word later. What will the dictionary entry say?

  a. More than one disorder has been diagnosed in this client.
  b. Some of the same symptoms have been reported by family members of the client.
  c. The client was suffering from a serious condition that is life threatening.

d. The word appears to be made-up and probably is used by someone suffering a psychotic disorder.

7. Rosenhan and his colleagues presented themselves as patients with just one symptom—hearing a voice say "empty," "hollow," and "thud." What diagnosis were these pseudopatients given? What is the implication of Rosenhan's pseudopatient study?

8. In a survey conducted in a city of 20,000 people, researchers found that 200 of them had been diagnosed with ulcers during the past year. A total of 1,000 people reported having had an ulcer at some time during their life.

  a. What is the incidence of ulcers in this city?
  b. What is the lifetime prevalence of ulcers?

9. What is the most common crime for which a defendant pleads "not guilty by reason of insanity"?

  a. rape
  b. murder
  c. assault
  d. bank robbery

10. Which of these symptom groups is most likely to be found in someone with *ataque de nervios?*

  a. crying, trembling, fainting
  b. delusions, hallucinations, and insomnia
  c. chest pain, memory loss, and profuse sweating
  d. rapid heart beat, amnesia, and loss of appetite

ANSWERS: 1. a. Dysfunctional or personal distress **b.** Deviance from social norms **2. a.** Behavioral **b.** Cognitive **3.** Right-wrong or M'Naughton definition **4.** d **5.** b **6.** a **7.** Schizophrenia. Labels can influence our perceptions of behavior. **8. a.** 200 cases in a year **b.** 1,000 is the lifetime prevalence (5%) **9.** c **10.** a

ANXIETY, SOMATOFORM, AND DISSOCIATIVE DISORDERS

One day while driving home, Deb realized that her heart had suddenly begun racing; she was dizzy, short of breath, and sweating profusely. Afraid that she might pass out, she rolled down the car window to let cold air rush across her face. Over the next several months, these attacks occurred more frequently— the laundromat, the grocery store, the bank, almost everywhere. She opted to drive side streets to and from work out of fear that she might be caught in traffic during an attack. Deb began to think she was "going crazy" or was about to die. As she read the obituaries in the newspaper, she thought the deceased were lucky because "they didn't have to go on anymore." Eventually she was unable to leave home; she was even afraid to walk across the backyard to her neighbor's house. *Could symptoms like a racing heart and profuse sweating indicate a psychological disorder?*

In this and the following sections, we focus on specific types or categories of psychological disorders. In doing so, we might list some symptoms you may see in yourself. Like medical students who sometimes believe they have the diseases covered in their textbooks and courses, you may conclude you have one or more of the disorders discussed in this chapter. Be aware of this tendency to diagnose yourself, and don't conjure up

anxiety
General feeling of apprehension characterized by behavioral, cognitive, or physiological symptoms

phobia
Irrational fear of an activity, object, or situation that is out of proportion to the actual danger

agoraphobia
Avoidance of public places or situations in which escape may be difficult should the individual develop incapacitating or embarrassing symptoms of panic

unnecessary worries. If you have troubling symptoms, however, do not hesitate to discuss them with a teacher, a counselor, or a therapist. These professionals can help you evaluate the severity of your symptoms and determine whether you need treatment.

The disorders described in the first part of this section are related to anxiety. People with anxiety disorders maintain good contact with reality, are not grossly disturbed, and usually are not hospitalized. Their symptoms, however, can be disturbing and may interfere with day-to-day living. After discussing the anxiety disorders, we will turn to the somatoform and dissociative disorders.

Anxiety Disorders

Giving a speech in class, waiting to take an exam, interviewing for a job—what do these experiences have in common? Perhaps you feel apprehensive and uncomfortable in these situations. Does the word *anxious* come to mind? At moderate levels, anxiety is normal; it often provides the motivation needed to give an outstanding speech, "ace" an exam, or get a good job. High levels of **anxiety** or a general feeling of apprehension, however, are distressing and interfere with effective functioning. Severe anxiety that disrupts a person's life indicates the presence of an *anxiety disorder*. According to one survey, 19% of men and 31% of women have had at least one anxiety disorder at some time in their lives (Kessler et al., 1994).

But how do we recognize anxiety? There are three categories of indicators: behavioral, cognitive, and physiological. The behavioral indicators include shakiness and stuttering. Physiological signs like a rapid heart rate and dry mouth reflect sympathetic nervous system activation (see Chapter 2). Cognitive signs include difficulty concentrating and thoughts or beliefs that can fuel the anxiety (such as "I'll make a fool of myself when I give my speech").

Phobias. As we saw in Chapter 5, a **phobia** is an intense, excessive fear of an activity, object, or situation. The fear in a phobia is out of proportion to the real danger, and it is difficult to overcome. If your concern about facing fear-arousing stimuli leads to efforts to avoid those stimuli, you may have a phobia. The DSM-IV organizes phobias into three categories: *agoraphobia*, *social phobia*, and *specific phobia*.

Agoraphobia (literally "fear of the marketplace") is the most common phobia treated in mental health clinics. Most people with agoraphobia are women who avoid

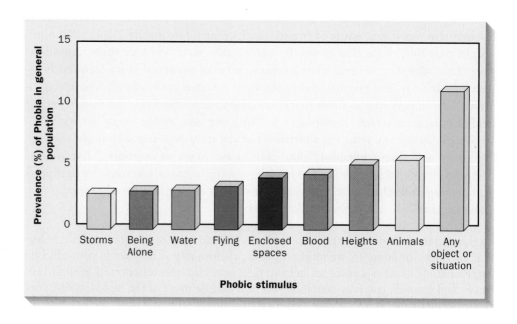

FIGURE 12-3 Specific phobias are not uncommon. In one survey, the lifetime prevalence for specific phobias was 11%, with fears of animals being the most common of the specific phobias.

Source: Curtis et al., 1998.

public places or situations from which it would be difficult to escape if they developed embarrassing or incapacitating symptoms such as dizziness or vomiting. They prefer the safety of a private place, quite often their home.

Different phobias tend to develop at different ages. Agoraphobia usually begins in one's twenties; **social phobias,** such as fear of speaking in front of a group, usually emerge between late adolescence and early adulthood (15 to 25 years of age) (Schneier & Johnson, 1992). **Specific phobias**—fears of particular objects or situations—often begin between ages 5 and 9 (Ost, 1987). Figure 12-3 depicts the prevalence rates of some of the social and specific phobias. Examples of specific phobias are the fear of blood (*hemophobia*), fire (*pyrophobia*), and heights (*acrophobia*) (see Table 12-2).

social phobia
A fear related to being seen or observed by others

specific phobia
Any phobia other than agoraphobia or the social phobias, including the fear of specific animals, of elements of the natural environment, and of such things as blood, injections, or injury

TABLE 12-2

Common Specific Phobias, by Type

Phobias	Focus of the Fear
Animal type	
Ailurophobia	Cats
Arachnophobia	Spiders
Cynophobia	Dogs
Entomophobia	Insects
Musophobia	Mice
Natural environment type	
Brontophobia	Thunder, thunderstorms
Frigophobia	Cold weather
Nephophobia	Clouds
Phonophobia	Loud noises
Photophobia	Light
Blood-injection-injury type	
Belonophobia	Pins and needles
Hemophobia	Blood
Odynephobia	Pain
Parasitophobia	Parasites
Poinephobia	Punishment
Situation type	
Cainophobia	Novelty
Claustrophobia	Closed spaces
Ochlophobia	Crowds
Scotophobia	Being looked at
Gephyrophobia	Crossing bridges
Other	
Catoptrophobia	Mirrors
Kakorrhaphiophobia	Failure
Logophobia	Words
Triskaidekaphobia	Number 13

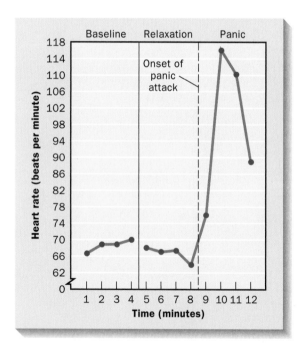

"I'm facing my fears in alphabetical order. How about you?"

panic disorder
The most severe anxiety disorder, characterized by intense physiological arousal not related to a specific

More than 50% of people with a blood-injection-injury phobia report a history of fainting. In contrast to the typical phobic reaction, their blood pressure drops dramatically when they are unable to avoid situations such as having blood drawn. Many victims of a blood phobia share the fear with a close family member, which may result from similar or common stressful experiences or genetic factors that predispose them to faint (Ost, 1992).

How do phobias develop? On the basis of their study of Little Albert (see Chapter 5), John B. Watson and Rosalie Rayner (1920) proposed that phobias are learned through classical conditioning. A phobia may result when a formerly neutral stimulus (such as a white rat) becomes associated with a fear-producing stimulus (such as a loud noise). Through this association, the neutral stimulus becomes a feared stimulus; that is, it is now the conditioned stimulus (CS) or phobic stimulus.

During World War II, London was subjected to heavy aerial bombardment. Despite the frequent occurrence of unconditioned stimuli (loud explosions), few Londoners developed phobias. The situation in London is one example of our tendency to develop phobias to some stimuli more readily than to others. According to the concept of preparedness (see Chapter 5), we are more likely to learn to fear stimuli that our ancestors had reason to fear, such as snakes, than nonharmful objects like flowers or stimuli that did not exist in our ancestors' time—for instance, aerial bombardments.

Phobias may also develop by observing (modeling) the behaviors and emotional reactions of others; this indirect form of learning is often called *vicarious conditioning*. Few people who fear mice or snakes have actually had adverse encounters with such creatures. They may have seen other people react fearfully in the presence of these stimuli, however, or perhaps they have heard discussions of the awful things such animals might do to humans. This type of modeling can be beneficial when it enables us to learn reasonable fears without directly encountering dangerous objects; still, it can lead us to fear stimuli simply because we have been exposed to the fears of others.

Panic Disorder. At the beginning of the section we met Deb, who experienced symptoms such as a racing heart, profuse sweating, and difficulty breathing while driving home. Do these symptoms suggest she is suffering from a psychological disorder?

Deb had several panic attacks, which are intense physiological reactions that occur even in the absence of an emergency. Within seconds the heart rate of a person with this disorder can accelerate by 50 or more beats per minute (see Figure 12-4). In addition to rapid heartbeat, victims also report sweating, dizziness, shortness of breath, and shaking.

An episode of panic typically lasts between 5 and 20 minutes, although victims perceive the duration of the attack to be endless (Rachman, 1998). Many victims believe they are "going crazy," losing control, or having a heart attack, yet there is no medical evidence of a heart condition. Panic attack victims seem frightened by the physical symptoms of their fear; thus, panic attacks probably represent "fear of fear" (Craske & Barlow, 2001). Frequent panic attacks are diagnosed as **panic disorder,** the most severe anxiety disorder. The rate among women is more than twice that for men (Eaton et al., 1994), with some differences in reported symptoms: women are more likely to report respiration-related difficulties (Sheikh, Leskin, & Klein, 2002). Panic disorder is often comorbid with other anxiety disorders, depression, substance abuse, and personality disorders (Craske & Barlow, 2001; Knowles & Weissman, 1995).

FIGURE 12-4 Rapid increase in heart rate during a panic attack. In the midst of a diagnostic evaluation at a clinic, a 33-year-old woman experienced a panic attack a few minutes after she had been asked to relax her whole body. The sudden and intense physiological changes of a panic attack were also evident in increased levels of muscle tension in her forehead.

Source: Cohen, Barlow & Blanchard, 1985.

About 50% of the people who suffer from panic attacks also experience agoraphobia (Eaton et al., 1994), which is what happened to Deb. Thus it is possible that some cases of agoraphobia develop out of the experience of panic attacks (Barlow et al., 1985). Most people with phobias can avoid the stimuli they fear, but victims of panic disorder are not so fortunate. Panic attacks can strike "out of the blue," so victims cannot hide. Perhaps this is why many victims of agoraphobia prefer to remain in locations like their homes, where they will not be embarrassed if they experience panic symptoms.

What causes such attacks? In patients with a history of panic attacks, the symptoms can be induced by an injection of sodium lactate (the amount of this chemical in the body increases after vigorous exercise). The sodium lactate leads to increased physiological arousal like that occurring during a panic attack. Two other findings also support a biological cause: (1) Panic disorder occurs at a higher rate among family members of victims than in the general population, and (2) victims respond well to antidepressant drugs. What's more, a number of tests called *biological challenges* have revealed that certain biologically related phenomena can bring on panic attacks. For example, people with a history of panic attacks experience panic attacks if they hyperventilate, inhale carbon dioxide, or breathe into a paper bag. These procedures raise carbon dioxide levels in the blood and brain. People who are prone to panic attacks may be especially sensitive even to a small increase in carbon dioxide, which the brain registers as the threat of suffocation thus triggering the autonomic nervous system into a full fight-or-flight response—often interpreted as a heart attack. Victims of panic disorder may have a highly sensitive suffocation monitor that signals a lack of useful air (Klein, 1993).

"Looks like your fears of people, speaking, computers, and all forms of transportation might limit your career opportunities."

Source: Reprinted with the permission of Psi Chi, The National Honor Society in Psychology.

Psychological Detective

Between 15% and 30% of people surveyed report experiencing at least one panic attack (Eaton et al., 1994). If so many people experience panic attacks, why do only some of these people develop chronic panic disorder? According to cognitive psychologists, a key factor is the way people interpret their symptoms. What kind of interpretations could lead an individual to develop panic disorder?

According to cognitive psychologists, panic attacks occur when the bodily sensations of anxiety are misinterpreted as signs of impending disaster. Rather than attributing the symptoms to stressors in their lives, victims of panic disorder view them as indicators of serious physical problems such as a heart attack (McNally, Hornig, & Donnell, 1995). This interpretation increases their arousal during and after an attack and makes them even more vigilant about physical signs in the future.

Generalized Anxiety Disorder. Chronic worriers may suffer from a condition termed **generalized anxiety disorder (GAD)** that typically begins in one's twenties or thirties. Their low tolerance for uncertainty and ambiguity plays havoc with decision making; victims of GAD exhibit a continuous need for more evidence before rendering a decision (Ladouceur, Talbot, & Dugas, 1997). The anxiety characterizing this disorder is often called "free-floating" because it is not brought on by one specific stimulus. People who suffer from GAD describe their worry about family matters,

generalized anxiety disorder (GAD)
Chronically high level of anxiety that is not attached to a specific stimulus

obsessive–compulsive disorder (OCD)

An anxiety disorder characterized by repetitive, irrational, intrusive thoughts, impulses, or images (obsessions) and irresistible, repetitive acts (compulsions) such as checking that doors are locked or washing hands

work, finances, and so forth, as difficult to control. A consistent finding from epidemiological research is that GAD occurs more often in women than in men, with a ratio of 2 : 1 (Craske, O'Leary, & Barlow, 2001). Generalized anxiety disorder is a highly comorbid condition that may increase vulnerability to other psychological disorders, such as depression, as well as increasing the use of health care services (Craske et al., 2001; Roy-Byrne & Kato, 1997).

Generalized anxiety disorder, along with some other anxiety disorders, may result from low levels of the inhibitory neurotransmitter gamma-aminobutyric acid (GABA; see Chapter 2). Anxiety often occurs when there is a high level of nerve impulses in brain circuits related to fear and vigilance. Elevated levels of GABA block this neurological activity; low levels allow it to occur, and the result can be what we term anxiety.

Obsessive–Compulsive Disorder.   "Did I turn off the stove?" "Are the windows closed?" Do thoughts like these run through your mind occasionally? If so, you are like most people. But some people are dominated by thoughts of this kind or worse. Intrusive, recurrent thoughts, impulses, or images that are unwanted, inappropriate and appear "out of the blue" are *obsessions* (from the Latin word meaning "to besiege"). The "battle in the mind" (Osborn, 1998) created by obsessions can cause unbearable anxiety that leads some people to feel they must do something to get rid of or reduce their occurrence. These people may check the stove or windows over and over each day. For example, a clerk spent up to two hours a day checking electrical appliances, doors, and windows in her house before she was able to leave (Rachman, 1998). These repeated, irresistible behaviors (such as hand washing) or mental acts (such as silent counting or repetition of words) that often follow obsessions are called *compulsions*. Performing these so-called "rituals," however, provides only temporary relief; not performing them leads to a significant increase in anxiety. Although obsessions and compulsions may occur separately, most people with **obsessive–compulsive disorder (OCD)** have both of them (Foam & Kazak, 1995). Table 12-3 lists some common obsessions and compulsions.

TABLE 12-3

Common Obsessions and Compulsions

The most common obsessions involve contamination and the fear of harming oneself or others. The most common compulsions involve checking objects (such as light switches or locks) and cleaning or washing.

Obsessions

- A young woman's recurrent impulse to strangle children and domestic animals was followed by the thought that she might actually have committed this horrible act.
- A young man had recurrent intrusive images of violently attacking his elderly parents with an ax. The subsequent thought that he might have actually attacked them included images of the bloody victims.
- A young woman's recurrent, intrusive impulse to burn her eyes with a lighted cigarette was accompanied by images of the act.

Compulsions

- A young woman repeatedly washed her hands to rid herself of contamination by germs. On every occasion, she washed six times without soap and six times with soap.
- A man opened letters he had written and sealed to make sure that he had written the correct things. He would rip open the envelope, reread the letter, and put it into a new envelope several times before mailing it.
- A woman in her forties complained that every time she entered a room, she had to touch the four corners in a left-to-right sequence.

Sources: De Silva & Rachman, 1992; The Harvard Mental Health Letter, 1998.

Mental health professionals use the words *obsession* and *compulsion* differently from the way we use them in everyday conversation. You may think a friend who watches dozens of basketball games is "obsessed." To a basketball fan, however, his behavior is desirable and enjoyable. People with OCD do not want or enjoy their obsessive thoughts or time-consuming compulsions; they perceive them as excessive and feel that they interfere with daily functioning. What's more, compulsive gambling and compulsive eating are often associated with some degree of pleasure. By contrast, the compulsions in obsessive–compulsive disorder are irrational and do not give rise to pleasure.

The lifetime prevalence of OCD is about 2% (Narrow et al., 2002). Among children and adolescents, the rate is higher among boys than girls (Number & Van Open, 1994); among adults, the disorder is more common among women. Across the entire lifespan, however, there is little difference in the rates of OCD among males and females. Although OCD tends to begin around age 20, its onset could be earlier; there are difficulties in accurately diagnosing OCD in children so some cases may be missed (Penzel, 2000). The disorder is sometimes accompanied by depression, eating disorders, substance abuse, or other anxiety disorders (Robins, Rae, & Narrow, 1998; Wonderlich & Mitchell, 1997). Consider this case of one adolescent's struggle with OCD:

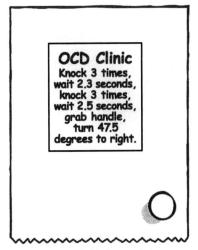

Source: Reprinted with the permission of Psi Chi, The National Honor Society in Psychology.

> For years, 14-year-old Charles has spent hours in the shower removing a sticky substance from his body. His mother knew the washing was crazy, but she joined her son's rituals because he would be miserable otherwise. She scrubbed household objects with alcohol. Charles and his mother heard about a treatment program, but he was wary of the required EEG test because a sticky paste would be used to attach the electrodes. "Stickiness is terrible. It is some kind of disease," he said. (Rapoport, 1989, pp. 82–86)

Behavioral psychologists view compulsions as learned habits that reduce anxiety. That is, the compulsive behavior has been associated with anxiety reduction through operant conditioning.

Psychological Detective

Charles showered repeatedly in an effort to remove a sticky substance from his body. After each shower, his anxiety was reduced. The reduction in anxiety is an example of an operant conditioning principle (see Chapter 5). Before reading further, identify that principle. Then identify the specific reinforcer involved and the behavior that is being reinforced.

Charles engaged in the behavior of showering, which led to a reduction of his anxiety. This sequence is an example of negative reinforcement: Showering behavior was reinforced by anxiety reduction. As a result, Charles is more likely to take showers in the future.

Obsessive–compulsive disorder runs in families; identical twins are more likely than fraternal twins to share the disorder. These findings point to an inherited biological predisposition (Andreasen & Black, 1995), which may involve abnormal levels of a neurotransmitter or abnormal functioning of certain parts of the brain. The neurotransmitter serotonin has been implicated in OCD because antidepressant drugs that affect this neurotransmitter are useful treatments (Penzel, 2000; Pies, 1998). Obsessive–compulsive disorder may involve elevated levels of activity in the frontal lobes and the basal ganglia (see Figure 12-5). This increased activity may account for the obsessions or merely reflect them; recall from Chapter 2 that the frontal lobes are involved in planning and thinking, an important component of obsessive–compulsive behavior. The basal ganglia play a role in motor movement and thus may be implicated in compulsions (Andreasen & Black, 1995).

FIGURE 12-5 Brain scans of a normal person and one with obsessive–compulsive disorder. Note the greater frequency of reds and yellows in the brain of a person with obsessive–compulsive disorder, indicating greater brain activity, especially in the frontal lobes.

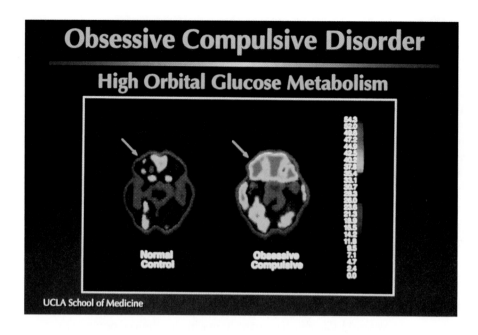

The study chart below should provide a helpful summary and review of the anxiety disorders.

STUDY CHART	
Anxiety Disorders	
Agoraphobia	Fear of being in places such as shopping malls or public transportation, where it might be difficult to escape if embarrassing symptoms occur suddenly. Sometimes occurs along with panic disorder.
Social phobia	Fears related to being in situations in which one might be subject to scrutiny.
Specific phobia	A large category of phobias other than those listed as agoraphobia or social phobia. These include phobias related to animals, the natural environment (storms, water), and blood-injection-injury.
Panic disorder	Recurrent panic attacks, which are intense physiological reactions in the absence of an emergency. There is also apprehension about the possibility of future attacks and concern about the seriousness of the attacks, which are often viewed as similar to heart attacks.
Generalized anxiety disorder	A high level of anxiety not tied to a specific stimulus. Symptoms include excessive worry about a number of events or activities.
Obsessive–compulsive disorder (OCD)	Typically a combination of disturbing, persistent thoughts, impulses, or images (obsessions) followed by irresistible behaviors (compulsions) that tend to reduce the anxiety.

Somatoform Disorders

somatoform disorders
Disorders involving physical complaints that do not have a known medical cause but are related to psychological factors

Somatoform disorders involve complaints of bodily symptoms (*soma* means "body") that do not have a known medical cause; instead psychological factors are involved. Do not confuse somatoform disorders with *psychophysiological disorders*, which have a medical basis; in the case of ulcers, for example, digestive juices erode the stomach lining. These disorders generally occur in parts of the body controlled by the autonomic nervous system, such as the digestive tract; by contrast, somatoform disorders usually affect body parts that are controlled by the central nervous system, such as the sensory organs or the limbs. Among the somatoform disorders listed in the DSM-IV are hypochondriasis, somatization disorder, and conversion disorder.

"IGNORE HIM. HE'S A HYPOCHONDRIAC."

Hypochondriasis. **Hypochondriasis** is a preoccupation with physical symptoms believed to indicate a serious illness; it occurs equally in men and women (American Psychiatric Association, 2000). People with hypochondriasis detect aches, pains, or bodily changes that many of us would ignore; they interpret these signs as proof that they are suffering from some dire though undiagnosed disorder. People with this diagnosis (as well as those with somatization disorder) tend to agree with statements such as "Bodily complaints are always a sign of disease" and "Red blotches on the skin are a threatening sign of skin cancer." (Rief, Hiller, & Margraf, 1998). Their beliefs are genuine; they do not voluntarily produce their symptoms. Despite repeated assurances of good health, they are never convinced and continually consult one physician after another.

Somatization Disorder. People with **somatization disorder** present vague but complicated and dramatic medical histories, usually beginning in their teenage years. In contrast to hypochondriasis, which centers on some specific disease, somatization disorder involves a large number of symptoms (for example, gastrointestinal, neurological, pain, and sexual complaints) (American Psychiatric Association, 2000). The symptoms cause significant distress that leads victims to consult physicians who inevitably fail to find a medical basis for the physical complaints. The disorder occurs more frequently in women than in men, although physicians may be less likely to recognize it in men.

Conversion Disorder. A loss or impairment of motor or sensory function that does not coincide with the organization of the nervous system is a **conversion disorder.** For example, a patient who reports paralysis of the wrist may still be able to move the fingers, even though the fingers and wrist are on the same nerve pathway. Sensory symptoms include blindness, deafness, and inability to feel sensations in some parts of the body, even though the sensory system is not damaged. Such symptoms are real to these individuals, who do not feel they produce them voluntarily. Nevertheless, there is no obvious medical explanation for the symptoms and the disability they produce.

This rare disorder is often a response to stressful situations such as war or the death of a loved one. For example, a group of Cambodian women all had unexplained blindness. When they were interviewed, they related horrifying tales of having been forced to watch relatives being tortured and killed during political conflicts in their native country (Cooke, 1991).

hypochondriasis
Somatoform disorder in which a person believes that he or she has a serious disease despite repeated medical findings to the contrary

somatization disorder
Somatoform disorder involving multiple physical complaints that do not have a medical explanation and do not suggest a specific known disease

conversion disorder
Somatoform disorder in which a person presents sensory or motor symptoms that do not have a medical explanation

dissociative disorders
Disorders affecting a function of the mind, such as memory for events, knowledge of one's identity, or consciousness

dissociative amnesia
Dissociative disorder that involves a sudden inability to recall important personal information; often occurs in response to trauma or extreme stress

dissociative fugue
Dissociative disorder involving amnesia and flight from the workplace or home; may involve establishing a new identity in a new location

dissociative identity disorder (multiple personality)
Dissociative disorder in which a person has two or more separate personalities, which usually alternate

Modeling may occur in some cases of conversion disorder (Mucha & Reinhardt, 1970). Naval aviators who developed conversion disorders during their stressful training were likely to have parents who had physical problems in the same body parts in which the aviators developed symptoms.

How can we explain the development of somatoform disorders? First, the symptoms may be a defense against the distress of difficult situations. Second, when we have physical problems, relatives and friends often offer attention and sympathy, and these reactions can act as reinforcers for continued presentation of the symptoms. For example, conversion reactions often disappear without treatment in hours or days, sometimes in response to changes in the availability of attention and sympathy.

Dissociative Disorders

Dissociative disorders involve a disruption in a particular function of the mind, such as memory or self-awareness, usually in response to extreme stress. These rare disorders are dramatic and have been the basis of plots for movies, books, and television shows. Dissociative disorders include dissociative amnesia, dissociative fugue, and dissociative identity disorder (multiple personality).

Dissociative Amnesia and Dissociative Fugue.   An individual with **dissociative amnesia** is unable to recall important personal information. The memory impairment is too extensive to be due to normal forgetting; it may involve a specific traumatic event, most of the person's life, or a stretch of time ending in the present. Dissociative amnesia occurs suddenly, does not affect storage of new information, and frequently ends as abruptly as it began.

Psychological Detective

When Ed took his friends for a ride, he drove too fast on a hairpin turn, and the car flipped over. Rescue crews found three dead passengers; Ed survived, sustaining several broken bones and chest injuries. After he recovered from his injuries, he had no memory of the accident. The memory loss was too profound to be attributed to ordinary forgetfulness. How can we explain Ed's failure to recall the events? Use the medical and psychodynamic models to explain Ed's failure to recall events surrounding the car accident.

According to the medical model, amnesia results from physical causes such as a head injury or ingestion of large quantities of alcohol. Memory loss in these forms of amnesia is often permanent. Ed did not suffer a head injury and had no alcohol in his body, so we must consider another explanation. The psychodynamic explanation tells us that amnesia may occur as a defense against or escape from the anxiety caused by a traumatic event. In Ed's case, it appears that his recall failure was caused by the trauma of seeing his friends killed and feeling responsible for their deaths.

When amnesia is accompanied by travel, the person is suffering from **dissociative fugue.** People with this disorder may leave a stressful environment and take up residence in a distant city, with a new identity and no memory of their past life. Recovery is often sudden, and the victim's recall of the episode is no better than a dream. Cases of dissociative fugue are fascinating but extremely rare; more typical cases, although still infrequent, involve wandering away from a natural disaster.

Dissociative Identity Disorder.   The presence of more than one personality in a single individual, **dissociative identity disorder** (*multiple personality*), is the most dramatic dissociative disorder. Although it was once considered to be extremely rare, mental health professionals report significant numbers of cases of dissociative identity disorder, which they argue indicates that the disorder is not rare but underdiagnosed. There has been a clear increase in the number of cases of dissociative identity disorder

Seventeen-year-old Cheryl Ann Barnes is reunited with her family after she disappeared from her Florida home in 1996; she was found a month later in a New York hospital where she was listed as Jane Doe. Although quite rare, cases of dissociative fugue often receive widespread media attention.

reported during the past decade (Coons, 1998). Some psychologists are cautious and note that this increase in diagnoses coincides with the recovered-memory movement, which has been implicated in a number of false reports of abuse (see Chapter 7) (Ofshe & Watters, 1994).

Most cases of dissociative identity disorder are associated with an early childhood history of sexual or physical abuse (Gleaves, 1996; Lowenstein, 1994). Children are ill-equipped to cope with the trauma of abuse and may split off new personalities in an attempt to deal with it, in much the same way some children invent imaginary playmates. There are usually three or four personalities, although more than 100 have been reported in a single individual.

The personalities in dissociative identity disorder often contrast sharply with one another. For example, in the classic case described in *The Three Faces of Eve* (Thigpen & Cleckley, 1957), Eve White was shy and inhibited. At one point during psychotherapy, she put her hands on her temples and pressed hard, as if she was experiencing a severe headache. She dropped her hands, smiled, and said in an unfamiliar voice, "Hi, there, Doc!" A few minutes later she introduced herself as Eve Black. In a subsequent publication by Chris Sizemore (Eve's real name), she revealed that she actually had 22 different personalities. These personalities always occurred in groups of three, always included a wife/mother image, a party girl, and a more normal, intellectual personality (Sizemore & Pittillo, 1977). Here is her description of the different personalities:

 The Three Faces of Eve

> Among these twenty-two alters, ten were poets, seven were artists, and one had taught tailoring. Today, I paint and write, but I cannot sew. Yet these alters were not moods or the result of role-playing. They were entities that were separate from the personality I was born to be, and am today. They were so different that their tones of voice changed. What's more, their facial expressions, appetites, tastes in clothes, handwriting, skills, and IQ were all different too (Sizemore, 1989, p. 9)

In most instances, it is not easy to identify cases of dissociative identity disorder. Typically, 6 to 12 years elapse between the first occasion on which a person seeks treatment and the eventual diagnosis of dissociative identity disorder (Lowenstein, 1994). During that time several diagnoses may be suggested; the most common are depression, schizophrenia, and alcohol or drug abuse (Gleaves, 1996).

Psychodynamic theorists describe multiple personality as resulting from early traumas such as sexual assault or physical punishment. They regard patients with this disorder as passive victims of unconscious processes that suddenly take over when the individual faces a stressor. One alternative explanation suggests that the presentation of multiple personalities is a learned role (Spanos, Weekes, & Bertrand, 1985). Movies,

STUDY TIP

Develop a chart to summarize anxiety, somatoform, and dissociative disorders. Define each type of disorder at an appropriate location of your choice within the chart.

Chris Sizemore is Eve of *The Three Faces of Eve* and *A Mind of My Own*. Her story is one of the best-known cases of dissociative identity disorder (multiple personality disorder). She is now cured and is an advocate for the mentally ill.

television shows, and books like *The Three Faces of Eve* provide vivid descriptions of people who have suffered from this disorder. People with dissociative identity disorder may have been reinforced for revealing those personalities. For example, some therapists are so intrigued with the symptoms of this disorder they may inadvertently reinforce their clients for revelations concerning other personalities. Some researchers have found that many of the symptoms of the disorder occur for the first time during the course of treatment (Ofshe & Watters, 1994). What's more, using hypnosis in treatment may create a situation in which suggestible individuals turn the therapist's questions about other possible personalities into a belief in their existence. On the other hand, dissociative identity disorder is viewed as an underrecognized and underdiagnosed response pattern that has similarities to posttraumatic disorder (Gleaves, 1996).

The Study Chart below should prove helpful; consult it frequently.

STUDY CHART

Somatoform and Dissociative Disorders

Somatoform Disorders

Hypochondriasis	Preoccupation with physical symptoms that are believed to indicate a serious illness despite repeated medical evaluations that find no evidence of a disease.
Somatization disorder	Presentation of a large number of gastrointestinal, pain, sexual, and/or neurological symptoms that do not suggest a recognized disease.
Conversion disorder	A loss or impairment of motor function (for example, paralysis) or sensory function (for example, blindness) that does not coincide with the organization of the nervous system, with symptoms that may constitute a response to a very stressful situation.

Dissociative Disorders

Dissociative amnesia	An inability to recall important personal information that is often related to a traumatic event and is too extensive to be the result of normal forgetting.
Dissociative fugue	A rare disorder that combines amnesia with travel away from a stressful environment.
Dissociative identity disorder (multiple personality)	The presence of two or more distinct personalities that often contrast sharply, associated with a history of sexual and physical abuse.

The disorders we have discussed so far rarely lead to hospitalization, although the symptoms can interfere with daily living. Other psychological disorders, which we discuss in the next sections, have more serious consequences.

REVIEW SUMMARY

1. Anxiety involves behavioral, cognitive, and physiological elements. **Phobias** are excessive, irrational fears of activities, objects, or situations. The most frequently diagnosed phobia is **agoraphobia.** The DSM-IV also lists **social phobia** and **specific phobia.** Classical conditioning and modeling have been offered as explanations for the development of phobias.

2. Frequent panic attacks (which resemble heart attacks) are the main symptom of **panic disorder.** Biological and cognitive explanations for this disorder have been proposed. A person with a chronically high level of anxiety may suffer from **generalized anxiety disorder.**

3. Most people who have the diagnosis of **obsessive-compulsive disorder** have both obsessions and compulsions.

Obsessions are senseless thoughts, images, or impulses that occur repeatedly; they are often accompanied by compulsions, which are irresistible, repetitive acts.

4. Somatoform disorders involve the presentation of physical symptoms that have no known medical causes, but psychological factors are involved. Among these disorders are **hypochondriasis, somatization disorder,** and **conversion disorder.**

5. Dissociative disorders involve disruptions in some function of the mind. In **dissociative amnesia,** memories cannot be recalled; in **dissociative fugue,** memory loss is accompanied by travel. **Dissociative identity disorder** (*multiple personality*) is characterized by the presence of two or more personalities in the same individual.

✓ CHECK YOUR PROGRESS

1. Identify the most likely diagnosis for each of the following conditions.

   a. Every day Brad thinks about hurting a family member. These thoughts are so repulsive that he begins counting backward from 1,000.

   b. Maria's 12 physical symptoms don't reflect any disease her physician has ever seen, and she is angry when the physician advises her to make an appointment to see a psychologist.

   c. A week after reporting for military duty, Dean cannot use his arm to fire a gun. Medical causes have been ruled out.

   d. Andrea reports symptoms such as a racing heart and difficulty breathing that last for 10–15 minutes several times a week. She thinks she is having a heart attack.

   e. Nick always seems to be on edge, is often restless, and just can't relax. His mind always seems to be focused on some new worry.

2. What is the difference between an obsession and a compulsion?

3. Psychophysiological disorders are likely to affect parts of the body controlled by which part of the nervous system? Somatoform disorders are likely to be found in parts of the body controlled by which part of the nervous system?

4. Which neurotransmitter has been implicated in the development of obsessive–compulsive disorder?

   a. Ach
   b. GABA
   c. Dopamine
   d. Serotonin

5. Angela is given an assignment to report back on the diagnosis of hypochondriasis with a special emphasis on the rate of diagnosis in men and women. When she has completed her report, what will she find?

   a. Women are diagnosed with the disorder more often.
   b. Men are diagnosed with the disorder more often.
   c. The diagnosis is made equally in men and women.
   d. Among children, girls receive the diagnosis more often; whereas, among adults men receive the diagnosis more often.

6. Researchers at the medical center are using sophisticated brain scanning devices to study the brains of people with obsessive–compulsive disorder. Which areas of the brain would they expect to be especially active in this group of patients?

   a. cerebellum and temporal lobes
   b. basal ganglia and frontal lobes
   c. corpus callosum and thalamus
   d. thalamus and hypothalamus

7. While watching a talk show, you hear the announcer describe today's guests as suffering from multiple personality. What is the current name for this disorder? It takes several years before a proper diagnosis is made; give examples of typical diagnoses made during the meantime.

8. Which of these individuals is suffering from the most common phobia treated in mental health centers?

   a. Dan, who suffers from zoophobia.
   b. Alice, who suffers from agoraphobia.
   c. Ben, who suffers from a social phobia.
   d. Darla, who suffers from belonophobia.

9. Ted is sitting in the campus center when he is suddenly overcome by an intense fear that he had never experienced before. His heart seems to be "racing out of control" and he wonders if he is having a heart attack. Ted's symptoms would be called

   a. fugue.
   b. a panic attack.
   c. a mood disorder.
   d. depersonalization.

10. An announcement from the Psychiatric Research Center seeks volunteers for research involving a "biological challenge." Because the center is willing to pay volunteers, you are interested but would like to know what is involved. When you call for more information, what will they tell you about the procedure?

   a. You may be asked to breathe into a paper bag as part of research on the cause of panic disorder.
   b. The research involves electrical stimulation of parts of the brain to determine which areas house repressed memories.
   c. A series of increasingly difficult physical tasks will be presented as a way of mimicking the stress that can cause heart attacks.
   d. You may be asked to sit still for long periods of time during which bursts of light will be flashed. This method is used to determine how the brain responds to fearful stimuli.

ANSWERS: 1. a. Obsessive–compulsive disorder **b.** Somatization disorder **c.** Conversion disorder **d.** Panic disorder **e.** Generalized anxiety disorder **2.** An obsession is a recurrent, intrusive thought, impulse, or image that is unwanted and inappropriate; a compulsion is a repeated, irresistible behavior or mental act that often follows obsessions. **3.** Autonomic, central **4.** d **5.** c **6.** b **7.** Dissociative identity disorder; schizophrenia, depression, and alcohol or drug abuse **8.** b **9.** b **10.** a

MOOD DISORDERS

Two years ago, Jim, a 62-year-old mechanic, tried to commit suicide by hanging himself; a neighbor found him just in time. Last week he told a co-worker, "There's no reason to live. I can't take it any more. I've got a gun and I'm going to use it." Jim has lived alone since his wife died three years ago; his two daughters live in another state. Fellow workers often detected signs that Jim had been drinking. One co-worker sought the advice of others, who seemed confident in their advice: "Don't worry. He is all talk. People who talk about suicide don't do it." *Do people who commit suicide give advance warning of their plans?*

Mood is like a brush that paints a wide swath across our lives. Minor changes in our mood are normal and add variety to life. One day we feel fine, the next we feel blue. These feelings are insignificant, however, compared with the depths of despair experienced by seriously depressed people or the wild elation of those who suffer mania. Mood disorders occur at both ends of a continuum ranging from severe depression to excessive euphoria. In this section we discuss (unipolar) depression and bipolar (manic-depressive) disorder, disorders that involve extremes of mood.

Depression

A lack of understanding of depression and the failure to recognize and treat this disorder costs $43 billion a year, primarily for treatment, absenteeism, lost productivity, and premature death (Hirschfeld et al., 1997). Clinical forms of depression are more severe than what we might call "the blues," so how do we recognize depression, and how common is it?

Symptoms. The symptoms of depression tend to fall into three broad categories: emotional, cognitive, and somatic (see Table 12-4). The most obvious symptoms of **depression** are sadness, a lack of interest in previously pleasurable activities, and reduced energy. Depressed people often describe themselves in unflattering terms such as inferior and unattractive. They do not see themselves as capable of completing intellectually demanding tasks. This negative self-evaluation extends to their views of the world and the future. They torture themselves with guilt over what they see as

depression
Mood disorder characterized by sadness; feelings of guilt; changes in sleep, appetite, and motor behavior; and sometimes thoughts of suicide

TABLE 12-4

Symptoms of Depression

Emotional

Excessive crying

Persistent sad or "empty" mood

Loss of interest or pleasure in most activities once enjoyed, including sex

Cognitive

Recurrent thoughts of death or suicide, or suicide attempts

Feelings of guilt, worthlessness, or helplessness

Difficulty concentrating, remembering, making decisions

Somatic

Weight loss or gain

Insomnia or hypersomnia

Fatigue or loss of energy

Psychomotor agitation or retardation

Chronic aches and pains that are not caused by physical illness or injury

past failures and inadequacies, and the future holds no promise of any improvement. What's more, they may blame themselves for negative events, including ones that have no connection to them, yet they rarely credit themselves for any achievements. This sense of worthlessness and hopelessness makes them vulnerable to thoughts of suicide. The essence of depression is captured in the following quotation: "I am now the most miserable man living. If what I feel were equally distributed to the whole human family, there would not be one cheerful face on earth. Whether I shall ever be better, I cannot tell; I awfully forebode I shall not. To remain as I am is impossible. I must die or be better" (Oats, 1977, p. 62).

Other symptoms of depression can occur in different and even opposite ways. Two forms of insomnia are frequently associated with depression: difficulty falling asleep (sleep-onset insomnia) and awakening early in the morning with an inability to return to sleep (see Chapter 4). Conversely, about 10% to 20% of depressed people greatly extend their sleep, perhaps to provide temporary refuge (Kupfer & Reynolds, 1992). Most people who are depressed lose their appetites (anorexia) and consequently lose weight; a few people eat excessively and gain weight. Depression is typically evident in *psychomotor retardation*: a slowed rate of speaking (in extreme cases, the person may stop speaking altogether), slow walking, and stooped posture. Symptoms such as wringing of the hands, pacing, and bemoaning one's fate, called *agitated depression*, can also be present, however.

Depression seems to occur in all cultures; the similarities in depression across culture are more apparent than the differences. Nevertheless, some differences are noteworthy. For example, depressed people in Western countries report guilt more often than people in non-Western countries (Marsella et al., 1985). Another common difference is the manifestation of the symptoms. Although "feelings" may be important in our culture, depressed people in cultures such as China do not necessarily "feel" depressed, but tend to report more somatic problems. One explanation for this finding is that some cultures have few words to convey emotions such as sadness (see Chapter 8 discussion of linguistic relativity hypothesis). In addition, different cultures locate feeling states in different parts of the body, which may explain why some cultural groups emphasize somatic complaints in the expression of depression (Matsumoto, 1996).

Prevalence and Course.   Depression strikes rich and poor, young and old, men and women, the famous (the quote above is by Abraham Lincoln) and the unknown. Approximately 6 percent of adults have experienced at least one episode of major

Abraham Lincoln exhibited numerous symptoms of depression.

Reprinted courtesy of the Library of Congress.

depression (Weissman et al., 1991). The onset of the first episode of a major depressive disorder often occurs in the late twenties (Judd, 1997). A milder, yet chronic, form of depression (*dysthymic disorder*) is so common it is known as the "common cold of psychological disorders." In some cases, major depressive disorder and dysthymic disorder occur together in what has been called *double depression* (Hammen, 1997; McCullough et al., 2000). Affected people are chronically dysthymic, and then occasionally experience a major depressive episode. As the episode passes, they return to their chronic level of dysthymia (moderate depression), rather than to a normal mood.

Depression does not strike only adults. Epidemiological data from U.S. samples reveal the following:

- 1% of preschoolers suffer from major depressive disorder.
- Among school-age children the rate is 2%.
- The rate is 5% to 8% among adolescents.

Diagnosing depression in children poses special difficulties because they are not adept at expressing sadness in language (Son & Kirchener, 2001). What's more, some of the typical signs of depression in adults (for example, appetite loss) are less common in children and adolescents. The symptoms of depression also change with age. For example, depressed adolescents may be angry rather than sad (The Harvard Mental Health Letter, 2001). Therefore, depression is usually inferred from behaviors such as apathy, withdrawal, delay or regression of developmental milestones, and failure to thrive that has no organic basis. Although school-aged children are able to internalize environmental stressors such as family conflict (often associated with depression), their inner turmoil tends to be expressed through somatic symptoms such as headaches and stomachaches as well as irritability (temper tantrums).

As you can see in Figure 12-6, in many cultures the rate of depression is twice as high among women as men (Nolen-Hoeksema, 2001); however, accumulating evidence suggests that this sex difference occurs in developed countries, rather than in developing countries, where the male to female ratio is closer to 1 : 1 (Culbertson, 1997). The

FIGURE 12-6 Sex differences in depression across cultures. The rate of depression among women is consistently higher than among men.

Source: The Journal of the American Medical Association.

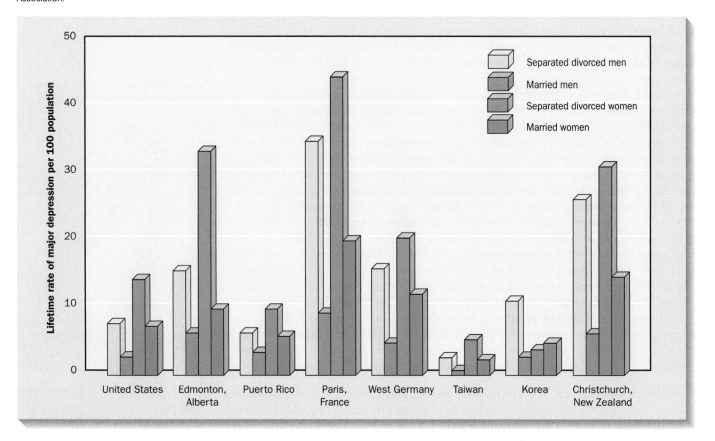

disparity in developed countries begins around puberty and continues throughout life (Weissman & Olfson, 1995). In children there is no sex difference in depression, but by about age 13, the rate of depression among girls begins to increase sharply; the rate among boys remains low. By late adolescence, the rate of depression among girls is twice that among boys where it remains (Nolen-Hoeksema, 2001). There are several points that explain the higher rate of depression among women. Depression occurs more frequently when a person engages in passive and dependent behaviors and focuses on the depressed feelings (rumination) instead of acting to overcome the depression (Nolen-Hoeksema, 2001). Given the traditional gender roles in most societies, women are more likely to assume a passive role. Sexual and physical abuse is another factor that puts women at risk for depression. Although marriage may create a protective buffer against depression, the advantage is greater for men than it is for women. Mothers of young children are especially vulnerable to depression. Finally, poverty is a path to depression, and the rate of poverty is especially high among women and children.

The rate of depression has risen dramatically over the past century. Surveys of people in the United States, Western Europe, the Middle East, and Asia yielded two major findings: (1) rates of depression have risen steadily for each successive generation since 1915, and (2) depression is beginning at an earlier age with each successive generation (Cross-National Collaborative Group, 1992).

What accounts for this "epidemic of depression"? Close family and community ties are important in preventing depression. For example, the Amish people have maintained their customs in rural farming communities for generations. Their supportive families and community provide comfort and aid in times of need. When an Amish family loses a barn to a fire, neighbors join together to rebuild it. Depression occurs among the Amish at about one-fifth to one-tenth the rate as it does among people in, say, the city of Baltimore (Seligman, 1989).

Although depression usually diminishes with time (typically within six months), episodes tend to recur. Most people who experience one episode of major depression will experience another one (Judd, 1997). Compared to patients with chronic medical illnesses such as heart disease, people with depression report more physical pain, feel less well, and experience more social limitations. Depression tends to be comorbid with anxiety disorders, substance abuse, and eating disorders (Cicchetti & Toth, 1998). Comorbidity is associated with poorer functioning and a longer course of the disorder than what is termed "pure" depression (Hammen, 1997).

The symptoms of depression are somewhat more likely to occur at certain times during the year. Although a majority of people notice mood changes related to the seasons, some are so susceptible to these changes that they develop a form of depression called *seasonal affective disorder* (*SAD*). SAD typically occurs during the fall and winter months (October through February) and remits in the spring (Bhatia & Bhatia, 1997; Saeed & Bruce, 1998). This "winter depression" is associated with increased sleep length, increased appetite, weight gain, fatigue, and social withdrawal. SAD occurs more often among women and is more likely to occur among people who live in northern latitudes (thus, it is not likely to occur in Florida, but likely to occur in Maine and Canada) (Rosenthal, 1998). The symptoms may be related to levels of the hormone melatonin, which is secreted by the pineal gland. In animals, *melatonin* seems to regulate hibernation. As the hours of light decrease with the approach of winter, the animal's body secretes more melatonin, which slows bodily processes in preparation for hibernation. Like hibernating animals, some humans also slow down as their melatonin levels increase. People who suffer from this disorder can be helped by being exposed to greater amounts of bright light during winter, a treatment known as *phototherapy*.

Suicide. The most serious complication of severe depression is the possibility of suicide. Consider the following statistics:

- In the United States, someone commits suicide every 17 minutes (approximately 31,000 deaths); 1.3% of all deaths are suicides (U.S. Census Bureau, 2001).
- Hungary has the highest rate of suicide; other countries with high suicide rates are Denmark, Finland, and Sweden. Italy, Spain, and Greece have low rates of

Phototherapy involves the use of fluorescent lamps (incandescent lights may damage the retina), which are 10 to 20 times brighter than ordinary indoor light. Patients suffering from Seasonal Affective Disorder have daily 30–45-minute therapy sessions from fall into the spring that typically lead to a reduction in the depression within two to four days. Tanning beds, where the eyes are generally covered and the skin is exposed to light, have no effect on the symptoms of SAD.

Suicide Prevention

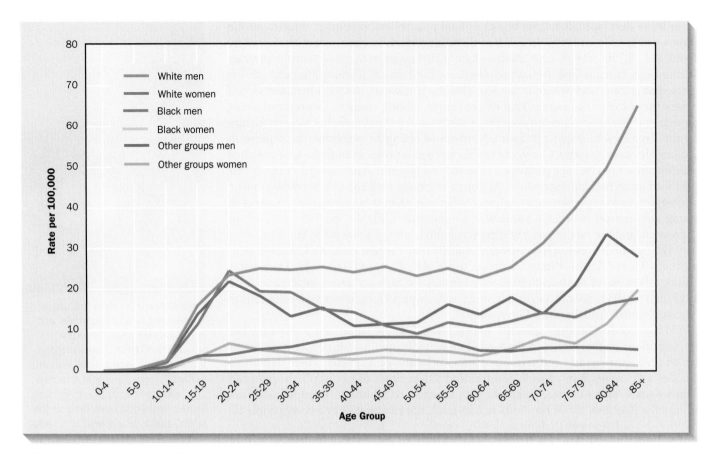

FIGURE 12-7 Rates of suicide per 100,000 for men and women. The "other" groups include people from the Asian American, Hispanic American, and Native American populations. Overall, the rate of suicide tends to increase with age, primarily as a result of the large increase in suicides among white men beginning at age 60.

suicide. Compared with other countries, the suicide rate in the United States is moderate (The Harvard Mental Health Letter, 1996).

- In the United States, more people die by suicide than from murder (U.S. Census Bureau, 2001).
- Married people have the lowest suicide rates; divorced people have the highest rates (The Harvard Mental Health Letter, 1996).
- In 1998, suicide was the third leading cause of death in the 15–24 age range, second among people age 25 to 34, and fourth among people 35–44 (National Center for Injury Prevention and Control, 2001).
- The majority of suicide victims were suffering from depression, alcohol abuse/dependence, or schizophrenia (The Harvard Mental Health Letter, 1996).
- In most Western countries women attempt suicide more frequently than men, but men succeed more often because they tend to use more lethal methods. A psychiatrist's chillingly blunt words make this point: "You can pump pills out of someone's stomach, you can't pump buckshot out of someone's brain." Suicide rates vary significantly with sex and race (see Figure 12-7); white men have the highest suicide rate. The overall suicide rate also tends to rise with age.

Myth or Science

Recall that Jim, the mechanic whom we met at the beginning of this section, described his suicide plan to a co-worker. The co-worker sought guidance and was told not to worry because "people who talk about suicide don't do it." Was this guidance correct, or should talk of suicide be taken seriously? Contrary to common belief, suicide is often preceded by a warning. About 80% of suicide victims give direct warnings like "I'm going to end it all" or indirect clues such as giving prized possessions to friends and relatives (The Harvard Mental Health Letter, 1996). Statements about hopelessness and helplessness are especially common signs of suicidal thinking (Rudestam, 1971; Wrobleski, 1989). Unfortunately, people who hear or see evidence of suicidal potential often overlook or deny its significance.

Suicide researchers and prevention centers have accumulated information to assess an individual's suicidal potential. Jim closely matches the profile of the likely suicide victim: An older white man suffering from depression who has made a prior suicide attempt and now has a plan, has recently experienced stressful life events, abuses alcohol, and has few sources of social support. You can see that Jim is at high risk for committing suicide.

What should you do if you suspect that someone you know might attempt suicide? You should not be afraid to ask, "Are you thinking about suicide?" If someone asked you that question, your likely response might be, "Are you nuts!" What should you do if your depressed friend's response is yes or a halfhearted no? "People who talk about or attempt suicide need immediate medical and psychological help" (Wrobleski, 1989, p. 45). Most suicidal people are ambivalent about committing suicide; they are experiencing pain, helplessness, and hopelessness. Help them understand that their current stressors make it difficult for them to think clearly.

Time is an important ally in the effort to prevent a suicide because people do not usually remain seriously suicidal for long. Surprisingly, suicide may be less likely when individuals are in the depths of depression. Helplessness and passivity sap motivation and energy so much that depressed people are unlikely to carry out their suicide plans. When the depression lifts and the person seems to feel better, suicide may actually be more likely. In the event that any of your friends talk about suicide, be sure that he or she knows that someone cares and encourage the person to seek professional help from a suicide prevention or crisis intervention center.

Bipolar Disorder

Two weeks ago, 20-year-old Will's mood switched from friendly to irritable. When he thought some money was missing from his room, he accused a friend of taking it. After determining he had misplaced the money himself, Will refused to apologize. Although he had no knowledge of music, he impulsively purchased an expensive guitar. As his need for sleep decreased, he spent hours making long-distance calls to friends and planning to write the definitive work on "existentialism, divine providence, and the collective unconscious." After deciding to reconcile with his girlfriend, he knocked on her door at 2 A.M. She refused to let him in, so he began shouting and pounding on the door. The noise woke neighbors who telephoned the police; they took Will to a hospital emergency room. While he was there, his speech was rapid, he shifted topics abruptly, and he was restless. A few weeks after his release from the hospital, he was extremely depressed (Andreasen, 1984).

Will experienced an episode of poor judgment, excessive activity, accelerated speech, and extreme euphoria known as **mania.** Manic symptoms can result from cocaine or amphetamine use or hyperthyroidism; therefore these possibilities must be considered when making a diagnosis and planning treatment (Werder, 1995). The knowledge that mood disorders run in families is helpful: Will's mother had been treated for depression, and an uncle was hospitalized several times for mania and depression. Will's episode of mania was a mood disorder; it was followed by depression, and the diagnosis was **bipolar disorder** (occurrence of episodes at both ends of the mood spectrum). *Cyclothymic disorder* is a less severe, yet chronic, form of bipolar disorder (American Psychiatric Association, 2000).

The depression and mania in bipolar disorder may occur simultaneously, but they usually alternate—often separated by periods of relative normalcy. During a manic episode, boundless energy replaces the fatigue of depression; sadness and despair give

Patty Duke, the actress, seeks to educate the public about bipolar disorder and its treatment. Before she was correctly diagnosed and treated with lithium, she attempted suicide several times, usually with pills. She also used alcohol and drugs to suppress her manic highs.

TABLE 12-5

Symptoms of Mania

Distractibility

Poor judgment

Inflated self-esteem or grandiosity

Decreased need for sleep (hyposomnia)

Increased energy, activity, and restlessness

Persistently elevated, euphoric, or irritable mood

More talkative than usual or pressure to keep talking

Increase in goal-directed activity or psychomotor agitation

Racing thoughts and talking fast, jumping from one idea to another

Excessive involvement in pleasurable activities that have a high potential for painful consequences

FIGURE 12-8 PET scans of the brain of a person who cycled from depression to mania reveal remarkably different patterns of activity associated with the two mood states. Activity levels are indicated by a spectrum ranging from blue (low) through green to yellow and red (high). It is not clear if the brain activity levels associated with depression and mania cause the mood disorders or whether they reflect underlying changes in mood (in which case they may be correlated with the mood).

Source: Nemeroff, 1998.

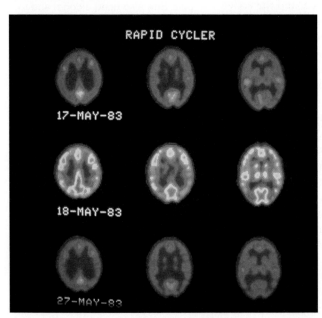

way to euphoria and elevated self-esteem. Depression often reduces the desire for sex; mania often brings uncharacteristic promiscuity (reflecting increased sexual drive or libido). During an episode of mania, people become highly sociable, although irritability lurks beneath the surface should anyone question their plans. They ignore painful or harmful consequences of their behavior and may incur huge debts, break the law, or make unwise business and personal decisions (see Table 12-5). Fortunately, bipolar disorder responds quite effectively to treatment with lithium (see Chapter 13), which was the treatment prescribed for Will.

Bipolar disorder is less prevalent than depression; it affects about 1% of the population with equal rates in men and women (Leibenluft, 1996). Most often, the symptoms begin in a person's early twenties (Werder, 1995), as they did for Will. An episode of depression usually occurs first; a manic episode may not occur until several years later, although mania is more likely to come first in men than in women (The Harvard Mental Health Letter, 2001). Like many other disorders, bipolar disorder often occurs with other disorders, especially substance abuse or dependence; among the other comorbid conditions are anxiety disorders, eating disorders and personality disorders (Miklowitz, 2001).

Causes of Mood Disorders

Biological Explanations. For several reasons, experts believe that biological factors play a role in the development of mood disorders. First, as noted earlier, the symptoms of depression tend to be rather similar across cultures, suggesting a common underlying biological cause. Second, certain drugs such as Elavil and Prozac reduce depression, and mania responds to lithium treatment. The effects of neurotransmitters seem to be reflected in the dramatic differences in the activity levels of the brains of people during depressive and manic episodes (see Figure 12-8). Third, mood disorders tend to run in families, which suggests genetic transmission. Nevertheless, researchers agree that rising rates of depression during this century are unlikely to result from genetic factors; psychological and social factors also must be considered.

One way researchers study possible genetic influences on mood disorders is to compare the prevalence of these disorders

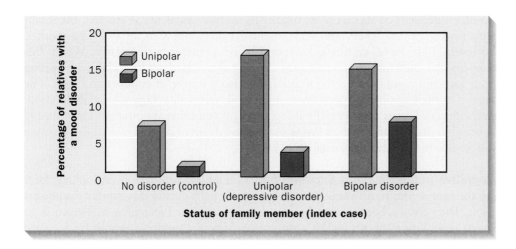

FIGURE 12-9 Prevalence of unipolar depression and bipolar disorder in families at different levels of risk. Being born into a family with a member who has a mood disorder raises the risk of having a mood disorder.

Source: Gershon & Nurnberger, 1995, p. 407.

in families with and without a family member with a mood disorder. Mood disorders occur more often in the first-degree relatives (parents, children, siblings) of family members with a mood disorder than among relatives of individuals who do not have such disorders (Gershon & Nurnberger, 1995). Compared with relatives of patients with unipolar disorder, relatives of bipolar patients exhibit higher rates of bipolar disorder but about the same rate of unipolar depression (see Figure 12-9). In general, the evidence for genetic transmission is stronger for bipolar disorder than for unipolar depression.

In their efforts to understand the role of genetic factors in mood disorders, researchers have also studied identical and fraternal twins. They begin by identifying a twin who has a mood disorder, called an *index case*. Then they determine whether the second twin in each pair (the co-twin) also has a mood disorder. A twin pair is said to be *concordant* when both twins have mood disorders. The **concordance rate** is the percentage of twin pairs in which both twins have the disorder. The concordance rate for mood disorders among identical twins is approximately 65 percent; the rate among fraternal twins is about 14% (Andreasen & Black, 1995). As mentioned, there is strong evidence for a genetic component to bipolar disorder. The concordance rate for bipolar disorder among identical twins is in the range of 60–80%; it is 20% for fraternal twins. If both parents have bipolar disorder, their child's chance of developing the disorder is approximately 75 percent (The Harvard Mental Health Letter, 2001).

These findings strengthen the belief that genetic factors are involved in depression. But what exactly is inherited? To answer that question, we need to know that two neurotransmitters, norepinephrine and serotonin, seem to play significant roles in depression (Nemeroff, 1998). Antidepressant drugs increase the availability of norepinephrine or serotonin at synapses in the brain. The increased availability of these neurotransmitters alters neural transmission and can lead to increased activity and a lifting of the depression. These neurotransmitters may also be involved in altering levels of certain hormones, which could lead to depression.

Explaining mood disorders as the result of abnormal levels of certain neurotransmitters seems to be simple and straightforward. This theory cannot account for an intriguing finding, however: Antidepressant drugs alter neurotransmitter levels almost immediately, yet depression may take as long as two weeks to lift after the start of drug treatment. What's more, the levels of certain neurotransmitters could change in response to environmental factors such as the disappointment after a major personal failure or after the death of a loved one. Thus, although people with mood disorders may inherit a tendency to develop these disorders, other factors need to be understood to complete the picture.

The Psychodynamic Explanation. The psychodynamic model emphasizes early childhood experiences as the foundation of adult behavior and emotional reactions.

concordance rate
Percentage of twin pairs in which both twins have a disorder that is of interest to an investigator

learned helplessness
Belief that one cannot control outcomes through one's actions; usually leads to passivity and reduced motivation and may cause depression

arbitrary inference
Conclusion drawn in the absence of supporting information

Source: Reprinted with the permission of Psi Chi, The National Honor Society in Psychology.

An infant depends on its caregiver, usually its mother. As its needs are met, the infant feels supported and loved, and attachment develops (see Chapter 9). The mother, however, must leave at times, temporarily or perhaps permanently. When this happens, the child may experience rage at being abandoned yet be ambivalent (feeling both love and rage) because the mother was also a source of comfort and love. The rage is turned against a more convenient and acceptable target—the child itself. According to Freud, this inwardly directed anger can cause depression. Later in life, depression may reappear when losses such as the death of a loved one or the loss of a job reactivate the earlier experiences of loss.

Cognitive and Behavioral Explanations. Suppose you have been looking for a job for over a year, to no avail. Some job seekers might decide they simply cannot get a job. They give up because they believe that no amount of searching will succeed. In short, if nothing they do makes a difference, why do anything at all? Under such circumstances, a psychological state known as **learned helplessness** may develop (Seligman, 1975/1992). Learned helplessness occurs when you believe you have no control over the reinforcements in your life, such as finding a job or getting a good grade on an exam. The result is often reduced efforts to attain those reinforcers. This model of depression explains the lethargy and lack of motivation seen in depressed individuals; one problem with this model, however, is that even in research situations designed to render people helpless, some individuals do not succumb. Hence there must be another variable that influences the development of depression.

A reformulation of the learned helplessness model, called the *hopelessness model*, focuses on people's beliefs about the situations in which they find themselves. Some people become depressed not because they lack control over a situation but because of the way they explain the situation. We differ in explanatory style—that is, the habitual way we explain good and bad events (see Chapter 13). Explanatory style is much more powerful than just the words a person uses. From the time we develop our explanatory style in childhood or adolescence, it serves as the mediator of whether we will suffer greatly from helplessness and possibly depression.

Explanatory style consists of three dimensions: permanent versus temporary, universal versus specific, and internal versus external. When bad events happen, we may view them as permanent or temporary. If you think about bad things in terms of "always" and "never," you have a permanent pessimistic style. Explanations may also be specific to the situation or universal, applying to all situations. People who rely on universal explanations for their failures often give up on everything when a failure strikes in one area. Finally, explanations may be either internal (we blame ourselves) or external (we believe outside forces are at work); people who use internal explanations find their self-esteem is lowered significantly.

One combination of the dimensions of explanatory style is especially self-defeating: permanent, universal, and internal. People with this very pessimistic style who encounter bad events are more likely to become depressed, whereas those who have the opposite "optimistic" style and experience bad events will tend to resist depression. Suppose you got back an exam with a big red F on it. How would you explain that F? Table 12-6 contains explanations based on the three dimensions of explanatory style. Research suggests that depression may be related to the tendency to use permanent, universal, and internal explanations for negative events (Sweeney, Anderson, & Bailey, 1986).

The hopelessness model has much in common with the cognitively oriented theories of researchers who view depression as stemming from problems in the way people think. Aaron Beck, for example, concluded that depression results from the way people think about themselves and about what happens to them. They often blame themselves for events, so they focus on the negative. Depressed people hold negative views of themselves, their current experiences, and the future. They find themselves in this predicament because they are prone to commit errors in logic, which perpetuate their negative views. For example, depressed people may decide that no one likes them because no one spoke to them on the bus on the way to work. In this case, they have drawn an **arbitrary inference**—a conclusion based on insufficient evidence. They may

TABLE 12-6

Explanations for Negative Events

How people explain events such as failing an exam varies quite a bit and may make some people more prone to depression.

	Internal	
	Stable	**Unstable**
Global	"My problem with exams has been test anxiety."	"I hit a deer this morning and have been unable to focus on anything all day.
Specific	"I have never understood biological concepts like neurotransmitters	"I didn't know a word on the first question and it kept haunting me."

	External	
	Stable	**Unstable**
Global	"Multiple-choice tests are not a fair way to assess my knowledge."	"No one does well on tests given right after spring break."
Specific	"Everyone knows this prof. loves giving impossible tests."	"The prof. didn't put any thought into this test because he was spending time on consulting.

also over-generalize, like the student who decides she will never get a good grade because she earned a C on her first exam.

Beck has devised a therapy that deals directly with these cognitive elements of depression. We discuss Beck's cognitive therapy in Chapter 13.

Multiple Causes.   To sum up, it appears that genetic factors play a role in mood disorders; clearly, however, they are not the only factors. As we have seen, factors such as explanatory style are also important components of depression. The levels of neurotransmitters may be influenced by a style of explaining negative events. One lesson is clear: The study of mood disorders leads us to recognize that there are no simple answers to questions about the causes of disorders; more often than not, biological, psychological, and social factors interact to affect the development and course of disorders. For example, researchers have suspected that stressful life events have been linked to the incidence of depression. Clarifications of this link, however, suggest that only some forms of depression are strongly related to stressful events (Brown, Harris, & Heyworth, 1994; Frank et al., 1994). What's more, stressful life events may also play a role in the frequency and timing of future episodes of bipolar disorder (Johnson & Roberts, 1995).

R E V I E W   S U M M A R Y

1. The symptoms of **depression** include sadness, reduced pleasure and energy levels, feelings of guilt, sleep disturbances, and suicidal thinking. The lifetime prevalence of depression is twice as high among women as among men; prevalence rates around the world are increasing.

2. Suicide, which is often associated with depression, is one of the leading causes of death in the United States. The risk factors for suicide include being male, being unmarried, and being depressed.

3. Bipolar disorder involves swings between depression and **mania.** The symptoms of mania include euphoria, increased

energy, poor judgment, decreased sleep, and elevated self-esteem.

4. Mood disorders tend to run in families, which suggests genetic transmission. Depression may involve low levels of norepinephrine or serotonin. According to the **learned helplessness** model, depression can also be brought on when people believe that they cannot control outcomes. A refinement of this model, the hopelessness model, suggests that typical ways of explaining negative events may be at the root of depression. Cognitive explanations focus on how errors in logic contribute to the development of depression.

CHECK YOUR PROGRESS

1. What have epidemiological surveys revealed about the rate of depression around the world?

2. Identify the symptoms of depression in each of the following areas.

   a. appetite
   b. sleep
   c. self-descriptions

3. Certain demographic characteristics are related to the probability of suicide. State the major predictor of suicide in each of the following demographic categories.

   a. sex
   b. age
   c. marital status
   d. psychological disorders

4. A psychologist reported on research to determine the extent of genetic influences on mood disorders. During the presentation, the psychologist said that "50% of twin pairs shared mood disorders." What term is used to describe this figure?

   a. bipolarity rate
   b. shared incidence
   c. prevalence rate
   d. concordance rate

5. Which neurotransmitters have been implicated in the development of depression?

   a. dopamine and GABA
   b. GABA and epinephrine
   c. norepinephrine and serotonin
   d. acetylcholine and norepinephrine

6. For 3 weeks, Rod has been unable to sleep more than an hour a day, yet he is energetic. He is developing plans for his own "Las Vegas on the Ohio River." When a friend asked about his plans, Rod berated him and physically attacked him. The police were called and took Rod to an emergency room, where a physician suspected bipolar disorder. The physician ran tests, however, to rule out physical causes such as

   a. angina.
   b. hyperthyroidism.
   c. Alzheimer's disease.
   d. barbiturate overdose.

7. Buddy graduated from college three months ago. His grades were generally good, in the B range, and he is well liked. His efforts to find a job have been unsuccessful yet he is optimistic. Using the explanatory model, write a universal-internal-permanent explanation of his situation.

8. A patient's records indicate that she is suffering from dysthymic disorder. Which of the following descriptions is most consistent with this diagnosis?

   a. The patient has a chronic form of moderate depression.
   b. The patient experiences swings in mood from depression to mania.
   c. The periods of "up" mood are more frequent than the periods of depression.
   d. A series of medical problems are masking an underlying depressive mood disorder.

9. Depressed people may jump to conclusions based on insufficient evidence. This flaw in thinking is called

   a. maximization.
   b. inexact labeling.
   c. base-rate fallacy.
   d. arbitrary inference.

10. If Sally is diagnosed as suffering from a form of mood disorder called SAD, which of the following might her psychiatrist say to her when they discuss treatments?

   a. "You need to increase your level of calcium intake."
   b. "Exposure to very bright light should reduce your symptoms."
   c. "Large doses of aspirin have been shown to have a positive effect on these symptoms."
   d. "An increase in total number of calories consumed and daily naps are highly recommended."

ANSWERS: 1. The rate of depression around the world is increasing and people are experiencing the first episode at a younger age. **2. a.** Either increased appetite or loss of appetite (anorexia) **b.** Increased sleep (hypersomnia) or insomnia **c.** Depressed people often see themselves as unattractive and incapable of completing intellectually demanding tasks **3. a.** The rate of suicide is higher among men. **b.** The rate of suicide tends to increase with age. **c.** Divorced people have a higher rate of suicide than married people. **d.** The rate of suicide is highest among people suffering from depression, alcohol abuse/dependence or schizophrenia **4.** d **5.** c **6.** b **7.** Universal: "I am able to deal successfully with difficult situations." Internal: "My success in dealing with difficult situations is due to my ability to stay calm and assess each situation accurately." Permanent: "My ability to handle situations does not vary from one course or challenge to another." **8.** a **9.** d **10.** b

SCHIZOPHRENIA

Although he was sometimes mischievous and moody, George usually appeared to be normal until the end of high school. At that time muffled sounds seemed to insult him, sudden movements were viewed as physical threats, and he saw a stove become "the Devil alive." After graduating from high school, George enlisted in the navy, where the symptoms continued. He thought the cook was Satan and food was poisoned. His babbling was difficult to understand: "Got one to seven—see, the life in the drain—it's all butaco." After George wandered from a marching formation, an officer took him to the hospital, where he was diagnosed as suffering from schizophrenia (Heston, 1992). *What are the symptoms of schizophrenia?*

The Swiss psychiatrist Eugen Bleuler coined the word schizophrenia, which literally means "splitting of the mind." **Schizophrenia** is a psychotic disorder that is characterized by positive symptoms (excesses) or negative symptoms (deficits). **Psychosis** is a general term for disorders in which severely disturbed people lose contact with reality and may require hospitalization.

Schizophrenia has been called "the cruelest and most devastating of the various mental illnesses" (Andreasen, 2001, p. 193). It strikes at a relatively early age (usually around 20), although deficiencies in attention and emotional responses are often noted in childhood. The symptoms frequently lead to significant social and occupational impairment at an estimated cost for treatment, lost wages, productivity losses, and disability benefits of over $100 billion a year (Black & Andreasen, 1994). Approximately 1% of the U.S. adult population has had the disorder (Andreasen, 2001; Carpenter & Buchanan, 1994). Although the rate of schizophrenia is approximately equal in men and women, it strikes men earlier and with greater severity (Beratis, Gabriel, & Hoidas, 1994). The overall death rate among victims of schizophrenia is higher than the expected rate, in part, as a result of increased rates of suicide (Brown, 1997; Meltzer, 1998).

Schizophrenia is often confused with dissociative identity disorder. The "split" in schizophrenia, however, is not among different personalities; it is a split from reality as well as a split between thoughts and emotions. As we discuss this disorder in detail, keep these two points in mind: Schizophrenia is not dissociative identity disorder, and it is far more prevalent.

Symptoms of Schizophrenia

Schizophrenia involves a range of symptoms, none of which is present in all cases. There may be disturbances in perception, language, thinking, and emotional expression. How do we make sense of this array of symptoms? One approach to classifying symptoms holds promise; it is based on two types of symptoms: positive and negative.

Positive Symptoms. The *positive symptoms* of schizophrenia are distortions or excesses of normal functions, such as fluent but disorganized speech, delusions, and hallucinations. While listening to the speech of a patient with schizophrenia, you may struggle to follow his or her pattern of thought; the disorganized speech is thought to reflect disturbances in the underlying thought processes (Barch & Berenbaum, 1996). The following excerpt from an interview illustrates an extreme form of disorganized speech:

> *Interviewer*: Have you been nervous or tense lately?
>
> *Patient*: No, I got a head of lettuce.
>
> *Interviewer*: You got a head of lettuce? I don't understand.
>
> *Patient*: Well, it's just a head of lettuce.

schizophrenia
Psychotic disorder characterized by positive symptoms (excesses) such as delusions, hallucinations, and fluent but disorganized speech or negative symptoms (deficits) such as flat or blunted affect

psychosis
Any disorder in which a severely disturbed individual loses contact with reality

Experts See Mind's Voices in New Light

delusion
An obviously false belief that is extremely difficult to change

hallucinations
Sensory experiences that are not caused by stimulation of the relevant sensory organ; may occur in any of the senses

The life story of John Nash (1928–) is presented in the film *A Beautiful Mind*. As a 21-year-old Princeton University graduate student this mathematical genius made a significant breakthrough in understanding game theory, which was recognized in 1994 by a Nobel Prize in Economics. The road to that Nobel Prize, however, was bumpy. At the age of 30 while a professor at MIT, he interrupted a lecture to announce he was on the cover of *Life* magazine (disguised as the pope). He claimed that foreign governments communicated with him through *The New York Times,* and he turned down a position at the University of Chicago because he said he was about to become Emperor of Antarctica. His wife had him committed to a mental hospital where he was diagnosed with paranoid schizophrenia. Beginning in the 1980s, the symptoms of schizophrenia began to taper off.

Interviewer: Tell me about lettuce. What do you mean?

> *Patient*: Well . . . lettuce is a transformation of a dead cougar that suffered on the lion's toe. And he swallowed the lion and something happened. The . . . see, the . . . Gloria and Tommy, they're two heads and they're not whales. But they escaped with herds of vomit, and things like that (Neale & Oltmanns, 1980, p. 102).

The ideas expressed by a person with schizophrenia can be like a train that has slipped off its track onto another track; this pattern of speech is called *loose associations*. As a result, it is almost impossible to determine what the patient means, despite the fact that the words are recognizable and generally in grammatical form. To complicate matters even further, some patients use neologisms, common words used in uncommon ways ("I wrote the letter with my writing toy") or newly created words ("I wrote the letter with my zemps"). Words may be strung together in ways that seem to follow grammatical rules, yet the words form an incoherent collection called a word salad. A simple question like "What brought you here?" can give rise to an odd response like "The, my, not, rode, for, new, cold, it, what, may, so" (Othmer & Othmer, 1989). Speech may also be characterized by *clang associations*, word connections dictated by sound similarity, not by logic or meaning. For example, one patient, when asked what he was doing, responded, "Eating wires and lighting fires" (Spitzer et al., 1994).

Among the most frequently observed positive symptoms are **delusions,** or false beliefs that cannot be corrected despite strong evidence to the contrary. Delusions can appear in numerous forms. Individuals with *persecutory delusions* (most common) believe that others are tormenting, following, or ridiculing them. Some delusions are bizarre, as is evident in the case of a patient who said she was "persecuted by a secret insect from the District Office" (Spitzer et al., 1994). A *delusion of grandeur* is a person's belief that he or she has special powers or abilities; for example, a computer programmer imagined the end of the world was coming and *he* determined which of his colleagues would survive in the afterlife by the keys he pressed on his keyboard. *Thought broadcasting* is the idea that one's thoughts are being broadcast to others. Imagine walking down the street and believing that every thought you have is shared with every person you pass. Delusions are real to the people who experience them, so it is difficult to convince patients that they are false. What's more, if you believe others are persecuting or controlling you, you may feel a need to protect yourself. Delusions have led some persons to take action against people or institutions perceived to be intent on causing them harm or interfering with their lives.

Cultural factors influence the content of delusions. For example, delusions of being controlled often involve reports of ghosts and witches in underdeveloped countries and nonindustrial areas; the mechanism of control in developed countries is more likely to be X-rays and lasers (Maher & Spitzer, 1993).

Schizophrenia often alters perceptions of the world. Objects take on unusual dimensions, and sensations seem to materialize from thin air. A frequent perceptual symptom is the hallucination (from a Latin word meaning "to wander mentally"). **Hallucinations** are perceptions that are not caused by stimulation of the relevant sensory receptors. They can occur in any of the senses, although *auditory hallucinations* are the most common. The person may hear voices that give orders, criticize, or offer ongoing commentary. *Visual* hallucinations, such as George's seeing a stove turn into a devil, are less common. Hallucinations seem real to the person experiencing them and can be quite frightening, as they were to George.

Negative Symptoms.   Negative symptoms are reductions or losses of function. These behavior deficits or defects include *poverty of speech* as well as disturbances in affect and volition (will). These symptoms are associated with more cognitive impairment and poorer prognoses than positive symptoms.

The speech of people with schizophrenia may be adequate in amount yet convey little information: Language that is vague, too abstract, too concrete, or repetitive is termed *poverty of content*. A restriction in the amount of spontaneous speech that is evident in brief and unelaborated replies to questions is called *poverty of speech*. Interviewers frequently find it necessary to prompt the person for additional information (Andreasen & Black, 1995).

Failure to experience any emotion is called *flat affect*; an inability to experience the typical range of emotions is called *blunted affect*. Disturbances in affect are evident in rigid facial expressions, few expressive gestures, poor eye contact, and a lack of vocal inflection. *Avolition* (difficulty making decisions) and *apathy* are characterized by a lack of energy and drive such that a person is unable to initiate or persist in tasks. Unlike the lack of energy in depression, however, the apathy associated with schizophrenia is not accompanied by sadness. A number of disturbances in motor movements and a lack of self-care also characterize some forms of schizophrenia.

Subtypes of Schizophrenia

The DSM-IV describes five subtypes of schizophrenia: catatonic, disorganized, paranoid, residual, and undifferentiated (see Table 12-7). Although the prevalence of schizophrenia is similar around the world, rates of diagnosis of the subtypes differ. For example, disorganized schizophrenia accounts for about 50% of the diagnoses of

TABLE 12-7

Subtypes of Schizophrenia

Subtype	Key Symptoms
Catatonic	Unusual motor symptoms ranging from rigidity to wild hyperactivity and occasional alterations between inactivity and excitement. Seldom seen today because drug treatments reduce or eliminate the symptoms.
Disorganized	Incoherent speech with highly unusual verbal associations along with flat or inappropriate affect (emotional expressions that are often the opposite of expected reactions). Patients often seem silly and childlike and may grimace, giggle inappropriately, and appear absorbed in thought. The onset of symptoms usually occurs during adolescence—the earliest onset of the subtypes. The symptoms do not seem to be reactions to stressful life events. The continuous nature of the disorder leads to a downhill progression that often results in long-term institutionalization.
Paranoid	Delusions of grandeur or persecution with possible auditory hallucinations. Has the latest age of onset of the subtypes. Develops in individuals who often have demonstrated good functioning before the relatively acute onset of symptoms. Has a generally good outcome and good recovery rates.
Residual	Delusions, hallucinations, and incoherent language are absent, but continuation of the disorder is evident in social withdrawal or odd beliefs.
Undifferentiated	Symptoms may include prominent delusions, hallucinations, and disorganized speech that do not fit other subtypes. Long-term outcomes of this subtype are highly variable.

Develop visual representations—a picture or icon—that will help you remember each of the five types of schizophrenia.

schizophrenia in Japan but only about 10 percent in other countries (Nakane, Ohta, & Radford, 1992). Such differences may be due to diagnostic, social, or cultural factors.

Each subtype of schizophrenia is characterized by a different set of symptoms, although distinctions among the types are not always clear-cut. Indeed, the undifferentiated subtype is a category for cases that do not fit into other subtypes. A patient may exhibit the symptoms of different subtypes of schizophrenia at different times during the course of the disorder.

Causes of Schizophrenia

The search for what causes schizophrenia is difficult because there are no physical tests for the disorder. What's more, researchers are not sure if schizophrenia results from a single process or several processes. There have been many false leads and potential breakthroughs. Currently considered to be among the possible causes are genetic factors, brain abnormalities, altered neurotransmitter levels, and environmental factors.

Genetic Factors.   When Beth was 3 years old, her father died in a mental hospital, where he was being treated for schizophrenia. Beth, who is expecting a baby, wants to know whether her family history means that her child is at risk for developing schizophrenia. To help answer Beth's question, let's suppose that we randomly selected a person from the general population. What are the chances that this person will develop schizophrenia? Suppose we randomly select another person from a family with a member who has been diagnosed as suffering from schizophrenia. Does the risk change?

We noted earlier that approximately 1% of the population develops schizophrenia, so the answer to the first question is about 1%. Because schizophrenia runs in families, the odds that it will occur in a person selected from a family with a member who has the diagnosis are greater than 1%. How much greater depends on the person's relationship to the family member with schizophrenia. Figure 12-10 lists the risk (odds) of developing schizophrenia for various family members. The risk increases with the degree of

FIGURE 12-10 Degree of genetic relationship and average risk for developing schizophrenia. The risk varies as a function of genetic relatedness to a person afflicted with the disorder as compared with the risk in the general population. The highest risk occurs among co-twins of identical (monozygotic) twins who suffer from schizophrenia, which suggests that genetic factors play a role in schizophrenia. The fact that the risk is not 100% for identical twins, however, suggests that non-genetic (environmental) factors also play a role.

Source: Gottesman, 1991.

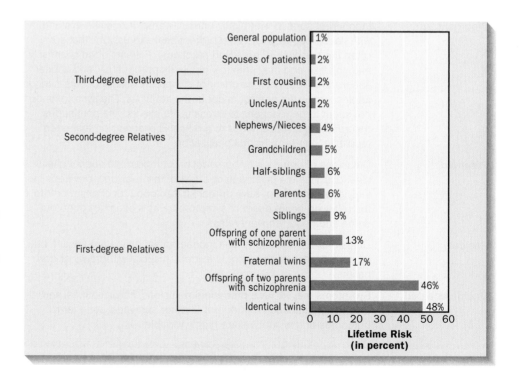

genetic relatedness (Gottesman, 1991). Thus having a brother or sister with schizophrenia raises the risk to 9%; the risk spirals to 46% for children of two parents with the disorder. Beth's baby has about a 5% chance of developing schizophrenia because the grandfather (Beth's father) had the disorder. The concordance rates (both twins diagnosed with schizophrenia) across several reports are 48% for identical twins and 17% for fraternal twins (Gottesman, 1991). This 3:1 ratio in the concordance rates for identical to fraternal twins strongly implicates genetic factors. In sum, this research has produced evidence suggesting that schizophrenia may be transmitted genetically.

We need to be cautious in interpreting these results because they may not be as clear cut as we presume. When children are reared by parents diagnosed with schizophrenia, we cannot separate genetic factors from the effects of being raised by parents with the disorder (environmental factors). For this reason, psychologists rely on studies of adopted children to distinguish the effects of genetics (nature) from those of the environment (nurture). In a study of children with at least one biological parent diagnosed with schizophrenia, rates of the disorder among the children were similar, regardless of whether they were raised by the biological parents or adopted parents (Wender et al., 1974). These results suggest that nature plays a more significant role than nurture in the development of schizophrenia. In fact, "Well-replicated findings from family, twin, and adoption studies indicate that there is a substantial genetic component to the predisposition for schizophrenia" (Conklin & Iacono, 2002, p. 33).

Psychological Detective

Is schizophrenia a genetically transmitted disorder? Can you identify reasons that genetic factors may not be the entire story? Twins are often reared in similar environments, raising the issue of nature versus nurture. What's more, if one twin has schizophrenia, the other (co-twin) twin does not always develop the disorder. If schizophrenia were transmitted entirely by genes, what concordance rate would you expect to find in identical twins? Why?

If genetic factors provided a complete answer to the cause of schizophrenia, we would expect a concordance rate of 100% among identical twins because such twins share all their genetic material (Conklin & Iacono, 2002). The less than 100 percent concordance rate for identical twins suggests a role for non-genetic factors (Moldin & Gottesman, 1997).

Brain Abnormalities.   A promising area of research on the causes of schizophrenia is the study of brain abnormalities. Several studies have demonstrated that some patients with schizophrenia have significantly larger cerebral ventricles—fluid-filled chambers in the brain—than nonschizophrenic people and therefore have smaller brain areas (Lickey & Gordon, 1991; Suddath et al., 1990). For example, limbic-area brain structures such as the hippocampus are smaller in some people with schizophrenia (Cannon & Marco, 1994). The limbic system plays a role in emotional response, memory, and other functions (see Chapter 2).

Are brain abnormalities associated with schizophrenia genetically transmitted? MRI pictures of the brains of discordant twin pairs—twin pairs in which one twin had schizophrenia and the other did not—have revealed clear differences in their brains. The ventricles in the twin with schizophrenia were larger than in the normal twin (see Figure 12-11). A difference in the ventricle size in identical twins could not be the result of genetic factors and provides further evidence that genetic factors are not the sole cause of schizophrenia. Both men and women diagnosed with schizophrenia show this pattern of ventricle enlargement; ventricle enlargement in men, however, is greater and may account for the common finding that the symptoms of schizophrenia are more severe in men than in women (Nopoulos, Flaum, & Andreasen, 1997).

FIGURE 12-11 MRI scans of the brains of identical twins, one with schizophrenia (left) and the other normal. The arrows indicate the ventricles (fluid-filled spaces in the brain). Note the difference in the size of the ventricles in these identical twins. One theory proposed to account for such a difference is the existence of a virus that infected one twin but not the other.

Source: Suddath et al., 1990.

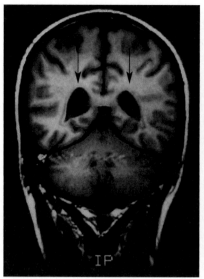 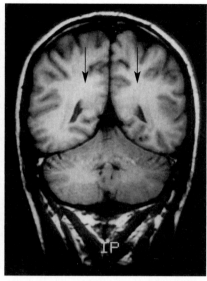

The exact cause of the differing size of the ventricles has not been identified; one proposed cause is viral infection very early in life (Torrey, 1991). An association of viral infections with schizophrenia was demonstrated in a follow-up of children born in 1966 in northern Finland. There was a strong association between the risk of developing schizophrenia and infections. According to the data, however, less than 6 percent of those in the sample with a diagnosis of schizophrenia had experienced infection. This finding suggests that viral infections may be one of many factors that could lead to the development of schizophrenia (Rantakallio et al., 1997).

Neurotransmitters.   Another focus of research is the role of neurotransmitters. Not long ago, patients could be seen roaming the halls of mental hospitals, behaving in erratic, sometimes violent ways, because available therapies were ineffective in controlling their behavior. Many patients were confined in straitjackets to prevent them from harming themselves and others. In the 1950s, antipsychotic drugs were developed (see Chapter 13); these drugs made most patients more cooperative and easier for the hospital staff to manage. The effectiveness of these drugs suggested another possible cause: biochemical abnormalities.

Available evidence suggests that the neurotransmitter dopamine plays a role in schizophrenia. Certain drugs, such as amphetamines and cocaine, can induce some symptoms of schizophrenia, and these drugs are known to increase dopamine levels in the brain. The brains of people with schizophrenia may have more dopamine receptors, or their dopamine receptors may be more sensitive than those of a person not suffering from the disorder. What's more, levels of dopamine activity may differ in different parts of the brain, and this could account for some of the variations in the symptoms of schizophrenia (Conklin & Iacono, 2002).

Of course, genetic factors may influence either dopamine levels or sensitivity to dopamine. The evidence, however, does not prove that schizophrenia is caused by biochemical factors alone.

Environmental Causes.   Genetic and various biological factors are not the only possible causes of schizophrenia. Consider the following: Schizophrenia runs in families, and identical twins are concordant for schizophrenia more often than fraternal twins. Yet 89% of all people with schizophrenia do not have a parent who suffers from schizophrenia (Gottesman, 1991).

The failure of genetic factors to provide a full explanation of why some people develop schizophrenia has fueled interest in environmental, including psychological, explanations. Stressful events and conditions have been shown to play a role in schizophrenia (Dohrenwend & Ergi, 1981). We know that schizophrenia is diagnosed

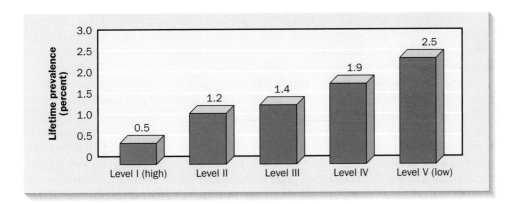

FIGURE 12-12 Socioeconomic status and prevalence of schizophrenia. (Socioeconomic status decreases from left to right.)

Source: Robins & Regier, 1991.

more frequently among people in lower socioeconomic classes than among those in higher classes (see Figure 12-12). Low-income people experience many stressors, including inadequate housing, substandard medical care, and poor diet. What's more, schizophrenia is more prevalent in urban areas than in rural ones—a tendency not attributed to differences in hospitalization policies (Torrey & Bowler, 1990). A study of the rate of schizophrenia in the Netherlands near the end of World War II suggests that prenatal nutritional deficiencies may play a role in the origin of some cases. Residents of the Netherlands endured severe famine as a result of the Nazi blockade of ports and other supply routes. Compared with people conceived at other times during the study period, individuals conceived at the height of the famine exhibited twice the rate of schizophrenia (Susser et al., 1996).

A series of studies has demonstrated a relationship between home environment and the risk of relapse for patients with schizophrenia. These studies have focused on *expressed emotion (EE)*, the degree to which family members' spontaneous talk about the patient is described as critical, hostile, or overinvolved. EE levels are assessed by interviewing family members and examining the content and vocal qualities of speech. A meta-analysis of 27 studies found that EE was a significant predictor of relapse among patients with schizophrenia, and an even stronger predictor of relapse among patients with mood disorders and eating disorders (Butzlaff & Hooley, 1998). Expressed emotion, however, is a controversial topic because it can be viewed as blaming family members for the disorder and its relapses. What's more, the direction of the effect is not clear: The family's emotional climate may be a reaction to the patient's symptoms rather than a result of those symptoms. For example, patients from families with high levels of EE are more likely to display odd and disruptive behavior within the family than patients from low-EE families (Rosenfarb et al., 1995).

Can stressors like poverty, urban life, or family conflict actually cause schizophrenia? Thousands of people have gone off to wars, suffered in major natural disasters, or been victims of violent crimes; few of them have developed schizophrenia. Researchers now believe that schizophrenia may result from several causes rather than a single cause.

Multiple Causes.   April 14, 1930 was a special day for one family in a small midwestern town—they were thrilled by the birth of four identical baby girls. The joy of that day eventually turned to anguish. Known as the Genain quadruplets (not their real name), the sisters would experience a turbulent family life. By the time they reached the age of 25, all four had been hospitalized with the diagnosis of schizophrenia. The probability of identical quadruplets all developing schizophrenia is estimated to be 1 in

Psychologists have studied the Genain quadruplets for more than three decades in an attempt to unravel the mystery of schizophrenia. All of the sisters were diagnosed as suffering from schizophrenia, although their level of adjustment and length of hospitalization varied.

1.5 billion births. Such a rare occurrence attracted the attention of the National Institute of Mental Health where staff members identified the sisters by the nicknames Nora, Iris, Myra, and Hester (N-I-M-H), which also represented their order of birth.

Over several decades, the Genain sisters were studied extensively by mental health experts, who attributed their common disorder to the interaction of several factors, including genetics and dysfunctional family life (Mirsky & Quinn, 1988; Mirsky et al., 1987). For example, their father was irritable, abusive, intrusive, and suspicious; he exhibited EEG abnormalities and reportedly suffered seizures. Their mother probably suffered from paranoid schizophrenia. Given this family background, it is not surprising that some of the sisters would develop problems. What struck researchers, however, were the variations in the onset and the severity of their illnesses. For example, Hester (last born and smallest) probably suffered the greatest brain insult at birth. She showed signs of schizophrenia as early as age 11, and was never able to function independently outside the home or institution. By contrast, Myra worked as a secretary for most of her life; she was married and had two sons and lives in her own home today. She did not show signs of schizophrenia until age 24. Hester's treatment by her parents reflected their view that she was the "moron type," whereas their treatment of Myra was much better. As the sisters approached their 66th birthday, they were studied once again, perhaps for the last time. The researchers concluded: "Although the genetic endowment of the Genians is presumed to be identical, the . . . expression of the disorder is relatively unique in each of the sisters. The outcome and life course of the Genain quadruplets remind us that any genetic model that could account for such diversity must include the participation of environmental factors, such as . . . brain injury at birth, differential expectations of and treatment by parents, and, most likely, the operation of chance factors" (Mirsky et al., 2000, p. 706).

In sum, it appears that no one inherits the specific symptoms of schizophrenia, although genetic factors play a role in a person's chances of developing the disorder. Despite past reports isolating a specific gene related to schizophrenia, the consensus of researchers suggests that multiple genes are involved in the disorder's development (Moldin & Gottesman, 1997). Researchers are beginning to converge on what they have called a neurodevelopmental model, which suggests that schizophrenia results from a combination of a genetic predisposition along with other factors. Irving Gottesman (1991) suggests that "what is inherited is a predisposition toward developing the disorder—a loading of nature's dice that increases the risk of developing schizophrenia" (p. 91). The child of a parent with schizophrenia is at higher risk for developing the disorder than the cousin of an individual with schizophrenia. The model suggests that schizophrenia is due to a disruption in forebrain development that occurs prior to or at birth in a person who has the genetic predisposition to develop schizophrenia. A brain lesion that occurs early in life remains dormant until around adolescence, when the signs of schizophrenia are likely to become evident. However, the model suggests that the loading of nature's dice provided by genetic factors is not enough to cause schizophrenia; there are other factors involved. Among the likely factors are birth complications and viral infections (Conklin & Iacono, 2002).

R E V I E W   S U M M A R Y

1. **Schizophrenia** affects approximately 1% of the population. Although it is often confused with dissociative identity disorder, the two disorders are different. Schizophrenia is characterized by a split between thoughts and emotions and a separation from reality.

2. The symptoms of schizophrenia are classified as *positive* (distortions or excesses) or *negative* (reductions or losses).

Positive symptoms include fluent but disorganized speech, **delusions,** and **hallucinations.** *Negative* symptoms include poverty of speech and disturbances in emotional expression such as flat affect.

3. The DSM-IV lists five subtypes of schizophrenia: catatonic, disorganized, paranoid, residual, and undifferentiated.

4. Schizophrenia tends to run in families; the risk of developing the disorder increases with the degree of genetic relatedness between an individual and a family member who has schizophrenia.

5. Evidence of various brain abnormalities, including larger ventricles, in people with schizophrenia suggests a possible biological cause. The neurotransmitter, dopamine, seems to be involved in the development of schizophrenia.

6. Environmental influences on schizophrenia include stress and hostile family communication. A predisposition to schizophrenia may be inherited, with the actual development of the disorder requiring the presence of other factors.

✓ CHECK YOUR PROGRESS

1. Identify the following symptoms of schizophrenia as either positive or negative.

   a. The patient hears voices in an empty house.
   b. The patient believes others are controlling his thoughts.
   c. The patient rarely smiles, does not change her tone of voice, and does not maintain eye contact.

2. On the basis of the following symptoms, identify the most likely subtype of schizophrenia.

   a. The patient grimaces and assumes unusual postures.
   b. The patient is suspicious and has delusions of persecution.
   c. There are no prominent symptoms, but the patient is withdrawn.

3. A sample of 1,000 people was randomly selected from the population. Which of the following represents the most likely number who have ever been diagnosed as suffering from schizophrenia?

   a. 1
   b. 5
   c. 10
   d. 25

4. If schizophrenia were entirely a genetic disorder, what concordance rate would you expect to find among identical twins?

5. What is the most common type of hallucination reported by people diagnosed as suffering from schizophrenia?

   a. visual
   b. tactile
   c. auditory
   d. gustatory

6. Which neurotransmitter has been most often implicated in the development of schizophrenia?

   a. Ach
   b. GABA
   c. Serotonin
   d. Dopamine

7. What evidence suggests that schizophrenia is not entirely genetically based?

8. During an interview, a patient says he has frequently seen a hand come out of the bathroom sink to grab a bar of soap. The psychologist who is conducting the interview most likely writes that the patient presents evidence of

   a. delusions.
   b. hallucinations.
   c. negative symptoms.
   d. loose associations.

9. What is the approximate risk of developing schizophrenia if both parents have schizophrenia?

   a. 1%
   b. 15%
   c. 20%
   d. 50%

10. What family variable is linked to relapse risk in people with schizophrenia who live with their families?

   a. poverty
   b. expressed emotion
   c. number of children
   d. sublimated emotion

ANSWERS: 1. a. Positive **b.** Positive **c.** Negative **2. a.** Catatonic **b.** Paranoid **c.** Residual **3.** c **4.** 100% **5.** c **6.** d **7.** The concordance rate for identical twins is not 100%, and some identical twins (one with schizophrenia and one without) have been shown to have different-sized brain ventricles. **8.** b **9.** d **10.** b

PERSONALITY AND SEXUAL DISORDERS

When he was younger, Chuck spent plenty of time in the principal's office for fighting. One night during Christmas vacation, Chuck left his house and stole decorations from neighbors' homes. Footprints in the freshly fallen snow led

personality disorders
Disorders characterized by long-standing, difficult-to-treat, dysfunctional behaviors that are typically first observed in adolescence

antisocial personality disorder
Personality disorder characterized by deceitful, impulsive, reckless actions that violate social norms for which the individual feels no remorse

the police to Chuck, who nonetheless denied knowledge of the incident. When he was 14, Chuck vandalized cars; when he was 18, he was arrested for dangling an acquaintance from a bridge. When asked why he committed such acts, he said that he was bored and wanted to "stir up some excitement." *Does Chuck's long-standing pattern of deviant behavior indicate that he exhibits a psychological disorder?*

Personality Disorders

Personality disorders are long-standing patterns of maladaptive behavior that are usually evident during the adolescent years and are resistant to treatment, which is seldom sought. Approximately 10% of the adult population may have one or more personality disorders. The high rate of comorbidity of personality disorders with other psychological disorders as well as with medical conditions complicates diagnosis and treatment (Oldham, 1994; The Harvard Mental Health Letter, 2000). In fact, two-thirds of people with one personality disorder have another and in some cases, several personality disorders (The Harvard Mental Health Letter, 2000). Furthermore, most people with personality disorders are convinced that if a problem exists, it lies not in them but in other people's reactions to their behaviors. For example, the key feature of *narcissistic personality disorder* is an inflated sense of self-importance and superiority. Narcissistic individuals are preoccupied with fantasies of success, power, beauty, or ideal love. They are sure that other people recognize their special qualities and are therefore envious. Expectations of attention, admiration, and compliance with their wishes are frequently expressed. Yet a lack of empathy leaves them unable to understand others' reactions to their behavior.

The DSM-IV describes 10 personality disorders, which are divided into three clusters (see Table 12-8). Personality disorders have been criticized for low reliability and questionable validity, especially in comparison to other psychological disorders. The definitions of the disorders have been described as ambiguous and overlapping, and the boundaries between normal personality and characteristics that would lead to a diagnosis are not clear. For example, how indecisive does someone have to be before being diagnosed with obsessive–compulsive disorder? What's more, most of these disorders are relatively new to the diagnostic system. Since the first diagnostic manual was published in 1952, only three personality disorders (paranoid, schizoid, and antisocial) have remained essentially unchanged (The Harvard Mental Health Letter, 2000). Although there are a number of personality disorders, more attention has been focused on antisocial personality disorder than the others. About 5 to 6 percent of adult men and 1 percent of adult women would meet the criteria for this diagnosis (Kessler et al., 1994; Robins, Tipp, & Przybeck, 1991). Consider Chuck, whom we described at the beginning of the section. Is his long-standing pattern of deviant behavior characteristic of a psychological disorder?

Chuck was eventually diagnosed as exhibiting **antisocial personality disorder;** in the past, he would have been called a *psychopath* or a *sociopath*. People exhibiting this disorder are often selfish, reckless, deceitful, impulsive, and remorseless. Robert Hare (1993), who has spent his career investigating these individuals, concluded that "lying, deceiving, and manipulation are natural talents" for them (p. 46). For example, one antisocial individual spotted a couple admiring a sailboat that had a For Sale sign on it. He introduced himself as the owner and invited them aboard for a closer look. They liked what they saw and handed him a deposit of $1,500. That was the last time they saw their money and the man (Hare, 1993).

The signs of disturbance seen in other disorders—anxiety, depression, delusions or hallucinations—are absent in antisocial personality disorder. Individuals with this disorder rarely seek professional help unless their goal is to obtain an excuse to be absent from work, to acquire drugs, or to avoid prison by submitting to court-ordered

TABLE 12-8

Personality Disorders and Their Characteristics

Odd or Eccentric Behavior

Paranoid	Tense, guarded, suspicious, tends to hold grudges and believes that others are untrustworthy.
Schizoid	Detached from social relationships, with a restricted range of expression of emotions, indifferent to both praise and criticism.
Schizotypal	Marked by peculiarities of speech, perceptions, appearance, and behavior that are often disconcerting to others; emotionally detached, socially isolated, and suspicious.

Dramatic, Emotional or Erratic Behavior

Antisocial	Manipulative, reckless, dishonest, impulsive, lacks guilt, habitually breaks social rules, childhood history of such behavior, often in trouble with the law as an adult.
Borderline	Cannot stand to be alone; intense, unstable moods and personal relationships; chronic, inappropriate anger, drug and alcohol abuse, suicide attempts.
Histrionic	Highly dramatic, seductive behavior, needs immediate gratification and constant reassurance, rapidly changing moods, shallow emotions.
Narcissistic	Self-absorbed, expects special treatment and adulation, envious of the attention others receive.

Anxious or Fearful Behavior

Avoidant	Socially inhibited, easily hurt and embarrassed, few close friends, sticks to routines to avoid new and possibly stressful experiences.
Dependent	Wants others to make decisions, excessive need to be taken care of, leading to submissive and clinging behavior, needs constant advice and reassurance, fears being abandoned.
Obsessive–compulsive	Preoccupied with rules and details, perfectionistic at the expense of flexibility; indecisive, stiff, unable to express affection.

Source: American Psychiatric Association, 2000.

treatment. They can appear so normal that psychiatrist Hervey Cleckley (1976) titled his classic book about them *The Mask of Sanity*.

Because antisocial individuals do not experience the warning signals of anxiety, they are prone to act impulsively, without regard for the feelings or well-being of others. They want immediate gratification, fail to develop emotional attachments, and have no remorse for their actions: "They leave in their wakes a huge amount of human suffering. The pain [these individuals] wreak on other human beings can be physical, or it can be the mental anguish often felt by those who try to form relationships" with them (Magid & McKelvey, 1987, p. 4). Yet these individuals can be charming and ingratiating when it is to their advantage. Serial killer Ted Bundy used his charm to lure dozens of young women to accompany him to isolated places; only one of them was ever seen alive again.

Many antisocial people do not come into contact with law enforcement agencies. These con men, unethical business leaders, and crooked politicians are less dramatic

Lauraine (bottom), a 28-year-old blonde and her younger half-sister Lenette, 22, were once half brothers, Cary and Burt from a small Minnesota town. Sex reassignment surgery was performed on the older sibling, Cary, at the University of Minnesota when he was 21. When he turned 21, Burt also had the surgery performed. Following surgery, court procedures made their sex reassignments legal.

but more numerous than the Ted Bundy type of killer. Nevertheless, our understanding of this disorder is based largely on studies of the unlucky or unsuccessful antisocial individuals found in prisons.

Cathy Spatz Widom (1977) devised a clever plan to identify antisocial people who are not in prison. She placed the following advertisement in newspapers: "Are you adventurous? Psychologist studying adventurous carefree people who've led exciting impulsive lives" (p. 675). A number of respondents to the advertisement met the criteria for antisocial personality disorder. Almost 50 percent of them had a history of heavy drinking and considerable experience with other drugs. Many had been arrested but had spent little time in jail, preferring court-ordered psychotherapy. Widom concluded that many people outside of prisons could be diagnosed as exhibiting antisocial personality disorder.

The childhood and adolescent years of people diagnosed with antisocial personality disorder as adults are marked by hyperactivity, impulsivity, attention problems, and neuropsychological impairment (Lynam, 1998). Nevertheless, many of them tend to engage in fewer criminal activities after age 40 (Hare, McPherson, & Forth, 1988). The specific reasons for this decrease are not clear. Perhaps they continue their antisocial activities but have developed better strategies for staying out of prison.

Because people with antisocial personalities do not conform to social norms, researchers have turned their attention to the socializing agent that is primarily responsible for instilling social norms in the young: the family. They have found that during childhood, many antisocial people were subjected to inconsistent discipline or no discipline at all. As in Chuck's case, their future course was evident in early episodes of fighting, lying, stealing, and vandalism. Many children who are raised with little or no discipline, however, do not develop antisocial tendencies. Thus it appears that lack of discipline during childhood is not a complete explanation of the emergence of antisocial tendencies.

Psychological Detective

Over the years researchers have found that antisocial individuals have a low level of physiological arousal, a condition that is so uncomfortable that they will do almost anything to change it. As Chuck said, he was just trying to "stir up some excitement." How could researchers determine that an individual has a low level of arousal? How could they determine whether level of arousal is related to antisocial activity? Before reading further, design a study to gather evidence that might show that physiological arousal is or is not related to antisocial behavior.

Just such a study was conducted by Adrian Raine, Peter Venables, and Mark Williams (1990). They recruited 101 young men between the ages of 14 and 16 to take part in a program to measure heart rate and brain waves, which served as indicators of arousal. Assessing the relationship of physiological arousal to antisocial behavior required a longitudinal research design. The criminal records of the young men were checked when they reached age 24. The men with a criminal record at that age were more likely to have had low arousal levels when they were teenagers than the men with no criminal record. Using only the indicators of physiological arousal, the researchers correctly classified 75% of the men as criminal or noncriminal.

Sexual Disorders

The DSM-IV divides sexual disorders into several categories: gender identity disorder (transsexualism), the paraphilias, and sexual dysfunctions. In this section we discuss the first two categories.

Gender Identity Disorder.   Are you a male or a female? Although this seems like a silly question, for some people it is a serious matter. Beginning in childhood, some people believe their anatomical sex does not match their gender identity. Many cases of **gender identity disorder (transsexualism)** in childhood cease by the time the individual reaches adolescence, but some cases progress into what is known as transsexualism.

Transsexualism is a disorder in which a person is uncomfortable with his or her anatomical sex, views it as inappropriate, and wants to be a member of the other sex. This rare disorder occurs in 1 in 30,000 biological males and 1 in 100,000 biological females (American Psychiatric Association, 2000). One treatment, sex-reassignment surgery, involves surgically creating external sex organs that are characteristic of the other biological sex. Mental health professionals screen candidates for sex reassignment surgery to ensure that disorders like schizophrenia are not present. Once a patient is considered eligible for the surgery, hormone therapy can begin. This therapy develops the secondary sex characteristics and must be continued for life. For males wanting to be female, estrogen and drugs to inhibit testosterone production promote breast growth, soften the skin, reduce body and facial hair, and reduce muscle strength. Females wishing to be male are given testosterone to increase body and facial hair, deepen the voice, suppress menstruation, and reduce breast tissue. The next step is a "real life test" in which the individual lives as a member of the other sex for a year or more prior to the surgery (Miracle, Miracle, & Baumeister, 2003). Although evidence suggests that transsexuals who have undergone the operation are generally quite satisfied (Pauly, 1990), controversy surrounds the treatment because it is radical and irreversible.

Paraphilias. **Paraphilia** literally means "Love beyond the usual." People with paraphilias are sexually aroused by objects or situations that are considered unusual or bizarre by most people, ranging from animals to dressing in the clothes of the other sex. Most of these individuals are men; their unusual activity is typically harmless or involves consenting others. Some of these people, however, can be dangerous and may come into contact with legal authorities. Table 12-9 lists some of the more common paraphilias.

Fetishism. Derived from a French word for a magical charm, a fetish is an object that arouses sexual passion in some people. **Fetishism** is a sexual disorder in which an object or body part becomes associated with sexual arousal. A wide variety of objects may serve as fetishes: shoes, boots, fur, women's underwear, and rubber or leather products (Junginger, 1997; Mason, 1997). Some of these objects are associated with sexual activity; others are rarely associated with sexual excitement by most people. Fetishists may kiss, taste, or smell the fetish and masturbate while fondling it. Typically, a person with a fetish is no danger to others and pursues use of the fetish in private (Miracle, Miracle, & Baumeister, 2003).

Consider the case of a 32-year-old man who was sexually excited at a young age by pictures of women wearing panties. At the age of 12, he ejaculated for the first time while fantasizing about panties. Thereafter he began to steal panties from his sister and her friends. His preferred pattern of sexual excitement involved panties, which he used while masturbating. Dating made him uncomfortable because he feared that if he and his date became intimate, she would not understand his sexual practices (Spitzer et al., 1994).

Psychodynamic theorists see paraphilias as associated with early childhood experiences or, in some cases, as alternatives that arouse less anxiety than sexual encounters with adult partners. Behavioral psychologists, in contrast, believe that most fetishes, and probably many of the paraphilias, develop through classical conditioning. Perhaps the object that becomes a fetish was accidentally paired with sexual arousal and thus acquired the power to elicit arousal later in life. In laboratory experiments, psychologists have paired pictures of boots with slides of nudes (Rachman, 1966). The participant's level of sexual arousal was measured by a device placed on the penis. The results showed that the arousal caused by the nudes was transferred to the boots.

People who exhibit one of the paraphilias are sexually aroused by objects or situations that most people consider bizarre or unusual. Unlike lower animals, humans can be sexually aroused by a wide range of objects and situations. Some businesses cater to the needs of paraphiliacs by providing objects used in their sexual activities. The man pictured here is standing outside a shop that sells leather dominatrix costumes, often used by people practicing sexual masochism and sexual sadism.

STUDY TIP

Write a two-paragraph summary of the material on personality and sexual disorders—one paragraph for each category.

gender identity disorder (transsexualism)
Sexual disorder characterized by a person's belief that he or she was born with the wrong biological sex organs

paraphilia
Sexual arousal by objects or situations not considered sexual by most people

fetishism
Paraphilia involving sexual arousal by unusual objects or body parts

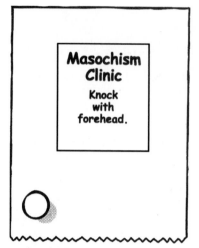

Masochism Clinic
Knock with forehead.

Source: Reprinted with the permission of Psi Chi, The National Honor Society in Psychology.

TABLE 12-9

Paraphilias

Autopedophilia: Sexual arousal by imagining oneself as a child or being treated as a child.

Autoscopophilia: Sexual gratification from looking at one's own body, particularly the genitals.

Avoniepiphilia: Sexual arousal from wearing diapers.

Exhibitionism (indecent exposure, flashing)**:** Repeated exposure of genitals to unsuspecting strangers, usually women and children. The exhibitionist may masturbate while exposing his genitals but usually does not pursue further sexual activity. Exhibitionists seem to desire surprise or shock in victims but are usually not physically dangerous to them.

Fetishism: Sexual arousal associated with nonliving objects, called fetishes, such as stockings, shoes, or boots. The fetishist often masturbates while fondling the desired object.

Formicophilia: Sexual arousal associated with bugs or other crawling creatures.

Frotteurism: Sexual arousal as a result of rubbing against or touching a nonconsenting person. The behavior usually occurs in crowded places like busy sidewalks or on public transportation. Victims may not protest at first because they cannot believe that such provocative acts are occurring in a public place.

Klismaphilia: Sexual arousal resulting from receiving or giving an enema.

Mysophilia: Sexual arousal that involves the presence of or use of filthy or soiled objects.

Narratophilia: Sexual arousal from listening to erotic stories.

Necrophilia: Sexual pleasure from viewing or having sexual contact with a corpse.

Partialism: Intense sexual attraction to specific body parts (most often legs or feet, and excluding genitals, breasts, and buttocks).

Pedophilia: Sexual activity with a child who has not reached puberty. Attraction to girls is twice as common as attraction to boys.

Pictophilia: The need for sexual pictures for sexual response.

Sexual masochism: Sexual arousal that involves being humiliated, beaten, bound, or made to suffer in other ways.

Sexual sadism: Sexual arousal associated with the physical or psychological suffering of victims.

Transvestic fetishism: Sexual arousal associated with cross-dressing; that is, dressing in the clothes of the opposite sex.

Voyeurism (peeping)**:** Sexual arousal as a result of observing unsuspecting individuals, most often strangers, who are either naked, in the process of undressing, or engaging in sexual activity. The voyeur usually does not seek any sexual liaison with the observed person.

Zoophilia: Sexual activity with animals.

Sources: American Psychiatric Association, 2000; Money, 1984, Miracle, Miracle, & Baumeister, 2003.

REVIEW SUMMARY

1. **Personality disorders** are long-standing dysfunctional patterns of behavior. A person with antisocial personality disorder displays few of the signs usually associated with psychological disorders, such as anxiety. They are often described as deceitful, impulsive, and remorseless. Low levels of arousal may play a role in the development of this disorder.

2. **Gender identity disorder (transsexualism)** is a sexual disorder in which a person believes that he or she should have been a member of the opposite sex.

3. **Paraphilias** are disorders involving sexual arousal in unusual situations or in response to unusual objects. **Fetishism** is a paraphilia in which a person is sexually aroused by an object such as boots. One of the explanations for fetishism and perhaps other paraphilias is classical conditioning.

CHECK YOUR PROGRESS

1. Of 100 randomly selected people, approximately how many are likely to meet the diagnostic criteria for one of the personality disorders?

    a. 1

    b. 3

    c. 5

    d. 10

2. What are the key symptoms of antisocial personality disorder? In what ways do antisocial individuals appear to be quite normal?

3. What are the key symptoms of transsexualism?

4. Give the name of each of the following sexual disorders.

    a. Sexual activity with a child.

    b. Sexual contact with animals.

    c. Sexual contact with dead bodies.

    d. Sexual arousal from rubbing against a person.

    e. Sexual arousal from receiving or giving an enema.

    f. Sexual arousal related to boots or fur.

ANSWERS: 1. d **2.** The individual with antisocial personality disorder is described as irresponsible, deceitful, manipulative, and remorseless. People with this disorder do not, however, exhibit anxiety, depression, hallucinations, or delusions. **3.** A transsexual is a person who has no genetic abnormality yet believes he or she has the sex organs of the wrong sex. **4. a.** Pedophilia **b.** Zoophilia **c.** Necrophilia **d.** Frotteurism **e.** Klismaphilia **f.** Fetishism

CHAPTER 15

Social Psychology: The Individual in Society

CHAPTER OUTLINE

So far we have considered the behavior of individuals independently of the groups to which they belong. In this chapter our focus expands to the individual as a member of various groups, including society as a whole; we describe the domain of social psychology. We examine the ways we view others and their behavior; interpersonal relations such as attraction, friendship, love, helping others, and aggression; social influences on behavior; and how the individual functions as part of a social group. As you read this chapter, you will encounter familiar terms and concepts from previous chapters. In a very real sense, social psychology is psychology in action. It applies what you have already learned to real-life behaviors in social settings.

SOCIAL PSYCHOLOGY AND CULTURE

Several students in your psychology class are discussing a new research finding. The results are exciting and seem to add considerably to our understanding of patterns of human interaction. You find the research particularly interesting because it was conducted in a foreign country. After further discussion, one of your classmates suggests that the results are presented in an ethnocentric manner. *What does the term* ethnocentric *mean?*

The study of social psychology is nearly as old as scientific psychology itself. The results of the first social-psychological experiment were published in 1898, just 19 years after Wilhelm Wundt founded the science of psychology (see Chapter 1). In that experiment Norman Triplett (1898) found that the presence of other people could enhance or facilitate the performance of a behavior requiring skill, such as bicycle racing. This effect, known as *social facilitation*, is still being studied by social psychologists. Social psychologists also study aspects of human interaction such as the formation of impressions, the development of attitudes, the effects of group pressure, the bases of interpersonal attraction, and the causes of prejudice and discrimination. Thus **social psychology** may be defined as the study of the causes, types, and consequences of human interaction.

As you read this chapter, keep in mind that the human interactions we are discussing do not occur in isolation; they occur in a specific cultural context. As you are aware, cultures can be very different; hence it should not surprise you to find that the results of a research project conducted in one culture may not be the same when the project is conducted in a different culture. Unfortunately, researchers are sometimes guilty of **ethnocentrism;** they disregard cultural differences and see other cultures as an extension of their own, "superior" culture. As Smith and Davis (2004) point out, such researchers "interpret research results in accord with the values, attitudes, and behaviors that define their own culture and assume that these findings are applicable in other cultures as well" (p. 149). Because culture can influence the type of research problem we choose to investigate, the nature of our research hypothesis, and the selection of the variables we choose to manipulate (the independent variable; see Chapter 1) and record (the dependent variable), researchers must guard against ethnocentrism (Matsumoto, 1994).

Consider the issue of individualism and collectivism. **Individualism** is defined as placing one's own goals over those of the group, whereas **collectivism** is defined

social psychology
Study of the causes, types, and consequences of human interaction

ethnocentrism
Belief that one's own country or culture is superior to all other countries and cultures

individualism
Placing one's own goals above those of the group

collectivism
Placing group goals above individual goals

Social facilitation occurs when the presence of other people enhances an individual's performance.

as placing group goals above individual goals. The degree of individualism or collectivism in a culture can influence many aspects of behavior, such as interpersonal relations, self-concept, parenting practices, self-esteem, and emotional expression (Kim & Choi, 1994; Triandis, 1995; Triandis, Brislin, & Hui, 1988).

Because cultures vary so widely, social psychologists need to conduct cross-cultural studies to determine whether the results of research conducted in one culture can be *generalized* to other cultures (Smith & Bond, 1993). Even with cross-cultural studies, however, you must learn to be a good psychological detective. In addition to ascertaining effects of culture, you need to ask about the conditions under which the research was conducted and, even, the nature of the research participants. For example, many psychologists rely on college students as participants because they constitute a convenient population for drawing a sample. What about a study from another culture that used college students as participants? Are college students in Iran or South Africa comparable to those in the United States? (Closer to home, we can ask if college students in different parts of the United States are comparable to one another. Remember, the United States is composed of different subcultures.) Questions such as these are difficult to answer. Yet they must be addressed if we are truly committed to developing a general body of knowledge.

HOW WE VIEW OTHERS AND THEIR BEHAVIOR

Last week you attended a party and made several new acquaintances, including Antonio and Roberto. Something about Antonio attracted other people to him immediately; he was the life of the party. By contrast, Roberto blended into the background; you hardly knew he was there. You left the party with very definite but different impressions of each of your new acquaintances. *What factors influenced your impressions of Antonio and Roberto?*

Impression formation is the process of developing an opinion about another person. In addition to forming impressions of others, we also make judgments, called *attributions*, about the reasons for or causes of this person's behavior. In this section we discuss these two processes and their effects, as well as the larger category, *attitudes*, that includes both impressions and judgments.

Impression Formation

The process of impression formation requires an actor and a perceiver. As the perceiver, you form an impression about the actor. The views and thoughts of the perceiver and the appearance and behaviors of the actor influence the impressions that are formed. Let us take a closer look at each of these dimensions of impression formation.

Aspects of the Perceiver.   Have you ever made a snap judgment about someone you just met? We do not enter into interpersonal relationships with a completely blank mind; we bring preconceived ideas or stereotypes to every situation. A **stereotype** is a set of beliefs about members of a particular group (Aronson, Wilson, & Akert, 2002). Stereotypes can be either negative or positive. Examples of negative stereotypes are "Jocks are dumb" and "Film stars are temperamental." "Beautiful people are good people" is an example of a positive stereotype (Feingold, 1991, 1992).

Why do we form stereotypes? In Chapter 3 we saw that the nervous system is not capable of processing all the sensory information to which we are exposed at any given time. To reduce this "information overload," we create perceptual categories, such as "red objects," "square objects," "sweet objects," and "loud objects." The same logic

impression formation
The process of forming an opinion about another person

stereotype
Set of beliefs about members of a particular group

If we view beautiful people as good, the "beautiful is good" stereotype may be influencing our attitudes.

applies to the formation of stereotypes. If you put people into categories, you have fewer items of information to deal with—you can think about a small number of categories rather than a large number of individuals (Kaplan, Wanshula, & Zanna, 1992). Those categories are stereotypes.

Obviously a lot of information about an individual is lost when he or she is viewed as part of a category. Take the "beautiful is good" stereotype as an example. When we meet an attractive person, we may unconsciously put him or her in the beautiful-is-good category and assume that he or she possesses all the positive characteristics associated with that stereotype (Patzer, 1985). Does your personal experience support this stereotype?

Understanding Prejudice and Acing Acronyms

Psychological Detective

Continued interactions with people should demonstrate that individuals in a given category do not necessarily share the same personality traits. Yet stereotypes persist, often in the face of contradictory evidence. Why do we continue to hold stereotypes? Write down at least one reason before reading further.

There are two reasons for the persistence of stereotypes. First, if we believe that a group of people (such as community leaders) possesses certain characteristics, we may selectively note behaviors that are consistent with that characteristic (such as volunteering to serve in the chamber of commerce) and fail to notice behaviors that are inconsistent (such as driving under the influence of alcohol). The second reason that stereotypes are durable involves the effects of our own reactions and behaviors on the individuals in question. Do you treat attractive people and unattractive people differently? Perhaps you treat individuals in ways that elicit behaviors consistent with your stereotype. For example, grade school teachers who are told that the children in their classes are slow learners treat those children differently from the children they are told are gifted (Rosenthal & Jacobson, 1968; Smith, Jussim, & Eccles, 1999). These different instructor reactions result in different behaviors on the part of the students, even if the students are not different in any appreciable manner. When your behaviors influence others to respond the way you expect, a **self-fulfilling prophecy** is at work (McNatt, 2000).

self-fulfilling prophecy
Phenomenon whereby our expectations elicit behaviors in others that confirm those expectations

self-disclosure
An individual's decision to share personal information

Clearly the perceiver can and does play an active role in the process of impression formation. Certain characteristics of the actor, however, also play a prominent role in this process.

Aspects of the Actor.   Four features of the actor have been shown to influence impression formation. Those features are (1) physical appearance, (2) style and content of speech, (3) nonverbal mannerisms and nonverbal communication, and (4) the perceiver's prior information about the actor.

Appearance.   The "beautiful is good" stereotype assumes that attractive people have positive characteristics—they are witty and intelligent and have pleasing personalities (Feingold, 1991). Therefore attractive people can be expected to make better impressions. Research has shown that these expectations are borne out in reality (Dion & Stein, 1978); our first impressions of attractive people are more favorable than those of less attractive individuals. Despite the prevalence of this "beautiful" stereotype, however, research has shown that people also find *average* facial features to be quite attractive. In fact, research participants routinely rate a composite (average) face created by a computer blending other faces as more attractive than the individual faces that contributed to the composite (Halberstadt & Rhodes, 2000). What's more, the attractiveness of a face can be increased or decreased by changing its amount of correspondence with the average face (Rhodes, Sumich, & Byatt, 1999).

Speech.   *How* you do things makes a difference. With regard to impression formation, an actor's style of speech is important. Among the aspects of speech that are influential are speed, volume, and inflections (variations). For example, a New Yorker's rapid, clipped speech may not appeal to a native of Atlanta, whose slower style may make the New Yorker impatient. When we meet someone with a foreign accent, we tend to talk more slowly and more loudly. In addition, straightforward and clear speech is more appealing than speech that contains numerous qualifiers and hesitations, such as *like, maybe, kinda, I guess,* and *you know* (Erickson et al., 1978).

The content of speech is also important. Research on **self-disclosure,** the amount of personal information a person is willing to share with others, indicates that the more a person reveals, the more positive the impression others form. Although self-disclosure by one individual prompts self-disclosure by another, too much self-disclosure early in a relationship can create a negative impression (Miller, 1990). How have you reacted when people whom you have just met told you highly personal information? Your reaction was probably unfavorable because you were unwilling to disclose the same kind of information about yourself. Most people are not willing to share intimate experiences and feelings with others whom they know only casually. As the relationship develops, they are more likely to reveal private information. Whereas self-disclosure is valued in Western, industrialized cultures like the United States that stress individualism (especially on radio and television talk shows), it is not as highly valued in Asian cultures like Japan that stress collectivism.

Favorable impressions are also created by people who respond appropriately to what has just been said to them. Suppose you have just told a new acquaintance what your major is. How would you react if the response to this self-disclosure was silence or a comment on an unrelated topic? Would your impression be different if the other person had said something positive about your choice of a major?

Nonverbal Communication.   Instructors often say that the first class session in a course is the most important one. As a student, your initial impression of the teacher may greatly influence your enjoyment of that first class. The instructor's nonverbal communication plays an important role in determining this initial impression. Which course would you rather

Nonverbal communication can tell us a lot about other people.

take: one in which the instructor never makes eye contact with students and has unusual mannerisms (such as blinking rapidly, a behavior associated with anxiety), or one in which the instructor looks each student in the eye, smiles frequently, and has an easygoing, relaxed manner?

Mark Snyder and his colleagues (Snyder & Gangestad, 1986) have developed the Self-Monitoring Scale to measure the degree to which individuals manipulate the nonverbal signals they send to others in social situations and how well they are able to adjust their behaviors to fit the specific situation. The Self-Monitoring Scale is reproduced below; see how you score on this dimension.

Hands On

Self-Monitoring Scale

The following statements concern your personal reactions to a number of situations. No two statements are exactly alike, so consider each statement carefully before answering. If a statement is true or mostly true as applied to you, mark T as your answer. If a statement is false or not usually true as applied to you, mark F as your answer. It is important that you answer frankly and honestly. Scoring instructions and interpretive comments are found at the end of the chapter.

1. I find it hard to imitate the behavior of other people.
2. My behavior is usually an expression of my true inner feelings, attitudes, and beliefs.
3. At parties and social gatherings I do not attempt to do or say things that others will like.
4. I can only argue for ideas I already believe.
5. I can make impromptu speeches even on topics about which I have almost no information.
6. I guess I put on a show to impress or entertain people.
7. When I am uncertain how to act in a social situation, I look to the behavior of others for cues.
8. I would probably make a good actor.
9. I rarely need the advice of my friends to choose movies, books, or music.
10. I sometimes appear to others to be experiencing deeper emotions than I actually am.
11. I laugh more when I watch a comedy with others than when alone.
12. In a group of people, I am rarely the center of attention.
13. In different situations and with different people, I often act like very different persons.
14. I am not particularly good at making other people like me.
15. Even if I am not enjoying myself, I often pretend to be having a good time.
16. I'm not always the person I appear to be.
17. I would not change my opinions (or the way I do things) in order to please someone else or to win his or her favor.
18. I have considered being an entertainer.
19. In order to get along and be liked, I tend to be what people expect me to be rather than anything else.
20. I have never been good at games like charades or improvisational acting.
21. I have trouble changing my behavior to suit different people and different situations.
22. At a party I let others keep the jokes and stories going.
23. I feel a bit awkward in company and do not show up quite so well as I should.

attribution
The process of assigning causes to events and behaviors

24. I can look anyone in the eye and tell a lie with a straight face (if for a right end).

25. I may deceive people by being friendly when I really dislike them.

Source: Snyder & Gangestad, 1986.

Prior Information.   Information that is available to you before you meet someone can affect your impression of that person. For example, if a label is applied to an individual, it may stick, regardless of its accuracy. A classic study by psychologist Harold Kelley (1950) illustrates this point. The students in a class were told they would be hearing a visiting lecturer. Half of the students received a written description that portrayed the lecturer as "warm." The rest received a description that portrayed the lecturer as "cold." After the lecture the students who had read the "warm" description had a more favorable impression of the speaker than the students who had read the "cold" description.

Stereotype Activation.   Although researchers have gathered considerable information about the nature, content, and origin of stereotypes, they know relatively little about the effects of stereotypes (Spencer, Steele, & Quinn, 1999). What reactions do people have when they are the target of a stereotype that has been activated? The answer to this question depends on whether the stereotype is negative or positive. The activation of a negative stereotype can cause the target person's performance to decrease. For example, increasing the awareness of minority or low socioeconomic status resulted in minority students (Steele & Aronson, 1995) and students with low socioeconomic status (Croziet & Claire, 1998) scoring lower on standardized tests (see Chapter 8). Because of the undesirable outcomes, the term *stereotype* threat is often used to describe such effects (Croziet & Claire, 1998). On the other hand, Shih, Pittinsky, and Ambady (1999) found that the activation of a positive stereotype can *enhance* performance. They activated the stereotype of Asian-American mathematics excellence and found that test performance of Asian-American students increased significantly when compared to a group of Asian-American students who did not have this stereotype activated. Research of this nature appears to offer answers to behavioral differences in numerous situations, such as group testing, where stereotypes can be activated.

Social Judgments: Attributing Causes to Behaviors

In addition to forming impressions of others, we seek to discern the causes of their behavior. **Attribution** is the process by which we decide why certain events occurred or why a particular person acted in a certain manner (Ross, 1998). Several factors influence our attributions. Among them are internal versus external causes, consistency, consensus, and our role as actor or perceiver in the situation.

Internal Versus External Causes.   In attempting to determine the cause of a particular event or behavior, we first decide whether it was due to internal factors, such as personality traits (see Chapter 11), or to external, situational factors, such as the stressors a person is experiencing. Because the determinants of many social events and behaviors are unclear, these attributions are not always automatic or trivial.

Psychological Detective

Consider each of the following events:

1. Your best friend made an excellent grade on her mid-term exam.

2. An automobile was stolen from the parking lot of a fancy restaurant.

3. An anonymous benefactor made a large donation to the local hospital.

Write a likely explanation (attribution) for each event before reading further.

What causes did you assign to each of these situations? Here are some possibilities:

1. Your best friend earned an excellent grade on her mid-term exam. Was her grade due to effort (internal cause) or an easy test (external cause)?

2. An automobile was stolen from the parking lot of a fancy restaurant. Did the theft result from a premeditated plan (internal cause) or peer pressure (external cause)?

3. An anonymous benefactor made a large donation to the local hospital. Was the donation prompted by the desire to help sick people (internal cause) or by the need to have a large tax deduction (external cause)?

Deciding whether the cause of an event or behavior is internal or external has a major impact on the attributional process. If we decide that the behavior has an internal cause, we attribute it to the individual in question; if the behavior has an external cause, we attribute it to the environment. According to Harold Kelley (1967, 1971; Gilbert, 1998), factors such as *distinctiveness*, *consistency*, and *consensus* influence our decisions about internal or external causes.

Distinctiveness. *Distinctiveness* refers to the extent to which a person's responses vary from situation to situation (for example, Roman likes this modern painting, but not that one). The greater the variability, the higher the distinctiveness.

Consistency. Has this behavior occurred before? Our confidence in making attributions regarding internal or external causes is greatest when the behaviors we observe are *consistent*. For example, suppose that one of the roommates from two doors down the hall on your dormitory floor just came in from class and you hear him yelling at his roommate about the mess in their room. Was the student's angry outburst a reflection of a nasty disposition (internal cause), or does his roommate provoke similar reactions in everyone (external cause)? Unless we have seen the angry student's reactions or the roommate's behavior in similar situations, consistency will be low, and we will not be especially confident in our attribution of a cause.

Consensus. Have others also observed this behavior? *Consensus* refers to the reactions of other people to the external object or behavior in question. If everyone agrees that the roommate is a messy slob, there would be a high degree of consensus. If the angry student is the only one who accuses his roommate of being a slob, there would be a low level of consensus. When consensus is high and everyone views the behavior or object in the same manner, we tend to make external attributions; when it is low and no one agrees about the behavior or object in question, we tend to make internal attributions.

The percentage of internal attributions in an individualistic society, such as the United States, increases dramatically starting at about age 11, whereas internal attributions increase only slightly in a collectivist society, such as India (Miller, 1984). The converse pattern is true for external attributions.

Attributional Biases. We are not as objective as we might think when we make attributions about the causes of behaviors, events, and situations. Various biases can and do influence our attributions. Some of those biases are described in the following pages.

Myth or Science

One of the most prominent myths in our society concerns the belief that individuals can control chance. Dice players believe that throwing the dice in a certain manner results in a high number, whereas throwing the dice in a different manner results in a low number. In one study, college students believed that once a particular number had been rolled with the dice, the person who rolled could roll that number again (Fleming & Darley, 1990). This feeling of control is not limited to dice; it has also

fundamental attribution error
The tendency to attribute behaviors to internal causes

been shown for picking lottery numbers (Langer, 1977) and flipping a coin. Despite such widespread belief in one's ability to beat the odds, such behavior is only an illusion of control. In the long run, an unbiased coin always averages half heads and half tails. Fair dice yield high and low numbers regardless of how they are thrown. A particular selection of lottery numbers has no bearing on those actually selected. Why does this illusion persist? Every once in a while a person is reinforced with an appropriate number on a roll of the dice, a lottery ticket pays off, or a coin toss ends as predicted. Behavior does not change the odds. As we saw in Chapter 5, partial reinforcement can cause people to repeat a behavior for a long time.

The Fundamental Attribution Error.　　Fritz Heider (1958) pointed out that people tend to pay more attention to the behavior and characteristics of an actor than to the situation in which the behavior occurs. This tendency biases them toward making internal attributions. Think back to the Psychological Detective on page 632. When you wrote explanations about your friend's mid-term grade, the automobile that was stolen from the parking lot, and the anonymous benefactor, did you focus on the individuals more than on the situations? This internal attribution bias, which occurs even when strong situational determinants are not present, is termed the **fundamental attribution error.** It becomes especially pronounced when the actor's behavior is unclear and ambiguous (Vonk, 1999).

Imagine that you have volunteered to participate in a psychology experiment. You arrive at the designated testing room and find it decorated like a television studio. As you enter the room, you are randomly designated as either a contestant or a quizmaster. The quizmasters prepare several general questions, which the contestants try to answer. Without fail, the contestants find themselves unable to answer the questions. When the quiz is over, the intelligence of the quizmasters and contestants is rated. Quizmasters are always rated as smarter than contestants.

Psychological Detective

Is this internal attribution accurate, or are there situational factors that have not been taken into account? If there are such factors, what are they, and why were they overlooked? Jot down some possibilities before reading further.

Recall that the participants were randomly assigned to either the quizmaster or the contestant role at the beginning of the experiment. The two groups should therefore have been comparable. What occurred next? The quizmasters created the questions that the contestants attempted to answer. This arrangement may have created a problem for the contestants. Who chose the categories of the questions? The quizmasters did. Why might this have created a problem? The contestants were forced to answer questions derived from the quizmasters' areas of greatest knowledge. Because the contestants' areas of greatest knowledge were different, they were placed at a disadvantage. (If you are an expert on sports trivia, it should not be surprising to find that your questions stump people who are not sports enthusiasts.) Yet in making their attributions, both the contestants and the quizmasters overlooked this aspect of the situation. The quizmasters repeatedly stumped the contestants, so they were seen as more intelligent; that is, an internal attribution was made. This experiment (Ross, Amabile, & Steinmetz, 1977) provides a clear example of the fundamental attribution error.

The Actor-Perceiver Bias.　　Any behavior that is observed by others can have two attributions—the attribution of the person who performed the behavior (the actor) and that of someone who witnessed the behavior (a perceiver). Are these two attributions likely to be the same?

STUDY TIP

Pair up to illustrate the actor-perceiver bias. Each student in the pair should develop two situations (using the sample situations on p. 635 as a guide). Then the pair should consider each of the four situations, with one student arriving at an interpretation appropriate for the actor, and the other student taking the part of the perceiver (switch off for each situation).

Consider the following situations, first from the standpoint of the perceiver and then from that of the actor:

1. A person stumbles and falls down a flight of stairs.

2. A middle-aged man is stopped for speeding.

If you adopt the role of the perceiver and then that of the actor in each of these situations, you should find a difference in your attributions. Perceivers are more likely to make internal attributions: The person stumbled because he or she is clumsy; the driver was stopped for speeding because he did not believe traffic laws applied to him. In the role of the actor, you are more likely to make an external attribution: I fell down the stairs because the heel of my shoe came off; I was speeding because my speedometer is not accurate. Thus the fundamental attribution error may be committed more frequently by perceivers than by actors.

The self-serving bias suggests that we are quick to accept credit for our successes but tend to blame our failures on factors beyond our control.

Self-Serving Bias.   Attributional differences between actors and perceivers lead to the prediction that perceivers make more internal attributions than actors. Another bias, however, may influence the attributions of the actors. So far we have not considered the impact of success and failure on a person's attributions.

Psychological Detective

Will an actor's attributions be different for successful experiences than for failures? Put yourself in each of the following situations:

1. Your short story has just been accepted for publication in a regional literary magazine.

2. Your psychology exam was just returned with a D on it.

Write down the attribution you would make in each situation before reading further.

Who was responsible for the *success* of the short story, and who is to *blame* for the D on the exam? Generally, we are quick to accept credit for our successes and equally quick to blame our failures on factors beyond our control. In short, we tend to make internal attributions when our behaviors are successful and external attributions when we fail (Sedikides et al., 1998). This attributional pattern is called the **self-serving bias.** The self-serving bias occurs more often in individualistic societies, such as the United States, but less often in collectivist societies, such as Japan, that stress interdependence, not independence (Markus & Kitayama, 1991).

Another aspect of the self-serving bias involves the **just world belief.** According to this view, we see ourselves as decent and capable human beings (Lambert, Burroughs, & Nguyen, 1999). Because we are good people, only good things happen to us; bad things happen to bad people. The just world belief leads to an attribution called *blaming the victim* (Stormo, Lang, & Stritzke, 1997). Because of their misfortunes, victims must be bad people who caused their own fate. For example, there is a tendency to blame rape victims (Bell, Kuriloff, & Lottes, 1994). Likewise, some media sources criticized Diana, Princess of Wales, as if she were somehow responsible for the car crash that took her life (Hafer, 2000); in fact, however, she was a passenger in the back seat.

It is easy to focus on just internal and external issues and lose sight of contextual and cultural factors when considering the process of attribution. Such judgments always take place within a specific context or cultural background, and researchers have shown that these factors can influence the attribution process as much as—if not more than—specific internal or external factors that are attended to (Branscombe et al., 1997). These researchers showed that the degree to which individuals identify themselves with the particular culture that is present affects the attribution process.

self-serving bias
The tendency to make internal attributions when we are successful and external attributions when we fail

just world belief
The belief that bad things happen to bad people and good things happen to good people

Likewise, the operation of the fundamental attribution error has been shown in several individualistic Western societies (Gilbert & Malone, 1995), but not in the more collectivist culture of India (Miller, 1984).

Attitudes

15.1

Earlier in the chapter we saw that impression formation involves the judgment of an actor's character by a perceiver. Because impressions are evaluative judgments, they could also be included in the larger category that we call *attitudes*. **Attitudes** are evaluative judgments, but they are not limited to judgments about people. We form attitudes about objects, people, and thoughts (Petty & Wegener, 1998). What is your attitude about AIDS, religion, soccer, abortion, opera, politicians, crossword puzzles, plastic surgery, and the death penalty? As these examples suggest, attitudes can be positive, negative, or neutral; they can also vary greatly in intensity. For example, some people feel very strongly about abortion; others do not. Some people are passionate about soccer; others find the game boring. You may have attitudes of differing intensity about a wide variety of subjects; and those attitudes influence many of your thoughts, behaviors, and interactions. For example, intense political attitudes influence our thoughts about society, our behavior toward others with dissimilar views, and the people whom we call our friends.

Components of Attitudes: Affect, Cognition, and Behavior. Let's say you love rollerblading. Just the thought of strapping on your "blades" brings a smile to your face. For you, there is no greater fun than rollerblading. You also know that rollerblading is excellent exercise and a great way to stay in shape. You have a positive attitude about it.

This description of rollerblading illustrates the three components of an attitude: affect, cognition, and behavior. You love the activity; it's great fun. These feelings highlight the *affective* or *emotional* component; they are an important ingredient in attitudes. The knowledge we have about the object or the focus of our attitude (in this case, rollerblading) constitutes the second, or *cognitive*, component of an attitude. You understand the health benefits that the activity can bring. Finally, attitudes have a *behavioral* component (Tesser & Martin, 1996). Our attitudes prompt us to do or say something. You strap on the "blades" and go outside to enjoy rollerblading.

Now, we don't want to leave you with the impression that these three components always work together perfectly. They don't; sometimes they clash. For example, let's say you love pizza (affective component); however, you have high cholesterol and understand (knowledge component) that eating pizza may be bad for your health. Which behavior will your attitude result in, eating pizza or avoiding it? The answer depends on which component happens to be stronger. If you are walking past a pizza restaurant at lunchtime, your emotions and feelings probably will be stronger than your knowledge that pizza may not be the best food for your health. In that instance, you have pizza for lunch. If you are at home trying to decide where to go for dinner, however, the knowledge component may be stronger, and you decide to go where you can eat a healthier meal.

Functions of Attitudes. Although it is easy to see that we all have attitudes, it is more difficult to understand why we have them and what their purpose is. Attitudes serve several distinct functions (Maio & Olson, 1995): ego defense, adjustment, and knowledge.

Ego Defense. Attitudes protect us from threats to the self or ego. If a person makes statements that we perceive as threatening, we might say, "He makes comments like that because he's a dumb jock (writer, bookworm, musician)." Attributing threatening statements to the type of individual making them allows us to avoid confronting the possibility that the statements are accurate.

attitudes
Evaluative judgments about objects, people, and thoughts that include affective, knowledge, and behavioral components

Adjustment.   Attitudes are used to maximize reinforcements and minimize punishments from the environment. People and behaviors that yield reinforcement are viewed positively; those that yield unpleasant effects are viewed negatively. For example, an individual who is being reinforced on a new job would be likely to say, "I am very impressed with the supervisors on my new job. They are friendly, fair, and understanding people."

Knowledge.   Attitudes can help bring order and meaning to one's world. For example, the following attitudes may help a person who is trying to understand an apparently unjust situation: "Most football players have skills that others lack. That's why they are paid such incredibly high salaries."

Measuring Attitudes.   Theoretically, it should be simple to measure attitudes—just ask individuals to tell you their attitudes. Self-reports are often used to measure attitudes, but this method is far from simple. The types of questions asked, as well as the way they are asked, can influence the responses. For example, some people may try to hide their true feelings about sensitive topics such as AIDS, abortion, or the death penalty. Therefore psychologists have developed several other measurement techniques. Among them are Likert scales and behavioral measures.

Likert Scales.   **Likert scales** are questionnaires that require participants to indicate the extent to which they agree or disagree with particular statements. As with other types of self-report, honesty of responses can't really be ascertained with these scales. See Figure 15-1 for examples of Likert scale items.
     The advantage of Likert scales is that they are easily quantified, which enables investigators to make comparisons among different groups of individuals. In addition, several items can be combined to form an attitude scale. For example, the question about recycling could be used in a scale that measured attitudes toward various aspects of environmental protection. Such scales can be developed to measure attitudes toward literally any topic.

Behavioral Measures.   The saying "actions speak louder than words" indicates that we place considerable value on the behavioral component of attitudes. For example, if we tell others that energy conservation is a good cause, we are expected to be willing to invest time and effort in conservation activities, such as planting trees or stuffing envelopes to raise funds for conservation.

STUDY TIP

Create a mnemonic device to help you remember the components and functions of attitudes.

There's a Sucker Born in Every Medial Frontal Cortex

likert scale
Questionnaire that requires individuals to indicate their degree of agreement or disagreement with a set of statements

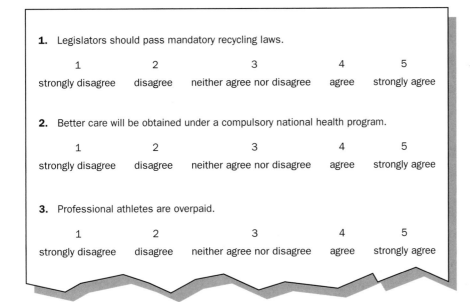

1. Legislators should pass mandatory recycling laws.

1	2	3	4	5
strongly disagree	disagree	neither agree nor disagree	agree	strongly agree

2. Better care will be obtained under a compulsory national health program.

1	2	3	4	5
strongly disagree	disagree	neither agree nor disagree	agree	strongly agree

3. Professional athletes are overpaid.

1	2	3	4	5
strongly disagree	disagree	neither agree nor disagree	agree	strongly agree

FIGURE 15-1 Examples of Likert scale items.

cognitive dissonance
Aversive state produced when an individual has two incompatible thoughts or cognitions simultaneously

The attitudes we express to others may not, however, coincide with our actual behaviors. For example, in a study of academic dishonesty (cheating), Stephen Davis and his colleagues (1992) found that over 90 percent of their college-student respondents felt that cheating is wrong. However, between 40 and 60 percent of the same participants reported they had cheated on at least one exam (Davis & Ludvigson, 1995). Clearly these participants' expressed attitudes did not coincide with their behaviors. Because expressed attitudes do not always coincide with behaviors, it is important to observe the behavior of participants in addition to obtaining self-reports of their attitudes.

How Are Attitudes Formed?   The process of attitude formation has been of interest to social psychologists for many years. *If* we understood this process, we could apply it in numerous real-life situations. For example, we could create favorable attitudes about particular politicians, toothpastes, and automobiles. In turn, those attitudes might lead to behaviors that would be financially rewarding to us. Because of the attitudes we had created, people would now be purchasing the toothpaste and automobiles that we manufactured and electing politicians who shared our views.

Learning.   Attitudes can be acquired through the process of classical conditioning (see Chapter 5), in which a conditioned stimulus (CS) comes to elicit a conditioned response (CR). When classical conditioning takes place, we also develop an attitude toward the CS; we either like it or dislike it. For example, assume that the sight of food (CS) has been paired with a mild electric shock (unconditioned stimulus, UCS). After this procedure has been repeated several times with several different types of food, what is your attitude toward the sight of food? It should be rather negative. This procedure is used in weight-reduction programs in cases of extreme obesity.

Operant conditioning can also serve as a basis for the establishment of attitudes. Behaviors that result in reinforcement produce positive attitudes, whereas behaviors that result in punishment produce negative attitudes. For example, children whose schoolwork is praised develop positive attitudes toward school; children whose schoolwork is continually criticized develop negative attitudes toward school.

Cognitive Dissonance.   In 1957, Leon Festinger proposed that a condition known as **cognitive dissonance** occurs when a person experiences an inconsistency between thoughts and behaviors. Because cognitive dissonance is an unpleasant or aversive state, we seek to reduce it and instead create *cognitive consonance*—the state in which behaviors and thoughts are compatible. Recall the example of the person who was concerned about cholesterol and high-fat foods but who loved to eat pizza. Here we have dissonant thoughts and behaviors. The dissonance in this situation could be resolved by finding reasons to distrust the medical advice about cholesterol or by finding new reasons to avoid eating pizza. In either instance, the individual would strengthen an attitude about an object or event in his or her environment. Thus the formation of new attitudes is involved in the reduction of cognitive dissonance. Dissonance appears to be a common phenomenon that occurs in both individualistic and collectivist societies in most parts of the world (Sakai, 1999).

Attitudes are at the core of interpersonal relations. We consider this topic in the next section.

R E V I E W   S U M M A R Y

1. **Social psychology** examines the causes, types, and consequences of human interaction.

2. Cultural differences, such as **individualism** (in which the individual's goals are most important) versus **collectivism** (in which group goals are most important), can influence the results of social psychological research. Researchers need to avoid **ethnocentrism** (viewing other cultures as inferior extensions of their own).

3. **Impression formation** requires an actor and a perceiver. The views of the perceiver, as well as the appearance and

behaviors of the actor, influence the impression of the actor that is formed by the perceiver.

4. **Stereotypes** are negative or positive sets of beliefs about members of particular groups. They reduce the amount of information that must be processed and are very resistant to change because we tend selectively to notice behaviors that confirm our stereotypes. What's more, our treatment of other people as prompted by our stereotypes often brings forth the very behaviors that we associate with our stereotypes of those people.

5. Some **self-disclosure** fosters a positive impression, but excessive self-disclosure early in a relationship may result in a negative first impression.

6. The process of **attribution** involves deciding why certain events occurred and why certain people behaved as they did. With internal attributions, behavior is seen as being caused by factors that reside within a person. With external attributions, the causes of behavior are viewed as residing outside an individual. We are more confident in our attributions when behaviors are consistent and have also been witnessed by others. The **fundamental attribution error** occurs when internal factors are emphasized to the exclusion of external or situational factors.

7. Perceivers' attributions may be biased toward internal attributions, whereas actors are biased toward external attributions, especially when failure is involved.

8. **Attitudes** are evaluative judgments (negative, positive, or neutral) that are formed about people, places, and things. Affect, cognition, and behavior are the three components of an attitude.

9. Attitudes can serve ego-defensive, adjustment, and knowledge functions. They can be measured by **Likert scales** and evaluation of observed behaviors. Learning (classical and operant conditioning) and reduction of **cognitive dissonance** lead to the formation of attitudes.

✓ CHECK YOUR PROGRESS

1. What factor makes social psychology different from other areas of psychology?

2. Viewing other cultures as inferior extensions of one's own culture describes
   a. ethnocentrism.
   b. cultural bias.
   c. nationalism.
   d. the just-world stereotype.

3. Placing the goals of the group above one's own goals is called
   a. collectivism.
   b. individualism.
   c. ethnocentrism.
   d. impression formation.

4. When your behaviors influence others to respond the way you expect them to respond, what has occurred?
   a. a stereotype
   b. an expectation
   c. a self-fulfilling prophecy
   d. a behavioral-outcome prediction

5. You spend a few minutes talking with a new acquaintance after class. He tells you several interesting things about himself, and you form a favorable impression of him. What process has facilitated impression formation in this case?

6. The process of deciding why certain events occurred or why a particular person acted in a certain manner is called
   a. ascribing.
   b. attribution.

   c. stereotyping.
   d. causality analysis.

7. The tendency to make internal attributions about others, even when strong situational determinants are present is known as the
   a. stereotyping effect.
   b. attribution illusion.
   c. internal attribution bias.
   d. fundamental attribution error.

8. Evaluative judgments about people, objects, or things are known as
   a. stereotypes.
   b. cognitions.
   c. attitudes.
   d. attributions.

9. The tendency to make internal attributions when we succeed and external attributions when we fail is called the
   a. self-serving bias.
   b. actor-observer bias.
   c. self-attribution error.
   d. fundamental attribution error.

10. A telemarketer calls and asks, "The JP45 is the best car on the road. Would you say you strongly agree, agree, disagree, disagree strongly, or are neutral?" What is this telephone surveyor doing?
    a. reducing cognitive dissonance
    b. inquiring about your level of knowledge
    c. using a Likert scale to survey attitudes
    d. relying on behavioral measures to identify stereotyping

ANSWERS: 1. Social psychology studies the individual as part of a group, whereas other areas tend to study individuals in isolation. **2.** a **3.** a **4.** c **5.** Self-disclosure **6.** b **7.** d **8.** c **9.** a **10.** c

attraction
The extent to which we like or dislike other people

INTERPERSONAL RELATIONS

Whenever Bonny has a problem that she cannot solve, she calls her best friend, Kathleen. Kathleen does the same. These two friends originally met over 20 years ago. Since then Bonny and her family have moved several times; they now live thousands of miles from Kathleen. Despite the distance and infrequent visits, their friendship remains as strong as ever. *What factors or behaviors serve to maintain friendships?*

During their lives, people form several kinds of interpersonal relationships. Some individuals become close friends; others remain casual acquaintances. The establishment of good interpersonal relationships is one key to a successful adjustment to society (Berscheid & Reis, 1998). In this section we examine the factors that cause us to be attracted to others (interpersonal attraction), as well as those that lead us to help or hurt others.

Attraction

Attraction refers to the extent to which we like or dislike other people. In this instance, our attitudes deal exclusively with others. How often do you find yourself saying, "I was naturally attracted to that person"? If someone asked you exactly what you meant by that statement, what would you say? What are the factors that attract us to others?

Proximity.   Proximity to others is positively related to the establishment of friendships; people who live or work near us tend to become our friends (Berscheid & Reis, 1998). For example, apartment dwellers are often attracted to individuals who live in nearby apartments (Nahemow & Lawton, 1975; see Figure 15-2). Likewise, police trainees who were assigned alphabetically to seats in a class reported having friends whose last names started with the same letter as theirs or with the adjacent letters (Segal, 1974).

Proximity is an important determinant of attraction because it encourages interaction and repeated exposure. The more frequent the contact, the greater the positive attraction; repeated contact turns a stranger into a familiar individual. (Just to make the picture complete, keep in mind that frequent contact can also intensify negative feelings. For example, repeated interaction with an annoying co-worker may increase dislike for that person.) Possibly you are a step ahead of us and you have already wondered about Internet relationships where there is considerable interaction and repeated

FIGURE 15-2   People who live in apartment buildings tend to have friends who live in nearby apartments.

Source: Adapted from Nahemow & Lawton, 1975.

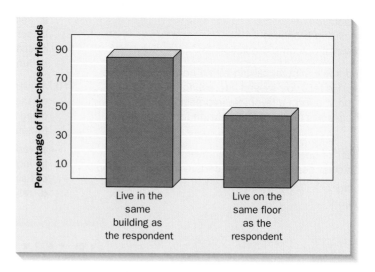

exposure (Aronson et al., 2002). It remains for research to determine if online relationships will survive face-to-face meetings.

Affect and Emotions. "Laugh, and the world laughs with you," wrote the poet Ella Wheeler Wilcox. Research supports her observation—a person's affect or emotional state can influence attraction (Zajonc & McIntosh, 1992). We are attracted to people who arouse positive feeling in us; we avoid individuals who arouse negative feelings. For example, what are you likely to do when you hear someone laugh? Most people join in the laughter, even if they don't know why they are laughing (see Chapter 6). The converse can be said for the effect of sad moods.

In addition to one's emotional state, the nature of our social interaction is an important ingredient in creating affect. For example, the type of opening line that is used in speaking to a stranger can determine attraction. Consider the following: You are sitting next to a stranger in the local laundromat waiting for your clothes to finish washing. Which of the following lines would elicit a positive response from you (Kleinke, Meeker, & Staneski, 1986): "Want to have a cup of coffee while we're waiting?" or "Those are some nice undies you have there"? Generally, direct opening lines are rated as more likable (positive) than cute or flippant opening lines (Kleinke & Dean, 1990).

Why are emotions and affect important to attraction? The principle of reinforcement (see Chapter 5) gives us a clue.

Reinforcement. Let's say that you're having a conversation with a new acquaintance. If that person pays you several compliments that make you feel good (positive reinforcers), you are more likely to be attracted to that person. Similarly, positive *affects*, such as laughing and smiling, also make us feel good. We like people who reward us and tend to dislike or avoid those who do not (Reisbult, 1980).

Similarity. We are also attracted to and make friends with people who are similar to ourselves (Berscheid & Reis, 1998). In addition to such observable characteristics as race, age, and sex, similarity of attitudes, beliefs, and values is very important in the development of attraction. For example, Theodore Newcomb (1961) found that attitude similarity played a major role in the development of friendships among transfer students living in a boardinghouse at the University of Michigan. Research has shown, however, that similarity may not be such a powerful determinant of attraction in all cultures. For example, because the Japanese culture recognizes and values status more highly than our equality-oriented American culture does, the Japanese are more attracted to individuals of superior status (Nakao, 1987).

Our feelings toward another person can affect our perceptions of similarity. In general, the more we like an individual, the more we perceive that person as being similar to us. For example, men overestimate the similarity between themselves and a woman in whom they have a romantic interest (Dryer & Horowitz, 1997).

Similarity can have positive benefits in a relationship. For example, the more similar a husband and wife, the lower the likelihood they will divorce, and the less their personalities change over time (Caspi & Herbener, 1990).

As we have suggested, being positively attracted to someone can lead to the development of a friendship. How does friendship differ from attraction?

Friendship

Unlike a casual relationship or chance attraction, a **friendship** is an interpersonal attraction that involves a set of rules, often informal, that must be followed if the friendship is to survive. Michael Argyle and Monica Henderson (1984) identified nine such rules:

1. Show emotional support.
2. Volunteer help in time of need.

friendship
Form of interpersonal attraction that is governed by an implicit set of rules

3. Strive to make a friend happy when in each other's company.
4. Trust and confide in each other.
5. Share news of success with a friend.
6. Stand up for a friend in his or her absence.
7. Don't nag a friend.
8. Be tolerant of (other) friends.
9. Repay debts and favors.

Friendships do not simply happen. Certain factors are important in the development of a friendship. In addition to the factors such as proximity, affect and emotions, reinforcement, and similarity that are important for establishing the attraction that underlies a friendship, self-disclosure is also an important factor.

Self-disclosure.   We saw earlier that self-disclosure influences the process of impression formation; it also influences the formation of friendships. We are more likely to form friendships with people who are willing to disclose information about themselves. Our level of self-disclosure evolves through several stages as a friendship develops. In the initial stage, we disclose relatively unimportant information. If these self-disclosures are reciprocated, subsequent disclosures will be more personal. Through this process the self-disclosures become progressively more personal, and the friendship becomes stronger. If the level of self-disclosure does not become more intimate or personal, the friendship stagnates. This is why we tend to have a group of casual friends who are in the category of "speaking acquaintances"; our level of self-disclosure with these individuals probably will not increase.

Love

Although most of us would agree that there is a difference between friendship and love, defining love is difficult. Is love the emotion that accompanies sexual attraction? Is it a stronger form of friendship that we reserve for our children, our parents, and other family members? Theorists have proposed that there are actually several types of love (Berscheid & Meyers, 1997). For example, a distinction is often made between passionate and companionate love (Hatfield & Rapson, 1993). **Passionate love** is a transitory form of love characterized by strong emotional reactions and arousal, sexual desires, and fantasies (Regan & Berscheid, 1999). Passionate love is another area in which researchers have found cultural differences. For example, German and American students place a higher value on romantic love than Japanese students do (Simmons, vom Kolke, & Shimizu, 1986). This difference may be due to the fact that Japanese women assume a more dependent role than American and German women or to the fact that love does not have as positive a connotation in Japan as in the other two countries. Similarly, American couples place a higher value on passionate love than do Chinese couples, who value companionate love (Ting-Toomey & Chun, 1996).

Companionate love is characterized by a long-term relationship and commitment. Even though most relationships begin with passionate love, companionate love must develop if the relationship is to survive.

The passionate-companionate distinction is not the only psychological model of love. For example, Clyde and Susan Hendrick (1992) propose the existence of six different types of love, giving them names derived from their ancient Greek equivalents:

eros—romantic, passionate love

ludus (loo´dus)—game-playing love

storge (stor´gay)—friendship love

mania—possessive, dependent love

pragma—logical, "shopping list" love

agape (ah´gah-pay)—all-giving, selfless love

passionate love
Transitory form of love that involves strong emotional reactions, sexual desires, and fantasies

companionate love
Long-lasting form of love that involves commitment

Despite the complexity of love relationships and the difficulty of defining them, researchers have identified a number of factors that influence love relationships. These factors include sex roles, the presence of children, and the degree of dependence of each partner on the other.

Sex Roles.   As shown in Chapter 10, boys and girls learn to engage in different patterns of behavior. These childhood sex roles influence their behavior as adults. The sex roles of men and women often reflect the stereotypes of maleness and femaleness prevailing in the culture in which they were raised. For example, Abbey (1982) found that men perceived the dating behaviors of women more sexually than women perceived those of men; friendliness on a woman's part was seen as reflecting a desire for sex. What's more, men in our society traditionally have been expected to initiate sexual activity, and women are expected to react to their advances. Research has verified this predicted pattern: Men made sexual advances, and women resisted (Muehlenhard & Hollabaugh, 1988). Although such sex role stereotypes are still prevalent, other research indicates that they are changing. For example, Robin Kowalski (1993) has shown that men who have accepted the changing roles of women in our society do not misperceive the dating behaviors of women.

Marital Satisfaction and Dissatisfaction.   A longitudinal view of the love relationship is provided through the study of marital satisfaction. Typically, marital satisfaction is described as a U-shaped function; satisfaction is high during the early years of marriage, decreases during the middle years, and increases during the later years. The decrease in satisfaction during the middle years of marriage is associated with having and raising children; the responsibilities of raising children can take a significant toll on a marriage (Cohan & Bradbury, 1997; Huppe & Cyr, 1997). Predictably, the increase in marital satisfaction during the later years is linked to the fact that the children have grown up and left home, thus enabling the partners to rediscover that which brought them together initially.

Unfortunately, some marriages go beyond mere dissatisfaction. In fact, nearly 15% of all marriages in the United States are characterized by persistent, severe physical violence (Holtzworth-Munroe, 1995).

Psychological Detective

Glenda is a battered spouse. For the past 7 years her marriage has been a nightmare. More often than not, she goes to work with several black-and-blue marks. It is difficult to cover the signs of the abuse she receives. Several of her friends have pleaded with her to leave her husband, but for some reason she cannot bring herself to make the break. Why does Glenda continue to stay in an abusive marriage? Write down some possible reasons before you continue reading.

Social psychologists have provided some insight into why such abusive relationships persist. **Interdependence theory** (Thibault & Kelley, 1959) takes into account the costs and rewards involved in a relationship, as well as the available alternatives. Here's how the theory works. Each person develops a **comparison level** (CL); this CL is the general outcome you expect from a relationship. Your CL is based on your past experiences and the experiences of others (such as your parents and friends) in similar situations. You are satisfied with a relationship when the outcomes are equal to or above your CL. You become dissatisfied when the outcomes fall below your CL. The more the outcomes in a relationship fall below your CL, the more dissatisfied you become. It is important to remember that different individuals may have very different CLs. We cannot assume that everyone sees the world exactly as we do.

When do you leave a relationship? It is predictable that we would leave a relationship when the outcomes fall below our CL. Surprisingly, this action seldom occurs; we

interdependence theory
Theory of interpersonal relationships that stresses the costs and rewards involved

comparison level
General outcome expected from a particular relationship

prosocial behavior
Behavior that benefits society or helps others

altruism
Helping behavior performed voluntarily with no anticipation of reward

continue to find ourselves in relationships that are not satisfying. Why? According to interdependence theory, we also develop a CL for alternative relationships. Given this information, we can say that we will leave a relationship when the outcomes for that relationship fall below our CL for relationships in general and our CL for alternative relationships.

Why does Glenda continue to stay in an abusive marriage? Although we would expect that the outcomes of this relationship are below her CL, the alternatives are even worse: Glenda has no family, her self-esteem is low (Blackman, 1990), and her educational training prepared her only for jobs that pay the minimum wage. There also may be cultural imperatives that place a premium on the intact family unit and view divorce as unacceptable. Thus the outcomes for the current relationship do not fall below Glenda's CL for the alternative relationships she perceives as available to her. To test your understanding of interdependence theory, try turning the tables and ask the question, "Why does Glenda's husband continue to batter?" What factors keep this behavior above his CL for other relationships?

Prosocial Behavior: Helping Others

Behavior that benefits society or helps others is called **prosocial behavior**. One of the most widely studied forms of prosocial behavior is altruism, or helping behavior that is performed voluntarily for the benefit of another person, with no anticipation of reward (Aronson et al., 2002). Examples of altruistic behaviors abound. Individuals have faced great danger to save others from situations such as drowning or being hurt in an automobile accident, burned in a fire, or injured in combat.

True instances of **altruism** are rare and difficult to document, because it is difficult to prove that an altruistic person is not rewarded in some way for his or her actions. Some theorists, such as Robert Cialdini and his colleagues (1987), feel that altruistic behavior always involves a reward of some kind. The reward may be extrinsic (money or praise) or intrinsic (a boost to the ego). Because it cannot be shown that intrinsic rewards are lacking, Cialdini and his colleagues question the existence of true altruism.

By contrast, Daniel Batson and his colleagues (1988; Batson, 1998; Batson & Moran, 1999) contend that altruism is a genuine phenomenon. The defining characteristics of altruism are empathy (an emotional reaction to the suffering of another person that produces the desire to help) and exceptionally small and uncertain rewards. When

Sights like this underscore the concept of altruism.

these characteristics are not present, Batson agrees with Cialdini that some selfish motive is involved and that true altruism is not being shown. Thus soldiers who cover an exploding grenade with their own bodies to protect their comrades are showing altruism, whereas a person who donates blood, wears a sticker announcing this fact, and receives the admiration of friends may not be altruistic.

Regardless of whether a reinforcer or a selfish motive is involved, individuals who display high levels of prosocial behavior have certain characteristics. For example, a study of female Japanese undergraduate students conducted by Takako Suzuki (1992) indicated that higher levels of prosocial behavior are positively correlated with empathy, social skills, and extraversion. The positive influence of empathy on prosocial behavior has also been shown in research on children (Bengtson & Johnson, 1992) and may even be related to parenting style (Dekovic & Janssens, 1992). These positive characteristics also are shown by individuals who have accepted the care of a spouse who is suffering from a long-term, chronic illness (Thompson & Pitts, 1992). Notice that we are using cross-cultural research to reach a generalized conclusion; prosocial people may be similar across cultures.

Situational and Personal Influences on Helping Behavior.　Most of us do not demonstrate prosocial behavior whenever an opportunity presents itself. We are reluctant to stop for hitchhikers on the highway; we give the cold shoulder to people asking for handouts on street corners; appeals from the Big Brothers and Big Sisters fall on deaf ears. Why? Research has shown that situational and personal influences may determine whether we are willing to help.

Much of the research on the factors influencing helping behavior has focused on the so-called bystander effect. We all hope that someone will come to our aid if we are in trouble—say, if we are being robbed. Unfortunately, this does not always happen. In a famous incident that occurred in 1964 in the Queens borough of New York City, a young woman named Kitty Genovese was stabbed to death. An especially horrifying aspect of her murder was the fact that the killer attacked the woman three separate times over the course of half an hour, during which time at least 38 people saw the attacks or heard the woman's screams. The killer was frightened off twice when people turned on their lights or called from their windows. On both occasions, however, he resumed his attack. None of the people who witnessed the attack came to the victim's aid, and no one called the police while she was being attacked. Why?

Two social psychologists, John Darley and Bibb Latané, provided some of the answers. Their laboratory studies demonstrated that individuals are more likely to give assistance when they are alone than when other people are present (Darley & Latané, 1968). As you can see in Figure 15-3, a person who appeared to be having a seizure was

Bystander Apathy

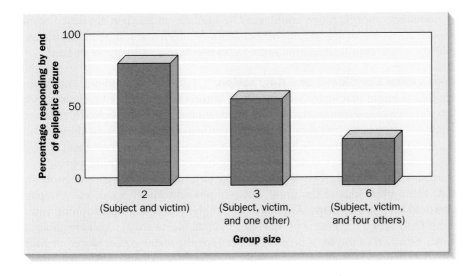

FIGURE 15-3　Effect of group size on the likelihood of helping the victim of an apparent epileptic seizure. As group size increased, the likelihood of helping decreased.

Source: Darley & Latané, 1968.

bystander effect
The tendency for a group of bystanders to be less likely than an individual to provide assistance to a person in trouble

aggression
Physical or psychological behavior that is performed with the intent of doing harm

hostile aggression
Aggressive behavior that is performed with the specific intent of harming another person

instrumental aggression
Aggression that causes harm in the process of achieving another goal

frustration-aggression hypothesis
The hypothesis that aggression is likely to occur when a person is frustrated

very likely to receive assistance when the person providing the assistance was alone. The finding that groups of bystanders are less likely than individuals to aid a person in trouble is known as the **bystander effect.**

Among the factors that determine the bystander effect are degree of danger, embarrassment, not knowing how to help, and diffusion of responsibility. Certainly there was a potential for great danger in the Kitty Genovese situation; the involved risks prevented many of the bystanders from coming to her aid. Likewise, it would be difficult to know how to help in such a situation.

Similarly, research has shown that people are less likely to help when the situation is perceived as serious. Most of us are not competent to help seriously injured people; we could do more harm than good. Likewise, most people are more reluctant to offer assistance in a foreign country. They fear that they will do something wrong. Such factors, however, should not prevent us from calling 911 for assistance.

Finally, when other people are present, the responsibility for acting is shared. Therefore the responsibility of each member of the group is lower than it would be for an individual. As a result of this diffusion of responsibility, each person is less likely to help the person in distress. This diffusion of responsibility is quite pervasive and is prevalent even on the Internet. In fact, one researcher (Markey, 2000) found that members of a chat group were less likely to assist each other as the size of the chat group increased.

Aggression

The converse of prosocial behavior is aggression. **Aggression** is any physical or psychological behavior that is performed with the intent of harming someone or something. This definition indicates that aggressive behavior is intentional; there is a deliberate intent to do harm. Deliberately hitting someone and yelling at an annoying driver are both aggressive behaviors.

At least two major types of aggression have been identified (Buss, 1961). **Hostile aggression** occurs when a person is angry or annoyed with someone else; the goal is to harm the other person (Berkowitz, 1994). Most murders tend to be impulsive, emotional acts of hostile aggression. **Instrumental aggression** is performed to achieve a goal. For example, a robber may attack a victim to steal something, not because the robber is angry with the victim, but because the aggressive behavior is instrumental in achieving the intended goal.

Biological Views of Aggression. *Ethologists* believe that at least some forms of aggression are inherited. Most territorial disputes among animals, however, do not result in physical damage or death. Konrad Lorenz (1966) believes that animals instinctively refrain from using their natural weapons, such as claws, horns, and fangs, to kill their opponents in aggressive conflicts. The conflict ends when the loser acknowledges defeat by displaying submissive behavior. Modern wars, in which thousands of people are killed, demonstrate that humans do not have a comparable instinct.

Environmental Conditions and Aggression. Although ethologists and biological psychologists argue that aggression is part of human nature, other psychologists stress the importance of environmental factors in producing aggressive behavior. Among the explanations they have proposed is the **frustration-aggression hypothesis** (Dollard et al., 1939). According to this hypothesis, an individual, when frustrated, is likely to act aggressively. *Frustration* is defined as being blocked from attaining a goal.

Consider an example. The decision to take a summer job as a construction worker seemed like a great idea at the time. The pay was reasonably good, and the physical labor would keep you in shape. After two days on the job, you are questioning your sanity. Your body aches, the heat is unbearable, and you feel as though you are about to die of thirst. Finally it's time for a break. You head for the water cooler stored in your car, only to find that you forgot to refill it this morning. No problem, a cool soft drink will

A hot summer day can encourage the display of aggression.

do just as well. But after three tries, you find that the vending machine is still returning your money. How will you respond?

The chances are quite good that you will direct some aggressive responses toward the machine. Some of those responses may be verbal; others, such as shoves, kicks, and hits, may be physical. Your frustration has led to aggression.

Since its publication in 1939, the frustration-aggression hypothesis has generated considerable research. Much of this research indicates that aggression results from a variety of frustrating conditions.

Psychological Detective

Put yourself in the following situation. You have been waiting in line for a long time to purchase concert tickets; you are now second in line. Your turn is next, but someone cuts in ahead of you. Is this frustrating? Will you act aggressively? Would you be less aggressive if you were twelfth in line when someone cut in? Write down your answers to these questions before reading further.

Mary Harris (1974) conducted this experiment in theater and grocery store lines. She found that cutting in front of the 2nd person in line resulted in more aggression than cutting in front of the 12th person. In other words, the closer you are to your goal, the more frustrated you become when you are blocked from attaining it. Harris concluded that aggressiveness is directly related to level of frustration: The greater the frustration, the greater the aggression.

After several decades of research on the frustration-aggression hypothesis, it became apparent that a third factor must be involved. Why does frustration lead to aggression in some instances but not in others? Anger seems to be the answer. If the frustrating event does not result in anger, the probability that aggressive behavior will be displayed is reduced.

Leonard Berkowitz (1984) contends that in addition to frustration and anger, cues for aggressive responding must also be present. Those cues elicit an aggressive response when frustration has caused anger. What are those cues? Visual images that suggest aggression may be one such cue. For example, video game images may be these cues—Anderson and Dill (2000) reported that playing violent video games was positively correlated with violence and delinquency in children. Likewise, studies have shown that there is a relation between viewing violence on television and engaging in violent behavior (for example, Geen, 1998). However, this relation may not be universal. Cultural differences (Levine, 1996) and personality differences (Bushman, 1996) are important factors in determining the effects of television violence.

Sexual Aggression.   As discussed earlier, many marriages are characterized by abuse and aggression, which is most often directed toward the wife. The dramatic increase in the incidence of rape indicates that such aggression and abuse are not limited to marital relationships (Goodman, Koss, & Russo, 1993a, 1993b). The extent of this problem is staggering. For example, crime reports from the Federal Bureau of Investigation indicate that in 2000, rapes occurred at the rate of one every 6 minutes. These are the known cases of rape; many others go unreported (Bachman, 1994).

Motivated by both scientific and social concerns, psychologists have investigated sexual aggression. What have they learned? What factors contribute to the increasing number of rapes?

The increased availability and tolerance of pornography, especially pornography depicting violence and domination, are correlated with the increase in sexual assaults. For example, one study found that sales of sexually explicit magazines were positively correlated with the rape rate in all 50 states; whereas a Canadian investigation (Marshall, 1989) found that rapists and child molesters viewed pornographic materials more often than non–sex offenders. Because pornography supports the myth that women enjoy sexual abuse and aggression, these findings should not be surprising (Dean & Malamuth, 1997).

What can be done to reduce sexual aggression toward women? One obvious answer would be to bring the creation and distribution of pornography under the control of state or federal laws. John Court (1984) reports that in countries in which pornography is controlled, the incidence of rape is lower. Other psychologists believe that increasing the public's awareness of women's true feelings about sexual aggression and the psychological devastation created by rape would also be an effective deterrent (Donnerstein, Linz, & Penrod, 1987). Does this view represent wishful thinking? Can a media-awareness campaign really have an effect? The answer may be yes. Alcohol and tobacco are not illegal, yet health concerns, highlighted by extensive media coverage, have resulted in a substantial decrease in consumption of both products.

Many unreported rapes fall into the category of date or acquaintance rape (Benson, Charlton, & Goodhart, 1992; Craig, 1990; Wiehe & Richards, 1995). In many instances date rape may be a result of misperceptions, especially on the part of the man. For example, research conducted by Tracy Bostwick and Janice De Lucia (1992) investigated perceived desire for sex. They presented their participants with several dating scenarios. Except for varying the party who asked for the date and the party who paid for it, the scenarios were the same. Even though there is no proven relationship between these behaviors and desire for sex, when the woman asked for the date and paid the bill, she was perceived as having a greater desire for sex than when the man asked and paid the bill. Likewise, men believed that sexual aggression was more justified when the man had paid all of the date's expenses (Cornett & Shuntick, 1991). In short, some women may be trapped in the dating relationship: If a woman asks and pays for the date, she is assumed to desire sex; if the man pays for the date, he may feel that he has the right to demand sex.

There are additional factors that contribute to the prevalence of date rape. The length of the steady dating relationship is positively related to men's perception of the acceptability of date rape: The longer the dating relationship, the more acceptable date rape is perceived to be (Bridges, 1991). Heavy alcohol consumption is another factor that often leads to date rape on college campuses (Abbey, 1991). Again, the explanations for this joint occurrence of alcohol consumption and date rape suggest that men often misinterpret the sexual desires of women and that men frequently use the supposed liberating effects of alcohol as a justification for sexual behavior (see Chapter 4).

To help college women deal with the threat of date or acquaintance rape, some authorities (Cummings, 1992) have advocated courses in defense training. Critics argue that such programs do not adequately prepare the women and thus give them a false sense of security. Other authorities (Lenihan, Rawlins, & Eberly, 1992) have explored the effectiveness of a date or acquaintance rape education program. Although such a program was effective in raising women's sensitivity to potentially dangerous situations, it had no influence on the men's attitudes. More effective solutions for this problem are needed.

Having looked at interpersonal relations, we next examine the effects of social influences on our behaviors. Have you ever bought something only to get home and wonder why you made that purchase? We will find out what makes a good salesperson in the next section.

REVIEW SUMMARY

1. **Attraction** is the extent to which we like or dislike other people. Attraction is determined by proximity, affect and emotions, reinforcement, and similarity.

2. **Friendship** is a form of interpersonal attraction that involves a set of unwritten rules.

3. **Passionate love** is characterized by strong emotional reactions, sexual desire, and fantasies. **Companionate love** is characterized by a long-term relationship and commitment. Several other types of love have been proposed. Sex roles can influence the love relationship.

4. **Interdependence theory** takes into account the costs and rewards in a relationship. Each person develops a **comparison level** (CL), or expected outcome, for the relationship. Dissatisfaction occurs when the outcomes of the relationship fall below the CL. People leave a relationship when the outcomes fall below their CLs for other relationships.

5. **Prosocial behavior** benefits society or helps others. **Altruism** occurs when a person helps others with no thought of reward. Because it is difficult to prove that no reward is present when a person behaves altruistically, the genuineness of this behavior has been questioned.

6. The **bystander effect** refers to the fact that people are less likely to provide assistance in an emergency when others are present than when they are alone. The bystander effect is attributable to potential embarrassment, fear of failure, and diffusion of responsibility.

7. **Aggression** is any behavior that is performed with the intent of doing harm. **Hostile aggression** occurs when the goal is specifically to harm another individual. **Instrumental aggression** occurs when someone hurts another person in the pursuit of another goal—for example, during a robbery. Biological views stress the inherited nature of aggressive behaviors.

8. The **frustration-aggression hypothesis** predicts that frustration, or being blocked from attaining a goal, results in aggression. In addition to frustration, the presence of anger and certain cues may be necessary for aggression to occur.

9. Physical and verbal attacks, as well as adverse environmental conditions, may also elicit aggressive behavior. A high level of general arousal can facilitate aggressive responding.

10. Current statistics underestimate the prevalence of sexual aggression directed toward women. Viewing of pornography is positively related to sexual aggression.

11. Many incidents of rape can be classified as date or acquaintance rape. Date rape appears to result from misperceptions, especially on the part of men, about the acceptability of sexual relations in certain situations.

✓ CHECK YOUR PROGRESS

1. What is attraction? Explain the factors that influence or determine whether we will be attracted to another person.

2. The interpersonal attraction that involves a set of rules, often informal, that must be followed if the relationship is to persist is called
   a. altruism.
   b. friendship.
   c. love.
   d. admiration.

3. Hendrick and Hendrick proposed six different types of love. Which name and description are mismatched?
   a. *ludus*–game-playing love
   b. *storge*–logical, "shopping-list" love
   c. *mania*–possessive, dependent love
   d. *agape*–all-giving, selfless love

4. What term refers to helping behavior that is performed voluntarily for the benefit of another person, with no anticipation of reward?
   a. altruism
   b. munificence
   c. interdependence
   d. humanitarianism

5. Your anger at your upstairs neighbor, who plays loud music at 3 A.M., has finally hit the boiling point; you are on your way upstairs to punch him in the jaw. This is an example of what type of aggression? The statement "Only a few people will be hurt in the accomplishment of this objective" is an example of what type of aggression?

6. In a busy shopping mall, a young man faints and falls to the ground. Several shoppers stare, but no one helps the man. This situation is an example of
   a. reactance.
   b. deindividuation.
   c. comparison level.
   d. the bystander effect.

7. What third variable often determines the nature and strength of the relation between frustration and aggression?
   a. anger
   b. experience
   c. familiarity
   d. interpretation

8. All of the following factors contribute to date rape except
   a. men paying expenses.
   b. alcohol consumption.
   c. males' misinterpretation of females' desires.
   d. brief dating relationships.

SOCIAL INFLUENCES ON BEHAVIOR

It's Saturday morning, time for your weekly trip to the local discount store. A large crowd has gathered around a display case. A handsome young man in a neatly pressed business suit and tie is encouraging the crowd to buy the brand-new Ronco Veg-O-Matic. "No more hassles with carrots, radishes, peppers, beets, or tomatoes—a perfect salad every time!" You listen to the sales pitch and even watch the salesman perform wonders with the Veg-O-Matic. You decide not to take advantage of his "wonderful introductory offer," however. There is something about him that just doesn't seem right. *Why was the salesman unsuccessful in his attempt to persuade you to take a chance on his product?*

Other people are constantly trying to influence us. Sales pitches are just one example of the numerous social influences and pressures on our behavior. In this section we examine three kinds of social influences: those designed to persuade us to change our attitudes and behaviors, to produce obedience, and to induce conformity.

Persuasion

Persuasion is the use of social influence to cause other people to change their attitudes and behaviors (Aronson et al., 2002). We are bombarded with hundreds of persuasive messages every day: Buy this car, join that group, support our cause, vote for this political candidate, give to that charitable organization. Some persuasive messages are effective; others are not. Social psychologists have identified four main factors that influence persuasion: source, message, channel, and audience. Let's take a closer look at each.

Source Factors.   Certainly the source of a persuasive message plays a role in determining whether the message changes our attitudes and behaviors. What is it about the source that is important in facilitating persuasion? Among the characteristics of sources that have been found to increase the impact of persuasive messages are expertise, attractiveness, and trustworthiness.

Expertise.   The greater the perceived expertise of the source of a message, the more persuasive the message (Chen & Chaiken, 1999). To demonstrate the importance of expertise, the following experiment has been conducted numerous times. First, participants are randomly assigned to one of two groups, and an initial appraisal of their attitudes on a particular subject, such as the dependability of American-made cars, is made. Then both groups read a message designed to change their attitude. The only difference is that the message for one group is attributed to a recognized expert (for example, *Road and Track*), whereas the message for the second group is attributed to a questionable source (for example, *Better Homes and Gardens*). After the message has been read, the participants' attitudes are measured again. The results indicate that the message from the recognized authority has produced significantly more attitude change. Assuming the attitudes of the two groups were comparable on the first measurement, any differences that appear in the second must reflect the influence of the perceived expertise of the source.

Attractiveness.   The source's attractiveness also influences the likelihood of persuasion; the more attractive the source, the more effective the message. The same physical factors that influence impression formation also influence persuasion (Dion & Stein, 1978). That is, the better your impression of the source, the more likely you are to be persuaded.

persuasion
The use of social influence to cause people to change attitudes or behavior

Would this salesperson be successful in convincing you to buy one of his used cars?

Psychological Detective

How would you conduct a research project to evaluate the influence of attractiveness on persuasion? Would it be possible to use the same research strategy that has been used to evaluate expertise? As you think about this research project, you might want to diagram your proposed study on a sheet of paper. Be sure to take all the important possibilities into account. When you are satisfied with your research design, continue reading.

To evaluate the influence of attractiveness, we would start with two randomly formed groups of participants and measure their attitudes. Then both groups would be given the same persuasive message, but the message would be delivered by individuals who differed in attractiveness. What other major influences must be controlled if our conclusions are to be valid? What about the level of expertise of the individuals who deliver the message? If we wish to measure only attractiveness, the degree of perceived expertise must be the same for both groups. What's more, the individuals delivering the message should be of the same sex. The ideal condition would be for the same individual to present the message to both groups. With a change of clothes, a pair of last year's running shoes, and mussed hair, the attractive expert would become less attractive. This research strategy is shown in Table 15-1.

TABLE 15-1

Design of an Experiment to Determine the Influence of Attractiveness on Persuasion

	Step 1	Step 2	Step 3	Results
Group 1 (attractive source)	Evaluate the attitude in question	Message presented by the attractive source	Reevaluate the attitude in question	Greater persuasion for attractive source
Group 2 (unattractive source)	Evaluate the attitude in question	Message presented by same source but unattractive	Reevaluate the attitude in question	Less persuasion for unattractive source

sleeper effect
Occurs when the message and its source become detached; messages from sources low in expertise, attractiveness, and trustworthiness may increase in effectiveness

Trustworthiness. A persuasive message may fail to produce a change in attitude even if it is presented by an attractive expert. It takes more than an attractive expert to persuade us; the source of the persuasive message must also be trustworthy (Smith & Shaffer, 1991). Most individuals are very conscious of the prevalence and intent of persuasive communications and are skeptical of the vast array of claims they are exposed to. To be persuaded, they must trust the source of the message.

One of the major factors contributing to trustworthiness is the listener's perception of whether the speaker stands to gain from acceptance of the message. When speakers do not have anything to gain from presenting a particular message, they are more likely to be perceived as trustworthy. For example, suppose a series of TV commercials features a famous athlete urging you to buy a certain type of running shoe. Is this a trustworthy source? Probably not. The more shoes that are sold, the more high-paying commercials the athlete will be hired to make. But what if the same athlete appears in a series of public-service announcements about AIDS? In the latter instance the athlete's credibility may be enhanced; in this role the athlete does not stand to gain from urging listeners to practice safe sex.

Recall the Veg-O-Matic salesman described at the beginning of this section. Why was he unable to persuade you to take a chance on his product? He was attractive; that's a point in his favor. What about his level of expertise? World-class chefs do not usually demonstrate products in local discount stores; thus the salesman's level of expertise is questionable. How trustworthy is the salesman? Because his only reason for being in the store is to sell as many Veg-O-Matics as possible, you immediately question his claims. His apparent lack of expertise and trustworthiness have greatly reduced his persuasiveness.

If a *sleeper effect* occurs, however, his message may be more effective than we have led you to believe. The **sleeper effect** occurs when the message becomes detached from its source. For example, over time an audience member may forget which person presented which message. In such instances messages from sources low in expertise, attractiveness, or trustworthiness increase in effectiveness and result in potentially flawed decision making. Thankfully, the sleeper effect does not appear to play a major role in everyday life (Pratkanis et al., 1988).

Message Factors. Features of the message itself also influence whether we are persuaded. Those factors include attention, drawing conclusions, and message acceptance.

Attention. To be persuaded by a message, you must pay attention to that message. This simple fact has led to the development of numerous procedures designed to attract attention, such as printing signs upside down or backwards, using vivid colors,

Advertisers use bright colors, unusual scenes, and unusual shapes to attract attention.

Reactance advertising tries to make consumers believe that their freedom to purchase goods and pay low prices is limited; hence, you buy their products so you will not feel that you have missed an opportunity.

using unusual music and sounds, and featuring sexually arousing stimuli. Unless the sights and sounds are the message, however, the story does not end here. The audience must attend to the message that accompanies these attention-getters.

reactance
The tendency to react in the opposite direction to a persuasive message when compliance might place limits on personal freedom

Drawing Conclusions.   Messages are designed to change our attitudes and thereby cause us to reach a particular conclusion. A basic research question concerns who draws the conclusion, the person delivering the message or the individuals receiving it. Should conclusions be part of the message, or should members of the audience be allowed to draw their own conclusions? The answer depends on the involvement of the audience. If the audience simply receives the message without being actively involved in processing it, explicitly drawn conclusions are more effective (Petty & Wegener, 1998). This situation fits the majority of television commercials. Conversely, when people are actively involved in processing persuasive messages, greater persuasion is achieved by allowing them to draw their own conclusions. For example, individuals who were in the market for compact disc players were influenced more by magazine ads that presented relevant facts and allowed readers to draw their own conclusions than by ads that presented the same facts and then stated conclusions (Kardes, 1988; Petty & Wegener, 1999).

Message Acceptance.   The fact that someone attends to a message does not ensure that it will be persuasive. How many times have you heard a televised speech and said something like "That's absolute nonsense"? For a message to be persuasive, it should not differ drastically from the attitudes of the audience. Thus during a recession, when people are losing their jobs, television commercials urging us to buy imported goods are less likely to be persuasive. Messages that do not differ from our beliefs too much appear to result in the greatest amount of attitude change (Petty & Wegener, 1998).

Reactance is another means by which message acceptance is manipulated. **Reactance** theory states that individuals tend to react rather strongly in the opposite direction to a persuasive appeal that has the potential to restrict their freedom (Brehm, 1972; Engs & Hanson, 1989). For example, most people are unlikely to react favorably to a proposal to raise taxes, regardless of the need for added revenue, because the resulting loss of income would limit their financial freedom. It should be evident that reactance is another name for what is popularly known as "reverse psychology."

Psychological Detective

Consider the ads we encounter every day on television, in newspapers and magazines, online, and in stores. Do those ads use the reactance principle to encourage us to make purchases? As you answer this question, try to think of as many specific examples as possible, and write them down before reading further.

We encounter reactance advertising every day in the form of proclamations such as "Sale! Everything Must Go," "Prices Will Never Be Lower," and "Limited Edition." Ads like these are designed to make us believe that our freedom to pay such low prices or purchase scarce merchandise is being restricted. It is expected that you will react to the threat of such restrictions by attending the sale or purchasing the scarce product.

Primacy and Recency Effects.   We noted in Chapter 7 that items that are presented first (*primacy effect*) or last (*recency effect*) are remembered best. If your audience receives two persuasive messages that oppose each other, would you prefer to have your message delivered first or last? The answer to this question depends on when the audience is required to act. If there is a delay between the presentation of the message and the required action, the first message is typically more effective (primacy). If action is required immediately after the message has been delivered, however, the last message has the advantage (recency). For example, suppose that you are the campaign manager for a political candidate. Your candidate and the opposing candidate are scheduled to debate the issues. Should your candidate speak first or last? If the election is a couple of weeks away, your candidate should speak first. If the election is tomorrow, your candidate should speak last.

Channel Factors.   Persuasive messages are presented through a variety of channels—printed words, spoken words, pictures, movies, and videos. The term *channel* can refer to any means by which a message is presented to the audience. Often two or more channels are used simultaneously. For example, television is popular with advertisers because it combines visual and auditory channels (French & Richards, 1996; Macbeth, 1996). Some channels, such as radio, television, newspapers, and electronic media, make it possible to present messages to large audiences.

Psychological Detective

Are persuasive messages more effective when they are delivered to a group or when they are delivered on a personal (one-to-one) basis? If a message can be delivered as effectively to a group as to an individual, much time and effort can be saved by delivering it to a large number of people simultaneously. Recall several situations in which you were the recipient of a persuasive message. Was the message more effective when you were by yourself or when others were present? Write down your answers to these questions before reading further.

Time and again, researchers have demonstrated that the person-to-person approach is more effective than appealing to a larger group (Maccoby & Alexander, 1980). Why? The same message is received in both cases. What factor of the one-on-one situation is lacking in a group presentation? When we are in a one-on-one situation, questions can be asked and answers given. In addition, the person who is presenting the message can extract a commitment from the receiver on the spot. This approach is known as the *foot-in-the-door* technique. We say more about this phenomenon later in this chapter.

The persuasive supremacy of one-on-one communication accounts for the recent growth of telemarketing, or direct telephone solicitation. The next time your phone rings and you find yourself being asked to subscribe to a magazine, switch long-distance telephone service, or purchase credit card insurance, see how many features of effective persuasion are present in the message you are receiving.

Audience Factors.   So far we have discussed the nature of the source, message, and channel factors that influence persuasion. The nature of the audience also influences persuasion.

The knowledge and past experiences of the receiver of a persuasive message are important. If the audience is naive and unaware that the message is intended to persuade—as in the case of young children watching Saturday morning television programs—the message is more likely to persuade. This effect is seen in the attempts of children to get their parents to buy the toys and foods they see advertised on TV. In general, the most persuasive messages differ only moderately from the attitudes of the audience.

Research has shown that audiences can defend themselves against persuasion. The most frequently used procedure is analogous to vaccination—giving people a mild case of a disease (such as measles) to inoculate them against that disease. With this method, the audience is exposed to a mild form of the persuasive message before the main or real message is presented. For example, exposing teenagers to a mild form of peer pressure to smoke, in anticipation of the pressure they will encounter later, has been shown to reduce the likelihood that they will smoke (Chassin, Presson, & Sherman, 1990). Inoculation effects work best when the audience is encouraged to develop counterarguments to the message being presented.

What We Attend to: The Central and Peripheral Routes of Persuasion.   What do you attend to when you are exposed to a persuasive message—the content of the message or the attributes of the person presenting the message? The answer to this question involves the nature of the message and the motivation to attend to the message (Chen & Chaiken, 1999; Petty & Wegener, 1999). If the message is relevant to you, then you are more likely to attend to the content of the message. Additionally, because some people enjoy thinking about the content of a persuasive message, this group of people is more likely to be motivated to attend to the message; these people are high in the *need for cognition* (Cacioppo et al., 1996). When you pay attention to the content of the message, the *central route* of persuasion is being used. If you find that the persuasive message is not especially relevant to you and you do not enjoy thinking about the content of a message, then you are more likely to attend to the attributes of the presenter (for example, credibility or attractiveness). When you pay attention to these attributes, persuasion is following the *secondary route* (Petty & Cacioppo, 1986).

Obedience

In Chapter 1 we met Keith, who was learning in his history class about the atrocities of war. He left the class wondering whether his psychology class would provide any answers to why people commit such terrible acts. The psychology instructor asked the students, "How much electric shock, from 0 to 450 volts, would you administer to someone as part of a psychology experiment?" This question refers to one of the most famous series of studies in the history of social psychology, a study of obedience to authority conducted by Stanley Milgram in the 1960s.

More than 800 townspeople in New Haven, Connecticut, served as the participants in these experiments. Upon arrival at the laboratory, each participant was greeted by two people—a rather serious-looking scientist (the experimenter) wearing a white laboratory coat and a middle-aged man who was actually a confederate of the experimenter. The scientist informed the participant and the confederate that they were about to participate in a study of teaching and learning and that one of them would play the role of the teacher. The confederate assumed the role of the learner; the real participant was the teacher.

The teacher read a list of pairs of words, then gave the learner the first word of a pair and asked the learner to identify the second word from among four words. Each time the learner gave an incorrect answer, the teacher was instructed to administer an electric shock to him. Before the session began, each teacher experienced a mild (45-volt) shock to appreciate what the learner would feel. Then the questioning began. As the session progressed and the learner began to make mistakes, the scientist (experimenter) demanded that the intensity of the shock be increased. The teachers followed these instructions until the learner had received a large number of what *appeared* to be very painful shocks. After the initial "shocks" were administered by the

STUDY TIP

Create a mind map or think link for the section on persuasion. Use different colors for the different parts or "stages" of your visual organizer.

FIGURE 15-4 The teachers (participants) in the Milgram experiment believed they were administering electric shocks to the learners when incorrect answers were given. (A) The machine that "controlled" the shock intensity. (B) Preparing the "learner" for the experiment. (C) The experimenter directs the "teacher" to administer the shock. (D) The "teacher" checks on the status of the "learner."

Source: ©1965 Stanley Milgram. From the film "Obedience," distributed by Pennsylvania State University, Media Sales.

A

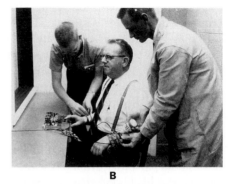

B

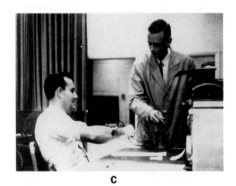

C

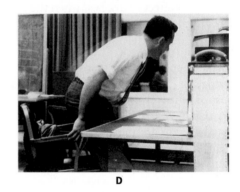

D

Obedience

teacher, the learner protested and also indicated he had a heart condition. In many instances the teachers became tense and faced a real conflict. They wanted to stop, but felt they could not. The stress they faced raised ethical issues about the conduct of this experiment.

When behavior is initiated or changed in response to the direct command of a person with authority, **obedience** has occurred. In the experiment just described, no electric shocks were actually administered to the learners, but the teachers were unaware that this was the case. All the teachers obeyed the instructions of the experimenter until the 300-volt shock level was reached. (The electric current in your house is 110 to 120 volts.) In one experiment, 65% of the teachers obeyed the experimenter's commands all the way to the 450-volt level (see Figure 15-4).

Why did the teachers repeatedly administer shocks to the learners? "Because they were told to" seems to be the best answer to this question. Before you say, "I'd never do that," bear in mind that Milgram's research involved more than 800 participants. Equal numbers of men and women continued to administer shocks up to the 450-volt level.

Now consider an even more horrifying situation. In 1978, hundreds of people in Jonestown, Guyana, poisoned their own children with cyanide-laced Kool-Aid and then poisoned themselves. Why did this tragedy occur? The most plausible answer is that a charismatic leader, Jim Jones, gave commands that were obeyed.

Research like Milgram's and events like the Jonestown and Waco tragedies lead us to conclude that people can be too obedient. Several factors, including proximity to the victim, proximity to the authority figure, and assumption of responsibility, influence how obedient we are. The closer the victim is to the participant, the lower the percentage of participants who obey a command to harm the victim. This factor is known as *victim proximity*. In the Milgram studies fewer shocks were administered when the learner was in the same room with the teacher. Likewise, the closer the person commanding obedience (*authority proximity*), the more obedient participants are (Blass, 1996). In the Milgram studies, obedience was greater if the experimenter was in the

obedience

Initiating or changing a behavior in response to a direct command of an authority

Obedience to authority can be incredibly powerful. In 1978 Jim Jones persuaded his followers to give cyanide-laced Kool-Aid to their children and then poison themselves.

same room as the teacher but decreased greatly if the experimenter telephoned the commands from another room.

Responsibility is also directly related to level of obedience. If the experimenter assumes responsibility for any harm that befalls the victim, as was the case in the Milgram studies, obedience is high. When responsibility is shifted to the participant, however, the likelihood of obedience drops dramatically. Similarly, if one of the experimenter's assistants defies the experimenter, the obedience of the teachers is reduced appreciably.

conformity
Initiating or changing a behavior in response to indirect social pressures

Conformity and Compliance

Imagine that you are a participant in an experiment. You and seven other students are seated around a table. You have been told that the experiment is on visual judgments. Your task is to determine which of three lines is the same length as a fourth line, the standard (see Figure 15-5). The person at the far end of the table answers first. Looking down the row, you see that you will be the next to last to answer. You think to yourself, "This is a piece of cake—the answer is obvious." Then something astonishing happens. All the students give the wrong answer; no one picks the line that matches the standard. Now it's your turn.

In the case of obedience, the *commands* to change behavior are clear, and the authority issuing the commands is obvious. In the case of **conformity,** there are *pressures,* often indirect, to change behavior and thoughts. The nature of the authority behind pressures for conformity is not as obvious as it is in commands for obedience. Think about the study just described. What would your response be under its conditions?

As with the obedience studies, many of us say that we would choose the correct line. However, Solomon Asch (1956), who conducted these influential studies, found that participants conformed to the rest of the group—that is, chose the wrong line—30% of the time. In case you have not already guessed, there was only one real participant in each group: the next-to-last person to answer. All the other students in the group were confederates of the experimenters. Asch (1955) also varied the number of confederates who were present; he found that as few as three people giving the wrong answer was sufficient to produce conformity. It was important that the confederates be *unanimous* in their wrong answers. If one of the confederates gave the correct answer, there was a significant decrease in the rate of conformity by the real participants. Having only one other person support you can wipe out most of the effects of group influence.

FIGURE 15-5 An example of the lines used in Asch's experiments. Although selecting the matching line might seem simple approximately one-third of the participants chose the wrong answer to conform with the group.

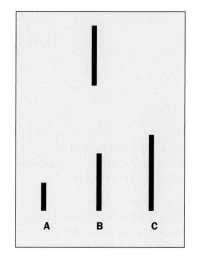

Psychological Detective

Let's examine the Asch studies to see if we have all the information we need to demonstrate that conformity has occurred. We tentatively concluded that individuals make wrong choices because other members of the group have made the same choices. This does not necessarily mean that conformity has occurred, however. What other information is required? How would you acquire that information? Write down your answers before reading further.

15.2

Additional data showing how the real participants perform under conditions that do not demand conformity are needed. Perhaps the line-judging task is rather difficult, and an error rate of over 30% is normal. To evaluate this possibility, Asch asked participants to judge the lengths of the lines when they were alone. He found their judgments were wrong less than 1% of the time. There is a big difference between 1% and 30%. Therefore it is reasonable to conclude that these experiments illustrated the effects of conformity. In an individualistic society, such as the United States, where conformity might be expected to be low, a conformity rate of 30% or greater is impressive. Conformity among people in other cultures, such as the Bantu of Rhodesia (now Zimbabwe) and the Fijians, is higher (Chandra, 1973; Matsuda, 1985).

Asch's classic studies soon gave rise to other research dealing with the effects of groups on judgments. Although group pressures do result in conformity, James Stoner (1961) showed that decisions reached by a group may be riskier than the independent decisions reached by individual members of the group. In many of the research projects conducted in this area, individuals were asked to read a situation in which the central character faced a potentially risky decision, such as conducting a lengthy and time-consuming research project to enhance a career. For a time, the results of such studies tended to support the notion of a **risky-shift phenomenon:** Groups make riskier decisions than individuals. This general conclusion was soon questioned, however.

Imagine changing the situation just mentioned. Instead of simply expending time and effort on an experiment that may enhance a career, the central character faces the decision of whether to sell a life insurance policy to invest in a risky but potentially very high-paying stock. What is your reaction to this situation? Most people would advise against selling the life insurance policy to play the stock market. What will the group decision be? Contrary to the risky-shift prediction, the group decision will be more strongly opposed to selling the life insurance policy than the individual opinions.

Findings like these prompted some researchers, such as Serge Moscovici and Marisa Zavalloni (1969), to propose that a group's influence is to strengthen or intensify preexisting attitudes, not simply to produce riskier decisions. In the case of the life insurance policy, the initial attitude was not to sell the policy; group discussion served to intensify this non–risk-taking attitude. In the case of expending time and effort on an experiment that may enhance one's career, the initial attitude might be favorable because there is nothing to lose. A group discussion would further enhance this preexisting attitude and lead to greater risk-taking. The effect of group discussion enhancing preexisting attitudes is known as **group polarization** (Pascarella & Terenzini, 1991).

As a group's cohesiveness or shared values increase, so does conformity on the part of its members. For example, as sorority members grow closer, they are more likely to share such behaviors as binge eating (Crandall, 1988). Yet the presence of just one person who resists the pressure to conform can reduce conformity by others. For example, the presence of a nonjaywalking confederate reduced jaywalking to 17%; when the confederate jaywalked, the number of jaywalkers rose to 44% (Mullen, Copper, & Driskell, 1990).

Culture also influences the likelihood that a person will conform. For example, when Asch's line-judging experiment was replicated, similar rates were found in cultures that have comparable views of conformity, such as those of industrialized Europe. However, in cultures that value conformity more highly, the rate of conformity rose

risky-shift phenomenon
The finding that groups make riskier decisions than individuals

group polarization
Phenomenon in which group decision making enhances or amplifies the original opinions of the group's members

appreciably (Whittaker & Meade, 1967). In all cultures, as the spirit of individualism increases, the rate of conformity decreases (Alwin, 1990; Remley, 1988).

When we conform, we yield to group pressures in the absence of direct requests to change behavior. Obedience involves a direct request to change behavior, but the request is in the form of an order. **Compliance** refers to behavior that is initiated or changed in response to a request, but the request is not a command or direct order. Compliance may sound rather simple: Requests are made, and behaviors result. It is actually more complicated than that, however, social psychologists have studied—and salespeople have exploited—numerous strategies designed to increase compliance. It is common lore among salespeople that if they are successful in getting a customer to comply with a small request, the chances of compliance with a larger request (a sale) are greatly increased. For example, if you can be talked into taking a test ride in a new car, the chances of your buying the car increase. This phenomenon is known as the **foot-in-the-door effect.** The converse procedure also is effective in securing compliance. In this condition, known as the **door-in-the-face technique,** the chances for compliance are increased by first asking for an exceptionally large response, such as a $1,000 donation to a charitable cause. This request is purposely so large that it will make most people want to slam their door (Cialdini & Trost, 1998). The refusal of the exceptionally large request allows the proposal of a smaller, more reasonable request, such as $10, the person is more likely to agree to.

Compliance also may be influenced by what another person has done for you. Consider the following situation. Suppose that a computer salesperson has come to your apartment to discuss a new computer system. She arrives with details about several systems based on your current and projected needs. How will you respond when she asks which configuration you want to invest in? With all the work that went into preparing these proposals for you, don't you feel obligated to purchase one of the packages she has prepared? This tactic for increasing compliance is known as **reciprocity.** With reciprocity, the person seeking compliance does something for you to make you feel obligated when he or she makes a request.

One of the most common examples of reciprocity occurs in supermarkets. Suppose that while doing your grocery shopping you see a person handing out free samples of chips and cheese dip. It is late in the afternoon, and a bite to eat would taste good; you accept the sample. How will you respond to a request to buy some chips and dip? The salesperson anticipates that your acceptance of the free samples will put pressure on you to make a purchase.

In sum, we have seen how social influences affect persuasion, obedience, conformity, and compliance in individuals. In the next section we examine the effects of group membership.

A woman hands out free samples to shoppers in hopes that they will reciprocate by buying some of this product.

compliance
Initiating or changing a behavior in response to a request

foot-in-the-door effect
Phenomenon in which a person who has agreed to a small request is more likely to comply with a subsequent larger request

door-in-the-face technique
People are first presented with an extremely large request, which they likely will refuse, and then they are presented with a more reasonable request that they are more likely to accept

reciprocity
Tactic for increasing compliance that involves doing something for others to create a feeling of obligation on their part

THE INDIVIDUAL AS PART OF A SOCIAL GROUP

Many college students pride themselves on their ability to play pool. Pool balls can be heard being racked and shot at all hours in the student center. Perhaps you are a campus pool shark. It is Friday afternoon, and you and a friend are playing a casual game of pool. Halfway through the game some friends from your dorm drop by and decide to watch the rest of the game. It is your turn to shoot. *Will the presence of your friends help or hinder your game?*

social facilitation
An increase in performance that occurs when other people are present

Most people have a strong need for affiliation; they enjoy being with others. Hence people frequently join and interact in groups like the group of friends just described. Being a member of a social group implies that there are membership criteria, responsibilities, privileges, and statuses. You are aware of your group memberships and responsibilities, as well as who does and does not belong to your group. The extent to which the members share the values of the group is known as *cohesion*. When there is high cohesion, group values are shared by all members. Low cohesion indicates that group values are not shared by all members and that conflict is likely.

In this section we examine group influences on individual behavior. We begin by looking at the effects of the simple presence of other people on the behavior of individuals.

Social Facilitation

Robert Zajonc (1965) proposed that the presence of other people increases arousal (general physiological or psychological excitement). Greater arousal increases the likelihood that the most dominant response for a particular behavior will be shown. If you have performed a task many times in the past, the correct response dominates, and the increased arousal causes you to perform even better when other people are present. As noted at the beginning of this section, the increase in performance that occurs when others are present is called **social facilitation** (Guerin, 1993). If, however, the task has not been practiced or learned very well and the correct response is not dominant, the presence of others tends to reduce the level of performance. This effect can be seen in the performance of children in a piano recital: Those who have practiced carefully perform as if inspired, whereas those who have devoted as little time as possible to practicing are plagued by wrong notes and memory lapses.

In the example at the beginning of the section, will the presence of your friends help or hinder your game of pool? As you now know, the answer to this question is "it depends." It depends on how good a pool player you are. If you are an above-average player, your performance should improve when others are present. If you are a below-average player, your performance should decline when others are present. As you can see from Figure 15-6, a study conducted by James Michaels and his colleagues (1982) verified this prediction. The accuracy of above-average players increased from making their shots 71% of the time when they were not watched closely to making their shots 80% of the time when friends were nearby. By contrast, the performance of the below-average players fell from 36% to 25% accuracy when their friends were watching.

Social facilitation does not always occur, however. If the pressure is too great, even professional athletes falter in front of their fans. Davis and Harvey (1992) found that major league baseball players have lower batting averages in critical situations.

FIGURE 15-6   The presence of others can improve your game of pool, if you are a good player. This effect is known as social facilitation. If you are a poor player, the presence of others may hurt your game.

Source: Michaels et al., 1982.

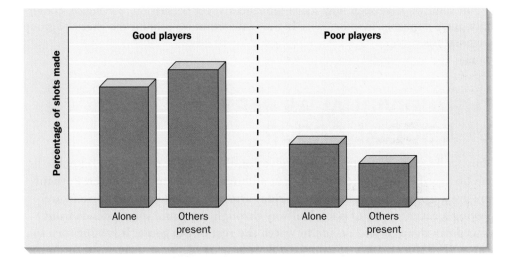

Social Loafing

The presence of others does not automatically guarantee that performance will improve. When one's individual efforts are being evaluated, social facilitation can be predicted to occur. When a group collectively works toward a common goal and individual efforts are not monitored or evaluated, however, social loafing is likely to occur.

Social loafing is the tendency to exert less effort when working on a group task if individual contributions are not evaluated. A French engineer, Max Ringlemann (1913), initially studied this phenomenon in the late 1880s. He found that when a group of men pulled a rope, each man exerted less effort than when he pulled alone. More recent laboratory research has shown that people clap and cheer louder when they believe they are alone (Hoeksema-van Orden, Gaillard, & Buunk, 1998; Shepperd & Taylor, 1999). Social loafing has also been shown in more complex tasks such as relay swimming performance (Everett, Smith, & Williams, 1992). What's more, Karu and Williams (1993) reported that men engage in more social loafing than do women, and that people in Western cultures are more likely to engage in social loafing than people in Asian cultures.

Social loafing can be reduced by making the task more involving, challenging, or appealing (Brickner, Harkins, & Ostrom, 1986). The coach of a good athletic team is well aware of social loafing and uses pep talks to counteract it. These motivational speeches are designed to challenge the team members to become more involved in the competition.

Audiences and Coactors

So far we have seen that the presence of other people may cause an individual to perform better at a task or to "goof off," depending on the situation. We need to add a clarification, however, about the other people who are present. In discussing social facilitation we assumed that the "others" constituted an audience. Sometimes the other people present are doing the same thing you are doing. In these instances they are called **coactors.** What happens when there are many coactors and few, if any, people in the audience? The answer is that the process known as *deindividuation* is likely to occur.

Deindividuation.   When everyone is doing the same thing (that is, when there are many coactors) and no one is watching (there is no audience), **deindividuation,** or a loss of personal identity and decrease in responsibility in the presence of a group, frequently occurs (Aronson et al., 2002). Deindividuation is the feeling of being lost in a crowd. Students at very large universities who complain about being a number instead of a name are experiencing deindividuation. Deindividuation often leads to uninhibited behavior. In some instances this behavior is positive, but the most frequent outcome is destructive or unauthorized behavior. The wild and destructive behavior of crowds after a major victory by the hometown sports team is an example of such behavior. Extra police and security guards must be hired to control the crowds.

Deindividuation has a powerful influence on the behavior of both adults and children. Some more extreme examples of deindividuation include the behavior of Ku Klux Klan members (they wear white sheets), military training (it is easier to kill an unseen, unnamed enemy), and mob behavior (most destruction and looting take place at night).

Fathali Moghaddam (1998) has proposed an alternate interpretation of the effects of deindividuation. Rather than losing themselves or experiencing diffusion of responsibility in such situations (Postmes & Spears, 1998), "deindividuated" individuals, Moghaddam suggests, have not abandoned all group norms and social controls; they simply have adopted new, antisocial norms and values. This view is supported by research on street gangs in which members, who might be seen as deindividuated, now obey a new code of behavior (Sanders, 1994; Sheldon, Tracy, & Brown, 1997).

social loafing
The tendency to exert less effort when working on a group task that does not involve evaluation of individual participants

coactors
Other people who are present and are engaging in the same behaviors as an individual at the same time

deindividuation
Phenomenon in which the presence of a group results in a loss of personal identity and a decrease in responsibility

The sheets and masks of the Ku Klux Klan hide personal identities and promote deindividuation.

In this brainstorming session, company executives pool their ideas concerning how to increase productivity.

Group Interactions and Group Decisions

There are many instances in which cooperation among group members is required. Families could not function, juries could not reach verdicts, and teams could not win games without interaction and cooperation among members. As we have seen, the presence of groups may result in riskier decisions or the strengthening of preexisting attitudes. The rest of this section explores several of the dynamics and processes of group interaction.

Group Formation and Effectiveness. When a group of unacquainted individuals is formed, certain predictable behaviors occur. First, the group will need a leader if it is to function effectively. Robert F. Bales (1950) found that two types of leaders emerge in a group. One leader is task-oriented; the business of the group is of primary importance to that individual. Another leader is socially oriented; he or she is more likely to show concern for the feelings and emotions of group members. What else do we know about people who emerge as leaders of groups? The individuals who become leaders typically talk more, talk first, and sit at the head of the table (Chemers, Watson, & May, 2000). Studies of leadership in India, Iran, and Taiwan have also emphasized the importance of task and social leadership (Smith & Tayeb, 1989).

Brainstorming. In some situations group leaders may defer their leadership role in an attempt to involve all the members of the group. Because of the different viewpoints and experiences that a group's members bring to a situation, it is reasonable to predict that groups should be more effective than individuals in solving problems (Hill, 1982; Kelly & Karu, 1999). Most research on this topic has dealt with the effects of a technique known as brainstorming. **Brainstorming** is a problem-solving technique involving the free expression of ideas by group members. Once ideas have been expressed, they lead to the generation of other, related ideas. Ultimately, the collection of ideas is pooled and a solution is achieved. For free expression of ideas to occur, it is important that brainstorming be conducted in an uncritical atmosphere. No ideas may be labeled as "dumb" or "stupid."

Psychological Detective

Brainstorming sounds impressive: Several individuals working together should be able to solve problems very effectively. This prediction has not proved to be true, however. Researchers have shown that the same number of individuals working independently actually generate more ideas than a brainstorming group (Madsen & Finger, 1978). Imagine yourself in a brainstorming session, and then imagine yourself trying to solve a problem by yourself. What is there about the brainstorming session that actually decreases the number of ideas generated? Write down some possibilities before reading further.

brainstorming
Free expression of ideas by members of a group to solve a problem

In a brainstorming situation everyone is encouraged to express opinions in an uncritical atmosphere. Problems may arise, however, when several people are ready to express their ideas. In a group, only one person can talk at a time, whereas many ideas can be generated simultaneously by individuals working alone. The presentation of ideas in the group setting may have a second unwanted effect as well. When one's train of thought is interrupted, it may be impossible to return to an idea that came to mind earlier. This situation often happens in groups but not when people work alone. Clearly brainstorming is not always the best way to generate ideas.

Groupthink.   Are there any other factors that might cause a group to be less effective than individuals? Yes—when maintaining harmony among group members becomes more important than carefully analyzing the problem at hand, the group's effectiveness decreases. The process of making decisions that tend to promote the harmony of the group is known as **groupthink** (Janis, 1972; 1982). Groupthink occurs most often in very cohesive groups that are insulated from other opinions and groups, feel that they are invulnerable, have a respected and directive leader, and are placed under time constraints to reach a decision concerning a threat to the group (Turner et al., 1992). In these circumstances groups tend to make premature and poorly considered decisions (Esser, 1998; Hogg & Hains, 1998). The first suggestion proposed by the leader is usually adopted, especially if there is little hope of finding a better solution. For example, analyses of the decisions to cross the 38th parallel during the Korean War, to invade Cuba at the Bay of Pigs in 1961, and to escalate the Vietnam War in the mid-1960s have concluded that these were poor decisions prompted by groupthink (Janis, 1972). The activities of the Klu Klux Klan and lynch mobs also reflect groupthink in action.

What can be done to avoid groupthink? Group members and leaders can take several steps to help avoid being snared into the groupthink trap. First, the leader should strive to remain impartial and nondirective. Second, opinions should be gathered from people outside the group. Finally, the group should use secret ballots when making decisions in order to ensure that group members express their true feelings (Zimbardo & Andersen, 1993).

Prejudice and Discrimination

Membership in a group such as a volleyball league team or a political action committee is usually voluntary. Some forms of group identification, however, are beyond our control. Most people are members of a variety of social categories of this type; they may be students, teachers, bricklayers, Italians, actors, rock musicians, alcoholics, Jews, or Catholics. When membership in such groups or categories determines how other people feel about us and act toward us, we are dealing with prejudice and discrimination. These are important aspects of interpersonal relationships and deserve a closer look.

Prejudice.   Think about the country you live in. Now think about several other countries. The chances are good that your feelings were more positive when you thought about your own country than when you thought about others. This occurs because the group to which we belong is the ideal against which other groups are compared and evaluated. Other groups naturally fall short of ours. When we make such comparisons between our nation or culture and others, we are being ethnocentric. Ethnocentrism is a form of prejudice.

Because the majority of psychological research is conducted in the United States, many of the results have been seen through ethnocentric eyes—that is, it has been assumed that the results produced in our culture are characteristic of other cultures. The results of cross-cultural studies are helping us remove these blinders. *Social loafing* provides a clear example of the influence of culture. We presented research results (see p. 661) that support the contention that people do not work as hard in groups as they do individually. These results, however, appear to be valid in *individualist* cultures where individual performance is valued. In *collectivist* cultures, such as China and Japan, where contributing to the group and group performance are valued, just the opposite is observed; research participants performed better in groups than individually (Gabrenya, Wang, & Latané, 1985).

groupthink
The tendency to make decisions intended primarily to promote the harmony of the group

Often our judgments of other individuals are based on only one characteristic—their social category or group membership. We do not need to know anything about the individual in question; all that matters is the category. Several examples of such group memberships were mentioned earlier; others are young, old, rich, poor, and intellectual. Judgments based solely on such characteristics are examples of **prejudice.** Ethnocentrism is an example of positive prejudice. Our thoughts about other countries and cultures probably reflect negative prejudice.

Psychological Detective

As we have described it, the negative or positive evaluation that is at the heart of prejudice is quite general. Still, we all know that prejudices can be very specific. They enable us to describe exactly why a certain person is desirable or undesirable. If prejudice creates a general negative appraisal, where do the specifics come from? Give this question some thought, and write down your answer and your reasons for selecting it before reading further. Here's a hint: The answer involves a topic discussed earlier in this chapter.

If you agree that these specifics are a set of beliefs concerning the members of a particular group, you already know the answer: We are dealing with stereotypes. Recall the examples at the beginning of this chapter: All actors are temperamental; all jocks are dumb. These general views can be directed toward individuals: The softball player in your history class is seen as a dumb jock; your friend the theater major is regarded as temperamental by the algebra instructor. Stereotypes are a major component of prejudice.

Discrimination.   The experience of prejudice frequently results in behaviors that adversely affect members of the targeted group; such behaviors are known as **discrimination.** In turn, prejudice can result in the belief that discrimination is acceptable; hence a vicious cycle is created (Bowser & Hunt, 1996). Discrimination can occur along many dimensions, including age, sex, religion, race, and political views. For example, for all the faculty members at a certain college to be men, despite the fact that many qualified women had applied for faculty positions, would be an instance of sex discrimination.

Sources and Functions of Prejudice.   Prejudice serves several functions and springs from a variety of sources. Here we examine both social and emotional sources and functions of prejudice.

Social Function.   Prejudice frequently justifies social standing or maintains self-esteem. For example, by holding a negative, degrading prejudice toward certain groups, individuals can rationalize mistreatment of (discrimination against) members of those groups. Consider the treatment of slaves, women, racial minorities, and people of different religions. Such discrimination implies the existence of two groups: "us" and "them," or *ingroup* and *outgroup* (Brewer & Brown, 1998). Members of the ingroup share common values, goals, and beliefs, whereas members of the outgroup are seen as different from members of the ingroup (Duck, Hogg, & Terry, 1995). The perception of ingroups and outgroups is relative, however; your ingroup may be our outgroup, and vice versa. What's more, the size of the ingroup influences the strength of members' feelings toward that group; smaller ingroups result in stronger favorable attitudes toward other members of the group. An example of the effect of ingroup size is frequently experienced when a small group of fans travels to a neighboring school for an athletic contest. Each member's ties to the group seem closer and stronger in the face of the large home crowd ("them").

prejudice
Judging a person on the basis of stereotypes about the group to which the person belongs

discrimination
Behaviors that adversely affect members of a particular group

Emotional Function.   Earlier in this chapter we saw that frustration can lead to aggression. When we are frustrated, who becomes the target of our aggression? Who can serve this function better than the objects of prejudice and discrimination, especially if they are competing with us for scarce resources? Are there prejudices and discrimination in the business world? What happens when there is a union strike and nonunion employees are hired? What would happen if a professor announced that there would be only four A grades in a class of 20 students? Which groups would be the targets of prejudice and discrimination in these situations?

Because it makes us feel superior, prejudice can also satisfy our emotional need for status. In fact, an increase in the feeling of insecurity often results in our judging others more harshly. For example, students who wrote a short essay about dying (designed to increase feelings of insecurity) showed stronger prejudice against members of outgroups (Greenberg et al., 1990). Prejudice is prevalent and can have quite negative effects. Can it be reduced?

How to Reduce Prejudice.   Prejudice and its outward manifestation, discrimination, are common occurrences that almost everyone has experienced in one form or another. Nearly five decades ago, Gordon Allport (1954/1979) proposed that "equal status contact between majority and minority groups in the pursuit of common goals" (p. 281) would reduce prejudice. His hypothesis predicts that close and extensive contact between group members will result in greater understanding because such contact shows that stereotypes are inaccurate. Before this hypothesis becomes workable, however, several additional qualifications are needed; otherwise, people may dismiss the inaccurate examples and actually strengthen their existing stereotypes (Kunda & Oleson, 1997). First, for contact to be effective in reducing prejudice, the parties in both groups must be of equal status. The importance of this factor is shown in the problems encountered in attempting to integrate public schools and urban neighborhoods. When one group is perceived as having lower social or economic status than another, it is difficult to overcome prejudice.

Second, contact is more effective in breaking down stereotypes and reducing prejudices when both groups are united in the pursuit of a common goal. For example, in the classic piece of research in this area, Muzafer Sherif and his colleagues (1961) demonstrated that competition between groups at a summer boys' camp resulted in strong prejudice and discrimination. But when the groups were forced to cooperate to achieve a common goal (starting the water-tank truck on which the camp's water supply depended), prejudice and discrimination decreased. In sum, cooperation that is successful in achieving a goal generally leads to reduced prejudice and discrimination.

When the city commissioned several different gangs to paint these murals, cooperation in this activity led to a decrease in prejudice and violence among the gangs.

 15.3

STUDY TIP

Make flash cards for the marginal definitions in this chapter—word or phrase on one side, and definition on the other. Then, sort the cards into groups according to whatever system of categories you think is applicable. Use this grouping technique to help you better recall the terms and definitions.

R E V I E W   S U M M A R Y

1. The use of social influence to cause other people to change their attitudes and behaviors defines **persuasion.** The expertise, attractiveness, and trustworthiness of the source of a message are important determinants of persuasion.

2. The most persuasive messages are those that attract attention, draw conclusions (if the audience is passively involved), differ only moderately from the attitudes of the audience, are the last message heard (if action is required immediately), and are presented on a one-to-one basis.

3. Naive audiences that are unaware of the intent of persuasive messages are more likely to be influenced by these messages. If the audience has previously been exposed to a mild form of the persuasive message, persuasion will be more difficult.

4. The cognitive approach to persuasion seeks to determine the thought processes that occur during persuasion.

5. **Obedience** is the initiating or changing of behavior in response to a direct command. In cases in which obedience will result in harm to another person, obedience increases with proximity to the source of the commands but decreases with proximity to the victim. If the source of the commands takes responsibility for any harm resulting from obedience to those commands, the likelihood of obedience is high.

6. Conformity results from indirect pressure on an individual to change his or her behaviors and thoughts. The authority behind these pressures is less obvious than in cases of obedience.

7. The decisions of a group may be riskier than those of individuals. This **risky-shift phenomenon** is attributable to the **group polarization effect,** in which the original attitudes of the group's members are enhanced during group discussions.

8. Compliance refers to behavior that is initiated or changed as a result of a request. The compliance technique known as **reciprocity** involves doing something for someone else to make that person feel obligated to do something in return.

9. The presence of other people increases arousal, which may result in enhanced ability to perform a desired response. This effect is known as **social facilitation.**

10. Social loafing occurs when people working on a group task that lacks individual evaluation perform at a lower level than they would if they worked alone.

11. When there is no audience and only **coactors** are present, **deindividuation** may occur. Deindividuation is the feeling of being lost in a crowd; it may lead to uninhibited behavior that is often unauthorized and destructive.

12. Two types of leaders emerge in a group. One leader is concerned with the tasks confronting the group; the other is concerned with the interpersonal needs of the group's members.

13. Brainstorming, or free expression of ideas by the members of a group, is often not as effective in solving problems as the generation of ideas by individuals.

14. The process of making group decisions that promote group harmony is known as **groupthink.** Groupthink may hinder effective solution of problems.

15. Prejudice is judging others solely on the basis of their group membership. Stereotypes about the members of certain groups are an integral part of prejudice. Prejudice may be reduced through contact among members of different groups. Such contact is most effective where status is equal and common goals are being pursued.

16. Discrimination consists of behaviors directed at members of a particular group that affect them adversely.

✓ CHECK YOUR PROGRESS

1. "The use of social influences to cause other people to change their attitudes and behaviors" is a definition of

 a. obedience.
 b. persuasion.
 c. brainstorming.
 d. discrimination.

2. Companies advertising motor oil often use race-car drivers as spokespersons because they are

 a. perceived as experts.
 b. perceived as trustworthy.
 c. attractive sources.
 d. able to attract listeners' attention.

3. What is the relationship between attractiveness and persuasion?

4. Attention, acceptance, primacy, and recency all pertain to which factor of persuasion?

 a. source
 b. channel
 c. audience
 d. message

5. What is the term for what we call "reverse psychology" in everyday life?

 a. reactance
 b. persuasion
 c. reaction formation
 d. unconscious motivation

6. The _____ occurs when the source of a message is forgotten and the effectiveness of the message increases.

 a. dissociation effect
 b. sleeper effect
 c. channel effect
 d. audience effect

7. Which term do psychologists use to describe situations in which behavior is initiated or changed because of a direct command of a person with authority?

 a. obedience
 b. compliance
 c. conformity
 d. persuasion

8. Giving in to indirect pressure to change your behavior and thoughts is called

 a. obedience.
 b. persuasion.
 c. compliance.
 d. conformity.

9. The extent to which members share the values of a group is known as

 a. cohesion.
 b. solidarity.
 c. belongingness.
 d. group identity.

10. An increase in performance caused by greater arousal is called

    a. social loafing.

    b. social idleness.

    c. social facilitation.

    d. social productivity.

11. All of the following would help reduce prejudice except

    a. heightened group awareness.

    b. equal status groups.

    c. pursuit of common goals.

    d. close and extensive contact.

ANSWERS: 1. b **2.** a **3.** The more attractive the source, the more persuasive the message. **4.** d **5.** a **6.** b **7.** a **8.** d **9.** a **10.** c **11.** a

SCORING For Self-Monitoring Scale

PAGE 631

Give yourself 1 point for every answer that corresponds to the following key:

1. F
2. F
3. F
4. F
5. T
6. T
7. T
8. T
9. F
10. T
11. T
12. F
13. T
14. F
15. T
16. T
17. F
18. T
19. T
20. F
21. F
22. F
23. F
24. T
25. T

High self-monitoring scores range from 15 to 22, whereas intermediate scores range from 9 to 14. Scores of 0 to 8 are in the low range. Individuals with high scores are sensitive to situational cues, can detect deception on the part of others, and know how to influence other people's emotions.

Credits

Photographs and Cartoons

Page abbreviations are as follows: (T) top, (C) center, (B) bottom, (L) left, and (R) right.

Chapter 1 Page 2: Liestte Le Bon, SuperStock, Inc.; p. 4: Getty Images Inc.—Hulton Archive Photos; p. 5 UPI/ CORBIS; p. 7: Federal Bureau of Investigation; p. 12: Jeff Greenberg, Rainbow; p. 14: Bob Daemmrich, Stock Boston; p. 17: Albert Bandura, D. Ross & S.A. Ross, Imitation of film-mediated aggressive models. *Journal of Abnormal and Social Psychology, 1963, 66.* p. 8; p. 22 (T) Psi Chi Newsletter 22, no. 1 (Winter 1996). Reprinted with the permission of Psi Chi, (B) Jesse Purdy; p. 25: Archives of the History of American Psychology—The University of Akron; p. 26 (T) Culver Pictures, Inc., (B) Getty Images Inc.—Hulton Archive Photos; p. 27 (T) Yvonne Hemsey, Getty Images, Inc.—Liaison, (B) Keystone, The Image Works; p. 28 (T) Roger Ressmeyer, CORBIS, (B) Candace B. Pert, Ph.D.; p. 30: (T) Courtesy of Wellesley College Archives, photo by Partridge, (C) Christine Ladd Franklin Papers, Rare Book and Manuscript Library, Columbia University, (B) T Courtesy of the Bancroft Library, University of California, Berkeley; p. 31 (T) AP/Wide World Photos, (B) Courtesy of Northside Center for Child Development, Inc.; p. 40: Alfred Pasieka/ Science Photo Library, Photo Researchers, Inc.; P. 42: (L) Chris Rogers , Rainbow, (R) Jeff Greenberg, Index Stock Imagery, Inc.; p. 49: Martin Rotker, Phototake NYC; p. 55: Richard Drew, AP/Wide World Photos; p. 56 David Young-Wolff, PhotoEdit; p. 57: AP/Wide World Photos; p. 61 R. Dahlquist, SuperStock, Inc.; p. 65: Creators Syndicate, Inc.

Chapter 2 Page 67: (T) Michal Heron, Pearson Education/PH College (B) Peter Menzel, Stock Boston; p. 68: Michael Rosenfeld, Getty Images, Inc.—Stone; p. 69: (L) Pete Saloutos, Corbis/Stock Market, (R) Hank Morgan, Rainbow, (B) Scott Camazine, Photo Researchers, Inc.; p. 70: Dan McCoy, Rainbow; p. 73: Bill Bachmann, The Image Works.

Chapter 3 Page 86: Cordon Art B.V.; p. 88: Laura Zito; p. 89: The Granger Collection; p. 91: Corbis RF; p. 93 (L) Charles Orrico, SuperStock, Inc., (R) M. Antman, The Image Works; p. 98: Carolyn Smith; p. 100 (L) Dick George, The Phoenix Zoo, (R) The Phoenix Zoo; p. 111: AP/Wide World Photos; p. 116: Gale Zucker, Stock Boston; p. 118: (T) Stephen F. Davis, (B)Catherine Karnow, Woodfin Camp & Associates; p. 119: (L) David Hundley, Corbis/Stock Market, (C) Mark E. Gibson, Corbis/Stock Market, (R) Carolyn Smith; p. 120: (T) Professor Joseph Campos, University of California, Berkeley, (B) M. C. Escher, "Sky and Water I," 1938. Woodcut, 17 1/8 in. 17 1/4 in. (c) 2001 Cordon Art B.V., Baarn, Holland. All rights reserved; p. 121: Jeff Greenberg, PhotoEdit; p. 125: Cyane Lowden; p. 128: PhotoEdit; p. 129: AP/Wide World Photos; p. 131: Stephen F. Davis.

Chapter 4 Page 132: Beth Ava, Getty Images, Inc.—Taxi; p. 134: SW Productions Getty Images, Inc.; p. 136: Sidney Harris; p. 139: Pater Vadnai, CORBIS; p. 141: Sherrianne M. Standley; p. 142: Michael Nichols, Magnum Photos, Inc.; p. 144: Monte S. Buchsbaum, M.D., Mount Sinai School of Medicine, New York, NY; p. 147: UPI Telephoto, CORBIS; p. 148: ZIGGY (c) 2001 Ziggy and Friends Inc./Reprinted with permission by Universal Press Syndicate. All Rights Reserved; p. 152: Aria (R) is a registered trademark of Respironics, Inc.; p. 154: From The Back to Sleep Campaign. National Institute of Child Health & Human Development, 2000; p. 159: National Library of Medicine; p. 162: AP/Wide World Photos; p. 165: Joseph J. Palladino; p. 168: National Institute of Health; p. 170: Davis Barber, PhotoEdit; p. 171: Illustration courtesy of Dr. Adolf Pfefferbaum of SRI International and Stanford University, with support from the National Institute on Alcohol Abuse and Alcoholism (NIAAA); p. 172: AP/Wide World Photos; p. 173: Courtesy of The National Library of Medicine, Bethesda; p. 175: Courtesy of Doug Hubbell; p. 176: Courtesy of Doug Hubbell; p. 180: White/Packert, Getty Images Inc.— Image Bank; p. 183: The Granger Collection.

Chapter 5 Page 186 (L & R) Joseph Palladino; p. 187: (B) Cartoonist Group— Reprinted with permission. All right reserved; p. 189: Jeff Greenberg, PhotoEdit; p. 192: Classic Videos in Psychology; p. 200: Nina Leen, TimePix; p. 201: Mary Kate Denny, PhotoEdit; p. 204: Lawrence Migdale, Stock Boston; p. 210: William Johnson, Stock Boston; p. 216: Tony Freeman, PhotoEdit.

Chapter 6 p. 220: Mark J. Terrill, AP/Wide World Photos; p. 222: Cartoonist Group—Reprinted with permission. All right reserved; p. 223: David Young-Wolff, PhotoEdit; p. 224: Harlow Primate Laboratory/University of Wisconsin; p. 226: U.S. Army Photo; p. 227: Bill Horsman, Stock Boston; p. 230: A. Ramey, PhotoEdit; p. 231: (T) CNRI , Phototake NYC, (B) Universal Press Syndicate ZIGGY (c) 2000 ZIGGY AND FRIENDS, INC. Reprinted with permission of Universal Press Syndicate. All rights reserved; p. 234: (L & R) AP/Wide World Photos; p. 240: AP/Wide World Photos; p. 244: AP/Wide World Photos; p. 251: Mark C. Burnett, Photo Researchers, Inc.; p. 255: (a) Getty Images, Inc.—Liaison, (b) Matsumoto, Paul Ekman, Ph.D., Professor of Psychology, (c) Alan Weiner, Laison Agency, Inc., (d) Christopher Briscoe, Photo Researchers, Inc., (e) Stock Boston; p. 260: (L & R) Michael Klausman, Paul Ekman, "Telling Lies," 2nd edition, W. W. Norton, 1992; p. 261: Bob Daemmrich, Stock Boston; p. 262: UPI, CORBIS; p. 266: AP/Wide World Photos; p. 267: (L) Mark Stevenson, Picture Perfect USA, Inc., (C) Steve Cavalier. Picture Perfect USA, Inc., (R) Kathleen Brown, Corbis Sharpshoot.

Chapter 7 Page 270: Steven Hunt, Getty Images, Inc.; p. 272: CORBIS; p. 275: William Hart, Getty Images Inc.—Stone; p. 279: George A. Miller; p. 287: George Zimbel; p. 289: Sean Adair, TimePix; p. 293: David Young-Wolff, PhotoEdit; p. 294: (L & R) Dr. Elizabeth Loftus; p. 295: Angela Maynard, Getty Images, Inc.; p. 296: Paul Sakuma, AP/Wide World Photos; p. 304: James D. Wilson/Woodfin Camp & Associates.

Text, Table, and Figure Credits

The publishers acknowledge the copyright owners for permission to reprint the following copyrighted materials:

Pages (xxii–xxvii), Study Tips: From *Keys to Success in College, Career and Life, 4/e* by Carol Carter, Joyce Bishop & Sarah Lyman Kravits. © 2002. Reprinted by permission of Pearson Education, Inc., Upper Saddle River, NJ.

Page 15, Figure 1-2: From McKinney BA, McAndrew, FT(2000). Sexuality, Gender, and Sports. *Psi Chi Undergrad Research 5,* 152–158.

Page 17, Figure 1-3: (B) From Bandura, Ross & Ross (1963). Social Learning and Personality Development, p. 8, fig. 1, 1963, 66, 3–11. Wadsworth. *Journal of Abnormal Social Psychology,* 1962. Reprinted by permission of the author.

Page 21, Figure 1-4: Source: Halpern (1991). Left-handedness: A Marker for Decreased Survival Fitness. *APA Psychological Bulletin 109,* pp. 90–106. Reprinted with the permission of Professor Diane Halpern, California State University, San Bernadino.

Page 31, Figure 1-6: www.nsf.gov/sbe/srs

Page 36, Table 1-5: Adapted from *The Psychology Major: Career Options and Strategies for Success* by Landrum, Davis & Landrum, p. 18. © 2000. Reprinted by permission of Pearson Education, Inc. Upper Saddle River, NJ.

Page 45, Figure 2-3: Adapted from *Psychology* by Shaver/Tarpy.

Page 48, Figure 2-6: From *Psychology: An Introduction 11/e* by Morris/Maisto. © 2002. Reprinted by permission of Pearson Education, Inc., Upper Saddle River, NJ. From *Biological Psychology* by Klein, Stephen B. © 2000. Adapted by permission of Pearson Education, Inc. Upper Saddle River, NJ.

Page 52, Figure 2-7: From *Human Anatomy 3/e* by Martini/Timmons/McKinley. © 2000, *Biological Psychology: An Integrative Approach* by Toates. © 2001, *Psychology: An Introduction, 11/e* by Morris/Maisto. © 2002. Reprinted by permission of Pearson Education, Inc., Upper Saddle River, NJ.

Page 54, Figure 2-8: From *Psychology: An Introduction 11/e* by Morris/Maisto. © 2002. Reprinted by permission of Pearson Education, Inc., Upper Saddle River, NJ.

Page 62, Figure 2-11: From *Psychology: An Introduction 11/e* by Morris/Maisto. © 2002. Reprinted by permission of Pearson Education, Inc., Upper Saddle River, NJ.

Page 62, Figure 2-12: From *Psychology: An Introduction 11/e* by Morris/Maisto. © 2002. Reprinted by permission of Pearson Education, Inc., Upper Saddle River, NJ. From Worchel & Shelibiske, *Psychology: Principles and Applications, 5/e,* 1994, fig. 2-5, p. 43. Reprinted by permission of Pearson Education, Inc., Upper Saddle River, NJ.

Page 72, Figure 2-20: From *Psychology: An Introduction 11/e* by Morris/Maisto. © 2002. Reprinted by permission of Pearson Education, Inc., Upper Saddle River, NJ.

Page 73, Figure 2-21: From *Psychology: An Introduction 11/e* by Morris/Maisto. © 2002. Reprinted by permission of Pearson Education, Inc., Upper Saddle River, NJ.

Page 74, Figure 2-22: Adapted from Kassin, *Psychology, 3/e,* p. 57, Fig. 2-15, 2000. Reprinted by permission of Pearson Education, Inc., Upper Saddle River, NJ.

Page 75, Figure 2-23: From *Psychology: An Introduction 11/e* by Morris/Maisto. © 2002. Reprinted by permission of Pearson Education, Inc., Upper Saddle River, NJ.

Page 77, Figure 2-24: (*A*) From *Psychology, 3/e* by Kassin, Saul. © 2000. Reprinted by permission of Pearson Education, Inc., Upper Saddle River, NJ. (*B*) Adapted from Greenfield, *The Human Mind Explained,* Henry Holt, 1996.

Page 82, Figure 2-25: From *Biological Psychology* by Klein, Stephen B. © 1999. Adapted by permission of Pearson Education, Inc., Upper Saddle River, NJ.

Page 83, Figure 2-26: From *Psychology: An Introduction 11/e* by Morris/Maisto. © 2002. Reprinted by permission of Pearson Education, Inc., Upper Saddle River, NJ.

Page 94, Figure 3-3: From *Biopsychology, 2/e,* by J. Pinel, p. 189, fig. 702. Copyright © 1993 Allyn and Bacon. Reprinted by permission.

Page 95, Figure 3-4: From *Understanding Psychology, 6/e* by Morris/Maisto. © 2003. Adapted by permission of Pearson Education, Inc.

Page 105, Figure 3-13: From *Psychology: An Introduction 11/e* by Morris/Maisto. © 2002. Reprinted by permission of Pearson Education, Inc., Upper Saddle River, NJ.

Page 109, Figure 3-15: From *Human Anatomy and Physiology* by Gaudin, Jones, Cotanche & Jones. © 1989. International Thomson Publishing. Reprinted by permission of the author.

Page 112, Figure 3-16: Adapted from *Psychology* by Shaver/Tarpy.

Page 122, Figure 3-22: From *Psychology: An Introduction 11/e* by Morris/Maisto. © 2002. Reprinted by permission of Pearson Education, Inc., Upper Saddle River, NJ.

Page 125, Figure 3-25: Adapted from *Psychology, 2/e* by Kendrick.

Page 126, Figure 3-26: From Stapel, D.A. & Kooman, W. 1997. Social Categorization and Perceptual Judgement of Size: When Perception is Social. *Journal of Personality and Social Psychology,* 73, pp. 1183. Copyright © 1997 by the American Psychological Association. Reprinted with permission.

Page 135, Figure 4-1: Adapted from The Tick-Tock of the Biological Clock. *Scientific American,* March 2000.

Page 136, Figure 4-2: The Suprachiasmatic Nucleus Has Connections to Visual Pathways. Illustration © Cynthia Turner 2002. Reprinted by permission of Artco, LLC.

Page 137, Figure 4-3: From Moore-Ede, M. (1992). *Twenty-Four Hour Society,* 1992. Reprinted by permission of Dr. Martin Moore-Ede.

Page 142, Figure 4-5: From *The Promise of Sleep* by William C. Dement, p. 31. Copyright © 1999 by William C. Dement. Used by permission of Dell Publishing, a division of Random House, Inc.

Page 143, Figure 4-4: Hauri, P. J. (1992). *The Sleep Disorders: Current Concepts.* A Scope Publications. Kalamazoo, MI: Up-john. Copyright © 1977 by the Upjohn

Company. Reprinted with the permission of Pharmacia & Upjohn, Inc. Kalamazoo, MI.

Page 146, Figure 4-9: Hartmann, E. (1987). *The Sleep Book: Understanding and Preventing Sleep Problems in People Over 50.* Glenview, IL: Scott, Foresman & Company. Copyright © 1987 by Scott, Foresman & Company. Reprinted by permission of Dr. Ernest Hartmann, Lemuel Shattuck Hospital, Boston, MA.

Page 147, Figure 4-10: Moorcroft, W. H. (1993). *Sleep, Dreaming and Sleep Disorders*, 2/e, p. 35. Latham, MD: University Press of America. Copyright © 1989, 1993 by University Press of America. Reprinted with the permission of the publisher.

Page 165, Figure 4-11: The Monitoring the Future Study, University of Michigan; Johnston, O'Malley & Bachman, 2000.

Page 170, Figure 4-12: Found in Jung, J.: *Psychology of Alcohol and Others Drugs*, p. 86. Sage, 2000.

Page 172, Figure 4-13: Substance Abuse and Mental Health Services Administration, 2000. *Summary of Findings From the 1999 National Household Survey on Drug Abuse.* (DHHS Publication No. SMA11-3466). Rockville, MD. October 12, 2001.

Page 177, Figure 4-14: From Horgan, C., Skwara, K., Strickler, G., The Schneider Institute for Health Policy, Brandeis University. *Substance Abuse: The Nation's Number One Health Problem.* 2002, p. 70. Princeton, NJ. The Robert Wood Johnson Foundation.

Page 177, Figure 4-15: From NIDA, 2001. *National Institute on Drug Abuse Notes 16* (5): 12, 2001.

Page 206, Figure 5-11: From *Introduction to Theories of Learning*, 6/e by Hergenhahn/Olson. © 2000. Adapted by permission of Pearson Education, Inc., Upper Saddle River, NJ.

Page 227, Figure 6-4: Abraham H. Maslow, *Motivation and Personality*, 2/e. © 1970. Reprinted by permission of Pearson Education, Inc., Upper Saddle River, NJ.

Page 232, Figure 6-5: From Hegarty, V. (1995). *Nutrition: Food and the Environment*, p. 292. St. Paul, MN: Eagan Press.

Copyright © 1995. Reprinted with the permission of AAAC/Eagan Press.

Page 233, Table 6-1: National Heart, Lung and Blood Institute—www.nhlbi.nih.gov/guidelines/obesity

Page 238, Figure 6-6: From *The Social Organization of Sexuality* by Laumann, Gagnon, Michael & Michaels. Copyright © 2000 University of Chicago Press. Reprinted by permission.

Page 246, Figure 6-9: From Levenson, R. W. Ekman, P. & Friesen, W. V. (1990). Voluntary facial action generates emotion-specific autonomic nervous system activity. *Psychophysiology*, 27, pp. 363–384. Copyright © 1990 by The Society for Psychophysiology Research. Reprinted by permission of Cambridge University Press.

Page 249, Figure 6-10: Illustration on pg. 56 by Robert Osti from *Emotion, Memory and the Brain*, by Joseph E. Le Doux in *Scientific American*, June, 1994.

Page 256, Table 6-3: Ekman et al., 1987. Universals and Cultural Differences in the Judgements of Facial Expressions of Emotion. *Journal of Personality and Social Psychology*, 52, pp. 712–717. © 1987 by the American Psychological Association. Reprinted with permission.

Page 257, Figure 6-13: "Emotion Flower" originally published in *American Scientist, vol. 89*, p. 349, July/August 2001. Reprinted by permission of Annette de Ferrari.

Page 260, Figure 6-14: From *Motivation: Theories & Principles 4/e* by Beck, Robert C. © 1999. Reprinted by permission of Pearson Education, Inc., Upper Saddle River, NJ.

Page 273, Figure 7-1: From Jenkins, J. G. & Dallenbach, K. M. (1924). Obliviscence During Sleep and Waking. *American Journal of Psychology*, 35. Copyright © 1924 by the Board of Trustees of the University of Illinois.

Page 285, Figure 7-8: Adapted from Hyde & Jenkins (1969). Differential Effects of Incidental Tasks on the Organization of Recall on a List of Highly Associated Words. *Journal of Experimental Psychology, 82*, pp. 472–481. © 1969 American Psychological Association. Reprinted with permission.

Page 285, Table 7-1: Adapted from Hyde & Jenkins (1969). Differential Effects of Incidental Tasks on the Organization of Recall of a List of Highly Associated Words.

Journal of Experimental Psychology, 82, pp. 473-481. © 1969 American Psychology Association. Reprinted with permission.

Page 294, Figure 7-10: Loftus, E. (1979). The Malleability of Human Memory. *American Scientist, 67,* p. 313. Reprinted with the permission of Dr. Elizabeth Loftus, University of Seattle, WA.

Page 304, Figure 7-11: From Chorover & Schiller (1965). Short-term Retrograde Amnesia in Rats. *Journal of Comparative and Physiological Psychology, 59,* pp. 73–78. Copyright © 1965 by the American Psychological Association. Reprinted with permission.

Page 308, Figure 8-1: Reprinted with permission from Shepard, R. N. and Metzler, J. (1971). Mental rotation of three-dimensional objects. *Science, 171,* pp. 701–703. Copyright © 1971 American Association for the Advancement of Science.

Page 317, Figure 8-8: From *Cognition 3/e* by Ashcraft, Mark H. © 2001. Adapted by permission of Pearson Education, Inc. Upper Saddle River, NJ.

Page 322, Figure 8-11: From Barron, 1958. The Psychology of Imagination. *Scientific American, 199,* pp. 150–166. Copyright © 1958 by Scientific American, Inc. Reprinted by permission of Dr. Frank Barron, Aptos, CA.

Page 372, Figure 9-6: From Morris, Charles G. (2001). *Psychology An Introduction, 11/e,* p. 399, fig. 10-2, Prentice Hall. Adapted from Bayley, 1956. © Society for Research in Child Development, Inc.

Page 372, Table 9-2: Frankenburg, W. K., Frandel, A., Sciarillo, W. and Burgess, D. (1981). The Newly Abbreviated and Revised Denver Screening Test. *Journal of Pediatrics,* 99, pp. 995–999. Copyright © 1981. Reprinted by permission of Mosby-Year Book, Inc.

Page 394, Figure 9-12: Reprinted and adapted by permission of the publisher from *Constancy and Change in Human Development* by Orville G. Brim and Jerome Kagan. Cambridge, MA: Harvard University Press. Copyright © 1980 by the President and Fellows of Harvard College.

Page 404, Figure 9-13: From *Development Across the Life Span, 2/e,* by Feldman, Robert S. © 2000. Reprinted by permission

Page 516, Table 12-3: Reprinted by permission of Oxford University Press and The Harvard Mental Health Letter.

Page 528, Figure 12-7: From *Abnormal Psychology: The Problem of Maladaptive Behavior 10/e* by Sarason/Sarason. © 2001. Reprinted by permission of Pearson Education, Inc., Upper Saddle River, NJ.

Page 538, Figure 12-10: The Origins of Madness, fig. 10, p. 96, from *Schizophrenic Genesis: The Origian of Madness* by Gottesman. Copyright © Irving I. Gottesman. Used with permission of Worth Publishers.

Page 548, Table 12-9: *Reprinted with permission from the* Diagnostic and Statistical Manual of Mental Disorders, Fourth Edition, *Text Revision. Copyright © 2000 American Psychiatric Association.*

Page 555, Figure 13-1: From *Out of the Shadows: Confronting America's Mental Illness Crisis,* by E. Fuller Torrey, 1997, p. 9. This material used by permission of Wiley-Liss, Inc. a subsidiary of John Wiley & Sons, Inc.

Page 563, Table 13-2: From Ellis, A. 1987. *The Impossibility of Achieving Consistently Good Mental Health. American Psychologist, 24,* pp. 364–375. Copyright 1987 by the American Psychological Association. Reprinted with permission.

Page 564, Table 13-3: Adapted from Andreasen, N.C., & Black, D.W. (1995). *Introductory Textbook of Psychiatry, 2/e* & Beck & Weishaar (1989).

Page 568, Table 13-4: From Meichenbaum, D. H. & Cameron, R. (1983). Stress Inoculation Training: Toward a General Paradigm for Training Coping Skills. In D. H. Meichenbaum & M. E. Jaremko (eds.) *Stress Reduction and Prevention,* 1983. Reprinted by permission of Plenum Publishing Corp. and Professor Donald Meichenbaum.

Page 569, Table 13-5: *Behavior Modification: What It Is and How To Do It, 4/e.*

Page 573, Table 13-6: From *Abnormal Psychology: The Problem of Maladaptive Behavior 10/e* by Sarason/Sarason. © 2001. Reprinted by permission of Pearson Education, Inc., Upper Saddle River, NJ.

Page 587, Table 13-9: From *Drugs and Behavior, 3/e* by Fred Leavitt. Copyright © 1995 by Sage Publications, Inc. Reprinted by permission of Sage Publications, Inc./Seeley, R.R., Stephens, R.D. & Tate, P. (1995). *Anatomy and Physiology, 3/e* St. Louis: Mosby-Year Book. Copyright © 1995. Reprinted with permission.

Page 588, Table 13-10: From *Abnormal Psychology: The Problem of Maladaptive Behavior 10/e* by Sarason/Sarason. © 2001. Reprinted by permission of Pearson Education, Inc., Upper Saddle River, NJ.

Page 595, Table 14-2: From Matarazzo, J. D., 1984. Behavior Immunogens. In B. L. Hammonds & C. J. Scheirer (eds.) *Psychology & Health,* pp. 9–43. Copyright © 1984 by the American Psychological Association. Reprinted with permission.

Page 599, Table 14-3: From Dohrenwend, B. P., Link, B. G., Shrout, P. E. & Markowitz, J. (1990). Measuring Life Events: The Problem of Variability Within Event Categories. *Stress Medicine, 6.* 179–189, pg. 182. Reprinted with the permission of John Wiley & Sons, Ltd.

Page 611, Hands On: From *Anger Kills* by Redford Williams & Virginia Williams. © 1993 by Redford B. Williams, M.D. & Virginia Williams, Ph.D. Reprinted in the US by permission of Times Books, a division of Random House, Inc. and in Canada by permission of Reid Boates Literary Agency.

Page 615, Figure 14-7: From Nowak, M. A. & McMichael, A. J. (1995). How HIV Defeats the Immune System, *Scientific American, 273,* p. 2. Reprinted by permission of Dimitry Schildlovsky.

Page 620, Figure 14-9: From Nezu, A. M., Nezu, C. M. & Blissett, S. E. 1988. Sense of Humor as a Moderator of the Relation Between Stressful Events and Psychological Distress: A Prospec-tive Analysis. *Journal of Personality and Social Psychology, 54,* pp. 520–525. Copyright © 1988 by the American Psychological Association. Reprinted with permission.

Page 640, Figure 15-2: From Nahemow, L. & Lawton, M. P. (1975). Similarity and Propinquity in Friendship Formation. *Journal of Personality and Social Psychology, 33,* pp, 205–213. Copyright © 1975 by the American Psychological Association. Reprinted with permission.

Page 645, Figure 15-3: From Darley, J. M. & Latane, B. (1968). Bystander Intervention in Emergencies: Diffusion of Responsibility. *Journal of Personality and Social Psychology, 8,* pp. 377–383. Copyright © 1968 by the American Psychological Association. Reprinted with permission.

Page 651, Table 15-1: From Snyder, M. (1974). Self-monitoring of Expressive Behavior. *Journal of Personality and Social Psychology, 30,* table 1, pg. 531. Copyright © 1974 by the American Psychological Association. Reprinted with permission; From Snyder, M. & Gangstad, S. (1986). On the Nature of Self-monitoring: Matters of Assessment, Matters of Validity. *Journal of Personality and Social Psychology, 51,* pp. 125–139. Copyright © 1986 by the American Psychological Association. Reprinted with permission.

Page 660, Figure 15-6: Michaels, J. W., Blommel, J. M., Brocato, R. M., Linkous, R. A. & Row, J. S. (1982). Social Facilitation and Inhibition in a Natural Setting. *Replications in Social Psychology, 2,* pp. 21–24. Copyright © 1982. Reprinted with the permission of Dr. James W. Michaels, Virginia Polytechnic Institute and State University, and Replications in Social Psychology.

Page 672, Table 16-2: From the U.S. Airforce, *Airforce System Command Design Handbook 1–3: Human Factor Engineering,* 1980.

Page 681, Figure 16-2: U.S. Airforce, *Airforce System Command Design Handbook 1–3: Human Factors Engineering,* 1980.

A

Abnormal Term used to describe behavior that is rare or dysfunctional, causes personal distress, or deviates from social norms, **502**

Abnormal behavior
concept of insanity, 503–504
criteria of, 501–502
defined, 502–503
models of, 504–506

Absolute threshold Minimum amount of energy required for conscious detection of a stimulus 50 percent of the time by participants, **89**–90

Accommodation Alteration of existing schemas to understand new information, **381**–382
In focusing, action of the ciliary muscles to change the shape of the lens, **94**

Acculturative stress The stress of adapting to a new culture, **600**

Acetylcholine, 56–57, 404

Achievement Manipulation of the environment according to established rules to attain a desired goal, **239**
motivation and, 239–241

Ackerman, Diane, 108, 110

Acquired immunodeficiency syndrome. *See* AIDS

Acquisition, 187

Acronyms A word formed by the initial letter(s) of the items to be remembered, **301**

Acrostic A verse or saying in which the first letter(s) of each word stand for a bit of information, **301**

Action potential Reversal in electrical charge of a neuron that occurs when the neuron fires, **62**–63

Activation-synthesis hypothesis Explanation of dreams that suggests that they result when the cortex seeks to explain the high level of neuronal activity occurring during REM sleep, **156**

Actor-perceiver bias, 634–635

Adaptation Loss of sensitivity to a stimulus by the receptors as a result of continued presentation of that stimulus, **88**

Adaptors, 262

Addiction, 165

Adjustment, attitudes and, 637

Adler, Alfred, 489

Adolescence The years between approximately age 12 and age 20, **387**

attitudes toward death, 408–409
cognitive and intellectual changes in, 389–390
commitments in, 392, 395
eating disorders in, 392
family influences, 392
identity in, 390–391
peer groups, 391–392
personality and social changes in, 390–392
physical changes in, 387–389
puberty, 387–388

Adoption studies
intelligence and, 350–351
schizophrenia and, 539

Adrenal glands Pair of glands located at the top of each of the kidneys; they release a range of hormones including epinephrine and norepinephrine, **50**

Adrenocorticotropic hormone (ACTH), 49, 50

Adrenogenital syndrome Condition caused by exposure to excessive amounts of androgens during the fetal period; can result in a female with genitals resembling those of males, **418**

Adulthood, early Period from approximately age 20 to age 40, **392**
attitudes toward death, 409
career development, 397
cognitive and intellectual changes in, 393–395
marriage and children, 395–397
personality and social changes in, 395–397
physical changes in, 392–393

Adulthood, late Period from approximately age 65 until death, **402**
attitudes toward death, 409
cognitive and intellectual changes in, 405–406
life expectancy, 404–405
personality and social changes in, 406–408
physical changes in, 402–405
retirement, 406–407

Adulthood, middle Period from approximately age 40 to age 65, **397**
attitudes toward death, 409
cognitive and intellectual changes in, 398
midlife crisis, 399
personality and social changes in, 399–400
physical changes in, 398
stress during, 399–400

Affect
attitudes and, 636
attraction and, 641

Affectivity, positive and negative, 680

Afferent (sensory) nerves Nerves that carry information from the receptors to the spinal cord and brain, **44**

Affirmative action, 673

Age, mental, 337, 338

Ageism Viewing elderly people in a negative manner, **406**, 407
cultural differences, 408

Age regression, hypnosis and, 161

Aggression Physical or psychological behavior that is performed with the intent of doing harm, **646**
biological views of, 646
environmental conditions and, 646–647
frustration-aggression hypothesis, 646–647
gender differences, 440–441
heart disease and, 612
hostile, 646
instrumental, 646
sexual, 647–648

Agitated depression, 525

Agitated dysphoria, 175

Agonists Drugs that enhance the effects of a particular neurotransmitter, **58**–59

Agoraphobia Avoidance of public places or situations in which escape may be difficult should the individual develop incapacitating or embarrassing symptoms of panic, **512**–513, 515, 518

Agreeableness, 470–472, 479–480

AIDS (acquired immunodeficiency syndrome) Viral disease transmitted via bodily fluids such as blood and semen during sexual relations or by sharing needles used by a person infected with the human immunodeficiency virus (HIV); the virus attacks the body's immune system, resulting in vulnerability to infections and diseases, which eventually cause death, 593, **613**–614

Ainsworth, Mary Salter, 378

Alarm stage, 596

Alcock, James, 128

Alcoholism/alcohol abuse Depressant psychoactive substance, also known as ethyl alcohol or ethanol, **166**
cultural differences and, 171–172
effects of, 168–171
factors that influence the use of, 171–172

myopia, 170
prenatal development and, 367–368
Alcohol use disorders identification test (AUDIT), 169
Alexithymia, 248–251
Algorithm A systematic procedure that is guaranteed to furnish the correct answer to a problem if it is followed correctly because the procedure involves evaluating all possible solutions, **312**–313
Allen, Andrea, 465
All Grown Up and No Place to Go (Elkind), 389
Allport, Gordon, 468, 665
Altered state of consciousness, 134
Alternate-forms method, 340
Altruism Helping behavior performed voluntarily with no anticipation of reward, **644**–645
Alzheimer's disease Degenerative brain disorder that results in progressive loss of intelligence and awareness, 348, **404**
Amabile, Teresa, 322
American Psychiatric Association, 506
American Psychological Association
ethics and, 20, 22, 192
first African American as president of, 30–31
first woman president of, 30
repressed memory and, 295
American Sign Language (ASL), 330–331
Ames room, 124, 125
Amish, depression and, 527
Amnesia Loss of memory that occurs as a result of physical or psychological trauma, **303**
anterograde, 303
dissociative, 520
dissociative fugue, 520
infantile, 297
retrograde, 303–304
Amniocentesis Withdrawal and analysis of amniotic fluid to detect genetic abnormalities in the fetus, **368**
Amniotic fluid, 366, 368
Amphetamines Stimulants that are used to treat attention deficit hyperactivity disorder and narcolepsy, 166, **173**–174, 529, 540
Amplitude Strength of intensity of a stimulus (brightness for visual stimuli; loudness for auditory stimuli), **92**
Amygdala, 247–248, 303
Amytrophic lateral sclerosis (Lou Gehrig's disease), 53
Anabolic steroids, 49
Anal stage The second stage of psychosexual development in which the focus of pleasure is the anus and conflict often occurs as efforts are made to toilet-train the child, **487**, 488

Anatomical sex, 417
Anderson, Craig, 216
Anderson, John, 291
Androgen insensitivity syndrome Failure by a male embryo to respond to male hormones, **418**
Androgens, 49, 388, 417, 419
Androgyny, 432
Angell, James Rowland, 25
Animal research, ethics and, 22–23
Anorexia nervosa A potentially life-threatening eating disorder occurring primarily in adolescent and young adult females; an intense fear of becoming fat leads to self-starvation and weight loss accompanied by strong beliefs that one is fat despite objective evidence to the contrary, **234**–235, 393, 505
Anosmia, 109
Anoxia Reduction or lack of oxygen, **369**
Antagonist Drug that opposes or inhibits the effects of a particular neurotransmitter, **59**–60
Anterior chamber, 94
Anterograde amnesia Inability to store new memories after a traumatic event, **303**
Antianxiety drugs Minor tranquilizers, such as the benzodiazepines, used to reduce anxiety, usually by increasing the ability of the neurotransmitter GABA to bind at synapses, **582**–583
Antidepressant drugs, 530, 531, 583
Antigens Foreign substances such as bacteria that trigger an immune response, **603**
Antipsychotic drugs Drugs that reduce the symptoms of schizophrenia by blocking dopamine receptors in the brain; the typical antipsychotic drugs work by blocking dopamine, whereas the atypical drugs (such as Clozapine) also block serotonin, **584**–585
Antisocial personality disorder Personality disorder characterized by deceitful, impulsive, reckless actions for which the individual feels no remorse, **544**–546
Anvil (incus), 104
Anxiety General feeling of apprehension characterized by behavioral, cognitive, or physiological symptoms, **512**
Anxiety disorders, 192
generalized anxiety disorder, 515–516
obsessive-compulsive disorder, 516–518
panic disorder, 514–515
phobias, 512–514
summary of, 518
Apathy, 537

Aphasia General term for problems in understanding or producing spoken and written language, **78**
Apparent motion Illusion of movement in a stationary object, 26, **121**
Appearance, impression formation and, 630
Appraisal
performance, 678–679
primary, 602
secondary, 602
theories of emotion, 265–266
Approach-approach conflicts, 227, 601
Approach-avoidance conflicts, 227, 601
Apraxia Deficits in nonverbal skills, **79**
Aqueous humor, 94
Arbitrary inference Conclusion drawn in the absence of supporting information, **532**, 564
Archetypes, 488
Ardrey, Robert, 222
Argyle, Michael, 641
Aronson, Joshua, 354
Asch, Solomon, 657–658
Assimilation Piaget's term for the process of incorporating information into existing schemas, **381**
Asylums, 551–552
Ataque de nervois (attack of nerves), 505
Ataxia Loss of motor coordination, **54**
Atherosclerosis, 608
Atkinson, John
Atkinson, Richard, 276–282
Atkinson-Shiffrin memory model, 276–282
Attachment Intense, reciprocal relationship formed by two people, usually a child and an adult, **377**
development of in children, 377–379
ethological theory, 377–378
experiment's on monkeys, 377
father's role in, 378–379
strange situation test, 378
Attention, perception and, 115
Attention deficit hyperactivity disorder (ADHD), 173–174
Attitudes Evaluative judgments about objects, people, and thoughts that include affective, knowledge, and behavioral components, **636**
components of, 636
formation of, 638
functions of, 636–637
measuring, 637–638
Attraction The extent to which we like or dislike other people, 640–641
Attractiveness, influence on persuasion, 650–651
Attribution The process of assigning causes to events and behaviors, **632**
biases, 633–634
consensus, 633

F

Facial expressions, 254–260

Facial feedback hypothesis Hypothesis that making a certain facial expression will produce the corresponding emotion, **258**

Fadeout, 351

Fagot, Beverly, 443

Fairies, 5–6

False negatives and positives, 90

Family influences, 392

Family responsibilities, gender differences and, 455–456

Family size, intelligence and, 352

Family therapists, 557

Family therapy, 573

Fan violence, 690–691

Fathers
attachment development and role of, 378–379
cultural differences, 379

Fausto-Sterling, Anne, 440

Feature analysis theory Theory of pattern perception stating that we perceive basic elements of an object and assemble them mentally to create the complete object, **117**

Fechner, Gustav, 89–90

Felkers, Kenneth, 392

Female sexual anatomy, 420

Feminization of poverty, 397

Festinger, Leon, 638

Fetal alcohol syndrome (FAS) Condition in some children born to mothers who drank during pregnancy, characterized by low birth weight, small head circumference, and mental retardation, **367**
prenatal development and, 368

Fetal tobacco syndrome, 367

Fetishism Paraphilia involving sexual arousal by unusual objects or body parts, **547**, 548

Fetus The developing baby from about the ninth week after conception until birth, **366**
checking the health of, 368

Fight-or-flight response, 50, 57, 596, 620

Figure-ground relationships Organization of perceptual elements into a figure (the focus of attention) and a background, **120**–**121**

Fixation Cessation of further development, resulting in behaviors that are characteristic of the stage of development in which the fixation occurred, 486–**487**

Fixed-ratio schedule, 206–208

Flashbulb memory Very detailed memory of an arousing, surprising, or emotional situation, **288**–**289**

Flat effect, 537

Fluid intelligence Intelligence involving the ability to view new relationships, solve new problems, form new concepts, and use new information, **394**, 405

Folkman, Susan, 602

Folk wisdom, 4–5

Foot-in-the-door effect Phenomenon in which a person who has agreed to a small request is more likely to comply with a subsequent larger request, 654, **659**

Forebrain Major division of the brain that consists of subcortical structures and the cerebral cortex, **73**–**74**

Foreclosure Uncritical acceptance of parental values and desires; hampers the development of a unique identity, **391**

Forensic psychologist Psychologist who applies psychology to law and legal proceedings, **37**, **686**–689

Forgetting, 281
curve of, 272–273
directed, 280

Formal operational stage Piaget's final stage of intellectual development, characterized by abstract thinking; achieved during adolescence or adulthood, 384, **389**

Fovea Indented spot in the center of the retina that contains only cones, **96**

Foxx, Richard, 570

Fragile X, 368

Framing The tendency for decision making to be influenced by presentation of negative or positive outcomes; decision making tends to be risk aversive, **320**–**321**

Fraternal twins Twins who develop from two ova fertilized by two different sperm; genetically related as siblings, **349**, 479–480, 517. *See also* Twin studies

Free association A psychoanalytic technique in which the patient is asked to say whatever comes to mind without censoring anything, **559**–560

Freeman, Walter, 589

Free recall Learning procedure in which material that has been learned may be repeated in any order, **272**

Frequency theory Theory stating that the basilar membrane vibrates at different rates to create the perception of different pitches, **105**–106

Freud, Sigmund, 11, 27, 156, 375, 414, 426, 481–483, 505, 532, 553–554
psychoanalytic therapy, 559–560

Friedman, Meyer, 609, 612

Friendship Form of interpersonal attraction that is governed by an implicit set of rules, **641**–642

Frontal lobes The largest lobes of the cortex; they contain a motor strip, Broca's area (speech), and areas responsible for decision making, **76**

Front-in-the-door effect Phenomenon in which a person who has agreed to a small request is more likely to comply with a subsequent larger request, **659**

Frustration-aggression hypothesis The hypothesis that aggression is likely to occur when a person is frustrated, **646**–647

Functional fixedness Inability to view new uses for familiar objects, **315**

Functionalism Approach to psychology that focused on the purposes of consciousness, **25**

Functional magnetic resonance imaging (fMRI) A modification of the standard MRI procedure that allows both structural and temporal images to be gathered, **70**, 248

Fundamental attribution error The tendency to attribute behaviors to internal causes, **634**

G

GABA (gamma-aminobutyric acid), 57, 516, 582

Gage, Phineas, 66

Gall, Franz Joseph, 65, 476

Galton, Francis, 336, 344–345, 347

Ganglion cells Cells in the retina whose axons form the optic nerve, **95**

Garcia, John, 195–196

Gardner, Howard, 346, 347

Gate control theory Theory of pain stating that the release of substance P in the spinal cord produces the sensation of pain, **113**

Gazzaniga, Michael, 81

Gender Social and psychological phenomena associated with being "feminine" or "masculine" as these concepts are defined in a given culture, 413, **414**
language and, 332–333
male vulnerability, 416–417
permanence, 428

Gender differences
aggression and, 440–441
AIDS and, 613, 614
biological, 435–436
communication and, 439, 440
depression and, 526–527
drug therapy and, 585–586
early analyses of, 436–437
emotions and, 262–263
family responsibilities and, 455–456
heart disease and, 608
helping behavior and, 439–440
impact of, 30–31

that conduct sound from the outer to the inner ear, **104**

Osteoporosis Condition in which the bones become thinner and more prone to fractures and breaks; typically appears in postmenopausal women, **398**

Oval window Structure that connects the middle ear with the cochlea of the inner ear; its movement causes fluid in the cochlea to move, **104**

Ovaries Female gonads, **49**

Overgeneralization, 564–565

P

Pain, 112
  hypnosis and the reduction of, 160
  theories of, 113
Painkillers, 60–61, 175
Paired-associate learning Learning procedure in which items to be recalled are learned in pairs. During recall, one member of the pair is presented and the other is to be recalled, **272**
Palmar or grasp reflex Reflex consisting of a very strong hold on any object placed in the palm, **369**
Pancreas An endocrine gland that lies between the stomach and the small intestine; the primary hormone released, insulin, regulates levels of glucose in the body, **48–49**
Panic disorder The most severe anxiety disorder, characterized by intense physiological arousal not related to a specific stimulus, **514–515**
Papillae Bumps or protrusions distributed on the tongue and throat that are lined with taste buds, **108**
Paralanguage Communication that involves aspects of speech such as rate of talking and tone of voice, but not the words used, **262**
Parallel distributed processing (PDP), 286–287
Parallel processing, 125
Paranoid personality disorder, 545
Paranormal phenomena, 127–130
Paraphilias Sexual arousal by objects or situations not considered sexual by most people, **547**, 548
Parapsychology, 128
Parasomnias Sleep disorders, other than insomnia and hypersomnia, which occur more frequently in children and often disappear without treatment, **152**
Parasympathetic division Subdivision of the autonomic nervous system that is responsible for returning the body to a resting or balanced state, **46**

Parenting styles
  cultural differences, 396–397
  role of, 396–397
Parietal lobes Lobes located behind the frontal lobes and containing the sensory cortex, **76**
Parkinson's disease, 55–56
Partial reinforcement Reinforcement that does not follow every target response, **205–206**
Partial reinforcement effect Phenomenon in which extinction of an operant response following partial or intermittent reinforcement takes longer than extinction following continuous reinforcement, 208–**209**
Participant modeling, 570
Passionate love Transitory form of love that involves strong emotional reactions, sexual desires, and fantasies, **642**
Pattern perception The ability to discriminate among different figures and shapes, **117**
Pavlov, Ivan, 26, 182, 183
Pavlovian conditioning, 182–184
Paxil, 56
Peer group Group of neighborhood children, classmates, or selected friends of the same age, **380**
  adolescent, 391–392
Pegword technique Use of familiar words or names as cues to recall items that have been associated with them, **300**
Penis envy, 487
Perception The process of organizing and making sense of sensory information, **87**
  attention and, 115
  binocular cues, 118–119
  constancies, 117–118
  current research/issues, 125–127
  depth, 118–120
  Gestalt principles of, 120–121
  hypnosis and, 160–161
  hypotheses and illusions, 122–125
  monocular cues, 119–120
  motivation and, 115–116
  of movement, 121–122
  pattern, 117
Perceptual constancies The tendency to perceive the size and shape of an object as constant even though its retinal image changes, **117**–118
Perceptual hypotheses Inference about the nature of stimuli received from the environment, **122–125**
Perceptual illusions Misperceptions or interpretations of stimuli that do not correspond to the sensations received, **123**–125
Perceptual speed, 437
Performance appraisal The evaluation of a person's functioning on job-related

tasks; this usually includes some formal assessment and feedback, **678**–679
Peripheral nervous system (PNS) Division of the nervous system that consists of neural fibers lying outside the brain and spinal cord, **43**
  autonomic division, 44
  parasympathetic division, 45–46
  somatic division, 43–44
  sympathetic division, 44, 45
Perls, Fritz, 562
Persecutory delusions, 536
Personal fable Feeling shared by many adolescents that one is not subject to the same rules as other people, **389**
Personality A relatively stable pattern of behaving, feeling, and thinking that distinguishes one person from another, **459**
  behavior consistency and, 465–467
  biological factors in, 474–481
  defined, 459–460
  development, 375–376
  evolutionary perspective, 480–481
  humanistic perspective, 494–497
  learning and cognitive perspectives, 491–494
  psychodynamic perspective, 482–490
  tests, 460–464
  trait approaches, 467–472
Personality disorders Disorders characterized by longstanding, difficult-to-treat, dysfunctional behaviors that are typically first observed in adolescence, **544–546**
Personality tests
  Barnum effect, 463–464
  California Psychological Inventory, 462
  Minnesota Multiphasic Personality Inventory (MMPI), 460–462
  projective, 462–463
  selecting police officers and use of, 675–676
  self-report inventories, 460–462
Persuasion The use of social influences to cause people to change attitudes or behavior, **650**
  attractiveness and, 650–651
  expertise and, 650
  message factors, 652–655
  source factors, 650–652
  trustworthiness and, 652
Pert, Candace, 28
Phallic stage The third stage of psychosexual development in which the genital organs become the focus of pleasure-seeking behavior, **487**, 488
Phencyclidine piperidine (PCP) Powerful hallucinogen that can have unpredictable depressant, stimulant, hallucinogenic, or analgesic effects, **175**
Phenylketonuria (PKU), 348–349

Pheromones Chemical odors emitted by some animals that appear to influence the behavior of members of the same species, **237**

Phobia Irrational fear of an activity, object, or situation that is out of proportion to the actual danger, **192**, 193, **512**–514

Phonemes The smallest units of sound understood as part of a language; there are approximately 200 phonemes in all of the languages around the world, but each language uses about 20 to 60, **327**–328

Photo lineups, 687–688

Photopigments, 96

Phototherapy, 527

Phrenology, 64–65, 476

Physical activity, benefits of, 622–624

Physical changes
  in adolescence, 387–389
  in adulthood (early), 392–393
  in adulthood (late), 402–405
  in adulthood (middle), 398

Physical development, in infants, 371–372

Physiological perspective View that behaviors and mental processes can be understood and explained by studying the underlying physiology, **28**

Physostigmine, 58

Piaget, Jean, 381–384, 389

Pineal gland, 48, 135

Pinel, Philippe, 552

Pinker, Steven, 329

Pinna, 104

Pituitary gland An endocrine gland located in the brain below the thalamus and hypothalamus; called the master gland because its secretions control many other glands, **49**

Placebo effect In drug research, positive effects associated with a person's beliefs and attitudes about the drug, even when it contains no active ingredients, **9**, 577

Placenta Organ that develops in the uterus during pregnancy; it produces hormones that maintain pregnancy, transmits nourishment to the fetus, and filters out certain harmful substances, **366**

Place theory Theory stating that the basilar membrane vibrates at different places to create the perception of different pitches, **104**–105

Plaques, 53

Plastic brain, 80

Plomin, Robert, 348, 360

Plutchik, Robert, 257

Polygenic heredity Principle of heredity whereby complex traits, such as intelligence and personality, are determined by many genes, **364**–365

Polygraph An electronic device (often called a lie detector) that senses and records changes in several physiological indices including blood pressure, heart rate, respiration, and galvanic skin response, **251**–253

Polysomnograph Instrument that amplifies and records signals associated with biological changes taken during a night in the sleep laboratory, **142**

Pons Structure of the hindbrain that connects the two halves of the brain; has nuclei that are important for sleep and arousal, **71**

Pornography, 647–648

Positive reinforcer Event or stimulus presented after the target response that increases the likelihood that this response will occur again, **200**–201

Positron emission tomography (PET) Imaging technique that involves monitoring the metabolic activity of the brain, **69**, 70, 436

Posterior chamber, 94

Postsynaptic membrane, 54

Posttraumatic stress disorder (PTSD) Set of symptoms that may follow deeply disturbing events; symptoms include reliving the event, difficulty in concentrating, sleep disturbances, anxiety, and guilt, **600**–601

Poverty, feminization of, 397

Poverty of content, 537

Poverty of speech, 536, 537

Precocious Developing motor and cognitive abilities at an early age, **372**

Precognition, 128

Preconscious, 483

Preconventional level Kohlberg's first stage of moral development (ages 4 to 10), in which standards set by others are observed in order to receive reinforcement or avoid punishment, **385**

Predictive validity, 340

Prefrontal lobotomy, 589

Prejudice Judging a person on the basis of stereotypes about the group to which the person belongs, 663, **664**
  how to reduce, 665
  sources and functions of, 664–665

Premack, David, 204

Premack Principle, 204

Premature ejaculation, 425–426

Prenatal development, 366–368

Preoperational stage Piaget's second stage of cognitive development, in which the child begins to think about objects that are not physically present, **382**–383, 384

Preparedness Theory that organisms are biologically ready or prepared to associate certain conditioned stimuli (CSs) with certain unconditioned stimuli (UCSs), **196**, 197

Presbycusis Middle adulthood hearing disorder involving reduced ability to distinguish sounds at higher frequencies, **398**

Presbyopia Farsightedness that normally develops during middle adulthood; stiffening of the lens results in difficulty in focusing on near objects, **398**

Presynaptic membrane, 54

Prevalence Number or percentage of people in a population that ever had a particular disorder during a specified period, **509**

Primary appraisal The first step in coping with stress; consists of determining whether an event is a threat, **602**

Primary reinforcer Stimulus that has innate reinforcing properties, **202**

Primary sex characteristics Characteristics directly related to reproduction, **388**

Priming memory Unconscious memory processing in which prior exposure to stimulus items may aid in subsequent learning, 286, **289**–290

Proactive interference Situation in which previously learned information hinders the recall of information learned more recently, **281**

Problem solving, 311–312
  approach to representing problems, 314
  methods, 312
  obstacles and aids to, 313
  rigidity, 314–315
  set effect, 316

Procedural memory Memory for making responses and performing skilled actions, **287**

Progesterone, 418, 420

Progressive relaxation Series of exercises consisting of alternately tightening and relaxing major muscle groups, **621**

Projection, 486

Projective test Psychological test that involves the use of unstructured or ambiguous stimuli in an effort to assess personality, **462**–463

Prosocial behavior Behavior that benefits society or helps others, **644**–646

Prosser, Beverly, 30

Prototype A specific example of a concept that is readily brought to mind; viewed as the most typical or best example of a particular concept, **311**

Proximity Gestalt principle stating that perceptual elements that are close together are seen as a group, **121**
  attraction and, 640–641

Prozac, 56, 59, 530, 583

Pseudohermaphrodite Individual who possesses two gonads of the same

Substance dependence More serious pattern of substance use than found in substance abuse; popularly called addiction and often characterized by drug tolerance and withdrawal symptoms when use of the drug is stopped, **165**

Substance P, 113

Substance use disorder, 164

Sudden infant death syndrome (SIDS) The unexpected death of an apparently healthy infant up to age 1 that is not explained by autopsy, medical case information, or an investigation of death scene, 153, **153**

Suicide, 408–409
 cultural differences, 527–528
 depression and, 527–529
 gender differences, 528

Suinn, Richard, 31, 689

Sumner, Francis C., 30

Superego In psychodynamic theory, the element of the mind that incorporates parental and societal standards in what is commonly referred to as the conscience as well as the idealistic ego ideal, 483, **484**–485

Suprachiasmatic nucleus (SCN), 135

Survey method Research method that involves collecting information from a selected group of people who are representative of a larger group, **14**

Survey research, 14–16

Suzuki, Takako, 645

Symbolic gestures, 261

Symbolic representation Using a mental thought or activity as a substitute for an actual object, **382**

Sympathetic division Subdivision of the autonomic nervous system that is responsible for mobilizing the body in times of stress, preparing organisms for "fight or flight," **44**

Synapse Site where two or more neurons interact but do not touch; neurotransmitters are released into the space in order to continue neural impulses, **54**
 clearing the, 58
 depolarization and excitatory, 61–63
 hyperpolarization and inhibitory, 63

Syntax The organization of words into phrases and sentences; thus, an understanding of word order to convey ideas, **328**

Systematic desensitization A behavioral technique based on classical conditioning that is used to treat phobias; the technique usually combines training in relaxation with exposure to imagined scenes related to a phobia, 192, **568**–569

Szasz, Thomas, 505

T

Tag questions, 439

Taijin kyofushho, 505

Tardive dyskinesia A serious adverse effect of antipsychotic drugs characterized by involuntary motor symptoms such as lip smacking, **584**

Taste
 how we taste, 107–108
 in infants, 370
 interaction with smell, 111
 in late adulthood, 402
 what we taste, 107

Taste-aversion learning Development of a dislike or aversion to a flavor or food that has been paired with illness, 194, **195**–197

Taste buds Structures that contain the taste receptors, **107**

Tay-Sachs disease, 364

Tectorial membrane Membrane located above the organ of Corti in the inner ear, **104**

Telekinesis, 128

Telepathy, 128

Television
 gender stereotyping and, 432–433
 influence on children, 380–381

Temperament, development of, 375

Temporal lobes Lobes responsible for hearing and understanding speech (Wernicke's area), **78**

Teratogens Any biological, chemical, or physical agent capable of causing birth defects, **367**–368

Terman, Lewis, 337, 342, 417

Terminal buttons Component of a neuron located at the ends of the axon where neurotransmitters are stored before being released into the synapse, **53**

Testes Male gonads, **49**, 420

Testosterone, 49, 236, 237, 366, 417–420

Test-retest reliability, 340

Thalamus Subcortical structure that relays incoming sensory information to the cerebral cortex and other parts of the brain, **73**–74

Thayer, Robert, 624

THC, 176

Thematic Apperception Test (TAT), 240–41, 463

Theory Explanation for a phenomenon based on careful and precise observations, **11**

Therapists, types of, 556–557

Therapy
 behavior, 567–572
 biomedical, 556, 582–590
 cognitive, 562–567, 574
 effectiveness of psychotherapy, 576–581
 group, 572–574
 history of, 551–553
 humanistic, 560–562, 574

 psychoanalytic, 559–560, 574
 self-help, 574–575

Thermoreceptors, 112

Thinking Manipulation of information in the form of mental images or concepts, **308**
 cognitive psychology and, 308–311
 creativity, 321–325
 decision making, 316–321
 language and, 331–333
 problem solving, 311–316

Thomas, Alexander, 375

Thomas, Clarence, 450

Thorazine, 584

Thorndike, E.L., 210

Thought broadcasting, 536

Three Faces of Eve, The, 521, 522

Thresholds, 89–90

Thyroid gland An endocrine gland located just below the larynx that releases hormones including thyroxine, which has widespread effects throughout the body via its effects on metabolic rate, **49**

Thyroid-stimulating hormone, 49

Thyroxine, 49, 388

Tinbergen, Niko, 202

Tip-of-the-tongue (TOT) phenomenon Condition of being almost, but not quite, able to remember something; used to investigate the nature of semantic memory, **287**–288

Titchener, Edward B., 25

Token economy A technique that reinforces desirable behaviors with tokens (secondary reinforcers) which can be redeemed for other reinforcers, especially primary reinforcers, **571**

Tolerance, drug Need for increasing dosages to achieve the same effect as earlier, smaller doses, **165**

Tolman, Edward C., 215

Top-down processing, 122

Training The deliberate and planned process by which employees are exposed to learning new experiences designed to teach new skills and improve job performance, **676**
 methods for, 677

Trait A summary term that describes the tendency to behave, feel, and think in ways that are consistent across different situations, **468**

Transcendental meditation (TM), 621

Transduction Conversion of stimuli received by the receptors into a form (patterns of neural impulses) that can be used by the nervous system, **88**

Transexualism, 236

Transfer-appropriate processing (TAP), 286

Part 2

Taken from:

Study Guide
by Scott A. Bailey
for *Psychology*, Fourth Edition
by Stephen F. Davis and Joseph J. Palladino

How to Use the Study Guide

This manual was created especially for you. The format of the manual conforms exactly to your textbook, *Psychology,* Fourth Edition, by Drs. Steve Davis and Joe Palladino.

Use this manual when you study your textbook and when you prepare for exams and quizzes. The two resources go hand in hand. Each chapter of the study guide contains a skeletal outline that was taken exactly from the corresponding chapter in the textbook. To get the most from each resource and from your psychology class, find a place to study where you can spread out all your material for the course.

Here are the elements that you will find in the chapters of this manual:

1. Chapter Overview. The first page of each chapter of the manual has the brief outline from the beginning of each respective chapter of the text.

2. Outline. The second page of each chapter begins a formal outline of the corresponding chapter from the textbook. Space has been provided so that you may jot down notes or questions that occur to you as you study the text.

> **a. Maximize Use of the Text.** The *Tip* section at the end of Chapter 6 of this manual, *Getting the Most from Your Textbook,* presents several ideas that help make the process of studying text material an active one.

3. Learning Objectives. At the end of each chapter outline is a list of questions and statements that relate to the content from the chapter. Having studied the chapter, you should be able to address each of these.

4. Naming Exercises. Exercises to test your knowledge of key names, terms, and anatomical structures are presented following the learning objectives in each chapter. The correct answers to these items are presented immediately following the practice tests. Naming exercises take one of two forms:

> **a. Labeling Exercises.** In Chapters 2 and 3, you will find figures that represent brain and neuron anatomy and the organs responsible for sensory awareness.

> **b. Key Word Exercises.** For every chapter except Chapters 2 and 3, you will find fill-in-the-blank exercises to test your knowledge of key words.

5. Practice Tests. Each chapter has a multiple-choice practice test. Take each of these after you have studied all the material from the relevant chapter. Answers and explanations are presented following the answers for the naming exercises.

6. Key Vocabulary Words. After the answers to the practice tests you will find each of the key terms from the chapter, presented in the order in which they appeared in the textbook. Use the space beside each term to define the term *in your own language.* In order to define the terms in language that is comfortable for you, you will have to understand the definitions from the book and process them. This process will lead to your comprehension of the terms. In addition to writing definitions of the terms, you may wish to create flash cards that have the terms on one side and their definitions on the other. Understanding the language of psychology is important in order for you to be able to understand the concepts that are built upon the language.

The pages of this manual are perforated to make them easy to remove. When you are preparing for a test, you may find it easier to carry only the pages that correspond to the chapters for which you are responsible. Another suggestion would be to remove and combine the naming exercises and practice tests relevant to the material for a forthcoming test.

The manual has been three-hole punched so that you can easily remove and insert the pages into your binder for the class. You will find that organizing your class notes, practice tests, and materials distributed by your professor (including assignments, quizzes, and tests) will be helpful when you need to refer to them in the future.

Tips for Success Topics. In addition to the chapter-related material, a dozen *Tip for Success* sections are included in this manual. The *Tips* are presented, one per chapter, at the end of the first 12 chapters. Start with the ones that will be of most use to you. The ambitious student will skip ahead and examine each tip within the first few days of the semester. Others will review them throughout the semester. They cover a range of topics, and represent ideas and techniques that can help you to be your best.

Please Send Your Comments. This study guide should help you master the content of your psychology course. If you have suggestions for changes to the manual, ideas for exercises that would make learning the material easier, or would be willing to share any other feedback, please send it to:

> Scott A. Bailey, Ph.D.
> Department of Psychology
> Texas Lutheran University
> 1000 West Court Street
> Seguin, Texas 78155
>
> Email: sbailey@tlu.edu

Good Luck! I hope that you find your introductory psychology course to be both challenging and informative. The concepts that you will learn from this course will be of great value to you for years to come.

CHAPTER 1

Psychology, Research, and You

Do You Know?

Do you know that psychology is an academic discipline that was founded upon careful scientific research? Since the establishing of a lab in Germany by Wundt in the late 1800s to the present, psychologists have sought causal explanations of human and nonhuman animal behavioral phenomena through empirical investigations. Whether working in applied settings such as clinics and counseling centers, in field settings such as crime scenes and wildlife refuges, or in traditional laboratory settings, psychologists seek to gather high quality data that will lend insight into myriad questions concerning behavior. Thus, counter to lay views on psychology, solid grounding in empirical research is central to the work of all psychologists. As you read your textbook, consider how psychologists might go about systematically studying each of the topics you study. Recall the passion for asking *why* that two-year-olds possess; psychologists similarly engage in a ceaseless quest to learn.

Notes from Class and the Textbook

Use the space provided in this outline to record notes from the textbook as well as from class lectures and discussion. Questions related to the *Psychological Detective, Hands On, Myth or Science* and *Study Tip* sections in the text have been presented in the outline; use the associated space to respond to the questions and to record your own comments about the issues.

I. Becoming a Psychological Detective

    A. Arthur Conan Doyle's Belief in Fairies

        1. The Law of Parsimony

    B. Guidelines for the Psychological Detective

Note: When a Psychological Detective feature appears in the text, you will see an icon of a magnifying glass. The magnifying glass icon will be used in the study guide outline to alert you to an opportunity to apply your critical thinking skills.

        1. What is the statement or claim and who is making it?

        2. Is the statement or claim based on scientific observations?

        3. What do statistics reveal?

        4. Are there plausible alternative explanations for the statement or claim?

Using the Guidelines for the Psychological Detective, analyze a statement or claim made in a current newspaper or magazine. How well does the statement or claim hold up under the scrutiny of these considerations?

II. Research Methods in Psychology

    A. The Case Study

    B. Naturalistic Observation

Point your Web browser at the textbook's Web page to see Live!Psych module 1.1.

    C. Correlational Research

Point your Web browser at the textbook's Web page to see Live!Psych module 1.2.

Create a scatterplot using the times of your current classes on the vertical axis (Y-axis), and the grades you are earning in each class on the horizontal axis (X-axis). Is there a pattern in your performance that suggests a relationship between time of class and how well you do? If there is a relationship, would it be characterized as positive or negative?

List several factors that could be responsible for an association between SAT scores and grade-point averages.

D. Survey Research

Why would a report on violent crimes from the police not necessarily reflect well the amount of violence that exists in society? How might the type of survey influence the kind of information that is collected?

E. The Experimental Method

Point your Web browser at the textbook's Web page to see Live!Psych module 1.3.

Why would it have been inappropriate for Bandura and his colleagues to assign only boys to the aggressive model condition and only girls to the nonaggressive model condition?

F. Statistics and Psychologists

Why is it necessary to summarize research data before disseminating them?

1. Descriptive Statistics

How do measures of central tendency and measures of variability for a given data set help contextualize and make individual data from the set more meaningful?

        2. Inferential Statistics

    G. Research Ethics

        1. Protection from Harm

        2. Confidentiality

        3. Voluntary Participation

        4. Deception and Intimidation

Create visual aids, such as icons or pictures, to help you remember the different principles of research ethics.

        5. The Ethics of Research with Animals

III. The Origins of Modern Psychology

    A. Wundt and Structuralism

    B. Functionalism

C. Gestalt Psychology

D. The Behavioral Perspective

E. Sigmund Freud and the Psychodynamic Perspective

F. The Humanistic Perspective

G. The Physiological Perspective

H. The Evolutionary Perspective

Point your Web browser at the textbook's Web page to see Live!Psych module 1.4.

I. The Cognitive Perspective

J. The Cultural and Diversity Perspective

Summarize the history of modern psychology in a short book. Write short, straightforward, one page summaries of each perspective to include in the book.

IV. Present-Day Psychology

V. Psychological Specialties

    A. Clinical and Counseling Psychology

    B. Other Specialties

List several ways that cultural issues can affect the development and conduct of psychological research.

    C. Emerging Specialties

Learning Objectives

After you have studied the chapter, you should be able to respond to the following statements and questions to convey your understanding of the material.

1.   Identify and describe several ways psychologists gather information about the problems they research.

2.   List, in order as they developed, the broad, thematic approaches characteristic of early psychology.

3. How do the perspectives (e.g., physiological, cognitive) psychologists adopt influence their approaches to their discipline?

4. What steps should one take when evaluating psychological research?

5. Name several different types of jobs that are held by psychology majors with bachelor's degrees.

Key Word Exercise

Fill in the blanks in the following statements with key words and terms from the textbook. Answer as many as you can without referring to your notes or to the book. If you have blanks after thinking about each item, try using your book. The answers are presented after the practice test.

1. Psychologists strive to design experiments that are void of _____ that may unintentionally influence the data they gather.

2. When describing research results, psychologists opt for the most _____ explanations, as they are the ones that rely on the fewest assumptions.

3. A _____ control group is one that illustrates the influence of having taken *any* medication in a drug experiment, even when the medication does not contain an active ingredient.

4. A *Sesame Street* definition of *hypothesis* is: an educated guess. More specifically, hypotheses are testable ideas that are carefully derived out of organized general principles called _____.

5. Correlations are relationships between sets of two variables in which changes in the level of one variable are associated with changes in the level of the other. The degree of relationship is expressed both in terms of the statistic r, and graphically with a _____.

6. _____ _____ was noted for emphasizing that perception of a whole differs from that of individual stimuli.

7. In spite of efforts to control extraneous variables, researchers are challenged by the fact that these unwanted influences on experimental data will persist. One way to reduce their impact is to distribute them among all the groups in an experiment. However, as they are typically unknown, one must use _____ _____, a technique that is employed in many experimental designs.

8. The _____ _____ was started by Pavlov and continued by Watson as an attempt to get psychologists to focus only on that which is overtly observable.

9. Though Harvard University refused to grant her a Ph.D. because of her gender, _____ _____ _____ was still elected as the 14th president of the APA.

10. The _____ _____ to psychology is one that many psychologists adopt because they use several approaches in their work.

Practice Test

Circle the letter that corresponds to the **best** alternative for each of the following items. Read each alternative carefully. The answers are presented at the end of this study guide chapter. Be sure to learn *why* each correct alternative is better than the others.

1. Proverbs are examples of:
   a. folk wisdom.
   b. falsifiable hypotheses.
   c. positive action words; their complements are converbs.
   d. universally applicable theories derived from cross-cultural research.

2. As discussed in the text passage on Arthur Conan Doyle's belief in fairies, *mediums* are:
   a. only slightly larger than smalls.
   b. the shirt sizes Doyle's Sherlock Holmes wore.
   c. descriptive statistics that share characteristics with both the mean and the mode.
   d. people who claim they can contact the spirit world and communicate with the dead during a séance.

3. *Bias* can unintentionally:
   a. cloud our observations.
   b. influence the questions we ask.
   c. influence the methods we use and the ways we interpret data.
   d. All of the above are true.

4. Which of the following statements is most parsimonious?
   a. Well-rested participants were more accurate than sleep-deprived participants.
   b. Accuracy of responding is impaired as a function of hormone cycle variations in sleep-deprived participants.
   c. Sleep-deprived participants were too fatigued to concentrate and consequently performed poorly in comparison to well-rested participants.
   d. Hormone cycle shifts, combined with the impact of overall fatigue, impaired the accuracy of functioning in sleep-deprived participants when they were compared to well-rested participants.

5. The experimental method is a preferred means of gathering information because it:
   a. is easy to use in most research contexts.
   b. can provide the basis for cause-and-effect statements.
   c. has a name that conveys credibility, and credibility is the primary goal of psychological research.
   d. is a fairly inexpensive technique when compared with other approaches (e.g., naturalistic observation).

6. Marie's research project indicated, with statistically significant data, that among first year college students, those who took introductory psychology scored higher on a problem-solving test than did a comparable group of students who did not enroll in introductory psychology. According to this statement:
   a. students should take psychology if they get the chance.
   b. psychology students are smarter than nonpsychology students.
   c. even though the psychology students did statistically better, they did not perform absolutely better.
   d. psychology students outperformed nonpsychology students at a level greater than would be predicted by chance alone.

7. A third-variable problem occurs when people attribute a causal link between:
   a. the second and fourth variables.
   b. experiments, but not within experiments.
   c. two variables that share a relation with another variable.
   d. administrations of the independent and dependent variables.

8. Which of the following was *not* offered in the textbook as a guideline for evaluating a claim?
   a. What do statistics reveal?
   b. In what resource are the data in question published?
   c. Is the statement or claim based on scientific observations?
   d. Are there plausible alternative explanations for the statement or claim?

9. Like all scientists, psychologists employ the scientific method to investigate phenomena. An aspect of this method involves:
   a. microscopes, beakers, and the like.
   b. summarizing findings into widely applicable laws of behavior.
   c. using theories to derive hypotheses which may be tested experimentally.
   d. challenging daily the claims made by popular press information sources.

10. Which of the following statements is true about the relationship between the case study and naturalistic observation?
    a. Data from both generalize well to other contexts.
    b. Both have limitations but are useful in developing research ideas.
    c. With both, participants are scarcely aware they are being studied.
    d. Naturalistic observation involves essentially several concurrent case studies.

11. Which of the following values is indicative of the strongest degree of relationship between two variables?
    a. $r = -0.8$
    b. $r = -0.2$
    c. $r = +0.1$
    d. $r = +0.75$

12. When conducting survey research, it is important to use a representative sample of the population of interest. In other words,
    a. it is important to survey everyone in the population.
    b. one must gather a population of participants that mirrors the population of actual interest.
    c. contacting state or national governmental representatives should yield an accurate reflection of the population.
    d. the participants should reflect the gender, cultural, and other significant attributes of the population of interest.

13. Within the context of the experimental method, the independent variable is to the dependent variable as ___ is to ___.
    a. measure; manipulate
    b. manipulate; measure
    c. experimental; control
    d. control; experimental

14. If an experiment has a comparison group that does not receive the effect of the independent variable, it may be said that the experiment has a(n):
    a. control group.
    b. extraneous variable.
    c. operational definition.
    d. representative sample.

15. A significant advantage of the experimental method over other techniques for gathering information is that the experimental method can provide the basis for making cause-and-effect statements. This is because when using the experimental method, one manipulates ___ variables, controls for ___ variables, and measures ___ variables.
    a. dependent; independent; extraneous
    b. extraneous; dependent; independent
    c. independent; extraneous; dependent
    d. dependent; extraneous; independent

16. Using the random assignment procedure is one way:
    a. to ensure a proper control group.
    b. to control for extraneous variability.
    c. to really mess up an experiment; all assignments should be nonrandom.
    d. to scramble the independent and dependent variables and to help guard against bias.

17. In Bandura's study of the effects of modeling on aggression, the dependent variable was:
    a. the population of nursery school children.
    b. whether participants were in the experimental group or not.
    c. the number of hits delivered by participants to the Bobo doll.
    d. systematic exposure to either the aggressive model or the nonaggressive model.

18. Descriptive statistics are to inferential statistics as ___ is to ___.
    a. summarize; analyze
    b. analyze; summarize
    c. central tendency; variability
    d. variability; central tendency

19. The ethical guidelines that all experiments must meet concern all but which of the following issues?
    a. protection of subjects from harm
    b. the quality of the experimental design
    c. confidentiality of participants' names and identities
    d. whether subjects are debriefed after participating in an experiment involving deception

20. Much of what we understand about behavior has been learned from experiments involving animal subjects. Partially to address concerns about the use of animal subjects in medical and psychological research, the American Psychological Association has:
    a. promoted the animal rights movement.
    b. come out strongly in favor of experiments involving animals.
    c. adopted a set of principles to consider when designing an experiment.
    d. formed a task force called the Committee on Animals in Medicine and Psychology (CAMP).

21. Modern psychology represents a sort of blending of early philosophy and physiology. The first psychology laboratory did not exist until it was established by Wilhelm Wundt in 1879. Wundt was trained as a physician, but his mission in establishing the laboratory was to:
    a. describe the contents of the mind.
    b. study the purposes of consciousness.
    c. focus the study of behavior on that which was overtly observable.
    d. challenge the notion that conscious experience could be broken down into elements.

22. Sigmund Freud had a profound influence on psychology, although it is important to note that his contributions to the field have been highly controversial. It is interesting to note that Freud's background was:
    a. in neurology.
    b. greater than the sum of its parts.
    c. in the early school of thought in psychology: behaviorism.
    d. characterized by numerous unconscious sexual urges which led him to study psychology.

23. Early psychology was characterized by schools of thought such as Structuralism, Functionalism, Gestalt Psychology, and Behaviorism. Today, psychology:
    a. is in a school of thought known as the Cognitive Movement.
    b. is comprised of two major components: the Basic Movement and the Applied Movement.
    c. bears little resemblance to its earlier forms as its focus has shifted from behavior to consciousness.
    d. is a diversified field that is made up of several specialties, a growing number of which involve providing services to clients.

24. Clinical psychologist is to ___ as psychiatrist is to ___.
    a. Ph.D.; M.D.
    b. M.D.; Ph.D.
    c. less serious problems; serious problems
    d. serious problems; less serious problems

Answers to Key Word Exercise

1. biases	2. parsimonious	3. placebo
4. theories	5. scatterplot	6. Gestalt Psychology
7. random assignment	8. behavioral perspective	9. Mary Whiton Calkins
10. eclectic approach		

Practice Test Answers and Explanations

The practice test questions largely follow the order in which the material is presented in the textbook. The answers to the questions are given below, accompanied by a brief explanation of each. To develop your understanding of a concept more fully, locate and read the paragraph(s) or page(s) corresponding to the items in the text book.

1. a. Proverbs are forms of folk wisdom—a category of information that can provide explanations for every conceivable event, but can never be proved wrong.
2. d. Mediums are people who profess special abilities to communicate with those who have passed.
3. d. Bias, or preconceptions, can unintentionally influence the behaviors of researchers and participants.
4. a. Parsimonious statements (see law of parsimony) are simple explanations that rely on few or no assumptions.
5. b. Scientists prefer the experimental method because by systematically manipulating independent variables in experiments, while also using appropriate control conditions, it becomes possible to infer causal relationships from experimental results.
6. d. Statistically significant data are those that are sufficiently different than one would predict based on chance factors alone.

7. c. Changes in the levels of two different variables often co-occur because both share a link with a third variable, and it is the third variable that is responsible for the correlation. An additional example would be the changes that occur in language acquisition and shoe size as a function of changes in level of maturation. Maturation is responsible for the changes, rather than one of the other two causing changes in the other.

8. b. While it is important to consider the source of information one receives, the textbook focuses on critiquing the claim rather than the source for its communication.

9. c. The scientific method is a cyclical process that involves ever adjusting the specificity of theories by way of testing the hypotheses they generate.

10. b. Both are useful in helping develop research questions that may be addressed with the experimental method, but both also have shortcomings with respect to the validity and generalizability of the results they generate.

11. a. The correlation coefficient, r, may potentially assume any value between –1.0 and +1.0, inclusive. The *strength of association* is expressed by the value's proximity to a nonzero integer (+/-1); the *direction of the relationship* is indicated by the value's sign (+ or -).

12. d. Participants that comprise the *sample* in a survey project should reflect the diversity of the larger population that researchers are interested in studying.

13. b. Researchers manipulate independent variables, and measure dependent variables.

14. a. A control group is essentially an experimental group that does not receive the effect of the independent variable. Experimental and control groups are treated similarly in all other ways.

15. c. See explanation to #13, above. Note also that experimenters attempt to control, or hold constant, unwanted, or extraneous, variability.

16. b. One way to control for extraneous variability is to assign participants to groups randomly; this assures that each group is equally likely to have participants with any given characteristic.

17. c. The dependent variable is that which is *measured* in an experiment; Bandura measured hits.

18. a. Descriptive statistics summarize data sets; inferential statistics are analytic in nature.

19. b. Institutional review boards review proposals to determine that the potential participants will be treated ethically; IRBs are not organized to provide feedback on experimental designs.

20. c. The APA is concerned that animals be used in experimentation only after consideration of the seven principles that are presented on page 26 in your textbook.

21. b. Wundt's interest in establishing a laboratory was to describe the contents of the conscious mind.

22. a. Freud was trained as a neurologist. His training facilitated his recognition that the symptoms of one of his patients were neurologically impossible, and that the patient must have had a psychological rather than a neurological disorder.

23. d. Present-day psychology is a diverse field that is comprised of many specialties.

24. a. One must have a Ph.D. to be a clinical psychologist; psychiatrists are medical doctors who specialize in the medical treatment of illnesses.

Key Vocabulary Terms

Use the following list to write definitions *in your own words* for each of the key terms from the chapter. Translating the terms into language that is comfortable and familiar for you will facilitate your learning. For further study of these terms, go to the companion website for the textbook where you will find electronic flash cards that you may use to test your vocabulary.

psychology

bias

law of parsimony

placebo effect

scientific method

theory

hypothesis

case study

naturalistic observation

scatterplot

correlation coefficient

survey method

representative sample

experimental method

independent variable (IV)

dependent variable (DV)

operational definition

experimental group

control group

extraneous variables

random assignment

statistics

descriptive statistics

inferential statistics

measures of central tendency

measures of variability

informed consent

debriefing

structuralism

introspection

cognitive psychology

functionalism

Gestalt psychology

behavioral perspective

psychodynamic perspective

psychoanalytic therapy

humanistic perspective

physiological perspective

evolutionary perspective

cognitive perspective

eclectic approach

clinical psychology

psychiatrist

counseling psychology

research psychologist

ethnocentrism

cross-cultural psychology

school psychologist

industrial and organizational (I/O) psychologist

consumer psychology

health psychology

forensic psychologist

sport psychologist

neuropsychologist

Tip for Success: Goal Setting

So What Is a Goal, Exactly?

Webster's dictionary defines *goal* as aim or purpose. When put in those terms, it is difficult to imagine not having goals, for to not have goals would be to have no aim or purpose. In a broader sense, a goal is anything you could do, have, or be. Goal setting helps people to live meaningful lives and to attain the careers they wish to have. Let us try breaking these ideas of what goals are into three categories: those that should be accomplished within the next few days, those that should be accomplished within the next several months, and those that you hope to accomplish in some years to come.

Note that the language associated with the first two categories indicated that the goal should be accomplished *within* some allotted time frame. Depending on the specific circumstances surrounding certain goals, you may need to be more precise with respect to when the goal will be met. Other goals, however, fall into a category of things that may be done within a range of times.   Added precision regarding when the goal will be accomplished may be helpful in ensuring that the goal is, in fact, met.   The third category, on the other hand, was described with a fairly undetermined, indefinite range of time in mind. These goals are nearly always more abstract and therefore it is more difficult to schedule target completion dates for them.

In short, a goal is anything you could do, have, or be, and it may be done according to one of three time frames. For ease of reference, those time frames will be referred to as immediate, short-term, and long-term goals. Some people prefer to add another category, intermediate-term, that facilitates greater specificity for the more proximal long-range objectives. You should organize your goals in a way that is most meaningful for you.

Whose Goals?

First off, it is important that the goals you set are *your own goals*. If someone else imposes them on you, you may not have the sense of ownership you will need to proceed in striving to meet them. This issue is related to the concepts of intrinsic and extrinsic rewards. Intrinsic rewards come from within you—the positive feelings you get for doing a job well, meeting the expectations you set for yourself, and so on. Extrinsic rewards come from outside. Money and material items, praise from others, and various forms of entertainment are all forms of extrinsic rewards.

It is worth noting that behaviors that are intrinsically rewarding are far more persistent than those that rely on reward and recognition from outside.   The very act of achieving a goal you set out to meet is intrinsically rewarding. On the other hand, if others set your goals for you, you will likely depend on others to reward you when you meet them. If that reward is not forthcoming, your productivity will trail off predictably. Set your own goals and take pride in meeting them.

A Healthy Attitude Goes a Long Way

In addition to understanding *why* you should set goals, it will be helpful to consider *how* you will go about attaining your goals. A key to meeting goals is embodied in the attributes of a positive attitude. No doubt, your life experiences to date have helped you to understand that keeping your chin up, so to speak, is exceedingly helpful when you fall short of a mark. People who are able to persist in spite of their shortcomings are simply more successful at meeting their goals than those who get down on themselves when they do not succeed. The old adage, "'Can't-Do-It' never did anything," really fits here. Attitude may not be everything, but without a good attitude it is hard to do anything.

Sometimes you will fail. Setting goals that keep you working your hardest is the best way to ensure a high degree of productivity. If you fall short of your mark, take stock of what happened, re-evaluate the goals you are striving to meet, and proceed with the knowledge you gained from the experience.

Why Are Goals So Important Anyway?

Learning to set appropriate goals and to attain them is one of the most important things you can do, both in terms of making the most of your college experience and in terms of living a fulfilling life beyond your college years. However, it is not an easy task to set appropriate goals; and meeting the challenges you set for yourself can be difficult at times. In the end, though, the process of setting goals and striving to meet them is well worth doing and will put you in charge of using your time in ways that are rewarding and meaningful. Before describing some important things to consider when defining goals, it will be useful to discuss why goals are helpful.

Perhaps the most important reason to set goals is that they provide a focus for your attention and energy. If you know what you want to achieve, determining what to do at any given time is easy. On the other hand, if you lack the focus gained by setting goals, it can be hard to decide how to use available time. Unfortunately, when people have a hard time deciding how to use time, they often waste it. Eventually those wasted minutes and hours return to haunt us when we find ourselves pressed to accomplish something, such as studying for a test or writing a paper. One of the most disconcerting feelings people can have is the sense they get when they realize they are unable to produce their very best work because they did not plan appropriately. Setting goals and monitoring progress toward them is an excellent way to guard against this problem.

Another reason for setting goals has to do with the mixed blessing of independent living. Many college students find it exciting to begin living without having to report on their whereabouts to others. They feel liberated being able to come and go as they please, set their own hours, perform tasks and duties when they want to rather than as instructed by someone else. With freedom, though, comes responsibility. You will find it to be rewarding to determine, more or less, when you will do these things. You will discover also that it will be up to you to monitor your own progress and decision making. By learning to set and achieve goals, you will meet your responsibilities and be able to appreciate your freedom.

What are two good reasons for setting goals?

_____

_____

Greater Opportunities through Goal Setting

A word of clarification is appropriate here. The notion of setting goals for the reason of meeting responsibilities is only part of why you should embrace goal-setting as a way of organizing your activity. The other reason, which has been implied in the previous paragraphs, is that as you meet more goals you will gain greater opportunities. Those opportunities are extensions of the freedom you get for living responsibly—that is, for responsibly setting and meeting your goals. As a student, greater opportunities will enrich your experience and expand your choices for employment or for graduate or professional training following receipt of your bachelor's degree. Enhanced opportunities in the workplace typically mean more meaningful work and better pay. People who do not set and achieve goals simply do not have the same opportunities as those who do.

Some Specific Examples: Which Goals Go Where?

Let us illustrate these categories with more detailed descriptions. Immediate goals are those that you should list each evening for the following day. This exercise will make your mornings a little less hectic, and your memory of items from the list will allow you to begin planning for each day as you retire the preceding evening, and again as you get around the next morning. These goals constitute essentially a "to-do list." Be as specific as you can with these items; think in terms of filling 15-minute intervals. If you can learn to make use of the small chunks of time in your days, you will be more productive, and will have more discretionary time in your schedule. A failure to take advantage of the small chunks of time will likely lead to a sense of frustration with your schedule, and conflicts between your need to do academic work and your desire to engage in social activity.

Identify some Immediate Goals in the spaces below:

1. _____

2. _____

3. _____

Can you assign priorities to the items in your list?

The short-term goals you set for yourself will probably center on spending a certain amount of time preparing for classes, including writing drafts of papers and organizing notes to study for quizzes and exams. Additionally, you will want to include objectives dealing with proper rest, exercise, and opportunities to pursue extracurricular interests. It is worth noting that your college experience will be most memorable and meaningful if you can keep up with your academic responsibilities *and* participate in the life of your community, be it a residential campus, a church community, or your neighborhood. Interaction with others during your college years will constitute a significant percentage of your opportunities to grow and develop. However, be certain to keep track of the academic goals you set for yourself in this category. It is a tremendous feeling to be able to relax and go to bed early on the eve of an exam because you have prepared well along the way. By stark contrast, it is miserable and counterproductive to cram the night before an exam because you procrastinated.

What are four short-term goals you have set for yourself?

1. _____

2. _____

3. _____

4. _____

Did you list your short–term goals in order of priority?

The long-term goals you set for yourself will, in part, determine the short-term and immediate goals of days to come. If you select a given academic discipline as your major, for example, it is a long-term goal to meet the criteria for that major. That goal will influence the courses you choose, and the assignments, quizzes, and exams for the courses will in turn influence your immediate-range goals. As you progress through your academic career, your long-term goals may well change. That is all right. It is common for students to change their majors once or twice during the course of their academic careers. Just keep updating your goals and measuring progress toward them and you will be able to mark progress in your development as a scholar and as a responsible person living a meaningful life.

Identify three long-term goals:

1. _____

2. _____

3. _____

Do these reflect your range of interests?

Make Your Goals Challenging

If you have ever competed with someone who is just slightly better than you most of the time, you know how that interaction can really cause you to work your hardest and do your best. Think about how much you improve your debate, musical, athletic and other skills when you are challenged. The same principles apply to goal setting and attainment. If you set goals you can easily reach, you are bound to be bored. Set appropriately challenging goals, and you will experience significant growth and development.

Take Baby Steps

One of the most prized experiences humans have is attaining a goal. On the other hand, if you were to sit down to try to attain a long-term goal in an afternoon, say becoming a financially independent person with a meaningful career, you would throw your arms in the air before you were to get started. The real value of long-term goals is to provide focus. If you can measure the steps necessary to reach a long-term goal, and then work on each of them, one at a time, you will be less daunted concerning how to begin.

Starting Over

Maslow's hierarchy of needs, which is discussed in chapter six of your textbook (beginning on page 226), suggests that after meeting needs from basic levels, humans strive for increasingly abstract goals. These include belongingness, esteem needs, and self-actualization needs. Self-actualization refers to the need to develop one's full potential. If you are to reach your potential, it will be important for you to constantly monitor your progress on goals, adding new ones when appropriate. It is not enough to set a long-term goal—say completing graduate or professional school and establishing a career—you will need to renew your goals to help maintain your focus.

Make Your Goals Measurable

In order to make the most of the goal-setting process, you should strive to set goals that you can measure. This is easier for some categories of activity than it is for others. For example, it is easier to assess whether you achieved a goal or a particular mark on an exam or paper than it is to determine whether you improved your attitude toward your roommate. However, if you are creative, you can come up with ways to determine whether you are making desirable progress toward a given goal.

Try using an end-of-the-day log for charting progress toward goals. Such a log might include responses to the following questions:

1) What goals did I accomplish today? _____

2) Which short- and long-term goals did I make progress on today? _____

3) Which immediate goals did I not attain today? _____

4) How should I change my goals lists based on what I accomplished and did not accomplish today?

_____

Use Feedback

If the techniques you have developed for measuring progress toward your goals indicate that you are doing what you set out to do, you will surely enjoy the satisfaction of meeting your aims. If you determine that something is not going as you had hoped, this is useful too. Provided you are regularly evaluating your progress, you will be worlds ahead of where you would be if you did not attach measurable goals to your activity. Use the feedback you obtain to establish a fresh plan of action—whether that means to bear down and work harder, to punt, or to change horses.

More Remarks about Goal Setting

Goal setting is a critical component of leading a productive, satisfying life. However, it is not enough to merely set goals; you must implement activities that are targeted at meeting the goals, review whether the goals were in fact met, and constantly revise your goals in order to make the most of the process. A critical step in this process involves being able to locate the goals you set for yourself. Some people record their goals in daily organizers or calendars that they carry with them at all times. Benjamin Franklin is noted for having done this and being rather successful because of it. Others prefer to keep a notebook or computer file that can be accessed easily for regular monitoring of their progress. Do whatever works best for you. It is probably worth experimenting with a few different systems until you find a good fit for your style.

Consider the Following Goal-Related Questions

1) Why did you go to college?
2) Why did you enroll in a psychology course?
3) What about the other courses you are taking?
4) What career goal(s) have you established for yourself?
5) What kind of preparation will you need to meet your career goal?
6) What resources are available to help you answer these questions?

These questions should provide fodder for a good deal of thought. If you cannot answer each of them readily, relax and schedule some time to think about them. Make it a goal to answer these and other questions regarding your life as a student. Doing so will keep you on track to becoming the best student you can be. This is the key to gaining the most from your college experience.

Commit It to Writing

While it is helpful to simply think about goal setting, it is best to record your goals in writing. So get busy. Identify goals according to each of the timelines listed above and write them down. Tape the list to your bathroom mirror or put it on your dresser. Keep your goals list current and read it often.

CHAPTER 2

Behavioral Neuroscience

Do You Know?

Do you know that psychology has important implications for one of the fastest growing scientific disciplines—neuroscience? Neuroscience is a broad term that is used to represent any of several different academic and applied domains that are characterized as being focused in large part on the structure and function of the nervous system. Neuroscientists come from psychology, biology, biochemistry, physiology, anatomy, and medicine, to name some of the key areas. Inasmuch as important work in computer modeling of neuronal activity is being done today, it is appropriate to list computer scientists in the list of people interested in neuroscience as well. Indeed, the relationship between life science-based disciplines and computer science is reciprocal; each party benefits from the work of the other. The role for psychologists in this booming area cannot be understated. As research into the roots and causes of behavior becomes increasingly molecular, as when researchers focus on the implications of particular ion channels or transmitter substances for behavior, it is critical that the behavioral measures be carried out with the same experimental rigor and control as the more molecular components of the studies. Because psychologists are trained in the study of behavior, they bring a great deal to the interdisciplinary table of neuroscience. Without good behavioral emphasis as part of a project in neuroscience, one's capacity to make inferences about the implications for the study is severely limited.

Notes from Class and the Textbook

Use the space provided in this outline to record notes from the textbook as well as from class lectures and discussion. Questions related to the *Psychological Detective, Hands On, Myth or Science,* and *Study Tip* sections in the text have been presented in the outline; use the associated space to respond to the questions and to record your own comments about the issues.

I. Biology and Behavior

Point your Web browser at the textbook's Web page to see Live!Psych module 2.1.

II. The Nervous System

      A. The Peripheral Nervous System

            1. The Somatic Division

            2. The Autonomic Division

                  a. The Sympathetic System

Suppose that your tire blows out while you are driving at a high rate of speed. Which sympathetic processes would be in operation under this circumstance? Write down the processes you think of before reading on in your text.

b. The Parasympathetic System

Make flash cards with the name of an organ and either "sympathetic" or "parasympathetic" on one side, and the organ's function in that system on the other. You may wish to use Figure 2-3, on page 45 in your textbook, to guide your creation of the cards. Then, do flash card drills with a classmate in order to learn the functions of the organs when under the influence of both systems.

B. The Central Nervous System

1. The Spinal Cord

III. The Endocrine System

A. Major Endocrine Glands

1. The Pineal Gland

2. The Pancreas

3. Hypothalamus

4. The Pituitary Gland

5. The Thyroid Gland

6. The Gonads

7. The Adrenal Glands

On a piece of scratch paper, work from memory only to create an outline of the major endocrine glands. Summarize the function of each gland.

IV. Neurons: The Cells of the Nervous System

    A. Components of the Neuron

        1. The Cell Membrane

        2. Dendrites

        3. The Cell Body

Point your Web browser at the textbook's Web page to see Live!Psych module 2.2.

        4. The Axon

        5. Terminal Buttons

        6. The Myelin Sheath

Consider what you have learned about the function of the myelin sheath. What do you suppose happens when the myelin sheath degenerates? Write down a few answers before reading further.

    B. The Synapse and Neurotransmitters

        1. The Synapse

        2. Neurotransmitters

Parkinson's disease appears to result from low levels of the neurotransmitter, dopamine. One potential treatment for the disease would seem to be to simply administer dopamine to patients; however, this treatment is not successful in diminishing the symptoms of the disease. Write down a few reasons why this treatment does not work.

3. Dopamine

4. Serotonin

5. Acetylcholine

Point your Web browser at the textbook's Web page to see Live!Psych module 2.3.

6. Norepinephrine

Convert Table 2-1, found on page 57 in your textbook, into a visual organizer. Use learning strategies such as a mind map or a think link format, different colored pens, or any other strategy that will help you learn about the principal neurotransmitters, their effects, location in the nervous system, and their functions within the system.

Conduct the Orientation, Memory and Concentration Test on page 58 in your textbook. The directions for the test may be found with the test. Calculate your score after you complete the test and consider it in light of the criterion for determining whether someone has dementia.

7. Clearing the Synapse

8. Neurotransmitters and Drug Action

    a. Agonists

    b. Antagonists

    c. Neuromodulators

C. The Nature of the Neural Signal

V. The Brain: A Closer Look

A. Investigating Brain Functioning

    1. The Case Study Method

    2. Stereotaxic Surgery

    3. The Electroencephalograph

        a. Alpha Waves

        b. Beta Waves

        c. Theta Waves

        d. Delta Waves

    4. Computerized Brain Imaging

Imagine that a construction worker suffered a head injury that may have resulted in brain damage. Which of the techniques for studying brain structure and function (EEG, MEG, CT Scan, PET Scan, MRI, fMRI) would be appropriate to investigate the nature and extent of his damage? What would be the advantages and disadvantages of each technique in this situation?

 B. Major Components of the Brain

   1. The Hindbrain

   2. The Midbrain

   3. The Forebrain

Point your Web browser at the textbook's Web page to see Live!Psych module 2.4.

    a. Frontal Lobes

    b. Parietal Lobes

Reread the paragraphs from the bottom of page 76 and the top of page 78 concerning the myth that humans only use 10 pwecent of their brains. According to the text, what misunderstanding contributes to this myth?

    c. Temporal Lobes

    d. Occipital Lobes

e. Language and the Brain

C. The Plastic Brain

Can a person live with only half of a brain? What are the likely consequences of such a drastic intervention of the split brain surgical intervention? Consider this issue and write down your thoughts before proceeding.

D. The Split Brain

How would the split-brain operation influence your ability to perceive and describe a stimulus that is presented in your right visual field only? What if it were presented in the left visual field?

Point your Web browser at the textbook's Web page to see Live!Psych module 2.5.

Use the basic outline from page 40 of your textbook to create a detailed outline of the chapter. Compare your outline to the one in this study guide. Are your detailed outline and the study guide outline the same? If not, how do they differ? Consider the organization of these outlines as they relate to the material that is covered in the Behavioral Neuroscience chapter.

Learning Objectives

After you have studied the chapter, you should be able to respond to the following statements and questions to convey your understanding of the material.

1. What physiological processes are involved in sensing, processing, and responding? Which components of the nervous system are necessary for those processes to occur?

2. How are relictual (phylogenetically older) brains similar to and different from derived (more evolved) brains? Can you think of explanations other than evolution to account for the differences?

3. Imagine three neurons in a sequence: a sensory neuron, an interneuron, and a motor neuron. Describe what happens in the interneuron as it conveys information from the sensory cell to the motor neuron.

Labeling Exercises

It is helpful when learning the information from this chapter to study how some of the terms are used in the contexts of figures and tables. Having studied the chapter you should be able to fill in the missing information. The answers are given at the end of the chapter.

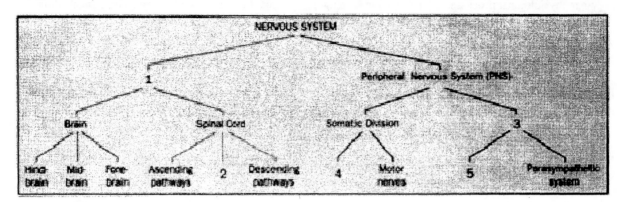

1. _____

2. _____

3. _____

4. _____

5. _____

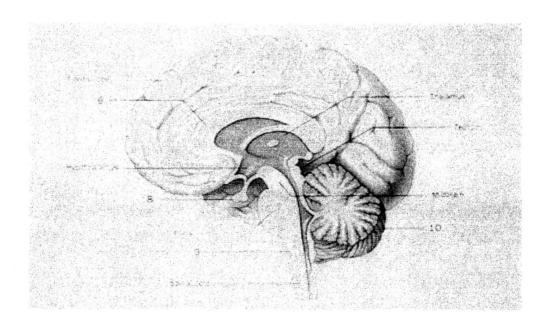

6. _____

7. _____

8. _____

9. _____

10. _____

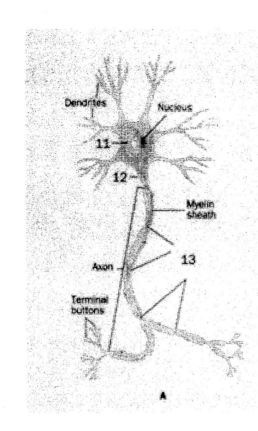

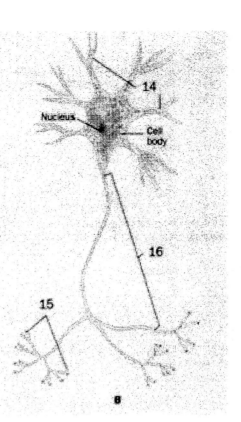

11. _____

12. _____

13. _____

14 _____

15. _____

16. _____

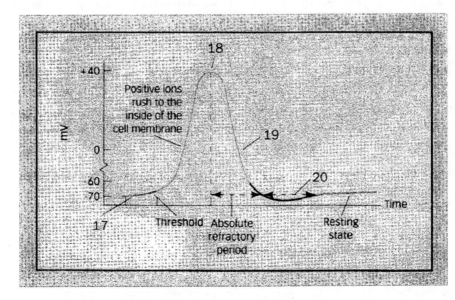

17. _____

18. _____

19. _____

20. _____

Practice Test

Circle the letter that corresponds to the *best* alternative for each of the following items.   Read each alternative carefully.   The answers are presented at the end of this study guide chapter.   Be sure to learn *why* each correct alternative is better than the others

1.   A common question asked by psychologists who adopt an evolutionary perspective is:
a.   How will I survive over generations?
b.   Why does a given behavior survive over generations?
c.   Which physiological and/or biological structures developed over generations?
d.   What role does a given structure or behavior play in survival and adaptation?

2.   Which of the following is least characteristic of a behavioral neuroscientist?
a.   interested in discovering the functional contributions of each brain structure
b.   likely to come from any of several disciplines, including psychology, biology, and medicine
c.   interested in researching ways in which the brain, as well as the rest of the nervous system, is influenced by changes in diet, use of psychoactive drugs, and learning.
d.   All of the above are appropriate descriptions of behavioral neuroscientists and their interests

3.   Environmental feature is to specialized cell as ___ is to ___.
a.   vision; audition
b.   space suit; toxin
c.   stimulus; receptor
d.   atmosphere; ambiance

4.   An important step between the sensing of raw stimulus information and responding to it is:
a.   positioning limbs for responding.
b.   processing the information for meaning.
c.   ignoring other raw stimulus information.
d.   focusing on the raw stimulus information.

5.   Quite literally, the central nervous system (CNS) is that portion of the larger nervous system that is located in the center of your body.   The peripheral nervous system (PNS) constitutes the remainder of the larger system.   The two major divisions of the PNS are:
a.   the brain and the spinal cord.
b.   the somatic and the autonomic.
c.   the forebrain and the hindbrain.
d.   the autonomic and the parasympathetic.

6.   The autonomic nervous system may be considered as operating on a continuum as its components are antagonistic.   That is, one component of the autonomic nervous system opposes the other for each function the system serves.   These components are known as:
a.   extremes.
b.   neurons and glands, respectively.
c.   the left-hand, and right-hand systems.
d.   the sympathetic and parasympathetic systems.

7.   Interneurons are cells:
a.   situated in the spinal cord between sensory and motor cells.
b.   that support the brain, and are technically not neurons at all.
c.   that enter neurons in order to promote more efficient activity.
d.   that die off after helping the brain turn over new cells during adolescence.

8. Psychologists are interested in the endocrine system because it impacts the nervous system. In some ways, its chemicals, ___, are analogous to neurotransmitters in that they are released from one location and influence another.
   a. hormones
   b. pheromones
   c. neuropeptides
   d. neuromodulators

9. Charles Scott Sherrington's discovery that a dog's reflex took too long:
   a. confirmed what cat lovers knew all along.
   b. was instrumental in learning about neural impulses.
   c. was exaggerated by the fact that his stopwatch was broken.
   d. occurred in the context of a brain stimulation experiment in the mid-1800s.

10. In general, signals are received by ___ and sent out by ___.
   a. axons; cell bodies.
   b. nodes of Ranvier; myelin.
   c. dendrites; terminal buttons.
   d. dendrites; nodes of Ranvier.

11. Glia cells comprise the myelin associated with about 50 percent of nerve cells. An interesting characteristic of the myelin sheath is that it has gaps, or ___, that break up the fatty covering of the axon.
   a. skips.
   b. dendrites.
   c. glia gaps.
   d. nodes of Ranvier.

12. Presynaptic cells are able to communicate with postsynaptic cells because of ___ that cross(es) the microscopic cleft that separates them.
   a. ions.
   b. myelin.
   c. anions.
   d. neurotransmitters.

13. After a signal crosses a synapse, it is important to clear the gap immediately to prepare for the next signal. This occurs in one of two ways:
   a. slashing and burning.
   b. flushing and rushing.
   c. breakdown and reuptake.
   d. All of the above are ways in which residual transmitter material is removed from the cleft.

14. Psychoactive drugs are those that impact the cells in the central nervous system. These drugs fall into two main categories: ___, that enhance the operation of a given transmitter, and ___ that block the action of a given transmitter.
   a. agonists; antagonists
   b. antagonists; agonists
   c. promoters; blockers
   d. helpers; blockers

15. Neurotransmitter is to neuromodulator as ___ is to ___.
   a. fast; local
   b. local; long
   c. widespread; fast
   d. long; widespread

16. When it is at its resting state, a nerve cell:
    a. has no charge.
    b. has a slight positive charge.
    c. has a relatively strong negative charge.
    d. None of the above; cells do not have charges, batteries do.

17. Depolarizing is to ___ as hyperpolarizing is to ___.
    a. negative; positive
    b. positive; negative
    c. less negative; more negative
    d. more negative; less negative

18. During the relative refractory period, a nerve cell is:
    a. hyperpolarized.
    b. merely depolarizing.
    c. not involved in ion exchange.
    d. at the peak in the course of its action potential.

19. If you were to suffer a closed head injury in an automobile accident, you would likely see a:
    a. Neuropsychologist
    b. Behavioral Geneticist
    c. Behavioral Neuroscientist
    d. Magnetic Neuroendocrinologist

20. The stories of "Tan" and Phineas Gage are:
    a. too poorly documented to be of lasting value.
    b. examples of the case study method for gathering information.
    c. entertaining ways of remembering some of the complex information on the brain.
    d. mere myths, but have nevertheless served to stimulate interest in brain functioning.

21. Brain structure is to brain activity as ___ is to ___.
    a. MRI; PET
    b. fMRI; MRI
    c. fMRI; CT/CAT
    d. EEG; CT/CAT

22. The hindbrain is, from an evolutionary perspective, the oldest portion of the brain. It makes sense, then, that this portion of the brain includes the structure that controls breathing, swallowing, and blood circulation. The structure that serves these functions is called the:
    a. pons.
    b. tectum.
    c. medulla.
    d. hippocampus.

23. If you accidentally drift, while driving a car, into the center section of a road or onto the shoulder of the road, you will likely be startled by the sound of your tires rolling on a different texture and making a lot of noise. The ___ is responsible for the startle response bringing you to full attention.
    a. sound of the road
    b. reticular formation
    c. ventromedial hypothalamus
    d. formation of the surface of the road

24. The limbic system regulates:
    a. the arms and legs.
    b. several branches of the PNS.
    c. heartbeat, respiration, and other vital activities.
    d. emotions and motivated behaviors including hunger, thirst, and aggression.

25. The thalamus is sometimes called a sensory switchboard because it:
    a. integrates and relays incoming information.
    b. resembles the appearance of an old time phone station.
    c. contains cells that convert raw stimulus information into neural signals.
    d. switches off and on, to conserve metabolic energy, rather than working constantly.

26. Phylogenetically newer brains are ___ than prehistoric brains.
    a. larger, in absolute terms
    b. smaller, in absolute terms
    c. the same size, in relative terms
    d. more wrinkled and crumpled on the surface

27. By selectively destroying or stimulating the tissue in living brains, researchers have:
    a. developed maps of the cortex.
    b. determined which parts we actually need.
    c. effectively discovered everything there is to know about the brain.
    d. None of the above. You cannot gain access to brain tissue without killing it.

28. Aphasia is to ___ as apraxia is to ___.
    a. vertebrate; invertebrate
    b. communication; nonverbal skills
    c. central nervous system; peripheral nervous system
    d. treatable with psychoactive drugs; incurable deficit of the brain

29. The split brain operation:
    a. was used to treat Phineas Gage after his accident.
    b. is a common procedure for treating migraine headaches.
    c. produces baffling results because brains continue to work normally in spite of tissue damage.
    d. affects dramatically the capacity for the two cerebral hemispheres to communicate with each other.

30. Which of the following is an example of functional asymmetry?
    a. Mean cell densities differ between hemispheres.
    b. The left hemisphere is more involved in speech, the right in spatial abilities.
    c. The surface anatomies of the left and right cerebral hemispheres are different.
    d. The motor strip of each respective hemisphere controls the behavior of the opposite side.

Answers to Labeling Exercises

1. Central Nervous System (CNS)
2. Interneurons
3. Autonomic Division
4. Sensory Nerves
5. Sympathetic System
6. Corpus Callosum
7. Cerebral Cortex
8. Pituitary Gland
9. Medulla
10. Cerebellum
11. Cell Body
12. Axon Hillock
13. Nodes of Ranvier
14. Dendrites
15. Terminal Buttons
16. Axon
17. Resting State
18. Action Potential
19. Positive Ions Being Pumped Out
20. Relative Refractory Period

Answers to Practice Test Questions

1. d. Psychologists are interested in behavior. Those who adopt the evolutionary perspective consider behavior as a function of the brain and biological structures that give rise to it.
2. d. Behavioral neuroscientists are interested in studying brain-behavior relationships. Work in this broad area of inquiry is done by researchers from several disciplines, and includes focus on a host of issues ranging from the effects of chemical agents on the nervous system to the ways in which the system changes as a function of learning.
3. c. The sensing process involves receiving stimulus information from the environment through receptors that have evolved to receive specific information—e.g., taste, touch.
4. b. Before any activity can transpire in response to a sensory experience, the information has to be processed.
5. b. The PNS may be further divided into the somatic and autonomic nervous systems.
6. d. The autonomic nervous system is comprised of the sympathetic and parasympathetic nervous systems.
7. a. Interneurons are located in the gray matter of the spinal cord and transfer signaling from sensory fibers to motor fibers or up the spinal cord to the brain.
8. a. Hormones are the chemicals of communication within the endocrine system.
9. b. Sherrington's discovery expanded on Ramón y Cajal's discovery of neurons being discrete units by adding that signals had to be transmitted from one cell to another for an impulse to travel through the nervous system.
10. c. Usually nerve signals are received by dendrites, processed in the cell body, and sent out through the terminal buttons.
11. d. The gaps between the glia cells that make up the myelin sheath are called nodes of Ranvier.
12. d. Neurotransmitters bridge the synaptic gaps that adjoin two neurons.
13. c. Depending on their type, neurotransmitters are either broken down or taken back into the presynaptic cells through a process called reuptake.
14. a. Agonists enhance the operation of a given transmitter, while antagonists block the action of a given transmitter.
15. b. Neurotransmitters are local, fast acting chemicals. Neuromodulators are longer lasting and cover more widespread regions.
16. c. At resting most nerve cells have net negative charges of approximately –70 millivolts.
17. c. As a cell depolarizes (becomes less polarized), it loses its negative charge. When a cell is hyperpolarized (hyper- is a prefix that means *more* or *excessive*) it has a stronger negative charge than it has when it is at its resting state.
18. a. During the relative refractory period, when it is difficult to get the neuron to fire, the cell's charge has dipped below its normal resting potential.
19. a. Neuropsychologists work primarily in human clinical settings and are trained to determine the characteristics of brain injuries and their resulting effects on adaptive behavior.
20. b. These case study examples are both key components to psychology's prehistory.
21. a. The standard MRI is used to gain structural information about the brain; PET tells researchers about the functional activity of the brain.
22. c. The medulla regulates these. Also it monitors blood chemistry and other survival promoting functions.
23. b. Before you have a chance to appraise what has happened, your reticular formation activates your brain.
24. d. The limbic system is a network of subcortical brain structures that regulates a variety of emotions and behaviors.
25. a. The thalamus receives incoming information and directs it to the cerebral cortex.
26. d. The wrinkled and crumpled appearance is the result of *convolutions* in the cortical layer of the brain. Effectively, the convolutions permit more cerebral mass to be contained within the skull. By analogy, you can put more notebook paper in a water glass if you wad it up.
27. a. The early surgical approaches to studying the brain were effective in mapping its functions.
28. b. Aphasias are deficits in communication, while apraxias are nonverbal deficits.
29. d. The split brain operation involves the severing of the corpus callosum, a bundle of fibers that connects the left and right cerebral hemispheres.
30. c. Functional asymmetry refers to differences based on what the two sides *do*. The left hemisphere is more involved in speech, the right in spatial abilities.

Key Vocabulary Terms: Use the following list to write definitions *in your own words* for each of the key terms from the chapter. Translating the terms into language that is comfortable and familiar for you will facilitate your learning. For further study of these terms, go to the companion web site for the text book where you will find electronic flash cards that you may use to test your vocabulary.

evolutionary perspective

natural selection

stimulus

receptors

central nervous system

peripheral nervous system

neurons

somatic division

afferent (sensory) nerves

efferent (motor) nerves

autonomic division

sympathetic division

parasympathetic division

homeostasis

reflex

hindbrain

medulla

pons

cerebellum

cranial nerves

midbrain

reticular formation

forebrain

corpus callosum

subcortical structures

cerebral cortex (cerebrum)

limbic system

thalamus

stroke

stereotaxic instrument

electroencephalograph (EEG)

positron emission tomography (PET)

computerized axial tomography (CT or CAT)

magnetic resonance imaging (MRI)

functional magnetic resonance imaging (fMRI)

dendrite

soma

axon

terminal buttons

myelin sheath

glia cell

nodes of Ranvier

multiple sclerosis

ataxia

synapse

neurotransmitters

synaptic vesicles

reuptake

agonist

antagonist

neuromodulators

opioid peptides

substance P

ions

resting state

depolarization

hyperpolarization

action potential

refractory period

brain asymmetries

aphasia

apraxia

endocrine system

hormones

pituitary gland

Tip for Success: Time Management

The Road Is Paved with Good Intentions

Goal setting was the topic in the first *Tip for Success* section. Another topic that is central to being successful is time management. Time management and goal setting go hand in hand. You may have noticed that the concept of time was mentioned in the section on goal setting. That was because it is not enough to have good intentions. If you want to be successful, you have to use your time to work toward achieving those intentions. Similarly, making yourself aware of time with clocks and calendars is of little value if you do not have goals. This section will focus on ways you can make the most of *your time*.

There Is Plenty of Time

That is right, there is plenty of time. Take a few moments to do the following thought exercise. Pick a task you wanted to do, but then used time as an excuse for not having done it. Now, imagine you are back in the setting for completing that task and assign a value to the task. Depending on the task, you may have to increase the value. Try setting the value at: $5...$50...$1,000...$1 Million...your life! A familiar saying goes, where there is a will, there is a way. If you want to do something badly enough, you can find the time just as you can find the resources.

The issue, then, is assigning priorities to the things you do, bearing in mind that you will need time to accomplish each of your goals, and using your time to work on your goals. You have probably heard someone say, "time is money." Consider this: there are 168 hours in a week. It does not matter which side of town people grow up on, how ambitious or lazy they are, who does their hair, or what kind of car they drive, everyone gets the same allocation of this priceless commodity. It is how people invest the commodity that determines their success.

If you require eight hours of sleep per night, then your 168 hours are down to 112. If you need more than eight hours, or like to sleep late on weekends, reduce the number accordingly. Next, subtract the number of hours you need to spend in school, preparing for classes (plan 2-4 hours outside of class for every hour spent in class) at work, eating, and so forth. How much time do you need to travel from one place to the next throughout the course of the week? Next, factor in time for exercising, reading, quiet reflection, attending to personal needs, doing laundry... The remainder is all you get for everything else you like to do: social commitments, hobbies, shopping, hanging out, or whatever. How you use *your time* is directly related to how successful you are at meeting the goals you set for yourself. Successful goal attainment will make you healthier, happier, and more likely to get exciting opportunities in the future.

Know Your Priorities

Being a student is costly. If you divide the cost of tuition at your school by the number of hours you are taking, you may be surprised at what it costs per hour for you to be enrolled. Given the costs, plus the fact that your education will determine, in part, how meaningful your life will be, it makes sense to make the most of your investment. Do not schedule appointments during your classes. If you do, you are telling yourself and others that there are things that are more important to you than planning with your future in mind. Using appointments and other excuses for missing class is a pet peeve for most professors.

Even though the hours you designate for studying are somewhat flexible, they deserve the same priority as your classes. Can you make the most of your investment in a class if you do not prepare for it? Do not allow a part-time job, your roommate's sudden need for a ride to the airport, or whatever, to prevent you from making the most of your education.

Forget About Time

Have you ever noticed what happens when you got a chance to talk with an old friend, were engrossed in a good book or movie, or got caught up in a game or working on a hobby? *Time flies*. How about the last half-hour before you get off work, when you are waiting for a call, or when you are stuck in traffic? *Time stands still*. How can both of these pearls of folk wisdom be right? The answer lies in how one's attention is focused. Time races away or stalls endlessly depending on what you are doing, and it is almost always at the wrong pace, right? Wrong. Time knows only one pace, no matter how you measure it. Worrying about time will merely serve to distract you from progress toward your goals. Focus on your goals; time will take care of itself. Now, it is usually helpful to work in designated units of time, so do not trade your watch for a sundial. But do not be a slave to your watch either.

Put Your Schedule Under a Time Microscope

It is important to study the ways you use your time. In academia there are regular opportunities to reorganize your schedule and use of time. In addition to taking advantage of the obvious opportunities at the beginning and end of each term, try to examine your efficiency at the middle of the term. You already have the resources you need to determine whether you are using your time effectively and efficiently. The table at the end of this section may be photocopied to do the exercise that is described below.

Photocopy the table at the end of this section, or make your own table. You will need enough copies to cover one week. Each cell corresponds to a 15-minute period in the day. Next, carry each day's chart with you and fill it out as accurately as possible. Write enough information in the cells that you will know how to figure out what you did at a given time. If you continue doing something through more than one block of time, simply draw an arrow to indicate continuation of the last activity. Do this for a week, then study the things you did and compare them with what you wish you had done. Assuming there is room for improvement, reread your list of goals and use your notes to plan a schedule for the next week. Carry each day's schedule with you, attending to whether the times you designated are appropriate for meeting your goals. Adjust your schedule as necessary to ensure that you are allowing for all the things you need and want to do.

If you are already fairly organized, challenge yourself by estimating how you will spend each block of time in the coming week. If you get close, congratulations! You are already aware of the advantages of keeping a schedule. If you do not get as close as you had hoped to, this exercise may help you find the stumbling blocks in your schedule. Repeat this process as often as it is helpful in getting you on track toward meeting your goals.

Threats to *Your Time*

It is important to always remember that the time you spend is yours. Sure, you have obligations, unexpected things come up, and there are occasions when you will not feel like you are in charge of how you are spending your time. Sometimes it is necessary to realize that even though you may not enjoy what you are doing, the activity may still be linked to goal attainment. Your time should always be spent in ways that are consistent with your goals, be they academic- or leisure-related. If you wonder whether you should be engaging in a given behavior, ask yourself whether you will be glad to have spent your time that way the next day...next month...in five years. It is surprising that we sometimes do things that seem really important at the moment, but thoughtful reflection would tell us to do something different.

The following list provides suggestions for combating common threats to effective use of *your time*. You may have different challenges to your schedule, or different solutions to the problems. What is important is that you give thought to making the most of every moment you get. Another adage, *time marches on*, reflects the importance of spending time wisely, for once a moment has passed, one cannot have it to spend differently.

1) **Know When You Are at Your Best.** Timing matters. Do you think more clearly after a good night's rest, or after you have been awake all day? If you are able to concentrate better in the morning, that is when you should study. If it takes 3 hours for your brain to begin working each day, you may be better off setting aside study time in the early afternoon. It is not always possible to study or work when your mind is operating at peak

efficiency. However, if you choose to study at times when you are better able to concentrate, your learning will be both more efficient and longer lasting.

2) **Save the Best for Last.** The Premack Principle, discovered by psychologist David Premack, suggests that more rewarding activities may be used to reinforce less rewarding activities (see Chapter 5, page 204 for more thorough coverage of the Premack Principle). Most people are familiar with that concept, even if they have never heard of the principle. For example, have you ever been told you can do something you want to do badly only *after* you do a household chore? It was effective, wasn't it? Use the principle on yourself for most everything you do. If you have a long list of things to study, start with the homework you are *least* excited about. If you need some incentive to make it through a set of responsibilities, establish a reward structure for yourself that will encourage you to work.

3) **Use Idle Time.** At any moment you may have to wait on someone or something for an undetermined amount of time. Waiting to meet with someone for an appointment, when your transportation plans are unexpectedly delayed, at a busy restaurant or cafeteria, or in a number of other circumstances is annoying. What is more, it chips away at your precious time. Take charge of how you use time by having something to do at any given moment. You will want to prepare according to how far from home base you will be. Bring a book (or more) with you when you travel in case your travel arrangements are altered. If you are headed to meet with an advisor, or your dentist, bring something that you can start and stop working on easily.

4) **Just Say No.** This is much easier said than done. However, if you consider each decision you make in terms of the goals you are striving to meet, it should be clear whether it is in your best interest to do something someone else asks of you. While they may be disappointed, most people will respect your need to protect time for working on your goals. The more clearly defined your goals are, the better able you will be to help others understand why you cannot always take on additional responsibilities.

5) **Be Clear About How You Use Your Time.** Sometimes the most respectful people will accidentally interrupt your activity because they do not realize *when* you are busy. Good communication can go a long way toward helping protect your time against disruptions, even if those disruptions are things that you would welcome at other times. Let people know when you are studying, whether by telling them which times are off limits, by hanging a "Do Not Disturb" sign on your door, or by donning a hat or jacket that acts as a signal.

6) **Monitor Your Effectiveness.** Sometimes in spite of good planning, you are unable to be as productive as you need to be. Sometimes you are plenty able to be productive, but allow yourself to get lazy. What would you pay yourself for the efforts you are exerting? Can you remember what you just read a few minutes ago? If the answer is no, you may want to refer to your goals list for something else you can do more effectively until you are better focused.

7) **Monitor Your Efficiency.** Perhaps you are plenty effective, but are not working as efficiently as you could be. Are you taking shortcuts where and when you should? Are you bogging yourself down by focusing too much on the details? In addition to asking yourself these few questions periodically, try this idea. Time yourself when reading a page from your textbook. As you read subsequent pages, check every once in a while to make sure you are not slowing down.

8) **Take One More Step.** Often when you are finishing a work session you have the necessary focus and additional energy to do a little more. Just as making one extra payment annually on a home loan will greatly reduce the cost of the mortgage, so too will taking one more step toward your goals when you have reached a targeted stopping point.

9) **Keep Your Word.** Some very important deals are sealed with nothing other than a handshake and a promise. Promises should be taken seriously, and should not be violated. Make promises to yourself and others as appropriate, and keep them. Do not let yourself or others down by failing to keep your word. If you adopt this attitude when making promises, they will serve as powerful motivators for striving toward your goals.

10) Don't Take Any Excuses. It is bad enough when someone else makes a promise and then fails to keep her or his word. If there is anything that is worse, it is when one lets oneself down. If you stick to your schedule as if it were a promise, you will surely be more productive and feel good about it.

Not a Paradox

It may seem contradictory that filling your schedule is the key to having enough time for relaxing, or whatever else you like to do. Many people find at the end of an evening, long weekend, or semester break, that somehow they failed to do all the work they had intended to do *and* they did not do all the other activities they had planned either. The fact is that if we do not have our time scheduled, it is easy to put off getting started on anything. As a result, too many hours get whiled away. By scheduling in everything that is important to you, you can be sure to have time for doing it. Whether its writing two pages on a term paper, playing tennis, listening to music, or propping your feet up in front of the TV, scheduling time for it and sticking to your schedule is the only way you will get it done.

Poor Time Management Is Linked to Stress

When we run out of time for completing responsibilities, we experience stress. While some stress may be helpful in motivating activity, too much stress can inhibit your ability to perform your very best. Often the sources of stress are linked to poor time management. It is clear to see that if you do not manage time effectively and experience stress as a result, it will become increasingly difficult to meet your goals, which, in turn, will create more stress. This cycle can negatively impact your attitude, behavior, and physical wellness. It is remarkable that poor time management can have such profound effects on these central issues in your life. If you desire to be happy, productive, and healthy, you will want to learn to take control of your time.

You Are Not Alone

Survey a group of successful people about the keys to their successes. Whether they are leaders in the student body, college professors, local business people, clergy, or others you may define as successful, each of them will identify the need to manage time wisely. Issues surrounding the ways that people use time are pervasive in our society. The company we keep and the people we look up to will influence us. Songs, books and plays, special seminars for business employees, and sections in bookstores are a few examples of places and ways we are exposed to comments on the usage of time.

Model your lifestyle after those who fit your definition of success. If you aspire to be a leader, but are acting like someone who is destined for a life of minimum wage jobs, something is awry. Do whatever it takes to learn to make the most of your time.

Time Microscope

Day:		Date:	
AM		PM	
Midnight		**Noon**	
12:15		12:15	
12:30		12:30	
12:45		12:45	
1:00		1:00	
1:15		1:15	
1:30		1:30	
1:45		1:45	
2:00		2:00	
2:15		2:15	
2:30		2:30	
2:45		2:45	
3:00		3:00	
3:15		3:15	
3:30		3:30	
3:45		3:45	
4:00		4:00	
4:15		4:15	
4:30		4:30	
4:45		4:45	
5:00		5:00	
5:15		5:15	
5:30		5:30	
5:45		5:45	
6:00		6:00	
6:15		6:15	
6:30		6:30	
6:45		6:45	
7:00		7:00	
7:15		7:15	
7:30		7:30	
7:45		7:45	
8:00		8:00	
8:15		8:15	
8:30		8:30	
8:45		8:45	
9:00		9:00	
9:15		9:15	
9:30		9:30	
9:45		9:45	
10:00		10:00	
10:15		10:15	
10:30		10:30	
10:45		10:45	
11:00		11:00	
11:15		11:15	
11:30		11:30	
11:45		11:45	

CHAPTER 3

Sensation and Perception

Do You Know?

Do you know that the subtractive color process is the one with which painters work when blending paints to create subtle hue differences in the objects of their attention? Because of this, subtractive color primaries are sometimes referred to as pigment or artists' primaries. Interestingly, subtractive colors can be used in combination with the Gestalt principle of closure to create the perception of continuous, blended color images using a field of small ink dots. A well-known example of this combination was created by French Neo-Impressionist painter Georges Seurat (1859-1891).

Seurat's famous painting, "A Sunday on La Grande Jatte-1884," created a dramatic effect on a canvas that now hangs in the Chicago Art Institute's gallery. You can view a reproduction of the painting over the Internet by linking to the Art Institute's Website (http://www.artic.edu/AA_Impressionist/pages/IMP_7.shtml). You are familiar with the effect, however, even if you have not seen the painting or a reproduction of it. The phenomenon Seurat pioneered by placing small dots of color on canvas is the same phenomenon that gives rise to the perception of whole images one experiences when viewing a video screen (e.g., television or computer) or reproduced images in books, magazines, and posters. Indeed, the pigment primaries, cyan, magenta, and yellow, plus black are used in the same way by common desktop printers to create the same effect. The concept of graphic resolution concerns the number of dots represented per standard unit (i.e., dots per inch, or dpi), whether in the form of pixels on a monitor or as specs of ink on paper. Examine mass-printed images with a magnifying glass and you'll see for yourself how subtractive color and the principle of closure interact to create images that appear convincingly uninterrupted.

Notes from Class and the Textbook

Use the space provided in this outline to record notes from the textbook as well as from class lectures and discussion. Questions related to the *Psychological Detective, Hands On, Myth or Science,* and *Study Tip* sections in the text have been presented in the outline; use the associated space to respond to the questions and to record your own comments about the issues.

Make flash cards of all the marginal definitions in the chapter (or book for that matter). Test yourself frequently on how well you can recall the definitions of key terms.

I. Sensation, Perception, and Psychophysics

    A. Sensation and Perception

    B. Psychophysics

    C. Thresholds

II. Sensory Systems

    A. Vision

Why is a 'red' rose everything but red?

Point your Web browser at the textbook's Web page to see Live!Psych module 3.1

    1.   How We See: The Visual System

Why are people not constantly distracted by the flashing on and off of their visual worlds when they blink?

    2.   The Visual Pathway

    3.   The Visual Receptors

Why should you expect your visual acuity to suffer when an item of interest is not in the center of your field of vision?

    4. Theories of Color Vision

How could you determine whether an animal can differentiate colors?

        5. Color Deficiencies

   B. Audition (Hearing)

       1.   What We Hear: The Auditory Stimulus

       2.   How We Hear: The Auditory System

Point your Web browser at the textbook's Web page to see Live!Psych module 3.2

       3.   Hearing Disorders

   C. The Chemical Senses: Taste and Smell

       1.   Taste (Gustation)

          a.   What We Taste: The Gustatory Stimulus

          b.   How We Taste: The Gustatory System

How, using only four basic tastes, can we explain the wide variety of tastes we are able to experience?

2. Smell (Olfaction)

    a. What We Smell: The Olfactory Stimulus

    b. How We Smell: The Olfactory System

Is there a relationship between the quality of smell in a work environment and the degree to which workers are productive?

3. The Interaction of Smell and Taste

D. Somatosensory Systems

1. Vestibular Sense

2. Kinesthetic Sense

3. The Cutaneous Senses

    a. Pain

Work with four other students, with each member of the group being assigned to one of the five senses. Provide brief overviews for one another on the senses.

III. Perception

    A. Motivation and Attention

        1.   Motivational Influences

        2.   Attention

Enlist two friends to create a dichotic listening task for you by situating themselves on each side of you and reading different passages of text at the same time. After 20-30 seconds of the task, write down as much as you can recall from what both people read. Study your pattern of recall; did you recall content mainly from one passage, the other, or a mixture of both? Rotate positions with your friends and repeat the experience until each of you has participated in the task. How do your patterns of recall compare with one another?

    B. Basic Perceptual Abilities: Patterns and Constancies

        1.   Pattern Perception

        2.   Perceptual Constancies

            a.   Shape Constancy

            b.   Size Constancy

        3. Depth Perception

4. Binocular Cues

Point your Web browser at the textbook's Web page to see Live!Psych module 3.3

5. Monocular Cues

C. Gestalt Principles of Perceptual Organization

Point your Web browser at the textbook's Web page to see Live!Psych module 3.4

1. Figure and Ground

2. Principles of Grouping

Draw your own pictures to represent the Gestalt principles of grouping.

D. Perception of Movement

Create a circumstance to experience the autokinetic effect. How long did it take to experience the phenomenon? Did the light appear to move as was anticipated in your textbook? How would you explain the effect to someone who has not studied the physiology of the eye?

E. Perceptual Hypotheses and Illusions

Explain why the grass really appears greener on the other side of the fence.

Point your Web browser at the textbook's Web page to see Live!Psych module 3.5

Create an outline summary of the basic perceptual abilities (patterns and constancies).

F. Contemporary Issues and Findings in Perception Research

     1.   Parallel Processing, Visual Search, and the Application of Basic Perceptual Research

     2.   Perception is Affected by Social Context

What do contextual stimuli contribute to our perceptual experiences?

IV. Paranormal Phenomena

     A. Skeptical Scientists

     B. A Believing Public

       1. A Final Word

Learning Objectives

After you have studied the chapter, you should be able to respond to the following statements and questions to convey your understanding of the material.

1. Describe the systems that receive sensory information about vision, hearing, taste, smell, body position, and movement. What do these systems have in common? How are they different?

2. How are the processes of sensation and perception related? What does each process contribute to one's ability to interact with the world?

3. How is perception affected by influences such as motivation and attention?

4. What roles do coincidences and chance occurrences play in beliefs about the paranormal?

Labeling Exercises

It is helpful when learning the information from this chapter to study how some of the terms are used in the contexts of figures. Having studied the chapter you should be able to fill in the missing information. The answers are given at the end of the chapter.

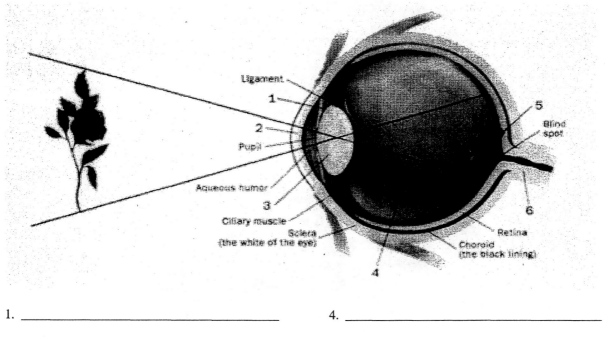

1. _____   4. _____

2. _____   5. _____

3. _____   6. _____

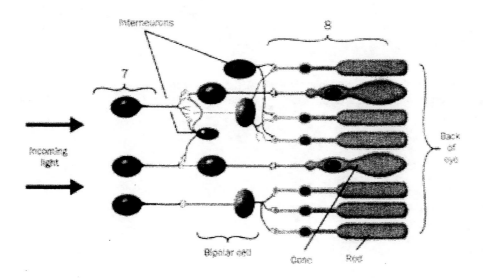

7. _____   8. _____

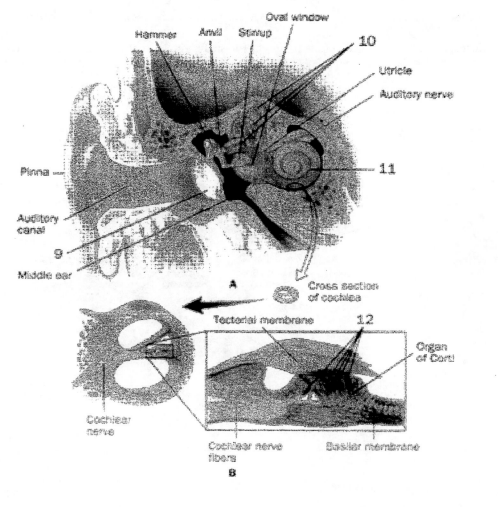

Figure labels (as shown): Hammer, Anvil, Stirrup, Oval window, 10, Utricle, Auditory nerve, 11, Pinna, Auditory canal, 9, Middle ear, A, Cross section of cochlea, Tectorial membrane, 12, Organ of Corti, Cochlear nerve, Cochlear nerve fibers, Basilar membrane, B

9. _____   11. _____

10. _____   12. _____

Practice Test

Circle the letter that corresponds to the ***best*** alternative for each of the following items.   Read each alternative carefully.   The answers are presented at the end of this study guide chapter.   Be sure to learn *why* each correct alternative is better than the others

1. Sensation is to perception as ___ is to ___.
    a. left brain; right brain
    b. right brain; left brain
    c. seeing something red; identifying something as an apple
    d. identifying something as an apple; seeing something red

2. A common feature of the basic sensory processes in that they:
    a. involve transduction.
    b. all work the same way.
    c. were each evolved from a common process.
    d. are all involved in sensing stimuli at a distance.

3. Frank is unaware that he is wearing too much cologne. His lack of awareness is probably due to:
   a. adaptation.
   b. transduction.
   c. Weber's law.
   d. the just noticeable difference (jnd) for olfaction.

4. An absolute threshold is:
   a. a dangerous level of sensory stimulation.
   b. the largest amount of stimulation a person can perceive.
   c. the minimum amount of energy required for conscious recognition.
   d. the smallest amount of stimulation that must be added or subtracted to be able to notice the difference 50 percent of the time.

5. ___ suggests that the threshold varies with the nature of the stimulus (signal) and background stimulation.
   a. Weber
   b. The jnd
   c. Experience
   d. Signal detection theory

6. Wavelength is to ___ as amplitude is to ___.
   a. brightness; color
   b. color; brightness
   c. saturation; purity
   d. brightness; intensity

7. The color of a car occurs as a function of:
   a. amplitude.
   b. saturation.
   c. radiant light.
   d. reflected light.

8. Chris is a theater technician. Her job involves manipulating the gels that go between light bulbs and the objects they illuminate on stage. A psychologist might say her job is:
   a. boring.
   b. dangerous.
   c. to manipulate radiant light.
   d. to attend to sources of reflected light.

9. When you mix primary paints together you yield a dark, yucky color. Mixing light primaries, however, produces white light. The processes underlying these differences are called ___ and ___, respectively.
   a. additive; subtractive
   b. subtractive; additive
   c. visual art; performing art
   d. performing art; visual art

10. Paintings by Ruby reveal:
    a. that elephants can see in color.
    b. that people well into their 80s can learn to mix paints and match colors on a canvas.
    c. radiant vistas typically involving sunsets and either rocky terrain or bodies of water.
    d. All of the above may be inferred or supported directly based on Ruby's paintings.

11. The photoreceptor cells, rods and cones, are:
    a. distributed equally throughout the retina.
    b. disproportionately located outside the retina.
    c. in the back of the retina, pointing away from the cornea.
    d. in the front of the retinal layer, positioned to receive light as it comes though the lens.

12. Color afterimages, such as seeing blue dots for awhile after someone takes your picture with a camera and a flash, are (were) explained well by:
    a. the fovea.
    b. the trichromatic theory.
    c. the opponent-process theory.
    d. Gestalt psychologists in the 1920s.

13. Which of the following was *not* mentioned in the text as a variety of color deficiency?
    a. dichromat
    b. achromatosis
    c. monochromat
    d. anomalous trichromat

14. In vision, the wave characteristic, *complexity,* corresponds to the saturation level of the hue. What does complexity correspond to in audition?
    a. hertz (Hz)
    b. decibels (db)
    c. timbre
    d. none of the above

15. In order to hear frequencies at the extremes of our range of sensitivity (20-20,000 Hz), the amplitude of the wave needs to be:
    a. higher.
    b. significantly lower.
    c. proportional to the wave's length.
    d. executed in the following sequence: elbow, elbow, wrist, wrist

16. In audition, changes in air pressure (sound waves) are translated into fluid waves when the *stirrup* causes movement of the:
    a. ossicles.
    b. basilar membrane.
    c. tectorial membrane.
    d. oval window of the cochlea.

17. Rock concert is to ear wax as ___ is to ___.
    a. gross; great
    b. soft; loud
    c. central deafness; sensorineural deafness
    d. sensorineural deafness; conduction deafness

18. Microvilli are:
    a. hairs that project from taste receptors.
    b. small clusters of houses in rural areas.
    c. the name for the hair cells on the basilar membrane.
    d. the small gaps between myelin cells on the auditory nerve.

19. When we smell, airborne particles come in contact with our ___, which, in turn, send signals into the CNS.
    a. nasal mucus
    b. olfactory bulbs
    c. thalamic nuclei
    d. olfactory epithelium

20. Inner ear is to muscles and joints as ___ is to ___.
    a. audition; kinesthesia
    b. aching; hearing
    c. kinesthetic sense; vestibular sense
    d. vestibular sense; kinesthetic sense

21. The ability to process more than one source of stimulation at the same time is called:
    a. synesthesia.
    b. schizophrenia.
    c. divided attention.
    d. paranormal perception.

22. ___ is the phenomenon that permits you to recognize a door as a door, even when you see it from its edge.
    a. Feature detection
    b. Shape constancy
    c. Binocular disparity
    d. Good continuation and direction

23. Depth perception, or the ability to see our world three-dimensionally, involves all *but* which of the following:
    a. binocular cues
    b. monocular cues
    c. binocular disparity
    d. retino-depth detectors

24. Which of the following grouping principles is responsible for your ability to fill in gaps in your visual world?
    a. closure
    b. proximity
    c. inclusiveness
    d. good continuation and direction

25. What do flashing road construction sign arrows and cartoons have in common?
    a. nothing
    b. reliance on apparent motion
    c. that only a small minority pays attention to them
    d. all of the above

26. Recall the Ebbinghaus illusion—the illusion that the perceived size of a circle in the center of a group of circles is influenced by the size of the circles that surround it. Staple & Koomen (1997) conducted an experiment using a variation on the Ebbinghaus illusion, using instead pictures of faces surrounded by faces of other objects. Which of the following produced the greatest magnitude of size contrast illusion? When the face was surrounded by:
    a. identical faces
    b. faces of people of the same gender
    c. faces of people of the different gender
    d. nonperson objects such as trucks and handbags

27. Clairvoyance, telepathy, precognition, and psychokinesis are all examples of:
    a. ESP.
    b. horse puckey.
    c. experimentally demonstrable phenomena.
    d. anomalistic psychological (or parapsychological) phenomena.

28. Which of the following, according to your textbook, is partially responsible for the fact that people commonly believe in psychic phenomena?
    a. influence by the media
    b. underestimating chance occurrences and coincidences
    c. many have had psychic experiences, or interpret their experiences as having been psychic.
    d. all of the above

Answers To Labeling Exercise

1. Iris	2. Cornea	3. Lens
4. Vitreous Humor	5. Fovea	6. Optic Nerve
7. Ganglion Cell Layer	8. Photoreceptor Layer	9. Eardrum
10. Semicircular Canals	11. Cochlea	12. Hair Cells

Practice Test Answers And Explanations

1. c. Sensation is the act of receiving stimuli from the environment; perception involves organizing and making sense of the information.
2. a. Transduction is the process of receiving stimuli and translating them into forms that can be used by the nervous system.
3. a. Adaptation is a loss of sensitivity to a stimulus by the receptors as a result of continued presentation of that stimulus.
4. c. The absolute threshold is the minimum amount of energy required for conscious detection of a stimulus 50 percent of the time.
5. d. The question in item 5 is the definition of signal detection theory.
6. b. Changes in perceived hue (or color) result from changes in wavelength whereas manipulating wave height results in shifts in intensity (or brightness).
7. d. Objects that do not emit light are sources of reflected light.
8. b. Radiant sources of light include light bulbs and the sun. By placing gels in front of a source of radiant light, one manipulates (selectively filters) the wavelength qualities of the light.
9. b. Mixing pigments is a subtractive process whereas mixing lights is additive. Note that the primaries for these processes are different.
10. a. Ruby is an elephant (see pages 99 and 100). Work with her has revealed that she chooses paint colors based upon colors in the environments in which she paints.
11. c. Interestingly, the photoreceptors point away from the front of the eye, rather than toward it.
12. c. The opponent-process theory explains the phenomenon of color afterimages.
13. b. The three types of color-deficient people are monochromats, dichromats, and anomalous trichromats.
14. c. Timbre is the acoustic property that has to do with purity of a sound wave. It is what is responsible for the difference in sound generated by two different musical instruments playing the same note.
15. a. In order to hear higher frequency waves, we need them to be of greater amplitude (i.e., louder).
16. d. As the ossicles move, the stirrup (the third middle-ear bone) causes movement of the oval window, which, in turn, sets fluid inside the cochlea into motion.
17. d. Rock concerts can cause sensorineural deafness; ear wax can cause conduction deafness.
18. a. Microvilli are the hairs that project from taste receptors.
19. d. The olfactory epithelium receives airborne molecules and transmits information to the olfactory bulbs.
20. d. The vestibular sense results from activity in the inner ear, whereas the kinesthetic sense stems from receptors in the muscles and joints.
21. c. Divided attention is the ability to process two or more sources of sensory stimulation.
22. b. *Shape constancy* permits the perception of an object's shape as constant despite changes in its retinal image.
23. d. Retino-depth detectors do not exist.
24. a. *Closure* helps us perceive incomplete visual stimuli as complete.
25. b. The illusion of movement in a stationary object is called apparent. Both examples rely on this.

26. a. The greatest effect was found when the picture of a face was surrounded by pictures of the same face.
27. d. Clairvoyance, telepathy, precognition, and psychokinesis are all examples of anomalistic psychological (or parapsychological) phenomena.
28. d. The reasons why people believe in psychic phenomena vary across individuals.

Key Vocabulary Terms

Use the following list to write definitions *in your own words* for each of the key terms from the chapter. Translating the terms into language that is comfortable and familiar for you will facilitate your learning. For further study of these terms, go to the companion Website for the textbook where you will find electronic flash cards that you may use to test your vocabulary.

sensation

perception

transduction

adaptation

Weber's law

just noticeable difference (jnd)

absolute threshold

differential threshold

signal detection theory

subliminal stimuli

wavelength

amplitude

saturation

radiant light

reflected light

accommodation

retina

bipolar cells

ganglion cells

blind spot

optic chiasm

rods

cones

fovea

trichromatic theory

opponent-process theory

color afterimage

monochromat

dichromat

audition

hertz (Hz)

decibel (db)

ossicles

oval window

basilar membrane

organ of Corti

tectorial membrane

place theory

frequency theory

conduction deafness

sensorineural deafness

central deafness

gustation

taste buds

papillae

microvilli

olfaction

vestibular sense

semicircular canals

utricle

kinesthetic sense

cutaneous sense

gate control theory

cutaneous receptors

divided attention

pattern perception

feature analysis theory

perceptual constancy

shape constancy

size constancy

depth perception

binocular cues

monocular cues

binocular disparity

figure-ground relation

proximity

similarity

good continuation

closure

apparent motion

perceptual hypothesis

perceptual illusions

visual search

extrasensory perception (ESP)

Tip for Success: Creating an Effective Study Environment

The Right Place at The Right Time

Think of *where* you would expect to go for each of the following services:
1) to get a manicure
2) to invest a large sum of money
3) to get a paint job on a valuable automobile
4) to get advice on native plants for landscaping
5) to have a delicate surgical procedure performed on you

The people who provide these services have very diverse backgrounds, but they all share at least one thing in common. Their work is done in environments that support their occupations. That is, they work in places that have conditions and resources that permit them to do their very best. Could you imagine: getting your nails done in a dark place without tables and chairs; handing your hard-earned money to someone on the street; getting your car painted outside on a windy day; going to a grocery store to determine which plants would be best for your yard; or having surgery performed on you in an old warehouse? While things might work out all right in each of those scenarios, the conditions are clearly not conducive to the services.

The principles that apply to professional services share things in common with those for establishing an effective study environment. You need the appropriate environment, tools, and access to the resources you may need if you are to make the most of your study time. Anyone would agree that beauticians, stockbrokers, autobody painters, horticulturists, and surgeons need to work in the contexts we usually associate with them. For some reason, though, perhaps because books are fairly portable, it is not uncommon to see students 'studying' in the darndest places. It is curious that students will walk right past the library en route to the busiest building on campus to study. If your goal is to socialize, why not leave the books at home?

List the last four places where you studied:

_____

_____

List four places you think would be ideal for studying:

_____

_____

Did you notice any differences? Why or why not?

_____

The Student Union Is a Great Place to Meet People

But it is a poor place to study, for exactly the same reasons. Because of schedule differences, different people pass through there at different times of the day: the environment is ever changing. Think about how goofy it would be if the professionals mentioned above were to do their same work, but to trade working places for a day. It would be more than disconcerting to hear the horticulturist talking about dirt and microorganisms in the surgery wing of a hospital. Or, what if the surgeon were on the floor of a stock exchange building, with her bright lights, instruments, and hair net, carving away on somebody? It is hard to imagine the brokers in the room attending to the changing of decimal points on the electronic tickertape.

The point is simple. Now that you have established goals, and have organized a schedule that will permit you to make the best use of your time, you need to focus on the places where you work at your most attention-demanding activity: studying. Do not be tempted to think that the portability of books means they are equally useful anywhere you might take them. The books may work equally well in a variety of places, but all they have to do is sit there. You will not work equally well in a variety of environments; find one or two places that will help you maximize learning efficiency. If you work when you should be working, and play when you should be playing, you will be much happier about both activities.

How can studying in a dedicated place help meet your academic and your leisure-time goals?

_____

_____

So Where *Should* I Study?

This may come as a shock: the library is probably the best building on your campus for studying. Think about it. It has the best collection of resources, such as books in every academic field, dictionaries, and likely also computers that can be used to find resources both on and off campus. Libraries are outstanding learning environments for other reasons, too. What comes to mind when you think of the library? Unless you have visited some mighty strange libraries, you probably think of a building that is fairly quiet, in which people work diligently and independently. There is little question concerning whether students who study in libraries are there to do homework. What about the student who sets up camp in the student union?

But, you might say, I do not need those things if I am reading novels for my literature class or working math problems. Or for some unexplainable reason, maybe you are not able to focus at the library. There are plenty of other places on your campus or in your community. What is important is that you identify a place or two that you can use to give your undivided attention (recall the passage in Chapter 3 that discussed the need to focus attention at times such as when driving in busy traffic).

List two or three places that might be good for studying that you have not yet tried.

_____

_____

Characteristics of the Designated Space

When you begin looking for a few places you can use for studying, adopt the criteria for evaluating good libraries. When you enter the context it should be immediately clear to you that you are preparing to concentrate. The place you choose should be quiet. You should have at your disposal, or bring with you, any resources necessary to make the most of your dedicated study time. The place you choose should also be well lit, and heated or cooled appropriately for your comfort needs. In short, aside from having the necessary resources, you need a place that anybody could go to and recognize as a good place to study.

The following are examples to help you get started thinking about where to study.

1) **Empty Classrooms.** Perhaps the best ones are those that you have regular class meetings in when they are not in use, but any empty classroom should be fine.

2) **Study Carrels.** These are distributed throughout the library, and perhaps in other designated spaces on campus. Study carrels can be great places to work because they limit your ability to be distracted and often provide shelving to organize your things.

3) **A Local Community Library.** If, with any regularity, your friends take you away from your studies, you no longer have a situation that is conducive to learning. Find a new one. Local libraries have many of the same characteristics as university libraries and can be great places to study. What is more, you are even less likely to be found in the public library than at your school's library.

4) **Bookstores, Coffee Shops, and Galleries.** These kinds of places are presently very trendy. If it is a business that sells drinks and snacks, but is also good for studying, the cost of a cup of coffee or a bagel is cheap in exchange for the opportunity to work there. Some businesspeople try to attract students and to maintain good study places.

Regardless of where you go, make sure it is away from distractions, including telephones and friends who do not take their homework as seriously as you do. If you have a cellular phone or pager, TURN IT OFF. You cannot possibly give your undivided attention to your academic goals if you are preoccupied with the phone, email, and the like. If someone needs to get in touch with you, they will. If you have a cellular phone or a pager, you probably also have an answering machine that will take messages for you. Let it do what it is supposed to do.

What three things are most likely to distract you during study time?

_____

_____

_____

Psychologists Study Environments

Classical conditioning (see Chapter 5) helps make an environment more or less effective for a given activity. As an environment becomes familiar, your perceptual systems begin to influence your brain in response to the environmental cues. Have you ever become suddenly hungry when you saw a restaurant advertisement or noticed the time (even though you were not hungry until then)? Environmental cues and temporal cues can influence behavior in powerful ways.

Use your knowledge of classical conditioning to your advantage. If a given context is most strongly associated, for you, with a behavior that is incompatible with focused attention on homework, avoid studying there. For example, the lounge may have many of the characteristics that are appropriate for a good study place, but you may feel compelled to turn on the TV or participate in some other distraction whenever you are there. Avoid tempting yourself. Likewise, your bedroom is designated as a place for resting; trying to study in bed will surely make you tired! Do not allow yourself to be lured into the bed with intentions of learning anything from a textbook.

The real value of identifying one or two places where you will do most of your studying has precisely to do with classical conditioning. Recall the attributes that make libraries effective for studying. That list is the result of conditioning; you have learned that libraries have certain characteristics. Your study places should serve to help you recognize immediately when you should be focusing your attention on homework.

What are some effective cues for letting you know you are in a place that is good for studying?

_____

_____

When One Is Not Enough

It is a good idea to identify two or three places where you can study. Imagine that you have scheduled time to work on your academic goals at your peak time for devoting attention, and that you have found your way to 'your' study carrel in the library. What will you do when someone else is there? What if the library is closed or exceptionally busy? Getting frustrated will only drain your energy and divert your attention from your studies. Smile and head for a quieter place.

Another good reason to have two or more designated study places is to provide some variation on long study days. You may find that you like studying in one place early in the day, but at another in the afternoon or evening. If you prefer to study in a business (e.g., coffee shop), you may need to find another location that has hours that permit you to start working earlier, or to continue later.

List Alternative Places Where You Could Study Effectively and Their Hours of Availability

Location: Time Available to You:

_____

_____

Be Mindful of Others

The previous chapter included a comment on good communication. People who are interested in doing things with you need to know when you will be available, and when you are busy. By making it clear that you will not be available until you finish your homework, people will be less inclined to interrupt you. This is especially important if you have a designated space in your room, or are known to be at a certain place when you are studying. An added bonus to communicating when you will be busy studying is that others may help protect your time.

Be aware that the best places for studying are effective because people respect them as places for quiet reflection. If you get restless, or get the urge to make a lot of noise, be courteous and leave before you ruin the environment for others. Also, avoid taking a project group from one of your classes to discuss the material in a place where people are usually quiet. You may be studying, but if your activity affects others, you are not being respectful.

CHAPTER 5

Learning

Do You Know?

Do you know that the principles of learning may be used to explain virtually all of the behaviors of you and others? Your text focuses on three important varieties of learning: classical conditioning, operant conditioning, and conditioning in the context of social cognition. For this Do You Know feature, special attention will be given to classical conditioning. However, examples of all forms of conditioning and learning are impossible to miss if you look for them in your everyday life—watch for them and begin thinking like a psychologist by identifying the key parameters that influence your and others' behaviors.

Classical conditioning principles are widely employed in the entertainment industries. One clear example concerns the use of music or other audio-visual cues to predict significant events in television and film. In the film, *Jaws*, a particular musical phrase was repeated each time a character in the movie was about to fall prey to the shark. After only a few pairings, viewers cannot help but become anxious when the music is played in scenes throughout the rest of the movie. In this case, the music is the conditioned stimulus (CS), the unconditioned stimulus is the attack, the unconditioned response is the feeling experienced after seeing a shark attack, and the conditioned response is the anxiety that is produced in anticipation of an attack when the music (CS) is played.

We have been hearing a lot about the roles that fast food restaurant restaurants may have played in creating an obesity problem in the United States. While many dismiss this notion as ridiculous, there may be value in considering the claim, especially from the perspective of conditioning and learning. Critics of fast food complain about the high amounts of fat in most of fast food menu items. Note that many of these items also use sauces and ingredients within high fat dishes, and that these sauces and ingredients have biologically significant taste properties—namely sweet and salty. One could easily argue that the paired tasting of fat and either sweet or salty (or both) flavors might well influence ones preference for the taste of fat because of its association with sweet and/or salt. If classical conditioning can be used to explain acquired anxiety to previously neutral music or other stimuli in films, is it not reasonable to think in terms of people having been conditioned to like the taste of fat because of its consistent association with biologically significant sweet and salty tastes?

Notes from Class and the Textbook

Use the space provided in this outline to record notes from the textbook as well as from class lectures and discussion. Questions related to the *Psychological Detective, Hands On, Myth or Science,* and *Study Tip* sections in the text have been presented in the outline; use the associated space to respond to the questions and to record your own comments about the issues.

I. What is Learning?

II. Classical Conditioning

    A. Basic Elements of Classical Conditioning

On page 186 in your text, the authors describe a demonstration of classical conditioning that involves popping balloons and watching people's responses. All you need for the demonstration will be several balloons and a sewing needle. If you don't have a sewing needle, a stick pin from your bulletin board will do; it is just not as dramatic. You may want to practice the demonstration before showing it to your friends. (Hint: if your balloon is under high tension, you could stick a piece of invisible tape on the balloon and run the needle through the tape.)

Think of your own examples of classical conditioning. To ensure that you understand each of the elements, be certain to identify the CS, UCS, UCR and CR. What do you notice about the qualities of the stimuli? Are the UCR and the CR similar in nature and strength? Think of examples in which the UCR and the CR are similar and others in which they are dissimilar.

B. Classical Conditioning Processes

    1. Acquisition

        a. Sequence of CS-UCS Presentation

        b. Strength of the UCS

        c. Number of CS-UCS Pairings

Point your Web browser at the textbook's Web page to see Live!Psych module 5.1.

    2. Extinction

    3. Spontaneous Recovery

4. Generalization and Discrimination

How do you anticipate Pavlov's dogs responded when an ellipse, that was associated with the absence of food, was gradually altered to look like a circle that had been presented as a signal for food?

C. Applications of Classical Conditioning: Phobias and Beyond

Consider Watson and Rayner's classical conditioning experiment with Little Albert. Consider the costs and benefits of that project. Would a proposal to conduct that experiment today be passed by the review board? Why or why not?

1. Classical Conditioning and Our Motives

D. Trends in Classical Conditioning: After Pavlov

1. Contingency Theory

2. Blocking

E. Evolution and Classical Conditioning: Taste-Aversion Learning and Preparedness

1. Taste Aversion

2. Preparedness

Diagram an experiment to test whether colors or tastes can more easily be conditioned to illness in birds.

3. Learning by Various Species

With a small group of friends, brainstorm and come up with at least five examples of classical conditioning in humans that were not presented in your textbook.

III. Operant Conditioning

A. Reinforcers: The Basic Concept of Operant Conditioning

1. Positive and Negative Reinforcers

Consider cheating in school as operant behavior. Can a positive reinforcer be used to encourage unethical behavior such as cheating? Describe the circumstances that would create an outcome such as positively reinforced unethical behavior.

2. Primary and Secondary (Conditioned) Reinforcers

B. Contingencies and Behavior

Point your Web browser at the textbook's Web page to see Live!Psych module 5.2.

Discuss the process of learning to drive an automobile (especially one with a manual transmission) in terms of *shaping*.

        1. The Premack Principle

C. Schedules of Reinforcement

A rat is being trained in a Skinner box. The responses by the rat are recorded on a graph called a cumulative record. What does a horizontal line on a cumulative record reveal about the rat's responding?

        1. Continuous Reinforcement

        2. Intermittent (Partial) Reinforcement

           a. Ratio Schedules

           b. Interval Schedules

D. The Partial Reinforcement Effect

E. Operant Conditioning and Stimulus Control

F. Punishment: The Opposite of Reinforcement

Drawing on what you know to be effective for training an organism to perform a response for positive reinforcement, consider what it would take to reduce the performance of a response using punishment. How can punishment be administered in order to maximize its effects?

Create an outline summarizing the basic points of the material on the Skinner box, shaping, and schedules of reinforcement.

IV. Cognitive and Social Perspectives on Learning

    A. The Role of Cognition

        1. Insight Learning

        2. Latent Learning

Create a visual organizer that shows behaviors with cognitive requirements (insight learning , latent learning, and so on) and their most important elements.

    B. Observational Learning

Learning Objectives

After you have studied the chapter, you should be able to respond to the following statements and questions to convey your understanding of the material.

1. Describe *learning* as an adaptive behavior that supports natural selection.

2. What role do sensory and perceptual processes play in learning?

3. What relationships exist between conscious awareness and learning?

4. Differentiate among classical, operant, and observational learning.

Key Word Exercise

Fill in the blanks in the following statements with key words and terms from the textbook. Answer as many as you can without referring to your notes or to the book. If you have blanks after thinking about each item, try using your book. The answers are presented after the practice test.

1. Reactions or reflexes that are elicited automatically when certain stimuli are presented are called _____ _____.

2. _____ is the training stage during which a particular response is learned.

3. When a sprinter has a false start because of hearing a loud noise other than the start gun, _____ is said to have occurred.

4. _____ occurs when a compound stimulus is paired with a US and the more intense (salient) CS elicits a stronger CR.

5. If you have ever become nauseated after eating an unfamiliar food, you probably developed a(n) _____ _____ as a result.

6. A(n) _____ _____ is a stimulus that has innate reinforcing properties.

7. A(n) _____ ___ _____ is a preset pattern of delivering reinforcement.

8. Reinforcement that follows every target response is called _____ _____.

9. Imagine that a child learns the laws regarding when to stop, and when to drive through intersections with traffic lights without ever driving. This would be an example of _____ _____.

10. Experiments have demonstrated that rats can remember a series of events. Thus, rats are capable _____ _____.

Practice Test

Circle the letter that corresponds to the *best* alternative for each of the following items.   Read each alternative carefully. The answers are presented at the end of this study guide chapter.   Be sure to learn *why* each correct alternative is better than the others.

1. A critical distinction between learned behaviors and those that become possible through maturation, is that learned responses:
   a.   are innate, or preprogrammed.
   b.   occur as a function of experience(s).
   c.   outlast those that are gained through maturation.
   d.   are acquired in strictly controlled laboratory conditions.

2. ___ ___ is to ___ ___ as stimulus-stimulus learning is to response-outcome learning.
   a.   Classical conditioning; operant conditioning
   b.   Operant conditioning; observational learning
   c.   Observational learning; classical conditioning
   d.   Operant conditioning; instrumental conditioning

3. A conditioned stimulus (CS):
   a.   is an automatically produced reaction.
   b.   is a stimulus that does not elicit a particular response.
   c.   is an event that automatically produces a response without prior training.
   d.   starts out neutral, but acquires the ability to elicit a response through training.

4. Unconditioned response (UR) is to conditioned response as ___ is to ___.
   a.   sight; sound
   b.   pleasure; pain
   c.   automatic; learned
   d.   None of the above; these terms mean the same thing.

5. The flinching people do when they see a long needle being stuck through a balloon results from learning, and is called:
   a.   magic.
   b.   extinction.
   c.   conditioned excitation.
   d.   a conditioned response.

6. Many phobias can be understood in terms of:
   a. operant conditioning.
   b. classical conditioning.
   c. observational learning.
   d. a psychological deficiency.

7. Watson's research with "Little Albert" demonstrated:
   a. what Holmes knew all along.
   b. that white rats can be conditioned to fear children.
   c. that emotional responses may be conditioned in humans.
   d. that children will act violently toward a Bobo doll after watching an adult do the same.

8. Which of the following is not a variable for determining the rate or quality of acquired responding?
   a. the strength of the US
   b. the strength of the CR
   c. the number of CS-US pairings
   d. the sequence of stimulus (CS & US) presentation

9. Spontaneous recovery is:
   a. more common in children than in adults.
   b. a phenomenon that is associated only with lab-based research.
   c. the reappearance of an extinguished CR after the passage of time.
   d. most often associated with patients suffering from mild psychological illnesses.

10. When a musician can recognize a note as "Middle C," rather than another note near "Middle C," this is an example of:
    a. generalization.
    b. discrimination.
    c. dishabituation.
    d. a learned goal (or learned incentive).

11. Contingency theory predicts that the better the CS is able to predict the occurrence of the US, the ___ conditioning will be.
    a. weaker
    b. stronger
    c. longer-lasting
    d. more resistant to extinction

12. ___ is a situation in which the conditionability of a CS is weakened when it is paired with a US that has previously been paired with another CS.
    a. Blocking
    b. Foreshadowing
    c. Overshadowing
    d. Latent Learning

13. An interesting feature of taste-aversion learning is that it:
    a. requires two CSs.
    b. is strong, but often short-lived.
    c. works well with novel and familiar CSs.
    d. occurs when the CS-US interval is lengthy.

14. The fact that some events go together naturally, and are therefore easily learned, is fundamental to the theory of:
    a. preparedness.
    b. easy learning.
    c. relative conditioning.
    d. conditioned associations.

15. A secondary reinforcer:
    a. always follows the CS in classical conditioning.
    b. concerns items of interest after basic needs have been met.
    c. can sometimes go unnoticed by the participant, but is nevertheless powerful.
    d. acquires reinforcing properties by virtue of an association with a primary reinforcer.

16. Hitting the snooze button on your alarm in the morning is:
    a. positively reinforced.
    b. negatively reinforced.
    c. not reinforced if you fall asleep again.
    d. only reinforced if you fall asleep again.

17. Shaping involves:
    a. reinforcement of the target response.
    b. reinforcement of activity other than the target response.
    c. reinforcement that does not follow every target response.
    d. reinforcement of successive approximations of the target response.

18. A cumulative record:
    a. is the peak response rate in a Skinner box.
    b. is a way of displaying results of conditioning trials.
    c. is another name for the acquisition strength of a trial.
    d. is usually released by a band after they have had several hits.

19. The two main types of intermittent schedules of reinforcement are ___ and ___.
    a. interval; ratio
    b. partial; complete
    c. positive; negative
    d. terminal; continuing

20. Conditioning in which we structure perceptual stimuli differently is called ___.
    a. latent learning
    b. insight learning
    c. serial enumeration
    d. perceptual learning

21. Negative punishers are:
    a. painful in nature.
    b. to be avoided at all costs.
    c. the same as positive punishers.
    d. pleasant stimuli that are removed.

22. The partial reinforcement effect:
    a. results from administering only a portion of a reward each time.
    b. is robust with respect to the quality of the reinforcer that is employed.
    c. describes the pattern of responding when one is on a FI schedule and only reacts part of the time.
    d. is reflected when extinction takes longer following intermittent reinforcement than after continuous reinforcement.

23. A stimulus that signals the participant that responding will be reinforced:
    a. is called a discriminative stimulus.
    b. is called a Boojum—as was used in the Snark experiment.
    c. would be Bob Barker yelling, "Come on down," for example.
    d. cannot last fewer than 15 seconds, or longer than 1 hour 25 minutes.

24. When older siblings help their younger siblings learn which behaviors will be punished, and which will be reinforced, the younger siblings experience:
    a. behavior modification.
    b. observational learning.
    c. synthesis of vicarious activation.
    d. prolonged extinction trials for acquired responses.

25. Behavior modification:
    a. is more easily done than said.
    b. was once a common treatment for the mentally ill, but is now considered unethical.
    c. has been defined as the application of the results of learning theory and the application of experimental psychology to the problem of altering maladaptive behavior.
    d. involves placing group housed clients in mental institutions in giant Skinner boxes and rewarding them on schedules as has been done previously with pigeons and laboratory rats.

Answers to Key Word Exercise

1. unconditioned responses	2. Acquisition	3. generalization
4. Overshadowing	5. taste aversion	6. primary reinforcer
7. schedule of reinforcement	8. continuous reinforcement	9. latent learning
10. serial enumeration		

Practice Test Answers and Explanations

1. b. Learning results from experience, whereas changes associated with maturation do not require environmental influence.
2. a. Classical conditioning involves learning about the relationships among stimuli. Operant conditioning involves learning response-outcome contingencies.
3. d. CSs start out as neutral stimuli, but take on meaning after being presented in conjunction with USs.
4. c. URs are automatic reactions that occur without training. CRs are expressed as a function of classical conditioning, or learning.
5. d. Flinching in anticipation of a "bang" when a needle passes through a balloon is an example of conditioned responding.
6. b. Phobias often result from classically conditioned cues associated with an unpleasant experience.
7. c. Watson's research, which would not pass today's APA guidelines, showed the ease with which emotional responses can by conditioned.
8. b. The strength of the CR might be used as an index of the degree of conditioning, but does not influence acquisition as it is the product of acquisition.
9. c. Spontaneous recovery takes place after a CR has been extinguished and there has been a break in conditioning and testing trials.
10. b. Discrimination is the occurrence of a response to a specific stimulus.
11. b. Contingency theory predicts stronger conditioning as a function of the CS's value in predicting the US.
12. a. Blocking refers to one CS impairing another's ability to acquire associative strength and value.
13. d. Taste-aversion learning can occur with CS-US intervals that were surprisingly long when the phenomenon was first discovered.
14. a. Preparedness refers to a theory of biological readiness to learn certain associations.
15. d. Secondary reinforcers are stimuli that take on meaning because they are associated with primary reinforcers.
16. b. An example of negative reinforcement is the termination of an alarm by pushing a button.
17. d. Shaping is also known as the method of (reinforcing) successive approximations.
18. b. A cumulative record is used to show the rate of responding in a conditioning trial.
19. a. Interval and ratio schedules are the two main categories of intermittent reinforcement schedules.
20. b. Insight learning involves the sudden grasp of a concept (the ah-ha experience) as a result of perceptual restructuring.
21. d. Negative punishment involves the termination of a satisfier (e.g., losing privileges).
22. d. The partial reinforcement effect describes the phenomenon of extended responding during extinction of a behavior that was reinforced only some of the time during acquisition.

23. a. A discriminative stimulus signals the participant that reward contingencies are in place for target behaviors.
24. b. Observational, or vicarious learning occurs when one models learning for another (either purposely or otherwise).
25. c. Behavior modification uses learning principles to decrease undesirable behaviors and increase desired ones. See discussion at the end of Chapter 6 in your textbook for more on behavior modification.

Key Vocabulary Terms

Use the following list to write definitions *in your own words* for each of the key terms from the chapter. Translating the terms into language that is comfortable and familiar for you will facilitate your learning. For further study of these terms, go to the companion website for the textbook where you will find electronic flash cards that you may use to test your vocabulary.

learning

classical conditioning

neutral stimulus (NS)

unconditioned stimulus (UCS)

conditioned stimulus (CS)

unconditioned response (UCR)

conditioned response (CR)

extinction

spontaneous recovery

generalization

discrimination

phobia

learned motives

learned goals (learned incentives)

blocking

taste-aversion learning

preparedness

operant conditioning

reinforcer

positive reinforcer

negative reinforcers

primary reinforcer

secondary reinforcer

shaping

cumulative record

schedule of reinforcement

continuous reinforcement

intermittent (or partial) reinforcement

ratio schedule

interval schedule

partial reinforcement effect

discrimination stimulus

punisher

law of effect

punishment

partial reinforcement effect

insight learning

latent learning

observational learning (modeling)

Tip for Success: Getting the Most from the Classroom

The time you spend in class can be very valuable. The classrooms, laboratories, and studios where your classes meet were designed for student learning. The lectures, demonstrations, and discussions you listen to, watch, and participate in were organized by your professors in order to facilitate your understanding of the course material. Your tuition provides you with access to professionals whose interests are the very courses you take, and to facilities that are meant to support your educational experience. What you make of the opportunities you have, however, will depend on how well you are able to extract ideas and information from your classroom experiences. This section offers several suggestions for helping you make the most of your classroom learning opportunities.

Why Notes Are Important

Your notes should represent your perspective on everything that happens in each class you take. Your notes for a given class will represent those elements from the subject that your professor thinks are of importance for students to know. Attend class regularly, pay close attention to the lectures, demonstrations, and discussions, and take thorough notes. The notes you develop as an active, attentive student will be invaluable to you in the future. As you receive assignments, quizzes, and exams back, 3-hole punch them and add them to your notes. Keeping course material organized and together is useful not only as you prepare for exams, but as reference material in subsequent semesters as well. Students are often surprised at how their notes from one class help them in other classes.

No matter how good your memory is, you will not recall everything from class. If your professor is really good at presenting difficult concepts, you may find it tempting to not write notes. Avoid that temptation. Too often, students find themselves frustrated when they do not recall how a given concept was explained in class. The very act of writing something down will help you remember it later. One thing is sure: if you write it down, you can always refer to your notes if you need to; if you do not write it down, you may realize too late that you do not understand a concept completely.

Be Prepared

When you go to a given class meeting, you should have a mindset that enables you to benefit as much as possible from the relatively brief opportunity. You can make an important investment in your career by simply preparing your mind for each class meeting. Learning how to do this, and making a habit of it, are the most effective ways for you to pursue your academic goals. Commit the following list to memory, and discipline yourself to do each step.

1. Know the Topic. Review your syllabus to learn what the topic of each day will be as you progress through the semester. If you have reading or homework assignments, do them. Completing assignments as you go, rather than 'whenever you get around to it,' even if your professor does not check to see if you are caught up, will keep you in touch with the class. At bare minimum you should flip through the pages from your text to review the variety of things you might expect to learn about.

2. Know the Environment. By merely showing up several minutes early, you can usually have your pick of chairs in a classroom. Choose a place in the room that will allow you to see and hear the instructor without having to strain. Any energy you have to spend focusing your attention will detract from your ability to think about the topic at hand. Sitting in the front, center portion of the classroom will allow your professor to see that you are committed to getting the most from your experience. Sitting farther away, or near people who chatter a lot, communicates that you do not think the professor has much of value to offer.

3. Have the Right Tools. Bring the book or books you may be discussing in class. It is rude to read these instead of paying attention, but it is good to be able to refer to your book if it becomes important to do so. Dedicate a 3-ring notebook, or section of a larger binder, to each class, and bring it with you to every meeting. Your notes from each class meeting will be your only reminders of what you did on a given day. By recording them in a well-designated place you will always know where to look when you need information for the class. The 3-ring format will permit you to add handouts from class, exams, and quizzes, etc. Always have *at least* one extra pen or pencil with you. If you are enrolled in a class that may involve performing statistical or mathematical calculations, bring a calculator with you each time as well.

4. Develop Your Own Shorthand. Having a system of abbreviations will help you keep up with comments from class. It is a good idea to keep a reference page in each notebook for the shorthand abbreviation system you develop. If a word is used regularly in your notes, use a standard abbreviation or devise a symbol that takes less time to write. Truncate words when possible. But, be sure to keep a glossary of abbreviations so you do not lose track of your system. If you consider that the time it takes to learn an abbreviation is far less than the time it will take to write the word(s) many times in longhand, you will quickly realize the value of using symbols and abbreviations.

You will want to translate these into your glossary. Look at the following examples, then record several other abbreviations that will save you time in class. Add to your glossary as you develop new shortcuts.

~ = approximately	b/c = because	e.g., = for example
i.e., = in other words	Q: = question	A: = answer
2 = to, too, two	4 = for, fore, four	+ or & = and
B4 = before	etc. = and so forth	→ = leading to
← = resulting from	Ψ = psychology	w/ = with
w/o = without	Δ = change	< = less than
> = more than	@ =at	√ = check
% = percent(age)	Σ = sum	

What are other ways you can simplify your note taking by using abbreviations and symbols?

Be Early, Be Interested, Be Courteous

Being early to and attentive during class shows your commitment. This will give you a few minutes to prepare (e.g., review notes, look through your text) or to discuss the class with your professor or other students. Being late is disruptive and gives the impression that the class is not a priority for you.

Having selected a seat that is front and center in the room, you are well positioned to give your utmost attention. Maintain eye contact with your professor whenever possible. If you are interested in your professor, your professor will be interested in you. Building on this relationship will help you develop and maintain a commitment to studying and doing good work.

To be eligible to teach the class, your professor studied the topic extensively in graduate school. The class you are taking is on a topic that is very important to your professor. If you discover your mind to be wandering, think about what it is that draws people to the discipline. Ask a question that will help your professor convey her or his passion for the subject. Another good way to keep on task is to take notes continuously. It is hard for your mind to wander if you are busy taking notes. Finally, do not close your notebook or put anything away until your professor has closed the class. Often some important points are made in the last few minutes; you cannot record them if you have already put your things away. What's more, closing your books is distracting to others in the classroom.

Approaches to Note Taking

Your notes have to be meaningful to you to be of any use. The most appropriate method for taking notes will depend on your style as a student, your professor's teaching style, the nature of the class, and other variables. Regardless of these things, your notes need to be organized. In addition to dedicating a whole notebook, or section of a larger binder, to each class, you will want to assign a piece of paper to each day. Put each day's date in the same place so that later it will be easy to track what happened by date. If you write on two or more pages, simply rewrite the date and number the page (2, 3, etc.), as appropriate.

Two common methods for taking notes are offered below. Experiment until you find a system that works for you. Take the opportunity to inquire with your professors about the methods that will work best for their particular courses.

1. The Outline Method. Some of your teachers will give highly structured notes that fit well into an outline. If the notes fit an outline format well, use that format. Some notes on using an outline, and a sample of the common outline format are provided near the end of this section.

2. The Cornell System. Another system for recording notes, that works well whether or not the notes follow an outline format, was developed by Walter Pauk at Cornell University. This system involves dividing each page of notes into three parts. See the end of this section for an example of a page. In short, the system uses a large box for notes on the right- hand section of the page, a narrower strip beside the main box for adding detail later on when you study your notes, and a section at the bottom of each page that spans the page's width where summarizing comments about the page can be made.

Things to be Sure to Include in Your Notes

Learning to take good notes takes time and practice. It is better to write too much than to write too little, but sometimes students work so hard to transcribe the class discussions exactly that they miss out on the main point(s). By developing a personally meaningful shorthand system, you will be able to spend less time scribbling in you notebook, and more time paying attention in class.

If you notice that something is reiterated, if your professor draws a picture or diagram on the board, or if you hear something in your professor's intonation that emphasizes a given point, make sure your notes reflect it. If a word is written on the board, write it in your notes.

If you are not sure what your professor is trying to communicate, ask. The chances are that if you are not following something in the class, others are also confused. Most professors appreciate it when their students ask questions; use questions to indicate your interest in class and to communicate that you are paying attention. Many times a question that you may ask will help your professor understand more about you and your commitment, and will also win favor with your fellow students.

Sometimes you understand perfectly well what is being said, but do not have time to record it before your professor moves on to the next topic. Raise your hand and ask that he or she repeat the comment. Again, this will underscore your commitment to getting the most from each class period.

Within a day of taking each set of notes, you should review them, filling in missing information, adding references to figures or text passages from your book, etc. You may even find rewriting your notes to be helpful. The sooner after taking a set of notes that you are able to review them, the better able you will be to fill in gaps, make references to the text, etc.

Notes on Using a Formal Outline

1. Typically there will be at least two points for each level of organization (if there is a I, there should be a II, if there is an A, there should be a B, and so on).

2. Note the numbering and lettering system; it is common to most outlines.

3. Use only key words and sentence fragments. The point of the outline it to record the main points; details are added when the outline is used as a basis for writing a paper or delivering a speech.

Sample Outline Format

I. Major topic (sentence fragment that reflects the main point of the topic or section)

    A. 1st important supporting point

    B. 2nd supporting point

        1. 1st detail to clarify I.B.

        2. 2nd detail relating to I.B.

            a. 1st small point relating to 2nd detail

            b. 2nd small point for 2nd detail under I.B.

                i. Minute piece of information about 3rd detail

                ii. 2nd minute piece of information

II. Second Topic

    A. 1st point

    B. 2nd point

    C. 3rd point

III. Third Topic

    A. 1st point

    B. 2nd point

Example of Layout for the Cornell Method

The table below represents a piece of 8.5" x 11" notebook paper:

	date (xx/xx/xx) - p.#

← ~2.5" →
 	
Cue Column
 	
Leave blank while in class.
 	
Add detail to this area when you review your notes. Draw diagrams, highlight terms and concepts, or refer to pages in the text book.
	Class Notes Section
	
	Use formal or informal outline format to record notes from class in this section. Include the following:
	
	        Drawings & diagrams
	        Key concepts & ideas
	        Q:s & A:s from class
	        Q:s to ask your professor
	        Other item, as appropriate

↑ 2" ↓	**Summary Area** Fill in this section after you review your notes. It should contain summarizing comments about the rest of the page.

CHAPTER 7

Memory

Do You Know?

Do you know that the basis of all memories is physiological? Through the years psychologists have developed several models of human (and nonhuman) memory systems. While these models have not always reflected the underlying physiological processes that are necessary for memory formation, they are not mutually exclusive with such processes either. Indeed, the function of memory modeling has largely been to organize phenomena that have been discovered and measured in well controlled laboratory studies. The models that have been developed by cognitive psychologists have not only contributed to understandings of different memory systems, but have also provided contexts for developing ever clearer perspectives on how memory works, including at physiological levels.

Cognitive neuroscience is an exciting, new interdisciplinary area of inquiry. As the name implies, people working in this area are interested in the biological underpinnings of cognitive processes. Models such as those presented in the memory chapter in your textbook have been very important in the quest to understand the conditions under which memories are formed. Aspects of research in this area have focused on mechanisms involved in encoding, storage, and retrieval of memorial information. While cognitive psychologists have been busy refining their models of memory to account for all of the phenomena that have been discovered through research, computer scientists have been busy developing artificial models that mimic the organic ones. Not surprisingly, information and ideas have flowed both ways during these related inquiries into memory. What is more, researchers trained in physiological methodologies have contributed information about neuronal activity to both groups while also borrowing ideas from the models in order to inform new approaches to their research.

Several interesting findings have developed as a result of inter- and cross-disciplinary interest in memory. For example, researchers in psychology and medicine documented very closely the outcome of H.M.'s bilateral hippocampal surgery. As a result, we have a clearer understanding of the anatomy of declarative memory and we have better models of human memory that account for the profound results of that experimental surgery. Studies of H.M.'s memorial deficiencies that resulted from the surgery have also helped distinguish declarative from procedural memory. Armed with the understanding that the brain regions involved in these distinct memory systems are likely to be different, neuroscientists have performed numerous experiments on both types of memory. Although our understandings are still developing, it seems clear that procedural memories are stored and maintained in more primitive brain regions, while declarative memories appear to depend upon more recently developed tissue.

Notes from Class and the Textbook

Use the space provided in this outline to record notes from the textbook as well as from class lectures and discussion. Questions related to the *Psychological Detective, Hands On, Myth or Science,* and *Study Tip* sections in the text have been presented in the outline; use the associated space to respond to the questions and to record your own comments about the issues.

I. Initial Studies

How many ways could an experimenter measure a participant's memory for nonsense syllables?

A. The Curve of Forgetting

Point your Web browser at the textbook's Web page to see Live!Psych module 7.1.

B. Recognition and Relearning

II. Traditional Models of Memory

A. Human Memory as an Information Processing System

Point your Web browser at the textbook's Web page to see Live!Psych module 7.2.

1. Encoding

2. Storage

3. Retrieval

Who was your fourth grade teacher? What process(es) did you use to retrieve the name?

Is there such a thing as photographic memory, or is it more likely that some people just have very good memories? Reread the section at the top of page 276 on Leonardo da Vinci and Napoleon Bonaparte.

Create a diagram of the human memory system. Include short definitions of each component of the system.

B. The Stages-of-Memory Model

    1.   Sensory Memory

What causes the sensation that one feels *after* having rubbed a hand against the edge of a desk, tapping fingers, or other form of sensory stimulation?

    2.   Short-Term Memory

Write down the three phone numbers from the *Psychological Detective* section. Why would it be easier to handle two versus three numbers?

Write down as many of the 15 words as you can. Did you perform better than 7+/-2? If so, why?

3. Long-Term Memory

    a. Forgetting

Point your Web browser at the textbook's Web page to see Live!Psych module 7.3.

III. Other Approaches to Learning and Memory

    A. The Levels-of-Processing Model

Compare the stages-of-memory and Craik and Lockhart models of memory. Which makes more sense to you, and why? Should a good model of memory include elements from each model?

    B. Alternate Approaches

        1. Transfer-Appropriate Processing

2. Parallel Distributed Processing

C. Different Types of Long-Term Memory

    1. Procedural Memory

    2. Semantic Memory

Write the answers to the *Psychological Detective* section questions. How many answers were just "on the tip of your tongue"?

Conduct the self-test of states' capitals that is presented on page 288 in your textbook.

    3. Episodic Memory

    4. Priming or Implicit Memory

Work with three other people—each person should provide a brief report on one of the four types of long-term memory. Brainstorm together to identify several examples of each type.

D. Retrieval

    1.   Retrieval from Short-Term Memory

Why is it necessary to *retrieve* information that is in our consciousness?

    2. Retrieval from Long-Term Memory

    3. Encoding Specificity

Consider the importance of context in encoding. How can you guard against having to depend upon contextual cues to aid your retrieval of information?

    4. Eyewitness Testimony

    5. State-Dependent Memory

E. The Repressed-Memory Controversy

F. Memory Illusions

IV. Techniques for Improving Memory

A. Influential Factors

B. Processing Strategies

Point your Web browser at the textbook's Web page to see Live!Psych module 7.4.

1. Imagery

2. Method of Loci

How can familiar songs, places on an often-traveled path, or rooms in your childhood home be used to help remember lists of information?

3.   Pegword Technique

4.   Grouping (Chunking)

5.   Coding

6. Acronyms and Acrostics

V. The Physiological Basis of Learning and Memory

   A. Amnesias

      1.   Anterograde Amnesia and the Hippocampus

Why do H.M.'s daily experiences consist exclusively of things he can maintain in STM, except for things he learned prior to 1953?

      2.   Retrograde Amnesia and the Consolidation Hypothesis

Learning Objectives

After you have studied the chapter, you should be able to respond to the following statements and questions to convey your understanding of the material.

1. What are some uniquely human aspects of learning and memory?

2. What contributions did Ebbinghaus make to the study of memory?

3. Compare and contrast the Atkinson-Shiffrin Model with the Levels-of-Processing Model.

4. What are some strategies and devices for improving memory?

5. What are amnesias? What have symptoms of amnesias contributed to our understanding of memory?

Key Word Exercise

Fill in the blanks in the following statements with key words and terms from the textbook. Answer as many as you can without referring to your notes or to the book. If you have blanks after thinking about each item, try using your book. The answers are presented after the practice test.

1. _____-_____ _____ is a technique that is often used to learn the vocabulary for a foreign language.

2. Identifying a suspect from a police line-up is an example of a _____ _____.

3. Information cannot be retrieved for a test unless it is first _____ and then stored.

4. Sperling elegantly gathered data on the capacity of _____ _____ by assigning tones, to act as signals, to each of three rows in a 12-letter stimulus matrix.

5. _____-_____ _____ is a relatively permanent store that depends on rehearsal or practice.

6. That people do better recalling information from a word list if they are instructed to rate the pleasantness of each word, versus counting the number of letters in each word, is evidence for the _____-_____-_____ _____.

7. Remembering how to rollerblade is an example of _____ _____.

8. Psychologists refer to memory of one's personal experiences as _____ _____.

9. People do not always know whether to tip waitstaff when eating out at a pizza place because the context does not exactly match the _____ for either a fast-food joint or for a restaurant.

10. Retrograde amnesia may exist for items that occur just prior to a traumatic event because _____ of the information concerning the items has not taken place yet.

Practice Test

Circle the letter that corresponds to the *best* alternative for each of the following items. Read each alternative carefully. The answers are presented at the end of this study guide chapter. Be sure to learn *why* each correct alternative is better than the others

1. Ebbinghaus used nonsense syllables in his studies of how associations between stimuli are formed:
   a. because they were short.
   b. because they were supposed to have no meaning.
   c. in order to encourage people from countries that spoke other languages to replicate his work.
   d. because generating the consonant-vowel-consonant sequence was easy to do with a computer.

2. A learning procedure in which material that has been learned may be repeated in any order is called:
   a. the recognition test.
   b. the free recall procedure.
   c. the serial learning procedure.
   d. the randomized recall procedure.

3. One of Ebbinghaus' most important findings was:
   a. the method of loci.
   b. anterograde amnesia.
   c. the curve of forgetting.
   d. the Atkinson-Shiffrin model of memory.

4. The difference between the time it takes to learn material once and the time necessary to learn it a second time is:
   a. called a savings score.
   b. commonly referred to as the difference score.
   c. usually shorter among children than with adults.
   d. is long unless the information is particularly salient.

5. The human information processing system has been characterized as having all *but* which of the following stages?
   a. storage
   b. retrieval
   c. encoding
   d. transferring

6. Leonardo da Vinci and Napoleon Bonaparte had in common which of the following?
   a. the capacity for eidetic imagery
   b. the capacity to form flashbulb memories
   c. anterograde amnesia due to a closed head injury (e.g., stroke)
   d. retrograde amnesia stemming from an open head injury (e.g., foreign object entering the head)

7. Which component of the Atkinson-Shiffrin model had the smallest capacity?
   a. sensory memory
   b. long-term memory
   c. short-term memory
   d. the environmental input channel

8. Information in short-term memory is usually lost after:
   a. 20 seconds or so.
   b. about 15 minutes.
   c. a good night's rest.
   d. new information is admitted.

9. The magic number that was proposed by George Miller was:
   a. three: many aspects of memory seem to involve the number three.
   b. not a single number, but span of numbers from about five to about nine.
   c. 8675309: a number that was later treated as a woman's phone number in a pop song.
   d. one. Three Dog Night described *one* as the loneliest number, but Miller thought it was magic.

10. Working memory was proposed:
    a. as a second phase of STM.
    b. as a treatment for broken memory.
    c. as a hypothetical construct to explain processing in LTM.
    d. by Ebbinghaus to explain improved recall for certain items.

11. Saving information for a specified period of time is to ___ as adding to the material to be remembered is to ___.
    a. storage; retrieval
    b. retrieval; encoding
    c. temporal encoding; summation encoding
    d. maintenance rehearsal; elaborative rehearsal

12. With respect to what is recalled (as opposed to what is sought in a memory task), old memories are to new memories as ___ is to ___.
    a. anterograde amnesia; retrograde amnesia
    b. retrograde amnesia; anterograde amnesia
    c. retroactive interference; proactive interference
    d. proactive interference; retroactive interference

13. The levels-of-processing theory states that which of the following relationships exists between processing depth and likelihood of recall?
    a. positive—as processing depth increases, probability of recall increases
    b. negative—as processing depth increases, probability of recall decreases
    c. no relationship—the probability of recall is independent of processing depth
    d. inverse—the probability of recall occurs as a mathematical expression equal to one over the depth of processing

14. The transfer-appropriate processing (TAP) model suggests:
    a. we process information in several subsystems simultaneously.
    b. that content is learned best when it is processed at deep versus shallow levels.
    c. we only transfer to memory that which is appropriate, as the model's name implies.
    d. the best learning and memory occur when the encoding and retrieval processes are the same.

15. Which of the following was *not* discussed in your text as a type of long-term memory?
    a. episodic memory
    b. personal memory
    c. semantic memory
    d. procedural memory

16. The tip-of-the-tongue (TOT) phenomenon is sometimes used to investigate the nature of:
    a. semantic memory.
    b. procedural memory.
    c. flashbulb memories.
    d. none of the above; TOT is strictly a phenomenon and hinders rather than helps investigators.

17. The topic of interest when discussing the role of prior exposure to stimulus items in aiding subsequent learning is:
    a. flashbulb memory.
    b. retrograde amnesia.
    c. anterograde amnesia.
    d. priming or implicit memory.

18. Multiple choice is to essay test as ___ is to ___.
    a. hard; easy
    b. recall; recognition
    c. recognition; recall
    d. semantic memory; episodic memory

19. A network of related concepts that are linked together is called a(n):
    a. schema.
    b. semantic network.
    c. flashbulb memory.
    d. eidetic memorial network.

20. State-dependent learning is closely related to the ___ hypothesis.
    a. flashbulb memory
    b. encoding specificity
    c. eyewitness memory
    d. repression of content

21. A distinction between "memory illusions" and true memories is:
    a. in their relative durations.
    b. in the time it takes to form them.
    c. that memory illusions are usually less detailed.
    d. that memory illusions are usually more detailed.

22. The serial position effect:
    a. is used extensively in determining how to stock shelves in the breakfast aisle in grocery stores.
    b. is most easily demonstrated in experiments that employ tasks including learning word pairs.
    c. refers to the tendency for people to show improved recall for items at the beginning and end of a list in comparison to items in the middle.
    d. refers to the phenomenon whereby participants perform better on recall tests of word lists when the words are from the middle rather than the end of the list.

23. John plays the game *Monopoly* frequently. He recently inferred from studying for his psychology class that he could use his memory for the game's board to his advantage. To his surprise, he finds it easy to recall terms when he associates them with places on the board. He is using a variation on:
    a. imagery.
    b. method of loci.
    c. pegword technique.
    d. flashbulb technique.

24. Acronym is to acrostic as ___ is to ___.
    a. word; saying
    b. saying; word
    c. opposite; same
    d. same; opposite

25. With respect to lost memories, anterograde amnesia is to retrograde amnesia as ___ is to ___.
    a. new; old
    b. old; new
    c. declarative; procedural
    d. procedural; declarative

Answers to Key Word Exercise

1. Paired-associate learning
2. recognition task
3. encoded
4. sensory memory
5. Long-term memory
6. levels-of-processing theory
7. procedural memory
8. episodic memory
9. schema
10. consolidation

Practice Test Answers and Explanations

1. b. Ebbinghaus chose to use nonsense syllables because he thought they would have no meaning. It turns out that these syllables sometimes do have meaning, and therefore may confound experiments.
2. b. The *free recall* procedure permits subjects to recollect information in any order they wish.
3. c. Ebbinghaus discovered the curve of forgetting when testing his own memory.
4. a. The savings score is the time saved by having learned the material previously.
5. d. The system involves three steps—encoding, storage, and retrieval—in that sequence.
6. a. Both men were reported to have had the capacities for eidetic imagery (photographic memory).
7. c. The short-term memory component of the model has the smallest capacity.
8. a. Information in STM lasts only 10-20 seconds before being lost from consciousness.
9. b. Miller proposed 7+/-2 (5 to 9) as the limit for normal STM capacity.
10. a. Working memory is considered to be a second component of STM in which attention and conscious effort are used to process material.
11. d. Maintenance rehearsal is used to keep information (e.g., a phone number) for a specified time. Elaborative rehearsal is used when expanding (elaborating) memory.
12. d. Retroactive interference involves new memories being recalled in place of old ones; vice versa for proactive interference.
13. a. The levels-of-processing approach states that greater processing depth results in improved recall.

14. d. The TAP model suggests that the best learning and memory occur when the encoding and retrieval processes are the same. This model, however, has been criticized.
15. b. The other three were discussed as types of LTM, as was *priming or implicit memory*.
16. a. Investigators sometimes use items the evoke TOT to study semantic memory as both TOT and semantic memory involve general knowledge.
17. d. *Priming, or implicit memory*, is unconscious memory processing in which prior exposure to stimulus items may aid in subsequent learning.
18. c. Multiple choice tests are examples of recognition tasks, whereas essay tests examine recall.
19. b. Semantic networks are clusters of related concepts.
20. b. State-dependent learning is an example of learning that supports the encoding specificity hypothesis.
21. c. True memories generally have more detail than memory illusions.
22. c. The serial position effect is the tendency for people to do better when recalling items from the beginning and end of a word list.
23. b. John uses a variation on the method of loci technique, in which familiar places on the game board become associated with items on a word list.
24. a. Acronyms are words in which each letter stands for something. Acrostics are verses or sayings in which the first letter of each word is important.
25. a. Anterograde amnesia is an inability to store new memories, while retrograde amnesia is an inability to recall information that was stored prior to a traumatic event.

Key Vocabulary Terms

Use the following list to write definitions *in your own words* for each of the key terms from the chapter. Translating the terms into language that is comfortable and familiar for you will facilitate your learning. For further study of these terms, go to the companion website for the textbook where you will find electronic flash cards that you may use to test your vocabulary.

memory

nonsense syllables

serial learning

paired-associate learning

free recall

recognition test

relearning test

savings score

encoding

storage

retrieval

sensory memory

short-term memory (STM)

working memory

long-term memory

maintenance rehearsal

elaborative rehearsal

proactive interference

retroactive interference

levels-of-processing

procedural memory

semantic memory

tip-of-the-tongue (TOT) phenomenon

episodic memory

flashbulb memory

priming or implicit memory

semantic network

schema

encoding specificity

state-dependent learning

serial position effect

mnemonic devices

imagery

method of loci

pegword technique

acronym

acrostic

amnesia

anterograde amnesia

retrograde amnesia

consolidation hypothesis

Tip for Success: Preparing for and Taking Exams

Under the best circumstances, tests are instruments that serve both teachers and students. Teachers rely on them for measuring student progress, and students use them for feedback on the depth and breadth of their understanding. Additionally, students can use tests to demonstrate their enthusiasm for a course. For many students, taking tests is the only way they communicate with their instructors.

Because tests are often closely linked to course grades, it is common for students to become anxious about them. Unfortunately, anxiety sometimes distracts students from focusing entirely on content when preparing for tests, and from performing their very best when taking tests. This section was developed as guide to preparing for and taking exams.

Things to Do Before the Test

1. Be Prepared. Preparation for a test can be overwhelming and should be broken into manageable units. Identify test days on your calendar, and set specific preparation goals that maximize your use of available time. By starting early, and proceeding only after mastering each unit along the way, you will save yourself a great deal of anxiety and frustration as the test day draws closer.

2. Be Early. Be early to every class meeting, but be especially early on test days. When you are running late, you will be more anxious. By being early you will be able to make full use of the time available for taking the test. It is unreasonable to ask for additional time on a test if you do not show up on time.

3. Stake Your Claim. You learned about state-dependent learning in Chapter 7 of your textbook. State-, mood-, and context-dependent learning can facilitate recall of information at test time. While the effects of any of these may not be whopping, anything that helps, counts. If your goal is to perform well, you will want to take advantage of anything that might facilitate your performance. In general, you want to maintain the same conditions at retrieval time as were in place when information was encoded. Consider the following suggestions:

> **a. Keep Your Physiological State Constant.** Do not drink 19 cups of coffee prior to an exam unless you drink that much coffee before regular class meetings. By changing your physiological state, you disrupt normal functioning, and may not be sensitive to feedback that would normally help cue recall. What is more, you will be distracted by the changes in your bodily activity.

> **b. The Same Goes for Mood.** There are data that indicate that some learning is mood-dependent. Thus, do not show up on test day angry, anxious, or otherwise discombobulated, unless you are that way on regular class days. Maintaining an even temper and stable mood will serve you well in many facets of life.

> **c. Keep Your Seat.** By keeping your normal classroom seat you are holding constant the contextual cues from the environment. Since those cues are part of a context where you think and learn about the course material, they may help improve your performance on test day.

4. Know Your Professor's Style. Whenever possible, review samples of the questions and other test items your professor has used in the past. Getting these may be as simple as asking her or him if there is a test file you may review, or if he or she would share some samples so you can become better acquainted with their style. Other students who have taken a course from your professor previously may also be of some assistance.

Get as much information as possible that will help you know how to prepare for the test. If there will be multiple choice items, will they focus on definitions, or should you know how to *apply* what you have learned? Will you have to solve analogy problems? In general, your preparations should match the type of text you will take. Learn to anticipate test items, and practice responding to them. Specific ideas for different categories of exam items will be given below.

5. Recognition Is Easier than Comprehension. Do not convince yourself that you understand material just because you recognize it. This goes for material from textbooks as well as for that which is presented in class. Good books make the most difficult material accessible to a student who is new to the field; good teachers can make challenging concepts seem easy to understand. Beware that even though you may take in material as you read or hear it, additional effort may be required to comprehend it fully. Challenge yourself to recall as much as possible about a given topic without cues from your textbook or notes.

At the Test: Objective Items

There is no substitute for understanding the material. The best thing you can do to improve your score is to study and thoroughly understand the material. Sometimes, though, you will be faced with challenging alternatives, or with an essay question that requires you to think differently than you had anticipated. Learn the following suggestions and use them as appropriate to help you during an exam.

1. Multiple –Choice Questions. This is a common variety of test item because it allows your instructor to probe your understanding at a variety of depths. The following tips may help:

> **a. Break Each Question into the Stem and the Alternatives.** Study <u>each alternative.</u> Sometimes the wording of alternatives reveals that they are poor fits for the stem. Sometimes there are alternatives that simply do not make sense. *After* reading each alternative, cross out those that you know are incorrect. If you do not identify a clear best answer, move on to the next item.

> **b. Avoid Absolute Statements and Extremes.** More often than not, answers that are absolutes or extreme statements are decoys, and should be avoided.

> **c. Beware of Jargon.** If an alternative is filled with complicated language, it may not be the right answer.

> **d. Use Your Familiarity with Prefixes, Suffixes, and Root Words.** When you are presented with an unfamiliar word, break it down and try to discover its meaning *in context*. Also, do not be afraid to ask your professor to define a word for you.

> **e. Study the Grammar.** Sometimes the grammar used in a multiple–choice alternative will help give it away as either the correct answer or as a decoy. Pay attention to grammar as it may provide helpful clues.

> **f. If You Must Guess.** Sometimes you simply cannot determine which answer is the best one. If you must guess, do so after eliminating one or two alternatives. Your chances of guessing correctly get significantly better with each alternative you are able to eliminate. If you are not penalized for guessing incorrectly, you should respond to each item.

2. True-False Items. Some professors use true-false items to test their students' mastery of detailed information. Consider the following tips for responding to these items.

> **a. Only Two Options.** A statement can be either true or false. If you do not know the answer, guess. With true-false items, you have a 50-50 chance of guessing correctly.

b. True Means Always True, False Means Always False. If a given answer is *true,* it must be true under every circumstance. Test the accuracy of statements by trying to think of examples of when the statement is false.

c. Qualifiers. If a statement is qualified (e.g., some, many, usually, frequently), this may be a cue that it is true.

d. Check Names and Dates. Details such as names and dates can easily be mixed up to test your knowledge of who did what, when.

3. Matching Sets. It is important to read directions carefully for matching sets, as the rules sometimes permit re-using alternatives, and sometimes there will be extra items. If you determine that every item will be used once, you have the advantage of being able to use the process of elimination to simplify guessing from among any remaining alternatives.

a. Look for Relationships. Often one column is devoted to terms, and the other to definitions for the terms. Determine whether this or another relationship is present in the set before proceeding as it may help in eliminating alternatives.

b. Save Time. It takes less time to read a long definition and scan a list of short terms for a match, than vice versa. If a matching set has lengthy definitions that are to be paired with short terms, read the longer items first.

c. Start with What You Know. If you are not confident of which alternative should go with a given item, skip it and come back to it later. The process of eliminating alternatives for matches you are confident about may make it easier to decide from among remaining alternatives later.

Comment on Returned Objective Tests

You will need to review your answers to determine which alternatives are correct. While taking an exam, jot notes beside each item to reflect your decision for an alternative. Make a list of the stems and alternatives that go together. This may require some digging in your notes or in the textbook. If your instructor will not let you take the exam home, ask if you can take notes from it; if so, you will be glad you have developed a shorthand system.

What can you do to improve your preparation for objective exams? How can you use your exams as learning tools after you get them back?

_____

_____

_____

Before the Test: Essay Items

Some professors give out a pool of essay questions from which they will choose the one(s) you will write on during an exam; if this is the case in your class, you have no excuse for not preparing thoroughly. Other times you may get some hints about particular content to focus on when preparing for the essay portion of an exam. Take note of these hints. If you have no direction from your professor, there are still some important things you can do to prepare.

As you study your text, you will note that some material seems to lend itself well to objective (i.e., multiple–choice, matching) items, while other material does not. If a portion of a chapter contains information that is more easily described in narrative text than in discrete definitions, or if there are important concepts or relationships between and among concepts, these items may be good essay item candidates.

Frequently students are able to anticipate the broad topic that will be addressed in essay questions. Practice reviewing the text and writing essay items of the same format and style that your professor uses. You will get better at this with practice.

Once you have generated a list of potential questions, write outlines for responses to each item. Include in your outline any key words or examples that would be useful for communicating your understanding of the topic or relationship. It is not necessary to write out your whole answer in longhand if you can include all the topics and elements in your outline. Study the outline to review for the exam.

At the Test: Essay Items

1. Know the Directions. Read the directions for the essay section carefully. Sometimes professors will expect grammatically correct answers; sometimes they are merely looking for lists. If you are unsure, ask. Attend to whether you are directed to answer each item, or a subset of the items. How many points is each item worth? It is a good idea to start working on the more valuable items first.

2. Jot Down Notes. Take a few minutes to make comments on scratch paper, or in the margins about things to include in each essay. If you observe that there will be overlap in your answers, you may wish to simplify them, and to refer to the content of one while writing the other. This will save you time and energy during the test.

3. Budget Your Time, and Stick to Your Schedule. Unless you have been granted unlimited time to work on your exam, you will need to attend to the time that you have available for writing on the essay item(s). If each item you are to answer is of equal length and complexity, distribute your time evenly. You may want to allocate more time to an item if it is weighted more heavily, or if your response to it will have more detailed information. Be sure to allow ample time to reread your essay. A careful review of your efforts should help minimize grammatical errors and word omissions.

4. Make an Outline. Borrowing from the list of things you wish to include, organize a brief outline or diagram that prescribes the flow of your response. Doing this will help keep you from having to erase, cross out, or reorganize major portions of your essay. Your professor will be more favorably impressed by a well-organized, succinctly written essay than one that is wordy and hard to follow.

5. Write Carefully. Write legibly and do not rush yourself. The organizational steps you have taken should help the essay flow smoothly onto your paper. Attend to your expression of ideas, keeping your reader in mind. Is your task to write for a well-informed or a naive audience?

6. Reread Your Essay. When you have finished writing your exam, re-read the essay questions as if you were a journal editor. If you write more than one essay, finish writing each one before moving on to editing your work. As you read, ask yourself the following questions: Are your ideas presented clearly? Did you make good use of transitional sentences? Are there any sentence fragments? Are there subject-verb agreement errors? Is the language gender- or culture-biased? Have you used effective examples to illustrate your points?

How can you improve the quality of your essays through preparation and planning before you begin writing?

_____

_____

_____

CHAPTER 8

Thinking, Language, and Intelligence

THINKING
Cognitive Psychology
Problem Solving
Making Decisions
Creativity

LANGUAGE
Language and Development
Thinking and Language

INTELLIGENCE
Cultural Views of Intelligence
The History of Intelligence Testing
Principles of Psychological Tests
Extremes of Intelligence
Kinds of Intelligence
Misuse of Intelligence Tests
Heredity and Environmental Determinants of Intelligence

Do You Know?

Do you know that it would be impossible to develop a culture-fair intelligence test? That is to say, an intelligence test void of bias cannot exist. When developing a test, the individual or group undertaking the task cannot help but build in language and examples from their own experiences. Even if a large committee of well-rounded people were to design a test, they could not possibly represent the diversity of life experiences that would characterize an apparently compatible group of people to be tested, and to hope the instrument could be used across cultures that use different languages, have different schooling systems, and so on would be futile at best. Intelligence is so intimately tied to experience that it is certainly impractical, and probably impossible to assess consistently across groups.

In spite of the inherent difficulties in assessing intelligence across cultures, and even though the concept of intelligence itself is difficult to define, testing can be quite useful in diagnosing and understanding individuals' intellectual capacities. Reliability and validity tests help guard against problematic test items, and the standardization process helps eliminate some sources of bias. As a result of these measures to eliminate unexplainable variation among scores, the tests produce reasonably consistent performance when they are administered repeatedly to the same people. Differences between cultures may also be consistent, and it is clear that the impossibility of culture-fair tests will make this difference impossible to eliminate. It is important to note, though, that while differences between cultures may result as artifacts of biased test construction, such differences represent probabilistic trends and not absolute differences in groups.

By analogy, consider the common claim that men are taller than women. While this is true based on the average heights of men and women, it does not hold that all men are taller than all women. There is significant overlap in the heights of men and women. As a result, some women are taller than most men, and most women are taller than some men. Similarly, culture-based differences in intelligence test performance do not define absolute differences for all members of the groups in question. Tests designed, however unintentionally, such that they benefit members of a given culture will be more difficult for those from outside the culture, and the reverse is also true.

Notes from Class and the Textbook

Use the space provided in this outline to record notes from the textbook as well as from class lectures and discussion. Questions related to the *Psychological Detective, Hands On, Myth or Science,* and *Study Tip* sections in the text have been presented in the outline; use the associated space to respond to the questions and to record your own comments about the issues.

I. Thinking

    A. Cognitive Psychology

        1. Images

How can researchers draw inferences about the mental processes involved in answering questions concerning the relatedness of stimuli, such as the pairs of three-dimensional objects shown in Figure 8-1 on page 308 in the textbook?

        2. Concepts

Study the geometric figures in Figure 8-2 on page 310 in your textbook. What rule groups items one and four together while excluding items two and three? After you have thought about the problem, check your response on page 356 in your textbook.

B. Problem Solving

1. Problem-Solving Methods

a. Algorithms

Solve the anagram on page 312 in your textbook. As you solve the problem, pay particular attention to the approaches you use in arriving at a solution.

Point your Web browser at the textbook's Web page to see Live!Psych module 8.1.

b. Heuristics

2. Obstacles and Aids to Problem Solving

3. Setting Subgoals

Solve the river crossing problem from page 313 in your textbook. How does your response compare with the answer presented in the textbook? How did you arrive at your response?

4. Approach to Representing Problems

Examine Figure 8-4 from page 314 in your textbook. How would you solve the problem? The answer is presented on page 356 in your textbook.

5. Rigidity

Point your Web browser at the textbook's Web page to see Live!Psych module 8.2.

Describe a solution to the problem presented in Figure 8-7, page 315, in your textbook. You may compare your solution against the one that is presented on page 356 in your textbook.

6. Set Effect

Work with two other people to create an outline of the basic problem-solving process. In your outline, label the steps according to the material that is presented in the text.

C. Making Decisions

    1. Seeking Information to Confirm a Solution

    2. Representativeness

You are to guess the outcome of the toss of a coin that has just landed heads-up five times in a row. What is your guess? Why?

    3. Availability

    4. Comparison

    5. Framing

Design icons or graphic images to help you remember each of the decision-making heuristics.

D. Creativity

    1. Defining Creativity

    2. Measuring Creativity

    3. Personal Factors in Creativity

4. Situational Factors in Creativity

5. Enhancing Creativity in Work

II. Language

A. Language and Development

1. The Acquisition of Language

2. American Sign Language

B. Thinking and Language

1. Using Language to Limit Thought

2. Language and Gender

Rewrite the sentences from page 333 in your textbook such that they are gender-neutral.

III. Intelligence

Write down several characteristics and behaviors that are shared by intelligent people.

A. Cultural Views of Intelligence

B. The History of Intelligence Testing

    1. The Stanford-Binet Intelligence Scale

    2. The Wechsler Scales

Create a timeline illustrating the history of intelligence testing.

C. Principles of Psychological Tests

    1. Reliability

    2. Validity

    3. Standardization

D. Extremes of Intelligence

    1. Exceptional Children

    2. Savant Syndrome

E. Kinds of Intelligence

    1. Spearman's Model

2. Sternberg's Model

3. Gardner's Multiple Intelligences

Describe the major theories of intelligence, illustrating with examples, as appropriate.

F. Misuse of Intelligence Tests

G. Heredity and Environmental Determinants of Intelligence

1. Hereditary Determinants

How could researchers interested in intelligence determine the contributions of genetic factors (heritability)?

2. Environmental Determinants of Intelligence

What is the relationship between birth order and intelligence? Read the passage on page 352 and consider the varieties of support that have been marshaled for and against notions that intelligence is negatively correlated with birth order.

Examine Figure 8-18. What components demonstrate the contributions of environmental factors to intelligence?

3. Explaining Differences in Intelligence Scores

Learning Objectives

After you have studied the chapter, you should be able to respond to the following statements and questions to convey your understanding of the material.

1. What are some problem solving and decision making abilities that differentiate humans from nonhuman animals?

2. How can we be mislead in problem solving and decision making?

3. What is creativity and how might its use be fostered in the workplace?

4. Describe the sequence in which language is typically acquired.

5. How are thinking and language related?

6. What are the implications of the fact that only humans devise ways of measuring their intellectual achievements?

7. What three principles apply to all psychological tests?

8. Discuss variations in intellectual ability in terms of extremes of intelligence.

9. Describe the models of intelligence (Spearman, Sternberg, Gardner).

10. What roles do heredity and environment play in determining one's intelligence?

Key Word Exercise

Fill in the blanks in the following statements with key words and terms from the textbook. Answer as many as you can without referring to your notes or to the book. If you have blanks after thinking about each item, try using your book. The answers are presented after the practice test.

1. _____ involves the manipulation of information in the form of mental images and concepts.

2. If you listed on your resume that you raised grain-consuming animal units, rather than saying you raised farm animals, you would be employing a kind of _____.

3. Chess players do not use _____ because it would take centuries to examine all the possible arrangements of the chess pieces.

4. Sometimes it is helpful when trying to solve a problem to break it into manageable intermediate _____.

5. Functional fixedness is a specific example of _____.

6. The fact that inducing positive feelings can enhance creativity is an example of _____ _____ in creativity.

7. _____ is an understanding of word order necessary to convey ideas.

8. The _____ _____ is calculated by dividing an estimate of one's mental age by one's chronological age and multiplying by 100.

9. The procedures for administering the SAT test are the same no matter where the test is given. This is because the test has undergone _____.

10. Describing a hypothetical experiment in which seeds are planted in different kinds of soil would be analogous to comparing _____ influences on intelligence.

11. _____ _____ was Charles Darwin's cousin, but is best known for his early work in the area of intelligence testing.

Practice Test

Circle the letter that corresponds to the *best* alternative for each of the following items. Read each alternative carefully. The answers are presented at the end of this study guide chapter. Be sure to learn *why* each correct alternative is better than the others.

1. When Scott Smith injected himself with curare, a poison that causes paralysis, he did so:
    a. because he had done poorly on an intelligence test.
    b. because people had criticized his cognitive abilities.
    c. to test whether he could think in spite of not being able to move.
    d. to test whether his paralysis would be passed on to his offspring.

2. Cognitive psychologists infer mental processes:
    a. from the observable behaviors of the people they study.
    b. based on little or no empirical data to support their inferences.
    c. in spite of the fact that by studying carefully, one can actually observe these processes.
    d. based largely on the reports offered by subjects regarding their notions about problem solving.

3. Interestingly, mental images are not exclusively visual in nature. Which other sensory modalities were presented in the text as being capable of evoking images?
    a. audition
    b. olfaction
    c. both a. and b.
    d. neither a. nor b.

4. High-imagery words are to ___ as low-imagery words are to ___.
    a. smell; hear
    b. nouns; verbs
    c. two pegs; meaning alone
    d. one syllable; multi-syllabic

5. A prototype is a specific example of a particular:
    a. model .
    b. concept.
    c. construct.
    d. classification.

6. "Doublespeak" or euphemisms may be cited as:
    a. evidence that our words determine our thoughts.
    b. examples of universal insults to the intelligence of others.
    c. often as necessary when one is describing problem–solving abilities.
    d. indices that careful selection of words can be designed to steer our thoughts.

7. Well-defined problems have all but which of the following characteristics?
    a. a clearly specified solution state
    b. a clearly specified beginning state
    c. a clearly specified set of steps for solving the problem
    d. a set of clearly specified tools or techniques for finding the solution

8. Samantha is trying to solve a problem by systematically evaluating all possible solutions until the correct one is found. That is, she is using:
    a. an algorithm.
    b. the availability heuristic.
    c. the trial-and-error procedure.
    d. the representativeness heuristic.

9. The familiar spelling rule, 'i before e except after c,' is:
    a. highly overrated.
    b. an example of a heuristic.
    c. effective only with five–letter words.
    d. more complicated than the algorithm that many use in the same circumstances.

10. Jim just used a dime to open the battery bank on his camera. In doing so he overcame:
    a. frigidity.
    b. poor framing.
    c. confirmation bias.
    d. functional fixedness.

11. The gambler's fallacy is the faulty assumption that independent events are linked: for example believing that four consecutive 'heads' tosses *will be* followed by a 'tails' toss. The gambler's fallacy is an example of:

a. the law of averages.

b. the set effect at work.

c. why gambling is evil.

d. a representative heuristic.

12. It is safer, in statistical terms, to fly in an airplane than it is to drive to the airport. People who debate this fact often cite a recently publicized plane crash to support their contention. In so doing, they:

a. use the availability heuristic.

b. violate the representativeness heuristic.

c. increase the likelihood of causing a plane crash.

d. deny the truth about why planes crash in the first place.

13. Terri is trying to talk her dad into taking her fishing tomorrow. After seeing the weather forecast, she realizes she will have to do some fast-talking. When she turned to her father and reported there was a 30% chance of sunshine for tomorrow she:

a. ignored confirmation bias.

b. told her father a boldfaced lie.

c. manipulated the framing of her report.

d. hoped he would use the representativeness heuristic.

14. Defining *creativity* is not easy. However, one characteristic of creativity is an ability to use ____ thinking.

a. random

b. diverging

c. emerging

d. converging

15. Tests of intelligence may not be appropriate for use in cultures other than the US because:

a. only US citizens are intelligent.

b. the tests cannot be translated into other languages.

c. intelligence is so hard to manipulate experimentally.

d. definitions of intelligence appear to vary widely across cultures.

16. Binet and Simon proposed the concept of ____ on the basis of having observed age–related differences in ability levels.

a. eugemcs

b. mental age

c. intelligence

d. chronological age

17. The smallest unit of sound in language is to the smallest unit of meaning in language as ____ is to ____.

a. phoneme; morpheme

b. morpheme; phoneme

c. syntax; grammar

d. grammar; syntax

18. Producing consistent scores is to ___ as measuring what is intended is to ___.
    a. reliability; validity
    b. validity; reliability
    c. standardization; validity
    d. reliability; standardization

19. A normal curve is:
    a. a characteristic of the forehead shape of someone with an average IQ.
    b. thrown with the first two fingers in perpendicular orientation to the seams.
    c. a bell-shaped distribution of scores with the majority clustered around the middle.
    d. produced when there is a strong positive relationship (correlation) between variables.

20. A person with mental retardation who manifests at least one remarkable ability:
    a. is said to have a learning disability.
    b. would have the rare savant syndrome.
    c. would be able to use a calculator extremely quickly.
    d. would probably be placed in a gifted and talented curriculum.

21. Which of the following is *not* part of Sternberg's triarchic theory of intelligence?
    a. social intelligence
    b. creative intelligence
    c. practical intelligence
    d. analytical intelligence

22. The proportion of intelligence that is attributable to genetics is called the ___ of intelligence.
    a. biology
    b. heredity
    c. chemistry
    d. heritability

23. If environmental variables were the key determinants of intelligence, which pair of people would score most similarly?
    a. fraternal twins reared apart
    b. identical twins reared apart
    c. adoptive siblings reared together
    d. adoptive siblings reared apart for six years, then reared together for six more years

24. Identical is to Fraternal as ___ is to ___.
    a. one ovum; two ova
    b. two ova; one ovum
    c. x chromosome; y chromosome
    d. y chromosome; x chromosome

25. In Gardners's model of intelligence, *g* refers to:
    a. genetics
    b. general intelligence
    c. the "thousand contributors to intelligence"
    d. the denominator in an equation that is used to predict native ability

Answers to Key Word Exercise

1. Thinking
2. doublespeak
3. algorithms
4. subgoals
5. rigidity
6. situational factors
7. Syntax
8. intelligence quotient
9. standardization
10. environmental
11. Francis Galton

Practice Test Answers and Explanations

1. c.   Smith demonstrated that thinking does not require sub-vocal mouth movements as had been thought previously.
2. a.   Many believe that the data cognitive psychologists use needs to be public and replicable.
3. c.   In addition to visual imagery, people are capable of evoking auditory and olfactory images.
4. c.   High-imagery words provide two pegs for hanging memories, whereas low-imagery words require memory for meaning alone.
5. b.   A prototype is a special case of a concept. For example, a carrot is a prototypical vegetable.
6. d.   Doublespeak is an acceptable or inoffensive term that is used in place of an offensive one.
7. c.   Specifying the steps to the solution would be to give away the problem.
8. a.   An algorithm is a systematic procedure that involves evaluating all solutions until one is found.
9. b.   'I before e, except after c' is a heuristic (or rule of thumb).
10. d.   Functional fixedness is the inability to see new uses for familiar objects (e.g., not recognizing that a dime can be a screwdriver).
11. d.   The gambler's fallacy is an example of the representativeness heuristic (a failing problem–solving strategy).
12. a.   The availability heuristic is a failing problem–solving strategy that involves estimating the probability of an event based on how easily it comes to mind (how available it is in one's memory).
13. c.   She manipulated the framing, or presentation of negative and positive outcomes.
14. b.   Creative solutions tend to be diverging, or moving in search of multiple answers.
15. d.   Definitions of intelligence vary widely across cultures.
16. b.   Mental age was proposed as a way of assigning people to categories based on test scores.
17. a.   Phonemes are the smallest units of sound that are understood as parts of language, whereas morphemes are the smallest units of sound that convey meaning in language.
18. a.   Reliability is the degree to which a test can yield consistent scores over repeated administrations; validity has to do with how well a test measures what it was designed to measure.
19. c.   A normal curve is bell-shaped with most scores in the middle of the distribution.
20. b.   Persons who have mental retardation, but who possess one or more remarkable abilities have *savant syndrome.*
21. a.   Social intelligence is not part of Sternberg's model.
22. d.   The heritability of intelligence is the proportion that is attributable to genetic factors.
23. c.   If environmental conditions were key in determining intelligence, people who were reared most similarly should score most similarly, regardless of parentage. However, it appears that genetics also plays a significant part in determining intelligence.
24. a.   Identical twins come from a single egg, or ovum. Fraternal twins come from separate ova.
25. b.   The *g factor* in Gardner's theory is generalized intelligence.

Key Vocabulary Terms

Use the following list to write definitions *in your own words* for each of the key terms from the chapter. Translating the terms into language that is comfortable and familiar for you will facilitate your learning. For further study of these terms, go to the companion website for the textbook where you will find electronic flash cards that you may use to test your vocabulary.

cognitive psychology

thinking

concepts

prototype

algorithm

heuristics

functional fixedness

set effect

confirmation bias

representativeness heuristic

availability heuristic

framing

creativity

phoneme

morpheme

syntax

intelligence

mental age

intelligence quotient (IQ)

reliability

validity

standardization

norms

normal curve

savant syndrome

heritability

identical twins

fraternal twins

Tip for Success: Learning Styles

In Chapter 8, *Thinking and Intelligence,* you learned about theories of intelligence. There are several theories of intelligence, each with different features and emphases. A common theme in them, though, is that intelligence is not a unitary, homogeneous entity. Prevalent theories such as Spearman's, Sternberg's, and Gardner's, propose that there are several types of intelligence.

Briefly describe Spearman's *g*.

_____

_____

What are the components of Sternberg's Triarchic Theory of intelligence?

_____

_____

_____

List the eight kinds of intelligence as proposed by Gardner:

_____

_____

_____

_____

_____

_____

_____

Given the widespread attention models of multiple intelligences have received in recent years, it is becoming clear that intelligence is complicated and involved, and is not a homogeneous, unitary entity as has been thought previously. It does not matter whether research supports each of these theories, one at the exclusion of the other, or other ideas altogether. It is important, however, that education and industry take stock of the fact that different people have different intellectual strengths--different intelligences--and that one's ability to excel in a given area will depend in part on her or his native abilities. By logical extension, people should, to some degree, be channeled into curricula in schools, and also into various career tracks, based on their type(s) of intelligence.

More specifically, different people learn and adapt differently, based on their abilities. In order to improve interest and performance in school, and, later on, productivity and satisfaction in a career, it is important that people discover their learning styles.

What Is Learning Style?

Take a few minutes to reread pages xxii through xxvii in the textbook preface. If you have not already done so, take the Pathways to Learning questionnaire on page xxiv. Note the extent to which each of your eight intelligences, according to Gardner's Model, are developed. If you show particular strength in one or two domains over and above the others, you may want to use this information to inform your approach to studying. Drs. Davis and Palladino have gone to great lengths to develop study suggestions that are tailored to four of the learning styles: verbal/linguistic, logical/mathematical, visual/spatial, and interpersonal. While anyone may certainly take advantage of each of the study tips presented in the book, you may want to pay particular to suggestions that fit your learning style profile most closely. For convenience, the study tips in the chapters are color coded; the legend for these is on the first page inside the cover of your textbook.

Why Are You in School?

Your answer to this question may vary depending on your learning style. Some people approach their classes with a perspective of finding a purpose for anything they learn. If they cannot find an immediate personal application for information, they would just as soon not learn it. Others are not so concerned with how information can be applied to their personal lives, and want to learn for the sake of learning. Some want to challenge the ideas they are exposed to by testing them in various situations; for them learning is solidified in experience-based activities. Still others are interested in how information can be applied to environments, cultures, and the larger world. It is as though these people view content through a filter that allows them to see how their knowledge can be used to benefit other people and places.

It is helpful to realize the variety of perspectives your classmates use. You may get more from a given class by approaching it from a perspective that is different than your normal one. Sharing perspectives with people who view course content in different ways can make a class more enriching for everyone. There is no best way to learn material. Each approach has its merits; the key is to learn to benefit from as many perspectives as possible.

Learning styles vary by individual. However, teaching styles are fairly consistent from one instructor to another, and do not often reflect the diversity of learning style strengths for a given class.

How can you benefit most from the classes you take in light of your unique learning style?

_____

_____

_____

Things to Consider

1. Get Out of Your Comfort Zone. Some of the most valuable experiences you will have will result from your willingness to try new things. Humans are creatures of habit, and tend to avoid uncomfortable situations. By trying new things and adopting different perspectives, you will discover exciting things about you and the world. You may even learn that a different career path fits your strengths and abilities better than the one you had been considering.

2. Adjust Your Learning Style. Your courses will be far more meaningful if you accept them for what they are. If you are enrolled in a class that has little application to your personal life, try to enjoy it as an opportunity to expand your knowledge base.

3. Be in Control. You are ultimately responsible for what you get out of your education. Do not allow yourself to get into a rut of thinking that your professor, the textbook, your classmates, or anything else is stifling your ability to get the most from the class. Nowhere is it stated that you cannot supplement your learning experiences by doing additional reading, or experiments, or by organizing discussion groups or trips to visit people or places that will expand your exposure to material. On the contrary, doing these kinds of things will help you develop your understanding of the topics at hand and give you a record of career-oriented activity to describe when pursuing options such as employment or graduate school; the skills one develops in independent projects are often highly desired.

4. Learn from Others. Often you will have opportunities to work with others in your classes in group projects. More frequently, you will have opportunities to discuss class material with others as you complete assignments and prepare for exams. As often as you can, team up and compare notes with people who take school seriously, but who have a different perspective than you do. You can learn from one another, plus you will develop appreciation for other ways of thinking as a result of collaborative learning.

5. Ask for Guidance. Think of your professors as learning resources. In addition to preparing for your daily class meetings, you may find it helpful to do additional work in order to gain the most from the class. Your instructor can help you identify interesting topics to explore in the library, resources to consult for further study on a topic of particular interest to you, and may even include you in her or his research if you show some interest and initiative.

CHAPTER 9

Development across the Lifespan

Do You Know?

Do you know that the average American child will have watched more than 25,000 hours of television before he or she graduates from high school? For years, researchers have debated what this vast exposure to television means for people's values, comfort with violence, and so on. A recently published longitudinal study by Huesmann, Moise-Titus, Podolski, and Eron (2003)* addressed some of the common topics in that debate.

The paper by Huesmann et al. revealed that childhood exposure to media violence for both boys and girls predicts aggressive behavior among the same population when they are young adults. Based on the study, such aggression is predicted irrespective of individual's initial childhood levels of aggression. The most influential programming was that in which the children can identify with one or more of the characters in the program.

The data from this project and others imply a relationship between the viewing of television violence and one's propensity to commit aggressive acts later in life. Given this probable link, plus the fact that television programming is increasingly explicit in nature, even on network (i.e., not cable) television, one might reasonably predict that we will see increased acts of aggression in the public and private lives of people in our culture in the years to come. Although definitive causal data are practically impossible to gather on this topic (we cannot experimentally control the lives of anyone, let alone many research participants for the length of time necessary to demonstrate the effects with proper control groups, etc.), we may be better off safe than sorry. Parents can exercise precautions by watching programming with their children and/or by imposing viewing restrictions by using ratings, perhaps employing technology to block access to some channels.

*Huesmann, L.R., Moise-Titus, J., Podolski, C.L. & Eron, L.D. (2003). Longitudinal relations between children's exposure to TV violence and their aggressive and violent behavior in young adulthood: 1977-1992. *Developmental Psychology, 39,* 201-221.

Notes from Class and the Textbook

Use the space provided in this outline to record notes from the textbook as well as from class lectures and discussion. Questions related to the *Psychological Detective, Hands On, Myth or Science,* and *Study Tip* sections in the text have been presented in the outline; use the associated space to respond to the questions and to record your own comments about the issues.

I. Basic Issues in Developmental Psychology

    A. Nature and Nurture

To what extent are musical ability, athletic ability, shyness, and activity level genetically determined? To what extent are they environmentally determined?

    B. Research Methods

        1. Longitudinal versus Cross-Sectional Studies

II. Development from Conception to Birth

    A. Heredity

Point your Web browser at the textbook's Web page to see Live!Psych module 9.1.

    1. Polygenic Heredity

    2. Determination of Sex

    3. Sex-Linked Traits

B. Prenatal Development

    1. Barriers to Prenatal Development

        a. Teratogens

        b. Drugs

        c. Smoking

        d. Alcohol

    2. Checking the Health of the Fetus

        a. Ultrasound

        b. Amniocentesis

C. Birth

Create flash cards for all of the terms defined in the margins of the section on development from conception to birth. With a study partner, test one another until each of you clearly understands the vocabulary.

III. Development in Infancy

    A. Sensory Abilities

        1. Voice Recognition

        2. Vision

        3. Taste and Smell

    B. How Newborns Learn

        1. Classical Conditioning

How could you demonstrate classical conditioning in a newborn? Outline a demonstration, naming the components of the conditioning paradigm.

        2. Operant Conditioning

3. Imitating Others

C. Maturation

    1. Development of the Brain

    2. Physical Development

IV. Psychosocial Development in Childhood

A. Temperament

B. Personality Development

    1. Sigmund Freud

    2. Erik Erikson

C. Attachment

    1. Ethological Theory

    2. The Strange Situation Test

D. The Father's Role

E. Day Care

F. The Peer Group

G. Television

What steps can parents take to ensure the television programming their children are exposed to is not detrimental?

V. Cognitive Development in Childhood

    A. Piaget's Theory

        1. The Sensorimotor Stage

        2. The Preoperational Stage

        3. The Concrete Operational Stage

        4. Challenges to Piaget's Theory

Summarize Piaget's stages of cognitive development in children. Underline or highlight important terms.

B. Moral Development

VI. Adolescence

    A. Physical Changes

    B. Cognitive and Intellectual Changes

        1. Adolescent Thought Patterns

    C. Personality and Social Changes

        1. Possible Outcomes of Identity Formation

        2. Adolescent Peer Groups

        3. Family Influences

        4. Making a Commitment

VII. Early Adulthood

    A. Physical Changes

    B. Cognitive and Intellectual Changes

Outline a research project that would help determine whether intellectual ability declines with age.

      1. Types of Intelligence

   C. Personality and Social Changes

      1. Intimacy versus Isolation

      2. Marriage

      3. Children

      4. Parenting Styles

      5. The Feminization of Poverty

      6. Career Development

VIII. Middle Adulthood

   A. Physical Changes

   B. Cognitive and Intellectual Changes

C. Personality and Social Changes

    1. Midlife Crisis

    2. Other Stresses during Middle Adulthood

What are some possible reasons for couples having greater marital satisfaction after their children leave home?

IX. Late Adulthood

    A. Physical Changes

Consider the five true-false statements on page 402 in your textbook. Commit to an answer for each item, then check your answers against the information presented in the subsequent paragraphs.

Page 403 in your textbook contains an exercise to simulate loss of sensory acuity. Get the suggested materials and try the exercise with a few friends, each of you taking turns in the simulation. Finally, discuss the questions presented in your text at the end of the Hands On section.

    B. Cognitive and Intellectual Changes

Create a timeline showing Erik Erikson's stage theory of personality development. Use different colors, or draw icons, to represent the different stages.

    C. Personality and Social Changes

        1. Retirement

        2. Aging

X. Death Dying, and Bereavement

    A. Attitudes toward Death

        1. Childhood

        2. Adolescence

        3. Young Adulthood

        4. Middle Adulthood

        5. Late Adulthood

    B. Confronting Death

C. Bereavement, Grief, and Support

Learning Objectives

After you have studied the chapter, you should be able to respond to the following statements and questions to convey your understanding of the material.

1. Discuss two primary research methods for studying psychological development. What are the advantages and disadvantages of each?

2. Give a few examples of how newborns and infants learn.

3. Discuss what happens to the temperaments of children as they mature.

4. Identify the steps of cognitive development that were suggested by Piaget. What does it mean that all humans develop cognitive abilities in roughly the same way?

5. Identify Kohlberg's proposed primary levels of moral development.

6. Differentiate between fluid and crystallized intelligences. What is the relationship between these as one develops across the lifespan?

7. What stages of Erikson's theory of psychosocial crises are typically addressed during adolescence, early, middle and late adulthood?

8. Identify and describe the five stages of dealing with death that were offered by Kübler-Ross.

Key Word Exercise

Fill in the blanks in the following statements with key words and terms from the textbook. Answer as many as you can without referring to your notes or to the book. If you have blanks after thinking about each item, try using your book. The answers are presented after the practice test.

1. _____ is a procedure that involves withdrawing fluid from the womb for analyses regarding genetic abnormalities of the fetus.

2. Emma, an infant girl, has learned to kick her leg in order to be reinforced by the movement of a mobile. She has demonstrated an ability to learn from _____ conditioning.

3. _____ is the developing of motor and cognitive abilities at an early age.

4. The _____ theory of attachment states that attachment evolved because of its adaptive value to the infant.

5. A form of social influence that usually includes classmates and neighborhood children, and can have both positive and negative influences on the development of a child, is called a _____ _____.

6. A _____ is common in some societies and is the key to manhood for boys.

7. Tomorrow, Mr. Johnston will have surgery on his eyes. This is because he has _____, a condition whereby his lenses have become clouded.

8. One form of dementia is _____ _____, a degenerative brain disorder that results in progressive loss of intelligence and awareness.

9. A(n) _____ _____ is developed by some adolescents in response to the expectations their parents have for them.

10. Peter is experiencing grief, the emotional changes that are associated with _____ following his mother's death.

Practice Test

Circle the letter that corresponds to the *best* alternative for each of the following items. Read each alternative carefully. The answers are presented at the end of this study guide chapter. Be sure to learn *why* each correct alternative is better than the others.

1. Which of the following statements would best characterize John B. Watson's view on the role of heredity in shaping human behaviors?
   a. There is no such thing as an inheritance of capacity, talent, temperament, or mental constitution.
   b. Key human characteristics develop depending mainly on training that goes on in the crib.
   c. It is a unique combination of heredity and environment that permits humans to develop their idiosyncratic abilities and characteristics.
   d. Given the complexities of the human nervous system, coupled with the rich nature of the rearing environment, it is impossible to know which is the greater of environment and heredity.

2. Nature is to nurture as ___ is to ___.
   a. Watson; Piaget
   b. Kohlberg; Erikson
   c. environment; heredity
   d. heredity; environment

3. It is important to note when studying people from different age groups that while they may share many demographic characteristics, they have not had the same life experiences. That is, they are from different:
    a. cohorts.
    b. cultural strata.
    c. phases and stages.
    d. socioeconomic groups.

4. Which sequence represents the order in which prenatal (before birth) development occurs?
    a. embryo, fetus, zygote
    b. zygote, embryo, fetus
    c. fetus, zygote, embryo
    d. embryo, zygote, fetus

5. The principle whereby complex traits are determined by many genes is called:
    a. genetics.
    b. behavior genetics.
    c. polygenic inheritance.
    d. the principle of deoxyribonucleic acid (DNA).

6. The placenta is important in prenatal development because it does all but which of the following?
    a. produces hormones
    b. transmits nourishment
    c. filters out certain harmful substances
    d. neutralizes the teratogenic effects of alcohol

7. The outline picture that is produced by projecting sound waves onto the fetus, uterus, and placenta is called a(n):
    a. sonogram.
    b. genetic diagram.
    c. amniocentesis scan.
    d. ultrasound procedure.

8. Which of the following is *not* one of the three stages of birth?
    a. labor
    b. anoxia
    c. delivery
    d. afterbirth

9. While it is initially poor, infant visual acuity improves to about 20/20 by:
    a. 3 weeks of age.
    b. 4 to 10 weeks of age.
    c. 6 to 12 months of age.
    d. the time the child reaches her or his second year.

10. Watson and Rayner demonstrated:
    a. that older infants can be classically conditioned to fear.
    b. the processes of meiosis and mitosis under strict laboratory conditions.
    c. the power of genetic influence in determining whether and what a child can learn.
    d. that "Little Albert" could learn to avoid painful stimuli by operating a manipulandum.

11. Erikson's theory of development stresses:
    a. attachment.
    b. psychosocial crises.
    c. psychosexual stages.
    d. the acquisition of morality.

12. Harlow's research with infant monkeys demonstrated:
    a. the role of contact comfort in attachment.
    b. that they all are raised with the same basic parenting style.
    c. the value of attending to the critical window during early development.
    d. little other than that the assumptions about humans generalize well to primates.

13. Which was not identified as one of three common parenting styles?
    a. permissive
    b. dictatorship
    c. authoritarian
    d. authoritative

14. Young Tim and his sister Carrie are having grain burgers for lunch. Each got the same amount, one patty, but when their father cut the patties to make them easier to eat, he cut Carrie's into more pieces than Tim's. Tim whined and complained that he got shorted, thereby demonstrating that:
    a. he had not yet reached the sensorimotor stage of cognitive development.
    b. he had not yet reached the preoperational stage of cognitive development.
    c. he had not yet reached the formal operational stage of cognitive development.
    d. he had not yet reached the concrete operational stage of cognitive development.

15. With respect to the development of full sexual maturity, girls are to boys as ___ is to___.
    a. menarche; nocturnal emissions
    b. growth of axillary hair; changes in skin
    c. primary sex characteristics; secondary sex characteristics
    d. secondary sex characteristics; primary sex characteristics

16. Presbyopia is to presbycusis as ___ is to ___.
    a. male; female
    b. female; male
    c. hearing; vision
    d. vision; hearing

17. Sarah is beginning to show symptoms of dementia. As a result of dementia, she:
    a. ceases to ovulate and menstruate.
    b. will experience memory loss and disorientation.
    c. may have to have corrective surgery to restore normal vision.
    d. will have to use greater caution in activity as her risk for bone damage will increase.

18. Ability to see new relationships is to ___ as ability to retrieve and use information is to ___.
    a. middle adulthood; late adulthood
    b. late adulthood; middle adulthood
    c. fluid intelligence; crystallized intelligence
    d. crystallized intelligence; fluid intelligence

19. An interesting characteristic of adolescents in Erikson's *intimacy versus isolation* crisis is that:
    a. the crisis is more common among boys than among girls.
    b. the crisis is more common among girls than among boys.
    c. boys usually develop strong autonomy before becoming intimate, while girls may never have a strong sense of autonomous identity.
    d. girls usually develop strong autonomy before becoming intimate, while boys may never have a strong sense of autonomous identity.

20. The feminization of poverty in the *U.S.* is ___ it is in other industrialized nations.
    a. less than
    b. greater than
    c. about the same as
    d. a less important issue than

21. The *hospice movement* is:
    a. cruel and inhumane.
    b. essentially an application of humanistic psychology.
    c. an interesting behavior shown by many middle-aged adults.
    d. more a way of using the workforce than providing service to those who need it,

22. The *personal fable:*
    a. includes self-centered ideas and a sense that one is invulnerable.
    b. the term psychologists use to describe the life stories told to them by aging people.
    c. is longer, but not near as loaded with moral messages than the ones recorded by Aesop.
    d. is demonstrated in the young adult woman who thinks she can "solve the world's problems" by becoming a psychologist.

Answers to Key Word Exercise

1. Amniocentesis	2. operant	3. Precocious
4. ethological	5. peer group	6. rite of passage
7. cataracts	8. Alzheimer's disease	9. negative identity
10. bereavement		

Practice Test Answers and Explanations

1. b.   Watson was a strict behaviorist who believed that the only thing that mattered was environment.
2. d.   Heredity is associated with natural, or biological issues, while nurture refers to training or upbringing.
3. a.   A cohort is a group of individuals born in the same period.
4. b.   Zygotes are formed by the union of a sperm and an ova; next, the embryo develops, then the fetus.
5. c.   As its name implies, polygenic inheritance involves many genes influencing traits.
6. d.   The placenta passes alcohol through to the developing baby in the same concentrations that are found in the mother's blood.
7. a.   A sonogram is a picture that is produced using the ultrasound procedure.
8. b.   Anoxia is a reduction in or lack of oxygen that can cause brain damage during the birthing process.
9. c.   Visual acuity usually develops to 20/20 by one year of age.
10. a.   They conditioned fear in "Little Albert," who was an older infant at the time.
11. b.   Erikson's theory of development focused on a series of psychosocial crises.
12. a.   Harlow's work was useful in demonstrating the need for contact comfort during early development. However, other forms of attachment between parent and offspring are important too.
13. b.   Dictatorship was not discussed as a parenting style.
14. d.   During the concrete operational stage children learn the principle of conservation-recognition that a physical change in a substance does not change the amount of that substance. Relax, Tim, most adults get too big a container when putting away leftovers.
15. a.   Menarche (the first menstrual period) marks full sexual maturity for a girl; the ability to ejaculate semen (often in nocturnal emissions) marks sexual maturity for boys.
16. d.   Presbyopia is farsightedness that normally develops in middle adulthood; presbycusis is a middle-dulthood related hearing disorder.
17. b.   Dementia is a general decline in intellectual ability that is associated with old age.
18. c.   Fluid intelligence concerns the use of new relationships, whereas crystallized intelligence involves the ability to use information that has been learned.
19. c.   Girls are less likely to develop autonomous identities prior to establishing intimate relationships.
20. b.   Because of the high divorce rate, coupled with the fact that children of divorced parents usually stay with their mothers, more women are impoverished in the U.S. than in other countries.
21. b.   Hospice, which is characterized by a philosophy of treatment for the terminally ill, is an excellent example of the application of (humanistic) psychology.
22. a.   Personal fable is a term used to describe the thoughts and behaviors of adolescents who act as though they do not have to play by the same rules as other members of society.

Key Vocabulary Terms

Use the following list to write definitions *in your own words* for each of the key terms from the chapter. Translating the terms into language that is comfortable and familiar for you will facilitate your learning. For further study of these terms, go to the companion website for the textbook where you will find electronic flash cards that you may use to test your vocabulary.

developmental psychology

nature

nurture

behavior genetics

longitudinal study

cross-sectional study

cohort

zygote

mitosis

embryo

chromosomes

genes

deoxyribonucleic acid (DNA)

polygenic inheritance

fetus

placenta

teratogen

critical period

fetal alcohol syndrome (FAS)

ultrasound procedure

sonogram

amniocentesis

anoxia

rooting reflex

palmar or grasp reflex

moro reflex

Babinski reflex

cesarean section

maturation

precocious

psychosocial crisis

basic trust versus basic mistrust

autonomy versus shame and doubt

autonomy

initiative versus guilt

industry versus inferiority

attachment

contact comfort

ethological theory of attachment

peer group

cognitive development

assimilation

accommodation

sensorimotor stage

object permanence

mental representation

preoperational stage

symbolic representation

egocentrism

concrete operational stage

conservation

preconventional level

conventional role conformity

autonomous moral principles

adolescence

puberty

pubescence

secular trend

primary sex characteristics

menarche

secondary sex characteristics

formal operational stage

personal fable

imaginary audience

identity versus identity confusion

identity achievement

foreclosure

negative identity

identity diffusion

moratorium

early adulthood

fluid intelligence

crystallized intelligence

intimacy versus isolation

middle adulthood

presbyopia

presbycusis

menopause

osteoporosis

midlife crisis

generativity versus stagnation

empty nest syndrome

late adulthood

cataracts

dementia

Alzheimer's disease

ageism

integrity versus despair

bereavement

grief

mourning

hospice

Tip for Success: Stress Management

Thus far, the *Tips* sections in this study guide have addressed goal-setting, strategies for making the most of your resources (e.g., time, textbook, classroom experiences, study environment), preparing for and taking exams, and identifying your learning style. Managing all these activities can be both challenging and rewarding. In order to strive for and reach your potential, it is important to think and feel your very best. Sometimes, though, the pressures associated with having a multitude of responsibilities may create stress that will keep you from performing optimally. This *Tip* section was written to help you understand stress, and to learn some ways of keeping stress levels at a minimum.

What is Stress?

Stress refers to that which produces pressure, strain, or tension. Often, stress occurs as a function of perceived or real restraints on time to perform some task or function. However, impending time is not always the source of stress. Think, for example, of the last occasion when you had to speak to a crowd, or perform an attention-demanding task.

Identify several sources of occasional stress in your life:

_____

Stress Is in the Eye of the Beholder

It is interesting to note that stressful events are different for different people. Sometimes you may find that the relative amount of stress associated with an item in your life changes. You, circumstances, or an interaction between both can cause you to be more (or less) stressed by a task or behavior. Why are things stressful sometimes and not stressful at other times?

An old saying is that *perception is reality*. If that is the case, then it might provide some insight into the reasons why events change with respect to the amount of stress with which they are associated. If that is the case, it means that you can control the amount of stress you experience at a given moment by learning to alter your perception in order to manage the potentially stressful circumstance.

This idea is probably not new to you, but it is important nonetheless. For example, you may have heard some interesting advice about using imagery to reduce stress while giving a public speech. Some say it is helpful to imagine that your audience is in their underwear. The idea is that they would have more to be embarrassed about than you, and that this should put you at ease. It is important, however, that you imagine that they, and not you, are the ones in underclothes!

The key message here is that your perceptions govern, to a large degree, whether something is associated with stress. Learning to take things in stride, and not to getting too worked up about them, will be helpful.

Not All Stress Is Bad

The Yerkes-Dodson law of motivation says that optimal levels of performance are associated with moderate levels of stress or anxiety about the event. If stress is too low, one is not sufficiently interested in the event. High levels of stress interfere with one's ability to perform well. You may have had this range of experiences when writing a paper or preparing for an exam. Students sometimes find it difficult to get interested in studying too far in advance. At the other end of the spectrum, they find it difficult to concentrate during the last minutes or hours for a large project that they have put off until it is too late. Somewhere in between is a happy medium: the amount of stress that is necessary to focus your attention without being distracting.

Some people say they work best under pressure. What is the role of stress when this is the case?

High Levels of Stress Can Impair Performance

The *Health Psychology* branch of the discipline covers many facets of the stress response. Please refer to that chapter for a thorough explanation of stress and stress-related issues. In brief, however, you should know that when one experiences stressors (anything that causes an organism to display the nonspecific stress response), a series of responses typically follows. That series of responses, known as the general adaptation syndrome, is associated with changes in vital organ functioning and biochemical activity that can be hard on one's body. Stress can increase one's susceptibility to disease and illness.

Therefore, then, not only do high levels of stress impair the level and quality of behavior, but they take a toll on physiology and physical health as well. Sufficiently high levels of stress suppress immune-system functioning and put one at risk of illness.

Maladaptive Responses to Stress

Imagine someone who has a high-pressure job, such as a salesperson whose income is based on commission. The circumstances of such jobs cause the people who have them to experience tremendous levels of stress. Unfortunately, they often turn to maladaptive behaviors to combat the stress, thereby exacerbating the problem. For example, smoking and consuming large amounts of caffeine cause one to become more, not less, restless. After a day of drinking coffee and smoking (both caffeine and nicotine are behavioral stimulants), some will even choose to "relax" with a few alcoholic drinks (alcohol is a central nervous system depressant)

Caffeine, nicotine, and alcohol all impair one's ability to get productive (i.e., REM) sleep. Thus, this pattern of drug use impairs a person's ability to get adequate sleep, which in turn produces feelings of fatigue. Fighting fatigue with caffeine and nicotine is a losing battle. As you can see, using drugs, whether to maintain alertness, or to relax, may produce more stress than it alleviates.

Some respond to stress by overeating or eating unhealthy food. Excessive sugar intake will cause wild fluctuations in energy levels. Consuming fats will lead to weight gain, and perhaps to obesity. Overconsumption of either fats or sugars causes people to feel bad about their bodies and about their health. These feelings lead to increased stress. As with the use of drugs, improper diet can have dramatic negative impact on one's health; this will lead to increased health-related stress.

What Can You Do?

Use your critical thinking skills to identify the *causes* that produce the *effect* of stress. Whenever possible, strive to reduce exposure to stimuli and circumstances that produce stress. By eliminating the cause, you will also rid yourself of the effect. For example, if working up to deadlines is highly stressful for you, learn to complete your work earlier so you are not pressured by time.

To do your best, you need to feel your best. This means taking measures to maintain good health, and to eliminate unwanted stressors from your lifestyle. Take the time to learn about behaviors and their effects that will contribute positively to your personal well-being.

List several things you can do to alleviate stress in your life:

CHAPTER 11

Personality

Do You Know?

Do you know that the concept of personality has been of interest to people for thousands of years, yet it still vexes psychologists as much as any other topic in the discipline? Your textbook defines personality as a relatively stable pattern of behaving, feeling, and thinking that distinguishes one person from another. On its surface, that definition is quite compelling, and to be sure, it is rather akin to definitions you might find in any other textbook. While there seems to be widespread agreement on the definition, it is important to note that these definitions do not lend to straightforward research questions that can be addressed such that they provide unambiguous data to clarify understanding of the concept of personality.

Whether considering the early approach of Hippocrates, the widely known one of Freud, or any of a large number of contemporary ideas, it is clear that tackling the task of understanding personality is difficult, and it is therefore likely that it will continue to puzzle researchers and theorists for generations to come. The difficulty, no doubt, stems from the very concept being hypothetical in nature, and not something that lends itself to measurement. Try the following thought experiment. Imagine two people whom you know reasonably well, and whom you consider to have very different personalities. Next, describe different tests that you might conduct on these two in order to probe their differences and underscore their personalities. If you had limitless resources and perfect compliance from your subjects, you would likely still fall short of definitive descriptions of their personalities. This is precisely because hypothetical constructs are not objective enough that they can be defined to the satisfaction of everyone. Not until personality is defined in objective, measurable terms will we be able to address the features that make us unique in ways that will be meaningful over time. Given the complexity of humans and human nature, it is difficult to imagine objective ways of defining personality that will work equally well in characterizing all people.

Notes from Class and the Textbook

Use the space provided in this outline to record notes from the textbook as well as from class lectures and discussion. Questions related to the *Psychological Detective, Hands On, Myth or Science,* and *Study Tip* sections in the text have been presented in the outline; use the associated space to respond to the questions and to record your own comments about the issues.

I. Analyzing Personality

    A. Defining Personality

    B. Assessing Personality

        1. Self-Report Inventories

        2. The Minnesota Multiphasic Personality Inventory

        3. The California Psychological Inventory

4. Limitations of Self-Report Inventories

5. Projective Tests

6. Limitations of Projective Tests

7. The Barnum Effect

Why do people accept feedback on their personalities from sources such as horoscopes, computer- and Internet-based programs, etc.?

8. Other Measures

C. Is Behavior Consistent?

1. Challenges to the Idea of Consistency

2. In Defense of Consistency

Does volunteering to work for charity provide evidence of the consistency of altruism over time? Why or why not?

3. Evidence of Consistency Based on Multiple Measures

II. Trait Approaches

Complete the "Big Five" Test on pages 467 and 468 of your textbook. The scoring key for the test appears at the end of the chapter in the textbook on page 499.

A. Factors in Personality: Raymond B. Cattell

B. Categorization of Traits: Hans Eysenck

What do people described as extroverts and introverts prefer doing? Write down a few answers before moving on to the next section.

C. The "Big Five" Traits

1. The Big Five and Job Performance

D. Alternatives to the Big Five

III. Biological Factors in Personality

    A. Early Biological Approaches

Trepanation, operating on the skull in order to facilitate blood flow in the capillaries of the brain, received mixed support as a medical practice. While it is illegal in the United States and Europe, it has its advocates. What are your thoughts on this controversial practice?

        1. Humors and Bumps

        2. Body Types

        3. Sensation Seeking

Complete the Sensation Seeking Scale that appears on pages 476 and 477 in your textbook. The scoring key for the scale appears at the end of the chapter in the textbook on page 499.

Write a paragraph describing what you have learned about yourself according to your scores on the Big Five Test and the Sensation Seeking Scale.

B. Twin Studies

How do you differentiate between a coincidence and an explainable event? Does the distinction change if the event is explained in terms of genetic versus environmental factors? Consider these questions in light of the similarities and differences in the behaviors of twins.

Point your Web browser at the textbook's Web page to see Live!Psych module 11.1.

C. Personality and the Evolutionary Perspective

IV. The Psychodynamic Perspective

A. Basic Concepts

1. Psychic Determinism

What, if anything, does it really mean when someone makes a *Freudian slip*?

2. Instincts

3. The Unconscious

B. The Structure of the Mind

   1. The Id

   2. The Ego

   3. The Superego

   4. Interaction of Id, Ego, and Superego

C. Defense Mechanisms

How could you test the idea that someone's id, ego, and superego are in conflict?

D. Stages of Psychosexual Development

   1. The Oral Stage

   2. The Anal Stage

Pair up with a study partner and act as Rotter and Bandura. In your role–playing exercise, reflect the theorists' perspectives on personality through a question and answer dialogue.

VI. The Humanistic Perspective

    1. Abraham Maslow

        a. Basic Needs

        b. Self-Actualization

    2. Carl Rogers

How can information from the Q-sort be used to study the relationship between one's real and ideal selves?

Learning Objectives

After you have studied the chapter, you should be able to respond to the following statements and questions to convey your understanding of the material.

1. What methods and tools have been developed to measure personality?

2. How are environmental and genetic variables involved in determining personality?

3. Describe the psychodynamic perspective on personality. Why has it been so appealing to people over the years? What are its shortcomings?

4. What has been contributed by the learning and cognitive perspectives on personality?

5. Identify the strengths and weaknesses of the humanistic approach to personality.

Key Word Exercise

Fill in the blanks in the following statements with key words and terms from the textbook. Answer as many as you can without referring to your notes or to the book. If you have blanks after thinking about each item, try using your book. The answers are presented after the practice test.

1. Psychological tests in which individuals answer questions about themselves, usually by responding *yes or no* or *true* or *false* are called _____-_____ _____.

2. The *Thematic Apperception Test* is an example of a(n) _____ _____.

3. _____ is a summary term that describes the tendency to behave, feel, and think in ways that are consistent across situations.

4. Sheldon's terms, *endomorph, mesomorph,* and *ectomorph,* came from an early approach to investigating personality based on _____.

5. _____ estimates suggest that genetics are responsible for between 20 and 50 percent of personality characteristics.

6. Freud's model for explaining personality development was based on his idea that people seek to experience pleasure in several parts of the body called _____.

7. _____ complex is to girl as _____ complex is to boy.

8. *Denial, projection, rationalization,* and *repression* are examples of _____ _____.

9. Freud's theory has been highly criticized by psychologists because it is not _____.

10. Bandura labeled one's expectancy about her or his ability to engage in effective behaviors _____ _____.

Practice Test

Circle the letter that corresponds to the **best** alternative for each of the following items. Read each alternative carefully. The answers are presented at the end of this study guide chapter. Be sure to learn *why* each correct alternative is better than the others.

1. Your friend just took a test with over 500 true-false items on it. Which of the following was it?
   a. the Self-Report Inventory
   b. the Thematic Apperception Test
   c. the Minnesota Multiphasic Personality Inventory
   d. the Generalized Personality Analysis (GPA) Questionnaire

2. A back translation is:
   a. a normal translation that is performed after the fact.
   b. a procedure used to ensure that adaptations of a test in another language are translated appropriately.
   c. a maneuver used by many Olympic platform divers that requires a combination of athletic agility and personality.
   d. done when someone is unsure what a person from another culture has done behaviorally, and describes it to someone back home who can make sense of it.

3. Projective tests involve:
   a. looking into the future.
   b. presentation of unstructured or ambiguous stimuli.
   c. assigning clients to projects and testing their abilities to do the work.
   d. overhead projectors that display images on huge screens for interpretation by subjects.

4. To say that someone has fallen subject to the Barnum effect is to say:
   a. they are depressed.
   b. they just had a good time at the circus.
   c. they actually believe in the work of Sigmund Freud.
   d. they just accepted a generalized description as an accurate statement.

5. Eysenck's theory posits that:
   a. personality consists of three basic traits.
   b. airplane pilots, musicians, and artists are basically the same.
   c. the id, ego, and superego are in constant battle with one another.
   d. that there are 16 personality factors (which may be measured using the 16PF scale)

6. The "big five" traits:
   a. were proposed by Cattell.
   b. were offered by Eysenck.
   c. are really just extensions of the three that Freud originally suggested.
   d. are gaining widespread support, and can be remembered using the acronym OCEAN.

7. Although there is a fair amount of debate about determinants of behavior, it seems clear that:
   a. genetics have insignificant influences on behavior.
   b. situational variables influence behavior in significant ways.
   c. it will always be impossible to know why people do the things they do.
   d. none of the above.

8. Which of the following did Hippocrates *not* consider as one of the four bodily humors?
   a. blood
   b. phlegm
   c. black bile
   d. vitreous humor

9. You and a friend were strolling through an antiques and curios store when you noticed a porcelain model of a human head with various labels that would have corresponded to parts of the brain that were theorized to control various behaviors. You realized that it was derived from the 1800's idea of ___ that was championed by Franz Joseph Gall.
   a. Oedipus
   b. phrenology
   c. mystic tea vessels
   d. the stream of consciousness

10. Skydivers, race car drivers, divers, and others who regularly seek stimulation from a variety of sources are known as:
    a. nuts.
    b. riskers.
    c. death wishers.
    d. sensation seekers.

11. The study of identical twins who were separated early in life:
    a. allows researchers to isolate the effects of nature from those of nurture.
    b. has been restricted to the U.S. states of Ohio and Minnesota because it is cruel.
    e. takes relatively little time and effort compared to studying fraternal twins the same way.
    d. is a common practice among developmental psychologists as such separation is commonplace.

12. Research comparing differences between identical twins reared apart, and those reared together,:
    a. has yet to be done in a systematic way.
    b. yielded similar results on many of the MMPI sub-scales.
    c. is by its very nature *longitudinal,* and therefore has not been completed.
    d. helped psychologists realize the greater similarity of fraternal versus identical twins.

13. The size of the genetic effect—estimated by what is called *heritability*—indicates that:
    a. Ohio twins outscore Minnesota twins.
    b. fraternal twins outscore identical twins.
    c. differences among most people are due at least as much to environmental influences.
    d. the parents of fraternal twins are often strikingly similar in comparison to other sets of spouses.

14. Freud's notion of psychic determinism:
    a. assumes that all behaviors result from early childhood experiences.
    b. developed out of the research that was first begun by phrenologist Franz Gall.
    c. is that one's sex determines the varieties of defense mechanisms on which he or she will rely.
    d. assumes that all behaviors result from resonating psychic energy that is in one's home, but cannot be measured.

15. Freud's model for understanding personality can be likened to a(n):
    a. iceberg.
    b. river barge.
    c. enormous cigar.
    d. canyon created by a river.

16. *Id* is to ___ as *ego* is to___.
    a. Maslow; Freud
    b. identical twin; fraternal twin
    c. steam locomotive; houseboat
    d. pleasure principle; reality principle

17. According to Freud, the *superego:*
    a. is an exceptionally good ego.
    b. is far above the surface of awareness.
    c. incorporates societal and parental standards.
    d. develops out of the ego as one resolves one's innate desire for the opposite sex parent.

18. By and large, the Neo-Freudians:
    a. were Freud's offspring.
    b. found Freud's idea of *ego* to be ridiculous.
    c. disagreed with Freud's focus on the *id* and sexual motives.
    d. All of the above are true about the Neo-Freudians.

19. A widespread criticism of Freudian theory:
    a. has not existed to date.
    b. is that it is largely untestable.
    c. was offered by the man himself at the close of his life.
    d. stemmed from Freud's having an unresolved Oedipal conflict.

20. A significant contribution to personality theory was offered by Julian Rotter, who:
    a. developed a scale to measure the *locus of control.*
    b. invented the idea of *sensation seeking* as a way of explaining his own behavior.
    c. was the first name relative of Julian Lennon, son of John Lennon (one of the Beatles).
    d. basically followed in the tradition of the behaviorists in emphasizing noncognitive factors.

21. *Reciprocal determinism* is an idea that was proposed by Albert Bandura:
    a. to compete with Freud's notion of *psychic determinism.*
    b. to explain the interaction of person variables, situation variables, and behavior.
    c. a psychologist who began his career in the automotive industry–the source of the term.
    d. when he observed that after children hit Bobo dolls the dolls retaliated by kicking the children.

22. Abraham Maslow, who is well known for having developed the *hierarchy of needs,* thought which of the following?
    a. Humanistic psychology was the "third force" in psychology.
    b. Cognitive psychology was the creation science of psychology.
    c. Humanistic psychology would bring the downfall of the discipline.
    d. His idea fit better with traditional Freudian ideology than with Humanistic psychology.

23. Carl Rogers is probably best known for his term:
    a. ego-ideal.
    b. self-actualization.
    c. unconditional positive regard.
    d. conditional reward contingency.

24. Research on the *self* in social contexts has revealed:
    a. that John Watson was right.
    b. that most people are antisocial in nature.
    c. little to nothing of lasting value to psychology.
    d. that there are significant cultural differences with respect to conceptions of the *self.*

Answers to Key Word Exercise

1. self-report inventories	2. projective test	3. Trait
4. body type	5. Heritability	6. erogenous zones
7. Electra; Oedipal	8. defense mechanisms	9. testable
10. self-efficacy		

Practice Test Answers and Explanations

1. c.   The MMPI is a test that scores people according to 10 different dimensions. It has been adapted for use in at least 22 languages.
2. b.   A back translation is performed when testing how well a term or concept from a test translated into another language. The term is translated back into the original language.
3. b.   Projective tests involve the presentation of unstructured or ambiguous stimuli and recording people's responses to the stimuli.
4. d.   The Barnum effect is based on P. T. Barnum's statement about the circus, there is a "little something in it for everybody." Here, it means that a generalized statement is accepted as an accurate description of one's personality.
5. a.   Eysenck's model suggests that personality is comprised of three basic traits: extraversion, neuroticism, and psychoticism.
6. d.   There is growing agreement about the five basic traits, although there is some disagreement about their labels. They are: openness, conscientiousness, extraversion, agreeableness, and neuroticism.
7. b.   Among other influences, it is clear that situational variables influence behavior in significant ways.
8. d.   The four bodily humors Hippocrates championed were black bile, blood, phlegm, and yellow bile.
9. b.   The model was based on Gall's idea, *phrenology,* which presumed that a lot could be learned about one's cognitive abilities and behavioral propensities by feeling the bumps on the head.
10. d.   *Sensation seeking* is the characteristic of engaging regularly in risky behavior, seeking thrills, and participating in novel experiences through the mind and senses.
11. a.   Though it is not easy to find such twins, researchers like to study identical twins that were separated early as it helps separate the environmental influences on development.
12. b.   University of Minnesota researchers compared 44 pairs of twins that were separated early in life, and found striking similarities between them in light of their comparability to twins reared together.
13. c.   Heritability research, including that done with identical twins reared together and apart, indicates that differences among most people are due at least as much to environmental influences.

14. a.   Freud's *psychic determinism* assumes behaviors stem from early experiences, especially conflicts related to sexual instincts.

15. a.   Freud's model of personality is often compared to an iceberg. See "The Structure of the Mind" section in your textbook.

16. d.   Freud's hypothetical construct (hypothetical construct is a fancy name for idea) *id was claimed to* operate according to what he called the pleasure principle. The *ego,* he said, was guided by reality.

17. c.   The *superego,* according to Freud, is the element that incorporates societal and parental standards in what is commonly referred to as the *conscience* as well as the idealistic *ego ideal.*

18. c.   The Neo-Freudians disagreed with Freud's focus on the *id* and sexual motives.

19. b.   Freud's theory has received much criticism since it does not lend itself to testing. Even when his ideas do lend themselves to testing, the results are mixed and do not support it well.

20. a.   Rotter developed a scale to measure *locus of control.* His research and ideas may be considered extensions of Skinner's, but Rotter's interests include cognitive components such as *expectancies.*

21. b.   Reciprocal determinism is Bandura's idea for explaining the interaction of person variables, situation variables, and behavior.

22. a.   Maslow thought that Humanistic psychology was the "third force" in psychology because it offered an alternative to psychodynamic theory and behaviorism.

23. c.   Rogers, a Humanist and a contemporary of Maslow, coined the term unconditional positive regard. He believed that growing up believing affection is conditional causes one to distort experiences.

24. d.   There are significant cultural differences with respect to conceptions of the *self.*

Key Vocabulary Terms

Use the following list to write definitions *in your own words* for each of the key terms from the chapter. Translating the terms into language that is comfortable and familiar for you will facilitate your learning. For further study of these terms, go to the companion website for the textbook where you will find electronic flash cards that you may use to test your vocabulary.

personality

self-report inventory

projective test

Barnum effect

trait

psychic determinism

unconscious

id

ego

superego

defense mechanism

oral stage

fixation

anal stage

phallic stage

Oedipal complex

Electra complex

latency stage

genital stage

social learning theory

locus of control

reciprocal determinism

self-efficacy

humanistic psychology

self-actualization

Tip for Success: Leadership Skills

At some level, everyone is a leader. By asking or answering a question, or otherwise redirecting the attention of your classmates and teacher, you are a leader in your class. Similarly, when you provide input to project group members, you are assuming a leadership position. When you are a leader, you shape your experience and help determine what your future opportunities will include. Sharing your insights is a sure way to ensure that your needs are understood. Alternatively, if you shy away from sharing your perspective, you may have to live with the consequences of others' interests and motives.

This *Tip* section will focus on ways you can shape your educational and career-related experiences by being a leader. There is no time like the present for you to begin shaping your life by assuming more leadership in your endeavors. The list that follows provides several suggestions for developing and maintaining leadership roles. Your ideas need to be heard. With a little effort, you will set in motion your future as a leader with a range of opportunities.

1. Be Willing to Make Mistakes. An old say goes, "nothing ventured, nothing gained." This saying fits a number of topics that involve taking risks. As a leader, you will be constantly making decisions that could result in failure. That is OK. Everyone falls short of her or his expectations from time to time. The hope is that, on balance, your advances will outweigh your setbacks.

Name three things that you avoided doing because you were afraid of making a mistake.

_____

_____

What was the worst thing that could have happened if you had made a mistake? What did you stand to gain?

_____

_____

2. Challenge Yourself. Take a few moments and think of several prominent leaders from history. What set them apart from everyone else? Most likely it was that they made significant contributions or accomplishments in their fields. The only way to make significant accomplishments is to take on challenging tasks. Identify a challenging goal, make a promise to yourself and others about the goal, and go for it! You will keep your interest in your endeavors peaked if you continue to take on meaningful challenges.

What challenging opportunities await you in your near future?

_____

_____

3. Leaders Are Role Models. By assuming leadership positions, you will have unique opportunities to help others and to share your insight into problems and issues. By maintaining your focus, you will encourage others to do the same. When things do not go as planned, keep your focus. Without having to divert energy, everyone will benefit.

4. Communicate Objective Truths, Make "I" Statements, and Be in Control. Leaders take ownership in their feelings and ideas. A very important leadership skill is to make statements that reflect either objective truths or personalized opinions. If you state something that is *not* an objective truth, preface it with *I think, I feel,* or *I believe.* Always resist passing judgment on others. Pointing fingers and placing blame only makes you feel bad and causes others to harbor resentment.

Only you have the power to decide how you will respond to what others do or say. When you place blame on someone else, you are indicating that you are out of control. If you begin to feel you are losing control, indicate that such is the case by making an *I statement* (e.g., I feel as though I am not in control of what is happening).

Think of three occasions when you have made statements that involved placing blame or pointing your finger at others. Write an *I Statement* that you could have made on each occasion instead.

_____

_____

_____

5. Focus on the Issue. By and large, your friends and colleagues are interested in succeeding at the endeavors they take on. If you are working together on something, and meet with frustration, do not blame others. Chances are they want to succeed too. Focus your attention on aspects of the problem that merit your attention rather than on other people who are also frustrated.

6. Give Credit to Others. The most satisfactory feeling that one can experience when something goes well is just that, a feeling. Have you ever noticed that many people like to brag, but that nobody likes hearing someone brag? This has a significant implication for those occasions when you meet with success in your endeavors. Rather than accepting responsibility for your successes, redirect attention to those whose efforts made your success possible. That will make them feel better and have more positive feelings about you.

Identify an accomplishment that you took credit for, even though someone else helped (even if he or she played a minor role that nobody was aware of):

_____

7. Have *Silent Pride*. Sometimes your successes are well deserved, and are due entirely to your own efforts. When things go your way and you are not able to redirect attention to others who played a role in the success, try being quietly humble. Being quietly humble, or having *silent pride,* will help others to see you more favorably and to wonder why you are not bragging. Since nobody likes to hear someone brag, this behavior will be intriguing. It is better to be intriguing than obnoxious.

Identify an example of someone bragging about her or his success at something. How would that occasion have been different had they adopted the silent pride response?

_____

8. Be Assertive. To *assert* is to state something positively. Being assertive means making clear statements about your ideas and feelings. Assertive comments and behavior typically come from those who are confident and respectful of others. Aggressive comments and behavior, on the other hand, are divisive and tend to break down relationships. Learn to control your aggression and to assert your position when appropriate.

9. Listen. When you adopt a position of leadership, it is important that you listen carefully to what others say. Failure to listen to, and respond to, others' comments reflects poor leadership. If you lead others, it is critical that you understand and represent their interests.

Identify the leadership skills you already practice. Which ones should you attend to?

_____

_____

CHAPTER 12

Psychological Disorders

Do You Know?

Do you know that diagnosis of psychological disorders is sometimes very difficult? Unlike many medical diseases that are diagnosable based upon a few defining symptoms, psychological disorders have less precise diagnostic criteria and therefore are more difficult to pinpoint definitively. What is more, some psychological disorders involve cyclical or periodic expression of symptoms, and unless the diagnostic criteria for all of the symptoms are viewed by the clinician or team that makes the diagnosis, persons with psychological disorders may not be properly diagnosed. A couple of familiar diagnoses will serve to illustrate examples of the importance of observing all of the features of someone's behavior in advance of performing diagnostic evaluation.

Dissociative identity disorder, which was previously called multiple personality disorder, typically takes several years to diagnose. This is not so much because the disorder's diagnostic criteria are so difficult to define, rather it typically takes several attempts to determine a proper diagnosis and course of treatment before it becomes clear that someone has the disorder. At one time the disorder was considered to be extremely rare, so clinicians did not necessarily consider it as a candidate when performing diagnoses. Instead, people were diagnosed with such disorders as depression, schizophrenia, and substance abuse disorder. Only after having gathered information on people for several years do patterns emerge that make it clear that the person in question may have dissociative identity disorder.

Another example of complicated diagnosis is with bipolar disorder, or manic depression as it was once called. Bipolar disorder is a mood disorder that involves the person's experiencing periods of depression and mania (the opposite of depression) in alternating fashion. Because people do not typically find manic phases to be maladaptive and undesired, it is not common for them to seek treatment when in that phase. Instead, only when people experience depression do they consider that they may need clinical help. If the clinician only witnesses the person in depressive phases, and is otherwise unaware that the person also experiences manic phases, he or she cannot offer the proper diagnosis. Because the treatments for (unipolar) depression and bipolar disorder are different, bipolar disorder may persist without effective treatment indefinitely until a more comprehensive diagnosis is made.

These are but a couple of examples of the complications clinicians experience when performing diagnoses. Inasmuch as the key criteria are typically behavioral in nature, it is not surprising that diagnosis is so difficult. As brain imaging techniques, cerebrospinal fluid assays, and other more objective tests of structural and functional abnormalities become part of the diagnostic evaluation, it is likely that the criteria for determining whether someone has a disorder, and if so which one, will become more precise.

Notes from Class and the Textbook

Use the space provided in this outline to record notes from the textbook as well as from class lectures and discussion. Questions related to the *Psychological Detective, Hands On, Myth or Science,* and *Study Tip* sections in the text have been presented in the outline; use the associated space to respond to the questions and to record your own comments about the issues.

I. Abnormal Behavior

    A. Criteria of Abnormality

        1. Statistical Rarity

        2. Interference with Normal Functioning

3. Distress

4. Deviance from Social Norms

B. A Working Definition

C. The Concept of Insanity

How often is the insanity plea used? What sources guide people's thinking about the frequency of use of the insanity plea? How often does it result in acquittal?

D. Models of Abnormal Behavior

1. The Medical Model

2. The Psychological Models

3. Culture and Disorders

II. Classifying and Counting Psychological Disorders

A. DSM-IV

Create flash cards with the names of the major categories of disorders listed in the DSM-IV. Put the disorder type on one side, and an example on the other side. Work with two other students. Have one call out either the disorder type or an example, and the other student give the other piece of information. Trade the cards around until each student can name an example of a disorder type when given an example, and vice versa.

    B. The Labeling Issue

    C. The Prevalence of Psychological Disorders

III. Anxiety, Somatoform, and Dissociative Disorders

    A. Anxiety Disorders

        1. Phobias

        2. Panic Disorder

Why do only some of the 15 to 30 percent of people who have experienced at least one panic attack develop chronic panic disorder? What role might cognitive interpretation of symptoms contribute to the likelihood that one will develop the disorder?

3. Generalized Anxiety Disorder (GAD)

4. Obsessive—Compulsive Disorder

What behavior is reinforced, and what is the reinforcer, when one feels less anxious after taking a shower? What principle of operant conditioning is in effect when each shower reduces anxiety?

B. Somatoform Disorders

1. Hypochondriasis

2. Somatization Disorder

3. Conversion Disorder

C. Dissociative Disorders

1. Dissociative Amnesia and Dissociative Fugue

How would the medical model account for Ed's amnesia concerning the accident? How would that explanation differ from one from the psychodynamic model?

2. Dissociative Identity Disorder

Develop a chart to summarize anxiety, somatoform, and dissociative disorders. Be sure to define each within your chart.

IV. Mood Disorders

    A. Depression

        1. Symptoms

        2. Prevalence and Course

        3. Suicide

Do people who are likely to commit suicide typically give signals concerning their intentions? Read the Myth or Science segment on pages 528 and 529 to learn more about the issue.

    B. Bipolar Disorder

C. Causes of Mood Disorders

    1. Biological Explanations

    2. The Psychodynamic Explanation

    3. Cognitive and Behavioral Explanations

    4. Multiple Causes

V. Schizophrenia

    A. Symptoms of Schizophrenia

      1. Positive Symptoms

      2. Negative Symptoms

    B. Subtypes of Schizophrenia

Develop visual representations that will help you remember each of the five types of schizophrenia.

C. Causes of Schizophrenia

  1. Genetic Factors

What can research with groups of twins, some reared together and some reared apart, tell researchers about the causes of schizophrenia?

  2. Brain Abnormalities

  3. Neurotransmitters

  4. Environmental Causes

  5. Multiple Causes

VI. Personality and Sexual Disorders

  A. Personality Disorders

How could a researcher measure physiological arousal? Design an experiment to study whether low levels of physiological arousal are related to antisocial behavior.

B. Sexual Disorders

    1. Gender Identity Disorder

    2. Paraphilias

    3. Fetishism

Write summaries, one paragraph each, to describe the material on personality and sexual disorders.

Learning Objectives

After you have studied the chapter, you should be able to respond to the following statements and questions to convey your understanding of the material.

1. What criteria must behavior meet in order to be considered abnormal?

2. What tools, methods, and techniques are available to diagnose and determine the prevalence of psychological disorders?

3. Discuss characteristics of anxiety disorders. How are they related to one another?

4. Describe the causes of mood disorders as they were presented in your textbook.

5. The word *schizophrenia* is widely known, but the disorder is not well understood. Why is it difficult to understand schizophrenia? What causes the disorder?

6. How can one use principles of learning (especially classical and operant conditioning) to understand personality disorders and sexual disorders?

Key Word Exercise

Fill in the blanks in the following statements with key words and terms from the textbook. Answer as many as you can without referring to your notes or to the book. If you have blanks after thinking about each item, try using your book. The answers are presented after the practice test.

1. The _____ _____ criterion for determining whether behavior is abnormal involves determining whether the peoples' behaviors are upsetting, distracting, or confusing to themselves.

2. According to the _____ _____, psychological disorders are learned and follow the principles of classical and operant conditioning.

3. _____ _____ _____ involves a chronically high level of anxiety that is not associated with a particular stimulus.

4. _____ is the number or percentage of newly diagnosed cases of a particular disorder in a given population.

5. In some cases major depression and _____ _____ occur together in a condition that is referred to as double depression.

6. What was once called multiple personality disorder is now known as _____ _____.

7. _____ _____ is the belief that one cannot control outcomes through one's actions.

8. A(n) _____ _____ is a conclusion that is drawn in the absence of supporting information.

9. Believing you are Santa Claus would be an example of a(n) _____.

10. An experiment involved MRI scanning of the brains of 'normal' people and persons with schizophrenia. Results indicated that the *thalamus* and surrounding regions in schizophrenic patients were significantly _____ than the same regions in 'normal' brains.

Practice Test

Circle the letter that corresponds to the *best* alternative for each of the following items. Read each alternative carefully. The answers are presented at the end of this study guide chapter. Be sure to learn *why* each correct alternative is better than the others.

1. The criteria for abnormality, as presented in your textbook, include all but which of the following?
   a. statistical rarity
   b. deviance from social norms
   c. interference with normal functioning
   d. adherence to rules for alternative fashion

2. Which example fits best the description of a *dysfunctional* family?
   a. The head of the household rarely functions before noon.
   b. Maids, gardeners, and cooks do all the work for the family.
   c. Typical familial interactions adversely affect the family's functioning.
   d. Both husband and wife get along well, but there are no children or pets.

3. Social norms are:
   a. guys named Norman that like to go to parties.
   b. behaviors such as keeping one's house well organized.
   c. difficult to follow for most people because of their elusive nature.
   d. guidelines (that are usually unwritten) that define the acceptability of behavior.

4. The U.S. public believes felony indictments involve the insanity plea ___ percent of the time, and that ___ percent of those pleas result in acquittal. Actually only about 1 % of cases involve the plea, and less than 1/4 of 1 percent are successful.
   a. 10; 80
   b. 50; 75
   c. 37; 44
   d. 89; 14

5. Psychological models for explaining abnormal behavior emphasize:
   a. the probability that underlying organic causes are at play.
   b. the likelihood that mental illness results from possession by demons.
   c. mental functioning, social experiences, and learning histories as having important causal links.
   d. all of the above.

6. Sociocultural variables apparently influence the likelihood that one will have a psychological disorder. For example, poverty is related to the prevalence of psychological disorders, and rates of psychological disorders are influenced by socioeconomic status. Another (category of) disorder that seems related to cultural variables is:
   a. bipolar disorder.
   b. phobic disorders.
   c. anorexia nervosa.
   d. obsessive-compulsive disorder.

7. A major reason people are diagnosed is:
   a. to be able to make predictions.
   b. so labels can be assigned to them.
   c. so that insurance companies can reimburse diagnosticians.
   d. to determine whether they were insane when they committed their crimes.

8. In the Rosenhan study in which 'normal' people entered hospitals and reported hearing voices:
   a. the people were admitted for an average of 19 days and were administered over 2,000 pills.
   b. while the people were taken seriously, they were not diagnosed as having any type of illness.
   c. the people were referred to a hearing specialist as it was determined their problem was not psychologically based.
   d. it was determined that the diagnostic criteria were very effective at discriminating 'normal' from those with mental illness.

9. The most frequently used diagnostic system for classifying mental disorders was developed by:
   a. Rosenhan and his colleagues.
   b. the American Psychiatric Association.
   c. the American Psychological Association.
   d. members of the American Psychiatric Association and members of the American Psychological association, under the leadership of Rosenhan.

10. An epidemiologist:
   a. is someone who study the bugs that cause mental disorders.
   b. is handy to have around if one experiences an epidemio infestation.
   c. studies the distribution and causes of accidents, diseases, and psychological disorders.
   d. has to have several years of training in brain scanning (e.g., MRI) in order to work effectively.

11. A *comorbid* psychological disorder is:
   a. one that develops initially with symptoms that one has died.
   b. a disorder that co-occurs with one or more other psychological disorders.
   c. a disorder that develops just as the symptoms of another disorder come under control.
   d. all of the above.

12. Phobias are:
   a. innate fears (not related to environment or experience).
   b. excessive fears that are categorized under anxiety disorders.
   c. more prevalent in third world than in highly industrialized countries.
   d. fears that develop as a result of eating diets that are proportionately high in saturated fats.

13. The most severe anxiety disorder(s) is (are):
   a. panic disorder.
   b. simple phobias.
   c. generalized anxiety disorder.
   d. obsessive-compulsive disorder.

14. Obsessions are to ___ as compulsions are to ___.
   a. OCD; GAD
   b. acts; thoughts
   c. thoughts; acts
   d. early onset; chronic syndromes

15. Somatoform disorders involve:
   a. physical symptoms with no known medical cause.
   b. the irrational repetitive creation (forming) of somas (bodies).
   c. medical symptoms that are known to result from psychological issues.
   d. peculiar behaviors that are targeted at reducing anxiety about repetitive thoughts.

16. Sally is forever going to the doctor and consulting pharmacists about what she can do to address a constellation of symptoms that most people would ignore. Sally probably has:
    a. OCD.
    b. cancer.
    c. hypochondriasis.
    d. anterior-lateral sclerosis.

17. A truck driver recently picked up Hans while he was walking toward town after crashing his car. Hans had absolutely no idea where he was, or for that matter where he had come from. After some careful investigative work, officials were able to determine that Hans had rented a car after flying to the U.S. from Europe. However, Hans could recall nothing of his adventure or the events leading up to it. Hans is likely suffering from:
    a. dissociative fugue.
    b. retrograde amnesia.
    c. conversion disorder.
    d. comorbid hypochondriasis.

18. Surveys of people in the U.S., Western Europe, the Middle East, Asia, and the Pacific Rim regarding depression have revealed which of the following?
    a. Depression is beginning at an earlier age with each successive generation.
    b. Rates of depression have risen steadily for each successive generation since 1915.
    c. Both a. and b., above, are true.
    d. Neither a. nor b. is true; depression is becoming decidedly less common world-wide.

19. The most serious complication of severe depression is:
    a. comorbidity.
    b. the possibility of suicide.
    c. that slowed heart rate can least to cardiac rest.
    d. that people with substance abuse disorders often also are depressed.

20. Bipolar disorder involves alternating cycles of ___ and___.
    a. OCD; GAD
    b. wash; rinse
    c. depression; mania
    d. somatoform disorder; conversion disorder

21. The *concordance rate* is:
    a. a measure of treatment efficacy for mental disorders.
    b. the percentage of twin pairs in which both twins have a disorder.
    c. an index of the proportion of the population that has a given disorder.
    d. usually 7/1 Os of a percentage point behind the 30-year mortgage rate.

22. Schizophrenia is a psychotic disorder. That is, it:
    a. involves the symptom of the afflicted person losing contact with reality.
    b. is most effectively treated with psychotherapies rather than drug therapies.
    c. inevitably results in a slow, painful death in which the individual is tormented by peers.
    d. is a violent disorder. As a result many people with schizophrenia have to be incarcerated.

23. Flattened affect is to hallucination as ___ is to ___.
    a. neurosis; psychosis
    b. psychosis; neurosis
    c. positive symptom; negative symptom
    d. negative symptom; positive symptom

24. Someone with antisocial personality disorder is:
    a. outcast, and transforms feelings of rejection into positive feedback.
    b. typically in late adulthood before symptoms develop sufficiently for diagnosis.
    c. characterized as deceitful, impulsive, and reckless and feels no remorse for her or his behavior.
    d. fun to be with at parties because even though others do not treat them well, they have what Freud referred to as strong unconscious needs to enrich the lives of others.

25. Transsexualism:
    a. is a particular form of paraphilia.
    b. is another name for homosexuality.
    c. is approximately three times more common in males than females.
    d. involves thinking like one gender, and acting like the other gender.

Answers to Key Word Exercise

1. personal distress	2. behavioral model	3. Generalized anxiety disorder
4. Incidence	5. dysthymic disorder	6. dissociative identity disorder
7. Learned helplessness	8. arbitrary inference	9. delusion
10. smaller		

Practice Test Answers and Explanations

1. d.　Adherence to rules for alternative fashion is not a criterion for abnormality.
2. c.　*Dysfunctional* is a term used to describe behaviors that adversely affect functioning.
3. d.　*Social norms* are guidelines for what is acceptable and what is unacceptable for a particular group.
4. c.　Surveys have demonstrated that people grossly overestimate the frequency with which the insanity plea is used, and the likelihood that people who use it will be successful.
5. c.　Psychological models reflect perspectives on behavioral issues. Medical models focus on organic causes (as they do with physical illnesses).
6. c.　Anorexia nervosa occurs mainly in Western cultures where thinness is considered a sign of beauty.
7. a.　Diagnosis is used primarily to make predictions about patterns in people's behaviors.
8. a.　People acting as if they had experienced hallucinations were diagnosed and treated as if they had mental illness.
9. b.　The American *Psychiatric* Association developed the Diagnostic and Statistical Manual of Mental Disorders (DSM). The DSM is in its fourth edition (DSM-N).
10. c.　Epidemiologists estimate the distributions and causes of maladies, accidents, and problems.
11. b.　Comorbid disorders are disorders that co-occur; often people who experience symptoms of one disorder also experience symptoms of additional disorders.
12. b.　Phobias are fears, often stemming from experiences that comprise a specific category of anxiety disorder.
13. a.　Panic disorder is considered the most severe anxiety disorder.
14. c.　Obsessions are repetitive thoughts; compulsions are acts (often targeted at allaying obsessions).
15. a.　Somatoform disorders involve physical symptoms with no known medical cause.
16. c.　Hypochondriasis involves the interpretation of normal bodily symptoms as indices that one is contracting dreaded disease.
17. a.　The symptoms of dissociative fugue include amnesia, flight from the workplace or home, and establishing a new identity.
18. c.　More people seem to be developing depression at earlier ages.
19. b.　People with severe depression are at great risk for suicide.
20. c.　People with bipolar disorder show symptoms of depression and mania, in alternation.
21. b.　Concordance refers to the percentage of twin pairs in which both twins have a disorder.
22. a.　Psychosis is any disorder in which a severely disturbed individual loses contact with reality.
23. d.　Negative symptoms are reductions in functioning, such as failing to show appropriate emotional responses. Positive symptoms are excesses or distortions in normal functioning, as with hallucinations.

24. c. Antisocial personality disorder is characterized by deceitful, impulsive, and reckless activity for which one feels no remorse.
25. c. Transsexualism is approximately three times more common in males than females.

Key Vocabulary Terms

Use the following list to write definitions *in your own words* for each of the key terms from the chapter. Translating the terms into language that is comfortable and familiar for you will facilitate your learning. For further study of these terms, go to the companion website for the textbook where you will find electronic flash cards that you may use to test your vocabulary.

dysfunctional

abnormal

insanity

medical model

psychodynamic model

behavioral model

cognitive model

sociocultural model

diagnosis

prevalence

incidence

anxiety

phobia

agoraphobia

social phobia

specific phobia

panic disorder

generalized anxiety disorder (GAD)

obsessive-compulsive disorder (OCD)

somatoform disorders

hypochondriasis

somatization disorder

conversion disorder

dissociative disorders

dissociative amnesia

dissociative fugue

dissociative identity disorder (multiple personality)

depression

mania

bipolar disorder

concordance rate

learned helplessness

arbitrary inference

schizophrenia

psychosis

delusion

hallucinations

personality disorders

antisocial personality disorder

gender identity disorder (transsexualism)

paraphilia

fetishism

Tip for Success: The Psychology Major

Psychology is a popular major at both the undergraduate and graduate levels. The diversity of psychology means that it holds something of interest for many students. Students who take an introductory psychology course are sometimes surprised when they realize that the discipline has implications for so many other academic areas, as well as for a range of career opportunities.

This last *Tip* section addresses some common questions and concerns for students considering a major in psychology. After reviewing this section, you may wish to make an appointment with a professor from your school's psychology department to pursue additional questions. The career services office, library, and the Internet are other places you can look for answers about a potential major in psychology.

Finally, a recently developed resource that provides a thorough review of issues surrounding psychology, including academic issues and career possibilities and considerations, may be of interest to you. The book is called *The Psychology Major: Career Options and Strategies for Success,* and was written by R. Eric Landrum and Stephen F. Davis (Dr. Davis is one of the authors of your textbook, so if you find the writing style in your textbook to be appealing, you will likely also appreciate *The Psychology Major*).

The following items may be of interest to you:

1. Psychology beyond the Introductory Course. The psychology curriculum varies from school to school. The courses offered in most psychology departments may be considered as extensions of the chapters from your introductory textbook. Here is a list of common courses:

a. Methodology: an introduction to the tools and techniques used by psychologists in their research. This course goes by various names, including Experimental Psychology, Psychological Methods, Psychological Research Methods, and so on. The methodology course is usually required for majors, and is considered an important part of the curriculum by graduate school admissions committees.

b. Statistics: topics include sampling, distributions, probability, descriptive, and inferential statistics. This course may be taught in the psychology department or in the math department at your school. It is usually required as a prerequisite for much of the upper-division psychology curriculum.

c. Developmental Psychology: a study of the physical, cognitive, and psychosocial processes of development. Some schools offer a lifespan development course; others offer separate courses that are based on age ranges.

d. Social Psychology: a study of how people think about, influence, and relate to one another. This class covers a range of interesting topics including altruism, group influences, and prejudice.

e. Abnormal Psychology: a survey of psychological disorders, their characteristics, and their origins. This course represents the aspect of psychology with which lay people are most familiar.

f. Cognitive Psychology: a study of cognitive and memory processes. Topics covered in this course may range from artificial intelligence to biologically based theories of memory formation.

g. Learning: an examination of theories, ranging from the classic to the contemporary, that have been developed to explain learning and related phenomena. The data that support theories in this area are typically from nonhuman animals.

h. Physiological Psychology: an introduction to the nervous system and its relationship to behavior and experience. Students of biology and physiology often take this course as well.

i. Psychological Testing: an introduction to theory underlying test construction, evaluation, and interpretation. This is an important course for those students who may be interested in working in school systems or with clinical populations. This course is sometimes called *Assessment* or *Tests and Measurement.*

j. Personality: a survey of psychological theories and research in the study of personality. Some instructors for this course emphasize theoretical issues; others focus more on research.

k. History and Systems: a study of the development of psychology. This course usually surveys psychology's historical roots in philosophy and the natural sciences. It is a senior-level, capstone course in many programs.

Compare this list with the course offerings in your school catalog. What additional classes are available at your school? Which courses are you interested in taking?

_____

_____

2. Getting Involved in Research. Most academic psychologists have research interests that are accessible to undergraduate students. If you convey your interest in helping with research, you may get an opportunity to become involved. Participating in research is arguably the best way for you to demonstrate initiative and commitment to your career. Establish a goal of presenting findings from a research project at a psychology convention. Attending and presenting data at conventions is a great way to meet others who share an interest in psychology, to get research ideas, and to learn about the latest developments in the field.

What topic(s) are you most interested in researching?

_____

_____

3. Getting an Internship. In addition to participating in research, you may want to do a psychology internship at a clinic, laboratory, school, or business in your town. Internships can be helpful in determining whether you should pursue a given line of study in psychology, and may even open up job opportunities if you decide to seek employment after graduation. If you are interested in doing an internship, consult a professor from your psychology department who can share with you the department's policies and procedures regarding student internships.

What careers in psychology would you like to learn more about?

_____

_____

4. Careers with a Bachelor's Degree in Psychology. People with academic training in psychology hold a wide variety of positions. Often, psychology-related careers require some level of graduate training, but there are many jobs that one can get with bachelor's level training in psychology. The following list indicates areas in which people who studied psychology at the bachelor's level have found meaningful employment.

a. Education and Teaching

b. Consulting and Statistics

c. Administration/Clerical

d. Professional Services

e. Sales

f. Health and Related Services

g. Research and Development

5. Careers with Graduate Degrees in Psychology. After completing your bachelor's degree, you may choose to pursue graduate education in psychology. There are a several options to consider if you are interested in graduate training. Are your interests in applied careers (e.g., industrial and organizational psychology, school psychology, counseling)? Are you interested in doing basic research in psychology or a related discipline (e.g., neuroscience)? Would you enjoy teaching as part of your career? The answers to these questions will have some bearing on your decision about whether to pursue graduate training.

Depending on which career(s) you are interested in, you may plan to complete a master's degree or a doctoral degree. Some undergraduate psychology majors attend professional schools (e.g., medical school, law school) after finishing their undergraduate work. Master's degrees and professional degrees are usually preparation for applied work, whereas a doctorate is required if one is interested in teaching at the college level and in some career fields (e.g., clinical psychology).

Will additional schooling be required for you given your present career interests? If so, how will you begin learning about graduate programs to suit your needs? If not, what can you do as an undergraduate student to improve your chances of getting the job you are interested in?

6. Identifying a Role Model or Mentor. Many of the most successful people gained their success by working with, or otherwise modeling themselves after, other successful people. Find someone who has the career in which you are interested. Ask that person if you can make an appointment to interview her or him in order that you can learn more about everything the job entails. Assuming you are able to get an appointment, plan your questions ahead of time and take notes during the meeting. The following are some items you may wish to address:

> **a. Educational Background.** Where did the person attend school? What subject(s) did he or she study? What were critical steps and turning points that helped her or him get the job? How long has he or she been in the position?

> **b. Job Characteristics.** What kinds of things constitute the person's daily responsibilities and activities? How much time does the person spend on career-related work each week? What are the advantages and disadvantages of that career as that person perceives them?

> **c. Is There Anything You Can Do?** Make certain to communicate your interest in learning outside the classroom. Indicate that you would like to participate in research, read and discuss journal articles, help out with filing, or anything else the person might suggest. Initially you may have less than glamorous responsibilities, but if you do good work and are reliable, you will gain greater opportunities. This may be the beginning of an instructive and mutually beneficial relationship.

CHAPTER 15

Social Psychology: The Individual in Society

Do You Know?

Do you know that the concepts of conformity and compliance extend into daily living of people who are well beyond the years that are typically considered to be most closely associated with peer influence? Social psychologists define conformity as initiating or changing behavior in response to indirect social pressures, whereas compliance is initiating or changing a behavior in response to a request. While it might seem that circumstances that lead to compliance would likely always be obvious, people often find themselves behaving in ways that they later call into question as a result of phenomena and effects that social psychologists study.

One interesting compliance phenomenon is the foot-in-the-door effect. Did you ever notice that telemarketers and other sales people, particularly those who make 'cold' contact such as in door-to-door sales, begin with small questions to get you engaged in conversation? Once you have begun dialog, the impact of the effect has it that it is more difficult for you to terminate the conversation than if you had denied it at the outset. It is important to know that if you realize you are falling prey to the foot-in-the-door effect, you recognize also that just because you were agreeable initially, you need not continue. Understanding that it is okay to discontinue a series of behavioral decisions that is leading in an undesirable direction may save you time and money.

Alternatively, if you understand how the effect works, it is also possible for you to use it to your own benefit. I once received a parking ticket for backing into a parking place on state property (something that I had no idea was against the law). Rather disturbed by having received the ticket, and armed with a good understanding of the foot-in-the-door effect, I set about to fight the ticket. My line of reasoning began with some very simple questions with which the judge could not disagree—these questions addressed concerns of safety, whether he had witnessed the vehicle and pedestrian traffic at the time of day that I parked (about 6:00 a.m.) and at the time of day I usually left (about 4:00 p.m.). Having gotten him to answer several consecutive questions affirmatively, I began developing my plea to have him drop the charges using language that would capitalize on the pattern of affirmative responding. When I got to my plea, he realized what I had been doing, smiled, and tore up the ticket. Now, I do not for a minute believe that the foot-in-the-door effect would have worked to get me off of many other charges, but it was quite effective in addressing a situation that I imagine would have otherwise cost me a significant amount of money.

Notes from Class and the Textbook

Use the space provided in this outline to record notes from the textbook as well as from class lectures and discussion. Questions related to the *Psychological Detective, Hands On, Myth or Science,* and *Study Tip* sections in the text have been presented in the outline; use the associated space to respond to the questions and to record your own comments about the issues.

I. Social Psychology and Culture

II. How We View Others and Their Behavior

    A. Impression Formation

        1. Aspects of the Perceiver

Why do stereotypes persist in spite of the fact that individuals in a given category do not share the same personality traits?

2. Aspects of the Actor

   a. Appearance

   b. Speech

   c. Nonverbal Communication

Complete the 25 item Self-Monitoring Scale that is presented on pages 631 and 632 in your textbook. Scoring instructions and interpretative comments for the true-false questionnaire are given on page 667 in your textbook.

   d. Prior Information

3. Stereotype Activation

B. Social Judgments: Attributing Causes to Behavior

   1. Internal versus External Causes

Use this space to record the attributions you assign to the three events presented in the Psychological Detective section on page 633 in your textbook.

        a. Distinctiveness

        b. Consistency

        c. Consensus

        d. Attributional Biases

Why do people sometimes possess illusions of control over chance circumstances? Read the paragraph beginning on page 633 in your textbook for insight into this issue.

        e. The Fundamental Attribution Error

Consider the attribution that quizmasters are always rated as smarter than contestants. Write down a few possible situational factors that may not be taken into account when one makes this attribution.

f. The Actor-Perceiver Bias

Read the Study Tip suggestion from page 634 in your textbook. Use the tip to develop your understanding of actor-perceiver bias.

Record your attributions concerning the hypothetical situations presented on page 635 in your textbook.

C. Attitudes

Point your Web browser at the textbook's Web page to see Live!Psych module 15.1.

III. Interpersonal Relations

    A. Attitudes

        1. Components of Attitudes: Affect, Cognition, and Behavior

        2. Functions of Attitudes

            a. Ego Defense

            b. Adjustment

            c. Knowledge

Create a mnemonic device to help you remember the components and functions of attitudes.

        3. Measuring Attitudes

            a. Likert Scales

            b. Behavioral Measures

4. How Are Attitudes Formed?

    a. Learning

    b. Cognitive Dissonance

B. Attraction

    1. Proximity

    2. Affect and Emotions

    3. Reinforcement

    4. Similarity

C. Friendship

    1. Self-Disclosure

D. Love

    1. Sex Roles

2. Marital Satisfaction and Dissatisfaction

What are some reasons that abused women (or men) stay in relationships with their abusive spouses?

E. Prosocial Behavior: Helping Others

1. Situational and Personal Influences on Helping Behavior

D. Aggression

1. Biological Views of Aggression

2. Environmental Conditions and Aggression

How do situational variables impact the likelihood that a given experience will be frustrating?

3. Sexual Aggression

IV. Social Influences on Behavior

    A. Persuasion

        1. Source Factors

           a. Expertise

           b. Attractiveness

Design an experiment to evaluate the role of attractiveness in persuasion. How is the experimental design similar to or different from one that looks into the role of expertise in attraction?

           c. Trustworthiness

        2. Message Factors

           a. Attention

           b. Drawing Conclusions

           c. Message Acceptance

What factors involved in persuasion are used by the advertising industry? List several examples?

d. Primacy and Recency Effects

3. Channel Factors

Is persuasion more effective in group or one-on-one situations?

4. Audience Factors

a. What We Attend to: The Central and Peripheral Routes of Persuasion

Create a mind map or think link for the section on persuasion. Utilize different colors for the different components of your organizer.

B. Obedience

C. Conformity and Compliance

What experimental control condition(s) were necessary for Asch to support his claim about conformity in the line experiment?

Point your web browser at the textbook's web page to see Live!Psych module 15.2.

V. THE INDIVIDUAL AS PART OF A SOCIAL GROUP

    A. Social Facilitation

    B. Social Loafing

    C. Audiences and Coactors

        1. Deindividuation

    D. Group Interactions and Group Decisions

        1. Good Formation and Effectiveness

        2. Brainstorming

Why are fewer ideas generated in group brainstorming sessions than when people work alone?

3. Groupthink

E. Prejudice and Discrimination

1. Prejudice

Where do prejudice-related comments and behaviors come given that most prejudices are general in nature?

2. Discrimination

3. Sources and Functions of Prejudice

a. Social Function

b. Emotional Function

4. How to Reduce Prejudice

LEARNING OBJECTIVES

After you have studied the chapter, you should be able to respond to the following statements and questions to convey your understanding of the material.

1. How does the presence of others, or being part of a group, influence individuals' behavior?

2. Discuss several factors contributing to patterns of social judgment or attributions.

3. What variables are important in developing and maintaining interpersonal relationships?

4. Differentiate between *persuasion, obedience,* and *conformity and compliance* as social influences on behavior.

5. Compare and contrast social facilitation and social loafing.

6. How do groups influence decision-making?

7. Discuss the development and maintenance of prejudice and discrimination from the perspective of a social psychologist.

KEY WORD EXERCISE

Fill in the blanks in the following statements with key words and terms from the textbook. Answer as many as you can without referring to your notes or to the book. If you have blanks after thinking about each item, try using your book. The answers are presented after the practice test.

1. Research on _____ - _____, the amount of personal information a person is willing to share with others, indicates that the more a person reveals, the more positive others' impressions are.

2. The internal attribution bias that involves attending more closely to a behavior than the context in which it occurs is called the _____ _____ _____.

3. Psychologists define _____ as a form of interpersonal attraction that is governed by an implicit set of rules.

4. _____ stresses the costs and rewards involved in interpersonal relationships.

5. Suzy becomes more aggressive when she is frustrated than when she is not frustrated. This trend supports the _____ - _____ _____.

6. _____ is the use of social influence to cause people to change attitudes or behavior.

7. Milgram's experiment, the Jonestown massacre, and the behaviors of Nazis in Germany all provide examples of people initiating or changing behavior in response to direct commands. This change in behavior is called _____.

8. A mechanic has offered to provide several checks on your vehicle free of charge while it is in the shop for an oil change. This is done in hopes that in exchange for this added service you will _____ and will have anything that shows up from the checks repaired at that shop.

9. The blindfolded tug-of-war experiment revealed what students who have worked on class projects with other students already knew. Both the experiment and real-life experiences reveal that _____ occurs when groups work on a task for which there is no individual evaluation.

10. Scott and Meri tried giving candy to trick-or-treaters last Halloween on the honor system. They put a few bowls of candy on their porch, and went to a friend's house for a party. Much to their chagrin, when they returned the candy and the bowls were gone. The likelihood the bowls were stolen was probably increased as a function of the _____ that occurred when the trick-or treaters donned their costumes.

PRACTICE TEST

Circle the letter that corresponds to the *best* alternative for each of the following items. Read each alternative carefully. The answers are presented at the end of this study guide chapter. Be sure to learn *why* each correct alternative is better than the others.

1. Jean studies *impression formation.* In other words, she is interested in:
   a. how people present themselves.
   b. how people form impressions about others.
   c. various techniques that are used in embossing paper.
   d. why people resist forming impressions on their first exposure to others.

2. A stereotype is:
   a. a brand of hi-fidelity equipment.
   b. a set of beliefs about members of a particular group.
   c. an individual's decision to share personal information.
   d. a bias toward members of one's group (i.e., the ingroup).

3. Carl and his friends went to watch the comedian-hypnotist at a local theater. The entertainer selected Carl as an "assistant". Soon, Carl was clucking like a chicken on stage, playing the role "the human plank", and being generally entertaining. He had not planned to participate, but when asked to, played the part well. Which of the following was at work in influencing his behavior?
   a. self-disclosure
   b. attribution theory
   c. the self-fulfilling prophecy
   d. the fundamental attribution of hypnotists error

4. In an experiment on ___, students in a class were given descriptions of a visiting lecturer that portrayed him as either *warm* or *cold*. After the lecture, those who had been told he was warm rated his presentation more favorably than those who were told he was cold.
   a. the self-serving bias
   b. cognitive dissonance
   c. the effects of prior information
   d. the fundamental attribution error

5. The tendency to make internal attributions when we are successful and external attributions when we fail is called the:
   a. self-serving bias.
   b. cognitive dissonance.
   c. unconscious motivation.
   d. fundamental attribution error.

6. Which of the following was **not** identified in your textbook as a component of *attitude?*
   a. affect
   b. behavior
   c. cognition
   d. environment

7. You just filled out a questionnaire on which you to rated the degree to which you agreed or disagreed with a variety of statements. The questionnaire employed:
   a. Likert scales.
   b. behavioral measures.
   c. minimum wage workers.
   d. the yes-no response scale.

8. An aversive state produced when an individual has two incompatible thoughts simultaneously is called:
   a. confusion.
   b. attitude clash.
   c. thought distraction.
   d. cognitive dissonance.

9. Proximity to others is ___ to the establishment of friendships.
   a. not related
   b. positively related
   c. negatively related
   d. all of the above

10. Which of the following was **not** identified as a contributing factor in attraction?
    a. IQ
    b. similarity
    c. reinforcement
    d. affect and emotions

11. Strong emotional reactions are to ___ as commitment is to ___.
    a. friendship; love
    b. passionate love; companionate love
    c. companionate love; passionate love
    d. compassionate love; dispassionate love

12. Altruism is one of the most widely studied forms of ___.
    a. prosocial behavior
    b. cognitive dissonance
    c. interpersonal attraction
    d. social influence on behavior

13. The tendency for a group of people to be less likely than an individual to provide assistance to a person in trouble is called:
    a. the bystander effect.
    b. the individual effect.
    c. the bystander intervention effect.
    d. the individual intervention effect.

14. ___ aggression is to the specific intent of harming another as ___ aggression is to harming others in the process of achieving another goal.
    a. Implicit; explicit
    b. Outright; concealed
    c. Instrumental; hostile
    d. Hostile; instrumental

15. Source factors that contribute to one's persuasiveness include all **but** which of the following?
    a. expertise
    b. attractiveness
    c. trustworthiness
    d. all of the above

16. ___ is another name for what is popularly known as "reverse psychology."
    a. Reactance
    b. Unconscious reversing
    c. Subliminal transference
    d. None of the above; psychologists do not describe the constellation of phenomena popularly described as "reverse psychology."

17. The *foot-in-the-door* technique is a good example of persuasion that:
    a. backfires when persuaders say things they should not say.
    b. gets cut off by the audience before the persuader's message has been heard entirely.
    c. is more effective in a face-to-face situation than with one person addressing many people.
    d. is based on another persuasion technique that involves telling lies in order to maintain audience attention.

18. In psychology, the term *confederate* refers to someone:
    a. acting for the experimenter.
    b. who fought for the South in the Civil War.
    c. who attempts to block the federation by subjects in an experiment.
    d. who realizes the goal of an experiment and produces meaningless data.

19. Asch's "line experiment" was designed to provide insight into:
    a. the phenomenon of conformity.
    b. factors contributing to one's persuasiveness.
    c. why subjects in Milgram's experiment acted as they did.
    d. a perceptual phenomenon that was originally studied by Gestalt psychologists.

20. ___ is a phenomenon in which group decision making enhances or amplifies the original opinions of the group's members.
    a. Reciprocity
    b. Risk taking
    c. Deindividuation
    d. Group polarization

21. People will wind fishing line more quickly when they are competing against others at the same task than when they are racing against the clock. This is an illustration of:
    a. social conformity.
    b. social facilitation.
    c. bystander intervention.
    d. a hypothetical construct.

22. The activities of the Ku Klux Klan and lynch mobs reflect ___ in action.
    a. group think
    b. social loafing
    c. outgroup bias
    d. none of the above

23. The free expression of ideas by members of a group to solve a problem is called:
    a. risky-shift.
    b. expressionism.
    c. brainstorming.
    d. free determinism.

24. ___ frequently results in behaviors that adversely affect members of a targeted group.
    a. Altruism
    b. Prejudice
    c. Groupthink
    d. Brainstorming